KING ALFRED'S COLLEGE
WINCHESTER

—

To be returned on or before the day marked
below:—

PLEASE ENTER ON ISSUE SLIP:

AUTHOR   HARRISS

TITLE King, Parliament & public finance
in medieval England to 1369

ACCESSION No.   19412

KING, PARLIAMENT, AND PUBLIC FINANCE
IN MEDIEVAL ENGLAND
TO 1369

KING, PARLIAMENT, AND PUBLIC FINANCE IN MEDIEVAL ENGLAND TO 1369

G. L. HARRISS

CLARENDON PRESS · OXFORD
1975

Oxford University Press, Ely House, London W. 1

GLASGOW   NEW YORK   TORONTO   MELBOURNE   WELLINGTON
CAPE TOWN   IBADAN   NAIROBI   DAR ES SALAAM   LUSAKA   ADDIS ABABA
DELHI   BOMBAY   CALCUTTA   MADRAS   KARACHI   LAHORE   DACCA
KUALA LUMPUR   SINGAPORE   HONG KONG   TOKYO

ISBN 0 19 822435 4

*Printed in Great Britain by
Butler & Tanner Ltd, Frome and London*

In memoriam
ARNOLD FELLOWS

Preface

I HAVE tried in this book to describe the emergence of public finance in England, to show this as an aspect of the development of a nation state, and to trace it as a theme in the political relations of the King and his subjects. Over the past half-century considerable research has been undertaken into the different elements of this story. Most notable has been the work of Tout on the royal administration, of Mitchell, Willard, Unwin, and Fryde on taxation, of Hoyt and Wolffe on the royal demesne, and of a host of distinguished scholars on the origins of parliament, while Gaines Post and Ernst Kantorowicz have made familiar the views of legists and schoolmen on the nature of the state. Only the detailed history of Exchequer finance has, perhaps understandably, remained unwritten. An attempt to draw from these distinct and magisterial studies a narrative of political development may seem presumptuous and over-ambitious; at least I hope it will not be thought misconceived. Much of the early work in this field was undertaken within the framework of constitutional history with its emphasis on the struggle between royal prerogative and popular liberties. Since then our view of medieval history has widened. These pioneers taught us that institutions develop a momentum of their own yet one which is broadly related to the needs of the society which they serve. Moreover, a growing appreciation that late medieval and early modern England shared a basically similar political structure and ideology has set such institutional developments within the broader context of the emergence of the state. A view of the state as both a territorial unit and a community in which ruler and ruled were bound by mutual obligations to act for the common profit appeared in the thirteenth century and attained its most eloquent expression in England in the sixteenth and seventeenth. During the later Middle Ages the concepts introduced by the schoolmen became the common assumptions of the political classes. How such ideas were applied within administrative and political developments, how they became rooted in political institutions and formed traditions of political behaviour, is the underlying concern of this book.

In a sense public finance stands at the heart of this development and uniquely illuminates it. In the last decades of the twelfth century there began a steady enlargement of the fiscal and administrative resources of the Crown and of the political consciousness of its subjects. By the end of the Middle Ages, indeed for the most part by the end of the period with which this volume is concerned, the institutions through which England was to be governed and administered until the Civil War had been brought into existence, while the gentry had decisively emerged as an element in the political community. This period of great political creativity, if also of great tensions, was dominated by the first attempt to organize the resources of the realm for war. War, waged for the preservation of the state, imposed a public obligation on all its members, which was framed primarily in fiscal terms. Taxation became national in incidence and was levied for the common defence of the realm. As the Crown became the symbol of the identity and perpetuity of the realm, so its hereditary resources were seen to constitute an inalienable fisc for the maintenance of its dignity and estate. Administratively a national office was needed to control the revenues of the kingdom and to distribute them in a more or less systematic fashion between the great charges of state and individual creditors.

In each of these aspects the emergence of public finance depended on the interaction of political interests and the concept of the common good. Thus taxation, though rooted in a recognized doctrine of public obligation, could involve political conflicts between ruler and ruled. The ruler normally secured taxes by the most politically economical means; he had, for instance, to weigh the low yield of customary levies against the likelihood of political opposition to prerogative exactions or novel theories of *raison d'état*. At every turn practical politics ultimately enforced a reconciliation of the interests of ruler and ruled which could be framed as a doctrine of their mutual responsibilities and obligations. Both were thus educated in political concepts and encouraged to harmonize their interests through institutions in which these concepts could be embodied. Crown, parliament, and Exchequer each came to incorporate the authority of the King, the rights of his subjects, and the common good of the realm.

I have dealt with these developments within two successive periods. The first covers the emergence of a system of public finance between the late twelfth century and the commencement of the Hundred Years War; the second deals with the pressures of war on that system up to 1369. Within the first period three themes have been kept distinct: the development of taxation, of the Crown fisc, and of the Exchequer as a national financial office. Each is discussed within a series of consecutive chapters although this involves some chronological recapitulation. Within the second period the discussion centres almost wholly on parliamentary taxation in its different aspects. At the end of the volume I have attempted a brief retrospect of the developments in parliament and public finance over the whole period. It is, of course, easier to generalize men's political ideas than to determine the springs of their political actions, and it would be foolish to suppose that over so long and intricate a period of national politics I have not missed or misinterpreted some of its political currents. Similarly I have found it difficult, except at a few specific points, to bring the piecemeal and often divergent evidence of economic trends into any detailed and consistent relationship with the political story. Any historian of this period is conscious how frail his conclusions must remain, and on almost all problems encountered in the following pages there is room for doubt and disagreement which even further research may never resolve. At best I can hope that this book will chart these developments in terms which appear credible to those whose expertise lies before and after and which will not mislead those who follow further some of the trails that I have pursued.

G. L. H.

Magdalen College, Oxford
April 1974

Contents

Abbreviations

B.M.	British Museum
Bull. Inst. Hist. Res.	*Bulletin of the Institute of Historical Research*
C.C.R.	*Calendar of Close Rolls*
C.F.R.	*Calendar of Fine Rolls*
C.P.R.	*Calendar of Patent Rolls*
Eng. Hist. Rev.	*English Historical Review*
Foedera	T. Rymer, *Foedera, Conventiones, Litterae,* ed. A. Clarke and F. Holbrooke, vols. I–III (London, 1816–30)
H.B.C.	*Handbook of British Chronology,* 2nd edition, ed. F. M. Powicke and E. B. Fryde (London, 1961).
Parl. Writs	*Parliamentary Writs,* ed. F. Palgrave, 2 vols. in 4 (London, 1827–34)
P.R.O.	Public Record Office
R.D.P.	*Report from the Lords' Committees . . . for all matters touching the Dignity of a Peer* 4 vols., (London, 1820–9)
R.S.	Rolls Series
Rot. Parl.	*Rotuli Parliamentorum,* vols. i–ii.
Rot. Parl. Hact. Ined.	*Rotuli Parliamentorum Angliae Hactenus Inediti, MCCLXXIX–MCCCLXXIII,* ed. H. G. Richardson and G. Sayles (Camden Soc. 3rd ser., vol. li, 1935)
Rot. Scot.	*Rotuli Scotiae,* 2 vols. (Record Comm., 1814–19)
S.R.	*Statutes of the Realm,* vol. 1 (Record Comm., 1810)
Trans. Roy. Hist. Soc.	*Transactions of the Royal Historical Society*

All other abbreviations used should be self-evident. Full detail of works cited in footnotes by short title only can be found in the List of Sources, pp. 531–43.

PART ONE

THE EMERGENCE OF PUBLIC FINANCE

CHAPTER I

The Origins of National Taxation

THE development of lay taxation in the west European monarchies during the thirteenth and fourteenth centuries meant the replacement of feudal and customary dues by public obligations. The aid or subsidy came to be levied at uniform rates on all free subjects and communities throughout the realm, it could only be secured for the public needs of the state not for the personal whim and wants of the monarch, and it could not be arbitrarily taken but had to be freely granted by a body representing the community as a whole.[1]

In England the first national lay subsidy of this kind, in which the twin elements of public necessity and public consent are both present, was the thirteenth levied in 1207. By the end of the thirteenth century taxes of this kind were a recurrent and standard element in government finance. But although the tax of 1207 may be taken with some confidence as a starting-point for considering national lay taxation, there is less agreement or certainty about where its roots should be sought. Some have seen the national lay subsidy as an evolution of the feudal aid,

---

[1] An extensive bibliography on all aspects of taxation will be found in J. Favier *Finance et fiscalité au bas Moyen Âge* (Paris, 1971). Some of the principal works on the development of taxation in England and France are: S. K. Mitchell, *Studies in Taxation under John and Henry III* (New Haven, 1914) and *Taxation in Medieval England* (New Haven, 1951); J. F. Willard, *Parliamentary Taxes on Personal Property, 1920–1334* (Cambridge, Mass., 1934); M. V. Clarke, *Medieval Representation and Consent* (Oxford, 1936); ch. XII; G. Post, *Studies in Medieval Legal Thought* (Princeton, 1964), ch. III; G. L. Harriss, 'Parliamentary Taxation and the Origins of Appropriation of Supply in England, 1207–1340', in *Gouvernés et gouvernants* (Société Jean Bodin, Brussels, 1965); F. A. Cazel, 'Royal Taxation in Thirteenth Century England', in *L'impôt dans le cadre de la ville et de l'état* (Brussels, 1966); G. Dupont-Ferrier, *Études sur les institutions financières de la France à la fin du Moyen Âge*, ii (Paris, 1932); J. R. Strayer, 'Consent to Taxation under Philip the Fair', in *Studies in Early French Taxation* (Cambridge, Mass., 1938) and 'Defence of the Realm and Royal Power in France', in *Studi in Onore di Gino Luzzato* (Milan, 1948); T. N. Bisson, 'Negotiations for Taxes under Alphonse of Poitiers', in *Studies Presented to the International Commission for the History of Representative and Parliamentary Institutions* (Paris–Louvain, 1966); J. B. Henneman, *Royal Taxation in Fourteenth Century France* (Princeton, 1971).

while others have discerned in it the practical fruit of a revived legal doctrine of the authority of the state. However we assess these influences, there can be little doubt that the appearance of public taxation in England in the thirteenth century was related to an emergent sense of nationality, which saw the King as the public head of a *communitas*. It was also consequent upon the growing administrative capacity of government and the increasing concern of governments with external relations. The development of these elements can be traced back to the reign of Henry II, and the tensions between them proved both fruitful and disruptive. The influence of Roman law concepts of the authority of the *princeps* and of the *respublica* is apparent both in the writing of public servants like Glanville and FitzNeal and in official documents. The growing administrative resources of the monarchy, including an emergent administrative class, met (but also partly created) the increasing military, political, and fiscal demands of the ruler. The increased power of the ruler, particularly in legal and fiscal administration, in turn forced subjects to seek safeguards for their rights in custom and legal doctrine and to evolve, as a counterpoise to the public authority of the King, a political identity as a *communitas*. Finally the steep escalation in the scale and costs of war between the rulers of incipient states compelled them to strain the old feudal forms of military and fiscal obligation and eventually to look beyond these to the wider political community for aid. The pattern of taxation faithfully reflected this atmosphere of experiment, immediate need, and changing legal and political concepts. New forms of taxation were introduced and old ones were revived, both encountering opposition and ultimately proving abortive, until a tax satisfactory in yield and incidence and with a legal basis acceptable to both ruler and ruled was evolved. Most of this chapter will be concerned with this phase of development, but because a form of public taxation—the danegeld—had earlier existed in the Anglo-Saxon and Anglo-Norman kingdom, and because feudal taxes continued into the thirteenth century, it will be desirable briefly to review the character of fiscal levies under the Anglo-Norman kings.

The basis of royal authority in the Anglo-Norman state was the personal fealty owed to the King by his vassals, and his

ultimate juridical sovereignty over all free men and all causes.[1]
Rulers thus obtained their revenues either through the authority
they enjoyed as great feudal lords in respect of their estates and
their rights over vassals, or through the exercise of their judicial
supremacy which yielded both profits from formal justice and
compositions and fines for the King's grace. When the pipe roll
of 1130 first gives a picture of the revenues accounted for at the
Exchequer, by far the two largest receipts are from the county
farms at over £11,000 and the *placita, oblata et conventiones* at
over £10,000, and these comprise three-quarters of the total
recorded revenue.[2] The Anglo-Saxon and Anglo-Norman
kings of course possessed, in the danegeld, a tax specifically
justified by and levied for the case of an invasion of the realm.
Under the Conqueror and Rufus it had been an effective
though exceptional levy, charged at triple the rate in 1084 and
double the rate in 1096. The recension of the *Leges Edwardi
Confessoris* of 1140–59 tells us that on the latter occasion the
Church exemption was suspended 'causa necessitatis'.[3] Its
emergency character had not been lost sight of when FitzNeal
wrote the *Dialogus*, although by then it had fallen into desue-
tude.[4] Even if both these sources are employing terms more
current in the mid-twelfth than the late eleventh century, they
clearly recognized the danegeld as a levy confined to a specific
emergency, the urgency of which might override private rights
and royal concessions. Partly to buy off the opposition to it
expressed at the beginning of the reign, partly perhaps in order
to turn it into the annual levy which it seems to have become
by the end of his reign, Henry I granted to magnates and
barons of the Exchequer pardons and exemptions from it,
which Stephen both confirmed and extended. As a result, the
danegeld, never a large tax when taken at the basic rate of

---

[1] For a recent discussion, see J. R. Strayer, *On the Medieval Origins of the Modern
State* (Princeton, 1970), ch. i.

[2] Summarized by Sir J. H. Ramsay, *A History of the Revenues of the Kings of
England*, i (Oxford, 1925), p. 60.

[3] *Die Gesetze der Angelsachsen*, ed. F. Liebermann, i (Halle, 1903), p. 636: 'a
baronibus auxilium requirente . . . concessum est ei (non lege statutum tamen
neque firmatum, sed hac necessitatis causa), ex unaquaque hida sibi dari quatuor
solidos, ecclesia non excepta'. See also, J. H. Round, *Domesday Studies*, i (London,
1888), pp. 82–4.

[4] *Dialogus de Scaccario*, ed. C. Johnson (London, 1950), pp. 55–6: 'quod fuerat
urgente necessitate bellice tempestatis exactum'.

2*s*. per hide, declined from £5,000 to little more than £3,000.[1] Its levy on only two occasions under Henry II and its abandonment after 1162 may represent 'an unrecorded baronial victory over the Crown'[2] but is equally in line with the general direction of the Crown's fiscal policy. For it was rather from their feudal and juridical revenues that the Anglo-Norman kings sought to finance their wars. As J. O. Prestwich has pointed out, the heavy and sustained war expenditure between the Domesday Survey and Tinchebrai was met 'in part by developments in judicial and financial organisation and in part by irregular exactions'.[3] This policy was determined not merely by the nature of royal authority but by the tappable sources of revenue. Feudal wealth was concentrated in the hands of a relatively small class of great landowners closely bound to the King by legal and political ties. The extraction of their wealth through fines, *conventiones*, *oblata*, forfeitures, the exploitation of vacant churches, and sheer seizure conformed more effectively with the King's political opportunities than the attempt to impose a widespread public tax. Communities paid *dona*, *auxilia*, *assisa communis* either by way of amercement or as supplements to the geld. Mostly these financial settlements, even where they had a public or feudal basis, were personal and arbitrary, determined by the King's 'vis et voluntas', his pleasure or ill will. Other financial measures, whether they be the selling of Crown lands, the surcharge on farms of the shires, or the debasement of the coinage, all illustrate the expediency which characterized the King's search for revenue when he faced extraordinary expenditure. At times of real need, it has been said, there was little that the Crown could not sell, and where it did not sell it could often borrow.[4] There is little sign that either kings or their subjects felt the need for a regular system of taxation, or conceived a basis for such in ideas of common need and common obligation.

[1] Ramsay, op. cit. i. 55–6; R. W. Southern, 'The Place of Henry I in English History', *Proceedings of the British Academy*, xlviii (1962), p. 133; H. A. Cronne, *The Reign of Stephen* (London, 1970), pp. 229–30.
[2] S. Painter, *Studies in the History of the English Feudal Barony* (Baltimore, 1943), pp. 73–9.
[3] J. O. Prestwich, 'War and Finance in the Anglo-Norman State', *Trans. Roy. Hist. Soc.*, 5th ser. iv (1954), p. 30.
[4] Cronne, op. cit., pp. 231–6; Prestwich, op. cit., pp. 36–7.

By the reign of Henry II the bureaucratic efforts of Exchequer officials and the first stirrings of legal theories of the state had begun to rationalize and extend this *ad hoc* system. But the Angevin kings still expended more effort in improvising new exactions from old feudal revenues than in evolving a new legal basis for taxation. The impression which their policy made on Gerald of Wales, even allowing for his customary hyperbole, is highly revealing.

Although their regular revenues were smaller than those of their predecessors, they took more care to make good the amount from exceptional sources, relying more upon occasional profits than upon steady income. Truly, wherever by any means something is to be gotten, there, of a surety, every effort will be made to thieve; unrestingly and delicately the robber prowls, on a chance that a weak spot will be found somewhere.[1]

What Gerald is describing is less a system of taxation than a system of plunder, but his remark receives authoritative support from the author of the *Dialogus*. Richard FitzNeal acknowledged in his prologue that much of the revenue of kings was derived 'not invariably by strict process of law, but sometimes it proceeds from the laws of the country, sometimes from the secret devices of their own hearts and sometimes from their mere arbitrary power'.[2] His recital of the revenues accounted for at the Exchequer shows that the pattern had not changed fundamentally since the days of Rufus and Henry I. Scutage was, indeed, becoming more frequent while danegeld had been levied for the last time—confirming the trend towards feudal and away from public modes of taxation—but it was still the shire farms, the *placita et conventiones*, the *dona, auxilia, communes assisae,* and later the *tallagia, nova placita et novae conventiones* which formed the staple sources of revenue. Of the revenues received into the Chamber we are only dimly aware but they were still more personal and occasional.

Under pressure of the wars against Philip Augustus the Angevin Kings sought to meet the rapid escalation of military

---

[1] Cited and translated by H. G. Richardson and G. O. Sayles, *The Governance of Medieval England* (Edinburgh, 1963), p. 376 from Giraldus Cambrensis, *Opera*, ed. J. S. Brewer, viii (R. S., 1891), p. 316.

[2] *Dialogus*, ed. C. Johnson, pp. 1–2. Cf. Richardson and Sayles, op. cit., p. 373; J. C. Holt, *Magna Carta* (Cambridge, 1965), p. 73.

expenditure by exploiting their feudal and judicial rights. Towards the end of Henry II's reign the pipe rolls registered a
steep increase in reliefs, amercements, and *oblata*; under
Richard I the eyre became more burdensome and a forest eyre
was introduced in 1198 and repeated in 1207; under John the
feudal incidents were pushed to even greater levels, and fines
and forced loans were made at the King's pleasure.[1] Even
where such demands were for sums of unprecedented magnitude, there was little possibility of challenging their legal basis.
The King's rights under feudal law were clear and accepted;
moreover, his right was not infrequently translated into a *con-
ventio* with the vassal which became the basis of legal enforcement by the Exchequer.[2] Only the notion that the amounts
exacted as his right should be 'reasonable' imposed any limitation on the essentially personal and arbitrary dealings between
the King and his vassals. In contrasting procedures 'by will'
with others 'by law' men were appealing more to a notion of
political morality than to any body of law which could be set
against the King's 'vis et voluntas'. Ultimately their only
sanction was the barren one of rebellion.[3] Thus the baronial
attempt in 1215 to subject both scutage and tallage to formal
consent proved a less effective restraint on the development of
these taxes than was their limited feudal incidence.

It was these customary and practical limitations which
prompted the Angevins to look to more novel forms of taxation
which should embrace all free men and yield a sum to match
the expenses of a long campaign. For such taxes the King
needed an authority beyond that of a feudal suzerain; he levied
them as a public authority, claiming responsibility for the safety
of the kingdom and obliging subjects to support him in defence
of the common good. These concepts become discernible in the
last quarter of the twelfth century. Richard FitzNeal may himself have disapproved of the methods of raising revenue which
he describes, but he goes out of his way to add that it was not

[1] J. C. Holt, *The Northerners* (Oxford, 1961), pp. 145–50; J. O. Prestwich, op.
cit., p. 20; Richardson and Sayles, op. cit., pp. 374–5.
[2] Holt, *The Northerners*, pp. 182 ff. For compositions even of the 1207 tax, see
S. Painter, *The Reign of King John* (Baltimore, 1949), p. 134.
[3] Holt, *The Northerners*, pp. 187–93; Holt, *Magna Carta*, pp. 75–9, 112: 'The
three years which immediately preceded Magna Carta laid bare the weakness of
the subject's defences against the feudal prerogatives of the Crown.'

for an official to question a ruler's acts; it was sufficient for him to guard this wealth safely for upon it depended the preservation of the kingdom. His remark reveals the existence of a new political mentality: not merely the conscious political amorality of the bureaucrat but an appreciation of the overriding importance of the preservation of the state in an age of increasing external wars.[1] The King's own interests and authority were coming to be identified with the needs of the kingdom, and from this flowed the notion of a reciprocal obligation of the ruler to defend the realm and of his people to support and contribute to its defence. Developments in military organisation reflected this. Henry II's Assize of Arms of 1181, which obliged all free men to equip themselves with arms according to an assessment of their income, marked the decline of the knight's fee as the effective basis of military service and its transformation into a unit of assessment.[2] Against threats of foreign invasion or domestic insurrection all *liberi homines* (whether feudal tenants, mercenaries, or communal levies) had a common duty to follow the King in arms,[3] so that FitzNeal can speak of a knight being called to service, either with or without payment, 'audita necessitate regis vel regni'.[4] By the end of the century the London interpolator of the *Leges Edwardi Confessoris*, who is notable for his views on the obligations of both King and community in the defence of the kingdom, believed that all free men should have arms and keep them ready to serve with the King 'ad tuitionem regni', and that shire levies 'pro commune utilitate' should be ready to serve 'ad honorem et ad utilitatem coronem regni . . . cum opus adfuerit in regno', and to defend the realm against external enemies.[5]

The need for a new public tax was first met by the reintroduction of the old danegeld in 1194 in the form of a carucage. But it was the thirteenth on movable property of 1207 which

[1] Thus FitzNeal observes that in time of war revenue 'effunditur ad conservandum statum regni'. *Dialogus*, pp. 1–2.

[2] M. Powicke, *Military Obligation in Medieval England* (Oxford, 1962), pp. 50–2, 54–6; S. Harvey, 'The Knight and the Knight's Fee in England', *Past and Present*, 49 (1970), pp. 31–43.

[3] Powicke, op. cit., pp. 30–1, 34–5.   [4] *Dialogus*, p. 111.

[5] *Gesetze*, ed. F. Liebermann, i. 655–6, and *Liebermann, Über die Leges Anglorum saeculo xiii ineunte Londoniis collectae* (Halle, 1894). See the discussion in J. E. A. Jolliffe, *Angevin Kingship* (London, 1955), p. 323, with further citations.

marked the real discovery of a uniform tax with a national incidence and a high yield which could be justified by the needs of the realm. It was, in Painter's words, 'beyond the range of feudal and seignorial rights and of English political tradition'.[1] We can best appreciate the novelty of this tax if we review the other experiments in taxation during these years. In what respects did scutage and tallage fail to satisfy royal needs? Why did the carucage prove abortive? What features of each of these taxes were also found in the new tax on movables, and were these derived from its predecessors? Should we, in fact, seek the ancestry of the new tax in the experiments with the traditional feudal and national levies or should we see it as an expression of the new influence of civil law? Though negotiated between the King and his barons, whose consent was formally rendered in the King's feudal court, did it yet give expression to a new political philosophy of the relations between ruler and ruled?

Neither the attempts by the first two Norman kings to exploit danegeld as an exceptional levy nor Henry I's success in making it an annual tax ensured its survival. Danegeld bore the imprint of a displaced system of military obligation, and with the introduction of tenurial service and the rapid spread of commutation, scutage began to feature as a regular source of revenue. But though by the beginning of Henry II's reign scutage reflected the more developed feudal character of society, as a tax it remained singularly restricted. Levied on the occasion of the summons of the host upon a schedule of knights' fees which was generally recognized to be out of date by 1166, there was little opportunity for the King to extend it beyond the circle of tenants in chief, to increase the rate of commutation, or to impose an additional charge. The Angevins attempted to do all these, but none of these expedients could turn scutage into a major tax and most of them provoked opposition. For the scutage of Toulouse in 1159, Henry II exacted a *donum* from sub-tenants, as he did from the towns, Jews, and moneyers.[2] In 1166 he instituted an inquiry into the

---

[1] Painter, *The Reign of King John*, p. 132.

[2] J. H. Round, *Feudal England* (London, 1895), pp. 277–9. This was described in one instance at least as an *auxilium*: *Pipe Roll 9 Henry II* (Pipe Roll. Soc., 1886), p. 9.

numbers of knights enfeoffed by his vassals, distinguishing between the 'old enfeoffment' before the death of Henry I and the new thereafter, and requiring the names of the enfeoffed knights. This information formed the basis for levying a feudal aid for the marriage of the King's daughter in 1168, charged at one mark to the knight's fee on both the old and new enfeoffment. The returns show that the attempt to collect the aid from these additional fees was, broadly speaking, a failure. Practically no one paid on the new enfeoffment.[1] This marked the end of Henry II's attempt to enlarge the *servitia debita* and of the attempt to extend scutage to rear vassals. It came to be recognized that this could only be done with the lord's consent. Custom likewise imposed a limitation on the rate of scutage which, until 1204, had varied between one and two marks. In that year, in a council at Oxford, John secured the grant of an 'aid' for the defence of Normandy which was levied as a scutage at the rate of $2\frac{1}{2}$ marks and in 1210 and 1214 scutages of 3 marks seem to have had an arbitrary or punitive element.[2] When in 1215 the barons demanded that no scutage or aid should be levied without the common counsel of the realm, they must have had in mind these scutages which in virtue of their exceptional size could be regarded as an 'aid'.[3] One further levy of this kind was a scutage of 2 marks sanctioned as an 'aid' by a great council in 1217. If the attempts to extend scutage to rear vassals and to increase its yield could only be carried through at the price of securing consent to it as an exceptional levy, a more remunerative device, practised first by Richard and then by John, was the exaction of fines for permission not to serve. Fines of 3 or 4 marks, in addition to scutage, were taken from the King's larger tenants in 1201, increasing as the reign progressed to an average of 10 marks per knight's fee. The additional charge, which was entirely at the King's will, was imposed selectively and was accompanied by permission for the tenant in chief to collect scutage from his tenants, upon whom the extra charge ultimately fell.[4] Thus the Crown had, albeit indirectly, found a way of tapping the

[1] S. K. Mitchell, *Studies in Taxation under John and Henry III*, pp. 165–8.

[2] For the grant of 1204, see Holt, *The Northerners*, p. 89 citing Matthew Paris, *Chronica Majora*, ii 484.

[3] Mitchell, *Studies*, pp. 20, 74, 125.

[4] Painter, *Studies*, pp. 126–8. On some occasions (1199, 1203) scutage was

wealth of the majority of landowners. Yet though scutage had
the advantage of being levied on the occasion of an expedition
without (in its basic form) the need for consent, it was never
a highly remunerative tax. John levied eleven scutages during
his reign, the average yield of which, including the fines, was
about £4,500.[1]

The decay of danegeld also prompted the Crown to secure
casual levies under the name of *auxilium* and *donum* from which
there eventually emerged the more defined *tallagium*.[2] Gifts and
aids from both towns and shires had already appeared before
1130 and both were being levied early in the reign of Henry II.
They were usually in connection with major military expeditions like the Toulouse campaign of 1159, the French campaigns of 1160-1, and the expedition to Wales in 1165.[3] Despite
the terminology and despite some element of bargaining and
agreement in the localities, there was probably little that was
voluntary about them. Since they coincided with the payment
of scutages, which tenants in chief might then levy upon their
tenants in the form of a *donum*, there was a tendency to restrict
such aids to the King's own lands and the cities and boroughs
whose conspicuous wealth the Crown was eager to tap. The
recognizable development of these aids into royal tallage began
in 1167-8 when expert assessors from the central financial
administration were sent out on circuits to levy the aid from
movable property on a uniform basis. Local communities could
either compound by an agreed payment (recovered thereafter
from the inhabitants) or—if agreement could not be reached
—were subject to a *per capita* assessment by royal officials.
There was a right of bargain but not of outright refusal.[4] Such
levies remained few and exceptional but slowly emerged as an
independent mode of taxation as they ceased to be identified
with the payment of scutage or even with the occasion of war.

collected from rear vassals by the sheriff: ibid., pp. 27-8, 58; cf. Mitchell, *Studies*,
pp. 42-3, 60, 73-4.
[1] Though some yielded very much more; that of 1205 for example produced
10,690 marks: Mitchell, *Studies*, p. 69.
[2] Mitchell, *Taxation*, p. 282; C. Stephenson, 'Taxation and Representation in the
Middle Ages', in *Mediaeval Institutions* (New York, 1954), p. 120; R. S. Hoyt, *The
Royal Demesne in English Constitutional History* (New York, 1950), pp. 112-23.
[3] Mitchell, *Taxation*, pp. 260-6.
[4] Ibid., pp. 238-51; C. Stephenson, *Borough and Town* (Cambridge, Mass.,
1933), pp. 160-6.

The 'aid' of 1168 was taken in conjunction with the feudal aid for marrying the King's eldest daughter; that of 1177 possibly for the marriage of his second daughter; in 1173 and 1174 the aid was for the King's expenses in suppressing the rebellion; only in 1186–7 was it identified with the scutage 'of Galloway', though an aid had been collected from London for the King's expedition to Ireland in 1171.[1] Already *tallagium* was the normal term for these levies on the royal manors, though the towns were still recorded as paying *auxilia* and *dona*, probably according to whether the levy was assessed or compounded.[2] With the intensification of the war in France, tallage, like scutage, began to lose its occasional character. A tallage necessarily formed part of the complex of taxes to pay the ransom in 1194 and thereafter it was levied yearly up to 1198, accompanied by a scutage. It was again levied continuously from 1202 to 1206. These years also saw attempts to increase its yield by insisting on *per capita* assessments, but although the intensification of the King's demands produced the largest yield from tallage in any comparable period, opposition to the attempt to turn it into an annual tax was strong and few of the levies extended to the whole demesne. Local communities opposed uncustomary exactions by bargaining, and individual towns and manors purchased exemption.[3] Nor was the annual yield very great: under Henry II it had been at most between £4,000 and £5,000. In the period of continuous tallage under John the numbers of counties and towns contributing to each levy declined, and the tallages from the shires in 1204–5–6 raised only between 3,000 and 5,000 marks.[4] Both these periods of continuous levy reflected the intensive military effort in France. After 1206 this declined and the only remaining tallage of John's reign, for the Irish expedition in 1210 (for which scutage was taken), again had the character of an exceptional

[1] Mitchell, *Taxation*, pp. 244–5.
[2] *Dialogus*, pp. 108–9; Mitchell, *Taxation*, p. 246; *Pipe Roll 2 Richard I*, ed. D. M. Stenton (Pipe Roll Soc., 1925) p. xix. London usually paid an *auxilium* (e.g. *Pipe Roll 3–4 Richard I*, pp. 137, 302; *Pipe Roll 5 Richard I*, p. 159) except in 1194 when it gave 1,500 marks 'pro benevolentia Regis et pro libertatibus suis conservandis et de auxilio suo ad redemptionem domini regis' (*Pipe Roll 6 Richard I*, p. 182). In 1195 the burgesses of Northampton paid 300 marks 'de auxilio assiso' (*Pipe Roll 7 Richard I*, p. 105; *Pipe Roll 8 Richard I*, p. 39).
[3] Mitchell, *Taxation*, pp. 286–313.
[4] Ibid., p. 239; Mitchell, *Studies*, pp. 68, 74, 82.

levy. Significantly, the yield, at over £8,000, was one of the heaviest. In this case all the towns compounded; indeed the King's first intention had been to raise the revenue by way of loan.[1]

Thus tallage displayed some of the features of the later lay subsidies, notably that it was levied on movable property of free tenants, touched both rural and urban wealth, and was an occasional levy on the pretext of a great and particular necessity which was very frequently identified with a military expedition. But though it was less feudal in character than scutage, it is difficult to conceive of it leading, by extension beyond its limited area, to the great national taxes.[2] Moreover, by the close of the twelfth century it was firmly established that tallage was levied by the prerogative of the King. The exercise of this right required neither counsel nor consent, even if custom and bargain might determine the amount. Although under Henry III tallage came to be levied only as part of one of the great general aids, it was on no occasion debated by the council. Even London, which had always negotiated an aid or gift, and had continued to do so long after other towns had come to render tallage, was finally brought within the framework of compulsory payment in 1255.[3]

The need for national taxation was further met in the late twelfth century by the attempt to revive the old danegeld as a new land tax, the carucage. Although the initial levy in 1194 was on the basis of the old assessment on the hide, in subsequent levies there were experiments with new actual assessments on the numbers of carucates (1198, 1217) and plough teams (1200, 1220). This involved the labour of county commissioners on a national basis, proceeding by inquest and sworn assessment. The novel character of the tax, its national incidence, and the fact that it was an exceptional expedient

[1] Mitchell, *Taxation*, pp. 319–20; *Studies*, p. 100. The last tallage of the reign in 1214 was to pay the indemnity to the clergy for the withdrawal of the interdict (*Studies*, p. 117).

[2] Compare the arguments advanced by R. S. Hoyt, 'Royal Demense, Parliamentary Taxation and the Realm, 1294–1322', *Speculum*, xxiii (1948), pp. 58–69 and 'Royal Taxation and the Growth of the Realm in Medieval England', *Speculum*, xxv (1950), pp. 36–48.

[3] Mitchell, *Taxation*, pp. 321–9 and above, p. 13, n. 2.

make it probable that it was taken after consultation in the council. Such at least is specifically stated in the writs for collection in 1194, 1217, and 1220, though evidence is lacking for the levies of 1198 and 1200.[1] Certainly the occasion for each levy was a specific, exceptional demand on the King. That of 1194, levied following the King's return, was for the discharge of his debts; that of 1198 must have been a contribution to Richard's campaign. John's only levy in 1200 was towards the relief of 20,000 marks promised to Philip Augustus for his French lands.[2] Under Henry III the carucage of 1217 was for the war against Prince Louis, that of 1220 'for the great and most urgent necessity of our debts and for the preservation of our land of Poitou'.[3] Carucage thus shared many features with the great taxes on income and movables—national incidence, assessment on actual wealth, consultation with the council— and was levied to meet great and exceptional needs of the King. Both its ancestry and use emphasized that it was levied for the safety of the King's person or his lands. Like the taxes on movables it was also received into a separate account by specially appointed custodians, and not included in the pipe roll.[4] But though it required a similar degree of trouble for its collection, its yield could not match that of the taxes on movable property. Whereas the thirteenth of 1207 yielded some £60,000, the carucages of 1200 and 1220 probably gave no more than £7,500 and £5,500.[5]

Finally the most novel taxes to be levied in the late twelfth century were those on revenues and movables: the tithes of 1166 and 1188, the fourth of 1193, and the more dubious seventh levied in 1203. The purposes of these were widely dissimilar. The first two were for the defence of the Holy Land and were not confined to the Angevin territories. The third was one of a number of expedients to raise money for Richard I's ransom and was auxiliary to the recognized feudal aid for this purpose. The last was an obscure levy which John took in connection with his campaign of 1203, partly perhaps as a penal

[1] Mitchell, *Taxation in Medieval England*, pp. 177, 194–5; Mitchell, *Studies*, pp. 122 n. 6, 130 n. 52.
[2] Mitchell, *Studies*, p. 32.
[3] Ibid., pp. 123, 130 n. 50 quoting the Close Roll.
[4] Mitchell, *Taxation*, pp. 12–22
[5] Painter, *The Reign of King John*, p. 129.

fine on the earls and barons who had allegedly deserted him. The first three of these at least were levied upon both income and movable property at a uniform rate and were paid by all men. Although the levy of 1166 was paid under personal oath, some form of assessment was employed in 1188 and 1194 and again in 1203, though personal compositions seem also to have been made on both these latter occasions. The twelfth-century levies were also, according to the writs for collection, the result of a decision taken by the King in council with his barons.[1] The emergence of these great, occasional levies on national wealth, under the influence of the Church, was a step of immense importance. National in incidence, and sanctioned after consultation for an exceptional need, they formed an obvious precedent for the national lay subsidy. But they had not been sought for the purpose of a secular war, nor had they been justified in terms of the needs of the realm.

All the forms of taxation developed in the latter half of the twelfth century had elements in common with the later lay subsidy, and each reveals the common pressure to evolve a tax to meet the increasing demands of external wars. Such a tax needed to be an obligatory response to the necessity of war, its yield had to be sufficient to meet the cost of an army, and thus it had to tap actual wealth by an assessed levy on a national basis. Any tax which met all these requirements would be a heavy burden on the subject, and in so far as it was wholly novel or extended what was customary it could only be levied under some form of agreement. Scutage was by definition most closely related to war, though tallage and even carucage were often associated with the occasion of a campaign. Carucage alone was national in incidence and assessed on actual wealth, but only tallage was levied on movables. None of these taxes of itself yielded a sum sufficient to finance a major campaign, and in each case the pressure for their extension or (in the case of carucage) reintroduction had induced the Crown to seek a measure of consent. It is clear, then, that although the Crown was actively exploiting its feudal and traditional taxes, and was

---

[1] The writs for the collection of the taxes of 1166 and 1188 are given by Gervase of Canterbury, *Opera Historica*, ed. W. Stubbs, i (R.S., 1879), pp. 198–9 and by Benedict of Peterborough, *Gesta Regis Henrici Secundi*, ed. W. Stubbs ii (R.S. 1867), p. 31. For a discussion of these and of the tax of 1194, see Mitchell, *Taxation*, pp. 123–5, 114–22. For that of 1203, see Painter, *Reign of King John*, pp. 130–1.

extending them to meet the requirements of new military demands, none of these taxes adequately met its needs. A new tax was needed, the cardinal requirement of which was that its yield should vastly exceed that of the existing levies. It was this which the new lay subsidy provided. It was levied upon all free men by a strict assessment of their income and movable property, authorized after discussion in council, and justified as being for the defence of the realm. It was clearly an exceptional measure.

Did the inspiration for this new tax come from feudal or civil law concepts? Some historians have argued that the key to so novel a levy was the consent which the King's chief tenants would give when asked to help their lord in his exceptional need. Aid of this kind transcended their feudal obligations; it depended on the good will and personal obligation of the vassal to his lord; and this free consent was the cardinal feature of the new lay subsidy. Thus S. K. Mitchell saw the problem as being

first [to] determine the source and character of the notion of consent and then follow the changes in the notion with reference to taxation down into the last quarter of the thirteenth century. The origin of consent is to be found in the feudal notion that in case of great need the lord has the right to ask his vassal for aid over and above the established dues and services. This in the feudal language was the gracious aid.[1]

He identified the thirteenth of 1207 as a gracious aid, noting that consent for it had been obtained from the tenants in chief, and concluded that only by this consent could such a levy have arisen out of feudal obligation.[2] This view was endorsed by Miss M. V. Clarke in her discussion of the growth of the doctrine of consent.[2] It has, however, been challenged by Gaines Post who has argued that the origins of national taxation lay in Roman law rather than in feudal custom. Taxation represented the superior right of the ruler to impose burdens for the common good when the necessity of the state demanded; it was this necessity which imposed on subjects the obligation to

[1] Mitchell, *Taxation*, p. 159.   [2] Mitchell, *Studies*, pp. 84–5.
[3] M. V. Clarke, *Medieval Representation and Consent*, pp. 253–9. 'The main contribution of feudal theory was to make concrete the doctrine of consent by relating it to taxation' (p. 259).

render aid and it might, though it normally did not, override consent. But where consent was given it was tacit, formal consent to the necessity such as was given by suitors to the judgement of a court.[1]

The theory that the later lay subsidy developed from the feudal gracious aid faces a number of difficulties. First, such references to the gracious aid as can be traced in the twelfth century (and by definition they will be few) mostly refer to the relations between lords and their vassals, not to the tenants of the Crown.[2] Glanville, in a passage often cited, asks whether a lord can exact aid from his tenants to maintain himself at war, and while he is clear that lords cannot do so against the will of their tenants, his opinion is that if the aid is sanctioned in the lord's court he can thereafter distrain for payment.[3] This is very much the situation as we see it in a case in 1207, but this and other cases suggest that the request for a gracious aid was either unprecedented or rare and was likely to encounter opposition.[4] Glanville, it should be noted, raises the question as a matter for discussion rather than as long-formulated custom, and there is some indication that such demands upon vassals may have been becoming more frequent by 1200 as the expenses of war pressed harder upon lords.[5] Neither Glanville nor any of the twelfth-century evidence refers to gracious aid granted to the King. On the royal demesne it is difficult to distinguish such a levy from the payment of tallage or to see any precedent for the request of 1207 except perhaps in 1204. Secondly, although the relation of the King to his realm and to his barons still remained strongly feudal in the early thirteenth century, the language of the writ for the levy of the thirteenth in 1207 was more national than feudal in tone. The levy was authorized by the common advice and assent of the council,

---

[1] G. Post, 'Plena Potestas and Consent in Medieval Assemblies', *Traditio*, i (1943), pp. 355–408; *Studies in Medieval Legal Thought*, ch. iii.

[2] Mitchell, *Taxation*, pp. 267 ff.; *Studies*, p. 84; C. Stephenson 'The Seignorial Tallage in England', in *Mélanges d'histoire offerts à Henri Pirenne* (Brussels, 1926), pp. 465–74; M. V. Clarke, op. cit., p. 253.

[3] Glanville, *De Legibus Anglie* IX, c. 8, ed. G. D. G. Hall (London, 1965), p. 112.

[4] J. C. Holt, *Magna Carta*, p. 103 n. 4 and cf. p. 219 nn. 5 and 6.

[5] As Holt remarks (*The Northerners*, p. 188), Glanville's statement is somewhat tentative; Glanville was at times stating 'opinions rather than certainties' (Holt, *Magna Carta*, pp. 202, 219).

was for the defence of the realm, and was to be assessed on all
free men through oaths taken before the King's justices. There
is no explicit evidence that this was regarded as a feudal
gracious aid, nor is it easy to see why the grant of such aid
by the King's feudal vassals should bind the free men of the
realm as a whole. Finally it may be doubted whether *auxilium*
was used here as a technical term which could either denote a
continuing identity between the gracious aid of lord and vassal
and the tax of 1207 or necessarily imply a notion of free consent. Indeed *auxilium* appears to have been a generic term
which could be applied to any kind of service and to every
kind of tax, but was more commonly used of novel levies whose
character and designation were as yet uncertain[1] The history
of taxation in the twelfth century shows its gradual replacement by more specific terms until by the end of the century it
is found comparatively rarely on the pipe rolls.[2] Both tallage
and carucage were at first designated '*auxilium*' and the only
significance its use had in 1207 was to emphasize the novelty
of the levy. Nor is it easy to feel confident that *auxilium* denoted
a charge levied only by consent. The *auxilia et dona* of the early
and mid-twelfth century could never have turned into the
arbitrary *tallagium* had they embodied a right of free refusal.

We may indeed wonder how precise and effective was the
notion of consent in the twelfth century. In practice, as we
have seen, consent offered little effective barrier to the extension of the King's feudal levies. As J. C. Holt has pointed out,
'the obtaining of consent was never any real difficulty to the

[1] Cf. G. Dupont Ferrier, *Institutions financières*, ii, ch. i; also 'Histoire et signification du mot "aides" dans les institutions financières de la France', *Bibl. École des
Chartes*, lxxxix (1928).

[2] Besides the *auxilia* for the marriage of the King's daughter and the ransom of
Richard, and the *auxilia* of the city of London (q.v. above, p. 13, n. 2), the other
references in the Pipe Rolls of Richard and John are principally to: (i) *commune
auxilium* which can describe a feudal gracious aid (F. Stenton, *The First Century of
English Feudalism, 1066–1166*, Oxford, 1932, pp. 172, 276), but is found as an
arbitrary exaction early in the reign of Henry II (Clarke, op. cit., p. 261; Mitchell,
Taxation, p. 286) and in the Pipe Rolls of Richard and John is frequently used for
the sum by which a community compounds for amercements before the justices
(e.g. *Pipe Roll 2 Richard I*, p. 2; *Pipe Roll 4 John*, p. 157; *Pipe Roll 9 John*, p. 10),
this being the old *communis assisa* (*Dialogus*, pp. 47–8); (ii) *auxilium* is applied to the
cornage payments of the free men of Westmorland and Cumberland (*Pipe Roll
8 Richard I*, pp. 23, 97; *Pipe Roll 9 Richard I*, pp. 13, 181); (iii) *auxilium* is applied
to the carucage of 1194 (*Pipe Roll 6 Richard I*, p. 126) and the carucage of 1198
(*Pipe Roll 10 Richard I*, p. 166; *Pipe Roll 5 John*, p. 30).

Angevin kings'.[1] Consent was very frequently secured for the formulation of new laws and new judicial procedures by which customary and traditional rights would be abrogated. We should not, in fact, give more force to the notion of consent in the field of taxation than it had in the field of law and feudal custom. 'When John sought aid for which there was no customary warrant, he did so openly, admitting that he was doing so for special reasons and asking for compliance as an act of grace on the part of his subjects.'[2] Such consent was of the nature of *concordia*, agreement or acceptance of the King's actions. It was necessary for the King or lord to obtain it, particularly in taking a man's goods, for the rights of the free man could not be broached without his consent; to do otherwise was to proceed by arbitrary will. And the securing of this *concordia* was best done in the lord's court, so that his tenant might be bound by its judgement. *Magna Carta* elaborated the means by which the common counsel of the realm might be given in the King's court for the assessment of an aid; but it nowhere spoke of a right of consent. For the obligation of King or lord to proceed by way of consent (or more properly consultation and agreement) did not imply the right of the free vassal to refuse. Both Mitchell and Miss Clarke admitted that the feudal gracious aid was not easily refused: the vassal was obliged to come to his lord's assistance in time of great need; 'only a false or disloyal vassal would refuse necessary aid'.[3] It is difficult indeed to find cases of successful refusal either of royal or seigneurial demands for aid of any kind, though composition was plentiful.

Neither the term *auxilium* nor the notion of consent, therefore, was applied either exclusively or in any special sense to the gracious aid and the thirteenth of 1207. No special ancestry links the national lay subsidy to the feudal gracious aid; indeed the latter lacked any wide basis in feudal custom and may have been the product of the strains of late-twelfth-century warfare on feudal resources. Although no specific feudal tax gave birth

[1] J. C. Holt, *The Northerners*, pp. 191–2.   [2] Ibid.
[3] M. V. Clarke, op. cit., p. 253; Mitchell, *Taxation*, p. 161. But cf. Hoyt in *Speculum*, xxv (1950), p. 44 who would seem to hold that the vassal had an absolute right of refusal to render gracious aid. As will appear, I do not think that the refusal of aid to Henry III by the *magnum concilium* derived from this supposed feudal right of free refusal of an aid.

to the lay subsidy, feudal taxation at the end of the twelfth century was adapting to meet the demands of new patterns of warfare and new notions of political obligation. It is significant that 'feudal' consent as described by S. K. Mitchell and M. V. Clarke bears very many of the signs of the 'legal' consent of the civil lawyers. Notions of necessity and emergency were being applied to traditional taxation, and new forms like the crusading tenths and the fourth of 1193 were teaching men to think in terms wider than the personal relationships on which feudalism was based. These changes alone might have produced a tax based on national obligation by which the wealth of the kingdom could be mobilized. What Roman law did was to provide rulers with the theoretical justification for such a levy, along with the legal basis for obliging their subjects to contribute when the needs of the realm demanded. At the same time it offered the subject more precise grounds for defending his rights against arbitrary seizure than was available to him in custom. For obligation and consent had as their common basis the concept that the state served the common profit of ruler and ruled; a concept to which the facts of war and government were daily giving increasing relevance.

The later twelfth century saw a marked advance towards a theory of public authority in which the ruler represented the realm. The doctrine, derived from Roman law, had already proved influential in shaping the jurisdictional structure of the Church. It provided secular authority with an incipient notion of *raison d'état* along lines which Saint Thomas was to define more explicitly in the next century.[1] For the twelfth-century lawyers already regarded the state as natural and, to a degree, sanctified. In Roman law, the *principatus* with its *princeps* was a feature common to all peoples; a basic element in the *ius gentium*. The Law of Nations was itself an aspect of the Law of Nature, in its turn derived from the Law of God. Thus the state was both natural to man and acceptable to God; and its government must take as its end the maintenance of the moral law. The essential role of the state in the natural and divine order therefore justified its preservation, and in the twelfth century this could still not be taken for granted. In most places

[1] For this see Gaines Post, *Studies in Medieval Legal Thought*, ch. iv *passim*, and particularly pp. 262–3, 291.

the realm, under the effective authority of a single ruler, was only just emerging. Even in England, which in this respect enjoyed a longer tradition, the century before Henry II's accession had witnessed foreign invasion and civil disorder. The safety and preservation of the realm was the constant and foremost preoccupation of the ruler, and it was not surprising that the notion of a public authority which might transcend private rights in defence of the common good found expression first as a doctrine of emergency. From the early twelfth century the canonists had familiarized the notion that necessity over-rode the law, and could even abrogate the Church's own privileges,[1] and in 1179 the Third Lateran Council permitted the clergy to accede to lay taxation in cases of urgent necessity.[2] Since such a necessity derived not from the whim of the ruler but from a threat to the common good for which the state existed, a ruler could require support from his people. As we have seen, for the London interpolator of the *Leges Edwardi Confessoris* early in John's reign this was already a common-place in regard to the obligation to bear arms. In the next half-century fiscal obligations were to be formulated in the same terms until they could be given clear definition in the words of Saint Thomas:

Where princes do not possess sufficient means to provide against hostile attack . . . it is just that the citizens should contribute what is necessary to promote the common interest. So a prince who fights for the interests of his country may make use of the resources of the community and lay a charge on the community either through the normal forms of taxation or, if such are insufficient, through indi-vidual contributions.[3]

As the passage indicates, war was already the most usual pre-text for appeal to the plea of necessity. In the twelfth century this was not consistently so; yet it is significant that the two levies on all lay and ecclesiastical revenues throughout Christen-dom made at the appeal of the Pope in 1166 and 1188 were for the preservation of the crusading state in its hour of need.

---

[1] *Studies in Medieval Legal Thought*, p. 258, citing Hugh of St. Victor; and cf. above, p. 5 n. 3.

[2] Ibid., pp. 81, 440 n. 18.

[3] *De Regimine Judaeorum*. The translation cited is that by J. G. Dawson in *Selected Political Writings*, ed. A. P. D'Entrèves (Oxford, 1948), p. 92.

Moreover, when a tax of this kind was first levied in a secular context in England, the occasion was a threat to the safety of the realm by the capture and imprisonment of its head. The inadequacy of the feudal aid to meet this emergency was symbolic, for the King's peril jeopardized his realm. It is interesting that Richard's appeal from prison for the money to meet his ransom was couched in terms of his necessity.[1]

The ruler, then, had the initial right, indeed duty, to proclaim the emergency; an emergency which gave him a right to receive support from his people. Such an emergency had to involve the common good and could not be of the ruler's mere contriving. By the thirteenth century the phrase 'evident and urgent necessity' attested its legitimate usage.[2] To whom was it evident? Not to the ruler alone. The appeal to the common good was basically democratic. The twelfth century already held firmly to the doctrine that the just ruler ruled for the good of his people, the tyrant according to his own will, and the principle 'quod omnes tangit ab omnibus comprobetur', if not yet applied in the realm of public law, bore witness to the element of consent in Roman legal thought. Reinforcing in feudal monarchies the notion that departure from custom could only be legitimized by common consent, it meant that the case of necessity had to be attested and agreed by the realm itself. The consent of all had to be given to a necessity which touched all.

The plea of necessity, therefore, implied both obligation and consent. Not consent to a tax, to a free alienation of one's goods or rights, but to the plea of necessity by which those rights might legitimately be overridden in the name of the common good. Once he had accepted the plea of necessity the subject was under obligation to render aid; he could not refuse. He could, indeed, question the necessity, but this was not easy, particularly as war became more discernibly between kingdoms

---

[1] Roger of Hoveden, *Chronica*, ed. W. Stubbs, iii (R.S., 1870), pp. 209–10: 'Quem autem in necessitate nostra promptum inveniemus in suis necessitatibus amicum nos reperiet et remuneratorem.' Hubert Walter, when he attempted to secure a grant of 300 knights for Richard in the council at Oxford in 1197, according to the author of the life of Saint Hugh, 'regias proposuit necessitates': *The Life of Saint Hugh of Lincoln*, edited and translated by D. L. Douie and H. Farmer, ii (London, 1962), p. 98.

[2] G. Post, op. cit., p. 258 n. 31 collects a number of examples of its usage.

and could be seen to have decisive effects for their inhabitants. Although at first sight curtailing the subject's right of free consent, the plea of necessity in fact provided greater security against arbitrary demands by the ruler, for it placed the subject's right of consent within the framework of a specific legal obligation rather than an undefined notion of traditional usage.

Such was the theory of taxation formulated by the civilians and canonists. How consciously it underlay the thirteenth of 1207 hardly matters, for these notions were clearly permeating political thought and feudal custom at the time, and were to exert even greater influence as national taxation became more frequent in the thirteenth century. For in 1215 many of the problems inherent in these theories had not yet been raised, and were only to achieve laborious definition over the next century and a half. Much debate was to take place before the case of necessity was fully defined, and in the early thirteenth century this stemmed in part at least, from the difficulty of separating the necessity of the King from that of the realm. As we have seen, feudalism recognized the vassal's obligation to aid his lord in extraordinary need, and the English monarchy was still in many respects feudal, as in the military service due from its subjects and in the tenure of overseas lands under the suzerainty of the King of France. A situation which could furnish occasion for prolonged disputes over the obligation of an English vassal to serve overseas presented comparable difficulties when it came to urging the case of national emergency.[1] Did an expedition to Poitou constitute a 'necessity of the realm' which could justify the levy of a tax in England? If the case was pleaded in terms of the defence of the King's rights, was the King's necessity synonymous with that of the realm? Kings undoubtedly saw the opportunities and advantages which Roman law gave them of identifying their own interests with those of the realm: John in a summons to a great council in 1205 did not hesitate to identify the 'magna et ardua negotia' of his war against Philip with the 'utilitas communis' of the realm, just as the writ for the assessment of the thirteenth coupled 'the defence of our realm' with 'the recovery of our

[1] For the disputes about service overseas, see I. J. Sanders, *Feudal Military Service in England* (Oxford, 1956), pp. 52–4; J. C. Holt, *Magna Carta*, pp. 64, 216.

rights'.[1] However, the equation was not to remain acceptable to subjects for very long.

Another problem inherent in an obligatory national tax was whether the case of emergency could still be pleaded when the threat to the realm became recurrent rather than exceptional. The sense that it could not remained strong throughout the first decades of the thirteenth century and drove kings to meet recurrent war expenditure through the levy of annual scutages and tallages rather than national taxes. More distant was the problem of what body had the authority to give the approval of the realm to the King's plea of necessity; for the moment the sufficient answer was that this should be sought from the widest possible circle of the King's immediate vassals. The common counsel of the realm which clause 12 of *Magna Carta* affirmed as necessary for imposing an extraordinary aid was to be sought by summoning all tenants in chief at a fixed day and place to proceed by the counsel of those then present. Clearly this was in no sense expected to rubber-stamp the King's wishes. Notice was required of the business under discussion, and the debate and dispute which took place over the grant of 1207 and in the assemblies of Henry III's reign indicate that it was expected both to scrutinize the King's demands and to make a significant act of authorization. As such its decision would have to be unanimous, or virtually so. Was such agreement binding on dissentients and absentees? In practice, surely, yes. Although this is not necessarily implied by the provision in clause 14 that the business should proceed even if all those summoned had not come, and although the levying of the tax at times encountered opposition on the ground that the individual had not given his consent, a notion that common agreement gave the authoritative approval of the realm to a decision which touched the common good could not be reconciled with freedom of individual refusal.[2]

[1] Stubbs, *Select Charters*, pp. 277–8; cf. Post, op. cit., p. 384; Mitchell, *Studies*, p. 85 n. 1. It is interesting that the Statute of Pamiers (quoted by Holt, *Magna Carta*, p. 65 n. 6) released the count's knights from obligation to follow him to war outside the realm 'si comes non necessitate sua aut terre sue, set pro voluntate propria vellet juvare aliquem vel aliquos in guerra'.
[2] On this Mitchell (*Taxation*, pp. 191–2) and Clarke (*Medieval Representation and Consent*, pp. 256–7) take different views. Although the phrase 'commune consilium regni' does not seem to have been applied to the council at Oxford in 1207, it

Thus notions of public obligation, though still imperfect in many respects, were sufficiently present in the first occasion of national taxation to suggest that these rather than feudal custom were its source. Feudal taxation, itself adapting to new requirements, paved the way; but the decisive advantage of the lay subsidy was its immense yield. It was precisely this that signalized it as a new kind of taxation. For a tax of this kind could only be levied from the whole realm as an occasional measure to meet a common need. This preserved it from hostile reaction, whereas the persistent attempt of the Crown to exploit its customary and feudal rights provoked an attempt to set limits to the development of the prerogative. The King was thus encouraged to seek a wider authority for taxation than that of a feudal lord, namely as the embodiment of the realm and the agent and spokesman of its needs. But he could only do this in co-operation with the community of the realm, represented as yet by his free vassals. The thirteenth century was to see Crown and people merge together as a community. To this development the fact of taxation and its theoretical basis would make a not unimportant contribution.

---

was used of the council of barons in 1194 which authorized the disseisin of Count John (Roger of Hoveden, *Chronica*, iii, pp. 236–7).

CHAPTER II

The Growth of National Taxation,
1217–1290

In the seventy-five years following the Great Charter, national taxes on movable property became an accepted and familiar, if still occasional, element in royal government. The first stage in this process, completed by 1237, saw the aid on movables emerge as a well-defined tax, distinguished from feudal and prerogative levies by the requirement of consent, and demanded only as an exceptional measure. Although this development took place primarily in response to royal needs, baronial influence helped to establish the terms on which the King's plea of necessity should be adjudicated and the form of consent rendered to it. For, despite the omission of cap. 12 and cap. 14 from subsequent issues of *Magna Carta*, the principle that such aids should be taken only by the common counsel of the realm expressed through a large assembly of magnates was consistently maintained.[1]

In the early thirteenth century the King's right to levy different types of taxes was being rapidly defined. A distinction was being drawn between those customary, or 'prerogative' levies which did not need consent and the innovations or extensions of custom which did. Among the former the King's right to tallage his demesne at will was clear, even though custom forbade him to do this with unreasonable frequency. The development of a legal notion of the royal demesne based on this right, and the inducement to exploit its economic resources were expressed in the increasing use of *per capita* assessments in place of the old compositions.[2] *Auxilia* and *dona* no longer had a place in these dealings; by 1255 even London was brought to acknowledge that it answered for *tallagium* not

---

[1] For appeal to this principle in Henry III's reign, see J. C. Holt, *Magna Carta*, p. 288.

[2] R. S. Hoyt, *The Royal Demesne in English Constitutional History*, pp. 116, 202–6; Mitchell, *Taxation*, pp. 340–3; B. P. Wolffe, *The Royal Demesne in English History* (London, 1971), pp. 23–4.

auxilium.[1] The two terms were no longer interchangeable as in the twelfth century, for *auxilium* had come to be associated with consent. Scutage likewise became clearly distinguished from aids. The consent which John had sought for that of 1204 was doubtless exceptional, and *Magna Carta* cap. 12, lacking any sanction in custom, never became written law. If the amount of scutage was still expected to be reasonable, a close examination of the occasions on which it was taken under Henry III left S. K. Mitchell in no doubt that it was consistently treated as a feudal right, for which no consent was required.[2] Here again the very tensions between Henry and his magnates over war and foreign policy reinforced definition. Their refusal of financial aid for the King's expeditions contrasted with their acknowledged duty to render the *servitium debitum* or scutage. The latter was recognized explicitly by the barons in 1232 and 1254 and affirmed by the King in 1242 and 1253. In 1233 when the King wanted to levy a scutage for the campaign against Richard Marshal, but lacked the right to do so, he apparently envisaged seeking consent.[3] When in 1242, following the magnates' refusal of aid, Henry took a scutage for the Poitou campaign, the attempt by the Exchequer to levy this on all knights' fees, which if successful would have turned scutage into a national tax, was spuriously justified as having been granted 'per commune consilium regni'.[4] On this occasion, as previously in 1229 and 1230, the ecclesiastical tenants in chief were allowed to grant an *auxilium* to the King in lieu of scutage —without forming a precedent to the King's detriment. The importance of consent for innovations and its sharp differentiation from prerogative right is evident in all these examples.

On four occasions, however, an aid was levied by means of

---

[1] Mitchell, *Taxation*, pp. 324–8.

[2] Mitchell, *Studies*, pp. 339–46. Magnate consent was sought in 1217 for an aid levied as a scutage to pay the indemnity to Prince Louis and in 1229 when scutage was levied at the rate of 3 marks. These were both said to be assessed by the common counsel of the realm, and the scutage of 1230 for Poitou was assessed by the magnates with the army. In both 1229 and 1230 ecclesiastical tenants were allowed to treat their payments as 'aid' (Holt, *Magna Carta*, pp. 219–22; Mitchell, *Taxation*, pp. 180–93).

[3] Mitchell, *Studies*, p. 206.

[4] Ibid., p. 235, citing T. Madox, *History and Antiquities of the Exchequer*, 2nd ed. (London, 1769) i. 681, note. p.) In 1242, as in 1229, the rate was at 3 marks, probably another reason for alleging consent.

a scutage. On the first two of these, in 1217 and 1235, this was to meet royal debts for which the magnates were under no obligation to assist the Crown. In both cases this was granted at a great council, and though called a scutage in the writs, it was levied as an *auxilium* or *donum* on those clergy who did not hold by knight service.[1] This was its essential character. The aids of 1245 and 1253, however, were recognized feudal obligations, for which the King did not normally have to ask consent. Henry does seem to have obtained consent from a great council if only in the form of consultation and agreement for at least two reasons. On both occasions the magnates had refused the King's request for an aid on movables, and the levy of the feudal aid was perhaps at their suggestion and certainly with their agreement. Moreover, as in 1217 and 1235, the aid was extended to the knights' fees of rear vassals and not merely those of the *servitium debitum*. Both levies were probably employed for the expenses of the Gascon campaign.[2] Thus in the thirteenth century taxes which in any way extended the King's customary feudal and seigneurial rights came to be designated *auxilia*, a term implying that some form of consent was required. Of the taxes which were acknowledged to require consent, carucage ended its brief history with the clerical levy of 1224, and both that and the lay carucages of 1217 and 1220 were termed *auxilium* or *donum* and were granted by magnate assemblies.[3] So too were the three grants of the aid on movables in 1225, 1232, and 1237; likewise on every subsequent occasion when the King's request for aid was refused (in 1242, 1244, 1248, 1253, 1257, and 1258) this was done by a full assembly of magnates.[4]

By what authority did the magnates render consent on behalf of the realm? Aids fell on classes over whom the King did not have tenurial rights: on subjects rather than on tenants. The

---

[1] That of 1217 was for the indemnity to Prince Louis, that of 1235 for the expenses of the marriage of Henry III's sister Isabella (Mitchell, *Studies*, pp. 122, 208).   [2] Ibid., pp. 240, 253.

[3] Ibid., pp. 122, 130, 153–6. The writ for the collection of the carucage of 1220 states that 'concesserunt nobis sui gratia communiter omnes magnates et fideles totius regni nostri donum nobis faciendum' (Stubbs, *Select Charters*, p. 349), but the knights of Yorkshire claimed that the local magnates had not been consulted and knew nothing of it (Holt, op. cit., p. 288).

[4] Mitchell, *Studies*, pp. 222, 239, 249, 254, 261. References to these occasions in Matthew Paris, *Chronica Majora* are: iv. 180, 366–8; v. 20–2, 334–7, 623, 682.

consent alleged from the knights to the extended scutage of 1242 followed the precedents of 1217 and 1235 in the assumption that the lords' consent comprised that of their rear vassals. In the early thirteenth century a ruler could still normally assume that the agreement of the magnates would bind all classes in the realm. The consent which the magnates in the great council gave to the aids on movables of 1232 and 1237 was treated in the writs of collection as binding on all classes down to and including the villeins.[1] Similarly the writs for the collection of the carucage of 1220 interpreted the common counsel of the realm as obliging 'all magnates and lieges of the whole realm'.[2] For all these types of aid, therefore, the consent of all those who paid them was presumed to have been sought and obtained. If this was a practical precaution and assisted collection, it was also evidence for the nature of consent and the authority of the assembly which gave it.

The consent which was presumed to have been obtained from classes not present at the great council defies legal definition. In no sense were the magnates delegates of the community, as in private law an attorney held delegated authority from his client to accept as binding the verdict of the court. Attorneys were becoming common in private and public courts of thirteenth-century England,[3] but there was as yet no hint that even tenants in chief could be represented by attorney at the King's council. Yet clearly there was a notion that the great council could lawfully oblige other classes to pay taxation in virtue of its and their consent. Perhaps the inspiration for this came rather from the matters involved than from the status of its members. The magnates were not in any explicit form attorneys or representatives, but they were able to claim that, as a body, they could treat of the great affairs of the realm. Their claim to voice the 'commune consilium regni' may be traced back to the last decade of the twelfth century and was a response to the growing political and administrative unity of the realm under the vigorous policies of the Angevin kings.[4]

---

[1] The aid of 1225 was said to have been granted by the free men and all of our realm (Stubbs, *Select Charters*, pp. 350, 356, 358).

[2] Ibid., p. 349.

[3] In 1234 a council at Westminster had permitted any who owed suit of court in seigneurial courts to appear by attorney (*C.C.R.*, *1231–4*, p. 551).

[4] Above, p. 25 n. 2.

During the thirteenth century the claim of the *magnum con-cilium* to voice the assent of the realm to 'magna negotia regni', which touched the interests of the subject, was widely accepted.[1] If we are anxious for a definition we must call this political consent, for the consent of the magnates to extraordinary taxa-tion was inseparable from their right to concern themselves with the affairs of the realm. For although the extraordinary aids of the thirteenth century were granted only by the King's immediate vassals, the fact that they were demanded for the needs of the realm gave them a public and national character. Taxation was part of the 'magna negotia regni'.[2] In times of controversy this meant that it could appropriately be used as a lever to induce the King to heed baronial demands for con-sultation, since the granting of taxation was an expression of the political harmony between King and subjects. The first clear sign of this was given in 1225 when in return for the King's gift and concession of the Charters by his own free will, all classes of the realm gave him a fifteenth of their goods in return.[3] Mag-nate resentment against the King's familiar council came to a head in 1233–4 with the demand for the expulsion of the foreigners under threat of deposition.[4] In 1237 the King's re-quest for a further aid was agreed to only in return for a promise to reconfirm the Charters and to admit three of the magnates to the council. The more elaborate scheme of reform in 1244 likewise had for its basis the reconfirmation of the Charters and the imposition of a council of the magnates' own choosing, together with the appointment of a Chancellor, Justiciar, and Treasurer, a demand to which the magnates

---

[1] Two examples of local resistance to royal demands on the ground that these had not secured the assent of the magnates were the opposition of the Yorkshire knights to the levy of the carucage of 1220 (Holt, *Magna Carta*, pp. 287–8) and the opposition of local communities to the collective liabilities imposed by the Assize of Arms of 1253 'because new and great changes in the law should not be intro-duced without the consent of the baronage' (Matthew Paris, *Chronica Majora*, v. 369, cited by M. R. Powicke, *Military Obligation in Medieval England*, p. 90). The need for consultation on *ardua negotia* was generally recognized in papal and im-perial circles in the mid-thirteenth century; see A. Marongiu, *Medieval Parliaments*, trans. S. J. Woolf (London, 1968), p. 34.

[2] Thus in 1242 when Henry summoned his magnates to grant him an extra-ordinary aid, it was 'de arduis negotiis statum nostrum et totius regni nostri specialiter tangentibus' (*C.C.R., 1237–42*, p. 428).

[3] Stubbs, *Select Charters*, p. 350.

[4] Ibid., pp. 324–5.

returned in 1248 and 1255.[1] Three years later the scheme of reform which invested the magnate council with authority for the government of the realm named a commission of twenty-four to treat for an aid to the King. Thus the King's obligation to govern justly and well, expressed alike in the confirmation of his subjects' liberties and in the taking of counsel with his magnates, was paralleled by the subjects' obligation to assist royal government by the granting of aid.

Consent, then, could only be a consequence of counsel. Both were an aspect of that participation in the business of the realm which the magnates claimed as the King's natural counsellors and which they sought to define by claiming to represent the community of the realm in relation to the King who was its acknowledged head. Such were the broad principles behind the magnates' grants of taxation up to 1237, but did their refusal to grant further aids in the following twenty years effect a decisive change in the nature of the aid, the character of consent, and the solidarity of the *magnum concilium*? S. K. Mitchell argued that it did. In his view the sustained baronial refusal ensured that the aid should be occasional, not customary; it established the principle of real consent; and it consolidated the *magnum concilium* by the need to maintain a corporate refusal in the face of the King's demands.[2] Mitchell's central point—that the corporate refusal of aid by the magnates changed consent in form to consent in reality—faces a serious difficulty. If the magnates had established a right of real consent, or free refusal, under Henry III it is difficult to see why this was not exercised to escape the annual levies of the years 1294–7 which threatened to turn the tax into a customary obligation. In fact, far from disappearing, the subject's obligation to aid the King in his need became more rigorously defined as the century progressed. The barons' success in resisting Henry III's demands reflected not the development of a novel right to refuse aid but their ability to place their own interpretation on the King's

[1] Stubbs, *Select Charters*, pp. 327, 328, 329; R. F. Treharne, *The Baronial Plan of Reform 1258–1263* (Manchester, 1932), pp. 52–5.

[2] S. K. Mitchell, *Taxation in Medieval England*, p. 163, and later (p. 220): 'The barons' success in refusing taxes also . . . repeatedly prevented the establishment of an aid of this kind as an obligatory due. It thus retained the original character of a gracious aid with the *added* trait that it could be refused' (my italics).

plea of necessity. This was the product of the particular circumstances in which taxation was asked and refused.

The notion that taxation was part of the great business of the realm was sharpened by the development of the doctrine of necessity. By the second decade of the thirteenth century the papacy was appealing to this doctrine to demand contributions for a Crusade to defend the Holy Land since this concerned the common good of the Church.[1] For secular taxation necessity could be pleaded to meet a threat to the safety of the state or its ruler and such a plea obliged all subjects to contribute their wealth or services for the common-good. Rulers were quick to appreciate that this placed a powerful weapon in their hands and demands for taxation came to be made in these terms as a matter of course. The two lay carucages of Henry III's early years were war taxes: that of 1217 to meet the cost of the civil war and the indemnity to Prince Louis, that of 1220 being demanded 'for our great necessity and the most urgent pressure of our debts and also for the safeguard of our land of Poitou'.[2] In 1224 the King had summoned the magnates to discuss the recovery of his and their inheritances in France, the former of which he identified with the lost dignities and pristine rights of the Crown of England.[3] That the fifteenth granted in 1225 for the protection of Aquitaine testified to the acceptance of this as a necessity of the realm is borne out by Archbishop Langton's negotiations with the clergy to secure a corresponding grant in 1226 in which he bade them recognize 'what great necessity faces the King in these days'.[4] Likewise

[1] E. Kantorowicz *The King's Two Bodies* (Princeton, 1957) p. 235.

[2] Mitchell, *Studies* pp. 122, 125; the writ for the collection of the 1220 carucage is printed in *Select Charters*, p. 349.

[3] Roger of Wendover, *Chronica*, ed. H. G. Hewlett, ii (R.S., 1887), p. 282.

[4] For the writ of collection of the tax, see *Rotuli Litterarum Clausarum*, ed. T. D. Hardy, ii. 75; also, F. A. Cazel, Jnr., 'The Fifteenth of 1225', *Bull. Inst. Hist. Res.* xxxiv (1961), pp. 67–81. The Pope had urged the clergy to make a general contribution corresponding to the grant of the laity in view of the King's needs in Poitou. Langton's letter stressed the case of the King's necessity: 'cum ecclesia secularium principum in necessitatibus sponte communicat, necessarium eis subsidium liberaliter impendendo, non est libertatis preiudicium, sed officium potius caritatis . . .' (F. M. Powicke, *Stephen Langton*, Oxford, 1928, p. 158 n. 2) and to the bishop of Salisbury Langton wrote: 'nos igitur, pensantes quanta necessitas immineat diebus istis domino regi . . . in suis necessitatibus liberaliter subvenire praeter auxilia quae totiens ei fecimus. Nichilominus tamen in hoc necessitatis articulo quintadecimam mobilium bonorum nostrorum ei duximus concedendam . . .' (*The Register of Saint Osmund*, ed. W. H. R. Jones, ii (R.S., 1884), p. 58).

in 1232 Matthew Paris tells how Henry's debts for his recent campaign in Gascony 'compelled him of necessity to ask for a general aid'.[1] The notion of necessity was thus currently associated with these demands, although the King's needs were more often cited than those of the realm and the recovery or defence of his rights or inheritance was not distinguished from the defence of the realm.

Indeed, the concept of the realm was not sufficiently strong or defined for 'necessity' to be used only in the context of *raison d'état*. Though war and the financial burden which it entailed were usually cited to justify an appeal to subjects for aid, in 1237 Henry pleaded the Crown's indebtedness arising partly from mismanagement and partly from the heavy marriage expenses of the King and his sister.[2] Thereafter, in 1242, 1248, 1253, and 1254, Henry's demands were all for aid for prospective or actual expeditions to Gascony or, in 1244, for discharge of the debts incurred in the previous campaign.[3] Even so the feudal character of the royal lands in France made it less plausible to invoke national obligation for their defence than in the case of England. Opposition to service overseas as part of the *servitium debitum* went back to the previous reign when the Unknown Charter had tried to restrict this to Normandy and Brittany. Henry indeed described the object of his campaigns as the recovery of his inheritance and rights, and the growing consciousness of the *status* of the King and the rights of the Crown encouraged the notion that even such overseas possessions were part of the Crown of England.[4] Certainly Henry was appealing beyond feudal obligation when he informed the citizens of London in 1243 that he was fighting in Poitou 'pro commoditate regni', just as when he told the baronage in 1248 that the recovery of his rights in Gascony 'also concerns you'.[5] When in 1254 he again asked for help in defending his land of Gascony he declared that it stood in such

---

[1] Matthew Paris, *Chron. Maj.* iii. 211; *Select Charters*, p. 324.

[2] Matthew Paris, *Chron. Maj.* iii. 380–1.

[3] Ibid. iv. 185, 362; v. 20, 440; Mitchell, *Studies*, pp. 224, 241, 249, 253, 261.

[4] Henry's demand in 1242 was 'ad hereditatem suam et jura sua perquirenda in partibus transmarinis quae spectabant ad regnum suum Angliae' (*Chron. Maj.* iii. 185; *Select Charters*, p. 360). Cf. G. Post, *Studies in Medieval Legal Thought*, ch. viii, esp. p. 385.

[5] Matthew Paris, *Chron. Maj.* iv. 242; v. 21: 'Ad jura sua quae etiam vos contingunt adquirenda in partibus transmarinis.'

danger from the King of France that 'without the common aid of our realm we are not strong enough to defend it'.[1] Yet the concept of a national war, waged for the defence of the realm, to which all men should contribute for the common good, was never attained under Henry III. This was due less to any deficiency in the theory than to the fact that Henry's expeditions were mainly overseas, were undertaken on his own initiative, and were at a relatively light cost.[2] The realm of England was never itself endangered or compelled to mobilize its resources in its defence. Until it was no binding obligation to grant aid could develop.

It was precisely because the plea of necessity was never exclusively identified with a war in defence of the realm that the magnates were able to challenge and refuse the demands for taxation. They were able to exploit not only the ambiguity of the King's plea of necessity but the ambiguity of their own position as both feudal vassals and, collectively, representatives of the realm. As his feudal vassals they owed military service (or scutage) with their quotas of knights and pecuniary aid on the feudal occasions. Twice at least they took their stand on the fulfilment of their service. In 1232 the earl of Chester reminded Henry that he and other magnates had done military service with the King and were not bound by law to give aid for the discharge of the King's military debts.[3] In 1254 the magnates declared their willingness to come with their men to serve the King in person if he was in danger, but refused a grant of aid on this plea.[4] When Henry met with the initial refusal of aid in 1242 he attempted first to secure grants on an individual basis and then strictly enforced military service on tenants in chief, with an attempt to levy scutage on fiefs of rear vassals.[5] Again, in 1253, Henry distrained his barons for service in Gascony.[6] Thus throughout the reign the performance of feudal

---

[1] 'Sine communi regni nostri Angliae auxilio defendere non valemus': Prynne, *Brief Register*, i. 3–4 (cited by B. C. Keeney, 'Military Service and the Development of Nationalism in England, 1272–1327', *Speculum*, xxii (1947), p. 543 n. 55).

[2] The refusal of the magnates to grant an aid in 1242 while the truce with Louis IX was still in being underlined the defensive nature of the concept of necessity. For a general conspectus of taxation under Henry III which emphasizes its lightness, see F. M. Powicke, *The Thirteenth Century* (Oxford, 1952), pp. 31–7.

[3] *Chron. Maj.* iii. 211; *Select Charters*, p. 324.   [4] *Chron. Maj.* v. 424.

[5] Ibid. iv. p. 181–2; Mitchell *Studies* pp. 233–5.

[6] Mitchell *Studies*, p. 254.

military service remained the most constant expression of
baronial obligation to assist the King in war, even though there
was a decline of the service quotas under the influence of persistent service overseas. Secondly the magnates were ready on
two occasions to grant a feudal aid when they were unwilling
to grant a national one. Both the aid of 1245 for the marriage
of Henry's eldest daughter and that of 1253 for the knighting
of Prince Edward were asked for and used for military expeditions, and each of these was levied on rear vassals.[1] Thus
the magnates were prepared to go out of their way to render
their feudal dues to the King while maintaining their refusal to
grant aid on behalf of the realm. They were able so to do because the campaigns in Gascony could still be treated as the
King's war which involved his feudal tenants, rather than as
national wars obliging all subjects for the common defence of
the realm.

Just as the barons did not regard the King's wars as constituting a necessity of the realm, so they contested the plea that
his debts constituted a necessity. Aid to discharge royal obligations incurred under exceptional circumstances had been
granted on a number of occasions. Those for Richard I's ransom, for the relief paid to Philip Augustus in 1200, for the
indemnity to Prince Louis in 1217, and for the dowry of
Henry III's sister, Isabella, in 1235 had been levied under
different forms (on the last two occasions as an aid on knights'
fees). In 1237 Henry asked for a national aid to discharge debts
arising from his marriage and the mismanagement of his
officials. Earlier, in 1232, the magnates had denied their
obligations to meet the King's war debts both on the ground of
their performance of military service and because he had
foolishly wasted his money,[2] and they only granted aid in 1237
on condition that it was set apart to be spent on necessary uses
in the realm.[3] This marked a change of emphasis in the purpose

[1] Matthew Paris, *Chron. Maj.* iv. 362, says that aid was originally demanded in
1244 for the expenses of the Scottish war, though according to other sources it
was to discharge debts from the campaign of 1242–3 (Mitchell, *Studies*, p. 239).
The aid of 1253 was associated with the Gascon expedition proposed in October
1252 which the magnates had opposed (*Chron. Maj.* v. 335).

[2] *Chron. Maj.* iii. 211; *Select Charters*, p. 324: 'pecuniam suam ita inaniter effu-
derunt quod inde pauperes omnes recesserunt, unde regi de jure auxilium non
debebant'.

[3] *Chron. Maj.* iii. 381: 'in usus regni necessarios reservetur expendenda'.

of the aid which was to become increasingly marked in the refusals by the magnates over the next decade. In 1242 they refused to make a grant because the money collected in 1237 had not been spent under the agreed form of supervision, and they asserted that it should have been spent for the use ('utilitas') of the King and realm as was necessary.[1] In 1244 it was said that the aids which had so often been granted to the King had yielded no profit ('profectum') to the King or the realm, a comment which receives support from the requirement of the 'Paper Constitution' that the money granted by all for a particular purpose and for the benefit ('commodum') of the lord King and the realm should be spent according to what would seem best to expedite.[2] Thus the magnates related their refusal of aid to their demand for reform, arguing that the misuse of aid granted for the common profit released them from further obligation until the King should have accepted baronial officers of state.

The recognition of the essential character of the aid as being for the 'utilitas', 'commodum', 'profectum' of the King and the realm had important implications. The needs of the kingdom were associated with those of the King as of equivalent importance; moreover in claiming to adjudicate these needs in terms of the common profit, the magnates acted as representatives of the community of the realm, not as individual tenants in chief. Such adjudication had to be a corporate act,[3] and it implied authority to impose a binding decision on the whole community—to pay or not to pay—to which the collection writs of 1225, 1232, and 1237 had already testified. Thus by the middle of the thirteenth century the magnates had gone a long way towards defining the occasion, procedure, and authority under which national aids should be granted. In 1254, when they had again refused the King's plea for a national aid but had agreed to render their individual military service, the regents put the

---

[1] Ibid. iv. 186; *Select Charters*, p. 361: 'pecunia illa expenderetur ad dicti regis et regni utilitatem, cum necesse esset'.

[2] *Chron. Maj.* iv. 363, 367: 'si aliqua pecunia eidem concederetur, per dictos duodecim expenderetur ad commodum regni'; 'pecunia ab universis specialiter concessa et ad commodum domini regis et regni expendatur secundum quod melius viderint expedire'.

[3] The corporate nature of the refusals by the magnates in the *magnum concilium* in 1242, 1244, and 1245 is, of course, emphasized in Matthew Paris's narrative (*Chron. Maj.* iv. 182, 362, 372; *Select Charters*, pp. 326–7).

plea of necessity explicitly before knights summoned as representatives of their shires, but to no avail.[1] If this was an attempt to seek approval of a national emergency at a wider level its failure only reinforced the authority of the magnates.[2] In 1257 and 1258 the great council again refused the King's plea for an aid for his Sicilian commitments. We are not told on what grounds it was debated; but it is not difficult to guess that the baronage refused to recognize that the King's debts and promises constituted a necessity which touched the common good of the realm as well as the King, or that this was a genuine need, not one which sprang from Henry's own folly.

The baronial refusal of aid was therefore not based on any new-found corporate unity or newly developed right to refuse the royal demands, but on the right of the *magnum concilium* to adjudicate these demands as part of the business of the realm. In judging them to be unjustified they took as their criterion the profit of the realm, and cited the exclusiveness and the incompetence of Henry's government as evidence that the aids had not been and would not be used for the common good. Their adjudication was only possible because they insisted that the granting of aid was a national and not a feudal obligation; that in granting or refusing it they were acting on behalf of the realm and for the good of the realm and that, as part of the 'magna negotia regni et regis', taxation was the appropriate vehicle for criticism of royal government. Such a stance could only be taken so long as the needs and profit of the realm were not wholly equated with war. The King's war, regarded as a war waged in defence of the King's rights, was not yet a national war which bound the whole realm. The King was, indeed, moving towards this conception, but the magnates were still able to maintain that the wars in Gascony and Poitou imposed on them at most a personal and feudal obligation. Indeed their readiness to admit their feudal obligation in terms

[1] *Select Charters*, p. 366: 'quale auxilium nobis in tanta necessitate impendere voluerint. Et tu ipse militibus et aliis de comitatibus praedictis necessitatem nostram et tam urgens negotium nostrum diligenter exponas.'
[2] So regarded by M. V. Clarke, *Medieval Representation and Consent*, p. 313, but challenged by Mitchell, *Taxation*, pp. 214–18. Mitchell's argument seems to ignore the fact that the magnates' offer of feudal service implied a refusal to treat the King's plea as a national necessity and that it was this for which the regents were seeking acceptance in approaching the localities through representatives.

of grants of feudal aids enabled them to forestall the plea of national necessity. The fact that under Henry III England was never subjected to the military and economic strains of the reigns of John or Edward I thus had a profound influence on the development of national taxation. In the absence both of pressure from the ruler to meet recurrent military needs and reaction from the subject against continuous demands the extraordinary and occasional nature of national taxation could be freely recognized. Consent did indeed take the form of an adjudication of the plea of necessity for which aid was demanded, but because under Henry III this necessity never attained the compelling character of *raison d'état*, consent did not become formal or legal assent to necessity but retained the character of feudal *concordia* and political *consilium*. Consent was never overridden by urgent necessity; instead the character of consent, refusal, and necessity could be slowly explored in the context of a constitutional dialogue between King and baronage in which neither side was powerful enough to shout the other down. Such a situation, however, was exceptional and temporary; it could not be maintained into the coming era of testing struggles in Wales, Scotland, and Flanders, of deliberate appeals to national sentiment, of large paid armies, and parliaments containing representatives. None the less the definition given to the purpose and nature of taxation, and the political consciousness which debate over it had developed under Henry III, went far to determine its development in the following reign.

Only one of the four aids granted between 1269 and 1290 was national in both its purpose and incidence.[1] The twentieth of 1269–70 seems to have been for Prince Edward's Crusade. For the fifteenth of 1275 we have a formal *pronuntiatio* delivered by the Chief Justice, such as was to become common in later parliaments, which explained the reasons for the demand and

[1] It is worth noting, however, that the writ summoning representatives of the boroughs in 1268 was to a discussion and debate 'super arduissimis negociis nos et regnum nostrum statum et communitatem regni nostri et vos tangentibus' (G. O. Sayles, 'Representation of Cities and Boroughs in 1268', *Eng. Hist. Rev.* xl (1925), pp. 580–5) a phrase which recalls the writ of summons to the great council in 1242 (above, p. 31, n. 2). The grant was not, on this occasion, made 'communaliter', but separately by each section of the community (Mitchell, *Studies*, p. 288).

the purpose for which the money was needed. By 1275 this was already the habitual procedure for submitting the King's plea of necessity for adjudication by the magnates on behalf of the realm.[1] On this occasion they were told that Edward I had spent his own wealth and that of his father in the Holy Land so that he had of necessity to ask his subjects for aid. However, this was the first formal parliament since Edward's return and coronation in the previous year, and by convention the King could probably ask an aid to support his expenses in securing his kingdom. The writs for its collection, which describe the aid as 'for the relief of our estate', likewise suggest that the plea had been for the King's personal necessity.[2] The thirtieth of 1283, levied 'for the present expedition to Wales',[3] was the first national tax for war in the reign. The writs which summoned four knights from each shire and two burgesses from the cities to meet at Northampton and York contained the most explicit statement hitherto framed of the obligation to grant taxation for the common profit of the realm. The Welsh rebellion, the knights were told, disturbed the peace of the realm; its suppression had been agreed by the counsel of magnates, nobles, and all the community, and it was better that the King and his people should weary themselves at this time by labour and expenses to restore peace and tranquillity to the realm ('pro communi utilitate') than that the rebellion should continue to plague their successors.[4] Here the elements of national emer-

---

[1] Gervase of Canterbury, *Opera Historica*, ii. 281. M. V. Clarke, op. cit., p. 225, cites this as the first example of the *pronuntiatio* made in parliament, but its ancestry was of course much older. Matthew Paris, for instance, records the speech of William Raleigh, the King's clerk and confidant, to the *magnum concilium* in 1236 setting forth the King's reasons for asking aid, and his account of the council of 1242 provides another example (*Chron. Maj.* iii. 380; iv. 185).

[2] *Select Charters*, p. 422; *Rot. Parl.* i. 224. According to the Winchester annals it was 'causa suae novitatis', and the first tax granted to Edward II in 1307 seems to have had a similar character. Cf. G. Post, op. cit., p. 392.

[3] *Parliamentary Writs*, i. 13; *Select Charters*, p. 462.

[4] *Parl. Writs*, i. 10; *Select Charters*, pp. 457–8: 'propter quod negotium quod ad ipsorum versutiam reprimendam jam incepimus de consilio procerum et magnatum regni nostri necnon et totius communitatis ejusdem, ad praesens proponimus ad nostram et totius regni pacem et tranquillitatem perpetuam Deo concedente finaliter terminare, commodius etiam et decentius esse perpendimus quod nos et incolae terra nostrae ad ipsorum malitiam totaliter destruendam, pro communi utilitate, laboribus et expensis fatigemur hac vice, licet onus difficile videatur, quam huiusmodi turbatione per Walenses ipsos pro voluntate sua futuris temporibus cruciari . . .'

gency, acknowledgement of this by the magnates, and obligation on the realm to assist the King for the common profit were
embodied in language which anticipated the pleas of the next
decade. The occasion for the fifteenth of 1290 is rather more
obscure. In 1289, during the King's absence, the Treasurer had
put to the great council the King's request for aid to meet his
war expenses in Gascony over the previous three years, but the
magnates had refused to consider the request until Edward
returned to England.[1] It was not until the long parliament of
April to July 1290 that the magnates discussed the King's
demand. Whether this was still made on the same ground is
impossible to say, for the writs for its collection make no mention of its purpose, but in fact the grant of what was to be one
of the most onerous levies of the thirteenth century was really
purchased by a number of concessions. In May Edward had
secured from the magnates a grant of an aid *pur fille marier* at
40 shillings the knight's fee, but this was put in suspense; on
8 July the statute *Quia Emptores* was published to meet the
wishes of his tenants in chief. Ten days later, as the knights
arrived, Edward issued the edict expelling the Jews. Edward
may also have set before parliament the prospect of a Crusade,
since he had just sent his acceptance of the project to Pope
Nicholas IV.[2] All this points to the lack of any clear ground of
national necessity on which the demand for extraordinary
taxation could be based and the consequent difficulty of
obliging the subject to render consent.

There is every indication that for all these four levies consent
had been obtained, in the first instance, from the magnates to
whom the plea of necessity had been submitted. As J. G.
Edwards has shown, it was in this period between 1268 and
1295, and in respect of the King's demands for taxation, that
the writ requiring representatives to come 'with full power to
do what shall be ordained by common counsel' was evolved.[3]

---

[1] Thomas Wykes, *Chronicon*, in *Annales Monastici*, ed. H. R. Luard, iv (R.S.,
1869), p. 316.

[2] F. M. Powicke, *The Thirteenth Century*, pp. 265–8, 513. Walter of Guisborough,
Chronicle, ed. H. Rothwell (Camden Soc., vol. lxxxix), p. 227 had no doubt that it
was granted 'pro expulsione Judaeorum'.

[3] J. G. Edwards, 'The *Plena Potestas* of English Parliamentary Representatives',
Oxford Essays in Medieval History presented to H. E. Salter (Oxford, 1934), pp. 141–54,
and subsequently reprinted in *Historical Studies of the English Parliament*, ed. E. B.

But the evolution of this formula makes it clear that initially the representatives had been summoned merely to ratify the magnates' acceptance of the plea of necessity. In 1283 when representatives were summoned 'to hear and do what we shall cause to be shown to them', their grant was made 'according to what the magnates provided and agreed on in relief of this kind'; in 1290 the writs which explicitly required them to come 'to counsel and consent on those things which the earls, barons and nobles shall be led to agree upon' were issued when the magnates had certainly debated the King's request and, in all probability, agreed to grant a fifteenth. Thus while the summoning of representatives is a clear indication that the *magnum concilium* was no longer thought able to bind the whole realm in granting taxation, it is no less clear that it had been able to do this until quite recently.[1] But though in 1290 the magnates could still give an effective answer on behalf of the realm to the King's demand for a tax, the increasing demands made on the communities for money and services required that they should bind themselves by a more direct and active consent. The power of representatives to bind their communities could only be fully exercised if they themselves adjudicated the necessity and gave their agreement to it. Thus representatives had (by 1295) been brought into that common counsel of the realm along with the magnates to give (as the writs came to recognize by Edward II's reign) their consent to the necessity as part of their counsel. The magnates could have continued to give the counsel and consent of the realm to taxation only if they had been themselves the accredited attorneys of the communities; this they had never claimed.

Both the traditional procedure of submitting the King's necessity to the common counsel of the realm and the more recent tendency to enlarge the body giving that counsel were affected by developments in military organization and obligation. The practice of the King in seeking the agreement of his tenants in chief for undertaking war went back at least to the

Fryde and Edward Miller, i (Cambridge, 1970), pp. 136–49. The writs of summons are given in *Select Charters*, pp. 458, 473, 476, 481.

[1] This is not the view of Edwards who holds that at no time in the thirteenth century did the magnates claim or have power to give a corporate consent binding upon everyone. This, he thinks, was the view solely of the King and his ministers (op. cit., pp. 149 and 144).

twelfth century and was an expression of their normal and necessary *concordia*.[1] Here again the refusals by the magnates to give general support to Henry III's wars in Poitou, Gascony, and Sicily, on grounds of policy, brought into question the nature of this *concordia* and directly linked it with the obligation to render financial aid. Just as the King's demand for taxation in his necessity was submitted to the *magnum concilium* for adjudication, so the formulae of the writs of summons to the host attest the King's personal presence on the expedition, the cause of the expedition, and the fact of consent given by the magnates or the council. Here too the general endeavour of the magnates was towards making consultation mandatory. Their support for Henry's Welsh and Scottish campaigns reflected a greater willingness to acknowledge domestic than foreign obligations. As in taxation, the Welsh war provided Edward I with the need and occasion for seeking an expression of national *concordia*, which would go beyond mere baronial consultation. Before the first Welsh war the *magnum concilium* heard the case against Llewellyn and authorized Edward to proceed against him, and in May 1282 at a large gathering of magnates at Worcester Edward summoned the feudal host for August. The November writs which summoned assemblies to Northampton and York in the following year stated that the war was waged on the advice of the magnates and whole community of the realm, and at the Shrewsbury parliament in 1283 representatives were present to witness the trial of David.[2] The terms in which Edward's first Welsh campaign was authorized, popularized, and paid for thus marked an important stage in the development of national consent to war and taxation.

Developments in military organization during this period likewise had important implications for national taxation. Although the restriction of feudal obligations to small quotas paved the way for the introduction of payment at the highest levels, it was rather in defining and extending the obligation

[1] M. R. Powicke, *Military Obligation*, pp. 225–7.
[2] Ibid., pp. 227–9. Powicke concludes: 'by 1294 the Welsh wars had provided Edward with military and political victories, but also with a habit of seeking consent which it would be hard to disavow'. For the writ of 1282 see above, p. 40 n. 4, and cf. J. E. Powell and K. Wallis, *The House of Lords in the Middle Ages* (London, 1968), p. 207.

of the knights and free tenants that the middle decades of the century witnessed a significant advance. The Crown's attempt to create an effective pool of knights sprang not only from their importance in war and increasing wealth as a class, but from the decline of the *servitium debitum* and the objections of the baronage to overseas service. The first general distraint of knighthood in 1224 was issued in connection with the proposed expedition to Gascony; the second in 1242, which extended the category to twenty-librate holders, was likewise for the Gascon expedition of that year; the final expedition of the reign, that of 1253, involved at least two writs to distrain for knighthood. The following year may have seen a further attempt to secure service from this class, closely paralleled by their summons to discuss the grant of financial aid,[1] and the returns to the order of 1256 show that by then most of those liable to take up knighthood had in fact done so. Here again the Welsh wars of Edward I's reign suggested distraint of knighthood to meet both military and financial needs. In 1283 the writs which summoned knights and burgesses to provincial assemblies also summoned twenty-librate holders to muster at the same place for service in Wales, though in the event the representatives alone assembled and granted fiscal aid.[2] This imposition of military obligation on an income group in respect of their fealty rather than as feudal obligation testified to the King's authority over the realm in providing for its defence and instilled this class with a responsible awareness of national necessity. It provided further grounds for their association with the magnates in the *commune consilium regni*. But participation in the common emergency did not stop at the level of the knights. Although the reissues of the Assize of Arms during Henry III's reign added no further definition of military obligation, that of 1242 recognized the existence of mounted men at arms and archers, and the employment of both feudal and communal elements in the Welsh wars of the reign formed an important precedent for the extended service of the latter in a national army. Of equal significance were the duties of coastal defence which these levies were called on to perform, for these sprang

---

[1] M. R. Powicke, op. cit., ch. iv, *passim*; B. C. Keeney, *Speculum*, xxii (1947), p. 538.

[2] *Select Charters*, p. 458; M. R. Powicke, op. cit., p. 108.

directly from the threat of invasion and presented the notion of emergency in visible form. Here the coast array for East Anglia in 1264 marked an important departure, with its provision for selective service at the communal expense. If this and Simon de Montfort's radical scheme for a levy of four or five men from each vill to be maintained out of special taxes hardly constituted precedents of sufficient authority on which to build an effective communal force, it only awaited, as M. R. Powicke has remarked, 'a leader who would use and develop it, and money—lots of money—to pay for it'.[1]

Gradually, and under many influences, national consciousness and the institutions which expressed and nourished this were being born. The Crown was coming to stand for more than the person and interests of the King; it embodied the continuity and life blood of the realm. Wars might still be waged to defend the King's rights and suppress rebels,[2] but the King also had the obligation to defend the realm and call on his subjects for assistance in the name of the common good. The community of the realm on whom lay this responsibility, both in rendering military service and giving financial aid, was widening from the circle of tenants in chief to all free landholders. Consent to these burdens was consequentially enlarged both in the circle which gave it and in its nature. By 1290 all these developments were clear enough, even though they had not been exploited in concert, as they were to be before the century closed.

Such developments attuned with a growing interest in the theory of the state and an exploration of the mutual obligations of ruler and ruled. We have noted above that the doctrine of necessity familiar to the legists and the canonists of the twelfth century was already in use as a notion of political obligation when Saint Thomas defined the occasions on which a ruler might tax his subjects. When an emergency threatened the existence of the state the ruler might plead necessity to compel private rights to yield for the common welfare.[3] If in this pure

[1] M. R. Powicke, op. cit., ch. v, *passim* and p. 95.

[2] Although, as J. G. Bellamy has recently pointed out in *The Law of Treason in England in the Later Middle Ages* (Cambridge, 1970), pp. 56–7, it was Edward I who first defined the crime of levying war against the King and classified it as high treason.

[3] G. Post, *Studies in Medieval Legal Thought*, p. 318.

form the doctrine emphasized the overriding power of the
ruler, as formulated in the thirteenth century it was certainly
not a justification for arbitrary rule. The 'just' war, 'evident'
necessity, 'common utility' all set some limitation to the plea
of emergency and superior need.[1] Philosophically a reconciliation of the interests of rulers and ruled was framed by the
Aristotelians in terms of a mutual obligation to promote the
common good, a threat to which obliged the ruler to seek
and the subject to render aid.[2] A just war was one fought
for the common good, and only for such a war could the ruler
request aid. Necessity thus became the expression of the moral
responsibility which all citizens had for the preservation of the
state.[3]

Two questions emerged when this plea was applied in practice. First, who was to judge when the plea of necessity could
be justly invoked? Secondly, did the plea of necessity override the private right of property and sanction the taking of tax
without consent? In regard to the first, although the ruler had
the initial responsibility for proclaiming the case of necessity
and was encouraged to act and speak in the name of the realm,
a matter which concerned the good of all might claim to have
the approval of all. All theorists agreed that the power of the
prince was subordinate to the ends of the state, and for a
ruler to invoke the plea of necessity for his own benefit would
be an act of arbitrary and despotic power. The test of necessity
was thus its adjudication by the realm as being for the common
profit. Moreover, the principle *quod omnes tangit*, familiarized by
both civil and canon lawyers, implied that the ruler's plea of
necessity had to be submitted to counsel and consent in a
representative assembly.[4] As to the second question, whether

---

[1] Thus Henry of Ghent, writing 1272–96, asks whether a ruler can tax arbitrarily and answers that no ruler could levy an extraordinary tax except for
evident utility, evident necessity, or dire emergency. On any other terms a tax was
an arbitrary confiscation of property. Cited by Post, op. cit., pp. 295–7.

[2] Aquinas, *De Regimine Judaeorum* in *Selected Political Writings*, ed. D'Entreves,
p. 92; cf. Post, op. cit., p. 451.

[3] For the deployment of the term in demands for taxes by Alphonse of Poitiers
in the 1260s, see T. N. Bisson, 'Negotiations for Taxes under Alphonse of Poitiers,'
xiie Congrès Internationale des Sciences Historiques (Paris, Louvain, 1966), pp. 82–3.

[4] G. Post, op. cit., p. 15 and ch. iv, *passim*. This is forcibly expressed in *The
Song of Lewes*, ed. C. L. Kingsford (Oxford, 1890) in lines 894–5 and 929–
930:

the plea of necessity carried a right of expropriation of the subject's goods, it could be argued that it did, the private wrong inflicted on the subject being outweighed by the greater public good.[1] But the solution preferred was to make the ruler's right to the tax consonant with the subject's free consent. What did free consent mean in this context? Since it involved the subject's natural and legal right to his property such consent had to carry the force of a legal judgement; and as such it required the authority of the *magnum concilium* or parliament. Theorists might therefore view representatives as filling the role of proctors with full power of attorney to bind their communities, as suitors, to the verdict of a court. In practice their role was rather that of participants in the 'magna negotia regni' who bound themselves and their communities by their own judgement. This judgement of the plea of necessity was freely and critically rendered; none the less if they agreed that the necessity was 'evident', the representatives were obliged to render their consent, they could not arbitrarily refuse consent to a tax which the nature of the necessity required.[2]

In theory this adjudication of the necessity provided a clear check to and limitation on the ruler's arbitrary power. Any tax that was unnecessary was illegal, and the necessity had, by definition, to be judged in terms of the common profit and in law by the community who were affected. On any other terms

---

Et rex nihil proprium preferat communi
Quia salus omnium sibi cessit uni;

. . .

Cur sua consilia non communicabit
A quibus auxilia suplex postulabit?

A. Marongiu, *Il Parlamento in Italia* (Milan, 1962), p. 180, cites Clement IV, appeal to Charles of Anjou not to tax his Sicilian subjects arbitrarily but to submit his needs to the 'prelates, barons and community' to obtain their counsel and aid.

[1] See for instance Pierre Jaime's admission that the French King could levy taxes without consent for the defence of the realm, cited by J. R. Strayer, *Medieval Origins of the Modern State*, p. 54 n. 48. In 1285 Pope Honorius IV attempted to limit the occasions on which the King of Naples could impose *collectae* without consent. These occasions were mainly those recognized by feudal custom but also included the invasion of the realm. None the less the kings seem to have levied taxes on any plea of necessity and with no intention of allowing an assembly of those concerned to judge whether the request was justified or not. See Marongiu, op. cit., p. 331 (English edition, p. 149).

[2] G. Post, op. cit., ch. iii section 4 and pp. 307, 323 n. 37.

a tax was an arbitrary confiscation of property. But a war in defence of the realm was already considered *ipso facto* a just war, and on this ground taxation was being asked increasingly by rulers throughout Europe. Where the necessity was undeniable consent was obligatory. Such consent had to be freely given, but this freedom did not imply a right of uninhibited refusal: it was the free recognition of obligation. This notion of an obligation towards the common welfare thus bound both ruler and ruled in different ways, constraining the one to limit his demands, the other to accede to them. But such demands were by definition intended to be exceptional, for emergencies. What would happen if just wars became endemic, if the necessity became perpetual? This was the question posed in England for a few years in the last decade of the century.

CHAPTER III

The First Crisis over Taxation, 1294–1297

IN the crisis provoked by Edward I's war levies of 1294–7 the doctrine of necessity became the subject of public debate. Before 1294 both the demand for national taxation on the plea of a necessity of the realm and the consent to this by a national assembly containing representatives had been restricted to widely spaced occasions. The levy of taxation by these means in each of the three years preceding 1297 helped to confirm this as the normal method. The need for this taxation sprang from Philip the Fair's formal confiscation of Gascony in May 1294, quickly followed by the outbreak of rebellion in Wales and the formation of a Franco-Scottish alliance in October 1295. Edward himself invaded Scotland in March 1296 and expeditions were sent to Gascony in 1294, 1295, and 1296. In the latter two years the English coast was threatened by invasion. The danger to the realm was thus indisputable. Each of the taxes granted by the parliaments of 1294, 1295, and 1296 was stated as being 'in aid of the king's war which the king waged against the king of the French for recovery of the land of Gascony which the king of France had occupied', while the writ of summons to the parliament of 1295 described the business as being to avert the perils threatening the realm.[1] Lay opinion readily acknowledged the validity of these demands, and the absence of opposition probably made unnecessary any elaborate exposition of the case of necessity.

This was more pronounced in the concurrent demands for clerical taxation. Edward's previous demands from the clergy

---

[1] The headings to the enrolled accounts of the lay subsidies of 1294–6 are given in J. A. C. Vincent, *Lancashire Lay Subsidies* (The Record Society for . . . Lancashire and Cheshire, xxvii, London, 1893), pp. 186, 189, 195. The writs for the collection of these taxes describe them as 'in subsidium guerrae nostrae' (*C.P.R., 1292–1301*, pp. 103, 170; *Parl. Writs*, i. 51). Like Henry III in 1248, Edward was ready to assert that the war for the recovery of his rights in Gascony was something that touched all: 'quam istud factum tangit communiter' (*Parl. Writs*, i. 261–2 nos. 6 and 10). The writ of summons in 1295 is in *Select Charters*, p. 481.

in 1279 and 1283 for the Welsh wars and in 1290 on his return from Gascony had been made on the principle that the clergy shared with the laity the responsibility for the defence of the kingdom, to which they should contribute from their temporalities.[1] Clerical opposition to these taxes had been at times vigorous and partially successful. It was principally inspired by the concurrence of papal taxation on spiritualities which had been intensified by the new valuation of 1291 and the imposition of a sexennial tenth. This lent some plausibility to the excuse that the churches faced impoverishment by double taxation, but at the lay and clerical assemblies of 1283 the clergy had also objected to granting money for a purpose which implied the shedding of Christian blood.[2] It was plain that with any intensification of the royal demands, dispute over the legal and moral validity of clerical taxation for the defence of the realm was likely to erupt. There is no doubt that the case of 'evident and urgent necessity' was expounded to the assembly of clergy of both provinces in September 1294. Edward cited Philip IV's attack on Gascony not only to establish the justness of his cause and his desire for peace, but as evidence of the French threat to the realm of England and all classes of subjects. More explicitly than ever before the defence of the King's rights was identified with the safety and welfare of his people.[3] The Church was again reminded of its obligation to render aid

---

[1] H. S. Deighton, 'Clerical Taxation by Consent, 1279–1301', *Eng. Hist. Rev.* lxviii (1953), pp. 161–92, and in particular p. 163 n. 4 quoting Edward I's letter to Bishop Giffard of Worcester: 'Propter quae justius et rationabilius esse censetur, quod cleri communitas quae non minus quam tota plebs reliqua sub nostro regimine vivit, et nostra defensione et protectione in temporalibus et plerumque in spiritualibus protegitur et munitur' (Wilkins, *Concilia*, ii. 40–1); and again on p. 167 n. 1 for Edward's hastening letter in January 1285.

[2] Ibid., p. 166.

[3] Ibid., pp. 173–4. This is reflected in numerous sources. Thus Walter of Guisborough's *Chronicle*, ed. H. Rothwell, p. 249: 'Verum quia terre vestre Anglicane non sum nisi unus quasi malus custos et non tantum ipsa terra vestra immo tota Anglicana ecclesia iam in arto ponitur et movetur iniuste, nec continuare possumus quod incepimus nisi de eadem terra vestra nobis auxilium tribuatur, idcirco in presenti orationes vestras expetimus et vestrum auxilium implorantes'; and Peter Langtoft's *Chronicle*, ed. T. Wright, ii (R. S., 1868), pp. 212–14, reflects this, especially in the lines:

> Non pur co chescun à Deu prier dait
> Ke nostre rays Eduuard face bon esplayt,
> E pusse par nos aydes recoverir sun drayt.
> Si il fust utraé, cum ne voyl Deus k'il sayt,

along with the lay community; nevertheless only the threat of outlawry—the logical corollary, in Edward's view, of a refusal to acknowledge responsibility for providing for the defence of the realm—overcame the clergy's resistance.[1] Archbishop Winchelsea himself acknowledged the argument 'that the king cannot defend himself and you against the enemy without your aid' when he put the King's request for a further subsidy to the clergy in the following year, and promised Edward that in addition to the tenth which was then granted a further grant would be made next year if the necessity of war still existed.[2] Churchmen had, indeed, long accepted the obligation to contribute to taxation when the realm was in danger. In 1295 the clergy's only, ultimately ineffective, plea was the poverty to which they were speedily being reduced; but in 1296 they could oppose the King's argument from necessity with Boniface VIII's prohibition under *Clericis Laicos*. Relieved of the ultimate responsibility of opposing the King, Winchelsea again felt free to acknowledge the validity of the King's necessity when the debate was resumed in the November parliament. Edward, for his part, reasserted the great danger from the French and declared that if the clergy failed to meet their obligations, he would consider himself free from responsibility towards them.[3]

Le eglise de Engleterre si mal mené serrayt
Ke clerk ne lays homme dount vivre troverayt.

The writ of summons to the clergy, given in Bartholomew Cotton, *Historia Anglicana*, ed. H. R. Luard (R. S., 1859), pp. 247–8, refers to the threat to Gascony as 'quos communiter negotium istud tangit', and the letters of 21 October 1294 to the collectors of the tax speak of 'evidens et urgens necessitas', *C.C.R., 1288–96*, p. 396.

[1] Thus Walter of Guisborough, *Chronicle*, p. 249: 'Et iuste debetis domini karissimi et precipue ista ratione auxilium impertiri quoniam videtis comites barones et milites vestros quod non solum bona verum etiam corpora sua pro vobis exponunt et pro terra vestra non solum ad sanguinis effusionem immo frequencius ad mortem. Et vos igitur qui corpora vestra exponere non potestis, iustum est et rationi consonum ut de bonis vestris subveniatis'; also Bartholomew Cotton, *Hist. Angl.*, pp. 249–50.

[2] Deighton, 'Clerical Taxation', pp. 176–7.

[3] Ibid., pp. 180–1; Cotton's account makes it quite clear that the danger to the realm was expounded to the clergy and that aid was sought 'per quod terra defendatur' (*Hist. Angl.*, p. 317). In Langtoft's *Chronicle*, p. 288, Edward describes himself:

Jo suy chastel pur ws, et mur, et mesoun,
Et ws le barbecane, et porte, et pavylloun.

In consequence the Church's refusal of aid was followed by outlawry in March 1297. Thus the inescapable obligation to aid the King in time of great and imminent danger to the kingdom, an obligation which poverty might mitigate but could not totally excuse, and from which dispensation was claimed only by appeal to a superior authority, had been widely canvassed before the lay opposition appeared.

The same years brought the earlier experiments in lay representation to fruition. In 1294 representatives had been summoned to parliament in the same terms as in 1290: to consult and consent on behalf of their communities to what shall be agreed on by the magnates. But in 1295 the form of the writ was finalized as a demand for full and sufficient powers for representatives of the communities of the shires to do what by common counsel shall be ordained. The need for representatives to come with full powers and participate in common counsel was an inescapable concomitant of the demand for the war taxation of these years of emergency.[1]

So much is clear; but the implications are more disputable. Did the representatives' power to bind their communities by their assent imply a power to refuse that assent; and did the power to participate in common counsel confer a right to dissent from what had been ordained by the magnates? These are not easy questions to answer in the absence of explicit evidence about the proceedings of these early parliaments, but the role of these early representatives was probably very circumscribed. As we have seen, consent was requisite because taxation infringed the property rights of the subject; but this was in the name of a superior public right—the common good—and it is to this, the necessity which overrode their private rights, that the representatives rendered their assent. Consent was thus an acknowledgement of a recognized obligation and implied no uninhibited right of refusal. The obligation could only be evaded by challenging the plea of necessity. In theory the opportunity to do this came when representatives met the King and the council: they could then judge the alleged danger to the realm to be unreal or claim that the necessity did not touch the common good, but only the King's private interest. But in practice the case was predetermined, for the authorization of

---

[1] Above, pp 41–2.

the necessity lay with the magnate council, a body which could still speak for the community of the realm.[1] This council then laid the case of necessity before the representatives to receive their assent, which, though legally necessary and administratively useful for collecting the tax, was probably largely formal.[2] Yet even when they had accepted the necessity and thus obliged themselves to grant aid to meet it, the representatives could protect the rights of their communities by insisting that the tax should be proportionate to the King's needs and should not impoverish the subject by depriving him of the means of subsistence, while at the same time they might seek redress for their grievances.

Although the summoning of representatives to parliament did not mark any fundamental shift in political power, the knights were not a negligible element either in politics or war. Edward I was imposing increasing military obligations on men of this rank and the burden of war levies of all kinds was being justified in the localities as being for the common needs of the realm. It was the obligation to take up knighthood and to perform military service which most immediately affected this class. Pressure for the former went back to Henry III's reign, and Edward I's appreciation of their military role was shown in his summoning of individual knights to attend the King in the Welsh wars, and in the general order to the sheriffs to summon all twenty-librate holders to appear at Northampton early in 1283. In February 1295 Edward ordered an inquiry into those qualified for knighthood, requiring them to be ready for service at the King's wages. This was followed in January 1296 by an array of all £40 freeholders to ensure that they were appropriately equipped and in November by a distraint of knighthood for £30 freeholders.[3] If the basis of this service was the common fealty and allegiance due to the King, no custom or law defined its extent. Edward's summons to all £20 land-

---

[1] Cf. W. O. Morris, 'Magnates and Community of the Realm in Parliament, 1262–1327', *Mediaevalia et Humanistica*, i (1943), pp. 58–94; G. Post, *Studies in Medieval Legal Thought*, p. 331.

[2] S. K. Mitchell, *Taxation in Medieval England*, p. 228 emphasized that the assent of the knights of the shire was supplementary to that of the magnates; that it gave additional authority, while not supplanting or challenging the authority of the magnates. This interpretation is consonant with the language of the writs of summons which do not include the words 'ad consentiendum' until the reign of Edward II.   [3] *Parl. Writs*, i. 267, 278, 280.

owners to attend him for service overseas in Flanders was an innovation, the legality of which was bound to be questioned, particularly since it was accompanied by no promise of payment. It is significant that the writs emphasized that service was to be in the King's presence and was for the safety and welfare of the realm.[1] The equipment and service of a knight was a heavy financial burden and its imposition on the plea of necessity was to arouse opposition in the summer crisis.[2]

Appeal to the common obligation to defend the realm in time of danger likewise featured in the writs to tenants in chief and in the commissions for raising foot levies, though with less emphasis since in both cases service was rendered in respect of precise customary and legal obligations. Though tenants in chief continued to be summoned *per servitium debitum* throughout the reign, the attenuated quotas and narrow limits of feudal obligation necessitated an appeal in wider terms. By 1282 Edward appears to have believed that the key to enlarged service was to be found in the offer of wages, but the campaign of this year seems to have produced among the magnates a reaction against the idea of contractual service and few if any took the King's wages in the remainder of the reign.[3] Enlarged contingents were provided on a voluntary and unpaid basis for later campaigns in response to royal writs which invoked the general fealty and allegiance of tenants and their special obligation to defend the realm, as in the Scottish campaign of 1296. Such writs might depict in emotive terms the ravages of the Scots or the threats of the French King to subdue the realm, and the atmosphere of military danger which they fostered certainly spread beyond those summoned for service.[4] But appeal, inducement, and obligation met a firm barrier when used in demands for overseas service. Although the feudal summons was sent out for service in Gascony in 1294, in the event those who went served under contracts for wages, while

[1] *Parl. Writs*, i. 281–2, 285–6, 288: 'cum corpore nostro ad partes transmarinas ad Dei nostri et ipsorum honorem ut speramus et pro salvacione et communi utilitate regni nostri'.

[2] On the expense of a knight's equipment and the general reluctance to assume knighthood, see N. Denholm Young, *Collected Papers on Mediaeval Subjects* (Oxford, 1946), p. 63; *History and Heraldry* (Oxford, 1965), p. 20.

[3] M. Prestwich, *War, Politics and Finance Under Edward I* (London, 1972), ch. iii.

[4] *Parl. Writs*, i. 275–7; B. C. Keeney, 'Military Service and the Development of Nationalism in England', *Speculum*, xxii (1947), pp. 541, 545.

in 1297 the writs which 'affectionately required and requested' service 'for the salvation and common advantage of the realm' met with almost universal opposition, despite the subsequent offer of wages.[1]

Communal service was, by remote tradition, compulsory, but it was service of a very restricted kind. In essence, it was the defence of one's locality from external foes or (more often) internal disorders. The assizes to arms of Henry III's reign and the Statute of Winchester of 1285 had extended it to the unfree classes but had not otherwise enlarged its scope. Their effect had rather been to particularize the kind of service required from different classes on the basis of assessments of rents and chattels. From 1230 commissioners had performed the task of assessing the people to arms, foreshadowing the later commissions of array and establishing the principle that the inactive should contribute to support those who served.[2] These efforts at securing a selective and better-equipped force were the prerequisite for using the shire levies as part of a national army; yet there was little overt recognition of this new role. Service for an extended period and beyond the boundaries of one's shire, perhaps outside the borders of the realm, went beyond the customary limitations. Only in the coastal shires and along the northern and Welsh borders were there more definite traditions of defence, requiring all to take up arms against the invader for prolonged periods at communal expense.[3] The threat of invasion in 1295 provoked commissions of array addressed to the northern and eastern shires, and for the remainder of the century the northern counties bore a heavy burden, though with the Scottish wars the offer of pay became more usual.[4]

---

[1] *Parl. Writs*, i. 265–6, 282; M. Prestwich, op. cit., pp. 76, 85.

[2] Above, pp. 44–5, and M. Powicke, *Military Obligation in Medieval England*, pp. 85–8.

[3] M. Powicke, op. cit., p. 126. The commissioners of array for the North and the coastal areas during the invasion scare of 1295 were instructed 'omnes et singulos ad custodiam et defensionem partium illarum compellere possit quociens necesse fuerit' (*Parl. Writs*, i. 270–1). The 1264 array of Norfolk and Suffolk at the expense of the community was probably of the same kind (M. Powicke, op. cit., p. 92). In the first Welsh war the men of the border counties were willing to do service beyond what they owed (M. Prestwich, op. cit., p. 71).

[4] Thus the arrays of September 1299 and April 1300 were both at the King's pay: *Parl. Writs*, i. 326, 342.

The use of communal levies in national defence was only made acceptable by the offer of wages, but the point at which these should commence was open to question. In the latter part of the century it became the practice for the King's wages to be paid from the point of leaving the county or sometimes from the point of muster; but this still left a certain obligation for the equipment and payment of local wages to be borne by the community. This combination of compulsion and payment in general made it unnecessary to appeal to obligation or to seek consent. The writs of array certainly recited the threat or occasion of an invasion, but contained no appeal to support the King in his and the realm's need, nor did they invoke the common profit. In these formal documents the King held firm to the principle of compulsion. Only where he sought Welsh soldiers for the French wars—as in May 1297—were the commissioners instructed to demonstrate how much the King had performed for the common profit, for the safety 'of us and them and all the realm' and to ask for service 'in as amiable and courteous a way as they knew how'.[1] Yet even in compulsory arrays the commissioners probably had to induce men to serve by using verbally the arguments from necessity which figured in their own letters of commission, and there is occasional evidence that the commissioners entered into negotiations with local communities to obtain some form of consent to military service.[2]

These experiments in enlarging military obligation were only beginning to have widespread effects in 1297, but their character was already well defined. Edward needed a national army comprising a well-equipped cavalry and a large proportion of foot-soldiers, able to operate for prolonged periods on or beyond the borders of the realm. It was raised through a combination of compulsion, obligation, and inducement; by appeal to necessity and by the offer of pay. Both meant a greater burden on the subject, the first directly, the second through the need for money which the King would seek from parliamentary taxation. The national need, the common profit were being pervasively invoked to justify the subject's loss.

[1] *Parl. Writs*, i. 283.
[2] Keeney, op. cit., pp. 540, 546. See *Parl. Writs*, i. 320 no. 16; 326, no. 5; 369 nos. 7–10; 370 no. 13.

This was brought home on the widest scale by the heavy prises of the years 1296-7. One of Edward's first actions on the outbreak of war in July 1294 had been to seize all wool, wool fells, and leather on the basis of which he extracted the grant of a heavy export tax from the merchants, quickly characterized as a *maltolt*. This action had been justified by reference to 'the certain and urgent necessity', and the subsequent tax was claimed to have been ordained through the counsel of the magnates for the defence of the realm and the whole people.[1] Further seizures of wool were ordered three years later, in April and July 1297, when Edward turned to the direct exploitation of the wool trade; all those who had wool for sale were required to deliver it to certain merchants specially appointed by the King to buy it.[2] Payment for their wool was promised from the tax but, as the magnates complained, subjects were thereby tallaged arbitrarily and compelled to redeem their own.

Over the fourteen months preceding July 1297 three great national prises had been ordered for victualling the army.[3] This was a rare if not wholly unprecedented occurrence and the King's right to exact prise of this kind had never been defined. The legality of prise 'ad opus regis' was unquestioned in 1297, and from 1215 onwards complaint and remedy had largely concentrated on enforcing payment and prohibiting illegal extensions of the right of prise by royal officials, usually for their

---

[1] Bartholomew Cotton, *Hist. Angl.*, pp. 245-6: 'Cum nuper ob certam et necessitatem urgentem tibi praecipimus . . . per nos et magnates regni nostri, praelatos, comites et barones et per consilium nostrum pro defensione regni et totius populi nostri ordinatum esset . . .'—a clear example of the council of magnates authorizing emergency measures.

[2] *C.P.R., 1292-1301*, p. 299; *Parl. Writs*, i. 394-5. This is discussed by G. O. Sayles, 'The Seizure of Wool at Easter 1297', *Engl. Hist. Rev.* lxviii (1952), pp. 543-6 and E. B. Fryde, 'The Financial Resources of Edward I in the Netherlands, 1294-8', *Revue Belge de Philologie et d'Histoire*, xi (1962), pp. 1182-4.

[3] The list of these is given in *A Lincolnshire Assize Roll for 1298*, ed. W. S. Thomson (Lincoln Record Soc. xxxvi, 1944), p. lxxiii and Appendix III. They are discussed on pp. xxix-xxxi and lii-liii. The writs which authorized prises for Gascony in 1296 were careful to order that payment should be made but did not justify the prise in terms of necessity (P.R.O. E 101/585/1, 556/1) although the King's instructions to the Exchequer and the Wardrobe emphasized both the necessity and urgency of the demand (P.R.O. E 159/170 m. 122d). Following the crisis of 1297 the writs ordering purveyances employed more propaganda to imply that subjects had an obligation to assist in the defence of the realm by contributing goods and supplies. See M. Prestwich, *War, Politics and Finance under Edward I*, p. 131 citing P.R.O. E 101/552/4, 8; E 101/585/5.

own benefit.[1] The Statute of Westminster, 1275, had imposed penalties on purveyors who accepted bribes and provided damages against those who, having received allowance for their purchases, withheld money from their creditors. Nothing limited the King's ancient and indisputable right to take prises for his household, though these were local in extent and specialized in kind. The widening scope of prises of merchandise first evoked protest in the Petitions of the Barons in 1258, and the ensuing years of civil war saw prises levied on whole counties as a means of supplying the royal army. It was this type of national or semi-national prise which made its reappearance as part of Edward's war levies, but on a scale not envisaged in 1258. They were 'well organised, widely spread impositions to meet exceptional circumstances, so arranged that no designated area of the country should escape. They did not differ in nature from the ancient prises, but they did differ in degree.'[2] Such heavy periodic seizures were a serious burden on whole areas and all classes, for though they were to be taken from all men 'saving their resaonable sustenance', they may have touched the goods even of the unfree. Moreover, those able to secure personal exemption thereby increased the burden on their neighbours.[3] Even so, the charge in the Remonstrances that such prises impoverished the subject was made in regard to non-payment for the victuals taken, and it is against this and the abuses by royal officials that greatest complaint was made in the commissions of 1298.[4]

All these measures shared a common characteristic: they were extensions on the plea of national necessity of previous occasional obligations. Lay and clerical taxation, hitherto restricted to infrequent emergencies, was now being demanded regularly for a continuing necessity. Feudal, personal, and local summons to arms were being transformed into a general obligation to military service for long periods in defence of the realm and with pay at the King's option; purveyance for the royal household was becoming the basis for prises of large

---

[1] The best discussion of the preceding enactments on prise is by W. S. Thomson, *A Lincolnshire Assize Roll*, pp. lxvi–lxxix.

[2] Ibid., p. lxxix.

[3] Ibid., pp. lii–liv. See also M. Prestwich, op. cit, pp. 128–9.

[4] Thomson, op. cit., pp. lviii–lix. The terms of the commission ruled out protest against the right of prise itself.

quantities of victuals for the royal army. The opposition of 1297 was directed against the extension of all these types of public and feudal obligations on the plea of national needs. Dispute was not restricted to direct taxation or to the right to grant those taxes. It did not, in the first place, involve parliament at all, although it strengthened the role of parliament as the body which, supremely if not yet uniquely, represented the community of the realm and could speak for its common profit.

Although Edward I's disputes over lay and clerical taxation in 1297 were conducted separately, so that the opposition of magnates and prelates never coalesced, the fact that they were argued in much the same terms is of great importance. For Pope, Church, and King necessity appeared the central issue of clerical taxation. When, under royal outlawry, the clergy submitted in the spring of 1297, they purchased their pardon with the grant of a fifth which was represented as an acknowledgement of their obligation to defend the Church and the realm from the threat of invasion.[1] By mid-July, under mounting difficulties, Edward sought a reconciliation with Winchelsea on a personal basis, both King and archbishop holding to their positions. In Edward's mouth the danger to the realm was depicted in lurid terms: he spoke of his enemies thirsting for English blood. Immediately after the reconciliation he renewed his demand for money. Already when Winchelsea summoned convocation to consider it he must have known of the concessions of *Romana Mater Ecclesia*, and when it met on 10 August Boniface had in fact qualified *Clericis Laicos* to the extent of permitting taxation of the clergy for the needs of the kingdom, in a case of imperative necessity of which the King himself was to be judge. The debate in convocation, however, followed the pattern of the preceding November. The archbishop carefully rehearsed the King's great necessity, but the clergy felt prohibited from making a grant on account of the papal bull, though they asked to seek permission from Rome. But if Edward

---

[1] Deighton, op. cit., pp. 183–4; H. Rothwell, 'The Confirmation of the Charters 1297', *Engl. Hist. Rev.* ix (1945), p. 23 citing *C.P.R.*, *1292–1301*, p. 237. See likewise Walter of Guisborough, *Chronicle*, p. 288; who says that the clergy, 'timentes iram regis maximam et coniecturantes grave periculum imminere, ordinaverunt se deponere velle in ede sacra quintam partem bonorum ecclesiasticorum illius anni ad tuicionem ecclesie Anglicane et defensionem urgentissime necessitatis ut sic iram regis evaderent et sententiam in bullam latam non incurrerent'.

was to maintain the position that the clergy had a legal obligation to contribute to an acknowledged necessity, he had to
forbid this and any consequent sentence of excommunication
under the terms of *Clericis Laicos*. Reverting to his position
earlier in the year, he declared that in a situation of such great
necessity he intended to seize the goods of the Church by
royal authority, though on a sufficiently modest scale not to
warrant the charge of oppression.[1] The ordinance of 20 August
in which he justified this act to the clergy by an elaborate
exposition of the doctrine of necessity has been described by
H. Rothwell as coming 'as near the scholastic expression of the
doctrine as a political document well could'.[2] Indeed, Saint
Thomas had spoken in the *De Regimine Judaeorum* in almost precisely the same terms. A ruler could impose contributions from
his subjects provided these were not excessive. If he were fighting for his country, and for the common profit, he could levy
normal aids and even special levies provided these were not for
mere greed of money or immoderate expenditure.[3] In the
King's view the clergy's acknowledgement of the case of necessity obliged them along with other subjects to contribute for the
common profit, and their refusal on any ground was illegitimate.

The same argument, we may assume, governed the King's
attitude to lay taxation; but lay protest first expressed itself
over military service. At the highest level it appeared in the
refusal of the Marshal and Constable to perform their services
in mustering the host on 7 July; but their specific objection,
that the summons was insufficient and that they could not
judge whether they owed service overseas, was symptomatic
of a more general restlessness over Edward's military innovations. This encouraged the two earls to identify their personal
grievances with those of the generality of the knightly class.
These were soon to be summarized in the Remonstrances

---

[1] Bartholomew Cotton, *Hist. Angl.*, p. 335. See the discussion in Rothwell, op.
cit., pp. 32-3; Deighton, op. cit., pp. 185-6.

[2] Rothwell, op. cit., p. 34. The document is in *Parl. Writs*, i. 396. It declares
the purpose of the war as being 'son reaume defendre e ses enemis rebouter e son
droit recovrer', and that if in 'ceste bosoigne qi est si grantz' the King fails, then
'tute seinte eglise e le poeple du mesme Reaume serroient en peril e destruccion e
perdicion'; hence the King asks for 'commune ayde des clerks et de lays de son
reaume . . . pur la dite necessaire emprise fere a meintenir'.

[3] *De Regimine Judaeorum*, quaes. 6 (*Selected Political Writings*, p. 92), cited by
Rothwell, op. cit., p. 19.

delivered to Edward probably in the negotiations at the end of July.[1]

This document brought together the grievances over taxa-tion, military obligation, and prises which had accumulated over the previous three years, and comprised an articulated attack on the doctrine of necessity. Although it was sponsored by the earls, it represented the grievances as being those of the Church, the earls, barons, and all the community of the realm. The appeal to *Magna Carta* and the complaint of the neglect of laws and customs and the loss of liberties in the third and fourth articles denoted a charge of fundamental misgovern-ment which the other articles particularized. The first and second articles expressed doubt whether the King could require his subjects to do service in Flanders, 'for neither they nor their predecessors nor forefathers ever did service in that land'. Even if subjects ought to do such service, they did not have the means to do so because of the tallages and aids and the prises of corn, oats, malt, wool, hides, oxen, cows, and salt meat that had been made without any payment. By reason of their poverty from these tallages and prises they likewise could not give aid to the King. The sixth article complained that the whole community felt oppressed by the tax on wool at forty shillings, and in the seventh their final complaint was that the King's absence would endanger the kingdom by inducing the Scots to invade.

This amounted to a twofold challenge to the King's plea of necessity. In the first place Edward was charged with im-poverishing his subjects with burdens so that they could support no further obligations. This was something more than a mere excuse. No king had the right to ruin his subjects, for this was contrary to their individual good, and thus to the welfare of the realm. Saint Thomas had required that public burdens should be distributed among the citizens in such proportions as would promote the common good, and medieval taxation was to show a consistent regard to spare the poor.[2] The King's orders for the taking of prises had, indeed, respected this, but his subjects

[1] J. G. Edwards, 'Confirmatio Cartarum and Baronial Grievances in 1297', *Eng. Hist. Rev.* lviii (1943), p. 151. In the following discussion I have used the enumeration adopted by Edwards on pp. 170–1.

[2] *Summa Theologica*, quaes. 96, art. 4 (*Selected Political Writings*, p. 134). The burden of taxation in the years before 1297 can be seen from the list of taxes

evidently took a different view of their effects. This was part of
the more fundamental challenge to the King's plea of necessity
on the ground that his war was unjust. The scholastic doctrine
of the just war was still in process of formation, but the triple
criteria applied by Aquinas—of due authority, sufficient cause,
and right intention—can be recognized behind some of the
specific criticism.[1] The justification of any war started from the
need to safeguard the community, but in the baronial view
Edward's expedition jeopardized his person and endangered
the realm. Again, a war waged in self-defence was evidently
just, whereas Edward was attacking a foreign realm. The
debatable character of the expedition may have fortified the
traditional baronial opposition to compulsory service overseas;
it enabled Boniface VIII to make a more strictly scholastic
criticism when, in protesting against the taxing of the clergy, he
remarked that if the King had gone campaigning in Gascony,
which was his land, to defend and recover it, that would have
been another matter.[2] The recovery of rights unjustly withheld
was acknowledged as justification for attacking an enemy.
But an attack on Flanders did not justify an aid in defence of
England.

That Edward recognized in the Remonstrances a threat to
the principle of obligation on which his war finance had been

---

compiled by Edwards, op. cit., pp. 158–9. For a recent discussion, see M. Prestwich, op. cit., pp. 179–81, 191–3. Walter of Guisborough's *Chronicle*, p. 289,
speaks of the prises of 1297 as 'multe oppressiones in populo terre'. The *Song of
Lewes* uses impoverishment of the community as evidence of evil counsel, a charge
which was to be repeated in the following century:

> . . . queque dura
> Argumenta fingerent, que communitatem
> Paulatim confunderent, universitatem
> populi contererent, et depauperarent (lines 564–8)

Likewise the poem known as 'The Song of the Husbandman' complains that 'to
sethe silver to the Kyng y mi seed solde': *The Political Songs of England*, ed. T.
Wright (Camden Soc., 1839), pp. 149–52.

[1] On the just war, see A. Vanderpol, *La Doctrine scolastique du droit de guerre*
(Paris, 1919) and R. Regout, *La Doctrine de la guerre juste* (Paris, 1934) and the later
discussion of their views in J. D. Tooke, *The Just War in Aquinas and Grotius*
(London, 1965), pp. 147–50, 181–3.

[2] Quoted by Rothwell, op. cit., p. 21. Whether or not Gascony was in every
sense part of the realm (cf. Matthew Paris, *Chron. Maj.* iv. 185 and above pp. 34–6),
the kings of England certainly had rights there which they could legitimately
defend.

built was apparent from the answer he made in the proclamation of 12 August. Edward began by affirming the justice of his war by scholastic criteria: it was 'to recover his rightful inheritance out of which he has been fraudulently tricked by the King of France, and for the honour and common profit of the realm'. The burdens he had laid on his subjects had been just and needful, 'because of the wars that have been raised against him in Gascony, Wales, and Scotland and elsewhere, against which he could not defend himself or his kingdom without the aid of his loyal subjects'. This affirmation of the just, defensive character of his wars was extended to the present expedition by the argument that if he should fail to defend his allies beyond the seas the kingdom itself might next fall into danger: though the present expedition might appear aggressive, the war itself was defensive.[1] Nor had he used the taxes for his own profit—'to buy lands or tenements or castles or towns for himself'—but for the common profit, 'to defend himself and them and all the kingdom'. He was not sparing of his own person or possessions but (echoing *De Regimine*) he could not meet the threat from his own resources and had to ask his subjects to bear this burden because of the great need at the present time. Finally, by his avowal that the present war was intended to secure a good and lasting peace, he not only underlined its righteous purpose but acknowledged that 'necessity' was an occasional plea, that he did not envisage perpetual emergency as a basis for continual taxation as was already being argued in some European kingdoms.[2]

The central issue in the crisis—whether the King could impoverish subjects by recurrent taxation to meet a continuing necessity—had been stated by the Remonstrances. This document was an expression of grievances, a testimony to misgovernment; it did not frame demands or attempt to define the limits of the plea of necessity or specify how taxes should be levied. However, on 30 July orders were issued for a prise of 8,000 sacks of wool and the collection of an eighth on movables, and these provided the general movement of discontent with specific grievances and focused it upon the legal principle of

[1] The text is given by Bartholomew Cotton, *Hist. Angl.*, pp. 330–4, and is in Rymer, *Foedera*, i. 872.

[2] E. Kantorowicz, *The King's Two Bodies* (Princeton, 1957), pp. 284–91.

consent to the necessity.[1] By then Edward's quarrel with the
Church had resolved itself into a conflict between jurisdictions,
while the legality of his demand for military service in Flanders
both from the tenants in chief and the £20 freeholders, since it
lay on the borderline of feudal and national obligation, could
be endlessly argued. Moreover, before sailing the King had
reached some kind of settlement with the clerical and knightly
classes even if not wholly with their leaders. It was not surprising, therefore, that the earls seized on the issue of consent
as a means of reuniting the opposition in defence of a principle
of general concern, which was also relevant to the major issue
raised by the Remonstrances.[2]

Both the King and the earls acknowledged that consent to
the levy of the eighth was necessary; they differed over whether
or not the King had secured that consent from the community
of the realm. That it was the scope, not the fact of consent
which was at issue was made clear by the earl of Hereford's
protest at the Exchequer on 22 August. Edward had secured
consent to the eighth from an indeterminate gathering of the
knights and others around him, probably on the plea that his
need for money was evident and urgent if he was to defend his
allies and save his people. This procedure was, in a measure,
defensible. Both King and magnates upheld the right of a
magnum concilium in a dire emergency to adjudicate and sanction
the King's plea of necessity on behalf of the realm and take
measures necessary for the defence of the common weal. In the
situation of midsummer 1297 the King could hardly have
summoned a full parliament. But whereas the King claimed
that the eighth had been granted by the earls and barons for
themselves and for the people, the earl of Hereford complained
that it had been granted neither by the magnates nor the
community.[3] In his view those who had gathered in the King's

---

[1] Rothwell, op. cit., pp. 30–2, 183–5.

[2] See B. Wilkinson, *Constitutional History of England, 1216–1399*, i (London,
1948), pp. 198–9.

[3] The King's statement ('les ditz Countes e Barouns . . . unt grante au Rei
pur eaux e pur le pueple') is in the *Forma ad informandum taxatores qualiter loqui
debeant ad populum* printed by Rothwell, op. cit., p. 31. Hereford's statement ('la
ou le dite utime par eux ne par la dite commounaute unques ne feut grante') is
printed by Edwards, op. cit., p. 156. On the general point, see the discussion by
Rothwell, op. cit., pp. 178–9, 185.

chamber to make the grant could not claim to represent the interests of the realm and were thereby unqualified to adjudicate a necessity which touched the common profit. That left the King as the sole judge of the necessity and gave the levy the character of a 'merchet or tallage at will' which threatened to make all into serfs. Edward had anticipated this argument in two ways. In the writs sent to the tax collectors early in August and in the proclamation through the sheriffs of 12 August he elaborately justified the levy by an appeal to the evident danger to the realm and the obligation upon himself and his subjects to offer their bodies and goods in its defence, seeking in effect an *ex post facto* assent to the plea of necessity.[1] Subsequently, in letters sent after the protest of the earls on 22 August, the King specifically disclaimed that the tax would be turned to the prejudice or bondage of any subject or made into a custom.[2] However much they differed in their interpretation of the facts, there was thus a good deal of common respect for the principles of legitimate taxation between King and opposition, and this was later to provide the basis for *Confirmatio Cartarum*. In contrast to the earls' articulated challenge to the legality of the eighth, all they could say of the prises was that, like the tax, they were intolerable, 'mie suffrables'. For the moment they had no legal or constitutional formula by which the king's feudal prerogative could be limited so as to prevent the impoverishment of subjects of which the Remonstrances had complained. The earls concluded by declaring their intention to redress these matters.

The protest of the earls on 22 August shows that they had for the moment turned away from the broader problem of the cumulative burden of war taxation to the specific one of the levies of 30 July, which they were seeking to proscribe as having been made without due consent. The document *De Tallagio* apparently relates to this process, although until it is possible to define its status and provenance its significance will

---

[1] See the *Forma ad informandum taxatores* in Rothwell, p. 31, and pp. 184–5 for the King's attempts to justify this form of consent; the proclamation of 12 August is discussed by Rothwell, p. 32 and by Edwards, op. cit., pp. 149–50, and a translation of the text is given by Wilkinson, op. cit. i. 214–19. M. C. Prestwich (op. cit., p. 240) cites a writ asking the Barons of the Exchequer to appoint men skilled in addressing the people to collect the eighth.

[2] The text is printed in *Trans. Roy. Hist. Soc.*, N.S. iii (1886), p. 289.

remain debatable.[1] In fact its form presents greater difficulties than its content. Its first clause, requiring consent to aids from all classes of free men, spelled out in terms of the practice of 1290-6 the principle of common assent to taxation which underlay the protest of the earls. The third clause abolishing the *maltolt*, the burden of which the Remonstrances had deplored, was to be carried forward into the less stark promise of *Confirmatio Cartarum*. It was the demand in the second clause, that prises be taken only with the assent of the vendor, that most sharply sets *De Tallagio* apart from the Remonstrances (where the complaint had been of non-payment) and introduces an unprecedented limitation of the prerogative. Two considerations may have been in the authors' minds. To the extent that it was directed against non-payment, *De Tallagio* was anticipating cap. 2 of the *Articuli Super Cartas* in legalizing resistance to illicit prises. To the extent that it reflected baronial unease about the legality of the great national prises, its adaptation of the safeguards provided in the first Statute of Westminster against non-royal prises may represent an oblique claim that the national prises were on the same footing as these and were not embraced by the King's prerogative. However we gloss it, *De Tallagio* offered no solution to the problem of prise though it probably affords evidence of the movement of baronial thought upon the problem since 22 August.[2]

The gathering strength of the opposition which Edward left behind on 24 August had, by mid-September, forced the Regents to agree to summon a parliament of all estates, and the defeat of Stirling on 11 September was to make military and financial aid a matter of urgency. The writs which summoned representatives on 15 September, though they continued to treat the eighth as valid, reiterated the promise that it would not be turned into a precedent and further offered a confirmation of the Charters.[3] This provided the basis for *Confirmatio Cartarum*, once the Regents had agreed to the withdrawal of the eighth and the grant of an aid in its place to meet the

---

[1] The problem of *De Tallagio* has been reconsidered in the light of J. G. Edwards's criticism in *Eng. Hist. Rev.* lviii by Rothwell, in *Eng. Hist. Rev.* lx, pp. 300-15 and by Wilkinson, op. cit., pp. 200-3.

[2] Compare the discussions of prises by Rothwell, op. cit., pp. 187-8 and by M. Prestwich, op. cit., pp. 129-30.

[3] *C.C.R.*, *1296-1302*, p. 129.

threat from the Scots. *Confirmatio Cartarum* was both more exacting than the Remonstrances and more sophisticated than *De Tallagio*. It was an attempt to resolve both phases of the dispute: the long-standing grievances which had found expression in the Remonstrances and the immediate issue of consent raised by the levies of 30 July. Against impoverishment by recurrent taxation on the plea of continuing necessity it sought safeguards in the notion of the common profit; against overriding prerogative action on the ground of urgent necessity it reiterated the doctrine of common consent. Not surprisingly it achieved a more apparent and immediate success in the latter; yet ultimately it was the linking of common assent and common profit as the criteria for sanctioning the necessity which proved of greatest importance.

The fear that, by long continuance, wartime burdens might be turned into customary payments and subjects be thereby impoverished and reduced to servitude was deeply embedded. It had been voiced by the magnates under Henry III, it had inspired the Remonstrances, and it had been adduced as evidence of the illegality of the eighth. Clause five of *Confirmatio Cartarum* recognized the danger that even aids and mises which subjects had granted of their own good will could become a bondage to them and their heirs, and formally promised that neither these nor prises would ever be drawn into a custom.[1] This acknowledged that aids were, by their nature, occasional, special levies; even more important, it coupled them with national prises—'prises qe unt este faites par my le roiaume'—thus taking the major step of freeing prises of this kind from the shadow of feudal prerogative right and recognizing them as a form of national taxation. The

---

[1] 'E pur coe ke aukune gentz de nostre roiaume se doutent qe les aides e les mises, les queles il nous unt fait avaunt ces houres pur nos guerres a autres busoignes, de leur graunt e de leur bone volente, en quele manere qe fez soient, peussent tourner en servage a eux, e a leur heyrs, par coe qil serroient autrefoytz trovez en roulle . . .' While the force of J. G. Edwards's argument (op. cit., p. 167) that 'en quele manere qe fez soient' refers to the illegal levy of the eighth must be admitted, I doubt if the whole passage refers exclusively to Edward's action then and in 1294. The threat of a tax becoming customary was one to which the barons were always alive. Thus in 1242 they 'dicunt quod per illa amerciamenta et per alia auxilia prius data, omnes de regno ita gravantur et depauperantur quod parum aut nihil habent in bonis' (Matthew Paris, *Chron. Maj.* iv. 186). Cf. Mitchell, *Taxation*, pp. 372–6.

implications of this were drawn out in clause 6. Here the King bound himself never, for whatever necessity, to take aids, mises, or prises of this kind except by the common assent of the realm and for the common profit of the realm. That the aids and prises specified were the new national wartime levies was made explicit by the reservation of the King's accustomed right to the ancient aids and prises. By associating aids with prises, *Confirmatio Cartarum* strove to emphasize their common nature as exceptional taxation levied to meet an emergency. Both King and magnates already accepted that aids levied in this context required assent, and *Confirmatio Cartarum* had confirmed that this should be the common assent of all the realm, for such assent was in fact a judgement that the aid was for the common profit of the realm. Now the magnates took the logical step of requiring common assent for the strictly analogous national prises; an assent which would likewise take as its criterion whether these were for the common profit. By this they may have hoped to limit their frequency and give adequate safeguards for payment. For though the form of this assent is not specified and there were no precedents for guidance, it seems clear that the magnates had left behind the notion of individual assent of *De Tallagio* and now envisaged a form of national assent where the voice of the whole community could adjudicate the common need and common profit. To what extent the magnates could still embody that voice was not defined. H. Rothwell has called this 'the greatest of Edward's concessions in 1297'; certainly it marked a notable extension of the practice of consent rendered in terms of the common profit.

The notion that such aids, mises, and prises had to be for the common profit was as important in *Confirmatio Cartarum* as the requirement of assent, but what did this mean? Both kings and their subjects were accustomed to invoke the common profit, but where Edward tended to equate this with the common peril, as justifying his subjects' obligations, the barons had asked for charters of liberties which should be for the common profit of the realm. *Confirmatio Cartarum* did nothing towards reconciling, or choosing between these interpretations; but by linking common profit with common assent it ruled out a unilateral declaration of necessity by the King and encouraged future parliaments to assess the King's plea of necessity not only in terms of military danger but in regard to the common welfare. It thus forged a link between the grant of taxation and petitions for the redress of grievances, both of which in different ways could be said—like the statutes of the reign—to be for the common profit of the realm. Finally in *Confirmatio Cartarum* Edward remitted the *maltolt* and promised not to reimpose it without the consent of the greater part of the community. Common assent would operate here in a different context; but it was significant that an indirect tax had been brought within the same framework of grievances and promises as direct taxes and other charges.[1] Nothing had been said in the document about military obligation, but on 5 November the earls received the King's pardon for not having gone with him to Flanders.[2] Nevertheless, aids, prises, and military service formed a trinity of charges the continued relevance of which was ensured by the war demands of the next half-century.

The crises of 1297 was important as much because of the check it imposed on the first development of the royal plea of necessity as for the terms in which the clash of royal and popular interests was disputed. *Confirmatio Cartarum* was a conservative document, designed as a restatement in general terms of the accepted conventions under which a ruler might expect to receive contributions for national war. These conventions, framed by legists and schoolmen, were that the necessity for which taxation might be asked must be occasional, it required assent, and it had to be for the common profit. *Confirmatio Cartarum* did not attempt to define these terms, though the controversy had been over usage and interpretation. Nor did it set forth the King's right to a tax in legitimate necessity, for this had never been challenged and was self-evident. Moreover, in endeavouring to restate the conditions under which the plea of necessity could be justly invoked, it could offer no protection against repeated taxation in a just cause. Necessarily it left this central problem unresolved. The only protection available to the subject was a denial of necessity on the ground of misrule. If the necessity was the fruit of misgovernment, if the previous

---

[1] The concession relating to the *maltolt*, is discussed below, p. 424.
[2] Edwards, op. cit., p. 166. *De Tallagio* had provided for the King to pardon both tenants in chief and £20 freeholders for not obeying the summons to serve in Flanders.

aid had been misspent, or if the King's demands threatened to impoverish his subjects or destroy their 'liberties', then in the name of the common profit the royal demand might be questioned and refused. It was on these grounds that the magnate opposition had withheld aid to Henry III and it was to this tradition that the Remonstrances appealed. But because by 1297 the plea of national necessity had acquired greater force and because appeal against the King to the common profit was acquiring a wider basis the dispute helped to clarify the principles of taxation and ensure that the argument and the phraseology of the plea of necessity, which had for the first time been extensively employed in political controversy, would become part of the political dialogue of King and subjects throughout the following centuries.

The war taxation of these years had two other consequences: it strengthened the King's financial control and it stimulated the presentation of grievances. Both were to be of profound importance in Edward I's latter years and we must briefly review their development up till 1297. Before 1290 all the extraordinary aids granted to the Crown were administered as separate and special revenues, and even that of 1232 which was placed under Exchequer control had been kept in a separate account. Usually special treasurers of the aid were appointed: when the King was absent, or a minor, as in 1193, 1203, and 1225, these needed to be important officials or magnates who could be held responsible for it; at other times, as in 1207, 1232, and 1237, Exchequer officials were named.[1] In the former circumstances disbursements were warranted by the council, and the treasurers were held responsible for seeing that the money was spent on the purpose for which it had been granted. More normally, when the King himself warranted payment, the responsibility for seeing that the aid was properly spent rested with him. Since the aid had been granted to meet his specific needs, it was normally in his own interest to see that this was done. Thus the extraordinary character of the aid ensured that, from the first, it was specifically appropriated and separately administered. This made it easier for subjects to keep

---

[1] Mitchell, *Studies, passim; Taxation*, ch. 1. J. F. Willard, 'An Exchequer reform under Edward I', *Essays presented to D. C. Munro* (New York, 1928), pp. 225–44 F. A. Cazel, Jnr., 'The Fifteenth of 1225'.

check on and criticize its expenditure and, as we have seen, the barons had justified their refusal of the King's demands in 1242, on the ground that the aids previously granted had been misused. Yet even when aids were stored in a separate account, as were those of 1232 and 1237, they proved a tempting source of ready cash for a weak-willed, prodigal, and indigent King. None of the external restraints which Henry III imposed on himself could avail against the authority of a specific royal warrant for expenditure, since treasurers of the aid who were royal nominees were usually not of sufficient standing to risk disobedience.[1] If—as in 1237—they represented the baronial opposition, their control of the tax amounted to a general limitation of the royal prerogative. Henry's offer in that year to store the aid in castle treasuries under the control of four magnates and to spend it by their advice thus implied a return to the conditions of the minority. In fact the King quickly repented of his offer and by November had transferred the aid to the care of the legate Otho.[2] Again in 1244, the magnates' demand that the aid should be placed in the hands of a committee of twelve was coupled with that for the election of the great officers of state.[3] Thus, it was only as part of a general restraint on the King's rule, justified by his incapacity to govern and the harm to the realm which this entailed, that the baronial opposition intervened to control expenditure of the aid. Their object was to ensure that the aid was spent on its prescribed purpose, and they sought to achieve this by the normal and traditional machinery of special treasurers.

No other disputes over the spending of taxes occurred in the thirteenth century. The aids of 1269, 1275, and 1283 were all placed in the charge of special collectors whose accounts show them to have disbursed their receipts on the Crusade and for the expenses of the Welsh war.[4] In 1290, however, came a change. After the years of emergency in Wales and Gascony,

---

[1] Mitchell, *Taxation*, pp. 54–60. It is significant that when Henry III borrowed from the aid of 1237 he agreed to make repayment from the ordinary revenues of the Exchequer (ibid., p. 218).

[2] Matthew Paris, *Chron. Maj.* iii. 383, iv. 188, 366–7. N. Denholm-Young, 'The Paper Constitution attributed to 1244', *Eng. Hist. Rev.* lviii (1943), pp. 414–19.

[3] *Chron. Maj.* iv. 362–3. A similar demand was made in 1255 when the King asked for a tenth (ibid. v. 493–4).

[4] Willard, 'An Exchequer Reform under Edward I', pp. 232–4. The fifteenth of 1275 was handled by the Riccardi. See R. W. Kaeuper, *Bankers to the Crown*, p. 106.

Edward was anticipating a period of domestic consolidation. The Exchequer, under his immediate control, was to be the central agency for the revenue of the whole kingdom. The reforms of William de Marchia strengthened the machinery of the Exchequer and enabled it to handle all the revenues of the Crown, including the aids, though it was found convenient for a time to enter them on a separate roll. Through his warrants the King would now spend the tax in the same way as he did any other Crown revenue. This was a development of profound symbolic and practical importance, for it witnessed to the political and administrative unity of the realm under the Crown.

The advent of a period of continuous war, unforeseen in 1290, made these extraordinary taxes a recurrent element in national finance, but at the same time led to the revival of the Wardrobe as an active war treasury needing direct access to taxation. The reconciliation of the Wardrobe's needs with the principle of Exchequer control of national revenues was achieved by the device of assignment. While the Wardrobe and its creditors were enabled to draw directly on these revenues the authorization for such payments and the ultimate oversight of them was in the hands of the Exchequer.[1] This answer to the traditional tension in the medieval state between the demand for flexibility and the demand for institutional control was eventually to show its defects. Under a King who sacrificed everything to the demands of war, the Exchequer was reduced to a cipher. But this only underlined how greatly the power of the Crown had been enlarged by its control of national taxation. Henceforth it was enabled, on a practicably indisputable plea, to receive sums of revenue many times greater than had been available from its estates and feudal rights. Both the need for taxation and the ability to deploy it through the Wardrobe and the Exchequer made criticism of or restraints upon its expenditure much less easy in the closing years of Edward I's reign than in the early years of his father's. All this marked a new stage in the emergence of national kingship. National taxation brought a sudden and enormous accession to the strength of the monarchy; but the nature of taxation helped to determine the character of that strength. It was no accident

---

[1] J. F. Willard, *Parliamentary Taxes on Personal Property, 1290 to 1334* (Cambridge, Mass., 1934), ch. ix; M. Prestwich, op. cit., pp. 156–8.

that the English monarchy in the next two centuries was aggressive, that it was strongest—financially as well as politically—when it was actively and usually successfully engaged in war.

The effect of national taxation on the political development of the community was more gradual if more enduring. The heavy and exceptional character of the national aid as levied in the first half of the thirteenth century made its grant a natural occasion for recovering or restating the rights of the subject. The aid was granted only after long debate in solemn assemblies which served to affirm the reciprocal obligations of subjects to aid the King and of the King to deal justly with his subjects. The confirmation of the Charters in 1225 and 1237 and the King's sworn promise to observe them in 1254 were all associated with grants of aids.[1] In addition to these solemn affirmations of liberties, the aid was made the bargaining counter for specific reforms of royal government. Throughout the first part of the reign the baronial demands had always invoked the profit of the realm, and in 1258 the Petitions of the Barons set forth in twenty-nine articles a variety of abuses of a legal and administrative nature for which redress was sought. If some of these touched matters such as feudal incidents contained in *Magna Carta*, others, like that on prises, revealed how the widening range of governmental action was affecting the rights of the classes below the baronage. The period of baronial government encouraged complaint by petition, for which redress might be provided either by a judicial eyre or through the council. Individual petitions for favour or redress speedily became a major part of the business of the early parliaments, and though their political content was small, this was a development of considerable latent importance. The community of the realm was finding its voice—though as yet in the form of individual voices—at a political level. If the magnates were to continue to speak for the realm, they could not neglect this expression and must indeed endeavour to harness its strength.

In the second half of the century, the Church also began to exploit the royal demands for taxation to present articulated *gravamina* on which it hoped to secure concessions. In granting

[1] The aid of 1254 was a feudal aid for knighting the King's son, but it was in place of the national aid demanded and was granted.

a clerical tenth in 1253, the clergy had joined forces with the magnates to demand a reissue of the Charters as a guarantee of the liberties of the Church,[1] and in 1280–5 this precedent was extended by a series of *gravamina* occasioned by Edward's demands for money for the Welsh wars over which lengthy debate was joined with the King's council. Although the clergy complained of the burden of taxation, they were more concerned to win concessions on ecclesiastical rights and liberties.[2] These clerical *gravamina* were not without influence on the development of lay complaints. The authors of the Remonstrances presented their grievances as those of the Church, the magnates, and all the community of the land, and asked the King to correct them 'for his own honour and for the salvation of his people'. In the ensuing articles the emphasis on the whole community was strong: it was oppressed by burdens, reduced to poverty, fearful of losing its liberties. These complaints were not associated with the grant of fresh taxation, and Edward's attempt to levy the eighth without seeking consent from the whole community looked like an attempt to evade a settlement of grievances as the price of a tax. In the event, on the same day as the Prince confirmed the concessions of *Confirmatio Cartarum*, the magnates and knights granted a ninth. Thus the baronial leadership began to justify its opposition to the Crown by seeking wider articulate support, using the grievances of the community to demonstrate royal misgovernment, citing the impoverishment of the people as evidence of notorious misrule, and seeking to secure redress as the condition for a grant of taxation. Such tactics were to be more widely used after 1300.

[1] *Chron. Maj.* v. 359–60.
[2] Clerical grievances in these years have been investigated at length by F. M. Powicke, *The Thirteenth Century*, pp. 479–83; E. B. Graves, 'Circumspecte Agatis', *Eng. Hist. Rev.* xliii (1928), pp. 1–20; H. G. Richardson and G. O. Sayles, 'The Clergy in the Easter Parliament of 1285', *Eng. Hist. Rev.* lii (1937), pp. 220–34; H. S. Deighton, op. cit., pp. 161–92.

CHAPTER IV

Parliament, Taxation, and Military Service, 1297–1337

THE years between the battle of Stirling and the opening of the Hundred Years War defined the composition and role of the English parliament for the remainder of the Middle Ages. This was achieved not by gradual or consistent growth but under the fierce pressure of political controversy and military needs. For much of this period parliament was not so much a political force in its own right as the agent for other political forces. Its concern with taxation, with military obligation and prises, even with the presentation of grievances, largely reflected the purposes and opportunism of King and baronage. As parliament slowly acquired institutional identity so the Commons' own field of action became defined. By the end of this period they were acknowledged to be an essential and integral part of any parliament, their assent necessary for the grant of lay subsidies and normal for legislation, their authority to present grievances on behalf of the community of the whole realm recognized. It is not easy to discern the stages by which the Commons achieved a corporate identity and acquired these powers, and doubtless this is largely due to the insufficiency of the records. After Ayremine's roll for the parliament of 1316 we possess no further roll of proceedings until that put together by another clerk, Henry Edinstowe, in 1331–3. Even this was a personal effort, and a regular record of parliamentary proceedings begins only in 1340. In that year the Commons for the first time ventured to take political action on their own.

The frequency of these early sessions was the most important factor in establishing parliament as an institution. In these forty years there were forty-four assemblies to which magnates and representatives from shires and boroughs were summoned. To a few other assemblies knights of the shires and burgesses from certain towns were summoned, and at rather more prelates and magnates alone were present; but full assemblies of all groups far outnumbered any other kind. The frequency with which parliament met varied considerably during this period. Almost half the total (twenty-one) of such full assemblies met in the first decade of Edward III's reign compared with only six in the last decade of his grandfather's. By the 1330s the habit of spring and autumn assemblies, even if these lasted for only a few days, and the uniform description of these as *parliamentum*, testified to the emergence of an institution with recognized political characteristics. Edward III accepted, used, and extended the role of parliament for much the same purposes as Edward I had promoted its growth at an earlier stage, before 1297. Parliament gave sanction and support to royal policy on behalf of the realm; it embodied the mutual obligations between ruler and ruled in the practical business of doing justice, dispensing favour, granting taxes. But after 1297 the parliaments which Edward I summoned for support in the Scottish wars, though they at times backed royal policy with the consensus of the realm, also saw acrimonious disputes and a progressive weakening of the harmony between Edward and his subjects. In the two decades following *Confirmatio Cartarum* parliament was moulded as much by the baronage as by the King, and in these early and infrequent assemblies there arose the notion of a community of all estates in parliament which could speak for the community of the realm, if need be in opposition to the King.[1]

The barons were part of that community, and could still at the beginning of the century be regarded as spokesmen for the community of the realm, particularly in political affairs. Upon them rested the formulation and leadership of opposition to Edward II before the parliament of August 1311 in which Edward conceded the Ordinances. Since the beginning of the reign there had been only two parliaments with representatives, but six great councils of prelates and magnates all of which were, in contemporary writs, called parliaments. It was in these that the baronial opposition was formed. Although sharpened

---

[1] W. A. Morris, 'Magnates and Community of the Realm in Parliament', *Mediaevalia et Humanistica*, i (1943), pp. 63–4; J. S. Roskell, 'A Consideration of certain aspects and problems of the English *Modus Tenendi Parliamentum*', *Bull. John Rylands Lib.* l (1968), p. 442.

by personal grievances and jealousies this opposition drew upon
a real and widespread feeling of misgovernment.[1] Originating
in the burdens imposed for Edward I's wars, and exacerbated
by the old King's obduracy and duplicity over the concessions
forced from him, this discontent was fed by the continuing
oppressions and lack of military success in the new reign. Complaints against the King's officials, illegal taxes, and lack of
redress which met Edward II at the parliament of April 1309
provided every inducement for the magnates to re-enact their
role in 1297 as spokesmen for the common profit.

The restraints which the Ordainers imposed on the King in
1311 made it advisable for them to muster the widest political
support, both by promulgating the Ordinances in a parliament
of representatives and by exacting oaths to maintain them in
the localities.[2] Indeed, the opposition sought to make parliament the principal agency for fettering the King's authority.
The assent of the baronage in parliament was made necessary
for the appointment of the King's ministers, for the restoration
of resumed grants, for the initiation of war, or the leading of a
royal expedition. Parliaments held once or twice a year were
to be the place not only for settling vexed questions of law but
for securing redress by petition against royal officials.[3] Although
the Ordainers probably had in mind a large, predominantly
baronial assembly whose unanimity would preclude factional
influence and afford protection against royal reprisal, the fact
that they sought a legitimate basis for opposition in their role
as spokesmen for popular discontent compelled them to enlarge
the composition of parliament.

The presence of representatives of the communities as
petitioners might add nothing to the essential character of
parliament as a court, and their role as witnesses of political
settlements might merely signify their tacit assent, but it was
in virtue of these two subordinate functions that they were
summoned to many of the full parliaments in the middle years
of Edward II's reign. Between 1311 and 1322 representatives

---

[1] This is discussed at more length in Chs. v and vii. J. R. Maddicott, *Thomas of
Lancaster*, pp. 99–102, has argued that the petition of 1309 may have been initially
framed at the Dunstable tournament preceding the April parliament.

[2] See M. V. Clarke, *Medieval Representation and Consent*, pp. 160, 166.

[3] Ordinances, cap. 7, 9, 14, 29. See J. G. Edwards, 'Justice in Early English
Parliaments', *Bull. Inst. Hist. Res.* xxvii (1954), pp. 41–6.

attended eleven times,[1] and on only five of these occasions were grants of taxes demanded and made. These assemblies marked the great political settlements of the reign: the compromises of 1313, the King's confirmation of the Ordinances in 1314, the promulgation of Lancaster's reform of the household in 1315, his reinstatement by the King at the Lincoln parliament of 1316, his own acceptance of the Treaty of Leake in 1318, the solemn decision for a major expedition to Scotland in 1319, the indictment, trial, and banishment of the Despensers in 1321, and the King's triumph over the opposition in 1322.[2] We know little of the Commons' activity in these assemblies but it is unlikely that they were always passive bystanders. Lancastrian propaganda made a vigorous appeal to the evils and burdens by which the people were 'afflicted and disinherited' and the logical counterpart of this unprecedented appeal to popular grievance was the expression of grievances by representatives in parliaments and their subscription to the baronial measures to secure reform. In 1322, as a means of proscribing the baronial appeal to notorious misgovernment, the King acknowledged that the assent of the community of the realm was necessary and normal for matters legitimately concerning the estate of the King and kingdom. This gave formal recognition to the full parliament as the body which, beyond any other, represented the whole community of the realm in matters which concerned the form and substance of the King's government in so far as they touched the rights and welfare of his subjects.

But if the Commons were thereby acknowledged to be an integral part of parliament, it did not of course ascribe to them an equal share with the magnates in discussion and decision on great matters of state. They remained primarily petitioners, but because they petitioned on matters of common grievance with a representative authority which was peculiar to themselves, their role was bound to assume ever increasing political importance. The other business of parliament in which their active power was recognized and, by frequent practice, enhanced,

[1] That is, knights and burgesses together and usually clerical proctors as well. Knights and burgesses were summoned separately on two other occasions. The two sessions of August and November 1311 have been counted as one parliament. *H.B.C.*, pp. 514-16.

[2] Morris, op. cit., pp. 76-86; M. V. Clarke, op. cit., p. 166.

was of course taxation. Fourteen lay subsidies were granted between 1297 and 1337, eleven of these falling in the thirty years after Edward I's death.[1] Taxation was thus frequent enough to become a normal act of government, and by 1334 the different rates between shires and boroughs became standardized as a fifteenth and tenth, collected on a fixed assessment for each county and vill. On the other hand it was not sufficiently persistent or continuous to threaten its occasional, emergency character. From the ninth granted in October 1297 'for the defence of the realm of England' after the battle of Stirling Bridge, every tax with one exception was for the war against Scotland. Each grant was made for a particular, declared emergency. This might be depicted in graphic phrases, recalling the murder, devastation, and destruction of homes and livestock which accompanied the Scottish raids, and presented—like the French war in 1297—as a threat to the English realm and Church.[2] Parliament was in this manner accustomed to the notion of an obligatory tax for a defensive war which constituted a necessity of the whole realm. There was never in these years any attempt to levy taxation without consent or to introduce the plea of perpetual or habitual necessity. Except in 1315–16 taxation was never levied for two consecutive years, as it had been from 1294 to 1296, and, of greatest significance, the periods of truce on the border between 1322 and 1327, and between 1328 and 1332, were free from taxation. Taxation was thus restricted to open war, and was always granted in a full parliament of all estates.[3]

---

[1] Namely in 1297, 1301, 1306, 1307, 1309, 1313, 1315, 1316, 1319, 1322, 1327, 1332, 1334, 1336. J. F. Willard, 'The Taxes upon Movables of the Reign of Edward I', *Eng. Hist. Rev.* xxviii (1913), pp. 517–21.

[2] B. C. Keeney, 'Military Service and the Development of Nationalism in England', *Speculum*, xxii (1947), pp. 541–5; R. Nicholson, *Edward III and the Scots* (Oxford, 1965), pp. 112 and 2–3.

[3] Willard, *Parliamentary Taxes*, ch. 1. The exception was the twentieth and fifteenth of 1307 granted for the expenses of Edward I's burial and the coronation of Edward II (*C.C.R., 1307–13*, p. 41). The beginning of a reign was to become the usual occasion for a grant on these terms; even so the articles of the barons in 1310 speak of it as 'en aide de vostre guerre d'Escoce' (*Annales Londonienses*, in *Chronicles of Edward I and Edward II*, ed. W. Stubbs, i (1882), p. 168). In this context it is significant that by 1316 the papacy no longer required the King to seek specific approval for a tax of the clergy on grounds of a necessity of the realm if the King was fighting within his own frontiers and for the common profit (see M. V. Clarke, op. cit., p. 333).

The fact that parliament gave its assent not merely to the King's demand for taxation but to the reasons for that demand implied its consultation and agreement on the issues of war and peace. It is fortunate that the record of one such consultation has been preserved from this period. Following the rupture of the truce with Scotland in 1332, the parliament held at Westminster in September granted the King a tenth and fifteenth for war, and lords and knights advised that other business should be curtailed to enable the King to proceed northwards with speed.[1] On his arrival at York in October Edward found that Balliol had proclaimed himself King. He therefore consulted with his magnates on what course to follow but they advised that 'the business was so weighty that it would be necessary to call a parliament'. To this parliament, in December, Edward put the alternatives: should he intervene in Scotland to assert his direct lordship over it, or should he support one of the contending parties to gain their recognition? There is little doubt that the King favoured the former course which opened up the prospect of an English invasion in strength. The decision in effect was whether to resume the war policy of his grandfather. For three days magnates, clergy, and knights of the shire and burgesses, meeting almost certainly apart, discussed the king's proposals. On Friday 11 December each estate recorded its separate answer and then the full parliament returned an evasive response, saying that there were insufficient magnates present to make a decision.[2] Edward had to reconcile himself, for the time, to a compromise policy. War involved the whole realm and no king could initiate it without the formal agreement of those who would have to support it. The proceedings of 1332 show that this could involve justification and debate in which each estate had an independent voice, and though the magnates still spoke with authority and could not easily be gainsaid, they no longer spoke for the whole community. We may assume that decisions over taxation were taken in the same way, the Chancellor's declaration of the reasons for the King's request being considered separately by the estates but with the knights joining the magnates to make a common grant.[3] The initiative for proposing the form and

[1] *Rot. Parl.* ii. 66–7.   [2] Ibid., p. 69; Nicholson, op. cit., pp. 99–101.
[3] There are records of the speeches of the Chief Justices in 1275 and 1316 and

Parliament, Taxation, and Military Service, 1297-1337   81

amount of the tax probably rested with the Lords, but as the
form of the tax became standardized after 1334 knights and
burgesses gradually came to deliberate together.[1]

Further evidence of the role of the Commons in the business
of parliament can be found in the *Modus Tenendi Parliamentum*,
now dated to 1321, which clearly draws upon an informed
knowledge of parliamentary routine.[2] Thus cap. xviii states
that the order of business was first war and the King's affairs,
second the affairs of the realm, and last the answering of
petitions. This was the sequence outlined in the charge to the
Commons recorded on the parliament rolls at a later date, and
it presumably formed part of the *pronuntiatio* when the author
was writing.[3] Although this reflected an order of importance
and not necessarily of sequence, it none the less emphasized
that in parliament the subject's obligation to render aid and
the King's obligation to render justice were correlative. The
subject's duty to contribute to the defence of the realm was
acknowledged in cap. xxiii of the *Modus* where the author
correctly states that apart from the feudal aids the King can
demand aid only for an actual war ('pro guerra instanti').
The subject's right to redress is recognized by the statement
(cap. xxiv) that all petitions should be answered before the

---

of the Chancellor in 1332 setting forth the cause of the summons (Gervase of
Canterbury, *Historical Works*, ed. W. Stubbs, ii (1880), p. 281; *Rot. Parl.* i. 350,
ii. 66; and see M. V. Clarke, op. cit., p. 225). The separate grants by the burgesses
are distinguished clearly in 1307, 1313, 1316, 1319, and 1322 (*Rot. Parl.* i. 442, 448,
450, 455, 456).

[1] The initiative of the magnates is indicated in their promise to the King in
1312 to put pressure on the Commons to grant a tax, which led some chroniclers
to describe it as granted by the magnates alone, see *Annales Londonienses*, pp. 211,
224, 227; Trokelowe, *Annales* in *Chronica Monasterii S. Albani*, ed. H. T. Riley,
iii (1865), p. 81; *Vita Edwardi Secundi*, ed. N. Denholm-Young (London, 1957),
p. 44.

[2] The character of the *Modus* has been discussed by M. V. Clarke, *Medieval
Representation and Consent*; V. H. Galbraith, 'The *Modus Tenendi Parliamentum*',
Journal of the Warburg and Courtauld Institutes, xvi (1953); W. A. Morris, 'The date
of the *Modus Tenendi Parliamentum*', *Eng. Hist. Rev.* xlix (1934); B. Wilkinson,
Constitutional History, iii. 323–31; J. S. Roskell, op. cit.; G. P. Cuttino, 'A Recon-
sideration of the *Modus Tenendi Parliamentum*', in *The Forward Movement of the Four-
teenth Century*, ed. F. L. Utley (Columbus, 1961), pp. 31–60; N. Pronay and
J. Taylor, 'The Use of the *Modus Tenendi Parliamentum* in the Middle Ages', *Bull.
Inst. Hist. Res.* xlvii (1974), pp. 11–23.

[3] *Modus*, cap. xi, xviii. The causes were to be declared 'primo in genere et
postea in specie'; for procedure in the later parliaments of Edward III, see below,
ch. xv, and also M. V. Clarke, op. cit., pp. 225–7.

end of parliament. This reflected a repeated demand of the Commons, and when in September 1332 the King wanted to march north immediately after parliament had granted the tax, he took pains to secure the assent of the knights. Moreover the grant of aid might be formally and legally linked with the amending of the ills of the realm. As early as 1301 and 1309 the grant of the tax is written into the list of grievances of the 'commonalty' as being conditional on their redress.[1] Perhaps at this date grants were not yet made by indenture, but the *Modus* tells us that both the King's request for aid and the response of parliament should be in writing. At a slightly later date the record of the charge and the indenture of grant both appear on the parliament roll.[2] The sparseness of our parliamentary records should not lead us to assume that grants of taxation so explicitly justified and debated were not matter of solemn record.

It has been argued that when the *Modus* leaves parliamentary procedure for the theory of representation, it must be treated as political propaganda, presenting an advanced and radical view of parliament and of the place of the Commons in particular.[3] More recently an examination of the manuscripts of the *Modus* has suggested that it was used, and probably compiled, as a quasi legal treatise of parliamentary procedure which continued to enjoy a professional, if not political circulation for well over a century.[4] If this establishes its 'authority and authenticity' as a technical tract, it leaves us with the question how far the author's views on the role of parliament as a political institution reflect ideas current at the time.

It is in this light that we should perhaps look again at cap. xxiii, 'De Auxiliis Regis', which has always been con-

[1] *Parl. Writs*, i. 105; *Rot. Parl.* i. 444: 'les laies gentz granterent au Roi le xxv denier par cieu condicion'. The relation between taxation and redress of grievances is discussed below, ch. v.

[2] *Modus*, cap. xxiii. Grants are first recorded as made by indenture in 1346 (*Rot. Parl.* ii. 159–60). The grant of foot-soldiers for the Scottish war made in the Lincoln parliament of 1316 was 'sub certa forma in eadem concessione contenta' (*Rot. Parl.* ii. 450), which seems to imply a written schedule, but I have not noticed any similar phrase relating to a money grant.

[3] Roskell, op. cit., p. 414, summarizing the views of Galbraith. J. R. Maddicott has argued for its connection with the Lancastrian opposition in 1321 (op. cit., pp. 289–92).

[4] N. Pronay and J. Taylor, op. cit.; J. Taylor, The Manuscripts of the *Modus Tenendi Parliamentum*', *Eng. Hist. Rev.* lxiii (1968), pp. 673–88.

sidered and often cited as one of the most unhistorical and provocative claims in the *Modus*. We have already noted that the accuracy of many statements in this chapter can be demonstrated and accepted: that aids were asked in full parliament and were for actual war, that request and response should be in writing and each estate should give its consent. There follows one of the author's most controversial assertions: that in granting and withholding—the reference is primarily to taxation but thereafter to all things which ought to be granted, refused, or done by [*per*] the community of parliament—the representatives have a greater voice than those attending by personal summons, since they represent the whole community of England and not merely themselves. There are two propositions here: first, that in matters which concern the full parliament the representatives speak with a greater voice than any lord, and secondly, that they do so because they and they alone represent the whole community of England. The author then reinforces the latter point by arguing that although the King could hold a parliament in the absence of the Lords if they declined to come when summoned, he could not do so if the representatives refused to attend on the ground that the King was not ruling as he ought, and specifically indicated this in certain articles. Here again the refusal of the representative element to come to parliament is justified by reference to a certain type of business, namely the presenting of articles demonstrating royal misgovernment. Thus, although the article is entitled *De Auxiliis*, it refers to two types of business performed by representatives, namely, assenting or refusing in matters brought before the full parliament, and testifying or petitioning about the ills of royal government. The hyperbole which the author employs to contrast the roles of the Lords and Commons, like the barely credible hypothesis of a wholesale withdrawal of either estate from parliament, may be a lawyer's rhetoric, but they also serve to underline an indisputable historic truth. The matters which were brought before a full parliament were those which touched the whole community of the realm, and what made the assent of a full parliament necessary for such matters was the authority of the Commons to speak for their communities. The Lords could no longer, in such matters, claim to represent the whole realm. For taxation this had been recognized under Edward I and the distinction between the grants of the non-representative and the representative elements was to be clearly drawn in the parliament of 1340. Political settlements and solemn treaties from the Barons' Wars to the Statute of York had been promulgated in full parliaments so that the whole realm might give its recognition. Moreover, under Edward II the barons had invoked and exploited the testimony of the realm to misgovernment as a justification for constraint upon the King. They had prompted articles of grievances in 1300 and 1309, and the Ordinances of 1311 had been promulgated in full parliament. Doubtless the Commons by themselves could not claim to represent the whole community of England as the author asserts, but it was an entirely defensible (though not entirely verifiable) assertion that in rendering the assent of that community the unanimous voice of the representatives had greater weight than the individual voices of the Lords. At the very least their assent had become a *sine qua non*.

If this section of the *Modus* bears witness to the force of the representative ideal, its general theme is that parliament is the focal point of the political relationship between Crown and subjects, the place where the mutual obligations of ruler and ruled are performed for the profit of the realm. It was there that the needs of the realm were formulated: by the King for war and other business; by the representatives of the whole realm for justice in matters of government which affected them. Both parties might put these in writing, in a statement of necessity or in articles of grievance, and the replies to both would be matters of record. The Commons derived their authority in assenting to laws, in granting taxation, and in presenting grievances from the fact that they represented the communities of the shires[1] and because they acted for the common profit of the realm.

If the *Modus* bears witness to how misgovernment stimulated claims on behalf of the Commons, the establishment of taxation as part of the normal, recurrent business of parliament strengthened the Crown. In the cause of a war which Edward II regarded as a duty and Edward III as an adventure to

---

[1] As in the taxes of 1307 and 1313: 'graunte . . . par Contes, Barons, Franks homes et les Comunautez des tutz les Contez du Roiaume' (*Rot. Parl.* i. 442, 448).

prosecute, the King could repeatedly extract taxes from his subjects, could identify his own war aims with the needs of the realm, and could deploy the greater part of national revenue as he judged best. In 1334 any further tendency of the lay subsidy to shrink was counteracted by stabilizing the quota for each county and each vill at a slightly higher figure than the preceding tax of 1332. This avoided delay in negotiating and collecting the tax and was a further step towards familiarizing the realm with the need for recurrent taxation. It may also have helped to shift the burden rather more on to the shoulders of the peasantry, though it is difficult to be certain about this.[1] Its yield, at over £38,000, was only equivalent to the cost of a short and modest campaign,[2] and though Edward III could draw on other and more lucrative revenues, this fact helped to identify each grant with expenditure on a particular emergency. It is difficult to measure with any exactitude how far the aids granted between 1297 and 1337 were spent on war, but Professor Willard's examination of the printed warrants in these years led him to conclude that, where the object of expenditure was specified, it was in most cases for war.[3] War expenditure had, of course, no easily definable limits. It might with reason

[1] For the incidence of the tax, see Willard, *Parliamentary Taxes*, pp. 77–81, 87–91. E. B. Fryde has argued in 'Parliament and the French War, 1336–40', in *Essays in Medieval History presented to Bertie Wilkinson* (Toronto, 1969), p. 256, that locally made assessments may have spread the burden to many poorer men who had been previously exempt, and cites evidence from Kent. In the districts of Horton and Stone in Buckinghamshire, however, the number of taxpayers remained steady from 1334 to 1336 and the new assessment followed the lines of the old (*Early Taxation Returns*, ed. A. C. Chibnall, Buckinghamshire Record Society, 1966, p. xiv). The Lay Subsidy in fact established itself as a tax on land rather than on personal property (ibid., pp. xv–xvi). J. F. Willard, *Surrey Taxation Returns*, Surrey Record Society, xviii (1922), p. viii, noted the tendency before 1332 for the number of tax payers to decrease.

[2] Thus the wages of men-at-arms, hobelars, and foot-soldiers in the Weardale campaign of 1327 (which was admittedly extravagant) came to £39,655, although the total cost was well in excess of this (Nicholson, op. cit., pp. 38–40). The subsidy of September 1334, for the Scottish war, 'was badly needed to pay for the previous campaign, let alone for the forthcoming one' (ibid., p. 170).

[3] Willard, *Parliamentary Taxes*, p. 244. These were the drafts in the form of letters close under the great seal. More numerous were the drafts under the Exchequer seal enrolled mainly upon the King's Remembrancer Memoranda Rolls. The references to these given by Willard which I have examined convey the same impression. Warrants under the privy seal are less numerous at this time but examples from Edward II's reign can be found in E 404/1/7, and for the Scottish wars of Edward III in E 404/3/17.

include payments for purveyance, for ships requisitioned and mariners impressed, for ordnance, horses, and repairs to fortifications, besides the wages of soldiers, craftsmen, and artificers. The great majority of warrants were for such expenses, though a smaller number can be found for gifts and personal purchases by the King.[1] Moreover, the practice of delivering large assignments on the subsidy to the Wardrobe or Chamber 'for the king's benefit', or 'for his affairs' makes it difficult to say whether some part of the taxes was applied to his domestic rather than military expenses.[2] The unhampered control which the King enjoyed over the disposal of the tax, and the identification of his interests with those of the realm in time of war, made a clear separation impractical. Yet usually it was precisely this concurrence of interests which ensured that the aid would be effectively spent on the purpose for which the King had asked it.

At no time was this more the case than when the King was conducting the war in person, when, as he might emphasize, he was risking his own body for the defence of his subjects. In 1309 Edward II ordered the Treasurer to reserve all revenue for the Scottish war and to make no payment without his personal command.[3] In the early years of his son's reign, with the King on the border and the Exchequer at York, the financial machinery was geared to the Scottish war, which received preference over all other charges.[4] Writs to the collectors, bidding them bring in the subsidy with all haste, spoke of the

---

[1] For war: *C.C.R.*, *1333–7*, pp. 13, 24, 27, 37–8, 47, 218, 447, 576, 604, 609, 629; for personal expenses: ibid., p. 370, and *1337–9*, p. 214.

[2] Willard, op. cit., p. 245. Tout, *Chapters in Med. Admin. Hist.* ii. 274 ff. Nicholson, op. cit., pp. 238–9, prints a receipt from the Keeper of the Wardrobe of July 1333 for the subsidy in the northern shires.

[3] E 404/1/5, 7 October 1309. In January 1319 he ordered that all money owed to the King should be applied to the war, *C.C.R.*, *1318–23*, p. 50.

[4] In 1327 the King suspended assignments on the customs and ordered the collectors to bring all their receipts to the Treasury while the Exchequer was told to distrain on all royal debtors (*Memoranda Roll*, *1326–7*, pp. 38, 102, 228–9, 250, 252, 266); in April 1333 Edward placed a temporary restraint upon payments from the Exchequer for the sake of the war (*C.C.R.*, *1333–7*, p. 30) and in 1334 he wrote to the Exchequer in urgent terms to send cash to him at Newcastle. See Nicholson, op. cit., pp. 38–40, 95, 170–4, 115, 241. In these circumstances there would seem to be little doubt that the taxes of 1327, 1332, and 1334 were expended on the Scottish war; except that in 1327 Queen Isabella used 10,000 marks of the subsidy to purchase lands for herself (*CCR.*, *1327–30*, p. 267).

King's urgent need of it for his affairs.[1] Edward III, indeed, used his Chamber for the receipt both of the subsidy and more often of loans contracted from foreign merchants for which the subsidy could be pledged. Normally payments into the Chamber were made 'for the king's secret affairs', or for 'divers arduous affairs closely touching the king'; it required the conservative obstinacy of the Exchequer, in refusing to honour pledges in this form, to elicit the statement that such loans and payments had been for the Scottish wars.[2] In fact Edward was already demonstrating how a masterful and single-minded ruler could exploit the resources of the reformed Exchequer to mobilize the wealth of the kingdom and pour it into his war treasuries. Moreover, as arbiter of the common good in the emergency, the King had every inducement to extend his prerogative rights beyond their domestic context to meet the demands of war. The complaint and resistance which such levies provoked might at first be directed against the notorious abuses or illegalities practised by royal officials, but at a higher level it might challenge the royal demands themselves in the name of the common welfare of subjects. The opportunity for such a challenge presented itself when the needs and profit of the realm were set forth in the demand for taxation. At this stage the redress of grievances and the grant of taxation became intertwined. How this happened we must now examine.

There were two principal impositions on local communities in these years: military service and prises. In both, the King's attempt to exploit and extend customary obligations on the plea of necessity provoked a demand for common assent on the analogy of parliamentary consent to taxation. The remainder of this chapter will be concerned with the obligation to military service; in the next chapter we shall consider prises in the wider context of the redress of grievances.

The Wars of Edward I had brought attempts to extend the military obligations of tenants in chief, the knightly class, and the local communities. For the first of these groups, the old *servitium debitum* was often (though not invariably) supplemented by requests for additional service justified by an appeal to common need and national danger. In 1300, for instance,

[1] *C.C.R.*, *1333–7*, pp. 9, 21, 286–7, 393.
[2] Ibid., pp. 393, 566, 576, 594, 596, 598; *1337–9*, pp. 4, 8–9, 14, 64.

magnates were requested to bring as many as they could of the better-armed men and horses of their retinues to serve in Scotland 'for the safety of the Crown and the great and common utility of the people'.[1] In 1302 tenants in chief were requested to bring a sufficient force of *armati* beyond their *servitium debitum* and in 1303 additional service was again requested for the common advantage of the realm.[2] In the last years of the reign the magnates may have come to see such requests as threatening an extension of their obligations and under Edward II their willingness to render such additional service at their own cost became an expression of their political support.[3] Outside the context of feudal military service Edward I's principal concern remained the enforcement of some general military obligation on the wide class of substantial freeholders. For the campaign of 1300 summonses were sent out on the basis of lists of those holding forty librates of land, requiring service to meet the common danger in respect of fealty to the Crown coupled with the specific promise of pay. If the King hoped by this to disarm the opposition encountered in 1297 he was disappointed; he was met by an explicit denial that any man owed service beyond his feudal obligations to his lord or as tenant in chief of the Crown, and though in *Articuli Super Cartas* Edward evaded the attempt to bind him never to demand it further, he did not again issue such a summons for the rest of the reign.[4] The widespread attempt in 1316 to summon for service with pay proved abortive.

The real effort to secure compulsory unpaid service came to centre on the communal array, although this could involve

---

[1] *Parl. Writs*, i. 327. The same phrase was employed in the writs for the summons to parliament. For descriptions of the ravages of the Scots and the threats of the French King to subdue the realm in writs of military summons, see Keeney, op. cit., pp. 541–5.

[2] M. R. Powicke, *Military Obligation*, pp. 99, 102, 115; M. Prestwich, *War, Politics and Finance under Edward I*, p. 89.

[3] Thus in the *Prima Tractatio* between the King and the magnates in 1312, they promised to grant 400 men-at-arms at their own cost for service in Scotland when the King next went to war with baronial assent; in 1319 tenants were to be arrayed by their lords for the Scottish expedition and were to be well armed and supplied for a month's campaign (Maddicott, op. cit., pp. 135, 245).

[4] *Parl. Writs*, i. 330. The Acland–Hood MS. containing a first draft of the *Articuli* is printed in *Hist. MSS. Commission, Sixth Report*, Appendix p. 344. For further discussion of this summons, see M. R. Powicke, op. cit., pp. 114–15; M. Prestwich, op. cit., pp. 88–9.

lesser knights as well as freemen. Edward I had familiarized the use of the array in the Welsh wars and then on a massive scale for service in Scotland. The basis of the array was, in effect, the communal obligations under the Statute of Winchester, though particularly after 1298 the offer of payment was frequently made in the writs to the commissioners. By 1298 there was already a long tradition that these levies received royal wages from the point at which they left their county, but even this failed to ensure service beyond the forty days of their obligation. The heavy toll of desertions and the unsuitability of massed infantry for operations in Scotland, probably more than the financial burden, had led Edward to abandon large-scale levies by the end of the reign.[1] Edward II's finances were in no state to support a revival of such levies and this could only be attempted through an extension of the principle of obligation. Under Edward II there were, broadly speaking, two ways in which communal levies could be brought into service as part of a national army at the cost of the county. First, the forty days' compulsory service under the Statute of Winchester could, under the threat of invasion of the realm or rebellion, be extended beyond the borders of the county. Secondly the provision of a certain number of soldiers of a specified quality or rank could be obtained from the shire, or the towns within it, equipped to serve for forty days at the cost of the community. For the first of these the Crown could usually rely on extending its statutory powers by an appeal to emergency, but for the second a form of consent, either local or, increasingly, national, was sought for what was evidently an additional form of taxation.[2]

Writs of array under the Statute of Winchester were issued in 1315, 1316, 1318, 1319, 1324, 1325,[3] and probably also in 1314 and 1322.[4] Most of these were specifically to meet the

---

[1] M. R. Powicke, op. cit., ch. vii; M. Prestwich, op. cit., ch. iv. On one occasion (1299) the commissioners were authorized to offer additional bounty to attract recruits if they encountered resistance on account of the bad money and inclement weather (*Parl. Writs*, i. 326).

[2] These were not absolutely distinct forms of levies. They overlapped both in the terms in which they were demanded and according to practical military requirements, but it is useful to separate them for the present discussion.

[3] *Parl. Writs*, ii, App. pp. 94, 478–9, 510–11, 525, 668, 735. In all these the service of all able-bodied men between the ages of 16 and 60 is specifically commanded.   [4] Ibid., pp. 431–4, 553.

threat of invasion. The writs of 1314, 1315, 1316, 1318, and 1319 were explicitly to counter Scottish raids, and frequently elaborated on the destruction these had wrought.[1] Those of 1324 mentioned the threat of French invasion but in February 1322 the levies were called out against the rebellious magnates, while in 1325 arrays were commissioned 'for the preservation of peace and for the secure defence of the people of our realm against their enemies', both foreign and rebels.[2] By this insistence on national emergency the Crown sought to override the local limitations of the Statute and oblige men to serve beyond their county boundaries in the common defence of the realm. On one or two occasions payment was for service made beyond the county, but in many cases the whole burden was borne by the community.[3] The elaboration of the plea of necessity was one means of securing acceptance of this extended obligation;[4] another was to assert that measures for the defence of the realm had been sanctioned by advice of the magnates, or the council, or even 'by the common counsel of the realm in parliament'.[5]

The fact that assent to parliamentary taxation had become firmly established as a corporate act on a formal occasion must have strengthened the tendency towards a similar form of assent to communal military service. As with taxation, the assent of the realm had first been sought from the magnates. The ninth of the Ordinances of 1311, which required the King to obtain the assent of the baronage in parliament for making war or going outside the realm, formalized a long tradition of baronial

---

[1] *Parl. Writs*, ii p. 479. The prologue to the writ of 1314 reports the penetration of the Scots into Yorkshire where 'homicidia, depredaciones, incendia, sacrilegia et alia mala innumera committere non desistunt'.

[2] Ibid., p. 735.

[3] Ibid., App. p. 94 (1315), p. 668 (1324). In 1314, however, the men of Northamptonshire, ordered to proceed to the defence of Berwick, were paid from leaving Northampton, and in 1316 payment was promised from county boundaries (ibid., pp. 433, 479).

[4] In 1315 and 1324 the writs expressly admitted that the requirements under the statute were insufficient for national defence. The writ of 1315 emphasized the obligation upon every subject to render aid in so great and arduous a necessity 'pro nostro et corone nostre honore et commodo et salvacione fidelium'. Thus likewise the writ of 1316: 'in tanto tam arduo negotio super salvacione sancte ecclesie et regni nostri defensione quisquam de eodem regno se excusare non potest'. This followed the phraseology of the writ summoning fifty-librate holders for service (*Parl. Writs*, ii 478).

[5] Ibid., p. 327 (1319), 668 (1324), 735 (1325).

agreement to or adjudication of the justice and reasonableness of the King's cause. By claiming it as the proper function of parliament the Ordinances helped to establish it as a concern of the whole realm. After 1311 Lancaster made it a prime element in his demands. Edward recognized the claim in 1313; it was realized in the Lincoln parliament of 1316, reaffirmed under the Treaty of Leake, given practical expression in 1319 for the Scottish expedition and used by the King in his period of triumph in 1322 and 1324.[1] In the November parliament of 1325 the baronage was again consulted on military projects and in the following decade the consent of the baronage in parliament became imperceptibly the consent of parliament as a whole. As we have noted, in 1332–3 Edward submitted his war policy to parliament which again discussed the Scottish war in 1335 and gave formal approval in 1337 to the war with France. On most of these occasions discussion and approval of the case for war was linked with the demand for money to fight it, and the King found it natural and convenient to extend the principle of obligation from the grant of money to the grant of soldiers. Nothing testified more clearly to the status of parliament as the voice of the realm than the fact that it became involved in authorizing and regulating these levies.

The commonest form of levy was to require that each vill should arm and support one foot-soldier for a given period. Militarily it was to be preferred to the array, but the lack of any legal or traditional basis for what was in effect a tax on local communities was shown in 1311 both by the terms of the writs which 'required and requested' service 'trusting in your benevolence' and by the attempts to gain *post facto* assent from the barons and the vills. The demand was, in fact, cancelled in favour of the usual array, at the King's pay.[2] In 1316 parliament for the first time made a grant of service in terms similar to a grant of taxation. It was placed on record amongst the *memoranda* that the magnates and community of the realm had granted to the King in aid of the Scottish war the service of one foot-soldier from each vill for sixty days from the place of muster, at the expense of the vill.[3] There is no doubt that the

[1] M. Powicke, *Military Obligation*, pp. 233–4.
[2] Ibid., p. 408. See Stubbs, *Const. Hist.* ii, 570; M. Powicke, op. cit., pp. 139–40.
[3] *Rot. Parl.* i. 351.

Commons participated in this grant, and in the same parliament the burgesses, as their contribution to the emergency, granted a fifteenth in similar terms. Finally in July a special assembly of the knights of the shires commuted the levy to a sixteenth.[1] The next occasion when parliament made a grant of this kind was in May 1322 when, in conscious imitation of 1316, the prelates, earls, barons, and community of the realm granted for the war one foot-soldier from every vill for forty days' service at the expense of the vill. As before, the King acknowledged that the grant was not to set a precedent.[2] Doubtless at such a moment parliament had little choice but to agree to royal demands; yet the force of parliamentary assent was such as to overrule local claims to exemption because the grant had been made 'by common counsel in parliament'.[3] By the end of Edward II's reign, therefore, the danger was real that parliament would be obliged to make grants of service as well as grants of taxation.[4]

How and why had parliament acquired this unenviable power? We have noted that, following the Ordinances, the baronage established the practice of giving assent to war in parliament, and that this could be made justification for the imposition of emergency measures, like the array. It was also extended to other forms of service. Baronial assent was implied in the writ of August 1316 which required service at their own expense from all those holding £50 in lands, and in August 1318 certain cities were requested and required to provide contingents for forty days' service at their own expense 'by the common counsel of the prelates, earls, barons, and nobles of the realm'.[5] In March 1322 an order to levy numbers of troops in the shires for service in Scotland was authorized in almost the same terms and was followed by a demand for service from the cities.[6] Appeal to the authorization of the emergency was followed in the writs by explicit declaration of the subject's duty

[1] *Rot. Parl.* i. pp. 450–1.
[2] *Parl. Writs*, ii. 573.
[3] *Rot. Parl.* i. 413 for this response given to the petition of St Osyth's priory. Cited by M. Powicke, op. cit., p. 153 n. 2.
[4] Thus Mortimer was alleged to have extracted from the Winchester parliament of 1330 a similar grant for service in Gascony (*Rot. Parl.* ii. 52).
[5] *Parl. Writs*, ii. 505. See Stubbs, *Const. Hist.* ii. 570; Powicke, op. cit., pp. 143–5.
[6] *Parl. Writs*, ii. 559.

to render aid when the realm was endangered.[1] Yet in the event the levy of 1316 had to be abandoned, that of 1318 though more successful encountered strong opposition, and those of 1322 (for which some counties offered commutation) were superseded by the more moderate grant of the May parliament.[2] Thus by the end of the reign, after experiments in various forms of military levies, it was coming to be realized that neither the plea of necessity on its own, nor even the attestation of this by the magnates offered an acceptable basis for national levies which touched every vill and were equivalent to a subsidy. What touched all required the approval of all.[3] Only a full parliament could provide the form of central assent which would be accepted as authoritative and binding for such grants. The same process which had made taxation the first prerogative of a full parliament was now helping to assert parliament's power over military levies.

In 1327 this amounted to an incipient power to authorize military levies, not to limit or control them. The first petitions from the Commons which sought to regularize the Crown's powers show that, as with taxation, limitations on military obligation were sought in custom and necessity.[4] Three grievances seem to have been stated. The first concerned compulsory military service abroad (in Gascony or Scotland) or 'in any other manner than men were bound by their tenure to do'. As phrased in the first of these petitions this was only applicable to those holding by military tenure; but the second

---

[1] The writ of 1318, for instance, ran: 'nost considerantes quod pro tanta necessitate fideles et subditos nostros ut in premissis manum apponant adjutrices, decet requirere et rogare . . .' (*Parl. Writs*, ii. p. 505). In 1322 the King required and requested 'quatinus in tam arduo negotio nos et nostrum ac vestrum et tocius populi regni nostri predicti honorem et salvacionem specialiter tangente de hominibus ad arma peditibus vel alio auxilio competenti juxta vestre beneplacitum voluntatis, considerata qualitate negocii velitis nos juvare' (ibid., p. 563).

[2] Powicke, op. cit., pp. 151–2, discusses the reception of the King's demands in 1322. Staffordshire commuted its obligation for a fine of £200 and Bedfordshire and Buckinghamshire theirs for 600 marks (*Parl. Writs*, ii. 557, 566). Other towns certainly made grants of troops at their own expense (ibid., p. 568).

[3] M. V. Clarke (*Medieval Representation and Consent*, pp. 160–1) pointed to evidence for the currency of this maxim in the middle years of the reign.

[4] *Rot. Parl.* ii. 8 nos. 9, 10, with the responses on p. 11; *Statutes of Realm*, i. 255–7. They have been discussed by Stubbs, *Const. Hist.* ii. 570; Powicke, op. cit., pp. 160–1; Wilkinson, *Const. Hist.* iii. 207–8; A. E. Prince, 'The Army', in *English Government at Work*, i. 360–2.

petition complemented this with the complaint that in arrays for overseas service the cost had been charged to the communities. It asked that for such service, 'which touched the King' the Crown should bear the cost. Secondly, the first petition asked that 'gentz de Commune' should not be compelled to go outside their counties except at the cost of the King. This, as we have seen, reflected much of the dispute of the previous two reigns; for though the Statute of Winchester restricted service to local defence, kings had used the local levies for national defence on the plea of emergency, paying only from the muster, if at all. Thirdly, the first petition asked that men should not have to arm themselves at their own expense beyond the requirements of the Statute of Winchester. The statute enacted on the basis of the King's response to these petitions that no man should be compelled to go out of his shire except where necessity required through the sudden invasion of foreigners, 'and then it shall be done as it has been in the past for the defence of the realm'.[1] This implicitly met the complaint of the military tenants, by admitting that the tenurial obligation for military service was confined to national defence and did not extend to overseas expeditions at the King's will; in so doing it opened the way for contractual service for the military classes. But at the same time it reaffirmed the obligation on the subject for the defence of the realm on grounds of both necessity and custom. This was to be expected; the Crown could hardly rescind the consistent policy of the previous thirty years in a period of critical danger. It should be noted that the statute said nothing about payment for such service. This had always been at the King's grace, and the practice had varied with circumstances. As A. E. Prince noted, within three months the King was ordering arrays for service on the borders to be paid only from the muster at Newcastle, and this continued to be the practice throughout the following decade.[2] The complaint in the second petition that communal arrays for overseas

---

[1] 1 Edw. III stat. 2 cap. 5; *Rot. Parl.*, ii. 11 no. 9.

[2] Prince, op. cit., p. 361. Owing to the tardiness of the array, however, the King was moved to authorize pay at the discretion of the arrayers in June (*Rot. Scot.* i. 225, 246). For the levies of 1333 and 1334–5, see Nicholson, op. cit., pp. 117, 179–80, 190, 194. Nicholson has pointed out that arrayed troops comprised a large element in the campaign of 1334–5, though a marked tendency towards desertion had to be counteracted by pay.

service had been charged to the communities was answered by the statute forbidding this in future;[1] and the request in the first petition that men should not be compelled to provide armour in excess of the requirements of the Statute of Winchester was granted but may have been in practice disregarded.[2]

The legislation of 1327 was important. Admittedly both petition and statute were conservative in that they sought definition in terms of custom and prerogative, but this was one of the first occasions on which public obligations were defined on the initiative of the Commons in parliament. This, moreover, was in terms of a necessity of the realm, strictly interpreted as a war to defend the realm against foreign invasion. The King thereby lost any claim to obligatory service overseas but the Commons had been compelled to admit that for national defence the King had a legitimate claim to service that was more than the local guard authorized by the Statute of Winchester. Under the pressure of national war, military obligation had been defined in terms remarkably similar to those governing fiscal aid; moreover, the fact that the necessity had to be one which touched the realm and not merely the King, implied some form of common assent or recognition which, on the analogy of taxation, parliament was supremely fitted to give.

The renewal of the Scottish war in 1332 brought a fresh attempt by the Crown to extend the obligation of military service.[3] The Statute of Winchester as promulgated in 1334, 1335, and 1336, extended to categories of £40 and £20 free-holders. Individual landowners were summoned on their allegiance to raise troops for the King, at his wages. Demands for quotas of men-at-arms and archers, to which in 1316 and 1322 assent had been given in parliament, were in 1327[4] and 1335 made in writs requesting cities and counties to provide hobelars and archers at local expense in respect of their fealty, allegiance, and affection, coupled with the assurance that this

---

[1] 1 Edw. III stat. 2, cap. 7; *Rot. Parl.* ii. 11 no. 10.

[2] Prince, op. cit., p. 362. 1 Edw. III stat. 2, cap. 5. *Rot. Parl.* ii. 11 no. 9.

[3] Prince, op. cit., pp. 350–1; N. B. Lewis, 'The Recruitment and Organization of a Contract Army, 1337', *Bull. Inst. Hist. Res.* xxxvii (1964), p. 5.

[4] The writs to the cities in 1327 laid emphasis on the present necessity, and those who refused or demurred at the King's demands found themselves summoned before the council. See *Foedera*, II. ii. 705; *Rot. Scot.*, i. 212; Nicholson, op. cit., p. 18.

would not be treated as a precedent.[1] Before parliament met
at York on 26 May 1335 representatives from some shires had
commuted this obligation to a fine, and this was followed more
generally after the beginning of the session. Thus a measure of
assent was accorded to what was a species of taxation.[2] An
initial and more specific approval seems to have been given by
the earls, barons, and 'communitates regni' to a revised quota
from the counties at a great council held at Nottingham in
September 1336. The troops were to be provided with victuals
and carriage for three weeks at local cost, the burden to be
graded by the size of communities 'to the less charge and
complaint of the people of the realm'.[3] The scheme was subsequently cancelled probably because it was commuted into the
grant of a tenth and fifteenth. The accentuation of Edward's
demands in 1337 as threats of invasion materialized on both
the northern and southern frontiers hastened recognition of the
affinity of these burdens to taxation and thus underlined the
need for consent. At the very beginning of 1337 the King
attempted to extract a financial grant for defence from four
representatives of certain coastal towns. Summoned before the
council they were treated to emphatic statements of the dangers
to the realm but, refusing to concede aid, were reminded of
their duty to arm themselves in defence of the realm.[4] A somewhat similar though broader experiment was practised with
more success later in the year. In August writs ordered the
convening of all classes, lay and clerical, rich and poor, in
county assemblies where members of the council harangued
them on the need for a grant. Although it was recognized that
these county assemblies had no power to bind their communities, the promises extracted in them facilitated the grant
of the triennial subsidy in the parliament of 26 September 1337
which furnished payment for the array ordered to muster at
Newcastle for the winter campaign.[5] At the earlier parliament

---

[1] 'In fide et ligeantia et dilectione quibus nobis tenemini firmiter injungendo
mandamus quod considerato tante necessitate articulo . . .': *Rot. Scot.* i. 328–30,
339, 345–6. See also, Nicholson, op. cit., p. 194.

[2] *Rot. Scot.* i. 345–50; *C.P.R., 1334–38*, pp. 131–3, 289; J. R. Strayer, *English
Government at Work*, ii. 10; Nicholson, op. cit., pp. 198–200.

[3] *Rot. Scot.* i. 459, 461, 469, 470–1.

[4] Ibid., pp. 474–5, 478.

[5] J. F. Willard, 'Edward III's Negotiations for a grant in 1337', *Eng. Hist. Rev.*
xxi (1906), pp. 727–31; W. N. Bryant, 'The financial dealings of Edward III and

of the year, in March, the Commons had actually granted quotas of men-at-arms and archers from the northern counties at the expense of all who held forty shillings and more of land, and later in the year this seems to have been extended to the southern shires.[1] Emphasis was laid on the parliamentary authority for this novel grant when at a local assembly at York in April magnates and others who had not been present in parliament were persuaded to contract for service in the forth-coming summer campaign.[2] Thus from the end of 1336 the King was moving away from compulsion towards seeking con-sent for military service of different kinds. In particular an effort was made to supplement parliamentary assent with that of the local communities, but the fact that military obligation was closely linked to taxation and both were justified by the danger to the whole realm ultimately enforced the supremacy and universality of parliamentary authority for levies which bound the subject on this plea. With the King's departure to the Low Countries in July 1338 this acquired added significance.

In this chapter we have examined the enlargement and recognition of the Commons' role as representing the com-munities of the realm, in response to the needs of government. Their voice was sought in differing measure for discussion of the great matters of the kingdom, for the levying of taxation, and for authorizing additional military service. We must now turn to their role as agents of their communities in presenting grievances rather than as agents of the government, and here the influence of the baronial opposition was to be more potent than the authority of the Crown.

---

the County Communities, 1330–60', *Eng. Hist. Rev.* lxxxiii (1968), pp. 766–8; M. V. Clarke, op. cit., p. 342; *Rot. Scot.* i. 501.

[1] *Rot. Scot.* i. 487, 495, 498. E. B. Fryde, 'Parliament and the French War', pp. 259–60, links this with the petition printed by Richardson and Sayles in *Rot. Parl. Hact. Ined.*, p. 269, but this set of petitions is probably to be ascribed to the parliament of February 1339 when a similar grant was made. See below, p. 248 n. 2

[2] N. B. Lewis, op. cit., p. 6.

CHAPTER V

Parliamentary Taxation and the Redress of Grievances, 1297–1337

IN discussing the granting of taxation and military service emphasis has been placed on the authority of parliament as a whole. Usually the military element in parliament—the magnates and knights—was ready to authorize fiscal and military levies as the most effective way of mobilizing the resources of the cities and vills for a national war. In this respect their interests marched with those of the Crown, particularly if war was successfully conducted. But for the first twenty years of the fourteenth century they were frequently ranged against the Crown on other issues which served to emphasize the distinct interests of magnates, 'buzones', and citizens. In this period we first see signs of the detachment of the knights of the shires from the magnates, and the coalescing of representatives in parliament.

The baronial opposition sought support from a full parliament of representatives for two purposes: to testify to the evils of misrule which could justify the baronial demands for reform, and to apply fiscal sanctions which could compel the King to make concessions and accept restraint. Baronial interests dominated and controlled the expression of grievances in parliament for the whole period between 1297 and the crisis of the Ordinances and continued to exercise powerful influence in the following decade. By the first decade of Edward III's reign, however, it is clear that the representative element had sufficiently emancipated itself from baronial control to organize and present its own petitions, though it lacked both the strength and desire to link these with the power to grant taxation. It was in the intervening period—roughly the last decade of Edward II's reign—that the most obscure, but perhaps the most important, development took place: the emergence of the independent voice of the Commons in presenting their own grievances. Although the outline of this pattern has become familiar from investigation of the petitions presented in parliament, there has been little attempt to connect these with grants of taxation. Yet the crises of the first decade of the century sprang ultimately from the demands of the King's wars and some of the heaviest burdens which these imposed were the subject of popular grievances. Prises, in particular, were a form of taxation, and complaint that the impoverishment of subjects by such charges was contrary to the common profit suggested a link with grants of taxation demanded on the same plea. Moreover, as has been emphasized, the subject's obligation to aid the ruler was paralleled by the ruler's obligation to redress the wrongs of his subjects. Taxation and the redress of grievance can therefore hardly be considered in isolation; indeed, when the evidence for each is read together, it helps to define in some important respects the position of the Commons in these early parliaments.

The crisis of 1300–1 echoed that of 1297. Although neither illegal taxation nor military service was an issue in 1300, grievances over fresh burdens of war were intensified by the breach of the King's promise of forest perambulations. When plans for a winter campaign in December 1299 had to be postponed, Edward summoned a parliament to meet on 6 March 1300 to provide a grant of taxes for the campaign.[1] He was met with demands for enforcement of the Charters by more stringent sanctions, for perambulations of the forests, and for restraints on prises. These were the main grievances in 1300, at least in so far as they were reflected in *Articuli Super Cartas*. The parliament granted a twentieth, though this was not collected in the remainder of that year. The first problem therefore is the relation between the King's concessions and the grant of the tax. In the absence of any narrative proceedings of the parliament, discussion of this must centre on an examination of the document itself. Like *Confirmatio Cartarum*, *Articuli Super Cartas* had two parts: in the first of these the King renewed and confirmed the Charters at the request of the magnates, while in the second he granted certain articles 'of his special grace for the redress of the grievances that his people hath sustained

---

[1] *Parl. Writs*, i. 82–4; Walter of Guisborough, *Chronicle*, p. 334; *Annales Wigorn.*, in *Annales Monastici*, ed. H. R. Luard, iv. 544; Nicolas Trivet, *Annales*, ed. T. Hog, p. 377.

by reason of his wars'. The document then explained that the
King had been moved to grant these 'for the amendment of
their [i.e. the people's] estate and to the intent that they
might be more ready to do him service and the more willing
to aid him in time of need'. To do service and to render aid
in time of necessity were explicit references to the King's need
for men and money for the war. It was precisely because he had
experienced difficulties in getting the autumn and winter campaign under way that Edward had called a full parliament,
with the expectation of launching a major campaign from
Carlisle at midsummer.[1] The King, therefore, had undertaken
to give redress from some of the burdens of war which his
people found oppressive or unjust in the expectation of receiving a legitimate grant for his war. Parliament did indeed
grant a twentieth, though no writs were issued for its collection
and it was superseded without having been put into effect
by the grant of a fifteenth in the following parliament of
January 1301.[2] From this history it seems probable that the
twentieth was granted under certain limitations which inhibited
its collection, a surmise strengthened by the fact that the
fifteenth of 1301 was granted on the specific condition that
certain grievances should be remedied and that it should not
be collected until Michaelmas.[3]

What deterred Edward from collecting the twentieth was
probably a requirement that he should accept the findings of
the commission to perambulate the forests which, following his
concession of the *Articuli*, he had sanctioned on 1 April 1300.
The parliament of January 1301 was, in fact, summoned to
receive and adjudicate the reports of the commissioners, and
the writs of summons ordered the return of the same members
who had sat in the preceding March.[4] This parliament was
intended to confirm and continue the business initiated nine
months before, the most important item of which was for
Edward the tax, and for his subjects the disafforestation. Even
so, the King had to wait a further nine months for the tax,

[1] F. M. Powicke, *The Thirteenth Century*, p. 692; J. E. Morris, *The Welsh Wars of Edward I* (Oxford, 1901), pp. 297–8.   [2] *Parl. Writs*, i. 105.   [3] Ibid.
[4] Ch. Petit-Dutaillis, *Studies and Notes Supplementary to Stubbs' Constitutional History* (Manchester, 1930), pp. 221–5; Willard, *Parliamentary Taxes*, pp. 22–3; Stubbs, *Const. Hist.* ii. 155–8; M. C. Prestwich, *War, Politics and Finance under Edward I*, p. 266.

during which time he had to ratify the disafforestations suggested in the reports, confirm the Charters, and give assurances
on payments for purveyances. These were, in fact, the major
grievances which had led to the concession of the *Articuli*, and
under the sanction of withholding the collection of the grant
the opposition had compelled him to give effect to its demands.
If it was scarcely surprising that Edward hesitated to seek
further parliamentary grants, it was proof of the strength, persistence, and skill of the opposition that they could defer the
King's urgent needs and military plans for so long. Consideration of their legal right to defer grants of taxation had better
be left until the analogous proceedings of the parliament of
1309–10 are discussed. The immediate questions are, first,
whether the whole crisis—and particularly the concessions of
the *Articuli*—represented a defeat or a victory for the King;
and, secondly, what were the respective roles of magnates and
Commons in it.

The view that the parliament of 1300 was a victory for the
King has been argued on two grounds: first, that though he
bound himself more strictly than ever to the Charters, he did
not repeat the additional clauses of 1297; secondly, that the
King secured some very substantial modifications of the original
demands. He introduced a saving clause protecting the rights
and lordship of the Crown in matters comprised in the *Articuli*,
he secured the withdrawal of demands for ecclesiastical sanction in support of the Charters, refused to permit actions
against the King's ministers in their official capacity, and established that the correction of prise complaints was a matter for
the King's special grace—'as a maladministration of the prerogative'—and did not fall within the Charters.[1] In all these
matters Edward took a successful stand for the prerogative; but
it is difficult to gauge how far this represented a defeat for the
opposition. There is, it must be remembered, little direct
evidence of what the opposition demanded: nothing like the
Remonstrances to set against the concessions of the *Articuli*.[2]

---

[1] H. Rothwell, 'Edward I and the Struggle for the Charters', in *Studies in
Medieval History Presented to F. M. Powicke*, pp. 328, 330. To these could be added
Edward's evasion of any surrender of his claim to summon forty-librate landholders
for obligatory military service.

[2] The only evidence is that indirectly presented by the Acland-Hood version of
the *Articuli*, analysed by Rothwell, op. cit.

Confirmatio Cartarum had been a very generalized and conservative statement of political conventions; to the magnates in 1300 it may have seemed insufficiently precise for their needs. The fact that the *Articuli* followed the same form as *Confirmatio Cartarum* showed that the latter had not been forgotten. Whereas the first part of each, the solemn reaffirming of the oaths taken by the King and his predecessors to maintain the rights and liberties of subjects, is the symbol of a permanent constitutional relationship, the second provides remedies strictly related to the occasion, a kind of superstructure to the Charters capable of expansion with the times.[1] The *Articuli* carried a step farther, and in more detail, the mode of seeking redress initiated in *Confirmatio Cartarum*.

In regard to the first part, it is indisputable that the provision of justices elected in the county court to hear complaints against infringements of the Charters represented a great advance on caps. i–iv of *Confirmatio Cartarum*, or on anything that had previously been promised in this respect. Moreover, the full text of the Charters was confirmed and the *inspeximus* issued in charter form, not as a letter patent as in 1297, 'convincing proof of the importance attached to the occasion'.[2] In these respects, then, the magnates in 1300 had bettered the guarantees of 1297. In regard to the second part, *Confirmatio Cartarum* had aimed to subject to common assent various national levies which had threatened to impoverish the subject. Had Edward disregarded these concessions? He had not attempted to levy a national aid without parliamentary consent, and had in fact submitted to criticism and exacting conditions as the price of a grant. Neither had he attempted to levy the *maltolt*. What of prises? The Remonstrances had complained of prises taken without payment, and *Confirmatio Cartarum* had required common assent for prises taken by the King's ministers which were not the ancient due and accustomed ones. Two national prises had followed: one in November 1297 for the Scottish war for which parliament had just granted the ninth; the other in April 1298 a few days after the

---

[1] W. Thomson, *Lincolnshire Assize Roll*, p. lxxxii.

[2] Rothwell, op. cit., p. 326; and cf. on p. 327: 'Justice, elective and summary for offences against the Charters in fields where there had previously been no redress save by royal grace, was a most notable concession.'

council had authorized the issue of writs to investigate the grievances complained of in 1297.[1] The magnates were at the time participating in council and personally engaged in the defence of the realm; their assent to these prises can hardly be doubted. Moreover it is significant that the commissions emphasized that payment for the goods taken should be made at the market rate and in 'earnest money'. This suggests that the baronage saw assent to prise as an instrument for ensuring payment, and as comprised within their general assent to the necessities of war. The question of whether goods had been taken without payment or promise thereof had formed the kernel of the inquiry in 1298, the returns from which, revealing evidence of extortion by royal officials, were probably in the minds of those at the parliament of 1300. If, in January 1300, Edward may have shown signs of reviving prerogative national prises,[2] the magnates may well have sought to define more strictly the limits of prise *ad opus regis* with a view to curtailing the excesses of officials and ensuring payment or redress to subjects.

Articuli Super Cartas is best read as complementing *Confirmatio Cartarum* on the question of prise. It limited prerogative prise to what was required for the royal household and looked back to the first Statute of Westminster to deal with the two endemic abuses of the purveyor who lacked proper authority for his demands, and the default of payment.[3] Only the authorized purveyors were to take prises for the household; they were to make payment to or reach an agreement with those from whom they took prise. All officials had to produce their warrants and if any took prises without warrant or against the will of the owner he was to be arrested by the vill and imprisoned, and if guilty treated as a felon. Purveyances made at local towns or fairs were to be specified in an indenture with the mayor or bailiffs which was to be delivered into the Wardrobe as a check on the purveyor. These clauses represented the most detailed and systematic attempt to regulate prise and eliminate

---

[1] Thomson, op. cit., pp. ix, xiii–xiv; *C.P.R., 1292–1301*, pp. 314, 344.

[2] A prise of victuals was ordered on 14 January 1300 (*C.C.R., 1296–1302*, p. 382). It seems to have been part prise, part request. Cf. Thomson, op. cit., p. lxxv.

[3] *S.R.* i. 137. Cf. Thomson. op, cit., pp. lxxxiv–vi; M. C. Prestwich, op. cit., pp. 265–6.

its abuse; above all they embodied specific guarantees of payment.

In the case of national prises the king was recalled to the need for common assent. The first subsequent prise of this kind was in the spring of 1301 for the anticipated summer campaign.[1] The January parliament had complained of 'prises wrongfully made without payment or agreement against the form of the statute last made', and in granting a fifteenth for the war it authorized it to be used to pay for prises.[2] Accordingly local communities were asked to aid the King by granting him a 'loan' of victuals for which payment was promised from the tax.[3] Only on the basis of such negotiation and assent were purveyances then authorized, although since the tax was not leviable until Michaelmas men even so refused to hand over their goods except to those named as collectors.[4] In October writs for a prise for the winter campaign sent to the northern sheriffs authorized them to make payment from their proffers and from the tax, while for the December prise in the south royal spokesman endeavoured to persuade shire assemblies to loan corn and victuals against the promise of payment from the third part of the fifteenth falling due at midsummer 1302 or to suggest what other security would be acceptable.[5] This insistent demand for payment in the localities was clearly the fruit of parliament's association of prise with the grant of taxation. Both in binding himself to formal guarantees in parliament and in negotiating prises in the shires the King was thus forced to proceed by common assent. Moreover, payment for prises was the most direct expression of the commonalty's interpretation of taxation for the common profit. Here above all the opposition

[1] *C.C.R., 1296–1302*, p. 433; Thomson, op. cit., p. lxxiv.

[2] *C.P.R., 1292–1301*, pp. 578–9; *Parl. Writs*, i. 104.

[3] M. C. Prestwich, op. cit., pp. 131–2.

[4] Willard, *Parliamentary Taxes*, p. 23. Edward secured advances from certain towns and communities either of money or goods on promise of payment. In the parliament of 1305 there were petitions from the community of Cumberland and the community of the city of Carlisle to have allowance on their payment of the fifteenth for goods taken by the King's purveyors. See *Memoranda de Parliamento*, ed. F. W. Maitland (R. S., 1893), pp. 84–5.

[5] *C.P.R., 1292–1301*, pp. 608–9; *C.C.R., 1296–1302*, pp. 572–4. See M. Prestwich, op. cit., pp. 131–2. Even when, in October, the Exchequer was suspending all other assignments on the fifteenth for the King's campaign, it ordered local collectors to pay for the corn taken, from the tax (E 159/75 m. 7 and see below, p. 205).

of 1300–1 was giving practical effect to the principles acknowledged in 1297.

The other major grievance in 1300 concerned the forests. The King's reluctance to concede a perambulation which would deal with claims for disafforestation undoubtedly aroused greater anger and distrust than any other issue since Edward's return. Although the problem had been present since the beginning of the reign, it had not dominated the outlook of the opposition in 1297 to the extent that it did in 1300 when it crystallized suspicions of Edward's good faith. Together with the need for taxation, it provided the principal reason for the reassembly of parliament in 1301, and the King's concession on disafforestation must be reckoned the severest and most material surrender forced on him at that parliament.[1] Thus in many respects the crisis of 1300–1 particularized and defined the issues raised in 1297, and because they were more detailed the *Articuli* were of more continuing importance than *Confirmatio Cartarum*. The Lincoln parliament of 1301 framed its demands on the basis of the *Articuli*, and the regulation of prises they contained was reaffirmed as late as 1322. Edward had striven with some success to maintain the rights of the Crown and limit the answerability of his ministers; but he had been forced to give to his subjects material safeguards against the power of the Crown and its ministers to impose levies at will.

The weakness of the King's position was shown not only by his concessions but in his prolonged dependence on parliament to furnish money for the war. The *Articuli* gave redress to the grievances of the people and were conceded on the promise of a tax. In January 1301 twelve further articles of grievances were presented on behalf of the whole community, the concluding one of which stated that providing all the foregoing demands were established, affirmed, and accomplished before Michaelmas next, the 'people of the realm' granted a fifteenth to be paid at Michaelmas, but otherwise nothing should be levied.[2] In 1301, as perhaps also in 1300, parliament was exercising the power to defer collection of a grant until grievances had been remedied. The coupling of taxation and redress of grievance in

---

[1] Petit-Dutaillis, op. cit., ii. 219–26. The disafforestation war revoked by the Ordinance of the Forest of 1306.

[2] *Parl. Writs*, i. 104.

so sophisticated and effective a political manner could only have been achieved by a resolute leadership with widespread and active support. The latter became apparent in the shires where prises were negotiated and perambulations took place; the former reflected the greater cohesiveness and perhaps embitterment of the baronial leaders who had confronted Edward in 1297. In 1300 the Charters had been reissued at the request of the magnates; in 1301 the articles which were the condition of the grant were described as a bill of the prelates and nobles of the realm. The baronial responsibility for securing the redress of the grievances of the community is undoubted; yet the fact that the articles of 1301 were presented by Henry Keighley, whom Edward later imprisoned, was symbolic of the association of the shires with the magnate opposition.[1]

It is hardly possible in these years to distinguish the different roles of magnates, parliamentary knights, and local gentry, and the important fact is rather that under pressure of royal demands for war, a capacity for united political action was being formed which would have important consequences in the immediate future and for the political education of the knightly class. The King's reluctance to seek further taxation until 1306, and then the bolstering of the plea of necessity with the legal levy of a feudal aid from tenants in chief, showed how fearful Edward had become of providing opportunities for the expression of complaints.[2] It was a long way from the confident assertion of the overriding claims of necessity in 1297.

Edward II, lacking the prestige and personality of his father,

---

[1] According to the graphic account in Langtoft's Chronicle, Edward coupled his demand for taxation for the defence of the kingdom with the proposal that a committee of twenty-six peers be set up who should judge whether he could assent to the petitions without dismembering the right of the Crown. The commission refused to accept this role and, according to the chronicler, for the moment the issue hung between peace and war (Langtoft, *Chron.* ii. 330–2).

[2] The memorandum printed by Pasquet (*Origins of the House of Commons*, pp. 234–6) from the Lord Treasurer's Memoranda Roll shows that the King's council asked for aid both 'de iure Corone Regis' and for the expenses of Bruce's rebellion and the war against the Scots who 'iam in illis partibus guerram movere presumpserunt'. The barons and knights discussed this and granted 'unanimiter' a thirteenth. It was described as 'auxilium misarum quas est facturus circa guerram predictam'. Edward's desperate need for money in these years is also reflected in the revival of fiscal prerogatives, scutage, and tallage, though neither yielded sums of any size. See M. C. Prestwich, op. cit., p. 184.

embarrassed by his debts and military commitments, and faced
with a united and largely hostile baronage, was quickly compelled to repeat the lesson his father had learnt in 1301. When,
in April 1309, he asked parliament for an aid, the 'lais gentz'
granted a twenty-fifth 'on condition that he took counsel to
remedy certain articles'.[1] The King's reply was not given until
July when, at a meeting of prelates and magnates alone at
Stamford the articles and responses were recited, and it was
only following this that the collection of the aid was authorized.
Although the interval was not so long as between the parliaments of 1300 and 1301, there was a clear analogy between the
two occasions. Just as in 1301 the collection of the aid had been
deferred until Michaelmas pending the enforcement of the concessions, so in 1309 collection was deferred until letters close
had been sent authorizing local officials to implement the
concessions.[2] Further, when in December 1309 the earls of
Gloucester, Lincoln, and Cornwall protested that the concessions of Stamford were not being observed, particularly in
respect of prises, the King suspended collection of the tax until
the February meeting of the council.[3] This council, in session
from February till April 1310, recalled that the twenty-fifth
had been granted by the community of the realm 'to be
released of prises and other grievances', but though it and the
previous tax (of 1307) had been levied, they had been foolishly
wasted, the war had not been advanced nor the poor people
relieved of prises and other burdens.[4] The result was the
appointment of the Ordainers in March, and not until April
was further collection of the tax authorized.[5] The baronial
opposition had thus, largely on its own initiative, compelled
suspension of the tax as a means of forcing the King to accept
surveillance. The barons acted on behalf of the community for
the redress of whose known grievances they professed to be
striving. Thus the tax granted by the 'lais gentz' in April 1309

[1] *Rot. Parl.* i. 443-4.
[2] Willard, *Parliamentary Taxes*, p. 25. Writs were sent out in August to cease the collection of the new customs, at the request of the 'communitas regni', to renew perambulations of the forest, and to give assurances that no recoinage was in prospect. *C.C.R., 1307-13*, pp. 170, 174, 225.
[3] Ibid., p. 189. The council had been summoned on 23 October 1309 (*Parl. Writs*, i. 40-1).
[4] *Annales Londonienses*, pp. 167-9.
[5] Willard, *Parliamentary Taxes*, p. 26.

had been deferred by them until their grievances were answered in July, then further deferred by the magnates alone until the remedies had been enforced at Michaelmas, and deferred again in December by the baronage with the King's assent until April when the King had accepted further demands.

In 1309 and 1301, and probably in 1300 also, parliament had shown little hesitation in placing conditions upon the grant of the tax and withholding the collection of it until these had been fulfilled. Both Edward I and Edward II had been obliged, at considerable cost and inconvenience, to accept this procedure; but while this action testified to the determination of the baronial opposition and its mastery of parliament, its legality was more uncertain. On each of these occasions taxation had been demanded for war and the plea of urgent necessity was acknowledged by parliament as obliging it to grant an aid and not merely promise to grant one.[1] Subjects were thereby fulfilling an obligation which even the *Modus* recognized as taking precedence over either the amending of general wrongs or the rendering of justice to individuals. But though the King was thus granted aid he was not put in possession of it until the conditions attached to it had been fulfilled. It was here that the element of doubt entered. The magnates seem to have withheld their assent to its collection until assured that the grievances had been remedied.[2] This they did in both 1301 and 1309, though in the latter year once the collection had begun it could only be suspended (in December) by the King's own authority. Yet on each of these occasions it could truthfully be said that this delay had increased the danger to the realm and that to this degree the barons were flouting their obligation to render effective aid to meet that danger. The legality of withholding from the King what had been granted to him for the common good could thus be questioned, and could only be justified by an appeal to the common good in

[1] *Parl. Writs*, 82–4; Langtoft, *Chron.* ii. 328–35; *Annales Londonienses*, p. 157. Thus in 1301: 'le pueple du Reaume ensy ke totes les choses suzdites se facent e seent establement afermez e acompliz ly graunte le xvme en luy del xxme einz ces houres graunte . . .' (*Parl. Writs*, i. 105); in 1309: 'les laies gentz granterent au Roi le xxv denier' (*Rot. Parl.* i. 444).

[2] Thus on 24 October 1301, a writ recited that appointment had been made to collect the fifteenth in three instalments 'according to the form of an ordinance by common consent provided and granted by the king and the earls, barons and others'. *C.P.R.*, *1292–1301*, p. 611.

terms of the welfare rather than the safety of the realm. This indeed was the force of the articles of grievances presented in the name of the whole community, for these opposed the subject's obligation to render aid to the King with the King's obligation to render justice to his subjects. Both in restraining the grant of taxation and in enforcing the redress of the grievances of the community, the baronial action led directly to the Ordinances.

These articles thus looked back to the Charters of Liberties of the preceding century rather than forward to the common petitions of the 1320s and 1330s, which were framed neither in the political context of baronial opposition to the Crown nor as an indictment of royal misgovernment, and did not transcend the Commons' traditional role as petitioners for the King's grace. But though popular grievances were skilfully exploited by the baronial opposition to restrain the King, they were not therefore less real. On a number of long-standing abuses, notably prise and the powers of the household courts, the Stamford articles looked back to 1300;[1] they also introduced a number of new complaints, two of which were significant as showing a specifically non-baronial origin. Article two complaining of the 'petty custom' of 1303 was met by a promise to refer this to the council for investigation; article six protested that the knights and burgesses who had come to parliament to seek redress of their grievances found no one to receive their petitions. The tone and content of both these petitions is sufficient evidence for the participation of the parliamentary Commons in the making of the Stamford articles. Both found their ultimate expression, with some modification, in the Ordinances of 1311: the second was enlarged and more clearly defined as the eleventh ordinance abolishing new customs and *maltolts*; the sixth was recited with more elaboration in article 29 which provided annual or half-yearly sessions of parliament for the answering of complaints and difficult cases.[2] In each case the developed content and phraseology of the Ordinances throw into relief the untutored directness of the original petition. But if such petitions were the work of the

[1] The comparison is well set out by Maddicott, op. cit., pp. 97–8.
[2] The latter is discussed by J. G. Edwards, 'Justice in Early English Parliaments', *Bull. Inst. Hist. Res.* xxvii (1954), pp. 41–5.

Commons, the responsibility for presenting common grievances rested with the barons. It is they, 'les bones gentz du roialme qui sont cy venuz au parlement', in whose name the petitions are framed, and the chroniclers are explicit that it was they who presented the petitions to the King.[1] Nevertheless in the tone and content of these petitions the voice of the Commons is more discernible than it had been in 1300. Clearly too the Commons must be numbered among the 'lais gentz' who had made the grant of the tax conditional on the King's acceptance of the petitions, though the fact that it was a magnate assembly which authorized the collection of the tax in July led the chroniclers to state that it was they who had granted it.[2] Thus the history of both grant and petitions shows the Commons furnishing active and vital support to the magnate opposition, though the responsibility for presenting demands and applying political pressure rested with the barons themselves.

The regulation of prise in the Statute of Stamford and the Ordinances provides one of the clearest indications of how, in the context of restraint on the Crown, the baronage aimed to redress popular grievance while preserving royal rights. The article on prise almost certainly arose from a petition of the Commons directed against royal officials who gave no payment or tally.[3] It was answered in the Statute of Stamford by

[1] *Rot. Parl.* i. 443. The petitions were also said to have been delivered to the King by the 'communalte de son roialme'. For the application of both this phrase and the more explicit 'bones gentz' to the magnates, see W. A. Morris, 'Magnates and Community of the Realm in Parliament, 1264–1327', *Medievalia et Humanistica*, i (1943), pp. 58–94. It was to the 'bonez gentz qi sunt venuz a ceo parlement' that Edward I showed the perambulations in 1300 (*Parl. Writs*, i. 114), and this was certainly the magnates. In 1300 the articles are recorded as being presented by the prelates and magnates alone, 'ex parte totius communitatis'. Declarations that in 1309 'articuli per comites et barones pro proficuo regni domino regi fuerunt propositi' are to be found in *Annales Londonienses*, p. 157, and *Annales Paulini*, p. 267.

[2] *Annales Londonienses*, p. 157, clearly implies that the grant in July was conditional on the King's acceptance of the Statute of Stamford: 'in quo parliamento comites et barones dederunt regi vicesimum quintum denarium ad guerram suam de Scotia, quam Robertus de Bruis injuste tenet; et quod prisae de cetero non capientur, ordinaverunt et statuerunt per statutum quod sequitur.'

[3] Writs sent out in June 1309 which recited the Statute of Westminster, I c.i declared how, 'from the grievous complaint of the people of our realm by their several petitions exhibited before us in our present parliament at Westminster, we understand that the people by frequent and various taking and carrying away of ... their goods and chattels by certain our ministers and others ... have been hitherto manifoldly oppressed and impoverished'. For the heavy prises of the years

a reaffirmation of the remedies of 1300, as being 'convenient for the king and profitable for his people'. In February 1310 the magnates cited the continuing extortions by royal officials from the goods of the Church and 'your poor people' without payment, as contrary to the Charter,[1] and the Ordinances issued in 1310 condemned all prises except for the ancient, due, and accustomed ones; all others were to cease. As in the *Articuli*, this related to the extension of prerogative prises; it did not challenge the King's right to national prises in a recognized necessity which since 1297 had been accepted provided that assent was given and payment was made. The 1311 Ordinance further reflected a growing distinction between prises as illegal seizures and purveyance as legal purchase in time of emergency.[2] It defined prises in these terms: 'if, under guise of any purveyance made to the use of the lord king or other, there should be taken corn, wares, merchandise or any other kind of goods, against the will of those to whom they belong, without payment of money to the true value if the owner is unwilling of his good will to give respite of payment', then the hue and cry should be raised, the offender seized and taken to the nearest royal prison and judged under the law as a felon.[3] This ordinance thus stood in direct succession to *Articuli Super Cartas*, and indeed to Westminster I and *Magna Carta*, reaffirming that payment for levies, not the curtailing of royal rights to either traditional or emergency prises, was the baronial aim.

Both in their subject-matter and in the manner of their

1308–10, see J. C. Davies, *The Baronial Opposition to Edward II*, p. 318; J. R. Maddicott, *Thomas of Lancaster*, pp. 103, 106–7.

[1] *Annales Londonienses*, p. 168. Compare the statement of the canon of Bridlington under this year: 'considerantes itaque regni proceres dominum suum regem Angliae alienigenas et quosdam Anglicos indiscrete sibi facere familiares, quos etiam praeposuit in officiis hospitii sui praecipuis, qui, se super hoc extollentes, victualia, res, et alia bona diversa ceperunt per patrias, valorem vel pretium non solventes; unde comites vehementer condolentes, clamoribus oppressorum remedium apponere statuerunt' (*Auct. Bridlington*, p. 36).

[2] The use of 'purvoiance' as a more acceptable term is found in writs after 1297 and figures, as apparently interchangeable with 'prise' in *Articuli Super Cartas* (M. C. Prestwich, op. cit., p. 131; Thomson, op. cit., pp. lxvi, lxxiv). The distinction has become explicit in a writ of 1 November 1310: 'et ausint auscun de vos sutzministres ne font mie les achatz ne les purveaunces en due manere mes par torteuouse prises a grant grevaunce de notre poeple a ceo qe nous avoms entendu' (*Rot. Scot.* i. 96).

[3] *Rot. Parl.* i. 282.

achievement the Ordinances marked the culmination of a long tradition of co-operation between magnates and Commons in opposition to the Crown. For the Commons this was the most effective way of securing redress from the burdens and grievances arising from royal administration; for the barons it offered the safest and most plausible justification for imposing constraints on the King. But though the magnates drew on their inherited capital as defenders of the common good, in 1311 they crossed the rubicon between reform of royal government and restraint of royal power. During the course of 1309–10 they had inched closer to so doing. In December they had prevented the King proceeding with the collection of the twenty-fifth; in the articles of February 1310 they had moved beyond the redress of the specific grievances demanded at Stamford to a declaration that the King's misgovernment was a dishonour to the royal power and a disinheritance of the Crown, and to the claim to safeguard the Crown by virtue of their allegiance. Continuity with the grievances and promises of the Stamford assembly was nevertheless maintained by the assertion that the taxes of 1307 and 1309 had been misused, the Crown impoverished, and the subject burdened.[1] Indeed the appointment of the Ordainers in 1310 to reform the estate of the Crown was described as being for the common profit of the realm and in accordance with the King's coronation oath. But this was the last act which could be justified as proceeding from the full wish and assent of the King, and the final Ordinances of 1311 evoked his declared opposition. The traditional procedure by which, through petition, confirmation of the Charters, and articles supplementary to them, the King had been induced but not compelled to grant redress now gave place to Ordinances enforced under baronial compulsion. Edward II had himself forced the issue by showing that he was not prepared to accept magnate participation in government as the price of effective action against the Scots. Thus the Ordinances, despite the ancestry of their particular reforms and their immense popular support, stood in the tradition of the baronial action in 1258 rather than in that of the parliamentary *communitas* which had secured the *Articuli* of 1300 and the Stamford articles.

---

[1] *Annales Londonienses*, p. 168.

During the decade following the Ordinances the magnates, in different groupings and in different measure, for long periods exercised control over royal government. Their attitude to the Commons consequently changed. They had now no interest in citing common grievances as evidence of misgovernment and no occasion to force the Crown to give redress; similarly their readiness to obstruct the King's expeditions to Scotland disappeared as they assumed responsibility for the prosecution of the war. The Commons found themselves forced both to present their own grievances and provide taxation under baronial pressure. Thus in the negotiations between the King and the earls which followed Gaveston's murder in 1312, the earls promised as part of their readmission to the King's favour that in the next full parliament they would press the Commons as far as they could for a suitable grant for the Scottish war. This undertaking became embodied in the subsequent agreement with the King and resulted in the grant of a fifteenth and twentieth in the parliament of September–November 1313.[1] The refusal of Lancaster to join the Scottish expedition and the King's defeat at Bannockburn meant that when a domestic settlement again permitted plans for renewing the war this was under the aegis of the baronial opposition. The parliament of January 1315 was again called on for an aid, and that of January in the following year was called on for the provision of infantry from the vills. Finally the parliament of May 1319 made the last of this series of grants for baronial expeditions against Scotland. Four taxes in six years was a heavier incidence than for any period except 1294–7; moreover, it coincided with a period of acute shortage if not famine and was accompanied by royal prises for war, and illegal exactions by royal and baronial officials. Finally, the north suffered severely from the incursions of the Scots.

As an addition to the effects of war and natural shortage,

---

[1] Ibid., pp. 211, 224, 227. The course of the negotiations is reviewed by Maddicott, op. cit., pp. 130–51. Once again the chroniclers bear witness to the decisive influence of the magnates in making the grant: 'ipsi magnates, Regis paupertatem considerantes, quintum decimum denarium bonorum temporalium per totam Angliam sibi concedebant' (Trokelowe, *Annales*, p. 81); 'comites et ceteri magnates terre dederunt regi in subsidium guerre sue vicesimum denarium totius Anglie' (*Vita Edwardi Secundi*, p. 4). For the grant, see *Parl. Writs*, ii. 116, *Rot. Parl.* i. 448, *Foedera*, ii. 238.

taxation might easily depress the peasant to the point of desti-
tution, as the 'Song of the Husbandman' from this period
bears witness.[1] The lesser landlords too may have felt, as did
the author of the *Mirror of Justices*, that the King held parliaments only for the purpose of obtaining aids and collecting
treasure.[2] As the redress of wrongs became secondary to high
politics and the needs of war, the magnates gradually ceased to
be spokesmen for the communities as they had been in the
crisis of the Ordinances. It is true that one chronicler thought
that Lancaster's quarrel with the King sprang from breaches
of the Ordinances regarding prises and the Marshalsea court,[3]
and the Commons could still look to the magnates to compel
observance of the sanctions of the *Articuli*. After the end of the
parliaments of 1315 and 1316 proclamations were issued
enforcing the regulations of the Statute of Westminster, the
Articuli, and the Ordinances.[4] Complaint in parliament was
met by commissions in December 1316 in Yorkshire to inquire
into non-payment for purveyances, and by proclamations
throughout the shires in June and November 1317.[5] For these
abuses legislation now provided ample remedy, and there is
some indication that by 1320 the King was taking steps to
ensure that this should be effective. Petitions in 1320, 1321, and
1322 were referred to inquiry by the Steward and Marshal
according to the provisions of *Articuli Super Cartas*.[6] Thus
baronial support for the war and readiness to implement the
existing legislation combined to make prise less of a political
issue in this decade.

1 *The Political Songs of England*, ed. T. Wright (Camden Soc., 1839), pp. 149–53.
For the general economic conitions in these years, see I. Kershaw, 'The Agrarian
Crisis in England, 1315–22', *Past and Present*, 59 (1973), pp. 3–50.

2 *The Mirror of Justices*, ed. W. J. Whitaker (Selden Soc., 1895), p. 155.

3 *Annales Londonienses*, p. 237: 'quia odium semper clandestinum fuit inter eos,
tum propter ordinationes confirmatas, quas ministri regis semper pro posse suo
fregerunt, nominatim de prisis et de marescalcia, et regem infringendo collauda-
verunt, tum propter mortem dicti Petri de Gavestone interfecti'.

4 For the writ of 11 June 1314 regarding purveyance, see ibid., pp. 234–6. On
10 April 1316 proclamations were issued forbidding the taking of prises contrary
to the statute and ordinances; this repeated the writ of 11 June 1309 (*C.C.R.*,
1313–18, p. 334).

5 *C.P.R., 1313–17*, p. 600; *C.C.R., 1313–18*, p. 477, *Cal. Letter Books, E*, p. 79.

6 *Rot. Parl.* i. 377–8 (nos, 68, 70, 92), 392 (no. 27), 400 (no. 79). A writ of 4 April
1322 ordered that article 2 of *Articuli Super Cartas* should be proclaimed at every
market day (*C.C.R., 1318–23*, p. 532).

The same could not be said about disafforestation, for Edward I's retraction of the concessions of 1301 still remained, and his son was to be equally tenacious in resisting limitations. But this had never been a major issue with the Ordainers and the burden of resistance to the Crown fell principally on the Commons. It was probably on their account that the promise of renewed perambulations was added to the observance of the Ordinances as a condition for the grant of the aid in 1315. So keenly were the communities aware of this concession that even though commissioners for the perambulations were appointed immediately following the grant in April, the tax collectors encountered resistance in the ensuing months on the ground that the conditions on which the tax was granted were not being observed.[1] Perhaps the Commons would have preferred to follow the precedent of 1301 in deferring the collection of the tax until the commissioners had reported and the King accepted the disafforestations. In any event it testifies to the respect for parliamentary authority within the shires and the practical force of the conditions of the grant; moreover, it fore-shadowed the development of political initiative by the knights in the following parliament at Lincoln.

Here once again parliament was called on to make a grant for the Scottish war in the context of a reaffirmation of Lancaster's authority.[2] Although the parliament opened late in January, the earl and other magnates did not arrive until 12 February when the cause of summons was proclaimed and the request for aid was made. On 17 February the King committed himself to the observance of the Ordinances, the perambulations of Edward I's time (though 'reserving his reasons' against these), and the appointment of the earl as chief councillor.[3] On 20 February, the last day of parliament, magnates and knights made their grant of a foot-soldier from every vill for service for sixty days at local expense, and the burgesses

[1] *C.C.R., 1313–18*, p. 224; *C.P.R., 1313–17*, p. 324; *Parl. Writs*, ii, App. pp. 89 92. The conditions of the clergy for the grant of a subsidy contain no reference to the forest.

[2] The chronology of the proceedings at the parliament of Lincoln was established by H. Johnstone, 'The Parliament of Lincoln, 1316', *Eng. Hist. Rev.* xxxvi, (1921), pp. 53–7. The full record of its proceedings made by William Ayremine is in *Rot. Parl.* i. 350–64. See also M. V. Clarke, op. cit., p. 227.

[3] Writs for the publication and observance of the Ordinances were sent to the sheriffs on 6 March (*C.C.R., 1313–18*, p. 328).

granted a fifteenth, writs being issued at once summoning the
servitium debitum to muster at Newcastle and ordering distraint
of knighthood for fifty-librate freeholders.[1] It is clear that as in
1313 the grant of the tax had been instrumental in promoting
the political settlement and the military expedition in the
interests of Lancaster; but there is also reason to think that
the knights of the shires were fighting for their own grievance,
the perambulations. It is clear that the Lincoln parliament had
seen vigorous complaints from the Commons about the failure
to give effect to Edward I's concessions, and when in acceding
to the baronial demands the King reserved his reasons against
the perambulations it was probably because he had already
agreed to a special council at Westminster on 1 May at which
this long-standing grievance should be finally thrashed out. On
20 February, the same day as the grant was made, writs summoned two knights from each shire to this council, 'with full
power to assent to what shall be ordained concerning the
forest'.[2] As in 1315, therefore, the tax had been granted in
anticipation of redress and, as before, failure to implement this
aroused obstruction to the tax. The muster at Newcastle had
been ordered for 8 July 1316 and though some progress appears
to have been made in levying the contribution of the vills, the
commissioners also encountered delay and perhaps opposition
so that by mid-June the levy had to be abandoned.[3] On
25 June the same knights who had come to the Westminster
council in May were resummoned to Lincoln on 29 July 'to
treat concerning the perambulations and the election of foot-
soldiers in each county'.[4] When it met, this assembly remained
in session for eleven days. Although shorter than most full
parliaments, this was a substantial period for negotiations over
one issue; two sheriff's returns refer to it as a parliament,[5] and
it undertook the one piece of business for which the assent of
the knights was essential, the grant of supply. The sixteenth
was not an adaptation of the levy of foot-soldiers, but a fresh
grant made to secure its remission and 'to obtain the aforesaid
perambulations in the form in which they were conceded by

---

[1] *Parl. Writs.*, ii. 157, 163–4.   [2] *C.C.R., 1313–18*, pp. 272–3.
[3] M. Powicke, *Military Obligations*, p. 143; H. M. Cam, 'Shire Officials' in
English Government at Work, iii. 170–1.
[4] *C.C.R., 1313–18*, p. 346.   [5] *H.B.C.*, p. 515.

the king's father'.[1] Coupled with the King's promise that perambulations of recently afforested lands should be made before
Christmas, this constituted an important victory in the long
battle over the forest. It may not be wrong to attribute this to
the stubbornness of the knights, for the baronial leadership had
lacked both the concern and steadfastness to implement the
perambulations.[2] Local resistance and, presumably, the corporate solidarity of the representatives in using their control of
taxation had forced this concession from the Crown. It was
this ability to use taxation to secure relief for their communities
which would prompt the claim in the *Modus Tenendi Parliamentum* that in granting taxation the knights had a greater
importance than the magnates in virtue of representing their
communities.

In the event Edward's promises of August, like those of
February and of 1315, had little permanent result, perhaps
because the Commons on their own lacked any means of
bringing pressure on the King's executive power—only the
magnates could do this, through the council. We can point to
no occasion in the next twenty years when the Commons used
their power over taxation to secure concessions from the King.
This may be partly because the absence of records makes this
one of the most obscure periods of parliamentary development,
but it also reflects the end of a long-standing alliance between
the shire knights and the magnate opposition and it heralds the
association of knights and burgesses in common political aims.
The waning influence of Lancaster and the rise of the middle
party put an end to the baronial practice of using parliament
to voice popular grievance and impose restraints on the King.
The aim of the middle party was to exert private and personal
influence over the King, seeking his co-operation by respecting
the integrity of royal power. After 1322 the Commons faced
the Crown alone, until they were enrolled to legalize the
revolution of 1327. Although they provided taxes for Scottish
expeditions under the aegis of the middle party in 1319 and of
the King in 1322, thereafter they were spared for the ensuing
decade except for one grant in the immediate emergency of
1327. From 1332 when the Scottish war was resumed, a
fifteenth from the shires and a tenth from the boroughs became

---

[1] *Rot. Parl.* i. 451.   [2] Petit-Dutaillis, op. cit. ii. 230.

the standard form of tax, levied after 1334 on a fixed schedule. Henceforth knights and burgesses habitually made their grants in common.

The growing unity of the lower house which this implied was also reflected in the procedure for petitioning for redress of grievances. At some time in the period between 1316 and 1327 the Commons began to present petitions in the name of the 'commune' and fashion them into a series of articles. In the following decade the presentation of a comprehensive petition of articles became frequent, indeed almost normal. None of these surviving lists of petitions was presented in a parliament where taxes were granted, and the only occasion on which conditions were attached to a grant was (as far as is known) the subsidy of 1332 for which the King remitted his demand for tallage. As the evidence stands, there is thus a complete divorce in these years between taxation and the redress of grievance. Nevertheless it was in this period that the 'commune petition' became the accredited vehicle for the requests and grievances of the commons of the realm.

There is little doubt that at the beginning of the century the presentation of petitions from the 'commonalte' was heavily influenced by, if not wholly dependent on, the magnates. On the other hand, we can be certain that even at this date the Commons were framing some petitions themselves although the identification of these is far from easy.[1] One of the earliest would appear to be the sixth petition in those of 1309 from 'the knights, and men of the cities and burghs who had come to parliament' complaining of the lack of opportunity for answering their petitions. The same groups, on behalf of their communities, presented a petition of 1320 against unlawful assemblies, and the substance of the complaint of 1309 was voiced again in the fifth petition of 1325.[2] The conviction that the Commons in parliament came on behalf of the shires and

[1] The subject has received a good deal of attention, notably from H. L. Gray, *The Influence of the Commons on Early Legislation*, ch. viii; M. V. Clarke, *Medieval Representation and Consent*, pp. 232–4; H. G. Richardson and G. Sayles, 'The Early Records of the English Parliaments', *Bull. Inst. Hist. Res.* vi (1928–9), pp. 75–7 and 'The Parliaments of Edward III', ibid. ix (1931–2), pp. 5–12; D. Rayner, 'The Forms and Machinery of the Commune Petition in the Fourteenth Century', *Eng. Hist. Rev.* lvi (1941), pp. 198–233, 549–70; W. A. Morris, op. cit.

[2] The petition of 1309 is given in *Rot. Parl.* i. 443; that of 1320 in ibid., p. 371; that of 1325 in ibid., p. 430.

boroughs of the realm may suggest that they adopted some of the petitions described as coming 'from the community of the realm' or 'from the community of England', though these originated from bodies outside parliament, including, in one or two cases, the magnates themselves.[1] The great majority of such petitions were neither demands for political reform nor suits for personal favour, but complaints about legal, administrative, and economic grievances, which were of general concern to the parliamentary classes. Some of these might form the basis of statutes. But though there is little doubt that isolated petitions were presented by the Commons in parliament from early in the fourteenth century, it is more doubtful whether they can be credited with the framing of the articles of grievances. It has been suggested that the grouping of petitions together was a convenient means of presenting them to the council and recording a sequence of answers,[2] but perhaps more important was the example of both baronage and Church. We have noted already the practice of adding to the charters a series of specific recent grievances, which was extended without reissuing the charters in 1309–10. In the same way the clergy in these years presented a sequence of *gravamina*, often in the same parliaments as the articles of the laity, and not infrequently linked with the grant of taxation.[3] It would hardly be surprising if the Commons had thought to imitate these practices; yet they lacked the status and political confidence to confront the Crown on their own.

The petitions of the 'commonalte' attested the need for reform, but it rested with the magnates to secure and enforce this. This is clear in the articles formulated in the first decade.

[1] Richardson and Sayles, op. cit., *Bull. Inst. Hist. Res.* ix. 7. In 1330 the responsibility of knights of the shire for presenting the grievances of their communities is clearly stated in a writ ordering the election of loyal and sufficient knights (*Rot. Parl.* ii. 443).

[2] Rayner, op. cit., pp. 552–4.

[3] The clergy presented grievances at the parliament of Lent 1300, Hilary 1301, April 1309 and a final comprehensive series in the *Articuli Cleri* of 1316, the first three of which and possibly the last coincided with articles on behalf of the 'communalte'. See Richardson and Sayles, 'The Clergy in the Easter Parliament of 1285', *Eng. Hist. Rev.* lii (1937), pp. 228–9 and cf. Stubbs, *Const. Hist.* iii. 479. In the January parliament of 1315 the clergy made their grant of a subsidy conditional on a number of demands including the observance of the Ordinances (*Parl. Writs*, ii, App. p. 92).

Those of 1300, 1301, and 1310 were explicitly described as coming from the prelates, earls, and nobles even though in 1301 the complaints were expressed 'on behalf of the whole community' and presented by a knight. The grievances of 1297 had been presented by the magnates 'and all the community of the realm', as were the petitions in the parliament at Carlisle in January 1307 and the petition for perambulations of the Forest in 1316. The articles of 1309 were 'presented by the community of the realm' at the Easter parliament, and received the King's answer at Stamford in July when the magnates alone were present. The prologue to the articles describes the petitioning body as 'les bones gentz du roialme qi sont cy venuz au parlement' which may well describe the magnates alone, or in conjunction with the Commons, but cannot describe the Commons alone. Moreover, as in 1310, and in other baronial complaints, redress was sought on behalf of 'the people who are much aggrieved'. The prologue thus leaves little doubt that they were sponsored by the barons, but the articles and responses contained detailed complaints over royal levies and the jurisdiction of the household officers and courts. Some of these had been the subject of redress in 1300–1, but amongst novel matters was the sixth article already referred to as being undoubtedly from the Commons, and the second against the new customs charges. It is suggested, therefore, that the articles of 1309 did in the main emanate from the Commons but were presented by the magnates.[1] The grievances of the Commons in the parliaments of 1315 and 1316 have not survived but they may well have followed this pattern.[2] As it is, the only remain-

[1] See above, p. 110 n. 1.

[2] In 1315 the answering of petitions was postponed from the January–March session until the second session between 13–30 April at which the Commons were not present; but the writs issued to the sheriffs on 20 April declared it to be the King's intention that the requests of Commons made at the time of the grant concerning the Ordinances, the Great Charter, the Charter of the Forest, and the perambulations and other matters concerning the welfare of the people which the King had conceded, should be observed (*Parl. Writs*, ii, App. p. 89). In 1316 one grievance was certainly brought to the King's attention 'par demonstrance des Prelatz, Contes, Barons, et autres Grauntz du Roialme somons a cel Parlement, et par grevouses pleintes du Poeple' (*Rot. Parl.* i. 353). In 1330 the complaint that previously elected knights had been maintainers of false quarrels 'et n'ount mie soeffret que les bones gentz poient monstrer les grevances du commun people' also suggests that traditionally this had been the magnates' role (ibid. ii. 443).

ing articulated grievances which were drafted in parliament are
a fragmentary set of 1324, a short series from 1325, and the
longer and much the most important set of 1327.[1]

Five of the petitions of 1325 are described as being from 'les
liges gentz' (in one case 'pur tote la commune') and concern
matters of principal interest to the upper landholding class; the
remaining petition from 'les gentz de la commune de vostre
roialme' concerns the privileges of the city of London. This set
of petitions seems to be the composite work of a number of
different interests in parliament[2] and the set of 1327 shares the
same characteristic in a more marked form. The political intention of the latter is, of course, evident. The deposition of
Edward II had been staged as an act of the whole community,
and the first parliament of the new reign was required to attest
the preceding misrule and underline the harmony of the
political classes in furtherance of the common good.[3] Politically
there was the tally of reward and proscription to make up.
Articles were received from the clergy and from the city of
London, alongside those from the prelates, earls, barons, and
community of the realm.[4] The first six petitions in the original
list were concerned with the political settlement, redressing the
wrongs of the Despensers, rehabilitating the memory of Thomas
of Lancaster and restoring the fortunes of his followers. The remainder touched common legal and administrative grievances,
a number of which reflected the particular interests of magnates and tenants in chief.[5] Two reflected the political strife of

[1] These are, respectively, C 49/5/25; *Rot. Parl.* i. 430; *Rot. Parl. Hact. Ined.*,
ed. H. G. Richardson and G. Sayles (Camden Soc., 1935), pp. 116–26 and the
parallel version in *Rot. Parl.* ii. 7–11. For a discussion, see D. Rayner, op. cit.,
pp. 554–7.

[2] Gray and Morris (loc. cit.) accept these are emanating from the parliamentary
Commons; Richardson and Sayles (*Bull. Inst. Hist. Res.* vi. 77 n. 2 and ibid. ix. 8)
do not. It is agreed that the uniform pattern of the petitions indicates that they
were drawn up in parliament.

[3] For this ideal and its appearance in the *Modus*, see M. V. Clarke, op. cit.,
p. 336.

[4] I have followed the text and enumeration in *Rot. Parl. Hact. Ined.*, pp. 116–26,
in preference to that in *Rot. Parl.* ii. pp. 7–11 as representing the earlier stage of the
document. It is clear that these were rearranged as a consolidated petition in
parliament before being presented as a *bille endentee* to the council (ibid., pp.
101–2). The London articles, likewise, show clear evidence of having been assembled from a number of sets (ibid., p. 104).

[5] Particularly numbers 14, 31, 33. Cf. *Rot. Parl.* ii. 10 n. 35. See J. M. W.
Bean, *The Decline of English Feudalism* (Manchester, 1968), p. 134.

the time: no. 8 referred to evil counsellors;[1] no. 13 asked that 'bones gentz et covenables et sages' to be chosen by the nobles with the assent of the 'commune' should counsel the King, and that under pain of dismissal neither they nor any other minister should maintain a party or cause so that the common law be disturbed.[2] Like other articles this was presented in the name of the 'commune', and the specific grievance was both re-current and widespread; it was the provision that the tradi-tional baronial remedy of an 'elected' council should have the assent of the 'commune' that marked a significant gesture to the political influence of the Commons. The further demand[3] that the King's concessions should be circulated under the great seal to the sheriffs, to be proclaimed in the shire courts where 'the community should be compelled to swear even as we have sworn to maintain the enterprise here begun' reveals how deeply the Commons had imbibed the precedents of the Ordinances and testifies to their vivid awareness of the inter-dependence of the community at Westminster and the com-munities in the shires. They sought to match the binding power of their promises to the King (on taxation) with those of the King's promises (for redress) which they carried back to their constituents. Yet the King's response to this, that the oath taken by the Lords would suffice, underlined that the Com-mons were merely petitioners; the responsibility for initiating and maintaining reforms the King would exercise only with the Lords.

The political settlement of 1330 reflected the magnate ideal of royal authority. The King was to govern his people 'accord-ing to right and reason' by 'the common counsel of the mag-nates of the realm'. This would obviate the risk of a faction dominating the King's ear, and the corollary of a magnate alliance with the people against the favourites. Harmony be-tween the King and the lords indeed characterized the first few years of Edward III's reign, strengthened by the demands of the Scottish war. The Commons tended to become isolated from politics, though by the same process to develop their own corporate sense. This is reflected in their petitions. During the

[1] Nos 4 and 5 likewise accuse Edward II of being led by 'malveise consail'.
[2] This is *Rot. Parl.* ii. 10 n. 33. The response was: 'Acorde est q'il soit fait. Il plest au Roi.' [3] Ibid. ii. 10, 12.

1330s the 'commune petition' becomes a normal and perhaps regular feature of each parliament. Although there is no formal narrative of any parliament between February 1334 and February 1339, three lengthy lists of 'commune petitions' survive for 1333, 1334, and 1339 before we reach the important petitions of 1340.[1] The fact that after 1332 no individual petitions were enrolled, and that in 1334 a procedure was laid down for preserving an official record of the petitions and responses, confirms that such petitions were an identifiable and regular feature of parliament even though they were not yet enrolled on the parliament roll as a matter of course. The form, too, is becoming stereotyped: most of the articles in these petitions commence 'prie la commune' and those of 1333 and 1339 have the response recorded at the end and are analogous in form to those of 1327.[2] Although these petitions contain articles in which the magnates speak for the realm or even present their own requests, the subject-matter now predominantly reflects the concerns of the non-baronial classes while the form of the petitions bears the imprint of their arrangement in parliament and presentation by the Commons.[3] It is in this decade, we venture to say, that the independent voice of the shires is first articulated at Westminster.

Complaints that petitions had been left unanswered at the end of parliament had been heard in the preceding decades and the *Modus* had asserted that the responses should at least be determined before parliament was dissolved.[4] In 1333 the Commons complained that 'bills presented by the commons'

---

[1] *Rot. Parl. Hact. Ined.*, pp. 224–30, 232–9, 268–72. Cf. Rayner, op. cit., pp. 557–559. E. B. Fryde considers that those of February 1339 should be assigned to the parliament of March 1337 but I do not share this view. See below, p. 248 n. 2.

[2] Gray, *The Influence of the Commons*, p. 215.

[3] The 1334 petitions were said to be delivered into parliament 'par gentz de commune' who seem to be distinguished from 'les bones gentz de commune' of the first petition for the confirmation of the charters, and 'les bones gentz' of article four; in both these latter cases the reference is probably to the magnates. Article one of the 1333 set, on the other hand, from 'la commune de vostre poeple Dengleterre' embraces the whole realm and in each set the petitions on purveyances speak of the impoverishment or burdens of 'le poeple' (1333, no. 5; 1334, no. 17; 1339, no. 1). That is not to say that there was any established procedure for the authorization or 'avowal' of these petitions by the Commons. On this point, see Rayner, op. cit., p. 201.

[4] J. G. Edwards, 'Justice in Early English Parliaments', *Bull. Inst. Hist. Res.* xxvii (1954), pp. 44–6; *Modus*, cap. xxiv.

had not been answered; and again in 1339 they asked that all petitions should be answered before the rising of parliament. There was every justification for the former complaint since the answering of petitions in the Lent parliament of 1332 had been postponed until September, but that parliament had been dissolved for an urgent campaign on the borders after only three days. The case was recognized to be exceptional and the reassembly of parliament first in December and then in January at York was to enable business to be completed, including the petitions of the Commons.[1] But there was no attempt in this decade, as far as we know, to induce the King to answer petitions by withholding the grant of aid. This is suggestive of the decline of magnate interests in parliament as a vehicle for pressure on the King and indicative of the almost wholly non-political content of the petitions of this decade.

Demands for reconstituting the council, for restraints on the royal power or prerogative, even complaints against evil councillors are markedly absent by comparison with the previous twenty years. Redress is sought, by the King's grace, from administrative abuses, the malpractice of justice, or the burden of royal levies. Remedies are through the clarification or enforcement of existing statutes, or additional controls on royal officials. If the content of these petitions reflects the preoccupation of the Commons with the ills which bore particularly on their communities, and the withdrawal of magnate concern to influence or constrain the King, there was one grievance which threatened to assume political significance in these years. With the renewal of the war in 1332 complaint against prise (which had been noticeably absent in 1327)[2] was likely to reappear.

This had already been a subject of complaint in the parliament of Michaelmas 1331 where the *Articuli* were re-enacted and the King's exclusive right to purveyance asserted.[3] If we may judge from the *De Speculo Regis*, written at about this date, Edward III was already incurring criticism for his purveyances and the parliament of September 1332 which hastily granted

[1] Richardson and Sayles, *Bull. Inst. Hist. Res.* viii. 73.

[2] Prises on a fairly wide scale had been ordered in 1327 for the Scottish campaign but they do not seem to have provoked protest (*Memoranda Roll, 1326–7*, pp. 24, 134).

[3] *Rot. Parl.* ii. 62; *S.R.* i. 265.

a subsidy for the war (thereby securing the withdrawal of tallage) designated it as being to 'enable the king to live of his own and pay his expenses and not to burden his people with outrageous prises'.[1] Moreover, when the Commons succeeded in presenting their petitions in the York parliament of January 1333 the second of their articles sought further restrictions on purveyors. Advancing beyond *Articuli Super Cartas*, they asked that men should be chosen in each county with the King's warrant to survey the activities of purveyors and punish infringements of the statutes. On the eve of a major campaign Edward was well advised to agree to the setting-up of 'justices of purveyors', unprecedented though this was.[2] Actually, in February the King contracted with Manent Francisci, of the firm of Bardi, to supply the armies, but Francisci's failure to deliver in sufficient quantity led to widespread purveyances in the Spring of 1333, though only about one-fifth of what was ordered was secured.[3] Accordingly on 4 March Edward issued writs appointing four justices in each of the ridings of Yorkshire and the counties of Nottingham and Derby.[4] Although the King's concession probably had little effect,[5] it was indicative of the Commons' concern over illegal prises, which was to emerge forcefully by the end of the decade under pressure from the immeasurably greater demands of the war with France. By the time the next parliament met in February 1334, Edward had secured his triumph over the Scots and the immediate need for purveyances had disappeared. The petitions did, none the less, make complaint that 'le poeple est molt greve par diverses prises' for non-royal households and asked that these should cease and that those for the King be taken as ordained by statute. Although for the final large-scale campaign in Scotland, that of 1334–5, the chronicle of Meaux complained of the burden of taxes and exactions,[6] the purveyances

---

[1] *Rot. Parl.* ii. 66; J. Tait, 'On the Date and Authorship of the *Speculum Regis Edwardi*', *Eng. Hist. Rev.* xvi (1901), pp. 110–15. For a further discussion on the text in the context of the King's 'own', see below, p. 179.

[2] *Rot. Parl. Hact. Ined.*, pp. 224, 228.

[3] R. Nicholson, *Edward III and the Scots* (Oxford, 1935), pp. 109–10, 113–15. For the commissions, see *C.C.R., 1333–7*, pp. 25–6, 27, 29; *Rot. Scot.* i. 229–30.

[4] *C.P.R., 1330–34*, p. 443.

[5] The Statute of 1336 made no reference to this and merely re-enacted that of 1331 which embodied the traditional legislation of 1300 (*S.R.* i. 276–7).

[6] *Chronica Monasterii de Melsa*, ed. E. A. Bond, ii (R.S., 1867), p. 373: 'Pro dicta

for Edward III's Scottish wars seem not to have provoked protests of the same depth and anger as those of the latter years of his grandfather. Above all there was no attempt to interpret such grievances as tokens of misgovernment for the purpose of political constraint on the King.

The forty years following the crisis of 1297 have long been recognized as formative of the character of the English parliament and, if the preceding analysis is correct, they witnessed the development of the principles of common assent and common profit which *Confirmatio Cartarum* had enshrined. The need for common assent to all forms of national taxation demanded that this assent be rendered in a full parliament where the Commons, who had the power to bind their communities to pay, could join in adjudicating the common necessity of the realm. Common necessity was closely allied to common profit, to which the Commons appealed in attesting the grievances of their communities. The peculiar authority of the Commons as representatives in the business of assenting and complaining helped to establish them as an essential part of a parliament which was recognized as the supreme expression of the 'communitas regni'. But though partners in this 'communitas' with the King and the magnates, the Commons were very much junior partners, and both magnates and King used the peculiar representative authority of the Commons for their own purposes. Up to 1311 the baronial opposition exploited the Commons' attestation of grievances to justify reform of royal government and utilized their power to grant taxation to force the King to accept reforms and eventually restraints. Such use of taxation and grievance for political constraint might pass beyond the bounds of legality; it depended on baronial leadership and had no relevance for the Commons' ability to assert their own interests. After 1311 this phase of close association with the magnate opposition came to an end; the King and the magnates separately and together used the Commons to provide fiscal and military supplies. Yet burdensome as were the grants of taxation and the communal levies of troops which parliament now authorized, these emphasized its authority to

---

autem guerra in Scocia, Anglia geldis creberrimis et exactionibus variis multipliciter est compressa'; cf. the discussion by Nicholson, op. cit., ch. xii.

sanction levies which touched the goods of the subject and
served to familiarize and define the principle of a necessity of
the realm for which they were demanded. They also helped to
characterize as illicit national prises and military service, which
were extensions of the prerogative. Whatever went beyond the
ancient right to household prise and local service under the
Statute of Winchester was thought to need assent. More particularly was this so when such levies were made without payment, and were thus identified as forms of prerogative taxation.
The King's readiness to provide payment was indeed the
condition of the toleration of this use of the prerogative. Payment thus safeguarded both the king's right and the subject's
goods. But if such levies or taxation itself did threaten the
welfare of the subject, then common assent to taxation provided the opportunity for criticism of royal government in the
name of the common profit. Although the Commons had not
yet been emboldened to do this on their own, their petitions
which they now formulated and presented on their own
authority uniquely voiced the grievances of the communities
of the realm. It only awaited a widespread sense of grievance
affecting the whole *communitas regni* for their petitions to include
demands for political reform.

CHAPTER VI

The Fisc

THE transition from feudal to national taxation during the period 1150–1300 was matched by a similar change in attitude towards the customary revenues of the Crown. There was of course less impulse to define the function of revenues hallowed by custom or the authority by which kings had long exacted them. But the emergence of a distinction between the Crown and the King brought subjects to view the King's feudal resources as the appurtenances of his office, with the function of maintaining its public status and role. It will be best to approach this development through the theory of the fisc, then to consider how this theory influenced the royal administration and finally to examine how the fisc became an element in the political relations of the King and his subjects.

The distinction between the Crown, the King, and the realm had begun to emerge in both England and France by the beginning of the thirteenth century.[1] The Crown symbolized the authority to rule with which the mortal King was invested and on which the existence of the realm depended.[2] Superior to both King and realm, since both in a sense depended on it, the Crown embodied the essential rights of the former and the

---

[1] The following account is based principally upon Gaines Post, *Studies in Medieval Legal Thought*; Hartmut Hoffman, 'Die Unveraüslichkeit der Kronrechter in Mittelalter', *Deutsches Archiv für Erforschung des Mittelalters*, xx (1964); F. Hartung, 'Die Krone als Symbol der Monarchischen Herrschaft im Ausgehenden Mittelalter', *Abhandlungen der Preussischen Akademie der Wissenschaften, Phil.-Hist. Klasse*, xiii (1940), especially pp. 6–19 dealing specifically with England; P. N. Riesenberg, *Inalienability of Sovereignty in Medieval Political Thought* (New York, 1956); E. H. Kantorowicz, *The King's Two Bodies* (Princeton, 1957); idem, 'Inalienability: a Note on Canonical Practice and the English Coronation Oath in the Thirteenth Century', *Speculum*, xxix (1954): H. G. Richardson, 'The English Coronation Oath', *Speculum*, xxiv (1949); idem, 'The Coronation in Medieval England', *Traditio*, xvi (1960), especially pp. 151–61; R. S. Hoyt, *The Royal Demesne in English Constitutional History, 1066–1272* (New York, 1950); idem, 'The Coronation Oath of 1308: the Background of "Les Leys et Les Custumes"', *Traditio*, xi (1955); W. Ullman, *Principles of Government and Politics in the Middle Ages* (London, 1961).

[2] Riesenberg, op. cit., pp. 98–9; Kantorowicz, *King's Two Bodies*, pp. 340 ff.

essential continuity of the latter. Such imprecise phrases as 'the honour and rights of the Crown', 'the estate of the Crown', 'the dignity of the Crown', 'the rights of the Crown of our realm' were designed to express this.[1] The nature of the Crown defined the functions of the King and his subjects. The King wore the Crown to signify that he was entrusted with all the public authority necessary for the preservation of the state and the fulfilment of its purpose. The attributes of the Crown—its dignity, honour, majesty—were made visible in his own royal estate, which on occasion might be treated as synonymous with the body politic, the *regnum* itself.[2] Thus the state of the kingdom depended on, and was made visible in, the state of the King. In this sense a doctrine of the Crown exalted the natural authority of the ruler.

Conversely, however, the state of the King was part of the state of the kingdom. The kingdom existed for the maintenance of the common good of the King and his subjects, and the King held his authority for the achievement of this end. His authority was defined by his duty to augment the rights of the King and kingdom and to eschew all that would diminish or destroy them. The King was not the *dominus*, the owner of the kingdom, with power to destroy it at will; rather he was the minister, the *tutor* of it, whose every action should be in conformity with the public good, the common profit.[3] This ideal of the harmonious partnership of ruler and ruled found symbolic expression in the Crown. The Crown became 'the juristic expression of the union of King and community of the realm'.[4] It stood for the good of the kingdom, indeed its very existence, and matters which touched the Crown were common to both the King and the community. Nor was this of merely theoretical importance.

[1] Richardson, *Speculum*, xxiv. 49–51; Riesenberg, op. cit., pp. 98–9. Bracton's statement on the rights which the King wielded in virtue of his Crown is discussed by Post, op. cit., p. 342, and see ibid. p. 397 for the decretal *Intellecto* and its statement of the 'iura regni et honorem coronae'. In the twelfth century kings frequently made appeal to the rights and dignity of the Crown in their disputes with the Church. See N. F. Cantor, *Church, Kingship and Lay Investiture in England 1089–1135* (Princeton, 1958), p. 78, and W. L. Warren, *Henry II*, pp. 431, 454.

[2] Post, op. cit., pp. 343, 367.

[3] Riesenberg, op. cit., pp. 62, 155–6, 178; Kantorowicz, *King's Two Bodies*, p. 190; Post, op. cit., pp. 281–3. For John of Salisbury's view of the King as a minister, see Post, op. cit., pp. 260, 355 and also p. 296.

[4] Ullmann, op. cit., p. 179.

Edward I's declaration to Gregory X in 1275 that he could do
nothing that touched the diadem of the realm without having
first consulted the prelates and barons was the most specific
acknowledgement that matters which touched the Crown (in
which the rights of the kingdom were comprised) were not to
be disposed of merely by the will of the King alone.[1] The
obligation on the ruler to take counsel when disposing of the
'iura regis et regni', like his obligation to obtain consent for
measures to deal with a necessity of the realm, had feudal
precedents as well as juristic roots.

The perpetuity of the Crown logically found expression in a
doctrine of the inalienability of whatever pertained to its
essence. This principle, derived directly from Roman law, was
appearing in the parlance of Western Europe from early in the
twelfth century.[2] At first it was expressed in somewhat unspecific terminology, in declarations that the royal 'majestas',
the 'honor regni' should be preserved 'illaesa et illibata'. Before
long it was applied to the lands and customary revenues of
the Crown which, together with the rights of the Crown,
comprised what was necessary to maintain the 'status regis',
the 'status coronae'. Thus emerged the notion of the fisc which
by the thirteenth century is conceived as enjoying a supra-
personal continuity independent of the life of the ruler.[3] By the
later Middle Ages theorists liken it to the soul of the realm, or
see it as the dowry of the *respublica*.[4] Such analogues emphasized
that the basic function of the fisc was to maintain the Crown
and thereby the state itself. This demanded the perpetual
preservation of its integrity. Only a dire necessity, which
threatened the very life of the state, could justify the alienation
of the fisc.[5] The corollary of these views was that the fisc was
not the private possession of the ruler, but was of common concern to the prince and the people. It served to maintain the

---

[1] Kantorowicz, *Speculum*, xxix. 500–1; *King's Two Bodies*, p. 361; Hoffmann, op.
cit., p. 458, with other examples pp. 435–9.

[2] Post, op. cit., pp. 399 f., 417 f.

[3] Kantorowicz, *King's Two Bodies*, pp. 176–7; Post, op. cit., pp. 371, 374,
417–19 where the words of Ralph de Diceto are quoted: 'fiscalia supprimentes, et
quae principis laederent majestatem, regiam indignationem incurrerent'. For the
public nature of the fisc according to Accursius, see ibid., p. 14.

[4] Kantorowicz, *King's Two Bodies*, pp. 212 ff.; Riesenberg, op. cit., p. 155.

[5] Cf. Innocent III's letter of 1200 to the guardians of Frederick of Hohenstaufen,
cited by Riesenberg, op. cit., p. 56.

public estate of the ruler, which in turn was constituted for the public good. If the people had an obligation to maintain the prince in a manner sufficient for his public dignity, he had an obligation to use these revenues for the common weal. Thus the prohibition against alienations of the fisc went, in theory, to the heart of that harmony between King and people, that identity of interest in maintaining the existence of the state and the common profit of ruler and ruled which it existed to promote.

The fisc has not been a term much favoured by the historians of Angevin England although some basic misunderstanding of the Crown's customary revenue might have been avoided if it had been preferred to the more usual 'royal demesne' or 'crown estate'. For as B. P. Wolffe has pointed out, the resources available to the Angevins through their political power as kings greatly exceeded their resources as landlords.[1] It was this prerogative authority over the resources of the realm and not their enjoyment of a restricted or immutable body of lands which constituted the fisc. The demesne lands, both those which figured as *terra regis* in Domesday Book and those acquired or held temporarily by feudal right, formed but one part of the fisc. The revenue derived from the King's feudal and judicial prerogatives and even from scutage and tallage was equally comprised in the fisc.[2] The fisc was thus less an estate or a defined revenue than the expression in land, legal rights, and administrative action of the King's status and authority. And the fact that this was so within the feudal kingdom of England made the reception of Roman law notions of inalienability and eventually of the public nature of the fisc that much easier.

A doctrine of the inalienability of the English royal fisc gradually emerged in the late twelfth and early thirteenth centuries. There seems little doubt that the impetus for this came from the Angevin policy of recovering and exploiting the rights of the Crown. The first phase of this was the extensive resumptions of royal lands in the years immediately following Henry II's accession. Lack of documentary evidence makes it difficult to be sure on what basis these were carried out, but Henry reputedly invoked the notion that such lands pertained

[1] B. P. Wolffe, *The Royal Demesne in English History* (London, 1971), ch. 1.

[2] For the use of the term fisc to cover the generality of the Crown's revenue, see Matthew Paris, *Chron. Maj.* iii. 219–20.

to the royal demesne or the fisc and some of the early resumptions explicitly affected lands which had been 'illicitly and unreasonably alienated'.[1] Whether Henry was acting on the basis of an oath taken at his coronation can only be a matter for surmise,[2] but a contrast between lands 'unreasonably' alienated and those alienated after due counsel does suggest that the Crown lands were regarded as the concern not merely of the King but of the realm.[3]

The second phase of Angevin policy, the fiscal exploitation of Crown lands and rights, was a reaction to half a century of heavy military expenditure and rapid inflation which began about 1180.[4] The insufficiency of their customary revenues compelled the Angevin kings to experiment with various forms of feudal and national taxation. They also attempted by various devices to increase the yield of the fisc, and though this was not in monetary terms strikingly successful, it served to confer on the demesne a legal identity and to establish the fisc as a political concept. The monopoly which the sheriff exercised over the collection of Crown revenue, once the bedrock of the monarchy's resources, was now seen as the impediment to its expansion. Within the fixed farm of the shire the sheriff collected not merely the farms of royal lands but annual rents like sheriff's aid, the profits of the shire and hundred courts, the view of frankpledge, and some smaller items. Separately accounted for were the assarts, purprestres (encroachments) and escheats, the amercements in the King's courts, and the fines and compositions made with the King in respect of feudal obligations. There were two ways in which the King could increase this revenue: he could either make the sheriff pay more for the farm or he could withdraw revenues from the sheriff to exploit them more profitably by other means.

The institution of first an 'increment' and then under John a 'profit' above the traditional farm, increased the yield by

[1] Hoyt, *Royal Demesne*, pp. 94–6; Richardson, *Traditio*, xvi. 154–5; W. L. Warren, *Henry II*, pp. 61, 368.   [2] Richardson, *Traditio*, xvi. 151–74.
[3] Ibid., pp. 157–8. V. H. Galbraith has pointed out (*Studies in the Public Records* (London, 1948), p. 127), that already from Richard I's reign the most solemn charters or perpetuities which alienated for ever royal prerogatives or demesne were fully dated and closed with a special formula taken from papal bulls.
[4] P. D. A. Harvey, 'The English Inflation of 1180–1220', *Past and Present*, 61 (1973), especially pp. 9–15.

about a third. But after four years the exaction of a 'profit' had to be abandoned, though both John and Richard on occasion compelled sheriffs to purchase the office by a large lump sum.[1] Amongst the shire revenues themselves the judicial and casual revenues offered the greatest opportunities for expansion. This was already appreciated by the author of the *Dialogus*, who records that the Eyre provided an instrument for inquiry into purprestres, escheats, and forfeitures, the revenue from which was additional to the farm of the shire. In the thirteenth century the declining concern of the sheriff with land revenues allowed him to be increasingly used as a collector of royal debts from fines and amercements levied in the Chancery, Exchequer, the Benches, and before the Eyre justices. This section of his account, known as the 'summonses' (summons of the Pipe and of the Green Wax), rose in value to exceed the farm and profit as the separate recording of these fines in estreats and their enrolment on the Originalia rolls of the Exchequer were systematized.[2] The revenue from escheats and wardships was likewise withdrawn from the sheriffs' hands in the reforms of 1232–4 and came eventually to be administered by separate officials within the counties, the escheators.[3] But most attention was devoted to the administration of the Crown lands. John began the practice of removing lands and boroughs from the sheriffs to lease them at higher rates to other farmers although such leases might not always be at the full value, for at all times grants of farms were an important way of giving favour or reward. Painter guessed that this might have added some £1,000 to their yield, and the value of these experiments was not lost on the Poitevins who resumed control of royal administration in the 1230s. In 1236 the last of the royal manors was removed from the hands of the sheriffs to be administered on short renewable leases under two 'keepers of demesne lands'.[4]

---

[1] S. Painter, *King John*, pp. 116–23; J. C. Holt, *The Northerners*, pp. 153–7; W. A. Morris, 'The Sheriff', in *The English Government at Work, 1327–1337*, ii (Cambridge, Mass., 1947), pp. 73–100; B. E. Harris, 'King John and the Sheriff's Farms', *Eng. Hist. Rev.* lxxix (1964), pp. 532–42; Harvey, op. cit., p. 10.

[2] *Dialogus*, p. 93; Hoyt, *Royal Demesne*, p. 95; M. Mills, 'The Reforms at the Exchequer (1232–42)', *Trans. Roy. Hist. Soc.*, 4th ser. x (1927), pp. 127–8; F. M. Powicke, *King Henry III and the Lord Edward* (Oxford), 1947)., pp. 96–8; W. A. Morris, op. cit., pp. 93–5; W. L. Warren, op. cit., p. 274.

[3] This is discussed below, pp. 151 ff.

[4] Painter, *King John*, p. 124, and Holt, *The Northerners*, pp. 153–7 for John's

The background to these administrative changes was the
regular inquisitions conducted through sheriffs and itinerant
justices into Crown lands. Investigation of 'illicit alienations'
helped to conserve the Crown's rights, but resumption followed
by re-seisin could also be used (e.g. in 1217) as a way of raising
the farm. The writs which ordered the investigation of alienations left little doubt that resumption was justified simply on
the ground that the lands were part of the demesne. The
demesne thus began to emerge as a separate administrative
entity in which the King's unlimited rights over the land could
facilitate intensive fiscal exploitation.[1] The concurrent development of tallage, as a tax on all lands of ancient demesne (the
terra regis of Domesday Book) in whosoever's hands they were,
as also upon lands temporarily in the King's hands by escheat,
further assisted this. Tallage was levied fourteen times under
Henry III but only twice thereafter; its rise and decline aptly
characterized this period of prerogative taxation which preceded the full acceptance of national taxation in the last
decades of the century.[2] Thus, as R. S. Hoyt has said, 'Under
John and during the minority of Henry III, the royal demesne
. . . emerged for the first time as a Crown endowment specially
subject to the unhampered royal will and annexed to the office,
rather than merely belonging to and disposable by the person
of the king.' Its evolution as an appurtenance of the Crown
may be traced in the change of nomenclature from 'royal
demesne' to 'ancient demesne of the King' to (by 1258–67)
'ancient demesne of the Crown'.[3]

From the very beginning of the thirteenth century kings
began formally to acknowledge that this implied some restric-

---

exploitation of the demesne lands and farms; Mills, op. cit., pp. 122–5; F. M.
Powicke, *King Henry III and the Lord Edward*, pp. 102–3.

[1] Kantorowicz, *King's Two Bodies*, p. 167; Hoyt, *Royal Demesne*, p. 146; Riensen-
berg, op. cit., pp. 14–15, 100; Hoffmann, op. cit., p. 441, thinks, however, that
these lands are not to be identified with the royal demesne. According to the St.
Albans chronicler Henry II's resumptions applied to 'all lands which formed part
of the demesne of his predecessors as Kings of England': *Gesta Abbatum Sancti
Albani*, i. 123, cited by Warren, *Henry II*, p. 61.

[2] Mitchell, *Taxation*, chs. v–viii and in particular pp. 356–7. The sources on
which tallage was levied in a number of shires in 1261 is printed in *C.C.R., 1264–8*,
pp. 534–40. The tallage levied in 1303 yielded a total of only £2,862 (Ramsay,
Revenues, ii. 71).

[3] Hoyt, *Royal Demesne*, pp. 135, 143, 163.

tion on its alienation. Early in John's reign the London interpolator of the *Leges Edwardi Confessoris* claims that the King is
bound to preserve the lands, honours, dignities, rights, and
liberties or the Crown of this realm and to recover the 'iura
regni, amissa et dilapidata'.[1] Henry III, however, is the first
King to appeal to a coronation oath in recognizably these
terms, although in 1216 Louis had declared that John had
sworn to preserve the rights and customs of the Church and
kingdom.[2] Not until the second half of the thirteenth century
did the English lawyers evolve a thoroughgoing doctrine of
inalienability, and then in regard to the prerogatives and
authority of the Crown rather than its lands. Bracton designated
certain franchises—those concerned with doing justice and
keeping the peace—as belonging to the Crown 'because they
make the Crown what it is', and hence as being inalienable.
Moreover, the perpetual character of the Crown deprived a
grant of such rights, however ancient, of any title. Time did not
run against the King, for the nature of the Crown outlasted
and defeated all temporal grants.[3] Under the influence of
Bracton, the Edwardian lawyers 'Fleta' and 'Britton' extended
this into a wholesale doctrine of inalienability which rendered
invalid all grants of liberties made by the King or his predecessors and obliged the King to resume them.

Royal policy followed some way behind these doctrines.
Kings made grants of franchises for life or in perpetuity, and
even Edward I's *Quo Warranto* proceedings, though they drew
on this legal background, admitted that holders of franchises
might plead a title of long user.[4] Kings might indeed invoke
the notion of a perpetual Crown to assert their rights over

[1] Liebermann, *Gesetze*, i. 635. I have followed most authorities in regarding this
interpolation as part of the archetype from which Rs/Ai derive, and thus dated to
post-1204 (Liebermann, *Leges Anglorum saec. xiii London, Coll.*, pp. vii, 77; 'A Contemporary Manuscript of the "Leges Anglorum Londoniis Collectae" ', *Eng. Hist.
Rev.* xxviii (1913), p. 742). However, H. G. Richardson (*Traditio*, xvi. 151–61), has
sought to detach it from its London connection and date it to early in Henry II's
reign. I am grateful to Professor J. C. Holt for advice on this point.
[2] Richardson, *Speculum*, xxiv. 48–56; Hoffmann, op. cit., pp. 426–32; Post, op.
cit., pp. 431–3.
[3] F. Pollock and F. W. Maitland, *A History of English Law*, i (Cambridge, 1895),
p. 518; Hartung, op. cit., p. 8; Kantorowicz, *King's Two Bodies*, pp. 10–11; D. W.
Sutherland, *Quo Warranto Proceedings in the Reign of Edward I* (Oxford, 1963), p. 13.
[4] Sutherland, op. cit., pp. 14–15, 128; Hartung, loc. cit.; Hoffmann, op. cit.,
pp. 431–2.

lands which were threatened by alienation. Thus in 1254 Henry III invested his son with lands and castles which were 'never to be separated from the Crown' and in 1261 he complained that the barons 'permit the King's son to squander what the lord King has given him as an endowment of the Crown of England, and which were conveyed to him so that they should not be separated from the Crown of England as appears by his charters'.[1] The same principle underlay the Dictum of Kenilworth which required that 'all places, rights, property and other things pertaining to the royal Crown shall be restored to the Crown itself and the lord King by those who detain them, unless they show that they possess them by reasonable warrant from the lord King or his predecessors'.[2] But like the illicit and unreasonable grants which Henry II had resumed a century earlier, the resumptions after the baronial civil wars were to apply only to alienations for which no adequate title could be shown. Those made under proper authority by the King and his council were not called in question. The principle of inalienability in the thirteenth century, it has been stressed, was not a legal rule which constrained the King. It was operated by the King against irregular alienations which were prejudicial to the estate of the King and his Crown.[3]

Even so, by invoking the notion of the inalienability of things which pertained to the Crown, the King was wielding a double-edged sword. With regard to the fisc Bracton had observed that, like the King's peace and jurisdiction, this was 'res quasi sacra'; it 'could not be given or sold or transferred by the reigning monarch to another, for it constitutes the Crown and belongs to the common good'.[4] Thus the fisc could not be

---

[1] Rymer, *Foedera*, I. i. 297. The same reservation was made in the grants of the Isle of Oléron (ibid., pp. 374, 388, 404). Cf. Hartung, op. cit., p. 10. The *gravamina* of Henry III are printed by N. Denholm-Young in *Collected Papers on Mediaeval Subjects*, pp. 127–9; this is item 20. Cf. E. F. Jacob, 'The Complaints of Henry III against the Baronial Council in 1261', *Eng. Hist. Rev.* xli (1926), pp. 559–68. [2] *S.R.* i. 13.
[3] Hoyt, *Royal Demesne*, p. 166; Hoffmann, op. cit., p. 444; Wolffe, op. cit., p. 45. When Edward I proposed to resume the vill of Stamford from Earl Warenne his advisers declared that he was bound to resume all rights unlawfully detached from the Crown even though they had been alienated by him before he became King (H. Cam, 'The Quo Warranto Proceedings', *History*, xi (1926), p. 145). This provides an interesting parallel with the reign of Henry II.
[4] Kantorowicz, *King's Two Bodies*, p. 168; Hoffmann, op. cit., p. 431 n. 50.

alienated (in the sense that there was no prescription against the Crown) and should not be alienated because it was a thing which pertained to the Crown for the profit of the King and kingdom.[1] Non-alienation expressed not merely the King's right and the King's duty, but the interest of the realm as a whole. Such considerations were not without effect on those who were charged with giving the King faithful service and profitable counsel. The first known councillor's oath, in 1257, prohibited councillors from consenting to any alienation of those things which pertained to the ancient demesne of the Crown.[2] The case of Master Simon the Norman shows that such men, though appointed by the King, might conceive a duty to resist his orders in order to preserve the rights of the Crown,[3] and it was upon this basis that the baronial opposition of 1258–60 sought to restrain the King's power to make gifts.

In submitting their case to Louis IX, the barons accused Henry III of so depleting the normal revenues of the Crown by prodigal gifts that he was unable to maintain his estate except by seizures from his people.[4] Condemnation of alienations which impaired the royal dignity was currently voiced by the papacy,[5] but restraint of royal alienations by subjects was more hazardous. In the *Song of Lewes* the King's choice of evil counsellors to whom he showed unreasonable generosity is criticized on the ground that he cannot be permitted to destroy the kingdom. But the poem has nothing to say on the restriction of royal grants and acknowledges Henry's own assertion that he should be as free to give his revenues as any of the lords who were his subjects.[6]

---

[1] Hoyt, *Royal Demesne*, pp. 162–3; Kantorowicz, *King's Two Bodies*, pp. 173, 343; Riesenberg, op. cit., p. 15.

[2] Hoyt, *Royal Demesne*, pp. 162–3; Kantorowicz, op. cit., p. 166. The full text is printed by J. F. Baldwin, *The King's Council in England in the Later Middle Ages* (Oxford, 1913), pp. 346–7. For the importance of the advice of the King's councillors for alienations in the late twelfth century, see Richardson, *Traditio*, xvi. 158. In 1275 Edward I declared that he was bound by his coronation oath to preserve uninjured the rights of the realm and not to do anything touching the Crown of the realm without requesting the counsel of the prelates and *proceres* (*C.C.R.*, *1272–9*, p. 198).

[3] F. M. Powicke, *King Henry III*, pp. 295, 781; Hoyt, *Royal Demesne*, p. 162.

[4] See *Documents of the Baronial Movement of Reform and Rebellion, 1258–1267*, ed. R. F. Treharne and I. J. Sanders (Oxford, 1973), nos. 37B, 37C.

[5] For Innocent IV's prohibition of alienations which impaired the royal dignity, see Riesenberg, op. cit., p. 116.

[6] The complaint put into the King's mouth in the *Song of Lewes* ll. 490–523 is

Such a proprietary view of the fisc would soon be outdated; already Aquinas could refer to the revenues of the realm as the King's 'stipendia', the fiscal attributes of his office, and by the next century a King would be viewed as trustee rather than *dominus* of the fisc.[1] For the present, although the barons were ready to condemn the King's prodigality, they were still hesitant about any outright challenge to royal authority. Some measure of resumption of royal lands seems to have been proposed at their meeting in Oxford in 1258 and the members of the council later took an oath not to receive themselves nor to permit the King to give away any part of the ancient demesne of the Crown.[2] Henry reacted strongly to this but in fact, though the grounds on which the Ordainers were later to restrain royal authority (namely, the King's dependence on evil counsellors, his prodigality, and the impoverishment of his estate and realm) could all be adduced in 1258, they were never co-ordinated to justify restrictions on the royal power in the name of the common profit.

If the baronial opposition evinced some hesitation about limiting the King's free disposal of the demesne, they felt markedly freer to criticize and restrain his gifts of feudal perquisites. This was because reliefs, wardships, marriages, escheats, and the temporalities of vacant sees and abbeys had long been regarded as occasional perquisites which were not attached permanently to the Crown as were its lands, and were thus unaffected by notions of inalienability. Revenue from such 'casualties' might take the form of 'offerings' or 'agreements' which testified to the King's freedom to bargain over his rights, and from the end of the twelfth century there is already evidence that they were considered more suitable as rewards than were gifts of desmesne manors.[3] A century later 'Fleta' lays down the principle that the King can bestow and lawfully alienate the lands which come to him as an escheat or acquisition as distinct

---

echoed in Henry III's complaints against the council in 1261 printed in *Documents of the Baronial Movement*, nos. 30, 31.

[1] *De Regimine Judaeorum* in *Selected Political Writings* ed. A. P. D'Entrèves, pp. 90, 92.

[2] *Documents of the Baronial Movement*, nos. 4, 29, 37B.

[3] Hoyt, *Royal Demesne*, pp. 102–3. The phrase in the *Dialogus*, p. 97, 'genus excidentium vel escaetarum', is translated by C. Johnson as 'class of casualties or escheats'.

from those of ancient demesne.[1] Bracton gives the reason for this when he describes some things as 'pertaining to the Crown on account of the privilege of the King and which thus do not belong to the common profit but can be given and transferred to another because if transferred this will be no damage except to the King himself'.[2] The first step to give administrative expression to this distinction was taken in the reforms which marked the inception of Henry III's personal rule in 1232.

Under the direction of Peter des Rivaux, who now became the general supervisor and custodian of all escheats and wardships, escheats were separated from the farm of the shires and pairs of escheators were appointed in nearly all shires. The policy aroused criticism in the parliament of February 1234 and later in that year Peter was replaced in his office by two escheators south of Trent, to whom a third was added in 1236, with responsibility for the shires north of Trent.[3] Henceforth the escheatries had a continuous, separate history. Moreover, Henry III showed a tendency to earmark such revenues for bestowal as personal favours or for the support of particular causes which he had at heart. One of the complaints in 1234 had been of the disposal of wardships and marriages to Poitevins and the first receipts from the escheators had been largely paid into the Wardrobe.[4] In 1241, perhaps as a temporary measure, Henry III made a more specific separation of such revenue, ordering that all fines from pleas held *coram rege*, all temporalities of bishoprics, and all revenue from the custody of escheats should be sent to and stored in the Tower of London under special keepers, to be reserved for his own use.[5] Temporalities had always been a potentially lucrative source of revenue, which in some years had yielded the Angevins around £2,000 and

---

[1] *Fleta*, Lib. III, c. 6, ed. H. G. Richardson and G. O. Sayles, iii (Selden Soc., 1972), p. 12; quoted by Hartung, op. cit., p. 8 and by Hoffmann, op. cit., p. 444 n. 120. The inquests of 1274 began by asking what manors the King held 'tam scilicet de antiquis dominicis corone quam de escaetis et perquisitis' (H. Cam, *The Hundred and the Hundred Rolls* (London, 1930), p. 248).

[2] Bracton, *De Legibus*, fol. 14, ed. Woodbine, ii. 58, quoted in Kantorowicz, *King's Two Bodies*, p. 170 n. 243.

[3] Powicke, *King Henry III and the Lord Edward*, pp. 105–8; E. R. Stevenson, 'The Escheator', *The English Government at Work, 1327–1336*, ed. W. A. Morris and J. R. Strayer, ii (Cambridge, Mass., 1947), p. 115. The escheators seem for a time to have handled temporalities as well.

[4] Stevenson, loc. cit.   [5] *C.C.R., 1237–42*, p. 277.

gave Edward I a calculated average of £1,700 p.a. throughout
the reign; under Henry III they tended to be paid indifferently
into Wardrobe or Exchequer, though during the periods of
greatest Wardrobe activity, from 1237 to 1242 and from 1255
to 1258, they became one of the major sources of its receipt.[1]
Under pressure of his debts, Henry on occasion made over the
revenue from these casualties to individual creditors, as well
as using some of it for projects, such as building, which reflected
his personal tastes and concerns.

Such revenue, though it fluctuated, was never negligible, and
it was not surprising that this field, where Henry's indulgence
and extravagances were most evident, should become the
focus for baronial criticism. This postulated a different use for
these revenues which perhaps reflected a different view of their
nature. When, in 1237, the King asked the barons to grant a
thirtieth, Richard of Cornwall rebuked him for his misgovernment and extravagance and added that Henry had collected
untold wealth from the vacancies of abbeys, earldoms and
baronies, wardships and escheats.[2] When they again refused a
tax in 1242, the barons observed that the King should have had
a large sum available from recent casualties if these had been
properly safeguarded.[3] This criticism was not wholly disinter-
ested: the complaint in the *Song of Lewes* is not so much against
royal prodigality as that the recipients are unworthy foreigners.
Instead the King is urged to use escheats and wardships to
honour his own men, who will be strong enough to aid him in
various ways.[4] Even so, the fact that the magnates were slowly
driven to criticize Henry's administration and ultimately forced
to take over the task of government in the name of reform led
them to challenge the view that the casualties were at the
King's personal disposal for his private interests, and to claim
them as a contribution to the needs of the realm.

The Provisions of Oxford forbade the Chancellor to seal any

[1] M. Howell, *Regalian Right in Medieval England* (Oxford, 1962), pp. 152–5.
The figure for Edward I's revenue has been calculated by M. C. Prestwich (*War,
Politics and Finance*, p. 178) on the basis of Howell's evidence.

[2] Matthew Paris, *Chron. Maj.* iii. 411.

[3] Ibid. iv. 186; Stubbs, *Select Charters*, p. 361. This criticism was distinct from
the reason for their refusal of the tax which was that, to their knowledge, the
previous grant had not been spent.

[4] *The Song of Lewes*, ll. 296–300.

gift of a major wardship or escheat without the assent of the
great council, a restriction of which Henry was to complain
bitterly in 1261.[1] Very probably the Provisions envisaged these
casualties as being comprised in the 'issues de la tere' which
were henceforth to pass through the Exchequer 'et en nule part
ailurs', for in claiming them for the uses of the kingdom, the
baronage had in mind that the most pressing need was to
reduce the King's debts and expenses, including those of the
household.[2] The Provisions of Westminster named a committee
to oversee the disposal of these feudal casualties, the proceeds
from which were subsequently paid to the Wardrobe and to the
earl of Gloucester for the satisfaction of royal creditors.[3] In
1261, the revenue from wardships, escheats, and tallages was
still under a separate commission charged explicitly with applying it to the payment of household debts and expenses.[4] Henry,
when he recovered power, did nothing to perpetuate these
arrangements, and in the following decade strove with some
success to keep this revenue separate and to reserve it, on
occasion, for the King's family.[5] By the end of the century the
King was again beset by debts arising from his overseas commitments, and Edward I, like his father before 1258, used wardships, escheats, and temporalities to satisfy his more pressing
creditors. Grants of the custody of these were made under privy
seal, though creditors seem to have viewed the wardships and
marriages assessed in the Exchequer, accepting or rejecting
them on their own calculations and in competition with others
who desired the grant.[6] Thus even when such revenues were
exploited to the full and were not dissipated as favours, they
were at the King's personal disposition for objects closest to his
heart.

Just as the revenues from the royal demesne were coming to
be distinguished from the King's fiscal prerogatives, so a distinction was emerging between the fisc itself and the patrimony
of the King. Under the influence of the Roman law distinction
between public and private property, the fisc in some European

[1] *Documents of the Baronial Movement*, nos. 5, 30, 31.
[2] Ibid., nos. 31 (cl. 12), 37C (cl. 7); Howell, op. cit., pp. 154–7.
[3] *Documents*, no. 12 (cl. 8, 14); Howell, op. cit., pp. 157–8.
[4] R. F. Treharne, *The Baronial Plan of Reform*, p. 181.
[5] Ibid., p. 369; Howell, op. cit., pp. 159 ff.
[6] Stevenson, op. cit., pp. 134, 136–7.

monarchies was recognized as an inalienable appurtenance of the kingdom in contrast to the private patrimony which the King could freely bestow.[1] Discussion of the *patrimonium* remained more common among the civilians than among English lawyers. Yet the distinction between the 'inheritance' and the 'acquisition', the former secured to the heir by primogeniture and the latter available for the endowment of younger sons, had for long acted as a constraint on the Anglo-Norman monarchy,[2] and it was the practical need to make provision for members of the royal family within the realm of England that led the monarchy to accumulate lands from which a patrimony could be formed.[3] These could be acquired by purchase, forfeiture, or the uncertainties created by the claims of collateral heirs.[4]

Henry III laid the foundation of the royal patrimony by the acquisition of the earldom of Chester, as the result of personal arrangements with the co-heiresses and the claimant to the title, William de Forz. The surrender of their titles to the King was effected by a private bargain, in due legal form, however much dictated by the demands of state and the persuasion of royal power.[5] Henry gave Chester to his wife, Eleanor, in 1243 and later, in 1254, to his son Edward. From the first he intended that it should remain in the royal family and be used for the support of its members. In 1254, as earlier in 1247, Henry strove to emphasize the inalienability of this estate by a prohibition against its separation from the Crown, but the latter charter also declared that it was to remain perpetually 'with the kings of England'.[6] Similarly Henry used the most important forfeiture of the reign, Simon's earldom of Leicester, to endow Edmund of Lancaster who, with the support of his father and brother, also secured the earldom of Derby forfeited by Robert

---

[1] Such a distinction was made in the laws of Alfonso the Wise of Castille (*Las Siete Partidas del Rey don Alfonso el Sabio*, II, Tit. xviii, Ley 1), while in France it derived from restrictions on the regnal succession: see R. E. Giesey, *The Juristic Basis of Dynastic Right to the French Throne* (Philadelphia, 1961). For the former reference I am indebted to Mr F. Fernandez-Armesto.

[2] J. C. Holt, 'Politics and Property in Early Medieval England', *Past and Present*, 57 (1972), pp. 17–20. [3] B. P. Wolffe, op. cit., pp. 52–3. [4] Holt, loc. cit.

[5] R. Stewart Brown, 'The End of the Norman Earldom of Chester', *Eng. Hist. Rev.* xxxv (1920), p. 45. Cf. K. B. McFarlane, 'Had Edward I a "Policy" towards the Earls?', *History*, l (1965), p. 146.

[6] R. Stewart Brown, op. cit., p. 52; Rymer, *Foedera*, i. 297.

Ferrers in 1269.[1] Edward I further exploited his position as King to enlarge his patrimony. The inheritance of Edmund's wife, Aveline, countess of Aumale, including the notable honour of Holderness, was retained after her premature death by a bargain with the claimant, and in 1293 Edward bought from Isabella de Redvers, countess of Devon, on her deathbed, the major portion of her inheritance including the Isle of Wight. In 1302 he purchased from the earl of Norfolk the reversion of the Bigod inheritance, should the earl die childless, probably intending it to be an endowment for the children of his second marriage.[2] Occasional forfeitures like the lands of Adam de Stratton in Berkshire and north Wiltshire were likewise used for the endowment of the Queen and the heir apparent and thus kept within the monarch's grasp.[3] The earldom of Cornwall had come into the royal family in 1227 and on the death of Earl Edmund in 1300 it escheated to the Crown and was retained in the King's hands. When in 1337 it was ultimately made the hereditament of the heir apparent, the charter contained no declaration of its inalienability as an appurtenance of the Crown but merely vested it in the heir apparent with reversion 'to us and our heirs, Kings of England'.[4] Although after its conquest Edward declared in 1284 that Wales was to be 'annexed and united to the Crown of this realm as part of the same body', when in 1301 Wales and Chester were conferred on his son Edward as a princely appanage, the grant was made 'to our son and his heirs, Kings of England in perpetuity'.[5]

Thus the thirteenth century saw the creation of a new royal patrimony, distinct from and overshadowing the demesne lands of the Crown. Whereas kings at first endeavoured to safeguard its identity by invoking notions of inalienability applicable to

[1] R. Somerville, *History of the Duchy of Lancaster*, i (London, 1953), pp. 1–11; W. E. Rhodes, 'Edmund, Earl of Lancaster', *Eng. Hist. Rev.* x (1895), pp. 31–40, discusses the endowment of Edmund at length; J. R. L. Maddicott, *Thomas of Lancaster, 1307–1322* (Oxford, 1970), p. 9.

[2] K. B. McFarlane, loc. cit. Edward provided for his daughters by marriages on favourable terms with the nobility. He also facilitated the acquisition of the earldom of Lincoln for Thomas of Lancaster his nephew and protected his interests in the last years of the reign (Maddicott, op. cit., pp. 4–6).

[3] R. B. Pugh, *The Crown Estate, An Historical Essay* (London, 1960), p. 6.

[4] *R.D.P.*, v. 358.

[5] *R.D.P.*, v, 10–11, 35–8; *S.R.* i. 55. See also *Litterae Walliae*, ed. J. G. Edwards (Cardiff, 1940), p. xlix, and Hilda Johnstone, *Edward of Carnarvon* (Manchester, 1946), pp. 55 ff.

Crown lands, its true character as a royal family patrimony was
realized in the grants of Cornwall, Wales, and Chester to the
heir apparent and in the employment of the other estates for the
endowment of the Queen and other members of the royal
family.

The Roman law concept of the fisc as a perpetual appurtenance of the Crown thus acquired relevance in England as the
monarchy was driven to exploit its feudal revenues and rights
in the half-century that spanned the year 1200. The terms in
which the fisc had been defined—as liable to tallage, and as
comprising inalienable rights and lands which could be resumed at will—emphasized that the initiative in its formation
had come from the King. At the same time the belief that the
King ruled for the benefit of the realm gave subjects an interest
in the preservation of the fisc which might be stirred if royal insolvency threatened the stability of the kingdom or imposed
burdens on them. In such circumstances subjects might be
moved to condemn, restrict, and even recall royal gifts which
diminished the capacity of the fisc to sustain the royal estate.
Yet under Henry III the notion of inalienability was still viewed
as an aspect of the royal prerogative rather than as an expression
of the common profit.

Before the close of the century the character of royal finance
fundamentally changed. Under Edward I the major thrust of
royal policy was towards exploiting national rather than feudal
revenues. War made national taxation a regular occurrence,
imposing on subjects the obligation to contribute their wealth
for the preservation of the realm. It could not fail to underline
the corresponding obligation on the King to contribute his.
Edward I acknowledged this in his proclamation at the height
of the crisis of 1297 when he claimed that he had not spared his
person or his own possessions in the present necessity.[1] Even
more specific was his message to the southern Convocation,
meeting in London in June 1298. The King, Convocation was
told, 'does not on this occasion intend to demand aid, nor at any
other time unless great necessity compel him, but to provide
from his own in this war as far as he is able'.[2] Thus it was in the
context of a national emergency, requiring his subjects to con-

[1] Bartholomew Cotton, *Historia Anglicana*, p. 33. See above, p. 63.
[2] *Registrum Roberti Winchelsey*, ed. R. Graham (Oxford, 1952), i. 260.

tribute their wealth, that the King first began to acknowledge that the fisc had public obligations. But this was only the logical extension of the function which theorists had all along ascribed to the fisc, namely to maintain perpetually the Crown and the kingdom. In the general crisis of royal finance which Edward I was to bequeath to his son the relevance of this became suddenly clear to the King's subjects and critics.

In assessing the role of the fisc in the early fourteenth century we must first ask how realistic was the concept that it should sustain the estate of the King and kingdom. Since its substance was perpetually changing and its fiscal value is undiscoverable, we can do no more than gain an approximate idea of its magnitude and of its ability to meet these charges.

We may begin with the first surviving statement of the Crown's customary revenues, made in 1284. Since this was unfortunately drawn up preparatory to the Statute of Rhuddlan which finally rationalized the sheriff's account, it does not provide a ready basis for comparison with later statements. Thus it preserves the notional total of £10,168. 3s. 1¾d. for the old farms of the shires before the removal of the *terrae datae* reduced these to £3,983. 16s. 11d. including the increment and profit.[1] There are likewise no separate estimates of the receipts from farmers of manors and fee farms, while some of the amercements separately listed would later be accounted for by the sheriff within his summonses. The statement estimates the ancient custom as £8,000 per annum but omits revenue from overseas territories of Ireland and Gascony. Some items, notably wardships, escheats, and temporalities, are almost certainly undervalued,[2] while others beside the old farms may include a notional or fictitious element;[3] nor is it clear whether some are rendered gross or net. The total given in the document, of £26,828. 3s. 9¼d., has therefore no validity as an estimate of actual revenue. Nevertheless if Miss Mills was right in estimating

[1] M. Mills, 'Exchequer Agenda and Estimates of Revenue, Easter Term, 1284', *Eng. Hist. Rev.* xl (1925), pp. 229-34.
[2] For these compare M. Prestwich, *War, Politics and Finance under Edward I*, p. 178.
[3] Thus one item reads: '[missing . . .] dampnatorum que debentur usque ad summam £2,000'. Comparison of some other items may be made with the estimate of 1324 printed as Appendix B item i.

the total of all shire revenues during the last decade of the century at some £13,000–£14,000 per annum, the addition to this of the customs and other 'revenues of the realm' may yet suggest that the notional total in the statement would be of approximately the right order for the value of the fisc.[1]

The next surviving statement of Crown revenues comes forty years later, in 1324, but it is unfortunately mutilated and can most usefully be considered along with evidence from the Exchequer rolls.[2] On this basis we shall attempt to assess the value of the fisc in the twenty years 1324–44, taking in order the annual renders at the Exchequer by royal officials, the Crown lands, and the casual revenue from feudal prerogatives. Finally we shall note the further development of the royal patrimony in the fourteenth century.

The sheriffs' proffers, comprising the reduced farm, the increment, and profit, brought in a clear total of approximately £3,458 p.a. during the decade 1327–37.[3] Though individual sheriffs might on occasion plead for further reductions in virtue of royal grants or the devastation of plague or war, there was probably no marked variation in this sum in the preceding or following decade.[4] The sums rendered by the sheriff for summonses were more variable, being particularly increased in the wake of general or forest eyres. In 1330–1 they totalled £847.17s., in 1332–3, £967. 19s. 2d., but in 1335–6 only £445. 9s. 5d.[5]

---

[1] Miss Mills based her estimate on the material collected for her Introduction to *The Pipe Roll for 1295, Surrey Membrane* (Surrey Record Society, vol. vii, no. xxi, 1924). Miss Mills, in two articles on the 'Adventus Vicecomitum' in *Eng. Hist. Rev.* xxxvi (1921) and xxxviii (1923), tabulated the sheriffs' proffers from 1254 to 1307. Between 1283 and 1297 these averaged over £6,000 p.a. but they do not represent all the revenue collected by the sheriff who, particularly in the last decade of Edward's reign, was paying large sums at source.

[2] Bodleian Library MS. North C.26, no. 4, tabulated below, Appendix B item i. Its value is tragically reduced by the disappearance of practically all the totals from the right-hand margin. I am indebted to Mr H. M. Colvin and Mr A. F. Butcher for this reference. I understand that the document is to be printed and described by Mr. Butcher.

[3] W. A. Morris, 'The Sheriff', in *English Government at Work*, ii. 75–8.

[4] For claims by the sheriff of Lincolnshire under Edward II for the release of £37. 11s. 11d. for wapentakes granted to the earl of Richmond see Morris, op. cit., p. 74 n. 3; and for a similar claim by the sheriffs of Nottingham and Derby for a reduction of £46 in 1348. *C.P.R., 1348–50*, p. 62: this despite the statute of 1334 that the ancient farm of the hundreds be rendered through the sheriffs where these are granted out (Morris, op. cit., p. 92).

[5] Calculated from Morris's figure on pp. 82–3.

Beyond these the sheriff might account for lands temporarily in the King's hands, forfeited chattels, or other special sources of income, including reliefs from tenants in chief or fines made in Chancery, though these were more commonly paid directly into the Exchequer, Wardrobe, or Chamber by the heirs or assigned to creditors or donees.[1] In the year 1342–3 the sheriffs rendered a total of £5,679. 18*s.* 3*d.* to the Exchequer.[2] Similarly the escheators themselves accounted for only the minor escheats, the more important lands and wardships being granted or farmed directly. This revenue seems to have been in steep decline: estimated at £700 p.a. in 1324, in the decade 1327–37 the southern escheatry averaged £300–£400 p.a. with perhaps a further £100 from the northern escheatry; but the total rendered to the Exchequer in 1342–3 was only £159. 13*s.* 1*d.*[3] The Exchequer likewise received revenue from some of the farms of royal manors and boroughs where these were not paid to members of the royal family, the Chamber, or the Wardrobe. In 1342–3 the Exchequer drew £2,901. 1*s.* 10*d.* from this source. Whereas in 1324 the Exchequer estimated its receipts from sheriffs, farmers, and escheators as £12,442. 12*s.* 3*d.* p.a., in 1342–3 the same officials rendered only £8,740 13*s.* 2*d.*, the decline probably being most marked in respect of farms of lands and escheats.

From the central departments of the Hanaper and Mint the Exchequer might at times draw a regular income. The Hanaper continued to yield some £800 p.a., as it had under Edward II.[4] The Mint may have yielded about 1,000 marks a year.[5] In

[1] Morris, op. cit., pp. 87 n. 3, 93–4 nn. 6, 7, shows that this revenue was mostly very small but might include occasional items of size such as the 500 marks owed for the custody of the lands of Richard Greystoke. The sheriff was usually only responsible for distraining for reliefs etc. See also Stevenson, 'The Escheator', *English Government at Work*, ii. 134, 140.

[2] P.R.O. E 401/370, 371. See Appendix B item ii. This does not include such fines from the Eyre as the sheriffs collected.

[3] Bodleian Library, MS. North C.26, no. 4; E. R. Stevenson, 'The Escheator', pp. 148–50; PRO. E. 401/370, 371. Below, Appendix B items i, ii.

[4] B. Wilkinson, *The Chancery under Edward III*, pp. 62–3; N. Pronay, 'The Hanaper under the Lancastrian Kings', *Proceedings of the Leeds Philosophical and Literary Society*, xii (1967), p. 74. In 1324 the Hanaper was estimated to produce £300 p.a. clear (Bodleian Library, MS. North C.26, no. 4); in 1342–3 it yielded £496. 14*s.* 11*d.* to the Exchequer (E 401/370, 371) and in 1348 Queen Isabella was granted £600 p.a. from the Hanaper in recompense of dower lands surrendered to Henry, earl of Lancaster (*C.P.R., 1346–8*, p. 217).

[5] After the first decade of the century the Mint yielded very little revenue until

addition to these some revenue from casualties appeared on the receipt roll in the form both of judicial fines and amercements and fines for wardships, reliefs, alienations, marriages, etc. In 1342–3 this revenue yielded £3,748. 14s. 10d. Finally the Exchequer drew some revenue from the temporalities of vacant sees and abbeys where these had not been assigned directly to royal creditors, and it received practically the whole revenue from the farms of the alien priories. Whereas temporalities rarely exceeded £1,000 in a year (£718. 6s. 3d. in 1342–3 and £917. 18s. 9d. in 1345–6), alien priories yielded £5,304. 7s. 7d. in 1342–3 and £4,181. 18s. 2d. in 1345–6, making them second in importance only to the revenue handled by the sheriffs.

The sum of all the Crown's hereditary revenues at the Exchequer was clearly subject to variation. The estimates of 1324 set the total of these at £60,549, but two decades later no revenue from Gascony (£13,000), Ireland (£1,424), the Contrariants' lands (£12,652), or Wales was available at the Exchequer, although it was receiving the farms of alien priories. Deducting these items, the Exchequer's revenue in 1324 was estimated as about £33,000 p.a. of which some £18,000 came from the ancient and new customs. This is not markedly different from the totals of £19,325. 16s. 1d. in 1342–3 and £15,721. 19s. 6d. in 1345–6 from the hereditary revenues other than customs, which can be compiled from the receipt rolls for these years.[1] A revenue of this order was in fact sufficient to meet the normal costs of the royal household and administra-

---

Edward III began his great recoinage in 1343–4. Thus the estimates of 1284 give a profit of £500 and those of 1324 the same figure, while noting that at the end of Edward I's reign it had produced £3,000 p.a. (Bodleian Library, MS. North C.26, no. 4). A. Beardwood ('Royal Mints and Exchanges', in *English Government at Work*, iii. 52–3) says that the Mint yielded little or no profit in the first decade of Edward III's reign, and even in 1342–3 it yielded only £316. 19s. 4d. to the Exchequer (E 401/370, 371). In 1345–6 the accounts of the keeper show a gross receipt of £1,827 and a net receipt of £811. 13s. 2d. (E 101/290/29), and it continued to have some value as a royal asset until 1362. For the fluctuations in business and the rates of royal seignorage, see J. Craig, *The Mint* (Cambridge, 1953).

[1] For summaries of revenue in 1324 and 1342–3, see below, Appendix B items i, ii; the figure for 1345–6 is given by Sir J. H. Ramsay, *Revenues of the Kings of England, 1066–1399*, ii. 293. The figure of £18,000 p.a. for the ancient and new customs is given as an average of the years 1303–7 by M. Prestwich, *War, Politics and Finance under Edward I*, p. 199; in 1362–3 the customs were estimated at some £7,700 for the half-year (below, Appendix B item iii).

tion with which the Exchequer was charged.[1] Taxation could thus be used wholly for the expenses of war. Moreover, what the Exchequer handled was certainly the lesser part of the resources available to the Crown. For the fisc could also be distributed as patronage and, along with the patrimony, provide support for the royal family.

The extent and value of the ancient demesne in the first half of the fourteenth century should not be underestimated. An extensive, though still incomplete, list of the lands and fee farms which belonged to the Crown can be compiled from the assignments of dower to Queen Margaret between 1299 and 1305, to Queen Isabella in 1318 and 1327, and to Queen Philippa in 1331 and 1359, and the endowments given to other members of Edward III's family. The dower lands assigned to Margaret in 1299, 1301, and 1305 were valued at £5,000 p.a.[2] Many but by no means all of these were transferred to Isabella in 1318 (to whom had already been assigned properties worth approx. £1,000 p.a.) to give her a dower of £4,500 p.a.[3] More extensive than either of these was the assignment of lands and rents to Isabella in 1327 valued at £8,722. 4s. 4d., though this again did not include all the properties in Queen Margaret's hands and should not be regarded as comprising all the Crown

[1] The main items of domestic expenditure at this time were the *hospitium* expenses of the Wardrobe, about £12,000 p.a., the Great Wardrobe about £3,000 p.a. (Tout, *Chapters*, vi, Appendix II), with the Works about £2,000 p.a. and wages and administrative costs at about £5,000 p.a. An estimate of peacetime expenditure in 1362–3 reckoned these items as totalling £23,304, though it added payments for the King's Chamber, the Queen, and the maintenance of garrisons on a peacetime footing, none of which was applicable in 1342. B. P. Wolffe (*The Royal Demesne in English History*, pp. 40 ff.) has warned against using the distinction between 'Ordinary' and 'Extraordinary' revenue on the ground that this has no contemporary validity, and see J. B. Henneman, *Royal Taxation in Fourteenth Century France*, pp. 18–19, for difficulties arising from its use by French historians. In fact the accounts of the Seneschal of Guienne at this period explicitly classify his receipts as 'Receptes Ordinaires', 'being the normal revenues of the duchy and the 'Fouages, subsides, donnes et foreynes receipts' which were clearly regarded as extraordinary (E 101/177/1). Contemporaries did distinguish clearly between revenue which came to the King by grant as gift or taxation and revenue which did not and this was the distinction which Blackstone had in mind.

[2] *C.P.R.*, *1307–13*, pp. 216–19.

[3] Ibid., *1313–17*, pp. 5, 38, 206, 276, 490, 639, 642, 668; ibid., *1317–21*, pp. 115–16; *C.C.R.*, *1313–18*, p. 373. She was also assigned the counties of Ponthieu and Montreuil worth £1,000 p.a. See Tout, *Chapters*, v. 277–8.

lands.[1] Although the total value of Isabella's dower was thus raised to 20,000 marks, this included £1,377. 13s. 4d. from Lacy lands and £1,533. 6s. 8d. from Contrariants' lands with a further £800 from the former Chamber manor of Burstwick. But most of the remainder, with some small exceptions, represented the ancient demesne lands of the Crown. If we are to estimate the yield of such lands it should probably be not less than £10,000–£12,000 p.a. and possibly as much as £15,000 p.a. This represented a substantial endowment but normally the Exchequer received only a small proportion of it as cash.

The major use to which it was applied was, as we have seen, the support of the Queen. This seems to have been an innovation of the fourteenth century. We are ill informed about the revenues of both Eleanor of Provence and Eleanor of Castille. The former seems to have been dependent on the King's household and occasional windfalls besides her French lands; the second was given a slightly greater landed estate in England, though much of it comprised lands taken from the Jews.[2] If in the thirteenth century the monarch had been reluctant to use the ancient demesne lands for the support of the Queen, this was reversed by Edward I's endowment of his second wife. Even so the Queen continued to receive advances from the King's Wardrobe probably equivalent in value to her dower lands, and until Margaret's death released her dower lands Isabella was dependent on the Exchequer for the balance of her income of 11,000 marks. It was only in the second quarter of the century that, with Isabella's grant of 1327 and the subsequent endowment of Queen Philippa and (until 1336) John of Eltham, half or more of the Crown lands came to be used for the sustenance of the royal family.[3] The fiscal value of these lands must have been realized to support these royal households: indeed as a land revenue office the Queen's household operated on a larger scale than either the Wardrobe or the Exchequer.

[1] *C.P.R., 1327–30*, pp. 66–9. These have been conveniently tabulated, together with their dispersal after 1330, by B. P. Wolffe, *The Royal Demesne in English History*, Appendix A.

[2] Hilda Johnstone, 'The Queen's Household' in Tout, *Chapters*, v. 267–70. For details of grants see *C.P.R., 1247–58*, p. 351; ibid., *1272–81*, p. 380.

[3] Thus leaving aside the lands of the Contrariants and other recent escheats, the revenue from demesne lands of the Crown in these endowments totalled £3,120 for Isabella, £2,765 for Philippa, and £1,400 for John of Eltham, a total of £7,285.

But Crown lands could also be utilized as political rewards. The farm of a royal manor, based on the extent, was itself a beneficial grant, and grants might be made at a reduced farm or in fee.[1] The bulk of these grants could be justified as rewards or repayment of services, political, military, or fiscal; few if any were permanent alienations. The Crown lands furnished a permanently replenished pool of patronage, but the distribution of this among the King's retainers, servants, creditors, and nobility was a matter of fine judgement both in sum and in particulars. The extent or value of this dispersal as patronage at any time is probably impossible to assess, and it is reasonably certain that no contemporary valuation of it was ever made. Probably the Exchequer was receiving less revenue from the demesne in 1342–3 than it had under Edward II or Edward I, but the basis of the demand that such grants should be resumed and contribute towards the expenses of the realm was conceptual rather than factual. When resumption did take place it was usually followed by the adjudication of grants in terms of merit.[2]

In disposing of Crown lands as dower or for service and favour the King exercised direct responsibility in a way that he did not for the deployment of the hereditary revenues received at the Exchequer. The same was largely true of the revenue from the King's feudal prerogatives and other 'casualties'. This revenue was, of course, highly variable both in its incidence and its yield, and the extent to which it was realized or exploited in fiscal terms depended very much on the King's personal decision. It is not at all easy now to assess how far this was done. Although the Crown's escheators had the task of searching out escheats and making an extent, they accounted only for minor escheats or for the larger ones until they had been granted or assigned elsewhere. Escheats and wardships were committed to farm or sold by bargain with the King or on the authority of the Treasurer. From a survey made of the first decade of Edward III's reign, E. R. Stevenson concluded that 'the chief use made of escheats seems to have been not to reward favourites but to pay individuals for real services'.[3] Even when the escheat was

[1] On these extents, see E. R. Stevenson, 'The Escheator', in *English Government at Work*, ii. 134–7; B. P. Wolffe, *The Royal Demesne in English History*, pp. 67–8.
[2] This is discussed below, ch. vii.
[3] Stevenson, 'The Escheator', pp. 110–13, 134–6. Thus in the estimates of 1324 it is said that 'tieles choses suffisont a acquiter les fietz di Roi' (Bodleian Library,

farmed at its extended value it was possible to make a profit, for the extent could be notional or undervalued by the escheator. The Walton Ordinances strictly charged escheators to render 'true and reasonable' extents for, like his predecessors, Edward III used escheats to provide security or repayment for loans and as retaining fees.[1] In such cases the farm was remitted either in whole or in part. It would probably be impossible to assess the value of this revenue even for a restricted period since the grants on the patent rolls do not specify their value; moreover, some of this revenue was at all times paid into the Chamber, since it was the result of a private bargain with the King. Comparatively little was received at the Exchequer in cash. Fines for licences to alienate, or crenellate, or marry, or entail were numerous though often of small value financially.[2] But here, as in the case of wardships, escheats, and reliefs, the work of the escheator and sheriff was less the collection of revenue than the location of it and if necessary distraint for payment.

Because this revenue was frequent if irregular, was levied from lay tenants in chief in virtue of personal bargains with the King or the Treasurer, and—probably to a greater degree than the Crown lands—served as patronage for those who had rendered political, military or fiscal services to the Crown, it was very much in the public eye. Probably neither the King nor the barons had a very accurate idea of its monetary value, but it was understandable that the baronial reformers of 1258–61 should have claimed this revenue as a contribution to the expenses of government.[3] In like manner the Ordinances of 1311 prohibited gifts from these casualties and recalled those previously made in order that they could be applied to discharge royal debts and maintain the King's estate in his household.[4] In

North C. 26, no. 4). A good example of the King's interest in the value of these casualties is provided by Edward's writ to the Treasurer in August 1337 instructing him to certify the value of the marriages of two wards and not to sell them without the King's special command (E 404/3/21).

[1] Stevenson, 'The Escheator', pp. 136–7 n. 1; Tout, *Chapters*, iii. 147.
[2] Ibid., pp. 138–40.
[3] See above, pp. 138–41.
[4] Ordinances, caps. 3, 7. Some major escheats like the Templars lands and the lands of Margaret of Clare were assigned to the Wardrobe in 1312–13. See Tout, *Chapters*, ii. 322–4.

1327 the Commons recommended that the revenue from escheats should be assigned to John of Eltham to support his dignity as earl of Cornwall,[1] but by 1340 under pressure of war they sought to apply them to more public charges. Their petition asked that the revenue from the 'great marriages and escheats' should, with other revenues of the realm, be assigned to support the charges of the realm and its defence under the surveillance of the Lords, and this was given effect in the statute of that year.[2] They reverted to this demand in 1343, though the King resisted any commitment in his reply and reasserted that such revenue was disposable at his will.[3]

When unfettered by baronial restraints, the King frequently received revenue of this kind into his Chamber, in whose records it was carefully distinguished from the lands held by the King 'de jure suo proprio'.[4] The administration of forfeited lands by the Chamber began in 1309–10 when many of the Templars' lands were transferred to Chamber officials and the clerk of the Chamber began to act as general keeper of all the Templars' estates. In obedience to the Ordinances writs were issued in November 1311 placing these lands under other keepers and directing that the issues be paid into the Exchequer. The King's revocation of these later in the month aroused complaint from the Ordainers and many of these lands were eventually assigned to the Wardrobe, though certain Templar manors remained part of the Chamber estate. This was not greatly extended until 1322 when the Contrariants' lands were systematically assigned to it as they escheated. But many of these remained under its charge for less than six months before being transferred to the Exchequer with the express purpose of furnishing revenue for the King's Scottish expedition. Harclay's lands likewise formed a bonus for the Chamber in 1323 but had disappeared from its receipt a year later.[5] Such political

---

[1] *Rot. Parl.* ii. 9.

[2] See Appendix A item i; *S.R.* i. 289–90, quoted below, p. 181, n. 1.

[3] *Rot. Parl.* ii. 141. See below, p. 182.

[4] Tout, *Chapters*, iv. 243; W. O. Ault, 'Manors and Temporalities', in *The English Government at Work*, iii. 34. The certification of Henry Greystoke for the Chamber revenues in 1356 grouped these as lands directly administered, fines and farms (E 101/392/18).

[5] Tout, *Chapters*, ii. 320–4, 341. The estimate of 1324 gives the value of the Contrariants' English lands as £12,652 (Bodleian Library MS North C.26, no. 4).

forfeitures by the upper nobility formed a special category. The King had the option of engrossing them as part of the royal patrimony or of using them as political bribes to create and ennoble a new family or restore the heirs of the old one. Thus many of the Lancaster, Warenne, Lacy, and Mortimer lands remained in the hands of Edward III to be used during the first decade of the reign for the endowment of the royal family. Subsequently they were distributed in 1337 to create a new peerage from among Edward's companions in arms: on the newly endowed families of Montague, Ufford, Clinton, Bohun, and Lancaster the Crown's political ascendancy was rebuilt.[1] Edward III continued to assign lesser forfeitures to the Chamber until in October 1349 he formally reserved to it all lands which fell to the Crown as escheat. Wards' lands likewise constituted a notable element in the Chamber estate between 1332 and 1348.[2]

Finally in this class of casualties there was the revenue from ecclesiastical temporalities. The revenues of a great bishopric could be substantial: in the first years of Edward IIIs reign a vacancy of three months at Durham yielded £1,410. 15s. 2d., one of ten months at Canterbury £1,314. 9s. 6d., and one of sixteen months at Norwich £1,152. 5s. 10d., and there were in addition the goods and chattels of the bishop, of scarcely less value than the temporalities.[3] But in Edward III's early years most of these sums were assigned in payment of the King's debts to his creditors and little cash from them reached the Exchequer. Vacancies of abbeys and priories, of less value than bishoprics, were usually compounded at a fixed rent. Glastonbury paid at the rate of 1,000 marks p.a., and the great monastic chapters of Ely (at £2,000) and Salisbury (at £1,021) stood at the head of a descending scale. Edward III never seems to have removed these revenues to his Chamber; they were paid at the Exchequer.[4] The only ecclesiastical revenues to which the Chamber laid claim were the lands of some alien priories, namely those within its principal holdings in Holderness and

[1] Tout, *Chapters*, iii. 37–40; Wolffe, op. cit., pp. 59–60.
[2] Tout, *Chapters*, iv. 243–5.
[3] Ault, 'Manors and Temporalities', pp. 23–9. Antony Bek's personal effects provided Edward II with 6,000 marks in 1311, all of which were assigned to the Bardi. See C. M. Fraser, *A History of Antony Bek* (Oxford, 1957), p. 229 n. 4.
[4] Ault, op. cit., pp. 19, 34.

the Isle of Wight; for the most part the revenues from alien priories were rendered as farms at the Exchequer.[1]

Thus by 1350 the Commons and the Crown had arrived at different views about the use of escheats, wardships and marriages, and to a lesser degree temporalities. The continual dispensing of grants of this revenue to those with access to the King was an element of the royal prerogative and an aspect of the King's rule with which the Commons did not normally claim to be concerned. But at times of heavy taxation and financial and political crisis suspicions were easily aroused that royal resources were being heedlessly dispersed through largesse. The Commons had little idea of the total value of such patronage, which they doubtless exaggerated, but its prerogative nature not only encouraged them to lay the responsibility for its dispersal directly on the King but to claim that as part of the fisc it should help to maintain the household or the King's wars. The crisis of 1340 produced the clearest statement of the view that such revenue pertained to the realm. To the King on the other hand such casualties, though they might often be granted in discharge of debts and services which were rendered as much to the realm as to the King, were pre-eminently an expression of his power to bestow favour in a personal and political context; alternatively he might claim such revenue for his personal expenses in his Chamber.

The Crown revenues rendered at the Exchequer, the Crown lands, and the casualties, which together comprised the royal fisc, were distinguished from the patrimonial lands of the royal family. The latter were kept firmly under the control of the King or his family and were not, other than in the most exceptional instances, either granted away or administered by the Exchequer. The policy pursued by Henry III and Edward I of acquiring a family estate by purchase, bargain, and forfeiture was continued in the fourteenth century though at a lesser rate. Some small manors such as Somerton (Lincs.) and Eltham, acquired from Anthony Bek, became part of the Queen's dower, and Isabella actually diverted 10,000 marks of the parliamentary subsidy of 1327 to the purchase of the lands of Robert de Montalt to form part of the endowment of John of

---

[1] Tout, *Chapters*, iv. 246–50.

Eltham.[1] But it was not until after the middle of the century that the monarchy again acquired lands by purchase on any significant scale. The forfeitures of Edward II's reign did not permanently enlarge the royal patrimony although some notable estates remained in the hands of the royal family for a generation and more. Knaresborough, Pontefract, and Tickhill, together valued at over £1,500 p.a., were granted to Queen Isabella in 1327 and passed thence to Queen Philippa in 1331. Only in 1348 was Pontefract restored to Henry earl of Lancaster in discharge of royal debts to him, and not until 1372 were Knaresborough and Tickhill granted to his successor in exchange for the honour of Richmond, and the whole Lancastrian inheritance constituted a royal appanage. Similarly the Warenne estates, which Edward II had acquired in fee from the last earl and Edward III had granted to William de Bohun, returned to the Crown to be used for the endowment of Edmund of Langley in 1347. But much of the Warenne, Mortimer, and Lacy lands went to endow the families whom Edward raised to the peerage in 1337, and by the middle of the century no sizeable estate had been permanently added to the patrimony of the Crown.[2]

But if the thirteenth-century patrimony had not been substantially enlarged its character had become more clearly defined. The convention that the patrimony should be confined to the King and the royal family was sufficiently established for Edward II's early grants of Burstwick, the Isle of Wight, and the earldom of Cornwall to Gaveston, to the detriment of the claims of Queen Isabella and Edward's half-brothers, to be regarded as a scandal.[3] After Gaveston's death Burstwick and the Isle of Wight were granted to the King's eldest son who, in 1312, had been invested with the earldom of Chester, though he was never created Prince of Wales. The Welsh revenues were frequently paid into the Wardrobe in these years. Queen Isabella received the issues of the county of Cornwall from 1317 to 1324 for the maintenance of the King's younger children, and they were restored to her along with Burstwick in 1327. Under Edward III Chester was assigned to Queen Philippa for the support of the young Edward until

---

[1] *C.C.R., 1327–30*, p. 267; Wolffe, op. cit., p. 235; Fraser, op. cit., pp. 220–1.
[2] Wolffe, op. cit., pp. 59–60   [3] Maddicott, op. cit., pp. 83–4.

granted to him two years later while on the death of John of Eltham in 1337 the Cornwall lands, which had been withheld when he was granted the title in 1330, were constituted a duchy and inalienably invested in the heir apparent.[1] In 1343 the Principality of Wales was granted to the Prince and his heirs, Kings of England. Thus, apart from Burstwick and the Isle of Wight which were administered by the Chamber from 1332 to 1355, the whole of the patrimony had been constituted an appanage for the heir. The only occasion on which Edward III alienated any piece of this patrimony was in 1338 when he was forced to sell Burstwick to William de la Pole to discharge his debts. Two years later when Pole's unpopularity made him vulnerable to charges of embezzlement, he was forced to restore Burstwick to the Crown. The vindictiveness with which Edward pursued the ruination of his principal financier may have been prompted by Pole's attempt to lay hands on this cherished royal estate.[2]

The lands which remained with the King were administered by the Chamber. As reconstituted in 1324 its estate included some notable properties both of the ancient Crown lands and the newer royal patrimony. Among the largest were Burstwick, Tickhill, Kenilworth, Rockingham, and lucrative manors like Langley Marsh, Glatton and Holme, Isleworth, and Chippenham. Although the total value of these Chamber manors cannot easily be established, it must have been more than the £2,000 which was returned as their gross issues in these years.[3] Many though by no means all of these properties were transferred to Isabella in 1327 but on her fall in 1330 some of these manors, among them Isleworth, Tickhill, and Langley Marsh were given to Philippa, while John of Eltham received Chippenham, Rockingham, and others until his death in 1337.[4] In consequence, when the Chamber estate was revived by Edward III

---

[1] Wolffe, op. cit., pp. 56–7.

[2] E. B. Fryde, 'The Last Trials of Sir William de la Pole', *Econ. Hist. Rev.* 2nd. ser. xv (1962), p. 21. Pole paid £22,650 for Burstwick and some of the Yorkshire manors of the Tickhill estate. Burstwick was worth about £800 p.a. and had rendered account at the Exchequer from 1330–2: see Ault, op. cit., pp. 20–1, 34.

[3] J. C. Davies, 'The First Journal of Edward II's Chamber', *Eng. Hist. Rev.* xxx (1915), p. 668; Tout, *Chapters*, ii. 348–55.

[4] The extent of Isabella's lands can be seen from the grant in *C.P.R., 1327–30*, pp. 66–9, and the views of account in *Cal. Memoranda Rolls, 1326–7*, pp. 251–2. See also Tout, *Chapters*, iv. 232 n. 1.

it comprised little more than Burstwick, the Isle of Wight, the manor of Corsham, and a few scattered estates of the Lancaster and Mortimer forfeitures; the total value of which was probably under £2,000.[1] The Chamber estate thus represented the residual lands of the monarchy which were not being used for the support of the King's family or as rewards for service, or were not received at the Exchequer. Since it was mainly composed of family lands and never attained a size sufficient to be the basis of financial independence, it had no constitutional significance.[2] What it does reveal is the determination of the King to keep the patrimony separate from the Exchequer and to reserve revenue for his personal needs. The dissolution of the Chamber estate, already foreshadowed in 1349, was effected in January 1356 when the King gave the order for the lands finally remaining under the Chamber to be returned to the Exchequer. The experiment of the Chamber lands was brought to a close for a number of reasons. The Chamber's comparative inefficiency in administering a landed estate meant that the cost became disproportionate to the yield; but perhaps more important than this was the withdrawal in 1355 of the manors of Corsham and the two large remaining estates, Burstwick and the Isle of Wight, for the King's eldest daughter Isabella. Only some individual manors, the yield of which was by comparison trifling, reverted to the Exchequer.[3]

The concept of the fisc as the inalienable endowment of the Crown had begun to acquire political currency at the beginning of the fourteenth century. Both then and now the difficulty of imparting definition to the fisc sprang from its debatable com-

---

[1] The last lands in the Chamber's hands had been returned to the Exchequer in March 1327 (*Cal. Mem. Rolls, 1326–7*, p. 252). For its revival see Tout, *Chapters*, iv. 291, and Ault, op. cit., p. 34. A list of the Chamber manors in 1344 is given in *C.C.R., 1343–6*, p. 303.

[2] Tout remarked of the reservation of the Contrariants' Lands to the Chamber that 'had the plan been thoroughly and permanently executed, future kings might have been rich and unrestrained autocrats' (*Chapters*, ii. 340). It is doubtful if he thought of the Chamber as a fiscal and administrative rival to the Exchequer; if he was thinking of the estates as providing a territorial basis for autocracy, his remark has some justification (cf. ibid. iv. 296).

[3] Ibid. iv. 301–5; *C.P.R., 1354–8*, pp. 185, 317. In January 1356 the keeper of the Chamber lands in the Isle of Wight was ordered to pay all his receipts since Michaelmas 1355 to Isabella (*C.C.R., 1354–60*, p. 165). By November 1356 Isabella had appointed her own receiver general for her lands in Holderness and Wight (*C.P.R., 1354–8*, p. 473).

position and its unknowable value. Our investigation suggests that what it yielded at the Exchequer in the first half of the fourteenth century was still just sufficient to maintain the normal domestic and administrative charges, though it is doubtful whether it could meet any of the demands of war. But the fisc was also distributed as patronage to those who rendered services to the King or had his favour, and a large part was used to support some members of the royal family. Beyond and distinct from the fisc there lay the patrimony, the private and family inheritance of the King used mainly for the endowment of the heir apparent. No formal political decision or clear theoretical distinction determined how any of these revenues should be used. But there was emerging a *de facto* pattern in the form of a spectrum ranging from the shire revenues administered by the Exchequer to the patrimonial lands which were normally withdrawn from it. Between these there were different views and varying practice about the use of the Crown lands and the prerogative revenues, and this was to erupt into controversy over the King's right or obligation to resume or restrain his grants of these. For we have now to examine how a royal right to resume grants prejudicial to the estate and dignity of the Crown was transformed into an obligation to resume them for the common profit of the realm.

CHAPTER VII

The Ordinances and the Demand for Resumption, 1307–1343

THE concept of an inalienable fisc attached to the Crown had stemmed from the monarchy's concern to protect and exploit its rights. Although theorists asserted that the fisc served the common good, the first explicit acknowledgement by the King that it should bear charges of state had significantly come at a time of unprecedented taxation for the common defence. In 1297–8 this had hardly been more than a passing phrase; a decade later it was to become part of an articulated programme advanced not by legists or royal spokesmen but by a baronial opposition which was consciously appealing for support to other classes in the realm. This development was far from straightforward, depending as it did on the coincidence and interaction of a crisis in royal finance and a crisis in the relations of the King and his barons. The Scottish war had not merely led the Crown into insolvency, it had forced it to exploit traditional prerogatives to furnish war supplies. Prises not only affronted subjects as a covert and illegal form of taxation; they demonstrated the inadequacy of the fisc to maintain the estate of the King and the Crown. By the reign of Edward II men had begun to see the royal estate as institutionalized in the household which, both as the instrument of purveyances and as a war treasury primarily responsible for heedless expenditure, thus came to be viewed as the symbol and source of royal misgovernment.[1] The crisis in royal finance directed attention to the institution where the King's prerogative was most directly and sensitively exposed to the criticism of his lesser subjects.

[1] The meaning of 'estate of the king' and 'estate of the realm', particularly in the context of the Ordinances of 1311 and the Statute of York, has given rise to much discussion and controversy. As against Lapsley's identification of the former with the King's household and the latter with the administration, I prefer, with Post, to read them as broadly correlative, though noting (as he does) that in these years the former is often used with reference to the household. In this context the household is seen not as the centre of the King's personal or prerogative rights but as reflecting the dignity of the Crown—it has a public function in that it concerns

Edward II's alienation of his baronage by his distribution of excessive favours to courtiers likewise involved the household and the fisc. To restrain and control royal patronage in their own interests, the barons had to transform a hitherto royal prerogative to alienate and resume the fisc into a constitutional limitation on the King. This they could only do by an appeal to a greater good than the King's rights, namely the common profit of the whole realm. At the highest level a doctrine of capacities offered some cover for action to constrain the person of the King in order to preserve the rights of the Crown. At a lower level the barons could justify their restraint of royal power by the benefits which subjects would receive from a proper use of the Crown's fiscal resources. In asserting that the fisc should contribute to the charges of government and defence and spare the subject they could command support from a wider political class. In this respect the Ordainers' programme was to be of lasting importance. For by disseminating in the shires ideas which had hitherto been largely theoretical, it made them the common property of the wider political class which was increasingly represented in parliament. These developments under Edward II we must now explore.

In claiming to restrain and correct royal misgovernment, the magnates appealed to two ideas both of which can be traced to the previous reign. They first appear in conjunction in the Boulogne declaration of February 1308 when a group of magnates agreed to redress and amend 'les choses que sount feites avant ces houres countre soen honeur et le droit de sa coroune' and also 'les oppressiouns que ount este feit et uncore se font de jour en jour a soen poeple'.[1] The barons who subscribed to the Boulogne declaration prefaced it by claiming that they were bound by their oaths of fealty to preserve the honour and rights of the Crown. As H. G. Richardson has shown, this phrase had been much in use in the preceding decade. It had figured in a

---

the kingdom and Crown as a whole. I have also followed Post in interpreting 'estate of the realm' as the *utilitas communis*. It is with these meanings that the terms are used in the following discussion. See G. Post, *Studies in Medieval Legal Thought*, chs. vi, viii; G. Lapsley, *Crown, Community and Parliament*, pp. 162–86.

[1] The words of this declaration, from Bodleian MS. Dugdale 18 fol. 80, are printed by N. Denholm-Young in *History and Heraldry, 1254–1310*, p. 130, and discussed by J. R. Maddicott, *Thomas of Lancaster, 1307–1322*, p. 73, and by J. R. S. Phillips, *Aymer de Valence* (Oxford, 1972), pp. 26–8.

number of Edward I's letters to the Pope and almost certainly reflected the wording of an oath (probably verbal) taken at Edward's coronation. In 1299, moreover, Edward had informed Pope Boniface VIII that the magnates were bound by their fealty to defend the dignity of the Crown.[1] The barons in 1308 could thus appeal to good authority for their assertion. These precedents further suggest that the phrase might have a specific application. Richardson has argued that the baronial duty to preserve the rights of the Crown could hardly be derived from the unspecific oath of fealty and must be ascribed to the councillor's oath. In the form given for this in 1306/7, which had an ancestry going back to 1257, the councillor swore[2]

qe vostre poyne, aide et consail a tot vostre poair donerez et mettrez as droitures le Roi, et de la Corone garder et meintenir sauver et repeler par la ou vous purrez sanz tort faire.

Et la ou vous saverez les choses de la Corone et les droitz le Roy concelez, ou a tort alienez, ou soustretz, qe vous le ferrez savoir au Roy

Et qe la Corone acrestrez a votre poiar, et en loail manere.

The councillor's responsibility for maintaining the rights of the King and Crown is here followed by the specific injunction to apprise the King of wrongful alienations. It seems probable therefore that the barons interpreted their declaration as requiring them (as natural and faithful councillors) to recover and amend such alienations.

Secondly the barons in 1308 claimed to redress the oppressions done to the people. Although the most notable precedent for acting in this capacity was the reform movement of 1258, the more recent and more relevant occasion was in 1297, when the barons had protested against the burdens of war levies, notably prise. Prise had, indeed, been the subject of acrimonious complaint, promised redress, and accusations of bad faith throughout the intervening years. Prises were in part the result of the old King's unwillingness to meet parliament and make further demands for taxation after the protests and limitations which he had endured in 1300–1. They were taxes in another form, as

---

[1] H. G. Richardson, 'The English Coronation Oath', *Speculum*, xxiv (1949), pp. 48–51.

[2] *Rot. Parl.* i. 218–19; J. F. Baldwin, *The King's Council*, pp. 346–9; see above, p. 137.

the magnates had pointed out in 1297; hence the demand that they should cease, that purveyances should be paid for, led back logically to the grant of taxation to provide the money. The parliament of 1309 accepted this, but even when taxation was granted for war and used to pay for war purveyances, there was still a demand that the revenues of the Crown should be laid under contribution before levies were made from the goods of the subject. This was required by the theologians and had been acknowledged by the King.[1] In citing the oppressions of the people the magnates were ultimately directing attention to the dilapidation of the Crown revenues, even if what they had primarily in mind was, almost certainly, fiscal and administrative reform rather than restraints on the prerogative.

Nevertheless it was with the estate of the Crown rather than the 'oppression done to the people' that the barons were primarily concerned in 1308. In April they made their famous declaration that homage and allegiance were due to the Crown rather than the King's person, thus emphasizing that there was an estate of the Crown which it was the King's duty to maintain and the barons' duty to compel him to maintain.[2] The dereliction of this duty and the damage to the Crown's estate is indeed seen as 'evil for the people at large and hurtful to the Crown', for the Crown is the symbol of the realm and all have an interest in it; but it is clear that their councillors' oath to restore the Crown's honour and rights was uppermost in the barons' minds. The threat to the Crown estate came from its enslavement by a favourite for his own advantage. Far from increasing the Crown's estate as a councillor should, Gaveston had disinherited and impoverished it, he had weakened it in many ways.[3] Nor were the barons thinking primarily, perhaps, of the financial consequences of the grants he had received. It was the

---

[1] See above, pp. 61–3.

[2] The text of this declaration has been printed from Brit. Mus. MS. Burney 277 by H. G. Richardson and G. O. Sayles in *The Governance of Medieval England*, pp. 417–18.

[3] Compare the Canon of Bridlington's account of the charges made against Gaveston in parliament: 'quod dominus Petrus coronam exheredavit et suo incitamento regem a concilio procerum regni sui amovit et sibi ligiantiam quorundam tanquam regi per sacramentum attraxit; et alia multa in coronae debilitamentum, et ligii domini sui et regni seditionem, multipliciter perpetravit', in *Chronicles of the Reigns of Edward I and Edward II*, ed. W. Stubbs, ii (R.S., 1883), p. 34.

political power which these grants gave him which they singled out for condemnation; it was the ability to command royal patronage through his exclusion of the magnates and monopoly of the King's ear, his ability to wield, to 'accroach' the royal power, that they feared; for, as they pointed out, this gave them no means of legal redress against him. Whereas the Crown's 'estate' should profit the realm it was being turned to the profit of a favourite. Hence in the context of their political judgement on Gaveston, they appealed to the people to attest his ill fame. Ultimately, however, the obligation to take action to save the Crown rested on them.

By asserting their responsibility for maintaining the estate of the Crown, even against the King, the magnates placed themselves in a hazardous position, for restraints on the prerogative could safely be effected only if the whole baronage remained unanimous. Gaveston's removal permitted a reversion to the less controversial demand for fiscal and administrative reform which could be justified by an appeal to the ills of the realm and for which the King's co-operation could be secured. For this the tide was running strongly in their favour. Throughout 1309 there was a rising volume of complaint against seizures by royal officials which was expressed in the Articles of Stamford and could be mobilized to force the King to accept reforms as the price of taxation.[1] The strength and confidence of the baronial opposition in 1309, which even led them to accept the recall of Gaveston, continued into 1310, and the same emphasis on securing royal co-operation in reforms underlay the petition which the barons presented to the King in February 1310. The barons it is true alleged the 'desheritaunce de vostre corone et damage de touz ceux de vostre roiaume', and since they were constraining the King by threats and force to accede to their demands they reaffirmed their duty by reason of their allegiance to safeguard the Crown; but the greater part of the petition was devoted to the poverty of the Crown.[2] The King could neither maintain his household nor his wars but was forced to practise extortion on his people through his officials. The taxes of 1307

---

[1] The parliamentary opposition to taxation and purveyances in these years is considered above, ch. v.

[2] *Annales Londonienses*, p. 168. Cf. J. C. Davies, *The Baronial Opposition to Edward II*, p. 362.

and 1309 had been misspent, the war not advanced nor prises paid for, even though this had been a condition of the grant. They attributed these evils to 'non covenable consail' and the remedy they proposed was an ordinance drawn up by themselves. Gaveston himself was not mentioned; the charge of accroaching the royal power had been dropped; there was no explicit demand for the removal of royal councillors. Instead emphasis was now laid upon redressing fiscal and administrative abuses, with the clear implication that this should be on the King's authority and with the assent and co-operation of the magnates.

This trend was carried further in the letters patent of 16 March 1310 which gave authority to the Ordainers and in the first six Ordinances issued three days later which were to form the guidelines for their work during the ensuing year.[1] Neither of these documents mentions the estate of the Crown, its honour or its rights. The barons were given 'plein poiar de ordiner lestat de nostre Hostel et de nostre roiaume' in such manner as would be for the honour and profit of the King and the profit of the people. The household did, of course, represent the estate and honour of the King; but the Ordainers' concern was primarily with its relations to the realm. For it was generally acknowledged, and not least by the King himself, that for the household to fail to pay its way was as dishonouring to the King as it was damaging to his subjects.[2] The baronial commission could thus be said to promote the honour and profit of the King without infringing the King's prerogative.[3] Of the six Ordinances, the fourth explicitly dealt with the responsibility of the household for the purveyances which had oppressed the people. Its declared aim was to provide the King with sufficient revenue to pay for his purveyances without resorting to illegal

---

[1] *Annales Londinienses*, pp. 169–70, 172–3.

[2] Thus in 1312 Edward II wrote to Pembroke, Despenser, and Sandal that complaints against his household debts bore heavily on him and ordered them to devise 'coment nostre dite meignee puisse mieltz estra sustenue'. See J. C. Davies, op. cit., p. 594, Appendix 123.

[3] This is, of course, rehearsed in the Statute of York and, as B. Wilkinson has pointed out, 'the powers and functions of the king were deliberately excluded from the reforms' proposed in the Ordinances of 1310 (*Studies in the Constitutional History of the Thirteenth and Fourteenth Centuries*, Manchester, 1937, pp. 229–30). The barons themselves promised that the commission 'ne tourne en prejudice du dist notre Seignor le Roi' (Davies, *Baronial Opposition*, p. 360).

prises, by ensuring that the customs and issues of the realm should come to the Exchequer for the payment of household expenses as a priority. The third Ordinance did indeed impose restraints on the King's patronage. Lands, rents, franchises, escheats, wards, and marriages were not to be given without the assent of the Ordainers, but the declared purpose of this was fiscal: to acquit the King's debts, relieve his estate, and more honourably maintain it.

The baronial proposal to reform the King's government and household thus sprang from the ills of the realm rather than from any claim to touch the estate of the Crown, and this was the basis of the authority which the Ordainers received from the King. Though their commission was in this sense limited, it none the less marked a radical encroachment of subjects on matters within the King's sphere of government. The estate of the household was clearly asserted to be a matter of concern not merely to the King but to the people of the realm. This sprang from its inability to pay its way, but it extended in consequence to household revenue and hence to the revenues of the realm. The household is explicitly seen as one of the public charges of the state: public in that its activities touched the people, and public in that it received its finance from the Exchequer. It could, indeed, claim to be the first charge on the Exchequer, for its function was to embody the King's honour and estate; but this only emphasized that in this respect the King himself was a public person and that his honour involved the welfare of the realm.

This was the real significance of these Ordinances, but we may notice some further points concerning the third Ordinance on gifts. This claimed the fiscal prerogatives of the Crown—wardships, escheats, etc.—for the maintenance of the King's estate and the discharge of his debts. We have seen that from the reign of Henry III there had been a tendency for King and barons to take formally different views on this. In view of the nature and importance of these revenues this was not surprising; for these were the principal source of rewards for favour and service. Consequently the baronial attitude was bound to be ambivalent, as it had been under Henry III. To eliminate the distribution of these revenues as patronage was not in their interest. Nor, really, was it practicable. Neither the Exchequer

nor the escheators could administer directly the miscellaneous
land revenue which came from the King's fiscal prerogatives.
The only practical way of dealing with these was by bargain
(as with temporalities and the sale of marriages) or leases (with
lands and wardships). The council might endeavour to get
the highest price for the former; the Treasurer might be instructed to extract the highest rent; but even when the lands
were leased at their extended value this concealed a necessary
profit to the lessee. The size of this profit could betoken the
favour (deserved or undeserved) which the recipient enjoyed,
but it might also be calculated in terms of the services he had
performed. Grants might be made in payment of debts for
service, in compensation of losses, or simply as deserved rewards.[1] Of all this the baronage was, of course, aware. The
financial yield of these prerogatives, though stressed in this
Ordinance, could never be exclusive. It did, however, provide
justification for the measure by which the magnates hoped to
contain the evil which they feared more, and which they had
outlined in the petition against Gaveston in 1308: the danger
of one favourite securing the monopoly of the pliant King's
ear. This could be prevented if all gifts had to have the assent
of the Ordainers. This is not to suggest that the magnates or
even the King were indifferent to the financial contribution
which these revenues could make to the King's estate; but the
magnates' foremost concern was that royal patronage should
be evenly distributed, and if to this end they had to limit the
King's traditional prerogative, they could best justify this as a
remedy for the financial ills which afflicted the realm.

If in 1310 the magnates had cautiously emphasized reform
and avoided touching the Crown estate, hoping to restrain the
King and reform the administration by co-operation, the events
of the following year hardened their attitude. Edward's commitment to Gaveston remained complete, and his removal of
himself and the Exchequer to York demonstrated his resolve to
exclude the Ordainers from any share in government. Lincoln's
death strengthened the intransigence of the magnates under
the leadership of Thomas of Lancaster. The full set of Ordin-

[1] Evidence relating to the use of escheats for these purposes during the reign of
Edward II is cited by E. R. Stevenson, 'The Escheator', in *English Government at
Work*, ii. ed. W. A. Morris and J. R. Strayer (Cambridge, Mass., 1947), pp. 135–7.

ances issued in September 1311 transformed the character and purpose of the baronial opposition. Fiscal and administrative reform took second place to personal and political demands, in particular the exile of Gaveston, the removal of evil counsellors from the court, and the restraint on the King's own movements. The article against Gaveston revived the charges and language of the declaration of 1308. He was accused of accroaching the royal power and, by binding his retainers by oaths of loyalty, of bringing the estate of the King and the Crown under his lordship. Edward's declaration that the new Ordinances were against his prerogative and that his consent to them was only under duress underlined the distance the movement had travelled since 1310.[1] The original Ordinances were reissued alongside these new ones; indeed the third and fourth Ordinances were rehearsed (c. 8, 10) with the intention of giving them effect, and stringent restrictions were placed on purveyors. But the new tenor of political conflict was apparent in Ordinance 7 which further limited the King's patronage. Its opening words—'pur ce qe la corone est taunt abeissee et demembree par diverses douns'—significantly recalled the petition against Gaveston in 1308. Such gifts as were 'au damage du roi et destresse de la corone' were to be repealed and were not to be given again except by common assent in parliament. Even though this only applied to grants made since the Ordinances of 1310, so direct a challenge to royal authority as the annulling of the King's grants involved reviving the concept of saving the estate of the Crown from the King first used in 1308.

The second point that calls for comment is that the Ordainers' authority to adjudicate grants was now extended and given more definition not only by the resumption of those 'au damage du roi et destresse de la corone' but by the power to punish recipients by judgement of parliament. The distribution and adjudication of patronage was thereby reserved for a public assembly for it concerned the whole realm.

[1] The Statute of York very clearly implies that the Ordainers had been guilty of moving beyond their original commission to ordain and establish the estate of the household and the realm (section 1) to restrain the royal power in blemishment of his royal lordship and contrary to the estate of the Crown (section 2). This distinction has been marked by Wilkinson (op. cit., p. 230), Lapsley (op. cit., p. 179), and Post (op. cit., p. 405). See also the comments by Davies (op. cit., pp. 369–71) and Maddicott (op. cit., p. 117).

Despite the harsher tone and political implications of the Ordinances of 1311, their broad intention remained to increase the wealth of the Crown and utilize it properly, and in the main it was on the ground of their responsibility for the welfare of the realm that the barons justified the fiscal and administrative restraints they imposed upon the King. The baronial appeal to act for the weal of the realm was well calculated. Not merely did the chroniclers see the Ordinances as designed to remedy oppressions and restore solvency,[1] but one at least gave voice to the conviction that it was the King's liberality with grants that had led him to impose taxes and incur debts.[2] The Ordainers themselves had been careful to avoid so explicit a connection, for their own interests were better served by ensuring an even distribution of royal patronage than by employing it for the payment of purveyances.

This intermingling of political and financial considerations is evident in the baronial handling of resumptions in the succeeding years. In pursuance of the Ordinances writs were issued in October 1311 to the escheators north and south of the Trent and to a number of sheriffs, ordering them to seize into the King's hands grants made since 16 March 1310.[3] The writs to the escheators specified fifty-two items of wardships, escheats, etc., and those to the sheriffs eighteen items of lands, hundreds, and bailiwicks. The lists furnish no estimate of their total value. The resumption applied to gifts made without the assent of the Ordainers,[4] and followed by the adjudication of whether

[1] 'Unde comites vehementer condolentes, clamoribus oppressorum remedium apponere statuerunt. Et adeuntes regem injustas et onerosas bonorum populi captiones eidem retulerunt, humiliter supplicantes ut super hujusmodi injuriis et oppressionibus populi praenotati remedium faceret optimum et vociferanti populo misericorditer subveniret' (*Auct. Bridlington*, p. 36); 'Facte fuerunt ordinaciones pro custodia domus domini regis ut sapiencius viveret ad evitandum tallagia et oppressiones populi communi consensu interveniente' (B.M. MS. Cotton Cleopatra D IX fol. 83ᵛ, in 'A Chronicle of the Civil Wars of Edward II', ed. G. L. Haskins, *Speculum*, xiv (1939), p. 77).

[2] 'Antiquos thesauros et preciosa iocalia in gazophilacio regis apud Westmonasterium, per suos antecessores a tempore a quo non extitit memoria salvo depositos, eidem Petro contulit et distribuit in proprium detrimentum et dampnum gravissimum sui ipsius et tocius populi anglicani; quia exhausto thesauro suo proprio statim indigebat auxilio populari tallagia que eis imposuit' (*Speculum*, xiv. 76). Clearly the belief that the King should use his own resources wisely for the common good before burdening his subjects was widely disseminated.

[3] *Calendar of Chancery Warrants, 1244–1326*, pp. 98–104.

[4] The articles for the enforcement of the Ordinances presented by Lancaster

these were to the 'damage et destresse' of the Crown. Here doubtless personal and political factors helped to sway the decision. Already in October the Ordainers had reserved adjudication on the grant of a wardship to Hugh Despenser until the next parliament, and in the following two months decisions were taken to resume the grants to Gaveston, Beaumont, and Emery de Frescobaldi. Stephen Segrave, however, recovered lands granted to him in respect of the King's debts and Robert de Clifford did likewise because his grants partly represented lands exchanged with the King.[1] Grants from the customs were likewise cancelled and the issues paid direct to the Exchequer in accordance with the Ordinances, but payment was later authorized from the Exchequer where such grants represented the Crown's debts.[2] At the same time the Exchequer was ordered to sell no wardship in future without the assent of the Chancellor and to ensure that those used in payment of royal debts were assessed at their true value.[3] But the effective enforcement of the Ordinances was too brief to provide more than this hint of how the baronial policy would have been implemented. Following the King's move to York early in 1312 the sheriffs were told that the Ordinances were to be observed only in so far as they were not prejudicial to the Crown, and by March 1312 numerous writs under the privy seal were ordering the restoration of grants resumed by the Ordainers.[4] The murder of Gaveston and Pembroke's defection from the baronial opposition restored the political initiative to the King and it was only after Bannockburn that Lancaster could reassert his authority to control the administration and the King. The Ordinances could still provide the legal basis for that authority for they had received the King's sanction, and both the Scottish danger and the economic and fiscal difficulties of the years 1314–16 gave credibility to the baronial claim to redress the ills of the realm by political and administrative reform. Gaveston's death, though it had embittered Edward

---

and Warwick ask the King to abide by the resumption except in the case of four grants made by agreement of the Ordainers (*Annales Londonienses*, pp. 198–9).

[1] Davies, *Baronial Opposition*, p. 592 Appendix no. 117; *C.P.R., 1307–13*, pp. 407–8; *C.C.R., 1307–13*, p. 386; *Annales Londonienses*, p. 201.

[2] *C.C.R., 1307–13*, pp. 386, 391, 401–2.

[3] Davies, *Baronial Opposition*, p. 551 document no. 15.

[4] *C.C.R., 1307–13*, pp. 406, 412–13, 415–16, 439, 447, 449, 451, 469.

and rendered co-operation between the King and Lancaster problematical, reduced the animus against evil counsellors and shifted the emphasis away from the reformation of the estate of the Crown.

The policy of resumption, renewed 'at the request of the magnates' in the parliament of 1314, began with the King's writs to the Exchequer in December to investigate all grants made contrary to the Ordinances,[1] and was put into effect by orders to the escheators in March 1315. These writs named forty-four properties which had been unaffected by the earlier resumption and which were now to be taken into the King's hands.[2] The enforcement of this showed, even more clearly than in 1311, that the adjudication of these was made as much on political as financial grounds. Mortimer's plea for the retention of lands granted to him illustrates this well. He claimed both that he had purchased lands from the Crown which were not part of the royal fisc, and that the grants he had received 'ne luy furent pas doner pur damage du Roi, mes pur son service fait et a faire'.[3] This interpretation of the letter of the Ordinance clearly raised principles of some importance. Adjudication was essential, but needless to say it was not easy. The baronial council might agree to the retention by the earl of Athol of lands given to him in lieu of his inheritance, but between March and May 1315 it fought a running battle with the King over the resumption of lands given to Henry de Beaumont which the King countermanded on the grounds that the lands were in payment of Beaumont's expenses in Scotland.[4] In May 1315, too, the King pardoned the debts of Henry Percy, on grounds of his faithful service,[5] though the previous pardon had been annulled. If grants for good service were to be accepted as legitimate it was clearly of crucial importance whether that service was to be adjudicated by the King or the council.

The work of the council in this respect during the year preceding the Lincoln parliament of 1316 was of considerable

[1] Davies, *Baronial Opposition*, p. 572 document no. 59. The order cited the original Ordinance of 1310 giving the magnates power to ordain the estate of the realm and household.

[2] *C.F.R., 1307–19*, pp. 240–1. See Davies, *Baronial Opposition*, pp. 402–5 for a discussion of the resumption.   [3] *Rot. Parl.* i. 305.

[4] *C.C.R., 1313–18*, p. 180; Davies, *Baronial Opposition*, p. 404.

[5] Davies, *Baronial Opposition*, p. 404.

significance. Not merely did the council adjudicate difficult
cases of resumption, some of which were reserved for settlement
in full parliament, but it authorized grants of various kinds, all
typical of the normal run of royal patronage. Though a detailed analysis of its work is impracticable here, it probably held
a balance between fiscal and political considerations. Thus the
Exchequer was ordered to realize the cash value of all wardships and marriages, and from those arising south of the Trent
the council ordered 1,000 marks to be paid into the Exchequer.
In April 1316 the Exchequer was ordered to take into the King's
hands all grants made for terms of years or at will and re-lease
these at greater profit. On the other hand the council confirmed
the pardon given to the executors of Anthony Bek for debts to
the Crown, and members of the council, not least Lancaster
himself, secured grants and pardons for themselves and their
followers.[1] The Lincoln parliament of 1316 was an attempt to
reaffirm and reinforce this conciliar control exercised inter-
mittently under Lancaster's leadership during the previous
eighteen months. In Lancaster's view it was to provide 'coment
vostre estat puist estre redresce et le gouvernement de vostre
roialme et de vostre hostiel meulz ordeignee'[2] as had the reform programme of 1310. This indeed meant a reduction of
household expenses and a purge of its members; but in co-
operation with and not by coercion of the royal power.

Although it is true that the economic and social problems of
1314–16 undermined any efforts at a restoration of effective
government,[3] it is also true that these years saw the most
sustained explicit subscription to the Ordinances during the
reign. At least in popular eyes, it seems probable that neither
Lancaster nor the Ordinances were discredited by the time of
the Lincoln parliament. Amongst the baronage, however,
Lancaster's rule was fast losing political credibility. The King's
refusal to co-operate with him, the earl's pride, and his growing
jealousy of the new courtier clique led him to withdraw from
the council after April 1316. This made it imperative to find a
different basis for controlling the King's propensity to fall under

---

[1] Davies, *Baronial Opposition*, pp. 405, 416–17; *C.C.R., 1313–18*, p. 166.

[2] Lancaster's letter of July 1317 is printed in *Adae Murimuth Continuatio Chroni-
carum*, p. 272.

[3] This point is emphasized by J. R. Maddicott, op. cit., pp. 183–5.

the influence of his new favourites. Pembroke and his associates wished to sustain, in essentials, the system of conciliar control of patronage that had obtained in the previous period. Although this control was to be exercised in the interests of the magnates and laid less emphasis on securing fiscal profit from such perquisites for the benefit of the Exchequer, these differences were matters of degree. Pembroke, as much as Lancaster, was opposed to allowing the King an unrestrained distribution of patronage and to the canalizing of this in the hands of one favourite. A controlled and diffused distribution of patronage by the council which could form the basis of a settlement with Lancaster remained Pembroke's aim. It has been convincingly argued that the famous indenture between D'Amory, Pembroke, and Badlesmere in November 1317 was an attempt to restrain D'Amory's cupidity by enforcing the principle that no gift worth more than £20 should be made without common assent.[1] Indeed during 1317–18 Pembroke and the moderates showed themselves ready to apply many of the measures of economical government envisaged by the Ordinances of 1310. They prepared to enforce a qualified resumption along the lines of 1315–16 and in February 1318, the lands formerly held by Queen Margaret were assigned to the Exchequer for household expenses.[2] What divided Lancaster from Pembroke and other councillors was partly Lancaster's personal hostility to the courtiers and partly his resentment at exclusion from the King's favour. Ultimately Lancaster's hostility frustrated Pembroke's efforts to restore the situation of 1315–16. These were the considerations behind the negotiations leading up to the Treaty of Leake in 1318.

Throughout these negotiations Lancaster reiterated, with little apparent flexibility, the doctrine of the Ordinances of 1311—that evil counsellors should be removed, that all gifts made contrary to the Ordinances should be resumed, that those who had received them should be punished, and that the profits from them should be paid to the Exchequer and used for the

---

[1] By Maddicott, op. cit., pp. 211–12 and subsequently by J. R. Phillips, op. cit., pp. 134–47; also in 'The "Middle Party" and the Treaty of Leake, 1318', *Bull. Inst. Hist. Res.* xlvi (1973), pp. 11–27. The grants to D'Amory and the terms of the indenture are well summarized by Davies, *Baronial Opposition*, p. 433.

[2] Davies, *Baronial Opposition*, p. 555 document no. 24.

maintenance of the King's expenses and wars.[1] His opposition stemmed from the collapse of the settlement of 1316. In his letter to the King in July 1317 he recalled the remedies proposed at Lincoln—how the King's estate could be redressed and the government of the realm and the household be better ordained—and the King's promise to observe them. Since then the King had surrounded himself with courtiers, to whom he gave his own wealth ('lour donez de vostre') so that little or nothing remained. Such gifts, if retained in the King's hands instead of being wasted, would place him in better state for the things he had to do.[2] There are good grounds for thinking that the rigidity of Lancaster's appeal to the Ordinances and his insistence on resumption were principally designed to foster opposition to the courtiers and force the maximum concessions from them. His attacks on Beaumont, Warenne, and D'Amory are evidence of his personal hostility and fears of their intentions. Ultimately it was this that caused the failure of the negotiations and led to Lancaster's exclusion from the council.

The negotiations with Lancaster initiated by Pembroke, Hereford, and a group of bishops at Pontefract in August and September 1317 and pursued at Leicester and Tutbury in April and June of the following year sought to make progress on the lines of a restoration of the *status quo* of 1314–16. At the September meeting Lancaster reserved his position to maintain the Ordinances and specifically the resumption of 'les choses qe ne sont mie duement alienes du Rey et de la corone', leaving aside the important question of how these were to be defined.[3] The rigidity of Lancaster's terms in the Leicester negotiations in April 1318 is explicable by the imminent danger from the Scots, but it is indicative of Pembroke's persistent desire to restore the government of 1314–16 that he should have agreed, even in principle, to the full implementation of the Ordinances of 1311.[4] Such conditions could never be accepted

[1] Knighton, *Chronicon*, i. 414: 'les ditez choses, terrez et tenementz etc. soient mises en si covenable garde que les usez veignent pleynement a lescheker le roy al commune profite de luy et de son realme, et dispenduz en la deffence de la terre'. See J. G. Edwards, 'The Negotiating of the Treaty of Leake, 1318', in *Essays Presented to R. Lane Poole* (Oxford, 1927), pp. 364–6.

[2] Murimuth, pp. 272–3.

[3] Maddicott, op. cit., pp. 208–9, 336–7 document no. iv. This document is also printed by J. R. Phillips, op. cit., p. 319, who dates it to April 1318.

[4] *Auct. Bridlington*, p. 54; Maddicott, op. cit., p. 216; Phillips, op. cit., pp. 159–60.

by the courtiers, but throughout the early summer of 1318 the military situation compelled the moderates on the council to make every effort to meet Lancaster's demands, for without his return to the government no measures against the Scots were possible. On 9 June the King was induced to order the Exchequer to initiate a resumption on the basis of those of 1311 and 1315, but with the additional requirement that profits from the resumed gifts should be chargeable to the donee or his assigns.[1] This may have been designed to put pressure on the courtiers to reach an accommodation with Lancaster, for hitherto they had presented an intransigent aversion to his re-entry into the council. Now, however, they were induced to commission the bishops to reach a new agreement with the earl on the basis of an adjudication of the resumed gifts similar to that practised in 1315. At Tutbury in June the bishops, while still accepting the principle of a total resumption of gifts contrary to the Ordinances, proposed an adjudication in parliament to distinguish 'queux choses estoient covenablement done et queu altrement'.[2] This Lancaster rejected, and the agreement reached with the bishops reaffirmed the resumption of all gifts since the making of the commission and provided that none was to be made henceforth without the consent of the baronage in parliament until the King's debts had been paid. Even this provided a slender basis for agreement since it did not close the door on further grants[3] or provide for the punishment of those who had received such gifts. But Lancaster remained determined on the removal of 'evil counsellors'. His distrust of these still stood as a barrier to his rejoining the council and even to coming to court. Some time before 21 July he finally secured a promise of their removal and followed this logically by his own proposal for a permanent council to hold office for a year.[4]

Lancaster had thus forced through a paper agreement for the restoration of his position in 1316. He had achieved this

[1] Maddicott, op. cit., pp. 218, 337 document no. v.

[2] Knighton, i. 413–14.

[3] This point was made by B. Wilkinson, 'The Negotiations Preceding the Treaty of Leake, August 1318', in *Studies in Medieval History Presented to F. M. Powicke*, p. 347 n. 1.

[4] Maddicott, op. cit., pp. 222–4; Edwards, op. cit., p. 371; Wilkinson, op. cit., p. 348; Phillips, op. cit., pp. 161–8.

through the divisions in the council. Pembroke and the bishops were ready to agree to a resumption and could hope to persuade the courtiers to accept this in principle if it were followed, as in 1315, by further grants by common assent. But if the courtiers were to be both deprived of their gains and excluded from influence over patronage they were left with no alternative but to fight. This they prepared to do in the latter part of July. For practical purposes this marked the failure of the attempts to bring Lancaster back into the council. His determination to exclude the courtiers from patronage and his inability to work with them was fatal to any attempt to restore conciliar government. Lancaster's hatred of them led him to miscalculate their influence with the King and the desperation with which they would defend their position. The mission 'ad mitigandum comitem' that went to Lancaster in the last week of July had one purpose—to avert war between Lancaster and the court, to settle the personal quarrel between them.[1] The Treaty of Leake marked a personal settlement, not a further basis for Lancaster's participation in government, for which the occasion had passed. At Leake Lancaster successfully mulcted the courtiers, or at least some of the more obnoxious of them, and did so for his own benefit, rather than the King's.[2] On the other hand he had not displaced them from the control of patronage and government. Politically the earl's face was saved by the formal subscription of the court to the Ordinances and the institution of the standing council. But it was clear that in both these respects the character of government would be determined by the court, for Lancaster himself had only token representation on the council and there was no specific reference to resumption or the removal of evil counsellors.

The political manœuvres of 1317–18 centred on the distribution of patronage. What induced Pembroke to approach Lancaster was the fear that the monopoly of patronage would fall to a small group or even to one of the courtiers as it had to Gaveston. Pembroke was attempting to maintain the distribution by common assent of the council which had operated since 1315, and he saw Lancaster as the architect and guarantor

---

[1] Cf. the views of Wilkinson, op. cit., p. 350; Maddicott, op. cit., p. 226; Phillips, op. cit., pp. 169–70.

[2] Maddicott, op. cit., pp. 233–7.

of this system. It was what the majority of the baronage and bishops understood to be the spirit of the Ordinances, if not their letter. The proposal in the Ordinances of 1310 for a total restraint of gifts and their assignment to the Exchequer had been designed to attract support for a conciliar programme of reform. In 1311 resumption had been added to counter the defiance of the Ordainers' authority by the court. In 1314–16, with the evil counsellors no longer a threat, the baronial implementation of the Ordinances had been pragmatic, seeking the King's co-operation for a controlled distribution of patronage to all elements of the baronage. When in 1317–18 Lancaster reasserted the Ordainers' demands for a complete restraint of gifts, for a wholesale resumption, and for the punishment and expulsion of the evil counsellors, he was returning not to 1315–16 (as Pembroke had hoped) but to 1311–12. Possibly Lancaster foresaw more clearly than Pembroke the dominance of the Despensers; possibly he was blinded by hatred of those who had displaced him. In the event his attempt to use the principle of the Ordinances to force out the court backfired; it was he who suffered political exclusion, leaving Pembroke to salvage what he could of his plan to return to 1315–16.

In fact for a time Pembroke was not unsuccessful. Conciliar control of patronage proved feasible during 1318–20. The confrontation with Lancaster may for a time have checked the ambitions of the courtiers, though their tacit victory prepared the ground for the final struggle. The parliament at York in October 1318 which confirmed the Treaty of Leake undertook an extensive review of grants, including those made to all the prominent courtiers. They were adjudicated, as in 1315, on grounds of merit. Some grants made for good service, for debts, for exchanges of land, etc. were allowed; in other cases the terms of the tenure were changed or a higher rent exacted; in others the grants were judged unsuitable and resumed. Individuals usually had to surrender a portion of what they had received, rarely everything.[1] At the same time parliament and the council were giving assent to further grants and even

---

[1] *Documents Illustrative of English History in the Thirteenth and Fourteenth Centuries*, ed. H. Cole (London, 1844), p. 9. For many illustrations, see Davies, *Baronial Opposition*, pp. 458–9.

formally requesting the appointment of the younger Despenser as Chamberlain.[1] The York parliament of May 1319 maintained this authority over grants, selling the Willoughby wardship and marriage to D'Amory for 2,000 marks, refusing Audley's claim to the earldom of Cornwall in right of his wife, and assenting to grants to Beaumont, D'Amory, and Edmund of Woodstock.[2] Between parliaments the permanent council constituted an essential element in the distribution of patronage, and in June 1320 the policy of economical government was still sufficiently effective for a review to be initiated of all royal lands and the revenues they were yielding.[3] During the summer of 1320, however, the growing influence of the Despensers was dividing the council, and though the October parliament of 1320 provided a last demonstration of the distribution of patronage by common assent, the award of Gower to Despenser led to a swift plunge into war.[4]

From this point resumption and the idea of restraint over patronage exercised by common assent for the good of the realm had no further relevance. The indictment of the Despensers and the Doncaster petition show the barons reverting deliberately to the form of the proceedings against Gaveston. The Despensers were charged with accroaching the royal power; to their evil counsel was ascribed the alienation of the King from his barons; against their tyranny no judicial process could avail and the only remedy was an 'award' by the barons. Although their evil rule was denounced as harmful to the realm and their notoriety adduced as evidence of their guilt, the baronage did not act as representatives of the realm to redress the common ills, but as lieges of the King, bound by their duty to correct the estate of the Crown and the estate of the realm.[5]

The fall of Edward II, the restoration to influence of the political heirs of Lancaster, and the renewed demands of the King for war taxation all contributed to a revived interest

---

[1] Cole, *Documents*, p. 4.   [2] J. C. Davies, *Baronial Opposition*, pp. 461–3.
[3] *C.C.R., 1318–23*, p. 196.
[4] J. C. Davies, *Baronial Opposition*, pp. 469–70, 472; Maddicott, op. cit., pp. 256–7.
[5] B. Wilkinson, 'The Sherburn Indenture and the Attack on the Despensers, 1321', *Eng. Hist. Rev.* lxiii (1948), pp. 23–7 Appendix v; G. L. Haskins, 'The Doncaster Petition of 1321', *Eng. Hist. Rev.* liii (1938), pp. 483–5.

in the Lancastrian critique of the function of the Crown revenues. The first indication of this is the tract *De Speculo Regis* addressed hopefully to the young Edward III.[1] As its title implies, its monitions drew heavily on a well-established genre and it would be unwise to adduce them as evidence of specific grievances current at the time. Thus the author urges the King to reduce the expenses of his household (which were, in fact, very moderate) on the ground that a king who did not live within his income would be led to plunder the revenue and property of his subjects.[2] If this merely restated the dictum of Aquinas and would have been familiar to the ears of Edward's grandfather, the tract does return with notable insistence to the effect of the royal debt accumulated from the two preceding reigns. The author's main complaint is of unpaid purveyances which ruin subjects and stir up social and political discontent through hatred of the King's ministers. His other target is indiscriminate royal generosity. Although the author acknowledges the conventional view that the King who rewards deserving and needy men is prudent and praiseworthy, he is more concerned to show that by gifts to unworthy and rapacious men, 'talis rex est depopulator reipublicæ et destructor regni et regiminis'. For not all the King's wealth, in land and movables, is sufficient to pay his inherited debts—scarcely indeed a third of them. The King should hold this before his eyes when suitors approach him, and tell them plainly that he cannot for the present give them anything.[3] Much of this—the complaints against prises as a source of discontent, the plea for economy in household expenditure, the insistence on the restraint of grants until the King's debts should be acquitted—directly echoes the Ordinances of 1311, though in the nature of his tract the author looks to the King to remedy these of his own accord rather than under baronial constraint. Almost simultaneously a Commons' petition in the parliament of 1332

---

[1] *De Speculo Regis Edwardi III*, ed. J. Moisant (Paris, 1891). The date of its composition has been argued by J. Tait, 'On the Date and Authorship of the Speculum Edwardi Regis', *Eng. Hist. Rev.* xvi (1901), pp. 110–15. The fiscal criticism is mainly concentrated in caps. 5, 7, and 8 of the tract.

[2] Op. cit., p. 157: 'Superfluitas expensarum est destructio regni, quia quando superfluitas expensas superabat redditus civitatum, et sic redditibus et expensis deficientibus, reges extenderunt manus suas ad res et redditus aliorum.'

[3] Ibid., cap. 7, p. 140.

employed the formula of the Ordinances in exhorting the King to live of his own and pay his expenses and not burden his people by prises.[1] The fact that the tract was plainly the work of a clerk illuminates the role of the Church in articulating criticism of purveyance and giving a lead to popular grievance against it. This was to become explicit in 1338–9 and provided fertile ground for Stratford's warning to Edward in the crisis of 1340–1 that he was losing the hearts of his subjects by oppressive burdens and the iniquities of royal ministers.[2] But what is of distinctive interest from the point of view of public concern with the fisc is that the author urges restraint of royal generosity, not merely in terms of the conventional virtue of moderation or of the divine threat to eternal life, but as part of the King's political responsibility for the welfare and maintenance of the *respublica*. For the dissipation of the fisc leads directly to the King burdening and impoverishing his subjects.

The same tradition was reflected in the Commons' petition in the parliament of 1340. The theme of this was the burden and impoverishment of the Commons by heavy taxation and fiscal corruption and incompetence. Following closely the remedies of 1311, the Commons demanded that those who had mishandled the taxes should be brought to account and that in future all manner of revenue—taxes, customs, marriages, escheats, and all other profits of the realm—should be entrusted to a committee of peers and spent on royal business and in defence of the realm. Against the evils of monopolist profits and prerogative levies which burdened and antagonized the community for the profit of the King and his associates, the petition appealed to an ideal of the common profit which should embrace, balance, and harmonize the interests of the King and of the realm for their common defence. It repeatedly emphasized that the proposed reforms would work 'to the profit of him and the discharge of his people'.[3]

---

[1] *Rot. Parl.* ii. 66.

[2] Tait, op. cit., p. 115 suggested that the author may have been Archbishop Simon Meopham. The author warns the King that his failure to discharge the debts of his father and grandfather will imperil their souls and his own; he also urges the King to be guided by clerical ministers. For clerical protests against purveyance, see below, p. 247.

[3] Appendix A item i cap. 2. Thus, too, in cap. 3 the revenues were to be used 'a les opes le Roi et en defence de sa terre'. For a full discussion see 'The Commons Petitions of 1340', *Eng. Hist. Rev.* lxviii (1963), pp. 625–54 and below, ch. xi.

The debt which the petition of 1340 owed to the Ordinances and the programme of Thomas of Lancaster is nowhere clearer than in the fourth clause relating to the Crown lands. This asked that the sheriffs should be instructed to inquire into all lands of the Crown (excluding those acquired by purchase or temporary escheat) which had been given, sold, or alienated since the time of Edward I. It proposed that all such gifts should be reviewed at the next parliament so that those which were adjudged 'unreasonable' should be revoked and remain in the King's hands 'so that the king might live of his own without charge to his people'. If the proposal for local inquisition and adjudication in parliament on the grounds of suitability recalled the resumption policy of the baronial 'moderates', the emphasis on the employment of resumed lands to alleviate fiscal burdens on the community reflected popular memory of the Ordinances and the propaganda of Earl Thomas. The demand for resumption may have been immediately prompted by the recent alienation of Burstwick to the hated William de la Pole or even the more distant endowments of the new earls in 1337, but while Archbishop Stratford may have deplored at least the former of these, he was probably aware that resumption had been the rock on which Lancastrianism had foundered. In the event this was the only major proposal of the petition not to be put into effect. Nevertheless the statute enacted in return for the grant of the ninth did appropriate not merely the aid but the casual prerogative revenue, from wards, marriages, and escheats, together with the ancient customs and revenues of the realm, to the safeguard of the realm against its enemies, in terms very similar to the third clause of the petition.[1] The idea that the fisc should contribute towards the charges of state had become popular orthodoxy, whatever reservations were felt about it by the baronial class.

Although Edward III had himself been quite ready to exploit his casual prerogatives for the furtherance of his military schemes,[2] it was no part of royal policy to acknowledge that

---

[1] *S.R.* i. 289–90: 'et qe touz les profitz sourdantz du dit eide, et des gardes, mariages, custumes, eschetes et autres profitz surdantz du roialme Dengleterre, soient mys et despenduz sur la meintenance de la sauve garde de nostre dit roialme Dengleterre, et de noz guerres Descoce, France, et Gascoigne, et nulle part aillours durantz les dites guerres'.

[2] Thus in August 1337 Edward ordered the Treasurer to certify to him the true

this more personal revenue ought to be applied to the charges of state. This became apparent in 1343 when the King, learning from the bitter lesson of 1340–1, had repaired his breach with Stratford and had begun to establish that close alliance with the magnates which was to ensure almost thirty years of political harmony. When the Commons entered their lone protest against the repeal of the statute of 1341 they also revived their demand for a restraint of royal gifts:

Item, q'il pleise a notre Seignur le Roi retenir devers lui Terres, Rentes et Eschetes et autres Profitz touchantz sa corone et droit, ensi q'il peusse de ce mieltz vivre, en descharge de son poeple, et pur mieltz meyntenir ses guerres et autres grosses Busoignes de son Roialme. Responsio: Le Roi est en volente de sauver le soen, selonc ce qe a lui serra avys par son bon Conseil mieltz pur son profit.[1]

Their petition, using the language of 1311 and 1340, rested on the assumption that the fisc and the King's feudal rights should be employed for the relief of the people by supporting the costs of war and administration. The King's own should help to relieve them of the burden of taxes and prises which, they complained in another article, threatened wholly to destroy them. But the King answered in the tradition of the thirteenth century that the safeguarding of his own was a matter for the King's 'will' (*volente*) with advice from his council as proved best for his own profit. He refused to bind himself either by promising to restrain his gifts or by undertaking to employ Crown revenues for the charges of the realm.[2]

This closed the first period of public debate about the nature and function of the Crown revenues. It had effected a radical change in the thirteenth-century practice of treating these as the sole responsibility of the King and had added to their traditional function of maintaining the royal estate the further obligation to relieve the burden which the King's needs placed upon the realm. A royal right to reclaim revenues alienated

value of the marriages of two wards and to make no sale of them without the King's special command (E 404/3/21).

[1] *Rot. Parl.* ii. 141.

[2] It is interesting to find Edward, in December 1343, specifically reserving the temporalities of the see of Norwich for his own use and forbidding the Treasurer to use them for assignment to Exchequer creditors (C 81/1331, no. 31), though by January they had been taken at farm (*C.C.R., 1343–46*, p. 265).

from the Crown had been developed into the right of subjects to impose on the King restraint and resumption of royal gifts for the common profit of the realm. These dramatic conceptual changes appeared in response to critical developments in the nature of political opposition to the Crown and in the exploitation of the resources of the realm. The thirteenth century had seen the formulation of a theory of the Crown as the perpetual symbol both of the King's honour and of the identity of the realm. From this flowed the notion of the inalienability of the royal fisc which supported the estate of the Crown. Primarily the responsibility of the monarch, it could become a matter of public concern if the fisc were insufficient to support the royal estate, notably as embodied in the household, so that this became a burden on the realm. The notion, seized upon by the baronial opposition to Edward II, that subjects could impose restraints on the King to preserve the estate of the Crown, gave a clear sanction for control of the Crown revenues in the name of the common profit. Moreover, the remarkable enlargement of the practice of taxation for the common profit tended to make this the criterion for the Crown's fiscal policies as a whole. The final emergence of a national system of finance under Edward I thus brought as its corollary a critique of royal management of finance in terms of national profit for which, by 1310, there was ground enough.

Such criticism would not have been formulated in political terms or, probably, have received public expression, had not a crisis in royal finance coincided with personal and political opposition to Edward II. The baronial demand for restraint and resumption of royal grants, first made in 1311 and then erected into the cornerstone of Lancastrian policy in 1314–18, was designed to counteract the monopoly of Crown patronage by a small group or a single favourite. It sought not so much to diminish patronage as to ensure its redistribution through the council on a broad basis. For the barons resumption was thus basically a political weapon, and the attempt to impose it on the Crown was justified in terms of their obligation to save the estate of the Crown from favourites who accroached its power or from the King who dissipated its resources. Either situation might justify the use of force to wrench power from the hands of the King and his associates. A more moderate approach was to persuade the King to accept restraint and resumption as a means of supporting the household and public charges. In this the magnates claimed to act as representatives of the realm and for its profit. But once they were in power, their use of resumption was neither exclusively penal (an embargo on all gifts) nor exclusively financial (the application of them to the King's expenses). It was pragmatic and selective. Resumption was used to strip obnoxious favourites of place and perquisites but was more commonly the prelude to adjudication of gifts on grounds of merit. Extravagant and undeserved generosity was wasteful and dangerous, but failure to reward real service, or the repudiation of gifts made for such, was equally dishonouring to the King and politically unwise. It was in these terms that the baronage understood good government; the balancing of political and financial considerations with a view to the good of both King and realm. This was the ideal held up to the faithful councillor.

The demand for resumption and restraint for a purely financial purpose sprang from those who suffered from the Crown's insolvency, its civilian and military creditors. It could draw on impeccable legal and moral authority, for a ruler was expected to use his own resources for the common good in time of need before burdening his people. Insolvency on a large scale, with consequent burdens on the subject, was commonly only the product of wartime, for the Crown's domestic expenditure was not on sufficient scale to produce a significant public reaction. Popular demands for resumption were thus the product of financial crisis and military burdens, and were fiscal in object. They were not necessarily correlated to baronial demands, though because they had a genuine impetus of their own they might provide powerful political support for a baronial movement. Above all they were given authority and coherence by the Lancastrian programme between 1310 and 1320 and lived on as an important strand in the critique of royal government presented by the Commons in the early years of the Hundred Years War. The fleeting success of this opposition in 1340, the fruit of widespread discontent, divisions amongst the magnates, and the King's desperate position, did not extend to resumption though it did secure the application of the Crown revenues and fiscal prerogatives for the charges of the realm. But Edward's reconciliation of the baronial factions deprived the Commons of essential political leadership while their energies were consumed in controversies over taxation and prerogative levies. The attempt to impose restraint and resumption on the King thus died away, or at least was denied political expression.[1] Public concern with the royal fisc might be sporadic in expression, but it remained part of a consistent and, thanks to the Lancastrian tradition, a known and defined doctrine of public finance, the counterpart to the concept of taxation. It was no accident, therefore, that as taxation, insolvency, and corruption again became matters of urgent political concern at the end of Edward III's reign, the concepts and language of 1310–20 again made their appearance as part of the Commons' critique in the name of the common profit of the realm.

[1] In the *Scalacronica*, written about 1355, Sir Thomas Grey complained that the King had granted away his lands so liberally that he scarcely retained the lands pertaining to the Crown and was forced to live on subventions and subsidies at great charge to his people (*Scalacronica*, ed. J. Stevenson, Edinburgh, 1836, p. 167); but his complaint cannot be related to any known protest by the Commons at this time.

CHAPTER VIII

Exchequer, Chamber, and Wardrobe to 1307

I N the preceding chapters we have traced the emergence of public finance in England as part of the wider development of the community of the realm under the Crown as its symbolic head. We now have to relate this to the development of administrative institutions of government. In this chapter we shall ask what effect the tendency towards an impersonal Crown had upon the mobile, personal, and often arbitrary government of the Angevin kings. The growth of state power presented the monarchy with a dilemma. For although the King could enlarge his fiscal and administrative resources by acting in the name of the Crown and for the needs of the state, those same needs threatened to engulf his own interests and to limit his role to that of an official of the realm. It has been argued that the monarchy reacted to the growth of a semi-autonomous bureaucracy by extending the household offices under its immediate control, seeking in particular to channel its newly acquired revenues through the Wardrobe. A conflict developed between the offices of state, representing and protecting the interests of the realm, and the household offices as organs of the prerogative, devoted to furthering the interests of the King. It was in these terms that T. F. Tout interpreted the administrative developments of the thirteenth century, believing that they reflected and held the key to the political struggles between the King's familiars and the baronage. The household, flexible, untrammelled by routine, and responsive to the royal will, was the natural instrument for autocracy; the great departments of state, national in character and already cherishing a tradition of autonomy, just as naturally served to impose baronial and constitutional restraint upon the King. Faced with baronial attempts to control the government, the King might retire into his household, and from this base he could govern independently of the Exchequer and Chancery. In Tout's view the size of the Wardrobe's revenue, and in particular that part which it received independently of the Exchequer as part of its 'foreign' receipt, gave a broad indication of the strength and freedom of the King's personal government.[1]

Since Tout wrote historians have sought an older ancestry for the rise of domestic offices in finance and have modified this view of their political significance. It has become clear that under the Angevin kings the Chamber played a role not dissimilar to that of the Wardrobe, and this has suggested that a household office of some kind was a necessity for personal monarchy in this period. Indeed the administrative work of Henry III has been seen as a revival of the Angevin system, and the reign of Edward I has been called 'the zenith of the Angevin conception of administration centred on the household'.[2] The King's use of his household and in particular his decision to draw money into it, away from the Exchequer, is seen to be a persistent feature of this type of government, being dictated not by political but by administrative and governmental needs. Moreover historians are now less willing to draw a distinction between the private and personal character of the household and the national character of the departments of state, emphasizing that both were equally under the King's control, equally responsive to his demands. The Exchequer had no independence wherewith to resist the King, nor any indefeasible control over the household.

In most points this revision has the merit of greater realism, but it may do less than justice to the changes which took place in one of the most formative periods of English history. There was a greater difference in quality between the government of Henry II and that of Edward I than this view seems to allow; and over the same period the relations between the King and the realm had likewise been transformed. It is doubtful whether the position of the Wardrobe under Edward I was in any way comparable to that of the Chamber under Richard and John.

[1] T. F. Tout, *Chapters in Medieval Administrative History*, vol. i (Manchester, 1920), deals with the Wardrobe up to Edward I and pp. 19–21 in particular summarize his views on the Wardrobe and the Exchequer; vol. ii, pp. 1–158 deals with Edward II and pp. 152 ff. with the 'autocracy' of the King's last years. J. C. Davies, *The Baronial Opposition to Edward II* (Cambridge, 1918), p. 198, shares the same view of the significance of 'exchequer' and 'foreign' receipt.

[2] S. B. Chrimes, *An Introduction to Medieval Administrative History* (Oxford, 1952), pp. 87–8, 120, 129.

Nor was Tout wrong in contrasting the personal and flexible character of the Wardrobe with the more rigid and bureaucratic Exchequer.

In the following pages we shall try to define the financial role of the household in the light of the general development of English government and administration between Henry II and Edward I, giving particular attention to its relationship with the Exchequer, its sources of revenue, and the nature of its expenditure. Tout's detailed work makes it possible to discuss this within a short compass, even though the resultant view will differ significantly from that which he argued.

EXCHEQUER AND CHAMBER UNDER THE ANGEVIN KINGS

Medieval government needed an administrative system which could safeguard royal rights by its routine and yet be responsive to the sudden requirements of personal monarchy. It had like-wise to satisfy the dual character of a monarchy which was already the centre of a political entity, the realm, but which was still essentially itinerant in its practice of government. These needs were met, in Henry II's day, by the rather dis-jointed operations of a number of physically separated organs of finance. The Exchequer, at Westminster, kept watch over what was due to the King while the Treasury, at Winchester, was responsible for receiving, storing, and paying out the King's money; these represented the routine element in financial administration. Locally the sheriff was still the collector of all the King's major revenues, for which he accounted at the Exchequer, but at times urgency and convenience led the King to order him to disburse money locally for the expenses of castle building, war, or the purchase of victuals, or to pay money direct to the Chamber. To the sheriff, as a fixed local agent through whom revenue could be anticipated, the Chamber formed an itinerant counterpart.[1]

The purposes for which Henry II used his Chamber have been investigated by J. E. A. Jolliffe.[2] Its most persistent use

---

[1] Cf. H. G. Richardson and G. O. Sayles, *The Governance of Mediaeval England*, chs. xi, xii especially p. 228.

[2] J. E. A. Jolliffe, 'The *Camera Regis* under Henry II', *Eng. Hist. Rev.* lxviii (1953); *Angevin Kingship*, chs. xi, xii.

was as a minor treasury for the King's immediate needs on itinerary, picking up odd debts and payments from local officials and occasionally receiving larger sums as a result of personal undertakings to the King from his greater tenants. Such receipts were both casual and diverse. On occasion escheated lands might be placed under the exclusive control of the Chamber, in respect of which it performed the functions of both Treasury and Exchequer. The Chamber was frequently responsible for the garrison and repair of royal castles, and when the King was on campaign it was the paymaster of the King's *exercitus* for which it might draw large sums from the royal treasuries or from taxes. Finally, Jolliffe has claimed that in particular circumstances, notably in the years before 1166 when Henry was preoccupied with restoring order and financial control, the Chamber was the King's personal instrument in disciplining recalcitrant debtors.[1] Thus the Chamber served at once the domestic, personal needs of the court and the governmental requirements of the ruler; it undertook on its journeys a wide range of operations which reflected the various, immediate acts of government which were required of the King.[2] While its character as a mobile, personal treasury is clear, and its central importance in itinerant personal rule is not in dispute, the scale of its operations under Henry II cannot be assessed. Jolliffe, while in no way minimizing its operations, saw these as 'at most ancillary to the traditional system', but for Richardson and Sayles its proximity to the King entitled it to be described as 'the centre and controlling organ of the financial system'.[3] This is probably to anticipate; what is certain is that for the military exigencies of Richard and John and for the latter's close and systematic exploitation of the financial resources of the Crown, the Chamber became the principal agent. For the defence of Normandy, up to 1204, the Chamber drew large sums from the treasury at Caen, from tallages, and occasional prizes of war.[4] In England, after that date, it became the hub of a system of government which

---

[1] H. G. Richardson, 'The Chamber under Henry II', *Eng. Hist. Rev.* lxix (1954), pp. 596–611, has made some substantial criticism of the evidence used by Jolliffe on this point.

[2] See Jolliffe's summary of its role in *Eng. Hist. Rev.* lxviii. 347.

[3] *Angevin Kingship*, p. 240; *Governance of Mediaeval England*, p. 239.

[4] *Angevin Kingship*, pp. 238–40; *Governance of Mediaeval England*, pp. 232–3.

depended on personal ties between the King and his servants as custodians of local revenues. Three great local treasuries under royal familiars usurped the predominance of the Treasury, lately moved from Winchester to Westminster, while some of the shrievalties were placed in the hand of household officials, who paid their issues to the Chamber and rendered account to it.[1] Despite the scope of these activities it remains true that the system of Chamber, castle treasuries, and 'familiar' shrievalties lacked the traditional safeguards of the Exchequer and was dependent on the loyalty and devotion of selected royal servants. Government had recognizably changed its character when the Chamber was used on this scale; it became 'familiar government', directed to 'whatever served the King's policy at the moment and engaged his special interest and concern'.[2] At all times this was the peculiar function of the Chamber, but it was only as part of government in which the King's personal interest and will systematically predominated— 'bold, resourceful autocracy' as it has been called[3]—that the Chamber became the central and controlling organ.

Although it is true that there was no restriction on what revenue the King might order to be paid into the Chamber,[4] some revenues were more likely to be diverted to the Chamber by the King's command. Since it was necessarily itinerant, the Chamber could not maintain a large permanent treasure, and the transport of treasure to it from the Treasury was the least efficient method of supplying its needs.[5] Hence the Chamber chiefly tended to anticipate revenue which could be drawn in large sums from individual receivers or local treasuries or which flowed to the King from the exercise of his prerogative or grace, or through his personal financial agreements.

The farm of the shire and, later, the profits which the sheriff answered for were normally paid into the Exchequer. Under

---

[1] *Angevin Kingship*, pp. 246–50 and ch. xiii. See also, Jolliffe, 'The Chamber and the Castle Treasuries under King John', *Studies in Medieval History Presented to F. M. Powicke* (Oxford, 1948), pp. 117–42.

[2] *Angevin Kingship*, p. 288.

[3] Ibid., p. 297.

[4] Jolliffe, *Eng. Hist. Rev.* lxviii. 359.

[5] The Chamber did, of course, draw large sums *in specie* from the royal Treasury by writ of *liberate*, though usually only when the King was in England. There are numerous references to the transport of treasure on the pipe rolls. See Richardson and Sayles, *The Governance of Mediaeval England*, pp. 231–2, 235–6.

Henry II payments to the Chamber were small and occasional,[1] but under John some shires were placed in the hands of the King's *familiares* who would pay the whole farm or some items of it into the Chamber.[2] Occasional debts from persons of standing, who might be farmers of royal lands or be under fine to the King, would appropriately be paid into the Chamber as pertaining to the King's grace or prerogative. In the same way fines for obtaining the King's good will or for 'having the King's justice' and occasionally *auxilia* and *dona* from the boroughs, all of which depended on the King's grace, were undoubtedly being paid into the Chamber under Henry II and formed an important part of its income under John.[3] Similarly, there was a tendency for the larger escheats to be withdrawn from the sheriff's charge and placed under special custodians answerable to the King. The institution of a special roll of larger escheats and debts under Richard of Ilchester in 1163, part of the general inquisition into royal rights of these years, foreshadowed the policy of 'attorning' some large escheated honours—those of Rayleigh and Boulogne—to the Chamber later in Henry's reign, a policy extended to embrace smaller escheats under John.[4] Escheats and wardships were committed to Chamber clerks, thus forming the beginnings of a 'Chamber estate'.[5] Temporalities presented a similar opportunity. Some important abbeys were placed under special custodians under Henry II, a practice extended under John,[6] who ordered the temporalities of Canterbury to be paid to the Chamber during 1205–6.[7] All these formed a particular type of revenue termed by Jolliffe 'the great and occasional

---

[1] T. F. Tout, *Chapters*, i. 103–5, giving references to pipe rolls; Jolliffe, *Eng. Hist. Rev.* lxviii. 7; *Angevin Kingship*, pp. 231 n. 1, 232 n. 1, 241; *Dialogus*, ed. C. Johnson, p. 80. Jolliffe also claims that before 1166 Henry drew large sums from sheriffs in an effort to enforce the payment of long-standing arrears (*Eng. Hist. Rev.* lxviii. 10–11, 14–15; *Angevin Kingship*, pp. 235–6) but cf. Richardson, *Eng. Hist. Rev.* lxix. 596–611.

[2] Jolliffe, *Angevin Kingship*, pp. 287, 289, 293. M. Mills, 'Experiments in Exchequer Procedure', *Trans. Roy. Hist. Soc.*, 4th ser. viii (1925), pp. 153–4.

[3] *Dialogus*, p. 120; Tout, *Chapters*, i. 105 n. 3, 106; Painter, *The Reign of King John*, p. 110.

[4] Jolliffe, *Eng. Hist. Rev.* lxviii. 11, 18–19; *Angevin Kingship*, p. 237.

[5] *Angevin Kingship*, p. 283. Tout, *Chapters*, i. 107, cites some cases of Chamber manors under Henry II.

[6] *Angevin Kingship*, pp. 283–4, 241; Tout, *Chapters*, i. 103 n. 2.

[7] M. Howell, *Regalian Right in Medieval England*, p. 57.

profits',[1] which reached the King by virtue of his prerogative
and often represented the result of his personal action. Largely
feudal and personal in nature and mainly the fruit of a specific
occasion rather than a normally recurring source of income,
they formed the natural means by which the King supplied his
immediate and personal needs.

Some recurrent sources of revenue, recognized as the prerogative rights of the King, also frequently came to the Chamber.
Revenue from the royal forests figures in the Chamber receipts
under Henry II and was of major importance in the years
1201–8.[2] The profits of the royal Exchanges and Mints were
placed in the hands of the King's familiars by John, to account
solely to the Chamber.[3] Loans, contracted on the King's personal authority, were a regular element in Chamber revenue.
Henry II's borrowings from the Jew Isaac and from the Fleming
William Cade were paid into the Chamber and repaid from
the revenues of the realm.[4] Within the context of Angevin
government, when administrative institutions were still fluid
and war and political crises added to the habitual conditions
of emergency in which kings operated, there could be no formal
distinction between the roles performed by the household and
the departments of state. To serve the King as both a personal
treasury and the paymaster for his household, castles, army,
and private pleasures, the Chamber needed to draw on the
widest range of revenue. Even so it found it easiest to draw upon
those revenues which sprang from the King's personal and
occasional action in virtue of his grace and prerogative, while
the bulk of the recurrent revenues were habitually paid into
the Exchequer. Even the latter might succumb to the demands
of John's 'familiar' government, and at all times this division
was 'a matter of convenience and habit, not of rule or right'.[5]
Nevertheless it is worth observing, for it helps to define the

---

[1] *Angevin Kingship*, p. 286. Examples of practically all the types of revenue
discussed here may be found in the excerpts from the pipe rolls of allowances for
payments to the Chamber printed in T. Madox, *History of the Exchequer*, i (London,
1769), pp. 263–5.

[2] Tout, *Chapters*, i. 106 n. 1; Richardson and Sayles, *The Governance of Mediaeval
England*, p. 235; *Angevin Kingship*, p. 241.

[3] *Angevin Kingship*, pp. 241–2, 294.

[4] Richardson, *Eng. Hist. Rev.* lxix. 605–7; Richardson and Sayles, *The Governance
of Mediaeval England*, pp. 233–4; Jolliffe, *Eng. Hist. Rev.* lxviii. 10.

[5] Jolliffe, *Eng. Hist. Rev.* lxviii. 359.

nature of the Chamber as an instrument for exploiting the King's fiscal prerogatives and it will become significant as government develops a momentum of its own and a financial machinery which will function for long periods in normal independence of the King.

EXCHEQUER AND WARDROBE UNDER HENRY III

With the accession of Henry III the 'familiar government' of the previous reign inevitably ceased. The reaction against John's rule and the circumstances of his son's minority stimulated the baronage to assert their corporate responsibility for good government, springing from their right to counsel the King and hardening into a theory of the council as guardian of the public good. Much of their criticism, in the next forty years came to be directed against royal finance; indeed a desire to assert the supremacy of the 'national' Exchequer over the 'private' Wardrobe has been seen as central to their plan of constraining the King and governing in his name.[1] Such a view is difficult to sustain. The emphasis which the baronial opposition placed upon the Exchequer as an agent for control and reform does indeed underline the central position it occupied in national finance by the middle of the thirteenth century. But it is important to stress that the Exchequer had attained this position through the action of the King and as the agent for the assertion of royal rights. However much Henry III may have been guided by the advice of familiars, the pattern of his government was not 'familiar' on the model of his father's.

The first forty years of Henry III's reign wrought a transformation in the character of financial administration. Although Henry lacked his father's restless experimentation and boldness of purpose in the pursuit of royal interests, his needs and revenues were constantly growing. Encouraged by the King, royal officials displayed an urgent and professional concern to preserve and enforce his rights and exploit Crown revenues. As under John, this stimulated an awareness on the part of subjects of their own rights and the claims of the common weal. What did this mean for the Exchequer? It meant that it became at once a more formidable and sophisticated but also a

[1] Tout, *Chapters*, i. 218–19; R. F. Treharne, *The Baronial Plan of Reform, 1258–1263*, pp. 27–30.

more public and national body. F. M. Powicke has pointed out that the Exchequer of Henry III's day was more intricate, more specialized, with more numerous responsibilities, than when Richard of Ely wrote the *Dialogus*.[1] With the appearance of new revenues and specialized financial officials, the Exchequer found itself the centre of almost perpetual transactions between the King's officials and his creditors from all parts of the realm. It was an 'open' place where the King's rights and the subject's obligations met in a perpetual and detailed dialogue.[2] Thus the growing administrative unity of the realm and the new political sense of community, as well as the more specific financial doctrines of the King and realm which we have considered, gradually produced a feeling that the Exchequer embraced the interests and concerns of the realm as a whole and that its revenues pertained to the realm.

The trend of the thirteenth century was, in fact, towards the consolidation of a national financial system embracing the interests and serving the needs of both King and realm, rather than towards the creation of 'household' government. The 'duality' of medieval government meant that kings still needed the household to meet the immediate exigencies of government or in circumstances where the sedentary Exchequer was impracticable, and in this respect Henry III's revival of the Wardrobe was certainly in the 'Angevin' tradition. But it scarcely played the part which the Chamber had in John's government. Henry used the Wardrobe less as a major instrument for the government of the realm, than as an *ad hoc* agent for matters which were of pressing concern to the King. It might serve, in the first instance, as the agent for political–administrative reform. Much as Henry II may have used the Chamber to enforce long-standing obligations from the shires in 1165–6, involving an attack on the existing sheriffs, so in 1232–4 the Wardrobe became the instrument for wresting the shires from entrenched interests in order to reform the whole system of the receipt of the royal revenues. It has been claimed, with reason, that the Exchequer reforms of 1232–6 were the most fundamental of the Middle Ages, initiating developments which were to be elaborated in detail in the fourteenth century.

[1] F. M. Powicke, *King Henry III and the Lord Edward*, pp. 89–92, 102.
[2] Ibid., p. 119.

These reforms wrought a drastic change in the position of the sheriff. Not only was the responsibility for wardships, custodies, and escheats transferred from him to a special official, while the demesne lands were likewise taken out of his hands to be let at farm, but for the parts of the old farm of the shire which remained in his hands he had to render strict account, both of the farm itself and of additional profits. The effect was firstly to detach certain revenues which could be more fully exploited by separate officials, and secondly to ensure that the sheriff derived no financial profit from his office but became a mere collector of Crown revenue.[1] The strengthening of the Exchequer's control over the sheriff was indicative of the centralizing tendency in the financial administration of the realm. Hitherto the sheriffs had on occasion been drawn into the sphere of familiar administration, delivering their revenues to the Chamber, and acting as minor treasurers entrusted with substantial expenditure at the King's command. Henceforth both their resources and discretion were curtailed and the King would normally utilize them through the Exchequer.

The withdrawal of revenues into separate 'foreign' accounts was ultimately as important in the creation of a national system of finance as it was for the exploitation of the royal revenue. For it was to the Exchequer that escheators, keepers of temporalities, farmers and custodians of demesne manors, castles, and honours, wardens of the royal forests, Justices of North and South Wales, and ultimately the receivers of aids and customs came to account. Nothing reveals more clearly the fundamental shift away from household government than the fact that, in separating these revenues from the shire, the government of Henry III should have still insisted that they came under the jurisdiction of the Exchequer. For many of these—notably escheats, temporalities, and forests—were prerogative revenues which were later to be regarded as being more at the King's personal disposal than were the revenues of the demesne lands which pertained to the Crown. But there is little doubt that the main object of the reform was to exploit the King's revenues and the King's rights, and for this Henry III and his household advisers accepted that the Exchequer was not only the most

[1] M. Mills, 'The Reforms at the Exchequer (1232–1242)', *Trans. Roy. Hist. Soc.* x (1927), pp. 111–33.

efficient instrument, but was responsive to the King's demands
and needs. It is also significant that the Wardrobe decisively
supplanted the Chamber as the principal household agency in
these years largely because it enjoyed a closer link with the
Exchequer.[1]

Within the context of the growing scope of revenue administration it was inevitable that the reforms of 1232–6 should result
in the creation of a national system, administered by the Exchequer, obedient to the King, and devoted to the enforcement
of royal right. There are no serious grounds for denying credit
for this to the King's advisers or for interpreting it as forced
upon them by baronial reaction to household government. Yet
there is no doubt that it was through the agency of the household that Peter des Rivaux initiated these reforms and that
the accumulation of offices and revenue in his hands during
1232–4 alarmed the barons and provoked the first serious
opposition of the reign. To Tout it seemed that 'the single
orderly control by a court official over both national and household finance' was 'an experiment in autocracy' and the reaction
against Peter was both personal and constitutional.[2] Chrimes,
however, sees no evidence of a struggle between ministers or of
conflict between the court and the officers of state. Financial
reform rather than autocracy was Henry's aim.[3] Such a view
may minimize the very real fear and antagonism aroused by
the unprecedented and unrepeated financial authority which
Rivaux wielded; but it remains difficult to interpret his control
of household and Exchequer, of shrievalties, forests, escheats and
wardships, Ireland, the Mint, the Jews, and numerous castellan-
ships as a model for permanent autocracy. Rivaux's tenure of
many of these was short; he was compelled to delegate authority widely; it was an *ad hoc* scheme of personal pluralism rather
than the model for an administrative empire.[4] To facilitate
investigation and reform these revenues were brought under the
personal control of one man, directly answerable to the King.

---

[1] Tout, *Chapters*, i. 178–9, 228.   [2] Ibid., p. 227.

[3] S. B. Chrimes, *An Introduction to the Administrative History of Medieval England*,
pp. 93–104.

[4] For the motive of the reforms, see Mills, op. cit.; for Peter des Rivaux's collection of offices, see Tout, *Chapters*, i. 218. It is difficult to accept that Rivaux's
fall destroyed 'the best chance of establishing a single orderly control by a court
official over both national and household finance' (ibid., p. 227).

For temporary, emergency measures of this type the household provided the ideal instrument for it was both flexible and uncontrolled. But ultimately the achievement of 1232–6 was to strengthen royal power through, not in opposition to, the financial control wielded by the Exchequer. The Wardrobe lay within this system in that it received its revenues almost wholly from the Exchequer and rendered account to it. The fact that Wardrobe accounts were enrolled on the Exchequer pipe rolls from 1224 and the warrants for its receipts from the Exchequer on the *liberate* rolls from 1226 is itself witness to how it now formed part of the national financial system.

The figures of the Wardrobe's receipts and expenditure give the best guide to its relative importance. Its normal revenue and expenditure were around £10,000 p.a. representing the living expenses of the household and the incidental expenses of government which the King and his administrative staff might incur on itinerary. It may, indeed, have exceeded this sum during the years of Peter des Rivaux's keepership, especially in 1232–4, for which no accounts survive, and it certainly did during the two Gascon expeditions of 1242–3 and 1252–4 when it served the King as a mobile war treasury.[1] At all times the Wardrobe might be called upon to finance military operations in which the King engaged or was directly interested. In 1224 it spent £1,000 on the siege of Bedford and in the following year undertook the cost of equipping Richard of Cornwall's Poitevin expedition. In 1228 it was involved in the Kerry campaign against Llewellyn and in 1229–30 drew up to £20,000 for the King's expedition to Brittany.[2] This prefigured its role during the period October 1241–June 1245 when its receipt and expenditure averaged around £20,000 p.a., though the increase was mainly concentrated in the period of active campaigning. The total figure for its expenses in 1252–4 is not known, but it probably drew very much less direct from the

---

[1] The totals of Wardrobe receipts for this period are tabulated by Tout, *Chapters*, vi. 74–6 from the pipe rolls, and the earliest accounts for 1224–7 are printed from the L.T.R., Foreign Accounts in vol. i, pp. 233–8. The gaps in the enrolled series (up to 1224, from 1227 to 1234, from 1252 to 1255 and from 1257 to 1258) are discussed ibid., p. 220. For Rivaux's treasurership, 1232–4, Tout used the evidence of the Liberate and Patent Rolls (ibid., p. 221); his discussion of the later accounts will be found on pp. 244, 266, 279, 301–2.

[2] Tout, *Chapters*, i. 194–9, 236.

Exchequer. But even when its operations were inflated by war expenditure, the level of its strictly domestic expenditure remained stable and the remarkably consistent level of its finances shows that it performed a defined and conventional role in the structure of royal government.[1]

The Wardrobe drew its revenue predominantly from the Exchequer upon royal warrant. It received some of it as prests authorized by writs of *liberate,* the remainder (usually less) from revenue collectors who returned to the Exchequer the acquittances they had received from the Wardrobe, for which the Wardrobe was then (by writ of *computate*) called to account. Through which of these methods the Wardrobe received its revenue was a matter of administrative convenience. It tended to draw the prests for its major expenses in large quantities of coin from the Exchequer, and to meet its immediate and individual commitments by drawing on, or pledging local revenues. This method of anticipating local revenues served well enough to meet the pressing needs of the King and his household in England, but it could not be readily adapted to the demands of a foreign campaign for which specie, warranted by writs of *liberate* for large sums, was still needed. The large sums delivered by the Exchequer to the Wardrobe for the Gascon campaign of 1242–3 have already been noted; for that of 1252–4 the sums received were insufficient to meet Henry's needs and he was in consequence driven to borrow on his personal credit from Italian and Cahorsin merchants, his brother, and a variety of lesser subjects.[2] Such stop-gap borrow-

---

[1] Tout, *Chapters,* vi. p. 249 emphasizes the general stability of Wardrobe finance after 1236; the first Gascon expedition is discussed on pp. 265–7, the second on pp. 270–2.

[2] A. Bond, 'Extracts from the Liberate Rolls Relative to Loans Supplied by Italian Merchants', *Archaeologia,* xxviii (1840), pp. 261–326. The repayment of loans of any size for the expenses of the Wardrobe and wages of war does not begin before 1246–7. In January 1254 repayment was ordered of 10,000 marks borrowed by Queen Eleanor 'ad negotia nostra et regi nostri utilitatem expedienda' (ibid., p. 266) and at the same time the Exchequer was borrowing from Richard of Cornwall and despatching this and other money to Henry. The evidence for Henry's borrowing in 1252–4, drawn from *Rôles Gascons,* i (ed. Francisque-Michel, Paris, 1885), is discussed by Tout, *Chapters,* i. 271–2. In nearly every case the loan was contracted on the security of the King's promise to repay at an appointed date or when the money was received from England; an exception is *Rôles Gascons* i, no. 4305 where a loan from Florentine merchants is charged on the clerical tenth in Worcestershire and Hertfordshire.

ing was occasioned by the deficiency of specie from England and the Exchequer's still rudimentary system of credit.[1] Moreover, in borrowing £54,000 for the Sicilian venture the King lacked the resources from which a loan of this size could be repaid and these commitments precipitated the financial and political crisis of 1257–8.[2] The requirement of the Provisions of Oxford that all issues of the realm should go through the Exchequer can hardly be read as reflecting baronial fears of the Wardrobe's capacity to secure an independent income of its own. The baronial government recognized the Wardrobe's need for a foreign receipt as legitimate and essential in its appointed role. Their concern was primarily to check Henry's irresponsible commitments, and in placing their hopes for good government in a nominated council they turned to the Exchequer as the appropriate agent for handling national finance and safeguarding the Crown's resources.

The Wardrobe habitually drew some of its revenue from local sources while on itinerary, as the earliest account for Henry III's reign shows. Issues from some sheriffs and bailiffs, from escheats and forests, from temporalities in the King's hands, from the Seal and the Exchanges, and from fines all came to it.[3] The crisis of 1258 did little to upset the traditional methods of Wardrobe finance just as it had little effect on the scale of its operations. The Provisions of Westminster had been careful to place wardships, escheats, and temporalities under the control of the Justiciar, Treasurer, and three others, and revenue from these sources was later specifically appropriated to the discharge of royal debts and maintenance of the household.[4] While this casual and prerogative revenue formed a normal and natural

[1] See in general, E. B. Fryde, 'Public Credit with Special Reference to North West Europe', in *The Cambridge Economic History of Europe*, iii, ed. M. M. Postan, E. E. Rich, and E. Miller (Cambridge, 1963), pp. 430–553.

[2] Treharne, op. cit., p. 51.

[3] Tout, *Chapters*, i. 190, 233–38, 301–2. It is significant that the tempory accumulation of revenue in the hands of Peter des Rivaux in 1232, as a prelude to reform, included escheats and wardships and the keeping of the forests. It was Henry's dispersal of these prerogative profits which according to Matthew Paris was the object of Peter des Rivaux's criticism and the starting-point of his reforms (quoted by Mills, *Trans. Roy. Hist. Soc.* x. 112).

[4] *C.P.R., 1258–66*, pp. 96, 336; above, p. 141. Specific authorization was given for the temporalities of Winchester to be paid direct to the Wardrobe in the period Michaelmas 1258 to Christmas 1260. See M. Howell, *Regalian Right*, pp. 157–8.

element of Wardrobe receipt, to be safeguarded and assured as a measure of good economy, it was not sufficient to supply the Wardrobe as a war treasury. For this it needed to command the revenue from taxation. *Ad hoc* payments from lay and ecclesiastical taxes into the Wardrobe started as early as 1224, but these were of no great magnitude and the first substantial payment from this source occurred in 1233-4 when Peter des Rivaux received £5,349 from the proceeds of the fortieth.[1] After 1237 there were, of course, no further lay subsidies to draw upon although the Wardrobe did receive money from the clerical subsidies and at the very close of the reign some proceeds from the crusading tenth.[2]

Taking the reign of Henry III as a whole the Wardrobe was not the vehicle of royal autocracy nor was it the object of political conflict. For the most part it functioned as a purely domestic treasury, charged with 'the necessary expenses' of the household including the armed retinue which surrounded the King. It might deal with particular exigencies, political and military, with which the King was concerned, but on only three occasions was it called on to play a major role, namely as a vehicle for Rivaux's fiscal and administrative reforms and as the war treasury for the two Gascon campaigns. By virtue of its closeness to the King the Wardrobe had this potentiality for becoming the seat of authority and royal finance for a limited period and particular end. Even so, both the political consequences of Rivaux's experiment and the financial chaos of the second Gascon war underlined its unsuitability as a permanent agent of government and finance. On the contrary, Henry III's reign showed the reliance of both King and ministers on the Exchequer as the central treasury for mobilizing the wealth of England and for transporting it overseas where, through the Wardrobe, the King might spend it on his war. Not only did Henry III abandon the ill-fated control of government through the household practised by his father, but the very 'duality' of medieval government which had made the Chamber an essential element in the rule of Henry II began to shrink. The scope for *ad hoc*, emergency, even arbitrary action by the itinerant King declined, as officials of Chancery and Exchequer multiplied in

---

[1] Tout, *Chapters*, i. 233-6, 221. In 1224 it drew £1,066 from the carucage on ecclesiastical estates.   [2] Ibid., p. 316.

the shires, attentive to royal rights and revenues. By the end of the reign the Wardrobe was fast becoming institutionalized, acquiring a defined and formal place within an administrative system dominated by the great departments of state.

EXCHEQUER AND WARDROBE UNDER EDWARD I

The absence of prolonged foreign wars had assisted this development under Henry III. Edward I by contrast was engaged, almost continuously, in a series of wars for which the Wardrobe was called on to serve as a mobile treasury, the war chest of the army on campaign. Because Edward's wars demanded the mobilization of the resources of the whole realm, the Wardrobe came ultimately to receive and disburse a larger proportion of the national revenues than the Exchequer. For the first three years of the reign its expenditure, at under £15,000 p.a., was comparable with that of the preceding reign; but the first Welsh war raised it to twice this sum in 1277–9. Thereafter, even in the intervals between Edward's major campaigns it hardly fell below this level. For the period of the Welsh war of 1282–4 it received over £100,000, for the two years 1288–90 when Edward was in Gascony over £140,000, and during the era of military activity which opened in 1294 it habitually received more than £100,000 each year.[1] Despite the absence of accounts for most years after 1300 it is certain that there was little decline in the scope of its operations during the long years of the Scottish campaigns. The Wardrobe accounts show that these increases in its revenues were wholly in response to its military commitments. The expenses of the *hospitium* remain remarkably stable even during the period of campaigns, at between £10,000 and £12,000 a year. Expenditure above this sum was wholly on the wages of bannerets, knights, and foot-soldiers on the household roll, the victualling and garrisoning of castles, and other incidental military and naval expenses.[2]

---

[1] The figures are taken from Tout's table, *Chapters*, vi. pp. 76–83.

[2] The domestic and military expenses of the household were frequently separated in the accounts and might even be separately accounted for. Regular household expenditure was contained in the annual roll of the household while the wages of war were recorded in the 'liber de necessariis' (see *The Book of Prests, 1294–5*, ed. E. B. Fryde (Oxford, 1962), pp. xvi–xix). A good example of a war account is that of Louth for 1282–4 printed in *Chronica Johannis de Oxenedes*, ed. Sir H. Ellis (R.S., 1859), pp. 326–36, where the expenditure is wholly on wages of war and castle building. The domestic expenses of the Wardrobe in this period are in the

The Wardrobe had become, in effect, the paymaster of the royal army, but neither the resources nor the mechanism for enabling it to play this role were at hand when Edward ascended the throne. For campaigns in Wales and Scotland, the difficulties of transporting specie were less than they had been for the Gascon campaigns of Henry III and the opportunities for local levies greater; even so Edward found it advisable to remove the Exchequer to Shrewsbury in 1277 and to York during the years 1298–1304. Large prests from the Exchequer by writs of *liberate* continued to form an important element in Wardrobe finance: £6,373 in Louth's war account for 1282–4, £14,000 in 1290, and £10,000 in 1291. In 1294–5 £55,453 at least can be shown to have been physically transported to Wales.[1] In England the Wardrobe continued to draw a variety of small sums directly from sheriffs, escheators, bailiffs, the Mint and Exchange, and other miscellaneous sources, and it might also draw upon these same officials for victuals and other supplies.[2] But what enabled the Wardrobe to maintain and enlarge its role as a mobile treasury and paymaster in the latter part of the thirteenth century was the development of taxation, the availability of credit, and the sophistication and efficiency of the Exchequer system of account.

Although lay and clerical taxation provided large sums of ready cash which could easily be transferred on royal warrant to

---

pipe roll (P.R.O. E 372/130 mm. 5, 5d) (see Tout, *Chapters*, ii. 115 n. 1). Neither are the expenses of the hospitium recorded in Droxford's account for 1299–1300 (*Liber Quotidianus*, ed. John Topham, Soc. of Antiquaries, 1787). These are given in the pipe roll as £10,968. 16s. (C. Johnson, 'The System of Wardrobe Account under Edward I', *Trans. Roy. Hist. Soc.* vi (1923), p. 60 n. 1). In 1297–8, save for £11,194 on the *hospitium*, £1,144 on alms, and £1,487 on the purchase of jewels, the remainder of the expenditure of £119,519 was on war (Tout, *Chapters*, ii. 119 n. 2). In 1300–1 the *hospitium* expenses were £9,570 against 'foreign' expenses of £67,721 and in 1303–4 £8,756 against £60,201 (Tout, *Chapters*, vi. 83). For a recent discussion of this, see M. Prestwich, *War, Politics and Finance under Edward I*, pp. 169–76.

[1] *Oxenedes*, p. 326; Tout, *Chapters*, ii. 58 n. 2, 97; Johnson, op. cit., p. 56; *The Book of Prests*, p. xv and Appendices A, D. Even in 1297 the bulk of the money needed for payments on the continent had to be transported in cash from England: see E. B. Fryde, 'The Financial Resources of Edward I in the Netherlands, 1294–8', *Revue Belge de Philologie et d'Histoire*, xl (1962), p. 1185.

[2] The Wardrobe's drawing on these local revenues is discussed by Johnson, loc. cit., and by J. C. Davies, *The Baronial Opposition to Edward II*, p. 183, and can be seen in the printed accounts for 1282–4 and 1299–1300 and in the *Recepta* section of the enrolled account for 1294–5 in *The Book of Prests*, Appendix A.

the Wardrobe, in the first part of the reign such taxes were infrequent. It was the institution of the wool custom in 1275, and its committal to the Riccardi of Lucca, that perpetuated the Wardrobe's role as a mobile treasury. From 1275 to 1294 the Riccardi provided a flow of cash to the Wardrobe on demand, to meet both its domestic and war expenditure. With an average receipt from the customs during this period of £9,950 p.a., supplemented by other Crown revenue both regular and casual, the Riccardi funded about £11,000 p.a. to the Wardrobe in normal years.[1] By solving the problem of liquidity which had always beset royal finance, the 'Riccardi system' reinvigorated the Wardrobe's traditional function in royal government.

The royal bankers were also inescapably involved in the Wardrobe's operations as a war treasury. They advanced most of the Wardrobe's receipts for the first Welsh war of 1276–7, and almost half of those for the more prolonged campaign of 1282–1283.[2] At the end of Edward I's operations in Gascony in 1289, they claimed to have advanced over £103,000 for the Wardrobe.[3] Royal resources, even from taxation, were barely adequate for the repayment of such sums and the strain placed upon the Riccardi by these urgent demands showed in their suspension of loans to other creditors in 1282–3 and in the size of the King's debt to them in 1290. But by then the era of wars appeared to be finished and Edward began to disengage from his increasingly troubled bankers, while his officials embarked on an attempt to stabilize the relations and functions of Exchequer and Wardrobe on a permanent basis.

In 1290 the order that henceforth all lay subsidies should pass through the Exchequer substantially reduced the Wardrobe's 'foreign' receipt.[4] A similar attempt to bring loans under

---

[1] R. W. Kaeuper, *Bankers to the Crown* (Princeton, 1973), pp. 125–8, 164.

[2] Ibid., pp. 177–91. The Riccardi advanced £42,709 out of a total Wardrobe receipt of £55,030 in 1276–8 (ibid., Table II, p. 128, but cf. discrepant figures p. 178). They received £74,599 from the fifteenth of 1275 (ibid., p. 106). In 1282–4 the Riccardi advanced £93,741 of a total Wardrobe receipt of £204,593 (ibid., Table II, cf. p. 183) but received only £30,188 in repayment from direct taxation (ibid., p. 190). The greater part of the thirtieth of 1283 appears to have been paid to the Wardrobe direct (*C.P.R., 1281–92*, pp. 70–1, 78, 147–8, 163, 223; *C.C.R.*, 1279–88, pp. 1, 8, 12–14, 17, 20, 29–30, 206; *Oxenedes*, p. 326).

[3] Kaeuper, op. cit., p. 96.

[4] J. F. Willard, 'An Exchequer Reform under Edward I'; idem, *Parliamentary Taxes on Personal Property, 1290–1334*, p. 231.

the sole authority of the Exchequer was made in 1294–5. Hitherto all loans had been paid into the Wardrobe; now their receipt
and repayment came to be recorded on the Receipt rolls.[1] The
effect of these measures was to restore the authority of the Exchequer as the central agency for national finance. There is
some ground for attributing this to Walter Langton who became
Keeper of the Wardrobe from 1290 to 1295 and then Treasurer
of England for the rest of the reign.[2] At the same time the development of writs of assignment, used after 1300 in conjunction with
tallies, enabled the Exchequer to keep track of the greater
part of national expenditure while still permitting the Wardrobe to secure revenue at source for urgent and necessary
expenditure.[3]

The renewal of war in 1294 caught both the King and his
bankers unaware. The Riccardi found themselves over-extended
in commitments to the papacy and fatally enmeshed in the
Anglo-French conflict.[4] Edward was forced to resume the
customs with no prospect of finding another firm to provide
advances or credit facilities on the continent. For the moment
this was less important, in that the revenue which flooded into
the Exchequer from the new wool subsidy, and the lay and
clerical taxes, could be channelled immediately through the
Wardrobe as cash payments for the war in Wales and Gascony,
and to Edward's continental allies. Almost £250,000 was
handled in this way.[5] But as the opening of the Scottish war
brought further commitments, and as the opposition of 1296–7
curtailed the levy of taxation, the King was forced to seek
credit and anticipate revenue to maintain the momentum of
his war plans. By 1298 the Frescobaldi had emerged as the
principal lenders to the Crown and the control of national
finance through the Exchequer was being distorted by the
extent to which the King was using Wardrobe warrants to
pledge revenue.

The strains imposed by war in the last decade of the reign

[1] R. J. Whitwell, 'Italian Bankers and the English Crown', *Trans. Roy. Hist.
Soc.*, N. S. xvii (1903), p. 219. No loans are recorded in the Wardrobe account of
1294–5.   [2] Tout, *Chapters*, ii. 106–7.
[3] Willard, *Parliamentary Taxes*, ch. ix; M. Prestwich, op. cit., pp. 157–8.
[4] Kaeuper, op. cit., pp. 209–20.
[5] E. B. Fryde, 'The Financial Resources of Edward I in the Netherlands, 1294–8',
pp. 1173–9, 1185; *Book of Prests*, pp. l–liii.

brought the flexibility of the Wardrobe into disrepute. It was probably not Edward I's original intention that the Wardrobe should usurp the pre-eminence of the Exchequer in the national system of finance. A letter written in the autumn of 1301, to which M. C. Prestwich has drawn attention, is indicative of the King's attitude at that date and of the Exchequer's limitations which forced Edward to exploit the Wardrobe.[1] Claiming that his troops were deserting and that his campaign had been brought to a halt owing to the insufficient sums he had received, the King proceeded to charge Treasurer and Chamberlains, 'on their fealty and as they cherished his honour and profit', to send money swiftly from what should be due from the Michaelmas proffers. The Exchequer could raise immediately only £1,000 by local loans (it was then at York), but it set on foot several measures to mobilize the financial resources of the realm. Agents were sent to the localities to hasten the collection of revenue both by the sheriffs and the collectors of the fifteenth and to send all sums over 100 marks as soon as they came to hand. At the same time it suspended all other assignments on the tax—amounting to £9,789. 16s. 5d.—and ordered the whole yield to be paid to the Exchequer. The strength of the Exchequer lay on the one hand in this administrative control over the revenue-collecting system of the whole country and on the other in its ability to render authoritative advice to the King on the financial resources of the realm. It could prepare detailed and accurate estimates of the costs of a campaign and inform him of its revenue in hand and its impending expenditure and obligations; it might also warn of the folly of borrowing without prospect of repayment, for on its capacity to honour obligations the King's credit ultimately depended.[2] Although the Exchequer was addicted to a daily balancing of revenue and expenditure there was in theory no reason why it should not itself pledge revenues for large cash loans to meet the King's demands; in a stable situation this would probably have happened. But at the head of an army which it was vital to keep in being for a decisive blow, Edward turned to the Wardrobe both as a mobile war treasury and as a credit-raising agency out

[1] P.R.O. E 159/75 mm 5d, 7, 10. Cited by M. Prestwich, op. cit., pp. 183, 204.
[2] Prestwich, ibid.; L. Ehrlich, 'Exchequer and Wardrobe in 1270', *Eng. Hist. Rev.* xxxvi (1921), pp. 553–4.

of sheer necessity. Nor was it so much the Wardrobe's ability to pledge the credit of the Exchequer as the scale of its operations and the rapidly growing deficit between Wardrobe expenditure and national revenue which jeopardized the delicate balance between Wardrobe flexibility and Exchequer control. These last years of the reign, in which the amount of cash handled by the Exchequer dropped dramatically as an increasingly wide range of national revenues were pledged by the Wardrobe, when the Wardrobe's own accounts witnessed such confusion that none of them after 1298 were audited at the Exchequer, and when the size of Edward's debts to foreign merchants dwarfed those his father had incurred to the Pope, made the Wardrobe the scapegoat for the old King's obstinate profligacy.[1]

It is easy to understand why Tout viewed the household, 'the special preserve of unrestricted prerogative' and the chosen instrument of the old King's last effort to carry through his policy, as a constitutional threat.[2] Writing under the influence of the Whig view of history, he saw the control of national finance by a prerogative agency as a recipe for tyranny. The demands of war did indeed reinvigorate the declining role of the household as the flexible, 'emergency' element of royal government, but this was for a restricted and special purpose. The supremacy of the Wardrobe in Edward's later years was so wholly determined by military needs that it is doubtful whether contemporaries regarded it as a constitutional threat, however much they were alarmed by the King's fiscal irresponsibility. There is an even more fundamental reason why the use of the Wardrobe in this context posed no ultimate constitutional threat. Vast as were the sums it handled and widespread as was its credit, its finances were, as we have noted, based largely on the new taxation levied on the plea of emergency and designated specifically for war. Because these revenues were occasional they gave no basis for any permanent usurpation by the

---

[1] As well as loans and lay taxes the Wardrobe in these years received the crusading tenth granted by Boniface VIII, the issues of Gascony, Scottish escheats, and revenue from the Irish exchequer (Tout, *Chapters*, ii. 111 n. 2). The state of Wardrobe finance in the last years of the reign is discussed ibid., pp. 119–21, and by Prestwich, op. cit., p. 221, and in 'Exchequer and Wardrobe in the Later Years of Edward I', *Bull. Inst. Hist. Res.* xlvi (1973), pp. 4–5. Prestwich reckons Edward I's debts by 1307 to have totalled 'at least £200,000'.

[2] Tout, *Chapters*, ii. 75–6, 121–9, 152–5; Chrimes, *Introduction to Medieval Administrative History*, pp. 150–1, is also critical of Tout's thesis.

Wardrobe of the Exchequer's control over national finance. In so much as these revenues were granted by subjects and were designated for a particular purpose, the utility of the Wardrobe as an agent of royal finance was ultimately dependent on parliament and the magnate council. Even the capacity to contract loans with the Florentine merchants was vulnerable to their opposition. Indeed the Wardrobe's difficulties in meeting the costs of Edward's campaigns in the last years sprang directly from the decline of revenue from taxation as the King's relations with his subjects steadily worsened.

There was, therefore, neither cause nor need for the magnates to attack the Wardrobe as an instrument of the prerogative. Its role as a war treasury was acknowledged as necessary both by them and by the King. Baronial hostility was directed neither at its personnel nor its activities but against the burdens and oppressions of war finance, and an arbitrary element in Edward's own rule. The doubts and discontents which were the inevitable consequence of military frustration and deepening debt made magnates and officials view Wardrobe finance with alarm and encouraged them to turn to the Exchequer as the traditional agent for reform. In the last years of the reign Langton made further efforts to keep the traditional revenues of the Exchequer out of the Wardrobe's hands,[1] but the effective reassertion of the Exchequer's centrality in national finance awaited the baronial reform movement of 1310–11.

[1] Prestwich, 'Exchequer and Wardrobe', p. 6, citing K.R. Memoranda Roll, E 159/78 m. 20.

CHAPTER IX

Exchequer and Wardrobe, 1307–1347

THE thirteenth-century view of the state as a community composed of King and subjects implied that royal government should be directed towards the common profit of the realm. In his latter years Edward I had equated this with the common danger, and had invoked the needs of common defence to enlarge the resources of the Crown through taxation and to bring national revenues under his immediate control by developing the Wardrobe as a war treasury. The excesses of this policy provoked the Ordinances of 1311. These proposed a programme of financial reform based on Exchequer control over all revenues and the use of the royal fisc to support the estate of the King. As a critique of royal misgovernment in terms of the common profit, the Ordinances made a deep impression on the community and ultimately produced the 'popular' programme of 1340 which sought to place all the finances of the realm under the control of a baronial council and the Exchequer. The political conflicts of Edward II's reign with which this reaction to royal misgovernment became linked encouraged T. F. Tout and J. C. Davies to interpret the Ordinances as an attempt to check autocracy based on the household. In their view the Wardrobe was a rival to the Exchequer, the size and importance of its expenditure qualifying it as an agent of national competence, while its subordination to the King's immediate control, its domestic staffing, and its possession of an independent 'foreign' receipt made it an instrument of personal government. The strength of the Wardrobe lay in its flexible, even chameleon-like nature; in response to the King's personal interests its competence could be enlarged to overshadow the Exchequer or be restricted to the administration and supply of the royal *familia*. Its proximity to the King and its undefined nature inhibited and baffled criticism. It could only be attacked indirectly—'without so much as naming it'—by cutting off its independent income and insisting that it draw all its revenues from the Exchequer.[1] This was what the fourth clause of the Ordinances attempted. In their view the size of its foreign receipt gave the measure of the Wardrobe's independence, of the 'legality' of its operations, and thus of the effective freedom of the King from baronial restraints.[2]

In fact it is doubtful whether the independence of the Wardrobe was a major theme either in the Ordinances or in the conflicts between King and baronage in the ensuing years. The only years in which its nominal foreign receipt exceeded that from the Exchequer were the two following the Ordinances, 1311–13, when Edward was estranged from the baronage and was almost perpetually on itinerary in the north; and this reflected not an increase in the independent income of the Wardrobe but the almost total suspension of its receipts from the Exchequer by a deliberate act of baronial policy. Faced with the King's defiance of the Ordinances, the barons asserted their control over the Exchequer, and this was largely successful; nor was the Wardrobe able to muster a foreign receipt as a sufficient substitute.[3] This makes it difficult to see why the fourth clause of the Ordinances should be covertly aimed at the Wardrobe's foreign receipt.[4] The object of the first group of clauses of the Ordinances was to provide the household with money rather than to deprive it. All the issues of the realm were to go to the Exchequer so that the King's debts could be paid and his honour and estate maintained. The prior claim of the household was thus acknowledged by the barons even while its place

---

[1] T. F. Tout, *Chapters in Medieval Administrative History*, ii. 228, commenting on cap. 4 of the Ordinances: 'without so much as naming the Wardrobe, these stipulations put a new legal barrier in the way of it acting as a rival treasury coordinate with the Exchequer.'

[2] Ibid., pp. 236–8, 275–6. Cf. J. C. Davies, *The Baronial Opposition to Edward II*, p. 198, for a summary of his view of the significance of the Wardrobe's independent position.

[3] Tout, *Chapters*, ii. 234–6. The earls of Pembroke and Hereford had appeared at the Exchequer to forbid the payment of 'nuls deniers ne autre tresor del vostre a nul homme par qui ils devenissent a les meyns l'enemy du Roiaume' (J. C. Davies, op. cit., p. 552 document no. 16). In the Wardrobe account for 1311–12 most of the Recepta Scaccerii was paid at Westminister by the hand of John de Oakham. Of the foreign receipt £2,022 represented the sale of victuals at Berwick and £1,060 was from the new custom, while £328 was gifts towards the Scottish war (P.R.O. E 101/374/15).

[4] B. Wilkinson, *Studies in the Constitutional History of the Thirteenth and Fourteenth Centuries*, pp. 236–7, was the first to express scepticism on this point.

within the national system of finance, under the control of the Exchequer, was asserted. If the financial independence of the Wardrobe was not a political issue in the eyes of the baronage,[1] was it any more so in the eyes of the King? Was the integration of the Wardrobe within the Exchequer system a distinctively baronial policy aimed at controlling the Crown or did it represent a development which the King himself accepted? To assess accurately the relations of Wardrobe and Exchequer within the framework of royal government we must review the magnitude, origins, and functions of the Wardrobe's foreign receipt, then consider the purposes of its Exchequer receipt, and finally examine the King's attitude to the Exchequer system as revealed in his warrants.

The foreign receipt of the Wardrobe was drawn from diverse sources. A proportion of it was always composed of 'book-keeping' entries (such as the estimated value of stores and, sometimes, undischarged debts) or represented sales of surplus victuals and stores.[2] There was, too, a fairly persistent revenue from small sums drawn occasionally from sheriffs, bailiffs, farmers, receivers, constables, and other land revenue collectors of the Crown in response to the King's immediate needs. Fines, mostly small sums levied in the Marshalsea but occasionally some of sizeable value which were the result of personal negotiation with the King, were likewise a fairly usual feature of this receipt, and 'gifts and aids' might likewise vary in size from token payments for the royal grace to substantial commutation of military obligation. Some of the Crown's large estates, notably North and South Wales, might render a receipt to the Wardrobe if they were not in the hands of the heir apparent. Revenues from escheats, from the temporalities of vacant sees, or profits from the sale of wardships might also on occasion come direct to the Wardrobe. Finally in the first quarter of the century the Wardrobe received, year by year, the issues of the Great Seal which averaged about £1,000 p.a. Thus the Wardrobe did command a normal, fairly regular independent income derived

---

[1] The barons' hostility to the political activities of its members is not, of course, in doubt. The desire for a purge of the household and the proscription of certain individuals largely inspired the demands of Warwick and Lancaster for the enforcement of the Ordinances. See Wilkinson, *Studies*, pp. 234–5.

[2] See Tout, *Chapters*, ii. 111 n. 2, 236 n. 2.

from the casual operation of the royal will over revenues which in practically every case pertained to the exercise of the royal prerogative or derived from the Crown's lands.[1] This accorded with the convention that such revenues should support the royal estate. The yield of these sources was not large; at most it might total a few thousand pounds, and taken with the often much larger fictitious element, might in any normal year account for a 'foreign receipt' under £10,000. It seems unlikely that the intention of the Ordainers was to restrict receipts of this kind which gave an inadequate basis for the political or financial independence of the household, as the period following the Ordinances showed.[2]

In certain years the Wardrobe did record a foreign receipt markedly higher than this. These were, 1307–8, 1309–10, 1321–2, 1322–3. In the first year of the reign the foreign receipt totalled almost £29,000, but most of this represented internal accounting, and the meagre receipts from external sources were exclusively from the revenues described above, nothing being received from loans or taxes. The only substantial sum in fact was the £2,466 received from the sale of Walter Langton's goods.[3] In 1309–10, however, the Wardrobe's foreign receipt did include some large sums from external sources, notably

[1] The early years of the reign provide examples of the appropriation of such revenues for household expenses. In 1308, for instance, the confiscated lands of Walter Langton and the Templars' estates were set aside at the Exchequer in a separate account for the payment of Wardrobe debts. See Davies, op. cit., p. 192 n. 3.

[2] Davies, op. cit., pp. 184–8, discusses the nature of the foreign receipt on the basis of the account book of 1309–10 and other documents. In the following year while the King was in the north the Foreign Receipt included many payments from northern revenues (E 101/374/6). In 10 Edward II the large sum of £3,223. 17s. 2d. was received from the Hanaper and £1,414 from a subsidy levied in Agenais and Bordeaux and delivered by the Bardi (P.R.O. E 361/2). The details of the foreign receipt in the years 1, 11, and 14 Edward II have been tabulated by Tout in *Chapters*, ii. 361–4. In 11 Edward II, of a total of £5,482 only £909 from the Hanaper and £900 from other sources external to the household was genuine foreign receipt. In 14 Edward II about £900 of the total of £2,674 represented money received from sources outside the household.

[3] Thus £19,750 was brought forward from the previous accounts of the Butler and Keeper of the Wardrobe, a further £1,950 came from the sale of victuals in the Wardrobe, and £2,900 from victuals in the hands of the bailiff of Holderness. The only other external receipt was £1,379 received from Henry Say, lately the King's Butler and receiver of the new custom. In 1311–12 the new custom is still recorded as yielding £1,060 to the Wardrobe (E 101/374/15).

£2,524. 6s. 8d. from the papal tenth and £9,689 from loans.[1] The latter mainly represented two sums, one of 10,000 marks from the Frescobaldi, the other of £1,400 from the City of London, the last in consideration of the King's confirmation of their charter. Other loans from the nobility seem to have been personal compositions for service in the Scottish war.[2] It is tempting to attribute the high foreign receipt of 1321–3 to the renewal of military conflict with the baronage and the final emancipation of the Crown from baronial control; to see the King at last openly challenging the doctrine of the Ordinances.[3] It is true that the main expenditure of the Wardrobe in these years was upon military operations against Lancaster and subsequently in Scotland. The account of Northburgh from July 1321 to April 1322 records a foreign receipt of £17,530 but little of this represented actual cash receipts.[4] The following account of Waltham, from May 1322 to October 1323, records the much larger foreign receipt of £31,565. But of this, sales of victuals and cloth account for over £15,000, and almost £1,600 more is credited from Northburgh's account. The real receipt, amounting to almost £15,000, included one large item, of £11,133 transferred from the King's Chamber, and two sums of about £1,300 from the Hanaper and from numerous bailiffs and local receivers. No money was received from loans and taxes.[5] One may say, therefore, that throughout the reign only very infrequently did the Wardrobe directly receive or pledge for loans any of the revenue from taxation. For most of the time its foreign receipt was modest in scale and was derived from the ordinary revenues of the realm. The Wardrobe thus possessed no independent resources which could make it a viable basis for royal autocracy. Indeed it is unlikely that either King or magnates ever thought of its role in these terms. They treated

---

[1] E 101/506/16. A total of £2,181. 3s. 7d. was drawn from local ministers and £892. 13s. 2d. was received from the issues of the great seal.

[2] Davies, op. cit., pp. 184–8.

[3] Tout, *Chapters*, ii. 275 speaks of the 'triumphant king throwing over the trammels of the Ordainers'.

[4] The main items were £3,725 from sale of victuals at Berwick, £3,734 from the *recta prisa* on wines, £2,214 in stores, and £1,871 from a clerical subsidy. A debt of £986 to Antony de Lucy for wages of the garrison at Carlisle, and a fine of £888 from the Peruzzi were also reckoned as part of the Foreign Receipt (E 361/2 m. 18).

[5] This account is summarized in Davies, op. cit., pp. 188–9 where its terminal date is wrongly given as 8 July.

the royal administration in its different functions and aspects as a whole, not contemplating the use of one part against another, as a particular vehicle for or barrier to the exercise of royal authority. Throughout the reign the Wardrobe continued to occupy the place assigned to it in the national system of finance, accepting the general oversight of the Exchequer; nor did this restrict the scale of its operations.

The King's demands were more directly reflected in the Wardrobe's receipt from the Exchequer, which for most of the reign up to 1323 far exceeded its domestic requirements. This was particularly true of the ten years 1314–23 in which its Exchequer receipt only twice fell below the figure of £30,000 for the year.[1] The only revenue from which payments of this size could be drawn was taxation, and the five lay subsidies collected in these years comprised two-thirds of the taxation of the whole reign. As we have seen, these taxes were granted for campaigns in Scotland for which the Wardrobe continued to act as a war treasury. This would naturally be so for the campaigns of 1314 and 1319 in which Edward participated, as also for the Boroughbridge campaign of 1322 and the ensuing Scottish campaign. But the Wardrobe was also the paymaster for Pembroke's expedition of 1315, the abortive campaigns of 1316 and 1317, and for the permanent costs of garrisoning and victualling the northern castles and retaining local captains.[2]

On the evidence we have reviewed the Wardrobe's expanded role was that of a war treasury dispensing national revenue under the Exchequer, not that of a domestic treasury safeguarding royal independence from a private income. If its operations precipitated national insolvency as they did in the last years of Edward I, this indeed aroused opposition, but the magnates never questioned the flexibility of the Wardrobe which made it so ideal a war treasury. During the middle years

[1] These were the years July 1318–19 and July 1320–1, both years without major expeditions. The figures are given in Tout, *Chapters*, vi. 84. The year 1307–8 when the Exchequer receipt totalled £49,648 was also clearly exceptional. Tout pointed out (ii. 235) that this represented nearly 5/7th of the Exchequer's income.

[2] Davies, op. cit., p. 189. The largest item of expenditure in the Wardrobe accounts for these years was the wages for 'those not of the household who were in castles and places of war'. This totalled £36,425 in 1316–17, £16,357 in 1317–18, £11,740 in 1318–19, £13,849 in 1319–20, £3,344 in 1320–1, and £13,189 in 1321–2. This last account also included £9,287 paid out for wages of the Boroughbridge campaign (E 361/2).

of the reign, when the magnates united briefly to prosecute the
Scottish War, Lancaster in 1316 and Pembroke in 1317 planned
campaigns in which the Wardrobe was to fulfil its traditional
role of war treasury, a function which was briefly translated into
reality in the one truly co-operative expedition of the reign in
1319. How far its character as a military cadre was a source of
political strength to the King is difficult to assess; doubtless this
depended very largely on his character, though the ability to
retain a large retinue gave a potent reserve of loyalty even to
Edward II.[1] But in attacking the personnel of the household
and seeking to control royal policy as a whole the baronage did
not seek to alter the administrative system. The effect of the
years of baronial opposition was thus to confirm, rather than to
question or jeopardize, the dual functions of the Wardrobe,
domestic and military, and to emphasize the priority which the
Exchequer should rightly give its supply.

The Ordinances had acknowledged that provision for the
household as an office of state should be the prime charge on the
Exchequer but the first evidence of steps to enforce this does not
appear until 1316. A warrant of November in that year refers to
an ordinance for the provision of money for the households of
the King and Queen and another of January 1317 to an
ordinance for this purpose recently made at York where both
the King and Lancaster had been in August 1316.[2] It is clear
that an annual sum or 'certeyn' was provided for each household, that for Isabella's being fixed at 11,000 marks p.a. until
she could be provided with a landed estate.[3] Some indication of
the thinking behind this is offered by the report of the deliberations of a council held in London at the end of 1316 which provides the earliest evidence for the preparation of estimates of
Exchequer revenue and expenditure, in this case for the first
half of 1317.[4] The council had before it estimates for the keeping

[1] This aspect of Edward II's household has remained almost wholly unexplored.
Miss E. A. Danbury's researches on the subject should add materially to our
knowledge about it.

[2] *C.P.R., 1313–17*, p. 564; E 404/1/7 24 January 1317.

[3] Ibid., pp. 115, 122–3; *C.C.R., 1313–18*, p. 380; Warrants for payments of the
'certeyn' to the queen are P.R.O. C 81/1394 no. 36b (20 March 1318), and
C 81/1671 no. 50.

[4] 'Edward par la grace de Dieu Roi Dengleterre Seignour Dirlande et Ducs
Daquitaine au Tresorier Barons et Chaumberleins de nostre Eschequier, Saluz.
Pur ceo que les bones gentz de nostre conseil a Loundr' nous ountz certifiez q'il

of the northern marches and the households of the King and Queen. Probably on its recommendation, the Exchequer was forbidden to make any payment or assignment other than to these charges unless express permission was given in the warrant. In the following January a number of warrants ordering payment to creditors notwithstanding this general prohibition are to be found in the Exchequer files.[1] The aim was thus to provide the household with an assured revenue at the Exchequer at a time of financial shortage, to protect its interests against those of other creditors. But this preference for the household was neither arbitrary nor uncontrolled; it was authorized by the council as part of an over-all policy. No clearer indication that the household was regarded by the baronage as one of the principal charges of state could be required than that it shared this preference with the guard of the marches. To preserve the safety of the realm and to maintain the dignity and estate of the King were generally acknowledged to be the principal duties of the ruler. The Keeper of the Wardrobe, Roger Northburgh, writing to the Lord Treasurer early in 1317 to ask for a further advance on the 'certeyn' of the household before Candlemas, was acutely conscious that the King would be 'decried' if the household failed to make payment for its purchases.[2] The same concern inspired

---

ount regardez queu somme de deniers se porra lever en certain a nostre oeps totes parez entre cy et la Nativite Seint Johan le Baptistre prochein avenir, et aussint les charges des paiementz que se coviendront faire en meisme le temps aussi bien pur la garde des Marches Descoce devers le North come pur les offices de nostre houstiel et del houstiel la Roine Dengleterre nostre treschere compaigne, vous maundoms et chargeons fermement enioignantz que pur nul maundement que vous est venutz ou que vous vendra desore de nous vous facez paiement ne assignement a nully de rien s'il ne soit en descharge de nos des ditz paiementz [illegible] maundement de nos feissant expresse mention de cest nostre maundement. Et ceo ne lesse. Don soubz nostre prive seal a Clipston le xxiii iour de Decembre lan de nostre regne disme' (P.R.O. E 404/1/6, 23 December).

[1] E 404/1/7, 13 and 20 January 1317.

[2] A fragmentary letter from the Keeper of the Wardrobe, Roger Northburgh, to the Treasurer dated 24 January 1317 begins: '. . . quant ordeinez feut nadgayres a Everwyk que nre seignur le Roy prendreit —— [sic] per an un certeyn pour les despens de son . . . si esteit ordeinez adounques que home ne prendreit mye tantque a ceste Chaundelleur forsque mille livres sur le dit certeyn . . .' Northburgh complains that this sum had not sufficed and that he had been forced to borrow to meet his expenses. Unfortunately the letter gives no indication of the annual sum provided (E 404/1/7 24 January 1317. Similar language was used in writs in 1309: see Madicott, *Thomas of Lancaster*, p. 103.

similar action in November 1318 when the Exchequer was instructed to impose a temporary restraint on all payments other than those already warranted and those in repayment of loans, as the King had appropriated all its revenue to the expenses of the household and 'autres bosoignes', 'issint qe nous ne soioms escriez par pays pur defaute de paiement ne noz dites busoignes arreries ne destourbees tantqe nostre estat soit mielz relevez'.[1] The writ of restraint was duly enrolled though the King made exceptions to it from time to time, as in January 1319 when the Exchequer officers were told to discharge debts to Robert de Grey provided they retained sufficient in hand for the expenses of the household.[2]

That the priority accorded to the needs of the household should be operated through the Exchequer testified to the control which it was now capable of exercising over the finances of the realm. It had aspired to this in the latter years of Edward I and the principle of Exchequer control had been asserted in the Ordinances and in the earl of Lancaster's demands during the negotiations of 1317–18; but it was in the two years 1318–20 that the first systematic effort to equip the Exchequer for this role seems to have been envisaged. Just as the Household Ordinance of 1318 sought to define the household's position as an office of state, so the Exchequer ordinance of 1319 took the first steps towards making it capable of exercising the wide competence with which the subsequent ordinances of 1323–6 would invest it.[3] The hearing of accounts was to be expedited, debts were to be collected, not respited, the records of the Treasury were to be arranged systematically for easy reference. Such measures related to the Exchequer's internal efficiency; others dealt with its role in the formulation and execution of financial policy. Twice a year, at the least, a statement of the issues and receipts of the Exchequer was to be laid before the

---

[1] Davies, op. cit., pp. 556–7, documents nos. 26, 28.

[2] *Red Book of the Exchequer*, ed. H. Hall, iii. 841; *C.C.R., 1318–23*, p. 53.

[3] Tout, *Chapters*, ii. 247; Davies, op. cit., pp. 557–9 document no. 29. The first indication of attention being given to the reform of the Exchequer comes in March 1312 but this was not so extensive as the ordinance of 1319 (Davies, p. 528). From 1315–16 there survive memoranda entitled 'De Agendis in Scaccario' which refer to the growing volume of business at the Exchequer and contain proposals for dealing with outstanding accounts and the collection of outstanding dues (E 101/332/22, 23).

council, as had already been done at the end of 1316. It is clear
that from the beginning of the century the Exchequer had been
able to produce estimates of expenditure for its principal
charges. From regular statements of half-yearly receipts it could
prepare estimates for succeeding years. In fact from 1324 we
have the first extant estimates of the annual revenue of the Exchequer. This covered all the recurrent sources of revenue and
was drawn up from the Exchequer rolls, apparently by aver-
aging receipts over a series of preceding years.[1]

By the use of such estimates and with the evidence of current
receipts and payments, some degree of financial planning and
control became possible. Thus a major charge of the Exchequer
could be allocated revenue for the forthcoming year and given
preference over the claims of other creditors, as had recently
been done for the royal households. In times of financial stringency the Exchequer's knowledge of its resources and liabilities
formed the basis for imposing a restraint on payments from
which only its most important creditors or charges would be
exempt. The 1319 Ordinance also provided for all warrants to
specify not merely the name of the creditor and the amount to
be paid but, in the case of assignments, the source of revenue.
Such day-to-day control over assignment played a major part
in sustaining royal credit, enabling the Treasurer to give varying degrees of security to creditors. Indeed the existence, tacit
or acknowledged, of a scale of preferences between creditors was
fundamental to financial planning.[2] In consequence the Exchequer became the clearing house for the competing claims of
the King and his subjects as each strove, through personal and
political influence, to secure payment or reliable assignment
for their dues. It was in this sense that the Exchequer emerged
as a national agency of finance, mirroring in its daily business
not merely the needs of the Crown but the interests of the political community. Significantly the Ordinance, in addition to

[1] Bodleian Library, MS. North C.26, no. 4 (see Appendix B item i). From the
document of 1305 printed by Willard ('Ordinances for the Guidance of a Deputy
Treasurer, 22 October 1305', *Eng. Hist. Rev.* xlviii (1933), pp. 84–9), it is clear
that the Exchequer could estimate the annual charge for the household and set
aside recurrent fortnightly payments to meet this. Summaries of royal finances
were also prepared in France during this period: see J. B. Henneman, *Royal
Taxation in Fourteenth Century France* (Princeton, 1971), pp. 64, 177.

[2] Cf. G. L. Harriss, 'Preference at the Medieval Exchequer', *Bull. Inst. Hist. Res,*
xxx (1957), pp. 17–40.

providing this control over assignment, forbade the Treasurer and Chamberlains (in charge of the receipt) to permit any unauthorized person to view the rolls or remembrances of the receipt, an evident precaution against the spying out of favourable assignment by the attorneys whom creditors might employ.

In these ways the document affords evidence that the Exchequer was the instrument of financial policy and the focal point of pressures of different kinds from the Crown and its creditors. Doubtless much that was here defined had developed over the previous three decades,[1] but this is the first evidence we have of an attempt to regulate and utilize the system. Too few warrants survive from these years to judge how far the Ordinance was put into effect, but in January 1320 the King ordered the Exchequer to change an assignment in favour of John de Somery from the shire revenues of Staffordshire to the eighteenth collected in the county;[2] in August following he strictly enjoined the Treasurer to make no payment or assignment to any creditor from the tenth except by the King's oral command, and the memoranda roll for 1319–20 contains a schedule defining the payments which the Exchequer could make for the following year on its own authority.[3] All this suggests that during 1320 there was a conscious effort to pursue a policy of financial control on the lines envisaged in the Ordinance; it bears out the view of Pembroke's policy as one of active involvement of the royal power in a broadly reformist and conciliar government, and there is evidence that Edward himself may

---

[1] The Exchequer had already had cause to restrain assignments under Edward I (see above, p. 205) and in October 1309 the King had imposed a restraint on all payments during the Michaelmas term except those he specially authorized for the benefit of those serving on the Scottish campaign: 'Vous mandoms qe des deniers qe sont ore a nostre ditz Escheker et qe vendront a ceste terme de la Seint Michel, ne facez nule manere de payement saunz especial mandement de nos, einz les facez garder por nos et por nos dites bones gentz qe irront en nostre service as parties desusdites. Et a ceux qe vendront a notre dit Escheker por demander paiementz qe leur y sont duz, facez assigner aucun certein iour por receivre meismes les paiementz quant vous entendrez que hom leur porra rienz paer, issint qe nos et noz dites bones gentz puissent estre serviz de ditz deniers en nos busoignes avandites. Don souz notre prive seal a la Grove le vii iour de Octobre lan de notre regne tierz' (E 404/1/5). In the same file there is a warrant (24 April 3 Edw. II) specifying the source of the assignment.

[2] E 404/1/8, 30 January 13 Edw. II.

[3] Davies, op. cit., pp. 559–60, documents nos. 31, 32.

have responded, at least spasmodically, with energy and in-terest.[1] Equally significant was the way this anticipated the Exchequer reforms effected during 1323–6.

The three Exchequer Ordinances of 1323, 1324, and 1326 completed the evolution of the medieval Exchequer.[2] They had the allied purpose of increasing its efficiency and asserting its control over the entire financial operations of royal govern-ment. The establishment of a whole series of foreign accounts withdrawn from the pipe roll and the Wardrobe account gave recognition to the growth of royal revenue and the need to bring its various sources under effective control. The Cowick Ordinance of 1323 consolidated on the roll of Foreign Accounts the accounts of the escheators and of the keepers of temporalities and lands in the Crown's hands, which had been withdrawn from the sheriffs in the previous century, together with the accounts of Ireland, Wales, and Gascony, and those of aids and customs. The extension and specialization of revenue admini-stration demanded increased vigilance: separate days for audit-ing these revenues were set aside, rules laid down to ensure that payments and allowances by revenue collectors were fully authorized, and measures taken to ensure that debts were remembered and collected. The responsiveness of the Ex-chequer's local officials was a vital consideration, and the Exchequer routine was based on the expectation of a return to its writs within three months.[3] With the Exchequer in command of the full range of public revenues, it was logical for it to be given direct responsibility for all expenditure. This was done by insisting that all expenditure was to be on the authority of royal warrants to the Treasurer and Chamberlains, which were to be enrolled.[4] The tallies issued to the Wardrobe at the receipt would thus provide a complete record of the sum for which it was called to answer. This did not limit the Ward-robe's essential flexibility. Its *de facto* independence of the Ex-chequer for part of its 'Exchequer receipt' remained. It could anticipate Exchequer revenue by drawing directly from local

---

[1] Maddicott, op. cit., p. 257.

[2] The Ordinances are printed in the *Red Book of the Exchequer*, iii. 848–969; they are admirably summarized by Tout, *Chapers*, ii. 259–67, and in *The Place of Edward II in English History*, 2nd ed. (Manchester, 1936), pp. 173–83.

[3] *Cal. Mem. Rolls, 1326–7*, p. xxii.   [4] *Red Book of Exchequer*, iii. 908.

receivers who would be credited with this sum when they appeared at the Upper Exchequer, and it could pledge Exchequer credit by giving a promissory bill in payment of services which the creditor presented at the Lower Exchequer for payment.[1] The Wardrobe needed to maintain this freedom to secure money and services as part of its normal domestic administration, as well as to meet the urgent and essential demands of a royal campaign.

Despite an element of professional rivalry, Exchequer and Wardrobe did not represent rival systems of government or administration. There was only one system through which the finances of the realm were received and spent, and it served the interest of both King and community that over this the authority of the Exchequer should be extended and strengthened. The Exchequer was emerging as an efficient financial organ not merely in keeping close watch on the King's revenues and officials but in serving the King's interests and commands. Its authority over the whole range of national revenue and financial administration was placed at the King's disposal; its ability to pledge and anticipate revenue extended his immediate financial resources; its capacity to restrain, direct, and order the priority of its expenditure gave him a range of options of some personal and political significance. In these matters its obedience to royal mandates was complete. Nevertheless the King's authority could not be exercised exclusively in the interests of himself or his household. He could give a legitimate priority to the household or to whatever else seemed to him to be of urgent and imminent need—his 'grosses busoignes'—but he did so within the

[1] Thus a comparison of Melton's account book of 8–9 Edward II (E 101/376/11, 14) with Northwell's for 11–15 Edward III (E 101/388/9), both of which give full details of the *Recepta Scaccarii*, show that the methods of receipt had not substantially changed. In both we can distinguish (i) receipts by Wardrobe officials from the Exchequer and local sources; (ii) receipts from loans paid direct to the Wardrobe or to its officials; (iii) receipts by Wardrobe creditors either at the Exchequer or from local revenues made on the authority of bills of the Wardrobe or letters of assignment by the Keeper. The amount of revenue actually collected by the Wardrobe at source was always fairly limited and its ability to pledge Exchequer credit either by negotiating loans or by delivering bills payable on Exchequer revenue was ultimately dependent on the capacity of the Exchequer to honour these. Thus the Wardrobe's debts over the period 1 December 1314 to 31 January 1316 totalled £6,514. 14*s.* 1*d.*, some of which were 'sine billis', others 'per billas', and others 'per tallias' (E 101/376/7). Usually a proportion of such debts were never discharged.

context of the Exchequer's responsibility for national expenditure as a whole. The Exchequer was his instrument but it also reflected the interests of the realm both in totality and in the persons of individual creditors. In this sense the Exchequer was national as well as royal while the King and his household were likewise but one element in the realm.

The reforms of 1323–6 did nothing to limit or constrain the King's authority over the resources of the realm and it is doubtful whether they seriously impaired the speed and flexibility with which his financial demands were met. Two illustrations may be given of the way in which Edward II could exploit the Exchequer's system in these years. Throughout the winter of 1322–3 he imposed a general restraint on payments, only dispensable on specific royal orders, and this formed one of the matters on which the Treasurer and Barons asked to know the King's will.[1] Even at a time such as this when money was short the King could still reserve for himself at the Exchequer a store of cash from which payment was to be made only at his express command and as a last resort: for in March 1323, needing 100 marks for the Wardrobe he sent the cofferer to get it from this store, providing him with the key.[2] With equal urgency, but on a different scale and for a different purpose, the King might order the Exchequer to meet his immediate demands, as when on 2 October 1326 Edward II commanded the Treasurer to deliver £20,000 to John de Langton for war expenses. Langton had this in his hands the following day; then two days later, as the King was already moving westwards, he sent back orders for a further £10,000. Of this the Exchequer provided £9,000 and Langton completed delivery of the whole sum to Edward at Chepstow by 20 October.[3]

Evidence of how close and immediate a control the King could exercise over the Exchequer's disbursements is provided by the warrants for issue of the first decade of the new reign.

[1] P.R.O. C 47/35/17, 2 December 1322; C. 47/35/21, 30 November 1322. C 49/33 no. 13 is an Exchequer memorandum of 16 Edward II of matters touching which the King's pleasure is to be known. The first item concerns dispensation from it for payments to 'les plus ovres ministres le Roi'.

[2] C 47/35/27.

[3] *Cal. Mem. Rolls, 1326–27*, pp. 15, 36. In July of the following year the collectors of the customs were ordered to bring all their revenues to the Exchequer notwithstanding any assignments made to other creditors to be used for the expenses of the Scottish campaign (ibid., pp. 228, 250).

The King warranted payments with a variety of emphasis determined by the status of the creditor and the urgency of the need. Apart from satisfying the needs of his household, his more express commands were employed on behalf of the Queen, his principal merchant creditors, the servants and creditors of the household, and captains of garrisons. Provision for the royal households, sometimes to meet an urgent shortage of cash, might be urged 'si que nous ne soioms descriez par defaute de paiement' or 'sicome vous aviez eschuire l'esclandre de nos et de notre dicte compaigne devers le poeple'.[1] Where a creditor was to receive recurrent payments for a large debt or standing charge, the Exchequer was ordered to give assignment where payment was secure, with the option of alternative sources if it failed.[2] If a previous payment had failed or a debt was long overdue, the King might order it to be paid 'hastivement et sans delai', so that the creditor should not have occasion to return to the King, and neither the King nor the creditor should be 'deservis'.[3] Where the King attached great importance to the business performed by the servant or creditor he would emphasize that 'notre entencion et volunte est qu'il soit hastivement paiez par cause d'aucunes busoignes dont nous lui avons especialement chargez'.[4] For debts to an important military creditor like William Roos of Hamelake, the King could order the Exchequer to receive his Wardrobe bills and discharge them in cash from the Treasury, emphasizing that he was showing 'plus especiale grace en celle partie', since this overrode a standing restraint on payments.[5] But while the King could thus manipulate Exchequer disbursements within a wide range of preferences for those whom he specially favoured, the real test of the Exchequer as the controlling authority over national finance was its ability to finance a national war. Could it effectively subordinate the interests of other creditors to the needs of the military machine, and could it keep the armies supplied with a flow of cash essential for the payment of wages and the purchase of victuals? How should these functions be co-ordinated with those of the Wardrobe as a war treasury in

[1] P.R.O. E 404/2 file 9, 18 April 1328; ibid., file 10, 22 June 1330; ibid., file 12, 19 December 1331.

[2] Ibid., file 9, 23 May 1328; ibid., 22 October 1329.

[3] Ibid., file 10, 5 July 1330; file 12, 15 December 1331.

[4] Ibid., file 14, 2 June 1332.   [5] Ibid., file 12, 24 January 1332.

the field? Edward III's campaigns in Scotland were marked by the revival of the Wardrobe's military role. After the initial campaign of 1327 the Wardrobe had fulfilled its restricted, domestic function, with its *hospicium* expenses consistently under £10,000 and its 'foreign' receipt well under a nominal £5,000 p.a. The campaign of 1332 and more notably those of 1334–7 enlarged its Exchequer receipt to first over £22,000 and then to an average of £42,000 p.a., though there was no increase in its foreign receipt.[1]

The Wardrobe's role as a field treasury was essentially to receive and disburse cash, but it could only fulfil this with the support of the Exchequer. The establishment of the Exchequer at York facilitated the transfer of large sums of specie which comprised a significant proportion of the Wardrobe receipt in these years. Otherwise the Wardrobe could draw on northern revenues, like subsidies and customs, and, more important, it could receive loans from the Italian merchants.[2] But here again the repayment of these and hence, to a large degree the negotiation of further loans, depended on the Exchequer. The Exchequer's command of national revenue both in providing cash for royal needs and in ensuring the satisfaction of important royal creditors can be illustrated from the warrants of these years. Several of these contain urgent demands for cash. In April 1334 Edward ordered the Exchequer to forward 1,000 marks to Newcastle to pay for purveyances;[3] in May he sent an usher of the chamber to collect 700 marks for the Wardrobe and to inform the Treasurer that he had received 300 marks from the customs of Lincoln.[4] In the following month, for so urgent and vital a matter as the payments to Beaumont and Balliol to seal the treaty of 12 June, the King ordered the Exchequer to send 1,000 marks to arrive at Newcastle 'on Tuesday next before nine o'clock at the latest'.[5] Equally important in the

[1] Tout, *Chapters*, vi. 86–9, iv. 96–7.
[2] Ibid.; A. E. Prince, 'The Payment of Army Wages in Edward III's Reign', *Speculum*, xix (1944), pp. 138–9; R. Nicholson, *Edward III and the Scots*, p. 238, notes that in 1334 the subsidy in the north of England was paid directly into the Wardrobe. E 404/3 file 17 contains a warrant of 12 May 1334 informing the Exchequer of the Wardrobe's receipt from the customs in Lincoln.
[3] E 404/3 file 17, 8 April 1334.
[4] Ibid., file 17, 12 May 1334; ibid., 18 June 1334.
[5] The writ is printed *in extenso* by Nicholson, op. cit., p. 241, and its context discussed on p. 115.

King's eyes was the Exchequer's ability to satisfy the merchants. Loans from the Bardi and Anthony Bache in 1332 were to be repaid, the former by assignment but the latter, with more urgency, in cash or—failing this—from the King's jewels.[1] In 1334 the Bardi who had paid Tawton, the Keeper of the Wardrobe, 400 marks were to be paid in cash 'from our treasure' without delay.[2] In July 1332 restraints were imposed on payments to other creditors so that the Bardi could receive their own dues.[3] Such restraint could be applied to a particular revenue or it could amount to a general stop on the Exchequer from which the King issued individual dispensations.[4] A general restraint of this kind was in force in June 1332 and was reimposed in February and April 1333 with the purpose of providing a large sum of cash to be sent northward to the Wardrobe.[5]

The years of the Scottish war show that within the system established under Edward II the Wardrobe could continue to function as a war treasury in the field, though in the lack of a detailed study it is difficult to assess how effectively the system supplied Edward's armies in Scotland. Nor was there any inherent difficulty in adapting this system to the French war; in fact the Wardrobe drew an Exchequer receipt for the two years of Norwell's account (1338–40) totalling some £108,000 in exactly the same ways as in the previous years.[6] Although Tout spoke of the Walton Ordinances as designed to put Exchequer and Chancery in leading strings and subordinate them to the Wardrobe, the crucial first section on warrants for issues was rather designed to adapt the existing system to the problem of the King's absence abroad.[7] The general purpose of the Walton

[1] E 404/2 file 13, 16 March 1332; ibid., file 14, 24 June 1332.

[2] E 404/3 file 17, 18 May 1334.

[3] Ibid., file 15, 7 July 1332.

[4] *Cal. Mem. Rolls, 1326-7*, pp. 228, 250; Nicholson, op. cit., p. 38.

[5] E 404/2 file 14, 21 May, 4 June 1332: 'et ne voudriens en nulle manere que ceste chose preist delai pour defaute de paiement, vous mandoms et chargeons que nien contrestant quecunque autre ordenance, facez faire paiement . . .' See likewise Nicholson, op. cit., p. 115.

[6] Tout, *Chapters*, iv. 104-6. The danger of conveying bullion overseas was partly met by giving Wardrobe debentures in payment of wages which were cashable at the Exchequer up to a total Wardrobe credit authorized by writ of *liberate* (see Prince, op. cit., p. 148). But the large cash supplies still needed in the Netherlands were to be furnished by loans and wool sales.

[7] Tout, *Chapters*, iv. 69 ff., with text at pp. 144-50.

Ordinances was to place the Exchequer on a war footing by eliminating any expenditure not warranted by the King, his regent in England, or one of the war commanders. Such warrants were to specify precisely the object of expenditure, even such phrases as 'pur les secres busoignes' under which the King had secured money for the Chamber being disallowed. Apart from fees and wages paid *de cursu* (and these were soon to come under the axe), the Treasurer and Chamberlains were to make no payments to creditors on their own authority. At the same time the Exchequer was rigorously to pursue and exact all debts, to disallow exemptions from taxes, and to repudiate any obligation to pay debts incurred before the beginning of the reign. This aligned the whole of the Exchequer's operations—in collecting and disbursing revenue—to the exclusive service of the King's war. If it lessened the field of discretion of the Treasurer and Chamberlains, it was the King's other subjects with claims on the Exchequer who had greater reason to complain. The Ordinance, as Tout acknowledged, clearly asserted the ultimate supremacy of the Exchequer in financial administration, and in requiring the Treasurer to report the King's debts and what revenue was anticipated 'to acquit and maintain his estate' reflected not merely the Exchequer's unique capacity to furnish the basis of any financial policy but its prime duty to maintain the estate of the household.[1] The Walton Ordinances thus bear witness to the belief of one experienced and energetic administrator that the Exchequer could be equipped to discipline and marshal the financial resources of the realm for war. Strengthened if constrained by the authority of the King, the Exchequer was expected to mobilize all the revenue of England for the war in Brabant. Though its officers might chafe under this yoke, and though they might complain that some of these restrictions were proving impractical and impolitic, yet it was not so much the King's close administrative control as his independent exploitation of national revenues which generated the conflict with parliament and the home council in 1340.[2]

Norwell's account for 1338–40 shows that the huge sum of £151,835 which he received as 'foreign' receipt came to him

[1] Ibid., pp. 73, 77. The phrase echoes the Ordinances of 1311.
[2] Discussed below, chs. x, xi.

from the advances on and proceeds of the wool sales through bargains concluded with the King's merchants, as well as from the sale of the Burstwick estate to de la Pole.[1] The revivified autonomy of the Wardrobe was merely an aspect of the King's daring bid to exploit wool taxation and split the profits, and its future as an independent agency stood or fell with the success of this scheme. This scheme directly challenged the doctrine acknowledged at the end of the thirteenth century and reaffirmed in 1311, that taxation for the common profit of the realm should be under the authority of the Exchequer. Even more decisive was the odium which became attached to the King's financiers and the dismay which greeted the revelation of his indebtedness. As in 1311, the Wardrobe became the scapegoat for the King's insolvency. The reassertion of Exchequer control over all revenues and the strict accounting of all who handled them was forced on the King in 1340, and during the following decade the wool subsidy was acknowledged to be a public tax granted by parliament. Although Edward was able, eventually, to repair the damage to his political authority inflicted by the opposition of 1340–1, the effect of this crisis on the system of national finance was decisive. Never again was the Wardrobe used as an instrument for the King's manipulation of the wool trade and an alternative to the Exchequer. The primacy of the Exchequer, established between 1290 and 1324, was reaffirmed. In the later wars 'the function of the Wardrobe seems much more that of a treasury with the army in the field, firmly controlled by the home treasury of the Exchequer than that of an independent and self contained office of finance, the rival if not the master of the financial office at home'.[2] Even as a war treasury the Wardrobe was coming to have a more restricted role, for its responsibilities were confined to the King's own retinue, while his captains—whose retinues helped to swell the accounts of 1338–41—indented separately at the Exchequer. For both the Scottish expedition of 1341–2 and the Breton expedition of 1342–3, the Wardrobe acted as a war treasury as the King eventually assumed command of each,

[1] Tout, *Chapters*, iv. 104–5.

[2] Ibid., p. 113. Tout regarded this crucial change as the work of Edington, Treasurer from April 1344 to November 1356, but it can also be seen as the logical culmination of the reforms of 1319–24. Cf. A. E. Prince, op. cit., pp. 151–3.

though in neither case was it financed independently through its foreign receipt. For the remainder of the decade that remained at less than £3,000 p.a. Even when the King went abroad for the Crécy-Calais campaign and the final campaign of 1359–60, in which the Wardrobe again fulfilled the role of a war treasury abroad, its receipt (though never on the scale of that of 1338–40) came entirely from the Exchequer with the exception of one large prest (of £32,129) from the Chamber.[1] All the expeditions sent to Gascony and Brittany in these years under individual captains were separately financed from the Exchequer.

The Chamber's role as a war treasury in these years was closely related to that of the Wardrobe. The extension of the activities of the Chamber in the years after 1333 have been reviewed by Tout. Pressed into the service of the King's wars, it became 'largely a channel through which war expenses were paid'. Payments were indeed made to it 'for the secret business of the king', and its freedom from account at the Exchequer emphasized that it was pre-eminently the storehouse of the King's personal wealth. Yet now that Edward's overriding pre-occupation was war, nine-tenths of its expenditure was on this. The full extent of Chamber revenue and expenditure cannot be known; but what is certain is that the revenue to meet these expenses 'did not come in any large measure from its landed estate' or from the King's fiscal prerogatives.[2] It came either from the Exchequer or from advances by the King's merchants and was predominantly derived from taxation. Although the Chamber maintained its freedom from rendering account to the Exchequer until after 1344, it was eventually obliged to account for its receipts from taxation, though for its revenue from lands it accounted solely to the King.

Thus by 1347 'the failure of the last attempt to assign the Wardrobe a new role or rather to revive on its behalf devices already tried earlier in the century left it to sink back into a modest position from which it emerged only when war, conducted by the king in person, called upon it to take again the great share in war administration.'[3] In the next two decades the way was open towards the further consolidation and co-ordination of the administration associated with Edington

[1] Tout, *Chapters*, ii. 90–1; iv. 110–11, 116; Prince, op. cit., pp. 152–60.
[2] Tout, *Chapters*, iv. 289–94.   [3] Ibid., p. 129.

and his successors. The control exercised by the Exchequer over the spending of all national revenues, its authority to require account, its capacity to pledge revenue in advance, and to provide security for loans gave the King complete command of national finance and placed in his hands a variety of options for awarding payment to those creditors and charges he favoured or found most pressing. If this represented an enlargement of the King's resources and authority, it was in response to the needs of the realm. The administration of national revenue through a national office in the interests of the whole realm made the King the chief interpreter of the common profit, notably in time of war. But in the last analysis the King's interpretation could not conflict with the political interests of his subjects. Specifically, he could not devote the resources of the realm to his personal profit or that of a group of intimates; nor could he use his authority to oppress his subjects. Such concepts were familiar to theorists but normally neither the King nor his subjects recognized any division between the King's personal and public interest in his dealings with the Exchequer. It was only under the stress of political controversy that the King might be accused of wasting the resources of the fisc or the taxes granted for war, of prodigality or mismanagement, and in consequence of impoverishing the realm. Underlying such criticism was the sense that the King was a trustee of the realm and in his relations with the Exchequer the greatest of its officers. Even the Wardrobe, traditionally the agent of flexible, personal government, was affected by this trend. The development of national war financed from national revenues was ultimately fatal to its role as an independent war treasury. It was left as 'domus magnificencie', the chief and most honoured charge on the Exchequer. The Chamber ceased to be an instrument of government; it was now no more than the King's personal treasury, the custodian of his jewels and, when appropriate, of his family lands. Its income met his personal expenses. The fount of rule and policy of course remained the King himself, but by the middle of the fourteenth century England was recognizably a national monarchy not merely in possessing a sense of identity, political cohesion, and centralized institutions of government but in the fact that the Kingship itself served the needs of the realm.

PART TWO

KING, PARLIAMENT, AND THE BURDENS OF WAR, 1337–1369

CHAPTER X

The Second Crisis over Taxation:
I The Crisis in the Country, 1337–1339

THE first open conflict with the Crown over taxation had been provoked by Edward I's intensive war effort of 1295–7 and his remorseless prosecution of the war against Scotland. The very similar, but more ambitious scheme of Edward III for an invasion of France from the north-east with continental allies produced the second financial and political crisis, of 1340–1. Although on this occasion the war against Scotland preceded the continental campaign, fears of an invasion on two fronts while the King was abroad formed the common background to both crises. On each occasion widespread discontent over the frequency of taxation, the burden of war levies, and the harsh and frequently illegal exactions of royal officials provided support for the political opposition. These burdens were inevitable concomitants of marshalling the resources of the realm for war, but they might be convincingly represented as oppressing and impoverishing the King's subjects, as evidence of misrule. Magnate opposition could in this way broaden its appeal, for such opposition was usually sectional, the work of those who were or who feared they were out of favour with the King. Thus the crisis of 1297 had originated in Edward I's quarrel with his two leading earls and with the archbishop of Canterbury, and that of 1340 sprang from a feud between rival groups amongst Edward III's councillors. Both crises developed as a broad attack on the character of royal government. Moreover, in 1340 it was all too easy to invoke the memories and language of the factional strife of Edward II's reign and the tradition of baronial support for popular grievances against the 'evil counsellors' of the King. In other ways, too, the developments of the intervening forty years revealed themselves. Most notable was the greater prominence of parliament with its defined procedures and increasing precedents; and within parliament the Commons had become more articulate, their support and intervention more important. Yet these forty years had also seen a corresponding increase in the resources of the Crown, financially from the addition of a tax on customs, and administratively by the development of techniques of public credit and a reformed Exchequer. The full development of the contract army made many of the middle landholding class associates in the royal enterprise, while nationalism, focused on the Crown, was brought to a higher pitch by persistent royal propaganda. Such developments gave Edward III the capacity to mobilize the resources of the realm for a national war, but his attempt to do this on an unprecedented scale made his failure the more catastrophic. The political repercussions were notable. For the first time in English history a major political crisis was fought out at every step in parliament and for the first time the Commons were agents for demanding and securing major changes in the structure of government. Edward III's war effort, as intensive as it was futile, proved to be a political catalyst. Its financial and political aspects call for detailed discussion if the occurrence and development of the crisis of 1340 are to be understood.[1]

Edward III's claim to the French throne in 1337 and his formal assumption of the title in 1340 formed a necessary element in the system of alliances with German princes and Flemish cities which he hoped would carry him into France. Such alliances were extremely costly to keep in being; E. B. Fryde has calculated that Edward had already committed himself to pay £124,000 to his nine leading allies by the end of 1337, and at the end of that year his agents in Brabant reckoned that they needed some £276,000 by Mid-Lent 1338 to meet their obligations.[2] Politically, as well as financially, a swift and successful campaign was highly desirable; after four years of

---

[1] The intricate story of Edward III's preparations has been unravelled in a number of notable studies on which the following account is largely based. References are to the following works: T. F. Tout, *Chapters in Medieval Administrative History*, iii (Manchester, 1928); E. Deprez, *Les Préliminaires de la Guerre de Cent Ans* (Paris, 1902); D. Hughes, *A Study of Social and Constitutional Tendencies in the Early Years of Edward III*; (London, 1915); G. Unwin, *Finance and Trade under Edward III* (Manchester, 1918); E. B. Fryde, 'Edward III's Wool Monopoly of 1337', *History*, xxxvii (1952), pp. 8–24; 'Financial Resources of Edward III in the Netherlands, 1337–40', *Revue Belge de Philologie et d'Histoire*, xlv (1967), pp. 1142–93, 'Parliament and the French War, 1336–40', in *Essays presented to Bertie Wilkinson*, pp. 250–69.

[2] *Revue Belge*, xlv 1146–7.

war the Scottish problem was still unresolved, and in a real sense the attack on France was seen as the precondition of a solution.[1] Edward had the support of the military classes for his new venture, but it did not lessen their concern for the defence of the north, and by inviting French coastal attacks or even invasion the King's absence increased the danger to the realm. Remembering Edward I's absence in 1297 men were acutely aware of this, but the precedent also held its lessons for the King. The discontent produced by the burdensome levies of a large-scale campaign could prove dangerous if exploited by a political opposition. A realm subjected to the strains of war needed effective and authoritative government, and during the absence of the King it was not easy for a council of ministers to resist political pressures on their own authority. Finally, a short, victorious campaign would provide an effective answer to papal diplomacy which on this occasion was prolonging negotiations with the French King and was bringing pressure upon Archbishop Stratford in the cause of peace.[2]

There is every indication that Edward was aware of these problems and that between September 1336 and September 1337 he initiated the measures which he hoped would provide an answer to them. Edward's planning during this year showed judgement and realism; it was only as his plans began to go awry that his actions betrayed an element of recklessness and blind obstinacy. The basis of Edward's war strategy was the capacity to mobilize the financial resources of the realm on a massive scale for a limited period, and for this he needed both a grant of taxation and the freedom to anticipate it through his own arrangements. This in turn depended on the recognition by the realm of the King's plea of necessity. That Edward obtained specific assent to the war from prelates, magnates, and Commons is certain not merely from what we may deduce from precedents but from subsequent explicit statements to

[1] This aspect is discussed by J. Campbell, 'England, Scotland and the Hundred Years' War in the Fourteenth Century', in *Europe in the Late Middle Ages*, ed. J. Hale, R. Highfield, and B. Smalley (London, 1965), pp. 184–216.

[2] Stratford had been one of Edward's principal negotiators with the French court during the Scottish war (Nicholson, *Edward III and the Scots*, pp. 156, 192) but throughout 1338 and 1339 he was under considerable pressure from both Pope and legates to prevent open hostilities (Hughes, op. cit., pp. 108–10; *Cal. Papal Letters*, ii. 564, 570; Deprez, op. cit., pp. 200, 206–9).

this effect.[1] According to Archbishop Stratford, answering the
King's attack on his administration in 1341, that decision was
taken in the parliament held at Westminster in March 1337.[2]
It was in this parliament that Edward conferred dignities and
lands on the magnates who were to be his principal companions
and commanders in the Low Countries during the following
three years. Following the parliament, and probably as a
result of its deliberations, the embassy of Bishop Burghersh and
the earls of Huntingdon and Salisbury set off for the Netherlands to enlist allies and to conduct the final negotiations with
France, in July, which led to the formal breach. From the indications we have of the analogous discussions in the parliament
of 1332 which preceded the Scottish war, it is highly probable
that the Commons were asked for their voice on these matters
even if the effective decisions were taken by the King and the
magnates. When they next assembled on 26 September 1337
the business of parliament was more immediately their concern,
namely the defence of the realm during the King's absence and
the grant of taxation for the expedition.[3] It was in terms of a
compelling necessity, to which assent had in effect been given
in the previous parliament, that they now granted a triennial
tenth and fifteenth, following which the King formally asserted
his claim to the French Crown.

The size of this grant was unprecedented; indeed the only
precedent for recurrent taxation was the years 1294–7 with
their bitter memories of hardship and crisis. The grant of a
triennial subsidy was thus not only a major security with which
the King could approach potential lenders but a considerable
political triumph, providing solid backing from the military
classes for the war and some assurance against the tensions and
demands aroused by repeated approaches to parliament. Yet it
reflected not only the magnitude of the envisaged operations
but, almost certainly, the Commons' expectation that this

---

[1] *Rot. Parl.* ii. 136, 157, 165, 231. Compare the discussion by Fryde, 'Parliament
and the French War', pp. 251–5.

[2] See Birchington: 'sicque per ipsum Philippum et non per vos guerra inchoata
iuxta deliberationem et consensum parliamenti apud Westmonasterium tunc ea
occasione convocati' (*Anglia Sacra*, ed. H. Wharton, i. 30). Stratford's account
associates this with the embassy of Bishop Burghersh and the earls of Huntingdon
and Salisbury and locates it before the council at Stamford in June.

[3] *R.D.P.* iv. 479–82.

represented a final effort which would be rewarded with victory and peace. Their disappointment was to be reflected in opposition to the further demands of 1339–40. Two things, apart from the good harvests of 1336 and 1337, may have assisted their generosity: first the fact that England had been conditioned to a state of emergency by the Scottish war but had not been exhausted by burdensome or widely unpopular levies; secondly, in the preceding weeks commissioners had held a series of local meetings with knights and landowners in the shires to put the case of necessity and get preliminary promises of contribution from them as individuals. It was clearly recognized that these assemblies of the county courts had no power to bind the community as a whole; for that the assent of the community of the whole realm could alone suffice; but the local assemblies served partly as propaganda, partly to negotiate a form of benevolence.[1]

Parallel with winning support from the knights, Edward had been negotiating with the merchants to secure a grant of wool. On 12 August 1336 he had imposed an embargo on the export of wool for the ensuing year, and in September an assembly at Nottingham which included knights and burgesses agreed to a subsidy of twenty shillings on the sack to be levied when export was resumed.[2] To exploit this the King needed the co-operation of a select group of wealthy merchants who could finance and operate a monopoly. The formation of this body of Contract Merchants had been mooted in 1336 when the minimum prices they were to pay for the wool were laid down; and in discussions at Stamford in June 1337, finalized and confirmed at a great council at Westminster in July, the scheme was adopted for purchasing and exporting 30,000 sacks of wool, making the King an immediate loan of £200,000 and paying him half the proceeds of the sale of wool as well.[3] The scheme was not impracticable, though it depended on the collection and disposal

[1] See above, p. 96, also W. N. Bryant, 'The financial dealings of Edward III with the county communities, 1330–60', *Eng. Hist. Rev.* lxxxiii (1968), pp. 766–8. It is perhaps to this procedure that Knighton (*Chronicon*, ed. J. R. Lumby, ii. 3) refers when he notices the aid from those with 40s. of goods and chattels 'quaesitum est a singulis per ministros regis praestito sacramento quantum possent bene dare'.

[2] *C.C.R., 1333–7*, p. 700; ibid., *1337–9*, p. 97.

[3] Fryde, 'Edward III's Wool Monopoly', gives the fullest account of this; see also his *Wool Accounts of William de la Pole* (York, 1964).

of the wool proceeding smoothly, and it was clearly liable to produce tensions between the monopolists and the wool growers and lesser merchants. But Edward had taken care to secure explicit approval of the scheme from the lesser merchants in the July assembly, and Archbishop Stratford as well as Edward's trusted agent Bishop Burghersh had been instrumental in negotiating it. At every stage, therefore, both in negotiating the lay subsidy and the wool scheme, Edward had proceeded by wide consultation and assent. To all appearance England was united behind the King's war policy when Burghersh and his embassy sailed to the Netherlands in November to prepare for the arrival of the wool and for the spring campaign to which the King's preparations were plainly geared.

The King's difficulties started almost as soon as the Westminster assembly had dissolved. The first signs that the King had turned in earnest to the mobilization of revenue for war were writs issued early in October for inquisitions into dues from chattels of felons and fugitives which, in the absence of eyres, had not been levied for a number of years. At the same time Edward claimed the levy of the scutage of 1327. Objections to both of these demands were voiced in the parliament of February 1338 and the King agreed to withdraw them as the price of a grant of wool, though he did not abandon the idea of using them at a later stage.[1] The parliament of February had been necessary partly to counter a new diplomatic peace offensive from the cardinals, partly to assist in salvaging the wool scheme which had foundered with the King's seizure of the wool shipped by the Contract Merchants at Dordrecht. Both these it did, and the setbacks which had attended Edward's financial schemes and his domestic control did not as yet diminish his military prospects or his confidence in the promise of all estates of parliament 'to aid him in this matter, each according to his estate and power'.[2] In the event the King did not sail to Brabant until July. The administrative arrangements for his absence had been made some time previously, though they were not formally issued until the eve of his depature.

[1] G. O. Sayles (ed.), *Select Cases in the Court of King's Bench* (Selden Soc. lxxiv, 1957), p. lxvi; H. M. Chew, 'Scutage in the Fourteenth Century', *Eng. Hist. Rev.* xxxviii (1923), pp. 39–40; Fryde, 'Parliament and the French War', pp. 260–1.
[2] Letter of Edward III from Antwerp, 24 July 1338, printed in Deprez, op. cit., p. 418.

A home council under his infant son Edward comprised the earls of Arundel and Huntingdon, and Lord Neville, with Richard Bentworth as Chancellor and Robert Wodehouse as Treasurer.[1] All could be reckoned loyal supporters of royal policy, and the particular interest which some of them had in the defence of the north suggests that Edward had not underrated the danger arising from his absence. Nevertheless the return of Chancery and Exchequer to London signified the concentration of effort in the Low Countries and the Walton Ordinances set out unmistakably the role of the home council in 'providing the money which the king was to spend and . . . carrying out implicitly all orders received from abroad'.[2] It was to be an executive agent of the King's will, with very limited responsibility and no real advisory capacity. In the context of Edward's plan of campaign this was reasonable: the financial arrangements had been completed and were dependent on the personal obligations between the King and his creditors; communication with him in Brabant was not difficult and the King probably did not anticipate a lengthy or geographically extended campaign; his most trusted councillors were in his camp and through the privy seal he could convey orders directly and authoritatively to the home government. The kingdom had been placed on a war footing and Edward doubtless felt it wise to retain in his hands the direction of the war effort as well as the campaign. What made this disastrous in the event was the failure of the King's financial arrangements, which delayed his campaign and produced mounting desperation and indebtedness in the royal camp combined with the growing discontent in the realm against royal levies and royal policies. Under these strains tempers became frayed in both Brabant and London, and misunderstandings bred jealousies and suspicions in the two councils. This situation provided the context of the parliament of 1339–40. To appreciate how this came about we must first review the failure of the King's financial policy, and then consider the domestic reactions to his war measures.

The high profits which the King and the monopolists hoped

---

[1] *C.P.R., 1338-40*, p. 112; Tout, *Chapters*, iii. 84. Wodehouse was Treasurer only from March to December 1338, an interval in the tenure of William de la Zouche from 1337 to 1340.   [2] Tout, ibid., p. 90.

to share from the Contract scheme of 1337 were at the expense of the rest of the community, and despite the immediate safeguard of minimum prices this was to store up trouble for the future. But it was the suspicions and bad faith between the King and the Contract Merchants which were most immediately in evidence as a result of the seizure at Dordrecht. The merchants who had advanced loans for their privileges were promised payment of their debentures from their own customs after the following August, only to be disappointed when the resumption of free trade was postponed for further monopoly schemes. In the parliament of February 1338 Edward negotiated the pre-emption of half the wool of the kingdom on condition that his subjects should be free to dispose of the remaining half. Payment for this was promised within two years. But unable to wait for the collection of this wool and unable to persuade the English merchants to enter any fresh agreement, the King offered it as security for a large advance from the Bardi and Peruzzi (to whom he was already heavily in debt), granting them a monopoly of exports until 1 August 1338. The attempt to collect the King's half of the wool met widespread obstruction and evasion, and on his arrival at Antwerp in July 1338 Edward found that only 1,584 sacks had preceded him overseas, while further advances from the Bardi had been suspended. The grant of wool in February had thus proved 'a lamentable failure', and Edward was forced to delay payment of further subsidies to his allies and thus effectively to postpone the campaign.[1]

The King now changed tack and adopted measures to facilitate the collection and export of wool from England while endeavouring to retain some benefit from his power to confer monopolies. Large reserves had accumulated during the lengthy suspension of exports, and the higher rate of subsidy (40s. for denizens and 63s. 4d. for aliens) that had been agreed with the merchants in the spring promised to yield substantial revenue. A scheme to collect the remainder of the King's wool on the basis of the assessment for the fifteenth was adopted in a merchant assembly in July at Northampton and the monopoly

---

[1] Unwin, op. cit., p. 197; Fryde, 'Financial Resources of Edward III', pp. 1148–50. Edward himself declared that he found 'scarcely 2,500 sacks' on his arrival and only slightly more than this had been successfully collected.

was enlarged by the issue of export licences to English and
foreign merchants and even to the King's own captains in
Flanders. For their benefit the general embargo on exports was
extended until March 1339 to the further detriment of the
holders of Dordrecht bonds. The most important of these new
monopolists was William de la Pole, who became mayor of
the newly established Staple at Antwerp and the lessee of
numerous Crown lands.[1] Others who had a share were John
Pulteney, Paul de Monteflorum, and William of Dunaforte.
These measures started to take effect in the autumn of 1338 and
during the following year produced a glut of wool which depressed prices in the Antwerp market and disappointed the
expectations of the King and his creditors.[2] Moreover, although
the council in England made efforts to collect the King's wool
by appointing special surveyors in the shires and ports, and did
succeed in shipping a large consignment from Harwich in
the early spring, this was wholly insufficient to meet the King's
pledges to his creditors old and new, and left nothing over for
his own use.[3] By May 1339 Edward was complaining that the
council was neglecting to satisfy the merchants and failing to
supervise the collectors, and that his financiers were threatening
to cut off their advances unless they received wool of the quantity and quality stipulated. The council, in reply, rebutted
these charges, placing the blame on the dishonesty of collectors and customers, and complained of its inability to control
officials who secured royal licences exempting them from the
council's jurisdiction.[4] This renewed failure to secure profits
from wool, while it poisoned Edward's relations with the home
council, drove him into further debts to the merchants, notably
de la Pole.[5] With his own troops deserting for lack of pay and

[1] Unwin, op. cit., pp. 198–200; Fryde, 'Financial Resources of Edward III',
pp. 1150–1. The King's indenture with Pole is in P.R.O., Parlt. and Council
Proceedings, C 49/7 no. 8.

[2] Over 40,000 sacks was shipped from England between the autumn of 1338
and the early months of 1340. The price fell to £6 per sack. Fryde, 'Financial
Resources of Edward III', pp. 1150–1, and *Wool Accounts*, p. 12.

[3] Hughes, op. cit., pp. 39 ff. and Appendix II; J. F. Baldwin, *The King's Council
in England*, p. 479 and n. 6. Fryde, 'Financial Resources of Edward III', pp.
1160–2, 1168, notes that Edward was actually *buying* wool abroad with heavy
losses in the winter of 1338–9.

[4] P.R.O. C 49/7 nos. 7 and 10. Between them Hughes and Baldwin have
printed the greater part of these documents.

[5] Edward had already borrowed £82,400 from the Bardi and Peruzzi prior to

the whole structure of his alliances endangered by the arrears of subsidies, Edward was forced to abandon all hope of a spring campaign and see his whole project 'on the point of perishing'.[1] When in the late autumn of 1339 he and his allies were finally ready to move, there was insufficient time to force the French to an engagement, and two years of diplomatic, military, and financial effort on an unprecedented scale ended in fiasco.

The wool schemes had yielded little but a harvest of hatred and recrimination. Edward deeply resented the humiliation of his indebtedness to his financiers, the advantages they had gained, and the duplicity with which, he was convinced, they had acted.[2] He was at loggerheads with his home council, suspecting them of half-heartedness for the Flemish campaign and jealousy of his military advisers. The monopolists, for their part, complained of the non-fulfilment of their agreements and were deeply uneasy about the extent of their loans and the depressed state of the wool market. They in turn were highly unpopular with those merchants whose Dordrecht bonds had been repeatedly deferred, and with both merchants and growers who desired the free disposal of their wool. Finally, the high export tax on wool left no margin for profit to the exporters who, in their inability to pass it on to the consumers, were forced back on paying lower prices to the producers. King, financiers, wool merchants, growers, and the council shared the conviction that the exploitation of the wool trade had been badly mishandled, though each placed the blame differently. When Edward turned to parliament in October 1339 for a further grant to extricate himself from his financial commitments a post-mortem of some kind on the fiscal expedients of the previous two years became inevitable for two reasons. First, the King's debts could only be discharged by further taxation of the wool trade; second,

---

December 1337 and they advanced another £71,522 to him in the Netherlands, mostly between July and Michaelmas 1338. After that his borrowing from them fell off steeply and it was William de la Pole who raised at least £111,000 for the King between June 1338 and October 1339, mostly from others. See Fryde, 'Financial Resources of Edward III', pp. 1146, 1153, 1158, and 'The Last Trials of Sir William de la Pole', *Econ. Hist. Rev.* xv (1962), p. 17.

[1] Fryde, 'Financial Resources of Edward III', pp. 1158, 1167, quoting P.R.O. C 49/7 no. 7.

[2] For Edward's persecution of Pole, see Fryde, 'The Last Trials of Sir William de la Pole'.

the grievances and resentments engendered by Edward's dealing with the merchants were aggravated by widespread re-action against war burdens and by the jealousies and differences between the home and war councils.

Hostility in England to the King's financial exactions and methods of government paralleled the collapse of his military and financial schemes abroad. Before he left the King had set up, by the Ordinance at Walton, an elaborate machinery for ensuring that his control was maintained from Brabant. The Exchequer was to make no disbursement, except for ordin-ary fees, without a warrant of privy seal, in which the reason for the payment was to be clearly stated, while rolls and counter-rolls of the warrants were to enable an audit to be taken at the year's end, in the Exchequer. As Tout pointed out, this machinery provided a means of deploying all the financial resources of the realm in the cause of the war.[1] The only ex-ception was the provision made for the defence of the northern border, where following the precedent of 1332–3 and 1337,[2] the earl of Arundel was given a similar control over the subsidy for the northern shires, independent of the Exchequer. In taking these special measures to ensure that the appropriation of the subsidy to the war was given effect, the King acted on his own authority and in his own interests. It was in the same spirit that Edward pledged the second and third years of the subsidy to the great financiers with whom he contracted loans, first the Bardi and Peruzzi and later William de la Pole. Edward thereby secured ready money to meet his commit-ments, and transferred to them the delays and difficulties of its collection, though he forfeited some of the yield by way of interest. Both the Walton Ordinances and these loans were a means of ensuring the King's personal control of revenue, of appropriating it for his own expenditure on war. In fact, this policy had two defects: first, there was confusion and vacillation between pledging revenue for loans and appropriating it under

---

[1] Tout, *Chapters*, iii. 69–79, with the text on pp. 144–50.

[2] On 27 January 1333 the abbot of St. Mary's York has been appointed receiver of the tenth and fifteenth of 1332 in the eight northern shires (*C.P.R., 1330–4*, p. 395). Edward had first established a separate command for the North with the early of Warwick's appointment in 1337. See N. B. Lewis, 'The Recruitment and Organisation of a Contract Army, May to November 1337', *Bull. Inst. Hist. Res.* xxxvii (1964), p. 4.

royal warrant; second, the King's interests conflicted with those of his subjects.

In the months before he sailed, Edward issued writs to the collectors to bring the tax to appointed centres 'for his urgent business', and maintained a careful check on what had been assigned and collected.[1] Most of the first year of the tax was indeed received in cash, and in the five months after the King's departure in July 1338, the Exchequer sent some £28,000 overseas.[2] Already at the beginning of 1338 some of Edward's creditors had received small assignments on the tax, and in April of that year the Bardi and Peruzzi received assignments on the second year for loans totalling £30,000. Further assignments in respect of loans were made by the King to Pulteney, the Bardi, and Pole.[3] These assignments exceeded what could be collected. Soon after his arrival in Brabant Edward was complaining that the Exchequer was failing to collect the tax, and particularly after December 1338 when Zouche replaced Wodehouse as Treasurer, the sums sent over from England fell rapidly.[4] By May 1339, moreover, the Bardi were experiencing difficulty in collecting their own assignments on the second year, and writs were sent to the collectors urging them to collect the arrears and deliver them to the Bardi so that the King should keep his promises.[5] Edward accused the council in England of making unauthorized assignments to other creditors to the detriment of the Bardi and others, and despite the council's explicit denial of this there may have been some truth in the charge.[6]

[1] *C.C.R., 1337–9*, pp. 213, 329, 372, 392. Assignments on the first year of the tax were made in December 1337 for the Wardrode and Great Wardrobe (ibid., pp. 214, 218, 221) and some of it was also pledged to John de Pulteney and to the Bardi for loans (ibid., pp. 232, 294, 309).

[2] Tout, *Chapters*, iii. 91.

[3] Ibid.; *C.C.R., 1337–9*, pp. 349, 400, 464, 467; Fryde, 'Financial Resources', p. 1143 n. 4. £6,000 from the third year of the tax was also assigned to York merchants (*C.C.R., 1337–9*, p. 365). The King's warrants ordered the Exchequer to assign the tax to the Bardi in July 1338 'in the counties which they will choose' (P.R.O. E 404/24, 21 July 12 Edw. III).

[4] Tout, *Chapters*, iii. 91. In a letter of 19 August 1338 Edward complained that the Exchequer had sent neither the balance of the wool (17,500 sacks) nor the money due from the tenth and fifteenth (E 404/25).

[5] *C.C.R., 1337–9*, pp. 175, 179.

[6] *Foedera*, II. ii. 1080. P.R.O. C. 49/7 n. 7 contains an item which refers to this retrospectively: 'Item, ils deivent dire coment ils font assignementz en Engleterre as diverses gentz sur les custumes et aillours a grandes sommes la ou autres sont

Edward was being driven to extreme measures to meet his commitments. Already in September 1338 he had ordered the Exchequer to suspend payment of the fees of ministers in the interests of the war, and in May 1339 he placed a stop on the Exchequer and revoked all assignments made before or after his passage overseas except those for the Bardi and the Scottish March.[1] So drastic a step, however necessary to safeguard his credit with the monopolists, could only aggravate the growing resistance to the King's policy at home. It was strenuously opposed and only reluctantly enforced by the council, who feared its repercussions on other Exchequer creditors and were doubtful of its practical benefit.[2] With the assent of the Bardi this was later mitigated in favour of some other creditors, notably Pole; and in September 1339 when Pole had emerged as the King's principal factor he was himself empowered to supervise all the issues of the realm, including the subsidy, and apply them to discharge the loans contracted by the King.[3] By using the whole mechanism of public finance in the exclusive interests of his monopolists, the King was provoking a public reaction. These financiers were widely suspected of mismanagement and embezzlement of the revenues, and were hated as the instruments of Edward's unpopular monopoly in wool. Further, the King was overriding the legitimate rights of his subjects, and this brought him into conflict with the council in England.

Personal jealousies and political rivalries of long standing

---

serviz et le (   ) riens, quele chose le Roi non tendist pas que se deust faire a son departir mais fust mis en certain espoir destre bien servi des issues de son roialme des laynes dismes et quinzismes et autres eides q lui estoient grantez. Le Respons. Nul assignement ne se fist pardecea sur les custumes dismes et quinzismes ne issues de la terre sinon par mandement nostre Seignour le Roi de la outre.'

[1] *C.C.R., 1339–41*, p. 155. *C.P.R. 1338–40*, p. 385. A similar suspension of the salaries of officials by Philip VI in 1345 likewise had to be speedily rescinded: see Henneman, *Royal Taxation in Fourteenth Century France*, p. 189.

[2] P.R.O. C 49/7 no. 7, printed by Hughes; op. cit., p. 240; and part of C49/7 no. 10, omitted by Hughes: 'Quant a ceste article est respondu que le repel est fait mes di cest repel nostre Seignour le Roi e poet estre petitement aide quant a ore, car les feodz ne deivent mye estre paiez avant la Seint Mich. et les assignemens que furent faitz des dismes et quinzismes a termes passes sont ia servis et les paiementz des assignementz de meismes les dismes et quinzismes del temps avenir ne se ferront mye avant la feste de Seint Andreu a plu tost et ce de premier paiement.'

[3] *C.P.R., 1338–40*, p. 394.

underlay this famous dispute, the repercussions of which lasted well into 1341; but the exchanges between the King and the council in the summer of 1339 centred on the reasonableness and legitimacy of the King's monopoly of revenue for the war. In one of these the council pointed out that it had to meet not only the domestic charges, but the cost of the fleets, of garrisons, of victuals, and of armies in Scotland and Gascony. In these matters it bore responsibility for the preservation of the kingdom, and this the King should consider when he complained that he was not receiving the profits of the realm.[1] Even had it so desired, the council could not have channelled all revenues to Brabant irrespective of other creditors, and from the time of Edward's arrival in Antwerp it was slowly driven to resist the King's importunate and increasingly autocratic orders for raising money.

The most provocative of these was the King's attempt to exploit his prerogative rights. The Walton Ordinances had repealed all personal exemptions from taxation, had forbidden the traditional granting of 'estallments' or respites of debts owed to the Crown, and had provided terms for the payment or composition of past debts, while placing a moratorium on all debts which the Crown itself owed. Although such measures were not unprecedented,[2] they touched powerful interests. A protest that estallments were the customary right of subjects

---

[1] P.R.O., Ancient Petitions, S.C. 8/95 no. 4740. This forms part of the same exchanges in C 49/7. 'Et pleise au conseil notre Sr le Roi es parties de dela qi lui sount a entendre qil n'ad riens des issues de sa terre charger les grantz paiementz et assignmentz que sont faitz a les marchantz de Bardes et de Peruch, William de la Pole, a les grauntz et autres qi sont devers notre Sr le Roi pour les gages de eux et de leur gentz, pour les fiez des Contes autrefoitz faitz, a certaine la Reine la Miere, a ma dame la Roine la compaigne, a mons Robert D Artoys, a la Contesse de Ulnesterr et as autres qi prendent lour fie a l'eschequier par graunt des Rois, dont riens ne vient a les mises q il covient mettre pour les gardes des Isles de Wight et de Gereseye, pour la garde de la ville de Suthampton, et des chastelx notre Sr le Roi en Engleterre, pour les gages des mariners des niefs notre Sr le Roi, pour les vitailles et autres curtoseies que hom fait et donne a les gentz des flotes, du North et del Suth, pour les gages a fiez des admirals et de lur gentz. Item pour la terre de Gascoigne pour la garde des villes et chastels en Escoce, pour les gages le Roi d'Escoce, pour les grantz custages et mises q l'en ad fait cavenar, cariage et pakker des leynes notre Sr le Roi, et autres mises er custages que renovelent et encrescent chescun iour, les queux custages et mises il covient prendre des issues de la terre et des aides grauntez a notre Sr le Roi et il apparra bien q il est servi d'une graunde somme des profitz de sa dite terre.'

[2] For orders to enforce the collection of all debts due to the Crown in 1327, see *Memoranda Roll 1326–7*, pp. 252, 266; *Red Book of Exchequer*, ed. H. Hall, iii. 937 f.

was made to the council at Northampton in July 1338 which renegotiated the wool grant of the February parliament. At that parliament Edward had suspended his demand for the debts arising from the chattels of fugitives and felons, but in September he ordered the Exchequer to make return of all debts owing to the Crown, specifically those from the profits of justice, and in October justices were instructed that all fines imposed on the eyre were to be speedily levied.[1] On neither matter did the home council act with much vigour; indeed it was still failing to repeal estallments after repeated royal commands in May 1339 when it was at last compelled to put them into effect.[2] It also offered prolonged resistance to Edward's order to suspend the fees of all ministers of the Crown who had other means of livelihood, from Justices and Barons of the Exchequer downwards. Although first received in September 1338, this order was not put into effect until May 1339, by which time the council had ensured that the fees had been paid up till the following Michaelmas and the threat of a breakdown of the administration had been averted.[3] Finally Edward thought to raise money on his feudal prerogatives. The Exchequer was told to investigate the practicability of levying tallage, the scutage of 1327, and the aids for knighting the King's eldest son and *pur fille marier*. In fact the practical difficulties and the discouraging precedents for these made them of doubtful value except as bargaining counters for a parliamentary subsidy, as the council pointed out.[4] But the project was not at once discarded, and the council's hesitancy must have increased the King's impatience.

The conflict between the King and the home council extended to the collection of revenue. Evasion, bribery, and embezzlement always took a toll of what any medieval King could extract by indirect taxation, and Edward's attempt to enforce collection in his absence formed in some ways the most

---

[1] Hughes, op. cit., pp. 63–4, 241.

[2] See Fryde, 'Parliament and the French War', pp. 261–2.

[3] Hughes, op. cit., p. 241; *C.C.R.*, *1337–9*, p. 467; C 49/7 no. 10.

[4] Hughes, op. cit., pp. 64–6, 74, 240, 245. For the opposition in parliament to the tallage of 1332, see Mitchell, *Taxation in Medieval England*, pp. 392 ff. Edward I's attempts to use tallage and a feudal aid in the last years of his reign had already shown 'that there was little future in prerogative forms of taxation' (M. C. Prestwich, *War, Politics and Finance under Edward I*, p. 222).

radical proposal in the Walton Ordinances. The local financial officials of the Crown—sheriffs, tax assessors, collectors and controllers of the customs—were to be elected by their communities who were to be answerable for them at their peril. This attempt to enforce liability on the communities proved highly unpopular. Edward's embargo on wool exports and his monopoly schemes were already alienating the wool merchants who principally served as collectors and controllers of customs, and when the writs ordering elections went out somewhat tardily in September 1338 they met with widespread obstruction, and in some instances Edward was forced to retract the order.[1] The home council complained with some justice that the removal of these officials from its control increased evasion and embezzlement, and before the end of 1339 the order had become a dead letter.[2]

It was in this context that personal rivalries found political expression. The King's principal advisers in Brabant, comprising the earls of Salisbury and Northampton and a group of bannerets and knights, were, like him, anxious solely for the successful prosecution of the war and impatient with the political difficulties of the English council. In administrative matters the King relied on his Keeper of the Privy Seal, William Kilsby, the author of the Walton Ordinances, and on Henry Burghersh, the able bishop of Lincoln. Distrust of Edward's councillors was initially located less amongst the home council in England than among the Stratfords: the archbishop, who had ceased to be Chancellor in 1337, and his brother Robert, bishop of Chichester, who as his successor had surrendered the seal to Bentworth with the publication of the Walton Ordinances.[3] It was not for this reason alone that Edward suspected the Stratfords of coolness towards the war policy. Though, as Edward later claimed, the archbishop had probably supported the initial decision to go to war, throughout

[1] Hughes, op. cit., pp. 68, 244; Tout, *Chapters*, iii. 94–6; R. L. Baker, *The English Customs Service, 1307–1343: a Study of Medieval Administration* (American Philosophical Society; Philadelphia, 1961), pp. 39–40.

[2] C 49/7 no. 10 article 3. Dr. Baker's contention that 'Edward III's inability to make the customs service honest rendered his situation hopeless from the very outset' supports the council's case for laying the blame for the shortage of money on the local officials, though it appears to neglect the more substantial fact that Edward's plans foundered on deeper political conflicts.

[3] Tout, *Chapters*, iii. 87–91.

1338 and 1339 he was under considerable pressure from both Pope and legates to prevent hostilities.[1] Moreover, the royal exactions of 1338-9 had further alienated him from the court, for in many places purveyors had entered Church lands and taxers had demanded contributions of the clergy's wool. In March 1339 Stratford wrote to the bishop of Bath and Wells bidding him defend the liberties of the Church, and two months later to the bishop of London in the same terms.[2]

By the summer of 1339, then, there was a deepening cleavage between the King and his council in England, and considerable discontent in the realm. A series of devices to exploit the wool customs had failed to provide Edward with an adequate revenue and had thrown him increasingly into the hands of monopolists, distrusted alike by the King and the council and hated by the lesser merchants who found themselves excluded by the King's policies from the profits of the wool trade. Edward had refused the home council responsibility for the government of the realm, limiting its discretion in finance and its authority over royal officials, and enforcing against its advice unpopular measures for raising money and restraining expenditure. For the needs of war he had threatened what ministers, the landed classes, and the men of the shires took to be their customary rights.

Finally, the shires had been burdened with purveyance and arrays on a scale comparable with 1296-7. The burden of these no longer fell mainly on the north but on the southern, eastern, and midland shires. Preparatory to the King's departure, commissions were issued in April-May 1338 in East Anglia, the south, and the east Midlands for the purveyance of large quantities of food. Arms and equipment were included in some commissions.[3] Although the terms of these commissions were circumspect, the illegalities which accompanied their execution inevitably roused complaint, and in July 1338 the

---

[1] Hughes, op. cit., pp. 108-10; *Cal. Papal Letters*, ii. 564, 570; Deprez, op. cit., pp. 200, 206-9.

[2] Hughes, op. cit., pp. 110-15.

[3] H. J. Hewitt, *The Organization of War under Edward III* (Manchester, 1966), pp. 68, 84 (citing *Foedera*, II. ii. 1021). Supplies were also purveyed for Gascony in this year (ibid., p. 62). P.R.O. C 47/2/31 no. 1 contains schedules for the extensive purveyances in the counties of southern England to supply the two fleets guarding the coasts in 1338. The overseer of these purveyances was William Dunstable.

King ordered detailed investigation of these.[1] Some counties paid large communal fines to be quit of purveyances and the parliament of February 1339 saw a chorus of protest.[2] The first of a sequence of articles presented by the Commons asked that the statutes relating to purveyors should be kept. The fifth article, after recalling the principal guarantees (that no goods should be taken without the assent of the owner or without payment), complained that purveyors holding commissions from the King had taken goods and money without payment and had assessed and levied from the people sums of money at will. It asked that such commissions should be repealed 'so that no free man should be assessed or taxed without common assent of parliament'. The echo of *Confirmatio Cartarum* is significant; in 1339 the Commons were quite clear that for levies which taxed the populace assent in parliament should be sought.

Edward recruited the army which he took to Brabant in July 1338 mainly by contract although in the southern shires some archers and foot-soldiers were arrayed to accompany him. The main purpose of the arrays, however, was to safeguard the coasts.[3] The fear of invasion from both north and south, which had haunted England since 1295, had been revived in an acute form. The absence of the King was itself an incitement to the enemies of the realm to attack. This had been urged, and had proved to be the case, in 1297; it had been widely feared even in 1335 when Edward III had wintered in Scotland; but his absence was now to be far longer, at a time when French naval

[1] Hewitt, op. cit., p. 59 (citing P.R.O. E 101/21/39); Hughes, op. cit., p. 96 (citing P.R.O. CW 247 no. 11274).

[2] *Rot Parl. Hact. Ined.*, pp. 267–72. Hughes, op. cit., pp. 194, 204–9. E. B. Fryde ('Parliament and the French War') would assign these petitions to the parliament of March 1337 but I am inclined to follow D. Rayner and the editors of *Rot. Parl. Hact. Ined.* in ascribing them to February 1339 both for the reasons they adduce and because the petitions on purveyances and military levies fit better the context of the latter year. Thus Knighton (*Chronicon*, ii. 3) leaves no doubt that the purveyances of 1338 aroused a storm of protest: 'Ex qua re ortus est ingens clamor in populo, et majus malum exinde provenisset si sanius consilium rex non accepisset.' Fryde shows (ibid., p. 263) how during the session of this parliament a commission was issued to inquire into the activities of William Dunstable whose purveyances in Yorkshire had produced a clamorous protest, and further inquiries into purveyances in Oxfordshire and Berkshire were made in the summer of 1339 (Hughes, op. cit., p. 96).

[3] P.R.O. C 47/2/31 no. 5 is a memorandum to array 2,000 men-at-arms and 4,000 archers from south of Trent and a further 4,000 men from Wales to assemble at Portsmouth at Whitsun.

forces were active in the channel and there was intelligence of French plans to invade.[1] Measures to alert defence along the southern coast had begun in September 1337; in the summer of 1338 arrays for the defence of the coasts were issued for all the southern shires, and the *Garde de la Mer* in the coastal strip was put into operation to cope with the French raids on ports from Harwich to Plymouth.[2] Although the only substantial damage inflicted was in Southampton, the French seem to have made at least contingency plans for an invasion in the Spring of 1339.[3] Parliament was summoned for February 1339 to provide against the double danger of invasion by the French and the Scots. Following the precedent of March 1337, Lords and Commons authorized the levy of quotas of men-at-arms and archers in each county and named arrayers. One of the Commons' petitions, probably presented in this parliament, had complained of the burden to local communities of finding wages and armour for troops in the recent arrays 'since the land was much grieved and charged by many taxes and other burdens'. This may have resulted in the provision that the cost of the troops was to fall not on the poor of the community but on the 'rich and powerful', which in subsequent instructions was interpreted as referring to any with more than 100 shillings of income or 10 marks in chattels.[4] Before the next parliament met in October this scheme had been called into operation for defence of the north, the writs of array again emphasizing that the charge should fall on the wealthier in the shire to spare 'the lesser people who are in many ways burdened by unbearable charges and the unjust exactions of ministers'.[5] That the council was ready to heed the concern of the Commons over the heavy burdens of war was of some importance in these crucial months.

[1] Nicholson, op. cit., p. 105; H. J. Hewitt, *The Organisation of War under Edward III*, p. 4; *Foedera*, II, ii. 1070.

[2] Hewitt, op. cit., pp. 5–6, 9, 49; *C.P.R., 1338–40*, pp. 134–9; Rymer, *Foedera*, II. ii. 1018. In Northamptonshire 5,200 foot were arrayed for the guard of the Lincolnshire coast (C 47/2/31 no. 9; Nicholson, op. cit., p. 2 n. 2.)

[3] The effect of the French raids on opinion in England may be seen in Knighton, *Chronicle*, ii. 3, 8–9 and *The Poems of Laurence Minot*, ed J. Hall (Oxford, 1897), pp. 8–10. The French invasion plan, reported to the parliament of 1346, is detailed in the *Black Book of the Admiralty*, ed. T. Twiss, i (London, 1871), pp. 426–7.

[4] *Rot. Parl. Hact. Ined.*, p. 269; *Foedera*, II. ii. 1070; Hewitt, op. cit., p. 12. Reductions were made in the numbers ordered to be arrayed in the commissions for Buckinghamshire and Bedfordshire in March 1339 (*C.C.R., 1339–41*, p. 55).

[5] *Rot Scot.* i. 573.

The council, as we have seen, was highly conscious of its
responsibilities for the defence of the realm, of the discontent
among all sections of the community, and of the King's increasing anger and suspicions at its inability to meet his
demands. In seeking the co-operation of the Commons for
plans of defence—by submitting the array to parliamentary
assent—it was gaining political support in the one matter
where the interests of all those dwelling within the realm tended
to be ranged against the party which had accompanied the
King on his foreign venture. For the Commons, in particular,
the protection of the realm for which they had explicitly granted
taxation was of more immediate concern than the success of
the expedition in Flanders. When Edward decided to approach
parliament for a further subsidy in October 1339 he therefore
faced not merely a Commons aggrieved by prises, taxes,
monopolist schemes, and prerogative actions, and a council
jealous, resentful, and on the point of revolt, but a tacit political
alliance based on the defence and welfare of the realm rather
than the prosecution of the French war.

The background to this political opposition was an un-
nerving deflationary situation in which three years of good
harvests, from 1336 to 1338, had produced an abundance of
goods, but shortage of cash and low prices had kept trade stag-
nant. The winter of 1338–9 was hard, but prices had still not
risen and the depressed economy gave rise to uncertainty and
forebodings.[1] The picture that can be constructed from the
chronicles and estate accounts is corroborated by verses datable
to 1338–9 which are exceptional in medieval literature in
having as their theme the effect on the realm of burdensome
taxation.[2] The poem is no mere lament or tirade; it is a coherent
indictment of the level of taxation as unnecessary and harmful
to the common good, and comprises the conventional points
of a charge of fundamental misgovernment. Both in language
and argument it strikingly anticipates the petitions of the
Commons in the Parliament of 1340 and serves to confirm that
these were representative of the opinions of the politically

[1] For an analysis of economic conditions in 1338–40, see Fryde, 'Parliament
and the French War', pp. 264–5; I. Kershaw, 'The Agrarian Crisis in England, 1315–22', *Past and Present*, 59 (1973), p. 47; E. Ames, 'The Sterling Crisis of
1337–9', *Journal of Economic History*, 25 (1965), pp. 496–522, discusses the effect of
war and embargo on the money supply.

articulate classes in the realm.[1] Most immediately noticeable is the wholesale swing of opinion against the King's expedition that had taken place since 1337 or even the parliament of February 1338. In the first verse the author blames those who caused the King to cross the seas and follows this with enunciating in the spirit of the Ordinances that 'a king ought not to go forth from his kingdom in manner of war unless the commune of his realm consent to it'. If this suggests that Edward's expedition was unjustified, no true necessity of the realm, the main burden of his attack is against the level of taxation as being fundamentally wrong, in that it impoverishes subjects especially the poor. The fifteenth runs in England year after year; the grant to the King of subjects' wool 'is not just law'; such demands which cause men to sell their possessions are not pleasing to God, for 'he who takes money from the needy without just cause commits sin'. Evidently the author is aware of the moral and theological limitations on taxation and appeals to them to establish a charge of misgovernment. He substantiates this by pointing to the likelihood of a peasant rising, traditional evidence of notorious oppression; then mitigates it by the equally traditional indictment of the King's evil counsellors and exculpation of the King himself.[2] More specifically in the context of 1338–40, he castigates the wool collectors who themselves get the wool in the King's despite, for 'not half the tribute raised in the land reaches the King; he does not receive the tax in its entirety just as it is granted to him', a complaint which the Commons directly echoed in 1340. Finally the author reproaches the great who make these grants to the King, for they are not burdened; he pleads for a more equitable distribution of taxation, to be levied on the mighty and to spare the lowly, in terms which recall the array authorized by the February parliament. If the author's discontent had a radical tinge, it was of the kind nurtured by theological notions of social justice on which popular protests against misgovernment fed. The poem thus reflects the mood of the lesser landowning classes in England. Disenchantment with the King's war and

[1] *Anglo-Norman Political Songs*, ed. I. Aspin (Anglo-Norman Text Soc., 1953), pp. 105-15. Cf. Fryde, loc. cit.

[2] For the persistence of these concepts into Tudor times, see M. E. James, 'Obedience and Dissent in Henrician England: the Lincolnshire Rebellion of 1536', *Past and Present*, 48 (1970).

with magnate leadership, resentment which might issue in resistance to the excessive burdens and autocratic tone of royal demands, bewilderment at the evidence of economic recession, fear of a peasant revolt, and bitter hatred of the financiers who were suspected of defrauding the King and diverting the taxes to their own enrichment: such, we can say with fair certainty, were the thoughts of those who assembled at Westminster in October 1339.

CHAPTER XI

The Second Crisis over Taxation:
II The Parliamentary Crisis, 1339–1340

I N Flanders the King's campaign was at last in prospect. On 19 August 1339 he had indented with the marquis of Jülich as principal counsellor, guaranteeing his losses,[1] and to pay his allies before they would move he had to borrow at least a further £60,000. Little or no revenue reached Edward from England in these months and the terms on which the King contracted these loans were ruinous indeed.[2] In his obstinate pursuit of military victory Edward now showed something like the recklessness of his grandfather. At the end of ten years' campaigning in Scotland Edward I had accumulated debts of some £200,000. When Edward III sent Stratford to tell the parliament of October 1339 that he needed £300,000 to release him from his debts, he was not exaggerating. Whatever inkling the Commons may have had of the King's predicament the writs of summons did nothing to prepare them to face the disastrous consequences of the King's policies. As in the previous February they were called to discuss the maintenance of internal peace and the defence of the north and the coasts.[3]

This conciliatory and oblique approach to parliament was deliberate. The writs of summons had been issued on 25 August 1339 soon after Edward's alliance with the marquis of Jülich. It was a step recommended by the home council as the best solution to the mounting financial difficulties although, aware after the February parliament of the volume of grievances, they had recommended that a bishop or some other councillor with the King should return to expound the King's needs.[4] Edward

---

[1] The document and an additional agreement of 21 August are printed by F. Bock, *Das Deutsche–Englische Bundnis von 1335–1342* (Munich, 1956), pp. 137–43. Tout (*Chapters*, iii. p. 99) gives the date wrongly as 19 May.

[2] Fryde, 'Financial Resources of Edward III', pp. 1167–75.

[3] *Rot. Parl.* ii. 104.

[4] Hughes, *A Study of Social and Constitutional Tendencies in the Early Years of Edward III*, p. 245.

chose a powerful embassy, consisting of Archbishop Stratford, Bishop Richard de Bury, and William de la Pole, and empowered them to make certain concessions to meet the anticipated demands of the Commons. Further, Edward made Stratford the effective head of the council in England, and associated this move with the repeal of the more obnoxious (and largely ineffective) measures of the summer which had emphasized the subordinate role of the home council.[1] A writ of 5 September once again permitted the council to grant estallments of debts to the Crown, to pay the fees of officials, and to warrant issues from the Exchequer, and empowered the Chancellor and Treasurer to supervise and, if necessary, remove royal officials.[2] These measures signified the abandonment of the policy of the Walton Ordinances. By giving Stratford real authority in England Edward was hoping, in effect, to commit him to the war policy and to ensure supplies for the French campaign. It was a shrewd move aimed at countering papal pressure on Stratford to use his influence for mediation, and at the domestic opposition, in whose eyes the archbishop was the traditional defender both of popular liberties and of the interests of the realm (and home council) against the *curiales*. Edward expected to buy Stratford with the grant of office, and to buy out the opposition with limited reforms under the aegis of Stratford's authority. He was prepared for a measured surrender in the expectation of definite gains.

In the first session of parliament Edward came very near to achieving his ends. Although the causes of summons had laid emphasis on domestic order and defence, Stratford's opening speech comprised a long account of the King's fortunes in Flanders, explaining why the campaign had been delayed so long, stressing the damage to the King's plans from the lack of supplies, and concluding that to get the campaign under way the King needed the sum of £300,000 or more. Since the King was unable to leave Flanders without offering some guarantee

---

[1] On 26 September, in the first week of the campaign, Edward named Stratford as principal counsellor to the duke of Cornwall. (*C.P.R., 1338-40*, p. 394) and see the royal letter given in *Chronica Adae Murimuth et Roberti de Avesbury*, ed. E. M. Thompson (R.S., 1889) p. 304. At the same time William de la Pole was made secondary baron of the Exchequer with the responsibility for repaying from the forthcoming subsidies all who had advanced money for the campaign (ibid.).

[2] P.R.O. K.R. Mem. Roll, E 159/116 m. 12.

to his creditors, the archbishop asked the Commons 'for the maintenance of the King and of his claim which he has undertaken by common assent of you all', to aid him and save his honour with a very great sum. Lords and Commons thereupon agreed that the King 'must be aided with a very great sum in this necessity or otherwise he will be shamed and dishonoured and he and his people destroyed for all time'.[1] This formal acceptance of the King's plea of necessity seems to have been a corporate act of the whole parliament, which was thereby obliged to grant an aid of some kind. Thus far the King's expectations had been fulfilled.

From this point the parliamentary crisis developed in two stages. In their response to how the King's needs should be furnished, Lords and Commons acted largely independently; in forcing reforms on the King they acted together. Lords and Commons certainly separated for their initial deliberations. The Lords' meeting was, in fact, a session of the council, and the parliament roll preserves the list of those who attended: thirty prelates, earls, and barons with all the justices and some others. They deliberated on 'how the king could best be aided with least charge and grievance to his people and greatest profit to himself'. Their solution was a tithe for two years on corn, wool, and lambs to which every man, of whatever state or condition, should be liable.[2] It is clear that the council was, in fact, proposing a form of tax for the Commons to adopt on behalf of the realm; for their choice had been influenced by the great shortage of coin in the realm and they themselves now made such a grant for their demesne lands. It was now time for the Commons to return their answer, which they did in a schedule addressed to the Lords. This began by acknowledging 'the great necessity of the king for an aid from his people' and avowed their will to give this as they had on previous occasions. But because the aid demanded was so great they did not dare assent to it without the counsel and advice of the commons of their countries. They therefore asked for an adjournment of parliament so that in the meantime they could make every effort in their localities to secure a good and suitable aid for the King.[3]

---

[1] *Rot. Parl.* ii. 103.   [2] *Rot. Parl.* ii. 103–4.   [3] Ibid., p. 104.

This is the earliest evidence we have of the procedure for making a grant and it illuminates the attitudes of mind of the Lords and Commons. The recital of the necessity of the King and the realm and the common assent then given to this was clearly a distinct and important stage, even though refusal was barely possible. The Lords, well informed about what the King required, deliberated over different forms of taxation and decided upon one which would best suit the King and the realm, although—representing no one but themselves—they could grant this only for their own estates. Doubtless this was communicated to the Commons whose own deliberations must have centred on how much they could grant without provoking reproaches and opposition in their localities. Although they could not refuse some aid, they were not to be intimidated or led by the Lords. Racked between the King's demands and the upsurge of local grievances, and aware of real impoverishment in the countryside, they temporized. Their request to refer back was unprecedented, but it demonstrated the power of local communities over their representatives.

In the shires one may assume that the King's demands would be weighed against local grievances, but in this session there had been no attempt to make redress of grievances the condition of a grant. Here again, though, Lords and Commons acted independently. The Lords, having made their grant of a tithe from their demesnes, followed this by expressing the wish that certain grievances should be remedied. They sought guarantees, under authority of parliament, that the *maltolt* recently imposed should cease and that neither the present nor any former grant should be used as a precedent. Their other demands concerned feudal incidents.[1] The Commons put in a slightly longer bill of 'graces' of their own. They complained of the *maltolt*—'increased without the assent of the Commons or the Lords'—and asked for release from a variety of fiscal burdens commonly covered by commissions of trailbaston (the murder fine, fines for escapes, the chattels of fugitives and felons, trespasses of the Forest), and for pardon of the two feudal aids, and of ancient debts before 1327; finally they demanded that purveyors who took without payment should be arrested as felons.[2] This both expressed the resentment at Edward's

[1] *Rot, Parl*, ii. p. 104.   [2] Ibid., pp. 105–6.

attempt to exploit feudal and prerogative revenues and asserted the growing tradition that all forms of financial levy beyond the strictly customary rights of the Crown should have common assent. The King was, indeed, prepared to concede many of these points. Earlier in the year the council itself had urged on the King the fruitlessness of these fiscal expedients except as bargaining counters for a parliamentary subsidy, and Stratford had returned with authority to remit debts under £10 and compound for larger sums owed, to offer a general pardon to communities for chattels of felons and fugitives and for escapes, and to release the scutage and aids.[1] This was expected to be sufficient to secure the grant of a subsidy. These concessions were eventually embodied in the first statute of 1340 which, broadly speaking, redressed those infringements of the rights of the subject which had attended the war administration since 1337.[2] Notorious purveyors were imprisoned and inquiries promised into their misdeeds. The only point in the Lords' and Commons' demands which was not substantially covered by Stratford's concessions was the *maltolt*, and this was subsequently to be granted as part of the final settlement. The fact that Stratford informed parliament of these concessions in order to secure a grant gave tacit recognition to the connection between redress of grievance and supply. This was particularly significant in view of the independent action of the Commons in deliberating, answering, and petitioning They had come a step closer to using taxation to apply political pressure, though their petitions, now formally distinguished from those of the Lords, still centred on common burdens.

The independence of the Commons' attitude was further demonstrated when parliament met in January 1340 with the expectation of receiving from them 'a good and agreeable answer concerning their promise at the last parliament to grant a suitable aid'. If the tithe proposed by the Lords was not acceptable, the Commons were told that they should suggest an alternative. The Commons indicated that they wished to discuss this together before making their answer. The parliament roll records this as given only on the last day of parliament, 19

---

[1] *Foedera*, II, ii. 1091.

[2] S.R. i. 281–9. For a summary, see Stubbs, *Const. Hist.* ii. 401–2, and G. L. Harriss, 'The Commons Petitions of 1340', *Eng. Hist. Rev.* lxxxviii (1963), p. 640.

February, although the substance of it must have been known by about the middle of the session. This was to offer (not to grant) the King 'in this necessity' 30,000 sacks of wool 'under certain conditions, comprised in indentures and sealed with the seals of the prelates and other lords; in case the conditions were not fulfilled they would not be bound to grant the aid'. Because these matters touched the estate of the King so closely, on the advice of the home council they were sent to the King and his privy council, together with the views of the home council, to receive his reply.[1] At the same time the Lords repeated their grant of the tithe from their demesne lands. Lords and Commons had thus continued to pursue different courses, the Commons having now attached separate conditions to a separate offer. That these conditions had been sealed by the magnates was probably more for authentication than to record support or even formal approval. What the advice of the home council was we can only guess; but the Lords by renewing their previous grant had tacitly dissociated themselves from the Commons.

The Commons had, indeed, taken a daring and startling step. Their previous promise of aid had now become an offer— on conditions. The nearest precedents were thirty years and more distant, but in 1309, as in 1301, it was not the grant itself but the collection of it which was deferred pending the King's acceptance of the conditions. The distinction is significant, for only the magnates could enforce restraint of the collection of a tax; and the fact that the Commons were attempting to use their own power of granting aids is further evidence that they were acting on their own. The dubious legitimacy of the Commons' action was manifest, for they had already acknowledged their obligation to give aid and had indeed promised to do so in this session; this was at once underlined by the council who, pointing to the pressing dangers of the situation, demanded how the Commons proposed to avoid these dangers and save themselves. After long discussion the Commons did in fact make a grant, of 2,500 sacks of wool 'as immediate security for a loan'. If the King accepted their conditions this was to form part of a larger grant; if not, it would remain

---

[1] *Rot. Parl.* ii. 107.

as a pure gift.[1] Once again it is clear that the Commons were thrashing out their own tactics, against the objections of the council, and with undoubted success; for the council was then forced to close the session and send the petitions of the Commons to the King.

The Commons had thus introduced a new stage between their recognition of the necessity and the grant of a tax. The power to decide how much they would grant was theirs alone, and by linking this power with a demand for the redress of their grievances they were emphasizing that the King's duty to provide redress and reform corresponded to their obligation to render aid. By deferring their formal offer of aid until the final day of parliament they underlined their long-held demand for their petitions to be answered before the close of parliament. The basis for the Commons' initiative in many of these respects had been gradually laid in the preceding thirty years, although they could hardly have exercised their power independently of the Lords before 1332. Undoubtedly they were assisted in 1340 by the exceptional situation of the King's absence and the divisions between home and overseas councils. Yet it would be hard to deny that in the parliament of January 1340 the Commons revealed a readiness to act independently of the Lords, which showed a consciousness of the strength of their support in the shires and a tactical appreciation of the opportunities of parliamentary procedure. In this respect the crisis of 1340 sees the first emergence of the Commons as an independent political force.

This conclusion is reinforced by an examination of the Commons' petitions presented in the session which opened on Wednesday 29 March. On the Saturday following the King sent to the Commons asking for an aid to be granted on the following Monday, 3 April, sufficient to discharge him from the bonds he had given to his Low Country creditors. On that day Lords and Commons joined in the grant of a ninth of corn, wool, and sheep conditional on the acceptance of their petitions. To these the King agreed, remitting them to a committee of

---

[1] Ibid., pp. 107–8. Dr. Fryde has pointed out ('Parliament and the French War', p. 268) that the offer of a tax in wool may have been thoroughly distasteful to Edward by 1340. If so this strengthens the suggestion that the Commons were flying in the face of advice from the council.

all estates empowered to frame statutes on such articles as were of permanent importance, those of more ephemeral concern to be issued as letters patent. These statutes had been drawn up by 16 April when they were rehearsed in letters patent. The rapidity of the settlement can only mean that all parties were prepared for it when parliament met, and since statutes and letters patent were indeed framed in direct response to the Commons' petitions presented in this parliament, it may reasonably be inferred that these petitions, or something very close to them, were what had been sent to the King in February.[1]

The form of these—a series of articles beginning 'prie la dite commune'—had become customary for the 'commune petition' in the preceding decade. Their arrangement shows some clumsiness and repetition and the language is homely and untutored. The statutes which were eventually framed upon the petitions show strikingly greater precision in language and arrangement. Evidently the petitions were not drafted with the assistance oɪ Chancery clerks; but if their tone suggests the authorship of the Commons alone, their content was more than the usual statement of grievances for which redress was sought through royal grace. For the first time the Commons were seeking political remedies for the correction of misgovernment which recalled the periods of magnate influence in 1310–18 or, more recently, in 1327–30. It seems likely that it was these demands which had touched the King's estate so closely that to answer them exceeded his ministers' discretion.

Cap. 1 of the petitions asked for the confirmation of the liberties of the Church and the redress of infringements of them in parliament at the suit of the plaintiff. There would appear to be no precedent for such a remedy, and the association of the Church's grievances with those of a body from which the clerical proctors were withdrawing is significant in its unexpectedness. It suggests a strong sense of common grievance

[1] These were first printed by A. W. Goodman in *Cartulary of Winchester Cathedral* (Winchester, 1927), pp. 131–3, and were translated by B. Wilkinson, *The Constitutional History of Medieval England, 1216–1399*, ii (1952), pp. 194–7. They are printed below, with a slightly revised text, in Appendix A. I have discussed some of the textual problems in 'The Commons' Petitions of 1340', where the argument for the substantial identity of the March petitions with those said to be sent to the King in February is set forth. Fryde, 'Parliament and the French War', p. 268, considers, however, that 'we can learn nothing about the grievances aired on this occasion' (i.e. in the January–February parliament).

between Church and parliament, such as is known to have existed in regard to the activities of royal purveyors. By contrast, the reference to the Charters was minimal, the demand being merely that they should be observed in those points to be redressed in this parliament. The elaborate local inquests secured in the *Articuli* of 1300 were ignored. Parliament was now seen as the proper court for redress of infringements. The solemn confirmations long favoured by the magnate opposition were no longer sought; the 'Age of the Charters' had finally passed.

Caps. 2 and 3 were primarily concerned with royal finance. Cap. 2 echoed popular suspicions that the recent taxes, while impoverishing the community, had largely failed to reach the King. It therefore asked the council to investigate and ensure that accounts for these had been rendered. Merchants, collectors, and ministers of any rank found guilty of mishandling these taxes since 1336 were to be punished. They were to receive no acquittance in the meantime and were to be debarred from office. All this was to be done under the supervision of a committee of magnates, elected by the magnates in parliament. Cap. 3 sought to control the spending of the taxes granted to the King in the future. All revenues—'taxes, customs, marriages, escheats and other profit of the realm'—should be reserved under the authority of a committee of peers ordained in this parliament, to be spent for the King's needs during the war, and not otherwise. This would be of assistance to him and a relief to his people, who could no longer endure such charges. In particular these peers were to have sole responsibility for the tax now to be granted for which they were to be answerable in full parliament. This clause declared that all the great matters of the realm were to be 'ordained, tried, judged and moved' by this magnate council. The election and composition of this council was further elaborated in cap. 5 which asked that those ordained to counsel the King and govern the realm should be magnates and lieges of the realm, that these should be elected from parliament to parliament, and should be ready to answer in full parliament. The petitions went on to envisage a continual council composed of these peers and others whom they would co-opt, who would continually supervise the business of the King and realm.

These chapters formed the kernel of the petitions. They

sought to withdraw from the King the administration of the realm, and notably the disposal of its finances, and place them in the hands of a permanent magnate council which would be answerable to parliament. In this the petitions stood in the direct lineage of the Treaty of Leake, the Ordinances of 1311, and the Provisions of Oxford; but in the context of 1340 this did not amount to so radical a displacement of royal authority. For this was to be a council of absence; and the intention of the petitions was to ensure that this should be invested with real authority for the government of England and the control of the revenues of the realm, so that these could be available to the King. Present circumstances gave point to this traditional remedy, for the policy of the council since the King's departure had been to placate the Commons and co-operate with them in easing the burden of purveyance and providing for the defence of the realm. Now the Commons sought to invest the home council with undisputed authority for the government of England during the King's absence, and to secure from it good and economical government which would spare the community arbitrary levies and unnecessary taxation.

The remainder of cap. 5 and cap. 6 dealt with the means for redressing particular grievances and placing restraints on royal officials and ministers. The remedies requested attuned with the general confidence placed in council and parliament. The council, or a committee of it, was to act as a high court to hear cases which were delayed in lower courts or in which justices were of different opinions, and any cases not disposed of were to be dealt with in the following parliament. It was to have jurisdiction over all ministers, who might be cited to appear at the suit of either the King or subjects, and if convicted were to be punished by judgement of the council of peers. The influence of the Ordinances of 1311 (caps. 29 and 40) is unmistakable here. All ministers and justices were to certify in parliament that they had not been guilty of taking bribes or delaying justice; and to render bribery inexcusable all ministers were to receive sufficient fees from the Crown. Some minor complaints about the administration of the law concluded the petitions.

Most of the measures demanded in the petitions were, in fact, conceded. In response to the second chapter, commissions were appointed in parliament to hear the accounts of those who had collected and received the former taxes.[1] The new tax—a ninth, granted in return for the concessions—was placed under the charge of magnate surveyors and two receivers, for north and south of the Trent. The second statute of 1340, echoing the words of the petitions, explicitly reserved the ninth, and other profits of the realm, for war, and this reservation was recited in the commissions issued to the two receivers.[2] Thus for the moment the King yielded up control of the finances to the council.

This council was set up by two ordinances issued while parliament was in session, appointing Archbishop Stratford and the earl of Huntingdon as chief councillors with the assistance of the earls of Lancaster and Warenne to deal with the great matters of the realm; and by letters patent of 27 May on the eve of the King's departure the councillors were empowered to exercise the feudal prerogatives of the Crown, to appoint and remove ministers, and to do whatever else was necessary for the maintenance and reform of the realm.[3] There is no evidence

---

[1] The Committee headed by Stratford and including two other bishops, five lay magnates, the Treasurer, and Robert Saddington was to hear the accounts of William de la Pole, John Charnels, Paul de Monteflorum, the Bardi, William Melchbourne, and others who had received the King's wools and goods. When Pole appeared before this committee on Wednesday 5 April, he was told that 'the King, the great peers of the land, and others for the Commons wished to be apprised of what had become of the goods he had received for the King on both sides of the sea'. Days were then assigned to him and others to come to account (*Rot. Parl.* ii. 114). Similar commissions to deal with the collectors were issued under the authority of parliament to three groups of magnates on 28 April (*C.P.R.*, *1338–40*, p. 507). Pole was still employed in rendering account on 21 July when he was removed from the office of second baron of the Exchequer (ibid., p. 551).

[2] 'Et qe touz les profitz sourdantz du dite eide, et des gardes, marriages, custumes, eschetes, et autres profitz surdantz du roialme Dengleterre, soient mys et despendus sur la meintenance de la sauve garde de nostre dit roialme Dengleterre, et de noz guerres Descoce, France et Gascoigne, et nulle partz aillours durantz les ditz guerres' (*S.R.* i. p. 290). On 20 April letters patent named collectors and magnate supervisors of the tax in each shire and the receivers were appointed on 12 May (*C.P.R.*, *1338–40*, pp. 499–504; *C.F.R.*, v. 178–9).

[3] *Rot. Parl.* ii. 114, 116; *Foedera*, ii. ii. 1125. The council's power to appoint ministers was also referred to in Statute 14 Edward III, I c. 5. It is not improbable that the councillor's oath ascribed to 15 Edward III printed by Baldwin (*The King's Council*, p. 352) relates to this council of absence. Its most notable feature is the promise 'de faire redrescer totes les choses meprises devers vous par quecunques vos conseilliers, ministres et autres vos subgiz en quecunqe manere qe ce soit auxi bien de temps passe come pur le temps a venir, et de mettre remeide et punissement selonc la qualite de lour mesprision'. This comprises precisely the authority demanded by the Commons' petition and the tenor of the whole oath strongly reflects the position which the council now occupied in Edward's absence.

that this council had been chosen in parliament or was answerable to it, but of its supreme competence in England during the King's absence there can be no doubt.

The remaining demands of the petition were mainly met by clauses in the first and second statutes of 1340. Redress of clerical grievances in parliament was provided by the fourth statute, and cap. 5 of the first statute set up the committee of the council to adjudicate delayed and difficult cases along the lines requested.[1] Caps. 6 and 16 of the first statute provided remedies for some of the judicial grievances. There is no doubt, therefore, that Edward was required to make a substantial delegation of royal authority as the price of receiving the grant of the ninth. This marked a very definite victory for the opposition, a clear demonstration of the power which the capacity to grant taxation gave to parliament when the King was in such desperate straits as was Edward in 1340. But we are still left with the question of the respective roles of Lords and Commons, and a final assessment as to who benefited from the King's concessions.

Some of the reasons for crediting the Commons with the compilation of these petitions have already been given. One further may be added. Cap. 4 of the petitions asked that before the next parliament writs should be issued for an inquiry into all Crown lands given, sold, or alienated since the death of Edward I, so that in the next parliament these might be reviewed and the lands resumed into the King's hands. Thus the King would be able to live without laying charges on his people. Although a resumption of gifts had figured among the demands of the Ordainers and had been strongly urged by Lancaster in the negotiations of 1317–18, it had since then passed from political currency. It had commanded support from the magnate opposition in the period 1310–17 primarily as a means of curbing Edward II's disposal of patronage to their rivals and its appeal as a means of securing relief from taxation had been wholly popular.[2] Its revival in the context of bitter complaint against the burden of taxation strongly suggests a wholly popular origin, particularly since Edward III's distribution of

---

[1] *S.R.* i. 282. The text is also given by J. G. Edwards, 'Justice in Early English Parliaments', *Bull. Inst. Hist. Res.* xxvii (1954), pp. 49–50, who discusses the case of Geoffrey de Staunton which was judged in this parliament (*Rot. Parl.* ii. 122–5).

[2] This is discussed more fully above, ch. vii, pp. 180–1.

patronage had been liberal and eclectic and the magnates stood only to lose from a resumption. Significantly, it was the only major demand in the petitions which received no response, and this suggests that it received no support from Stratford and the home council and was dropped. This strengthens the conviction that the remainder of the petitions expressed the wishes of the Commons, that these were substantially (if tacitly) endorsed by the magnate opposition, and that their support was necessary to secure the concessions from the King. The first two of these points have already been illustrated at some length in considering how the petitions related to the discernible grievances of the Commons and the council in the preceding period. Nor need it be demonstrated how the outcome was to establish Stratford and his associates in a position of commanding authority at home from which only the King's return to England in December shook them. But when was this alliance between the Commons and the home council formed? It became explicit in the third session. The tax granted by the magnates for themselves was withdrawn, and soon after the beginning of parliament the prelates, earls, and barons for themselves and their tenants, the knights of the shires for themselves and the Commons of the realm, and the burgesses granted a ninth on condition that the King accepted the petitions which they put before him and his council. Thereupon a large committee composed of prelates, earls, barons, twelve knights, and six burgesses was appointed in parliament to put the King's concessions into statute.

As we have already noted, the rapidity of the settlement once parliament had met and the extensiveness of the King's concessions indicates that this alliance between the Lords and the Commons must have been already formed when parliament opened in March. Indeed it is likely that it had taken place by the end of the previous session on 19 February two days before Edward's arrival in England. Although the Lords had done no more than attest the Commons' petitions in February, Stratford himself may have tacitly indicated his support for their demands, for it is difficult to believe that the Commons would have transformed their original grievances of October into a demand for a magnate council without assurance of support from above.

The archbishop was clearly the key figure in any attempt to align the opposition of the Commons and the home council, and as its new head he used his enlarged powers to establish confidence in it and win the co-operation of parliament. In two matters of central importance his success was striking. Already in the autumn session decisive action and had been taken against evil purveyors in answer to the Commons' complaints; now in the February session arrangements were made to supply the Scottish garrisons through contracts with individual merchants, thus removing the need for widespread purveyances at all. Moreover, it was explicitly stated that payment for these victuals was to be drawn from the lay subsidy reserved for the northern war.[1] Thus concrete recognition was given to the claim, implicit in *Confirmatio Cartarum* and explicitly made as recently as 1332, that aids granted for the common profit should be used to pay for purveyances. This must have done more than anything else to win over the Commons. Complementary to this was the initiation of a scheme for the defence of the north and the coasts. This matter had indeed been raised in the first session, but the Commons' unwillingness to add to the burden of the current arrays led them to reply that those who held lands there should be compelled to assume the obligations for their defence 'saunz charge de la commune'.[2] After their return in January, however, the Commons showed themselves far more ready to authorize a long-term plan for northern defence. Arrayers were named in the northern shires to lead companies of men-at-arms and archers to the muster at Newcastle. From there they were to go at the King's wages, which were to be raised from loans secured on the promised subsidy.[3] Parliament's authorization of this levy was to be explained to lay and clerical landholders at shire assemblies where, no doubt, the loans would be raised.[4] And in the final session of the parlia-

---

[1] *Rot. Parl.* ii. 109 nos. 25–27; *Rot. Scot.* i. 583. For the action against illegal purveyances in the October session, see Fryde, 'Parliament and the French War', pp. 266–7.

[2] *Rot. Parl.* ii. 104–5. In fact the scheme of February 1339 was still in operation, commissions being issued, even while parliament was sitting, for the array of the northern shires (*Rot. Scot.* i. 575–6). Parliament itself authorized the appointment of commissioners and decided that Holderness, despite its obligation for coastal defence, should be arrayed, taxed and give aid along with the rest of Yorkshire (*Rot. Parl.* ii. 105).

[3] *Rot. Parl.* ii. 110; *Rot. Scot.* i. 591.   [4] *Rot. Scot.* i. 583–4.

ment the Commons again authorized an array for the north; quotas were assigned to the leaders and order was given that every man 'de poer et de devoer' was to be ready to serve in the defence of the march when needed, while commissions were to be issued to array all 'sufficient' men of the northern counties. This was all conditional on the northern subsidy being spent on local defence and this was explicitly promised in the writs of array in mid-April which summoned men to arms under the Statute of Winchester. As we shall see, this reservation of the northern subsidy was strictly maintained.[1]

Thus under the leadership of Stratford both purveyances and arrays had been regulated by parliamentary authority and treated as charges on existing war taxation, not as additional burdens imposed by prerogative action. The wholesale acceptance of the subjects' point of view on these important matters was sufficient of itself to win the Commons over to Stratford; and in addition they needed his support for their wider political demands. For his part the archbishop might claim to have steered the realm past a crisis of confidence and to have restored credibility to the home government and home defence. His popularity at home provided a solid base on which to assert his authority against the King's privy advisers; but he must also have been conscious of its dangers. In asserting the primacy of home defence against the King's wars he was flying in the face of the King's own desires and plans; in seeking parliamentary authority for war levies he was calling in question important royal prerogative rights; above all in giving tacit encouragement to the Commons' further demands for a strengthened council and strict control of finance he was storing up the certainty of Edward's resentment and future vengeance. In securing his present position by an alliance with the Commons Stratford thus ran the risk of mortgaging his political future. But the archbishop was also caught in a further dilemma. His reinstatement with the King depended on his securing a new subsidy; if he did that all else might be forgiven, even to the extent of his support of the Commons' demands. But in doing so he would have to shoulder the unpopularity of a further extension of the war and the burdens which this entailed. To avoid the loss either of royal confidence or of popular support he

[1] *Rot. Parl.* ii. 115; *Rot. Scot.* i. 588–90, 597.

had to walk a political tightrope. If it gave way he would have to decide on which side to make his fall. For the moment, however, by securing the support of the Commons he achieved a result decisively in his favour. On every commission appointed in parliament there figured the names of himself and his principal episcopal and baronial associates.[1] Stratford himself returned to the Chancellorship in April.

The Commons must have supported the archbishop not merely as a matter of political tactics but out of conviction. The petitions of 1340, both in their broad outline and in detail, were heavily influenced by the Ordinances of 1311 and the Lancastrian tradition which stemmed therefrom. In 1340 Stratford himself was practically the last heir of that tradition. It is true that he had lent his support to the settlement of 1330 which emphasized the mutual responsibility of King and magnates for the government of the realm, but this was not inconsistent with recognition of parliament as a supremely authoritative body for certain functions which involved the consensus of the whole realm. The *Modus* had been written with this conviction and the crisis of 1340 translated some of its claims into political reality. These were the independent and decisive role of the Commons in assenting to or refusing taxation, the idea of a committee to deal with difficult questions, and the claim that the Commons had some political sanction in presenting articles testifying to the King's misrule. Each of these ideas had its origin in the persistent and inventive baronial opposition to Edward I and Edward II; but if the *Modus* marks one stage in their dissemination the petitions of 1340 marked a further advance by using these germinal ideas within the frame of a comprehensive scheme of government revolving around parliament. Parliament was the place in which the council was to be regularly chosen, to which it was answerable, and to which its uncompleted judicial business was to be referred. In parliament the custodians of the tax were to be appointed and were to answer for its management. Parliament was expected to meet regularly and was held to have a residual authority. The executive authority of the continual council was to be regularly renewed and supplemented by that of parliament into which it was periodically to merge. If it is correct to attribute these ideas

[1] Tout, *Chapters*, iii. 106.

to the Commons, this shows that within two decades the academic doctrine of the *Modus* had become the consensus of the mass of knights and burgesses who met the chastened King; in their eyes parliament had a major role in government and, since it represented the realm, spoke with an authority which could not pass unheeded. It was perhaps because he was aware of the force of these convictions that Stratford gave tacit recognition to the Commons' protest in 1340 and invoked their support in his hour of trial in the following year.

CHAPTER XII

The Second Crisis over Taxation: III Stratford's Administration, 1340

DESPITE all that has been written upon it, the crisis of 1340–1 has remained in some degree unexplained and its significance a matter of dispute. Although it evoked the language and drama of a great constitutional conflict, it was precipitated by a fit of royal temper and was concluded by what has been called 'an outrageous breach of faith'.[1] It has seemed to historians to form at best an appendage to the long magnate tradition of constitutional opposition to the Crown and to have left no abiding precedents. If it served to check an incipient despotism, this was born of the necessities of war and was typical neither of Edward's government nor of his relations with the magnates over the whole period of the reign.[2] There has thus been a tendency to treat it as a transient political storm, generated by the temperamental antagonism of a youthful and impetuous King and an ageing if still ambitious and politically adept archbishop. The issues of clerical privilege, choice of royal councillors, answerability of ministers, and trial of peers which were raised might be interpreted as rationalizations of this personal quarrel and of the further antagonism between Stratford and the King's confidants.

This ambiguous judgement on the crisis as a whole has been reflected in the various assessments by historians of the roles of the archbishop, the magnates, and the Commons. Although Stubbs did not see the conflict as springing from a clash of principles, he was clear that two principles of importance had received recognition. These were the right of peers to a trial by their fellows in parliament, and the responsibility of ministers to the nation and not to the King alone. Important as these milestones were, it was the advance of the Commons to political

---

[1] T. F. Tout, *Chapters in Medieval Administrative History*, iii. 140.

[2] For a comment in these terms, see E. Miller in *Historical Studies of the English Parliament*, i. 18.

maturity which marked the real importance of this parliament. 'Its proceedings', Stubbs' wrote in a characteristically memorable judgement, 'very distinctly mark the acquisition by the third estate of its full share of parliamentary power.'[1] Forty years after Stubbs's account, the subject was treated afresh, almost simultaneously, by Gaillard Lapsley and Dorothy Hughes.[2] Both were influenced by recent studies in the administrative history of the previous reign. For Lapsley, the central issue in 1341 was whether the King should govern through a council of magnates according to Lancastrian doctrine, or whether he could choose his advisers from whom he wished. By extension, should ministers be responsible to the council for implementing an agreed policy, or could ministers be dismissed, their conduct investigated, and their persons punished at the royal will? He saw it as the last attempt to set up a baronial oligarchy, the last gasp of the programme of 1258 and 1311. In this struggle the part of the Commons was incidental: their control of supplies induced the magnates to enlarge the traditional Lancastrian formulae to include parliament, but the Commons showed no real interest in these principles nor took any initiative in the proceedings. Stratford, about whom Lapsley had no illusions, was the manipulator of the individual interests of magnates and Commons for his own cause. Lapsley's analysis of the constitutional issues was sensitive and illuminating but it was limited by his starting his account with the King's landing in December 1340. Here Miss Hughes was on surer ground. She was able to emphasize that the crisis marked the culmination of opposition to a royal policy which since 1338 had been dedicated to the revival of a court party, the King's personal direction of the administration, and the overriding of privileges and franchises on grounds of necessity. Like Lapsley, she saw this opposition as organized 'chiefly in the interests of the baronial and ecclesiastical oligarchy', though Stratford received recognition as the chief opponent of royal autocracy.

In the third volume of the *Chapters in Medieval Administrative History*, Tout drew on both these accounts. His own deep

---

[1] W. Stubbs, *Constitutional History*, ii. 410.

[2] G. Lapsley, 'Archbishop Stratford and the Parliamentary Crisis of 1341', *Eng. Hist. Rev.* xxx (1915), pp. 6–18, 193–215 (reprinted in *Crown, Community and Parliament*, ed. Helen Cam and Geoffrey Barraclough (Oxford, 1951), pp. 231–72). Dorothy Hughes, *The Early Years of Edward III* (London, 1915), pp. 100–81.

familiarity with the developments of the preceding years led him to emphasize Edward III's acceptance of the principle of the magnate council in 1330 and the subsequent trend from about 1332 towards a revival of the household system, culminating in the Walton Ordinances. His interpretation of the crisis centred on the conflict between the magnate and curial parties, the former aided to victory by the development of notions of peerage and a revulsion against royal despotism. Although parliament provided the setting for the conflict, the leadership and initiative came from the barons, and theirs was the victory. They secured recognition for the view that the administration as a whole was responsible to the peers of the realm.[1] Tout thus reinforced the interpretation of Lapsley and Hughes.

In an article published shortly after Tout's volume, and subsequently in his *Constitutional History*, Bertie Wilkinson has argued for some modification of this account.[2] He sought to differentiate the ideal of co-operation between the Crown and the magnates contained in the 1330 declaration from the oligarchic and demagogic Lancastrianism of the preceding reign. Amongst personalities, he discerned a difference of view between Stratford and the magnates. The archbishop, heir to the older Lancastrianism with its cultivation of the people, never obtained full baronial support for his programme of restraint upon the King; what he did secure was their mediation in his personal quarrel, on the basis of their traditional demand for an aristocratic council. The radical movement in 1341 only developed, in full parliament, following the settlement of Stratford's personal quarrel. It sprang from the initiative of the Commons; but its success represented as much a violation of the aristocratic settlement of 1330 as had the King's curial and despotic government at the other extreme. The crisis determined whether the settlement of 1330 could survive these extremes; Edward's revocation of the concessions was thus a victory for moderation, recognized and accepted by the baronage. Thus, for all his constitutional language, Stratford appears

[1] T. F. Tout, *Chapters*, iii. 126 ff.

[2] B. Wilkinson, 'The Protest of the Earls of Arundel and Surrey in the Crisis of 1341', *Eng. Hist. Rev.* xlvi (1931), pp. 181–93; *Constitutional History of Medieval England*, ii (London, 1952), pp. 176–87. See also *The Chancery Under Edward III* (Manchester, 1929), pp. 102–13.

as a lone and somewhat irresponsible demagogue; the Commons as independent and radical, if ultimately ineffective.

Individual as these interpretations are, it will be clear that the general trend since Stubbs's day has emphasized the baronial interest in the quarrel and minimized that of the Commons. It has sought to differentiate sharply between Stratford's personal antagonisms and the aims and outlook of both magnates and Commons. In consequence historians have been in some difficulty to explain the depth of animosity between the King and the archbishop, to relate this to the constitutional issues, and to account for the political strength of the opposition.[1] For something more than Stratford's adept manipulation of the magnates or demagogic incitement of the Commons is necessary to explain how the full-scale 'Lancastrian' programme of Winchelsea and Thomas of Lancaster could be forced upon a King as vigorous and conscious of his prerogatives as Edward III.

That the Lancastrian tradition of Edward II's reign exercised a potent influence in 1340–1, both in the person of Archbishop Stratford and through the text of the Ordinances, is indisputable. But the crises of 1311 and 1340 exhibited marked differences both in the nature and aims of the magnate leadership and in its relations with the Commons. In 1310–11 the council had been forced on the King by the magnate opposition and, though justified in terms of popular clamour and grievance, was principally designed to remove Edward from Gaveston's influence. In 1340 the home council had received plenary power on the petition of the Commons who saw it as the means of rescuing the community from royal exactions, and as affording the best assurance for the defence of the borders and the maintenance of internal order during the King's absence. It is true that Stratford had used the discontents of both the home council and the Commons to re-establish his own position against the King's *familiares*, but the statutes and ordinances of 1340 embodied a reordering of royal government to reflect a constitutional ideal shared by the whole community. It is from this concrete constitutional achievement that any analysis of

---

[1] Thus M. McKisack, *The Fourteenth Century* (Oxford, 1959), p. 166, following Miss Hughes (op. cit., p. 105), finds the degree of Edward's hatred of Stratford 'somewhat inexplicable'.

the crisis of 1341 must proceed; for that crisis was fought over the validity of the settlement of 1340. In defending this settlement, Stratford could count on the support of those who had secured it—the home council and the Commons; he was defending their views and their interests; he was fighting their battle. The King thus returned in December 1340 to face an opposition with a coherent programme, and his one hope lay in dividing Stratford, the magnates, and the Commons and in dealing with each separately.

Two features of the constitutional settlement of 1340 are important.[1] First, it was secured by the common action of all estates in parliament and embodied concessions to Lords, Commons, and clergy. The first statute contained a series of detailed guarantees on abuses, such as an amnesty for past offences, the release of debts prior to 1337, the appointment of sheriffs in the Exchequer, the delivery of wardships to next of kin, and the proper behaviour of purveyors, all of which Lords and Commons had complained about in 1339. The fourth statute redressed the grievances of the Church, and the third guaranteed the King's subjects against claims arising from his new title as King of France. Thus the general effect of this legislation was to preserve the subject against royal exactions. The second important feature of the settlement was that it directly related these concessions to the grant of the ninth. Cap. 20 of the first statute gave effect to the grant and stated explicitly that it was made in return for the guarantees of the preceding chapters. The second statute then promised that because this tax was so unprecedented and burdensome, it should not be treated as a precedent, and that in future subjects 'should not be charged or burdened to make common aid or to sustain charge' unless by common assent of all estates in parliament. Read in the light of both the concessions in the first statute and the petition of February 1339 against prises (that 'no free man should be assessed or taxed without common assent of parliament'),[2] this would seem to refer to the exactions which had characterized the preceding years. The variety of these could only be embraced by an indefinite term but the vagueness of the statute here paved the way for future conflicts. Common assent in parliament might be seen as the only safeguard against charges

---

[1] *S.R.* i. 281–94.   [2] *Rot. Parl. Hact. Ined.*, p. 269.

at the King's will, but the King himself would predictably resist submitting his undoubted fiscal prerogatives such as feudal aids and purveyances to parliamentary assent. Moreover, the fact that the settlement of 1340 associated a series of specific concessions with the grant of a tax meant that any failure to implement either could easily generate a charge of bad faith and lead to a renewal of the conflict.

Much therefore depended on the success of the political settlement. Yet this had some disturbing features. In the first place, it had marked not a compromise but a very nearly total victory for the opposition. As Tout appreciated, when Edward left England in July Stratford ruled in his place: 'there was no longer a question of two ministries, for the court was dependent on the home government'.[1] The King had been humiliated and his resentment on finding that his dependence on Stratford profited him nothing erupted in his complaint to the Pope that he 'had placed the whole disposition of the kingdom' in Stratford's hands, on the understanding that he would ensure the supply of revenue to the King.[2] Thus the responsibility for making the settlement of May work was thrust on Stratford and his colleagues, and here arose the second difficulty. Stratford was bound to mitigate the burdens of war on the community, for so long as his enemies remained around the King he dared not risk losing popular support. Yet only a stringent use of his authority to provide the King's needs would dispel Edward's suspicion that he had conspired with his subjects to challenge royal authority. In this sense the means by which Stratford had secured his victory were incompatible with the ends which it was intended to serve. In fact the chances of satisfying both the King and the commons had been effectually prejudiced by the time Edward sailed on 22 June.

Local receivers and surveyors of the ninth for each shire were appointed on 20 April 1340 under the general supervision of the archbishop.[3] Although technically the receivers were answerable to the King, it is clear that control of the tax was firmly vested in the baronial council. Moreover, the provision of the statute that it should be wholly reserved for the war was embodied in the commissions issued on 12 May to the two

[1] Tout, *Chapters*, iii. 115.   [2] *Foedera*, II. ii. 1152.
[3] *C.P.R., 1338–40*, pp. 499–504.
K P P F—K

principal receivers north and south of Trent.[1] The warrants issued by Edward from the Tower during May show that a general suspension of payments had been imposed and that assignments on the current taxes were very closely controlled by the King and the council to ensure that they were employed for the purpose for which they had been granted.[2] The common resolve of King, council, and parliament that the new tax should be honestly and efficiently administered was soon forced to take account of some hard facts. The ninth of wheat, fleeces, and lambs had been granted for two years in the expectation of raising some £100,000 in each year but both its novelty and the high prices fixed for the sale of the produce meant that it soon ran into difficulties.[3] Instructions for the assessment, collection, and sale of the produce were included in the writs of 20 April, the collectors being instructed to send in their reports by 11 June.[4] The first half, for the first year, was due at All Saints, the second half at the beginning of February 1341. No earlier dates could be contemplated because of the need to await the harvest and shearing time. Yet the King's financial needs could hardly be delayed for so long. Edward had returned owing debts of more than £200,000 in Brabant, and it had been the pressing need to satisfy his creditors that had driven him to accept the conditions. The grant would indeed provide security for their repayment, but Edward was also anxious to resume his operations in France while his alliances were still in being. He had not made his surrender merely to clear off old debts.

Already by the end of May he had announced his decision to return to the Low Countries, and the next three weeks were

---

[1] *C.F.R.* v, 1337–47, pp. 178–9.

[2] P.R.O. E 404/4 File 26. The majority of the warrants relate to the clerical tenth. On 18 May the King sent a general warrant restraining assignments on this except by privy seals issued with the assent of the council. The prologue to this warrant expresses clearly the financial aims of the new administration: 'Nous savons bien que les eides que nous sount a ceste nostre darrein parlement grauntez en aide de perfourmer notre enprise sount molt chargeauntes a ceux de queux ils coviegnent estre levez et per tauntz si vorriens voluntiers que elles fuissent bien emploiez solonc notre poiar et quelles fuissent counserviez al ops pour quelles eles nous sount grantez cest assavoir de mettre notre enprise a fin honorable a nous et a notre roialme . . .' The warrant was also enrolled in K.R. Mem. Roll 14 Edw. III (E 159/116) rot. 108.

[3] E. B. Fryde, 'Parliament and the Revolt of 1381', in *Liber Memorialis Georges de Lagarde* (Paris–Louvain, 1970), p. 83.

[4] *C.F.R.* v. *1337–47*, p. 516.

occupied in preparations. Then on 20 June, on the very eve of the King's departure, Stratford resigned the seal. The official record attributed this to the archbishop's age and ill health,[1] but one chronicler believed it to be a final attempt to dissuade Edward from sailing on account of the danger from the French fleet.[2] Yet Edward's announcement of his departure in May had been coupled with the appointment of the council of absence headed by Stratford and he was later to aver to the Pope that the archbishop had supported his decision.[3] It is possible, however, that in the ensuing month Stratford came to appreciate the impossibility of his task, and the likelihood of a new financial crisis. For in the month preceding the King's departure the council had been induced to pledge the whole of the first year of the ninth to the King's allies and creditors in payment of their claims. Already on 17 May promissory assignments of £53,700 on the ninth in the southern shires had been delivered to Flemish and Italian creditors in repayment of their loans, and a series of other assignments followed the appointment of the council on 27 May.[4] On 12 May the King had engaged to discharge his arrears to the marquis of Jülich, totalling £30,000, from the subsidy in Cambridge, Huntingdon, and Bedfordshire, and the council issued the warrant for this on 8 June.[5] On 30 May £15,000 was assigned, principally to Walter de Mauny and Henry Burghersh, bishop of Lincoln,[6] and early in June a further £7,000 to English merchants from the northern subsidy.[7] On 21 June, the debts of Stratford himself and others for whom he stood surety were assigned on the ninth in Kent, where he was the principal receiver,[8] and on the following day warrants were issued for repaying the debts of all those of the nobility who were setting sail with the King and of 132 men of

[1] *Foedera*, II. ii. 1129.   [2] *Chronica . . . Roberti de Avesbury*, p. 311.
[3] *Foedera*, II. ii. 1125; *Cal. Papal Registers, Letters*, ii, *1305–42*, p. 585.
[4] *C.P.R., 1338–40*, pp. 532–3.
[5] Ibid., pp. 519, 526; *C.C.R., 1339–41*, p. 407. All the following assignments were warranted by the council apart from those noted below.
[6] *C.P.R., 1338–40*, p. 544. These were both warrants under the privy seal, though almost certainly with the approval of the council.
[7] Ibid., pp. 541–2.
[8] Ibid., p. 546; *C.C.R., 1339–41*, p. 423. On 14 June the citizens of London had secured repayment of a loan of £5,000 on the subsidy in Kent under the security of the archbishop (*C.P.R., 1338–40*, p. 534) and on 21 June an assignment of £1,000 on the second year of the ninth was delivered to the earl of Arundel (*C.P.R., 1340–3*, p. 23).

lesser rank, totalling about £29,000.[1] With what had been previously warranted, about £140,000 of the subsidy had been assigned for the repayment of past debts. Nor was this all, for before he sailed Edward had entered into agreement with the Bardi and Perruzzi who undertook to supply the household with 2,000 marks each month from 1 July until the end of the year and to discharge debts of over £28,000 on his behalf, for which they were assigned the whole subsidy in eight shires.[2] The fact that no assignments had been made on these prior to the King's departure suggests that the council had been party to this arrangement, which it formally warranted in August.[3] The satisfaction of past debts, even by nominal assignment, enabled the King to contract immediate new loans. Yet Edward's original plea for aid, in 1339, had been primarily to secure release from his creditors and there was no doubt that, in the words of E. B. Fryde, 'from the purely financial point of view the king needed a long respite from further continental warfare'.[4]

By the end of May the council recognized that money for renewed military operations could only come from a fresh grant and it had summoned a new parliament to meet on 12 July. Lords and Commons had already begun to discuss the difficulties in levying and selling the ninth when the royal envoys appeared to recount the King's victory at Sluys and explain his urgent need for further aid.[5] Edward was proposing to march on Tournai with the promise of Flemish troops and help from Robert of Artois; he told parliament that he needed money if his own forces were not to desert and his allies join the King of France to the perdition of 'our land, ourselves, our children and all lords and others'.[6] Faced with this demand,

[1] *C.P.R., 1340–3*, pp. 1–3; *C.C.R., 1339–41*, pp. 424, 523.

[2] *C.P.R., 1340–3*, p. 3; *C.C.R., 1339–41*, p. 528.

[3] *Rot. Parl.* ii. 121. Writing to the King in September, the council replied to complaints by the Bardi and Peruzzi and explicitly claimed that the sale of the King's wool and other matters had been ordained before his departure. See Westminster Abbey Muniments no. 12195.

[4] E. B. Fryde, 'Financial Resources of Edward III', *Revue Belge*, xlv. 1181.

[5] The victory at Sluys was announced in England on 28 June (Avesbury, pp. 312–14). On 15 July parliament decided that whatever produce of the ninth could not be sold should be committed to the keeping of four men from each vill (*Rot. Parl.* ii. 117, 120). The King's envoys, the earls of Arundel and Gloucester and William Trussell, reported on the same day.

[6] *Rot. Parl.* ii. 118.

and with the first year of the ninth already pledged, the council proposed a loan in wool. Members of the council, together with the King's envóys, pledged their own wool as a gesture, and thus persuaded the Commons to agree to the loan of 20,000 sacks of wool at an agreed valuation. Repayment of the wool was to be a first charge on the second year of the ninth. Even from the parliament roll it is clear that the Commons were deeply suspicious of this fresh demand and hedged their consent with stringent conditions. Not merely was the formal ratification of this loan required under the seals of all the magnates—those with the King as well as those in England— but copies of this were to be delivered to the knights of the shire to be reported in their localities. The Chancellor and Treasurer were to receive express instructions to make no assignments on the second year until repayment was complete, the wool was to be kept out of the hands of the financiers who had handled the previous wool sales, and its sale was to be negotiated with an assembly of merchants in August.[1] The grant was made, after long discussions, on 24 July[2] and parliament was dissolved two days later. By 13 August the council had made arrangements for the sale of the wool in nine counties to local merchants who undertook to make payments totalling £3,466 to the King at Bruges in September, while other merchants were summoned to Westminster on 21 August to negotiate the sale of the remainder.[3] Despite the hostility of the Commons, the council turned again to William de la Pole for a loan of 3,000 marks; for this further advance and in discharge of debts he received assignments of £10,000 on the ninth and the clerical tenth.[4] Following the completion of its initial arrangements, the council

[1] Ibid., pp. 119–21. In their letter of 30 July to the King, the councillors wrote that 'L'entente des grantz et communes de votre Roiaume si est que cest aide ne soit pas mys en mayns de tielx come voz autres lennes en est mys avant ces houres ou vous n'avez este serviz de riens a l'afferant.'
[2] Ibid., p. 122.
[3] Ibid., pp. 120–1; Hughes, op. cit., p. 98; *R.D.P.* iv. 524–5; Unwin, *Finance and Trade under Edward III*, pp. 207–8.
[4] *Rot. Parl.* ii. 121; *C.P.R., 1340–3*, p. 24; *C.C.R., 1339–41*, pp. 516, 619–20. The council also negotiated with the Bardi and Peruzzi for the discharge of debts to a number of merchants totalling £28,595. 15s. 2d. on the security of the ninth (*Rot. Parl.* ii. 121; *C.C.R., 1339–41*, p. 505) and on the same day (10 August) contracted to pay £5,132 to Pancius de Controne in repayment of debts (*C.C.R., 1339–41*, p. 438).

wrote to the King on 13 August to inform him that it now had
some expectation of sending supplies and earnestly begged him
to respect the engagements it had made. Their letter sought to
impress the King with their devotion to his military plans and
needs, and the energy and urgency of their attempts to raise
money; they hinted, too, at the difficulties they had encountered from the Commons.[1] There is no reason to doubt the
sincerity and accuracy of the authors; but they probably
realized that it was a desperate gamble to retain Edward's confidence and that the likelihood of anything like adequate
supplies reaching the King was very remote.

The general refusal to buy the produce gathered under the
levy of the ninth at the prices appointed, which was already
apparent by June, became so widespread that by the end of the
year only some £15,000 had been realized.[2] The council continued, indeed, to make efforts. New surveyors were appointed
in all shires on 24 August; a fortnight later the assessors and
vendors were accused of failing to levy the subsidy diligently
despite the King's urgent needs, and the receivers were summoned before the council to render account; when some failed
to appear they were again summoned in October.[3] It was not
long before widespread passive resistance on the one side and
determined government pressure on the receivers and vendors
on the other led officials to indulge in illegal seizures and
extortion and provoked the populace either to leave their holdings or to offer violent resistance. In September collectors were
assaulted in Somerset and in October the council received
reports of communities refusing outright to pay the sums
assessed on them.[4] It endeavoured to meet the double challenge
to its authority by threatening the assessors and vendors with a
judicial inquiry and at the same time ordering the sheriffs to
attend on them and enforce the collection of the tax.[5] In these
circumstances it was unlikely that the forced loan in wool
would prove any more attractive or enforceable. Between 18
September and the end of October there had been a total
failure to collect the loan in wool in twelve counties.[6] Again the

[1] *Rot. Parl.* ii. 122.
[2] Fryde, 'Parliament and the Great Revolt of 1381'.
[3] *C.C.R., 1339–41*, pp. 517, 635.   [4] *C.P.R., 1340–3*, pp. 52, 58, 96.
[5] *C.C.R., 1339–41*, pp. 585–6.   [6] Ibid., pp. 537–43, 548–9.

power of the sheriffs was put at the disposal of the purveyors of wool to punish those who concealed their wool; once again the council put pressure on the purveyors by threats of reprisals against their bodies and goods. There was violence as men plundered the houses where the wool had been stored while everywhere the habitual smuggling increased and growers evaded the levy by exporting their wool through alien merchants.[1] The council thus found itself faced with a growing and dangerous defiance in the country. Both parliaments of 1340 had been acutely aware of the economic distress in the shires, the weariness and hatred of the prolonged burden of heavy taxation and exactions, and the hostility to royal officials. The Commons had granted taxation with much reluctance and some delay, with an anxious eye on their constituents but some confidence in the council and the archbishop. It was this confidence which the open hostility of the countryside now put at hazard. In London it was thought that the shires would revolt if further pressure were applied.[2]

The failure of the home council to keep Edward supplied with money had brought his campaign to a halt by 27 September when he concluded the truce of Esplechin. He had failed to capture Tournai or bring the French royal army to battle and his allies were on the point of desertion. By Michaelmas he had returned to Ghent where he waited throughout October and early November for supplies with which to renew the war. Throughout this period the King's correspondence with the home council shows him in the direst financial straits: forced to borrow to pay off his archers, forced to pay his debts to his allies by grants of wool which he must already have despaired of seeing, forced to require his commanders like the earls of Derby, Northampton, and Warwick to enter prison in Malines as hostages for the debt of £9,450 which Edward still owed in

---

[1] *C.P.R., 1340–3*, pp. 30, 114, 148–9, 211; *C.C.R., 1339–41*, pp. 532, 538, 579, 616. Cf. F. R. Barnes, 'The Taxation of Wool', in *Finance and Trade under Edward III*, ed. G. Unwin, p. 158; D. Hughes, op. cit., p. 98. In September 1341 the council informed the King that, 'nous doutons de bon et hastif exploit aver des leynes et par autres busoignes qe touchent notre Sire le Roi et son poeple pardecea, est ordinez daver un Consail de lundy proschein apres la feste Seint Michel ou sera ordinez a leide de Dieu, punissement de faux ministres pour doner ensaumple as autres pour de mieutz servir le Roi qui n'ad este avant ces heures'. Westminster Abbey Muniments, no. 12195.

[2] *Croniques de London*, ed. G. J. Aungier (Camden Soc. xxviii, 1845), p. 83.

Malines from Easter 1340.[1] For its part, the council endeavoured to check the misrepresentations made to the King in
Flanders of its inactivity in levying the wools, pleading for his
forbearance and promising to correct its mistakes.[2] During
September and October the council, on the orders of the King,
renewed the assignments of many of those with the King whose
patents of 21 and 22 June had proved fruitless.[3] Resentment
against the council in London must have been widespread in
the army at Ghent but even at the end of October Edward did
not directly blame the council for the failure of supplies,
though he told them plainly that 'if all had done their duty we
should have been better aided and the levy of wools would not
have been so greatly delayed'.[4] But gradually the failure of the
council to send money was confirmed and what little it had
received it claimed to retain to pay the wages of the domestic
administration and household expenses. To Edward's eyes it
must have seemed that the situation of 1339 was recurring with
uncanny and alarming exactitude.[5]

It was small wonder that with his campaign in ruins, himself
dishonoured, his companions in jeopardy, and his debts now
astronomical, Edward bitterly regretted trusting the archbishop to see him through and deeply resented the surrender to
which he had been forced on his earlier return. By the middle of
November he was ready to accuse Stratford of treachery in
deliberately withholding supplies in order to jeopardize his
campaign and life.[6] As reports of the King's mind reached
England the council made a last desperate effort to meet his
demands. On 27 November it put into general effect an order

[1] E. Déprez, *Les Préliminaires de la Guerre de Cent Ans*, pp. 355 n. 1, 356; K. Fowler,
The King's Lieutenant (London, 1969), pp. 35–6. Two letters from the King cited
by Fowler (P.R.O. C 81/269/13359; C 81/270/13463) of 18 August and 9 October
reveal his difficulties in raising money in the Netherlands. In the first he reports that
his creditors are asking payment of 20% of his debts, that the two earls have had
to go bail for further advances, and that the army was threatened by desertions.
In the more urgent tones of the second he exhorts the council to further the collection of the 2,000 sacks of wool from the loan made to the King's use which he
had granted to the Bardi and Peruzzi for their debts and the similar assignment
to the two earls.

[2] Westminster Abbey Muniment, no. 12195.

[3] *C.C.R., 1339–41*, pp. 522, 528, 530, 532, 555–7, 559, 569–70.

[4] Deprez, op. cit., p. 356.   [5] *Croniques de London*, p. 83.

[6] This was what the envoys whom the King accredited on 18 November told
the Pope. *Cal. Papal Registers, Letters*, ii, *1305–42*, pp. 584–5.

which it had already applied selectively early in the month. All the collectors of the ninth were instructed to bring their receipts to a central receiver, William Edington, notwithstanding any assignments to royal creditors.[1] Thus the council retracted its policy and commitments of the early summer, but too late; for on 30 November Edward landed at the Tower and its members were dismissed or imprisoned. It marked the overthrow not merely of the structure of conciliar government set up by the settlement of May 1340 but of the fragile political harmony which Edward had then bought by his surrender. As so often, military failure opened the way to recriminations between King, ministers, and the realm all the more bitter because fed at the personal level by jealousies and ambitions amongst the royal councillors and at the political level by the dichotomy between military and civil administrations. The tensions bred of four years of exhaustive war effort at an unprecedented level do much to account for the shrill tone of the political controversy which ensued.

In the months following his return the King acted with a vigour born of long inactivity and frustration. His immediate task was to establish culpability for the failure to collect the ninth which he regarded as having caused the abandonment of his campaign. On 10 December commissions were issued in all shires to uncover the oppressions and deceits of the ministers in England, by inviting complaint against them.[2] Early in January the King ordered an examination of the accounts of all those who had handled the taxes.[3] The King still claimed to be seeking an account of these monies when parliament assembled on 23 April; but by then the commissions directed against royal ministers had broadened into general commissions of trailbaston in which all kinds of local officials and communities were induced, under threat of indictment, to compound with fines of up to 2,000 marks.[4] The city of London purchased

---

[1] *C.C.R., 1339–41*, p. 577.

[2] *C.P.R., 1340–3*, pp. 106, 111–13. On 13 January Parving, Sadington, and Scot were commissioned to proceed against the imprisoned officials on the basis of the 'common report and clamour of the people and divers petitions' (ibid., p. 110).

[3] *Croniques de London*, p. 87. The reference to household debts may be to the assignment of 510 sacks of wool in August 1340 towards the payment of £7,375 worth of household debentures of Queen Philippa (*Rot. Parl.* ii. 121).

[4] *Croniques de London*, p. 88; Tout, *Chapters*, iii. 129; Hughes, op. cit., pp. 116–17, 167–8.

pardon rather than submit to a general eyre.[1] In the new year the King in fact embarked on a major overhaul of the administration. Commissions were appointed to investigate smuggling, a clean sweep was made of existing royal officials in the shires and in the ports, and men who had not previously served were to replace them.[2] Investigations were ordered into the administration and revenues of Ireland and North Wales.[3] These inquiries went hand in hand with an effort to bring in as much cash revenue as possible. All farms and issues of the shires were to be paid in cash at the Exchequer and no payments made without the King's warrant, while the Exchequer was ordered to distrain on all outstanding debts to the Crown.[4] These measures were inspired by the King's profound mistrust of the home administration. They marked a reassertion of personal government, not only in the direction of finances and in the reliance on *curiales* among whom Kilsby was pre-eminent, but in the appointment of some household servants as officials in the ports.[5]

Edward's principal task was to enforce collection of the ninth, and the loan of wool. On 8 January he revoked all assignments made by the council, including those on the ninth, appointed new collectors, and ordered them to bring their receipts to London where Edington had been appointed sole receiver, answerable only to the King for payments.[6] A new assessment was set afoot, a date in mid-Lent set for its receipt, and new assignments issued to the King's most pressing creditors, principally the Bardi and the marquis of Jülich, and the soldiers who had returned with the King.[7] Meanwhile the King con-

[1] *C.P.R., 1340–3*, pp. 111, 223–4, 249; *C.C.R., 1339–41*, p. 659. Hughes, op. cit., p. 122.

[2] *C.P.R., 1340–3*, pp. 208, 213; *C.C.R., 1339–41*, pp. 607, 660, 663–4, 659. For a note on the changes of sheriffs, escheators, and coroners, see Tout, *Chapters*, iii. 122. There is a full discussion of the changes in the ports by R. L. Baker, *The English Customs Service, 1307–1343*, pp. 42–3. The investigations revealed that since 1337 smuggling had been on an extensive scale.

[3] *C.P.R., 1340–3*, pp. 206–7.

[4] *C.C.R., 1341–3*, p. 14; Hughes, op. cit., p. 123.

[5] Baker, loc. cit.

[6] *C.P.R., 1340–3*, pp. 78, 111. On 21 January writs to the collectors ordered them to send all money in hand to London, though this order had already been given in some shires on 11 December (*C.C.R., 1339–41*, pp. 592–3, 610–12). Payments of assignments on the ninth were suspended (ibid., *1341–3*, p. 14).

[7] *C.C.R., 1341–3*, p. 1; *C.P.R., 1340–3*, pp. 24–5. A series of writs to the two receivers of the ninth, Edington and Ellerker, are enrolled on the close rolls. To Edington: *C.C.R., 1339–41*, p. 601; *C.C.R., 1341–3*, pp. 5, 7–8, 19, 44, 49–50,

tracted some further loans and repaid some debts from the
security of the loan of wool.[1]
Nearly every one of these actions constituted a direct attack
on the administration of the council during the previous
twelve months. Politically the most important features of this
had been its co-operation with parliament and its responsiveness to public opinion. The council appointed in May had been
named in parliament and the scope of its authority defined and
enrolled for record; this had been done in direct response to a
petition of the Commons.[2] That council, comprising the archbishop and the earls of Lancaster, Arundel, and Huntingdon,
included the leading members of the home council in the preceding two years. The others named to attend on the regent on
the eve of Edward's departure in June—Henry Percy, Thomas
Wake, and Ralph Neville—had all as northern lords been
identified with the conciliar measures for the defence of the
border, and Wake had long enjoyed close ties with Stratford.[3]
Among those appointed to the Committees in the May parliament had been the earl of Arundel, who with Neville and Percy
had organized the defence of the north and the Dunbar
campaign of 1338, and the earl of Derby. Arundel, Huntingdon,
and Derby had all travelled back with Edward in June but
Arundel returned for the July parliament and thereafter
identified himself with the council of regency. He, Lord Wake,
and Stratford, as well as the Chancellor (Robert Stratford) and
the Treasurer (Roger Northburgh), were the leading members
of the council who signed the letters to the King of 30 July and
13 August informing him of the work of the parliament. The
last meeting of the full council held on 2 October comprised the
earls of Surrey, Arundel, Huntingdon, Hereford, and Pembroke
and Lords Bassett, Wake, Despenser, and Burghersh.[4] Those
identified with the work of the home council throughout the

55, 62, 68, 82–7, 94. To Ellerker: *C.C.R.*, *1339–41*, pp. 603, 608; *C.C.R.*, *1341–3*,
pp. 3, 16, 22, 62, 90, 98.
 [1] *C.P.R.*, *1340–3*, pp. 149, 157, 159, 166, 195. Cf. Barnes, op. cit., p. 161.
 [2] See above, pp. 262–4.
 [3] *Foedera*, II. ii, 1125; *Rot. Parl.* ii. 110, 113–14. Lord Wake was the son in law
of Henry Earl of Lancaster and had been one of Stratford's associates under the
earl's leadership since 1327. See K. Fowler, *The King's Lieutenant*, p. 25.
 [4] *Rot. Parl.* ii. 122; *R.D.P.* iv. 528. The earl of Arundel, Bartholomew Burghersh,
John de Stonor, William Shareshull, and Ralph Bassett were summoned to a

two years preceding Edward's dismissal of it were far from being merely Stratford's protégés; they numbered three of the leading earls, and an important nucleus of northern barons. They were a well-knit group who had probably gained, over the period, a certain *esprit de corps*.

Equally important was the work in which the members of the council had co-operated. The guard of the north, the guard of the sea, and the keeping of the peace were the three matters, together with the King's needs, to which the parliaments of May and July had given attention. In these parliaments Neville, Percy, and Wake had been commissioned to array the northern shires for the defence of the border as 'Chieftains of the King'; Neville and Bassett had been appointed to survey the temporalities of the archbishopric of York; Neville and Percy to take charge of the earl of Murray.[1] In the May parliament the committee dealing with the guard of the sea and coasts had included the earls of Arundel, Warenne, and Huntingdon, and the July parliament took measures for the defence of the Isle of Wight and authorized purveyances for the fleet.[2] With regard to the problem of public order, for more than a decade the Commons had been pressing for the appointment of local gentry and parliamentary knights as keepers of the peace rather than professional justices under magnate supervisors. The powers given to the latter in July 1338 had not been popular and the deterioration of public order after the King's departure had brought renewed criticism and demands from the Commons in the parliaments of February and October 1339. The May parliament of 1340 had turned its attention to the problem of order, and though parliament itself had not nominated to the peace commissions, gentry and lawyers were appointed to some special commissions.[3] The council had thus demonstrated in parliament its concern with defence and domestic order and had set precedents for the authorization of commissions of

---

meeting of the council on 4 September to meet messengers from the King (*C.C.R.*, *1339–44*, p. 621). The King's letters to the council in August had named in addition to the officers the earl of Arundel, Lord Wake, Nicholas de la Beche, John de Molyns, and John de St. Pol (C 81/269/13358, 9).

[1] *Rot. Parl.* ii. 113–14, 119.   [2] Ibid.

[3] Ibid., pp. 104, 113. See Hughes, op. cit., pp. 217–27; B. H. Putnam, *The Place in Legal History of Sir William Shareshull* (Cambridge, 1950), pp. 43–9; and the discussion below, ch. xvii. pp. 403–4.

array and purveyance in parliament. The council had also undertaken a major inquiry into the smuggling of wool. On the basis of the authority of the March parliament, commissions were issued in April 1340 to the earls of Arundel and Huntingdon and others in different localities to remove all collectors and substitute others.[1] Further measures were authorized in the July parliament to check the smuggling of wool and the evasion of customs, and the council ordered the closure of all ports pending further inquiries.[2] The council could not in 1340 evade responsibility for the supervision of officials as it had in 1338-9, and in late September it made a further attempt to tackle the problem by summoning before the full council certain sheriffs, mayors, and bailiffs of the customs ports and the collectors, with their rolls, for a major investigation.[3] It is doubtful whether all this resulted in much effective action, for a harassed administration, conscious of the impossibility of its task and aware of the strength of local resentment, was virtually powerless in the face of widespread collusion and resistance to the tax.

The King was certainly justified in his belief that the failure of the taxes of 1340 was due to obstruction and connivance by local officials, and his suspicions of undue leniency by the council were perhaps understandable, but Edward seems to have failed to appreciate the tense mood of the country. The commissions of oyer and terminer of 10 December 'touching alleged oppressions and extortions by the justices and any other ministers of the king', followed by the commission to arraign those taken into custody 'by the common report and clamour of the people', were in fact directed not against corrupt officials nor even at the council (members of which were named as commissioners) but were a blunt instrument for establishing communal culpability as the pretext for large-scale collective fines.[4] By the spring many royal creditors were receiving assignments on the fines in particular counties in discharge of the King's debts.[5]

---

[1] *C.P.R., 1338-40*, p. 507.
[2] *Rot. Parl.* ii. 120; *C.P.R., 1340-3*, pp. 89, 92, 94; *C.C.R., 1339-41*, p. 628. See R. L. Baker, op. cit., p. 41.   [3] *C.C.R., 1339-41*, pp. 624-7.
[4] *C.P.R., 1340-3*, pp. 110-11; Hughes, op. cit., pp. 167-8; Tout, *Chapters*, iii. 129; Putnam, 'The Transformation of the Keepers of the Peace . . .', *Trans. Roy. Hist. Soc.* 4th ser. xii (1929), p. 39.
[5] *C.P.R., 1340-3*, p. 147; cf. D. Hughes, op. cit., pp. 116, 167.

If Edward had contented himself with attacks on the two Stratfords there would almost certainly have been no crisis in 1341. But he seems to have interpreted the demands of the Commons in 1340 and the resistance to the ninth and the wool loan as a betrayal by the realm as a whole, and it was towards the people that the trailbaston commission was directed. It was this that gave Stratford the power to withstand Edward to his face. On 4 December the King had sent to him requiring him to go abroad to Louvain as a hostage for his debts; but the archbishop had already retired to Canterbury.[1] Whatever damage he had done to his popular reputation by his attempts to exact the ninth and the wool loan he now repaired by a re-cantation of his political acts and a pledge to devote himself to the defence of the people's liberties; these he delivered in the vernacular after sermons in his cathedral on 29 December and 21 February.[2] His action must have confirmed the King's belief that the archbishop had conspired with his subjects to undo him. The flagrant mass intimidation of the trailbaston thus rallied popular support for Stratford; but it also enabled him to appeal to the decisions of the parliament of 1340 as a safeguard against the apparently unlimited investigations of a prerogative commission. For in demanding an inquiry by the council into the actions and accounts of those who had handled the taxes, Stratford was recalling the King to the settlement of the March–May parliament and the investigations by the council during the summer.

To the support of the people, the parliament, and the council Stratford could also add that of the Church. Already in the first phase of the crisis, in the winter of 1339–40, Stratford had defended Church lands from purveyors, and the grant of a clerical tenth had been made conditional on the absence of further burdens. Concessions to the Church had figured in the statute of 1340 and Stratford had supported the Church in claiming exemption from the ninth. In July 1340 the council suspended its collection from all men of religion apart from those summoned to the parliament. One of Edward's first acts in January 1341 was to order it to be levied from all the lands of the Church, and Stratford sprang to the defence, ordering

---

[1] Hughes, op. cit., p. 105. *Litterae Cantuarienses*, ed. J. B. Sheppard (R.S., 1888), ii. 226–30.   [2] Birchington, in *Anglia Sacra*, i. 21, 23.

the excommunication of all officials who dared to lay hands on the Church's goods.[1]

The King's actions had thus done much to bring together an opposition, but what gave it cohesion was perhaps less the case of the archbishop, or even his personality—though he quickly became its figurehead—than the fact that Edward appeared to be reviving a type of government that had already provoked opposition in the preceding year. Moreover he was attacking the council which had been instituted as guarantor of the assurances and safeguards then secured and which still largely retained the confidence of parliament and the realm.

The points at issue were formulated in the King's message to the Pope of 18 November 1340, and Stratford's letter to the King of 1 January 1341. Though they were embroidered in the *Libellus Famosus*, Stratford's detailed reply, and Edward's second letter to the Pope of 14 March, these did not add any points of substance. Four principal matters were in dispute. First, and most important, was the nature and composition of the council, which had to be finally resolved now that the King had returned and dismissed from office the council of regency. In raising the cry against evil counsellors, Stratford appeared to be reverting to the Lancastrian programme of Edward II's reign. But though he cited Edward II's fate as an explicit warning, it was to the lessons of the present reign that he directed the King's attention. In a reference to the events of 1338–40 he recalled how, through certain councillors, the King had nearly lost the hearts of the people, but had then been delivered so that thereafter through the good counsel of prelates, peers, the great and wise of the council, he had so won the people's trust that they had granted him aid (the ninth) and his affairs had prospered.[2] In warning the King not to become dependent again on these evil counsellors, who sought their own profit rather than the King's honour or the safety of the realm, Stratford was recalling him to the magnate

---

[1] For this, see Hughes, op. cit., pp. 114, 156.

[2] Avesbury, p. 325: 'Et puis, sire, en vostre temps avetz ascuns consaillers par les qeux vous avetz a poi perduz les coeurs de vostre poeple; des qeux Dieux vous delivera, sicome luy pluist. Et puis, tauncqe en cea par bone avisement des prelatz, piers, grantz et sages du counsail de la terre, voz busoignez ount este mesneez en tieu manere qe vous avetz entierment lez coers de voz gentz qi vous ount eydez . . .'

council of 1340. Though he invoked the Lancastrian tradition that a magnate council alone had the interests of the realm at heart and could reconcile the claims of King and people, Stratford's ultimate purpose was probably a return to the harmony of 1330 rather than the imposition of a council on the King in the spirit either of the Ordinances or the demands of the Commons in 1340 for a council elected by peers.

Secondly, there was the question of the role and responsibility of the council. This was implicit in the King's charge that Stratford had betrayed his trust as a royal councillor.[1] His accusation embraced the whole period since 1337 during which the archbishop had been associated with the war policy. Briefly, Edward asserted that Stratford had twice given explicit promises to keep him supplied with money in Flanders, in 1337–9 and in 1340, and had twice failed him.[2] For this purpose he had committed the whole disposition and government of the realm to the archbishop who had then placed his own interests and profit before those of the King.[3] This echoed Stratford's own complaint against the King's *familiares*; indeed the charge of acting 'in status nostri detrimentum et dignitatis regiae laesionem' was peculiarly associated with evil counsel. Though it amounted to something less than treason, its history up to 1330 had closely associated it with a declaration of notoriety, either on the King's own testimony or by appeal to the people, as also with public trial.[4] Stratford was to turn both these to his own advantage by an appeal to public opinion and by demanding trial by peers. But in response to the explicit charge of causing the failure of the King's plans through lack of supplies, Stratford sheltered behind the corporate responsibility of the council. He declined responsibility for

---

[1] This is discussed by Lapsley, op. cit., pp. 262–6, though without reference to the historical background.

[2] *Foedera*, II. ii. 1147, 1152; *Cal. Papal Registers, Letters*, ii. *1305–42*, p. 585.

[3] 'Cui totius Reipublicae nostrae administrationem et summam rerum gerendarum a multo tempore duximus committendam'; 'quia sua non nostra negotia curantes et commoda propria procurantes'.

[4] See J. G. Bellamy, *The Law of Treason in England in the Later Middle Ages* (Cambridge, 1970), pp. 7, 55, 64–8. He interprets it as a crime very much akin to accroaching the royal power, i.e. utilizing the royal authority for the subject's personal ends. Bellamy would seem to be incorrect, however, in saying that Stratford interpreted this as an accusation of treason; that arose from the additional charge of inciting the people to rebellion. For charges on the King's record afforced by public notoriety, see ibid., ch. iii.

the failure of the monopoly schemes of 1337–9 on the ground that these had been approved by the whole council and handled by the King's financiers; in respect of the ninth he asserted that the whole yield of the first year had been pledged by the King and that the council was merely enforcing his explicit instructions, and had sent what little had been collected.[1] Stratford's defence was well grounded, even if it did not exculpate the council from its failure to enforce the collection of the ninth. But at the heart of this dispute were the conflicting views of the role of the council, which had become clear in the correspondence with the King in 1338–9 and had been left unresolved when the King returned to Flanders in June 1340. Was it to be merely the King's instrument for the furtherance of his war plans or was it to have some measure of autonomous responsibility for the government and welfare of the realm? The ghost of the Walton Ordinances still haunted the crisis of 1341.

Thirdly, there was the closely related question of where ministers were to answer for alleged misconduct. The King claimed that this should be to himself, perhaps in the Exchequer, the archbishop that he should answer only before the Lords.[2] Though he might assert that his rank as a peer entitled him to this, it was the logic of his political rather than of his personal position that prompted this claim. A public and above all a parliamentary trial could be turned into a defence of the home council's record and an indictment of the King's familiars which would rally his own associates and receive support from the Commons. Indeed the Commons' petitions of 1340 had asked that ministers should answer before the council of peers. Here Stratford inherited both a principle and the political backing for it, and the same could be said with regard to the general demand for accountability for the King's taxes. Soon after his return Edward had initiated an investigation into the accounts of those who had handled the ninth. In his letter of 1 January Stratford countered this by demanding an inquiry into whose hands the wool and money granted since the beginning of the war had come.[3] In widening the scope of the investigations, Stratford was not merely reviving the animus against the King's financial agents of 1337–9 but applying a demand that

[1] Birchington, in *Anglia Sacra*, pp. 30–1.
[2] *Foedera*, II. ii. 1147; Avesbury, p. 326.　　　[3] *Foedera*, II. ii. 1147.

had first been made in the 1340 petition and conceded when a committee had been set up for this purpose in May. That committee had included the earls of Arundel, Huntingdon, and Derby, and Lords Wake and Bassett.[1] It had still been hearing William de la Pole's account when Edward sailed in June, and the King had further agreed that the accounts of those handling the ninth should be audited in a similar way.[2] It was this agreement to a parliamentary audit that Edward repudiated when he instituted inquiries on his own prerogative.

Fourthly, there was the King's suspicion that Stratford had played the demagogue. For the archbishop personally this was the most serious charge of all. He had explicitly claimed responsibility for restraining the King in defence of the liberties of the common people and the clergy, in terms of his primatial function as keeper of the King's conscience.[3] Edward countered by accusing him of stirring up the realm to the point of rebellion with talk of royal exactions and tallages. It was this which prompted the charge of treason.[4] The inquiries of 1341 certainly played into the archbishop's hands by enabling him to pose as the defender of popular liberties, but this again was no more than the readoption of a role he had played from the end of 1339. In the writs ordering levies of the ninth, arrays, and purveyances the council had inserted exemptions for the poor and had reiterated its desire to save them from exactions.[5]

This literary polemic with its sequence of accusation, vindication, and counter-accusation thus ranged over the whole period from the commencement of the war; it opened an inquest into the failure not so much of a military campaign as of a system of government which had been fashioned to support it. It was an administrative failure in that basically the state lacked

---

[1] *Rot. Parl.* ii. 114.

[2] *C.P.R., 1338-40*, p. 551; Hughes, op. cit., p. 93.

[3] Avesbury, p. 326; for clerical excommunication of royal officials, see Hughes, op. cit., pp. 129-30.

[4] Thus, in the *Libellus Famosus* (*Foedera*, II. ii. 1148): 'Nequiter simulat se habere, et quasdam excommunicationum sententias in libertatis ecclesiasticae, et Magnae Cartae violatores in genere, dudum latas, ad sugillandam opinionem Regiam et praefatos ministros Regios diffamandos, ac seditionem in populo nobis commisso, proditorie suscitandam, et devotionem comitum procerum et magnatum regni nostri majestati regiae subtrahendam.' Stratford's answer to this is in Birchington, pp. 34-5. See also Lapsley, op. cit., pp. 244-5.

[5] Cf. Hughes, op. cit., p. 165.

the mechanism to enforce and control the fiscal arrangements which could ensure the very high receipts from taxation which the King needed; it was a political failure in that the King had alienated the political classes on whom the execution of his policy and commands depended; it was a personal failure in that the fund of affection, admiration, and good will from his ministers and nobility which Edward had started with, and still fundamentally retained, had turned into acrimonious jealousies and fears. To recover from the crisis Edward would have to recognize and repair each of these failures. The crisis concerned the quality of his kingship, nothing less. Stratford, certainly, had understood its seriousness, and perhaps the measure of his success and of the service he rendered to Edward was that the crisis of 1341 was the last in the reign in which accusations of rebellion and threats of deposition were employed.

CHAPTER XIII

The Second Crisis over Taxation:
IV Parliament and the Crown, 1341–1343

ONCE King and archbishop left their polemics and came to grips, Stratford's strategy was essentially defensive. He could expect support from an opposition of all estates, even more formidable than that in 1340, which derived its cohesion and principles from the May settlement. Thus Stratford's first success in forcing the King to summon parliament was not merely a vindication of the Lancastrian tradition but was due to his insistence that the King was attacking not him alone, or even the council, but the validity of the whole achievement of the previous May parliament.[1]

When parliament assembled, the King's one hope of retaining the initiative and enforcing his demands was to prevent the elements of this opposition uniting under the archbishop's leadership. This meant excluding Stratford from parliament and denying him the King's presence. The failure of this, marked by the formal admission of Stratford to the King's grace, on Thursday 3 May, was thus followed by the presentation of petitions from the Lords and Commons. Stratford's admission was secured by the lay magnates and signified their support for his charges against the 'evil counsellors'. Salisbury and Northampton brought him into the council; Arundel endorsed his attack on the evil counsellors, asserted the baronial right to aid and maintain the King in the great affairs of the realm, and backed his claim for trial by peers.[2] Stratford's admission to the council on 28 April entailed that he should be presented with the accusations against him and have the oppor-

---

[1] The writs of summons were issued on 3 March 1341, that is after the *Libellus Famosus* and Stratford's reply but before the King's assurance of safe conduct on 6 March and his letter to the Pope on the 14th.

[2] Warenne's protest is recorded in the *Croniques de London*, p. 90. It took place on 28 April. I have followed the chronology suggested by B. Wilkinson, 'The Protest of the earls of Arundel and Surrey in the Crisis of 1341', *Eng. Hist. Rev.* xlvi (1931), esp. pp. 187–8, 192–3. For the attitude of Arundel and Warenne, see also M. V. Clarke, *Fourteenth Century Studies* (Oxford, 1937), p. 128.

tunity to answer, and that if his answers failed to satisfy, the peers should ordain what should be done. The King put in writing twenty-two articles, on which the archbishop denied culpability.[1] Thus Stratford had secured what he had sought in January and February, namely that his case should be dealt with by the peers. It was doubtless the realization of this which provoked Kilsby and Darcy to arraign him by notorious defamation before the Londoners on Sunday and, probably, the Commons on Monday (29–30 April). Stratford seems to have hoped to clear himself by compurgation, offering to do so in council on Tuesday 1 May, where his chosen compurgators were named, and again before the King on the following day.[2] The *consiliarii* around the King would have none of this, but when Stratford then asked for a public hearing they shouted him down. Next day he humbled himself before the King and was readmitted to the King's grace, repeating his request for a hearing in full parliament on the things of which he was notoriously defamed. He was seeking an open attestation of his loyalty.[3] To this the King acceded in principle but postponed the appointment of auditors of the archbishop's case until the end of parliament.[4]

---

[1] *Croniques de London*, p. 90. It seems clear that in the first stages of the crisis the King had sought to convict the archbishop by the King's own record attested as notorious by the baronage and the realm. Stratford's detailed reply to the *Libellus Famosus*, his appeal to the people, and his claim for trial by his peers successfully countered this. A trial before the peers required both written accusations and the chance to answer them. See Bellamy, op. cit., p. 54.

[2] Birchington, in *Anglia Sacra*, p. 40. G. Lapsley (*Crown, Community and Parliament*, pp. 249–50) argued that Birchington had confused this with the committee recorded on the parliament roll as appointed on 3 May to consider the question of trial by peers. B. Wilkinson (op. cit., p. 183) would follow the chronology and accuracy of Birchington in holding this to be a different committee. The identity of the two committees would be natural since they were considering the theoretical and practical aspects of the same problem. For if Stratford was indeed seeking to proceed by way of compurgation he would probably have selected his compurgators from among those favourably disposed towards him, and the composition of the committee lends supports to this. The essence of compurgation was an avowal of belief in the innocence of the accused by members of his own order and, in political terms, this was equivalent to trial by Stratford's peers. The committee was composed of the bishops of London, Hereford, Bath, and Exeter; the earls of Arundel, Salisbury, Huntingdon, and Suffolk; Lords Percy, Wake, Bassett, and Neville.

[3] Birchington, p. 40; *Rot. Parl.* ii. 127 (8): 'issint q'il soit overtement tenuz pur tiel com il est'—hence the demand for a hearing 'en pleyn parlement'.

[4] *Rot. Parl.* ii. 131.

Stratford's personal quarrel with the King having been thus far settled, the business of the full parliament now commenced. Most immediate were a petition from the magnates and the appointment of a committee of Lords to report on the question of trials of peers. This was followed, some time before Monday 7 May, by the joint petitions of Lords and Commons which had been formulated in the previous week. On Monday 7 May the committee reported on the question of trials of peers; on Wednesday 9 May the King's answers to the joint petitions were received, judged unsatisfactory, and passed to a committee; concurrently the clergy presented their own petition of grievances. The King answered the clergy on Friday 11 May, but this again was not to their satisfaction and a committee which included lay lords was set up to work on this. Finally on Saturday the King's final answers to the Lords and Commons were agreed by the committee and accepted.[1] Thus a week of testing dispute had proved the alliance of Lords and Commons, and had forced from the King concessions which he later repudiated as derogatory to the estate of the Crown. How important was the contribution of Stratford to this? Did he, as has been claimed, form a party on grounds of common interest between the discordant elements of an opposition—an achievement located in the two days following his admission to full parliament on 3 May?[2] Or was there—as has been objected—no consolidated opposition to the Crown at all, and even among the Lords only half-hearted support for their demands?[3]

It must be emphasized that Stratford himself was in no position to lead the opposition in parliament. He stood accused by the King on certain charges and even at his formal reconciliation with Edward had not been permitted formally to purge himself. These charges stood throughout the course of the parliament. This may have been a deliberate tactic by the King, for with his case still *sub judice* the archbishop could not lead the opposition; and in fact he sat on neither of the committees appointed in this parliament.[4] Moreover, before 3 May Stratford had been excluded from full parliament, and until

[1] *Rot. Parl.* ii. pp. 127–31.
[2] Lapsley, op. cit., p. 252.   [3] Wilkinson, op. cit., pp. 188–90.
[4] That is, the committee to report on the trial of peers and the committee to consider the King's responses to the petitions (*Rot. Parl.* ii. 127, 129).

28 April from the council. It was precisely in this period that Lords and Commons were debating their demands which were formulated by 3 May.[1] Before 3 May they had probably been meeting apart to do so, and though they presented their demands in common, the individual articles were differentiated as coming from them jointly or from the Commons alone. Even if there was communication between them,[2] it seems clear that from when they first met Lords and Commons each had definite grounds for opposition and a clear programme of demands and that this was independent both of the archbishop's leadership and of the particular charges against him. The substance of this programme was the defence of those parts of the settlement of 1340 which the King's actions had threatened. Such unity as the opposition possessed had been generated in preceding months by the King's actions and Stratford's defence. Indeed Stratford's task was not so much to make a party as to avoid distracting by his personal case a party and a programme which already existed. Particularly was this true of the lay magnates. The nucleus of the opposition —those who sat on every commission appointed in this parliament—consisted of a group of eight magnates, four earls and four barons, six of whom had been Stratford's associates in the home council of 1338–40 and had assumed responsibility with him for the government of England after the King's departure in July.[3] In fact, both in terms of personalities and issues, the crisis of 1341 marked the culmination of the long-standing conflict between the home and privy councillors of the King.

It was in this respect that the Commons were likewise implicated. At the opening of parliament the King had been careful to affirm that he sought no further aid, but merely the

[1] Parliament had begun on Monday 23 April, but the Lords had not assembled until Thursday 26 April when the cause of summons was explained. A week followed, until Thursday 3 May, during which there were 'ascuns debatz mutz sur ascuns articles queux les Grantz et Communes de la terre demanderent de nostre Seigneur le Roi' (*Rot. Parl.* ii. 127 (6)).

[2] W. N. Bryant, 'Some Earlier Examples of Intercommuning in Parliament', *Eng. Hist. Rev.* lxxxv (1970), p. 55.

[3] These were the earls of Arundel, Huntingdon, Salisbury, and Northampton; Lords Wake, Percy, Neville, and Bassett. Salisbury and Northampton were closely associated with the campaign in Brabant and had returned with Edward in June 1340. Northampton had been present at the parliament of March 1340 but had taken no part in the ensuing administration, whereas the other six lords had served on many of the committees (*Rot. Parl.* ii. 113–16, 119, 122).

speedy and effectual collection of what he had previously been granted.[1] Similarly, Lords and Commons claimed that all things in the statute granted in return for the ninth should be observed, or they would not be obliged to pay the ninth or be charged in any other way.[2] Thus both sides sought to enforce the settlement of 1340 which each accused the other of failing to honour. The King sought his tax, the community its liberties.

The Lords adopted their traditional role as defenders of these liberties. The requests which they put to the King on Thursday 3 May to which, with one exception, he gladly assented, were for the most part an affirmation of traditional rights. The Charters were to be observed, the liberties of cities to be maintained, and none should be denied writs to enforce these. In asking that any breaches of the Charters should be declared in parliament and redressed by the peers and that any violator should be judged by the peers in parliament the Lords were going beyond the statute of 1340 or any other existing legislation, though such demands strikingly echoed the petitions of the Commons themselves in 1340.[3] Even so, the King accepted them, and all these requests became chapter 1 of the statute 15 Edward III.[4] The peers in parliament were thus constituted permanent guardians of the Charters, and this was substantially the role that had been sought for them by the Commons. Their other request, that peers should only answer trespasses alleged against them by the King before their peers in parliament raised some uncertainty in the King's mind, but he accepted the report of the committee in upholding the claim and this constituted chapter 2 of the statute. The King's assent

---

[1] *Rot. Parl.* ii. 127 (5).   [2] Ibid., p. 128 (16).

[3] Ibid., pp. 127 (7), 132 (50). Compare the petition of 1340 with regard to the liberties of the Church (cap. 1) and complaints against royal officials (cap. 5), printed below, Appendix A item i.

[4] The King had answered that any person who in future committed any offence against the Charter, the statutes, or the laws of the land should answer in parliament or wherever else he ought to answer at common law (*Rot. Parl.* ii. 130 (35)). The statute extended this to comprise any minister of the King or other person who, infringing the Charter, statutes, or laws, was to answer either at the King's suit or at the suit of the party where no remedy or punishment had previously been ordained, whether he had acted by commission or commandment of the King or by his own authority (ibid., p. 132 (52); *S.R.* i. 296). This was an important addition because it made the lesser officials of the Crown justiciable in parliament. It echoed the Ordinances cap. 40 and the Commons petition of 1340 section 5.

to the requests of the Lords opened the way to the six more detailed articled articles of the Lords and Commons. The prologue to these recalled the charters of liberties and the statute of 1340 granted for the ninth, complaining that these had been infringed and demanding that they be observed.[1] Most of the six articles sought particular remedies. The principal officers of state were to swear to maintain the laws, charters, and statutes; the concessions of 1340 respecting pardons and debts were to be observed and the infringements punished by the peers in parliament. Both requests provided additional sanctions beyond the 1340 statute, though both received royal assent.[2] Two other requests to which the King assented were for the repeal of the statute of Northampton which had authorized attachments before inquest, and for the repeal and amendment of the recent commissions of trailbaston.[3] Except for the last of these, on which a commission of inquiry was instituted,[4] all were woven into the statute of 1341. The general effect of these concessions had thus been to reaffirm existing legislation where it was felt to have been violated, and to provide redress by extending the role of the peers in parliament as judges of their own order, of illegalities of royal officials, and of general infringements of the Charters.

The two remaining articles were made specifically in the name of the Lords and Commons and dealt with the rendering of accounts and the composition of the council. Article 3 asked for a committee to hear the accounts of all who had received the King's money since the beginning of the war, this being essentially the demand that Stratford had made in his letter in January, and which the Commons had secured in the parliament of 1340. The King assented to this 'as has been ordained on previous occasions', and as before a committee of Lords and Commons was chosen in parliament.[5] The King had thus been

---

[1] *Rot. Parl.* ii. 128 (9).   [2] Ibid., p. 128 (10, 11).

[3] Ibid., p. 128 (13, 14). Significantly, the petition asked that commissions of trailbaston should be issued by parliament and hinted that only those under such authority were *droitureles*. For a further discussion of this point, see below, pp. 405–6.

[4] Ibid., pp. 133–4. For the limitations imposed on the trailbaston, see D. Hughes, *The Early Years of Edward III*, pp. 169–70

[5] *Rot. Parl.* ii. 128 (12), 130 (38). On 3 July the King had ordered the Exchequer to summon Charnels and Monteflorum to account 'in pursuance of the resolution of parliament' (E 159/117 m. 124) and the committee to audit and discharge the accounts of receivers of the King's wools, goods, and jewels beyond the seas,

forced to retract the order for an audit before the Exchequer but as a purely administrative measure this concession did not figure in the statute.

The central and most controversial demand by the Lords and Commons concerned the council. Because of the ills that had arisen from evil counsellors, the King was asked to appoint the great officers of state and household and the chief justices by advice of the prelates, earls, and barons in this parliament, and in future as need arose, 'according to the form of ordinances made previously'.[1] This in fact rehearsed almost verbatim cap. 14 of the Ordinances of 1311, and sought to establish as a permanent feature of the constitution the procedure which the King had accepted in 1340 for setting up the council of regency.[2] The chroniclers leave no doubt that what was at issue was the baronial claim to control the choice and appointment of the King's officers, and that Edward refused to compromise his exclusive right of choice when he replied initially to the petition.[3] The eventual compromise, probably worked out by the committee appointed in parliament, left the existing officers appointed by the King, but provided that when any of them should vacate office, the position should be filled by the advice of the Lords and council around the King and that on the third day of each parliament the King should take into his hands all such offices for five days during which such officers should answer complaints against them. Any of them thus 'attainted' in parliament should be dismissed and punished by

---

was appointed on 16 July 1341 (*C.P.R., 1340–3*, pp. 238, 313). Following his revocation of the statute on 1 October the King revoked this concession also, for on 18 October he ordered the Treasurer and Barons of the Exchequer to call to account all collectors of taxes since the beginning of the reign. (*C.C.R., 1341–3*, p. 294).

[1] *Rot. Parl.* ii. 128 (15).

[2] The petition of the Commons in 1340 had asked 'that such men be ordained to counsel him and govern his realm who are good and loyal men of the land and no others, to be chosen in this parliament and from parliament to parliament' (cap. 5). Text in Appendix A item i.

[3] The actual terms of the King's answer are not known, but Murimuth says 'quod majores officiarii regis eligerentur per pares regni in parliamento . . . sed de praefectione et electione officiariorum suorum non concessit' (*Adae Murimuthi Continuatio Chronicorum*, ed. E. M. Thompson, pp. 119–20). Baker, similarly, 'et maiores officiarii domini regis a paribus regni in parliamento eligerentur' (*Chronicon Galfridi le Baker de Swynbroke*, ed. E. M. Thompson, p. 73).

judgement of his peers.[1] This extended to the greater ministers
of the Crown the same principle of answerability before the
peers in parliament that the statute had already ordained for
lesser officials. An obvious precedent existed in cap. 40 of the
Ordinances, but the most direct model was the Commons'
petitions of 1340, where the answerability of ministers and
officials to the council and the procedure of complaint against
them were both explicitly set forth.[2]

In substance, therefore, the demands of the magnates and
Commons in 1341 contained nothing new: they were a return
to the settlement of 1340. As the chroniclers saw it, the King
was brought back to the letter of the Charters,[3] breaches of
which were now to be punished by authority of the peers in
parliament. But in 1340 the Charters were of less political
importance than the institution of conciliar government; and
whereas in 1340 this had been authorized in parliament for the
term of the King's absence, in 1341 the opposition sought to
give it statutory sanction and embody it in the constitution. It
was this that constituted the real threat to the royal prerogative;
hence Edward refused to concede the principle of baronial
nomination of his council, even though he had to accept that
his ministers should be answerable before the peers in parliament at the complaint of both subjects and King. Primarily
this was a matter for the magnates, yet it touched the Commons
too; indeed whereas the magnates failed to secure the right to
choose royal ministers, the answerability of ministers at the suit
of subjects in parliament gave the Commons a valuable weapon

[1] *Rot. Parl.* ii 131 (41); *S.R.* i. 296. See also Murimuth, p. 120, Baker, p. 74.
'Atteint' in the legal terminology of the fourteenth century 'signified that proper
legal process against the accused had been completed and he had been found
guilty' (Bellamy, op. cit., p. 50).

[2] Cap. 5: 'the said peers shall have full power on all occasions when they are in
session as stated, to bring to answer all the King's ministers, Justices, Barons,
Clerks of the Exchequer and the Clerks of the Chancery, and all other ministers
concerning their behaviour both at the suit of the plaintiff and at the suit of the
King by inquiry before them; thus any who are "attainted" of any misdeed or
have taken anything illegally for their office can be duly punished by the award
of the said peers.' Text in Appendix A item i.

[3] Thus Baker, p. 73: 'pecierunt quod magna carta et illa de foresta cum aliis
ecclesie et regni libertatibus forent ad unguem observata'; and Murimuth, p. 119:
'et maxime quod magna carta et carta de foresta et aliae libertates ecclesiae
servarentur ad unguem'. On 22 May the Exchequer had been ordered to cease
demands for all debts prior to the tenth year of the reign in accordance with the
statute of 1340 (E 159/117 m. 132 d).

for the redress of complaint and for compelling retribution if not reform. Although it is certain that in securing both common liberties and these political concessions the magnates took the lead in 1341—probably to a greater extent than in 1340—it is equally certain that the Commons had their own views on government and administration and a measure of political power which they could deploy in their support. They were allies rather than pawns.

The Statute of 1341, like its predecessor, was the price of the ninth. The further concessions of the King were now matched by the grant of an additional 10,000 sacks of wool to the 20,000 for which the second year of the ninth had been commuted. Parliament itself apportioned this levy between the counties on the basis of their assessment to the ninth, and attached to this grant a number of conditions which transferred its collection to the hands of men of the localities and set up commissions of magnates and others to hear complaints in each shire.[1] How far the expenditure of the new tax was determined in parliament is difficult to judge,[2] but the renewed effort to ensure its collection, minimize the burden of irregularities, and secure its audit marked a complete return to the position in May 1340.

So ended the parliamentary crisis which had begun with Stratford's return in October 1339. It had, in truth, been a tangled affair, the product of a diversity of grievances and circumstances. If in its final stages it had focused on the King's choice of council and control of government, this was because

[1] *Rot. Parl.* ii. 131, 133. Significantly these administrative conditions were included in the third statute, 15 Edward III. On 20 June 1341 two magnates were appointed in each shire to hear complaints arising from the levying of the tax (*C.P.R., 1340–3*, pp. 314–15). Nevertheless the wool was collected only with much difficulty and against some opposition. In July the King agreed that the further 10,000 sacks should not be levied until after 1 August. For illustration of these difficulties, see Barnes, 'The Taxation of Wool', pp. 159–62.

[2] The only grants of wool from the 30,000 sacks warranted by King and council in parliament were those to Bernard Ezii, lord Lebret on 4 June and subsequently (*C.P.R., 1340–3*, pp. 261, 263). Early in June the King made a series of such grants by letters patent, authorized either by privy seal or by the King, to military commanders such as the earls of Warwick, Derby, Gloucester, to continental allies such as the marquis of Jülich and the duke of Gueldres, and to creditors such as the Bardi and Peruzzi (ibid., pp. 223, 261–4). These could well have been agreed during the preceding parliament. It is perhaps significant that the next substantial series of grants of the wool were made during and immediately after the July council (ibid., pp. 247, 250, 257–60).

the dispute had been over the character of royal government. In pursuit of his military objectives Edward had displayed some of his grandfather's manic determination to override all obstacles, an obstinacy which blinded him to practical impediments and limitations, and a euphoric trust that his fortunes were about to turn. To organize the medieval state for war something of all these qualities was needed; but Edward in these years lost the support of the political classes and the populace for his enterprise. His taxation, prerogative levies, and exploitative monopolies redounded into a general reaction against royal government. This coincided with a division amongst the King's own councillors. The confidence which Edward placed in his companions and advisers with him 'in the field' led him to restrict the responsibility of the council at home and produced fear and resentment at the influence and favour of his *familiares*. Under the stress of fiscal and military failures, the gulf between the two councils widened. By the end of 1339 the home council found a leader in Stratford. Himself bitterly affronted by the influence of Kilsby, but genuinely alarmed at the tenor of royal government and steeped in the Lancastrian tradition, he could appeal forcefully to the doctrine of the baronial council as the guarantor against misgovernment by evil and unworthy counsellors. He could cite the grievances of the people as a threat to internal order, the draining of resources to Flanders as a threat to the defence of the borders and the coasts. The co-operation he secured from magnates and parliament gave him mastery in England in 1340. Edward postponed taking up the challenge to his authority to return to Flanders in the hope of a final successful campaign; his renewed failure only doubled the venom with which he attacked the archbishop on his return. None the less his attack was a momentous blunder of political psychology. For the arbitrary attack on ministers and the mass reprisal against the community through the commissions of trailbaston brought into play all the old Lancastrian reflexes. A full-scale hearing in parliament and the setting-up of a council to control the King and the government appeared for the moment as the magnates' only defence against the King's arbitrary favour and disfavour; to the Commons it had become, since 1339, their prime defence against arbitrary and penalizing exaction by royal officials.

The result was an almost total defeat for the King, virtually every aspect of whose government was made subject to the oversight of the baronage in parliament. This was a measure of how seriously the crisis had undone the conciliatory policy of the opening years of the reign and the gradual restoration of royal prestige.

Nevertheless neither King nor magnates wished to return to the conflicts or postures of the previous reign. Even when given statutory recognition, a council forced on the King could never be a solution, merely the means towards a solution. For the magnates that solution was the King's voluntary acceptance of them as his natural counsellors—the restoration to his grace and favour on an impartial, familial basis. For the Commons the desired solution was good government by the King himself. Thus the end of the crisis in 1341 posed for Edward the greatest test of kingship which he, or any King, had to face. Was he to let resentment and obstinacy lead back to the conflicts of his father's reign, or was he to restore the relationship with the nobility embodied in the settlement of 1330? His relations with parliament, indeed with the realm at large, were secondary to this. Unless that is grasped it is impossible to understand why the storm and fury of 1340–1 so completely subsided in the following years. For Edward soon showed his statesmanship by not merely reasserting his right to unimpeded rule but by a gradual reconciliation with the alienated magnates.

It is indicative of the depth of the divisions engendered by the crisis that its epilogue was spun out for a further two years. Although Edward probably acted with the council in authorizing the repayment of royal debts from the grant of wool, the summer saw him reassert his exclusive control of the administration but with the active support of only a section of the nobility. Probably some time in June he placed a stop on the Exchequer of all payments and assignments, reserving all issues for his verbal command.[1] This seems to have remained in operation until at least October and in respect of some

---

[1] E 404/4 Files 28, 29. A series of warrants from these months contain the phrase 'Coment que nadgairs nous eussions mandez par nos autres lettres que vous ne fuissiez nul paiement ne assignement a nulli saunz especial comandement de notre bouche.' I have not been able to find any writ ordering this action on the memoranda roll for this term.

annuities until the following March. Necessary as this was for ensuring repayment to his foreign creditors, it was also a means of bringing the Exchequer firmly under royal control and of favouring those whose support he was anxious to secure. A fortnight after the dissolution of parliament he summoned a council which met on 11 July. Only six earls and sixteen lords were summoned; they included none of the former council.[1] Amongst other matters it must have reviewed the prospects opened up by the disputed succession in Brittany, though for the moment the King's uncertain authority in England, the extent of his debts in the Low Countries, and the disturbing premonitions of a threat from Scotland ruled out any initiative overseas.[2] It was the last of these which came to dominate the King's plans during the autumn and nothing could have been more effective in promoting reconciliation between the King's party and the opposition.

The defence of the north during the King's absence had been of prime concern to the home council, many of whose members were themselves northern magnates. The return of Bruce was discussed at a council which met on 21 September and lasted until early October. At this council, unlike that held in July, most of the earls attended, and it was decided that the King himself should lead an expedition to Scotland at the end of the year.[3] On 7 October the earl of Derby was appointed the King's lieutenant of the army for Scotland and by 2 December he had taken up his headquarters at Newcastle upon Tyne.[4] This revival of royal concern with Scotland promised to provide the basis for the readmission to the royal camp of the dissidents of the summer, and this stage of the reconciliation may have owed much to the activities of the earl of Derby. As the most effective representative of the Lancastrian tradition, a great northern landowner, and a relation by marriage to Lords Wake and Beaumont, he had always enjoyed cordial relations

---

[1] *R.D.P.* iv. 532; *C.C.R., 1341–3*, p. 244. The six earls summoned were Gloucester, Salisbury, Devon, Oxford, Pembroke, and Suffolk.

[2] On Brittany, see J. le Patourel, 'Edward III and the Kingdom of France', *History*, xliii (1958), p. 187. For the repayment of debts, see *C.P.R., 1340–3*, pp. 243–50, 257–60. Other acts of the council are in *Foedera*, II, ii. 1168–9.

[3] Murimuth, p. 121. No writs of summons survive, but Murimuth remarks that 'habuit rex concilium comitum multorum'.

[4] Derby's expedition is discussed by K. Fowler, *The King's Lieutenant*, ch. ii.

with the home council and had been nominated to one of the parliamentary committees in the parliament of March 1340. His loyalty to the King was equally well attested, notably by his remaining with the earl of Warwick as hostage in Malines for the King's debts, to his own considerable expense. His absence from England for this reason throughout the parliament of April–May 1341 further recommended him for the role of peacemaker.

The Scottish expedition was not the only business of importance at this council. On 1 October Edward formally revoked his consent to the statute of 1341. His principal officers had sworn only conditional assent to it and the King now claimed that he himself had sworn not freely but because he needed taxation.[1] By the same token he might have had to reckon with a move by the baronial opposition to prevent collection of the tax, as in 1309. In fact his revocation was made with the assent of the magnates after debate in the council. Both sides acted wisely—the King in proceeding by assent, the magnates in recognizing that any attempt to control the practice of royal government by statute pointed back to Edward II's reign. Already in the summer the King had shown that he intended to resume his rightful power to govern and one of his first acts after revoking the statute was to order inquiry into the accounts of those who had handled the taxes to be resumed at the Exchequer.[2]

Two further aspects of the dispute remained to be settled. First there was the case against Archbishop Stratford, the arraignment of whom had been deposited with his enemy, William Kilsby. Second, the fate of Kilsby and other 'evil counsellors' had to be decided and consequent on this the future composition of the council. Even after the revocation of the statute, Edward had still to take account of Stratford's opposition. He felt it necessary to warn the archbishop in strong terms against issuing a formal excommunication in the provincial synod which immediately followed the council in October.[3] Whether Stratford himself had been at the council is uncertain, but if he felt betrayed several considerations held

---

[1] *Foedera*, II. ii. 1177; *S.R.* i. 297; *Rot. Parl.* ii. 131 (42). Cf. Lapsley, op. cit., p. 255; Wilkinson, op. cit., p. 190.
[2] *C.C.R., 1341–3*, p. 294.   [3] Ibid., p. 335; Murimuth, p. 122.

him back from a further challenge to the King. Without parliament and without magnate support he was in an incalculably weaker position; the realm was threatened by the Scots; above all he was still answerable at the King's pleasure on the charges brought against him, for Edward had refused to allow him to clear himself before the commission. Stratford accepted the revocation of the statute as the price of his final exoneration. On 23 October, in the Great Hall at Westminster before a vast crowd, King and archbishop solemnly made their peace. On the assurance of a chance to acquit himself of the charges, Stratford promised not to pursue his own charges against the *curiales*. In all this the earl of Derby is said to have been the principal mediator though it is clear that Edward himself was anxious for a reconciliation. Stratford's reconciliation with the *familiares* followed on 29 October when Kilsby and others journeyed to the archbishop's manor of Otford to receive the kiss of peace followed by what must have been a somewhat strained dinner.[1] Finally came Stratford's own restoration to the council: he was summoned to the meeting of the great council in February following the King's return from Scotland and by August he was again enjoying a measure of Edward's confidence.[2]

If both King and magnates were seeking a return to harmonious political association, Edward's insistence on his unrestricted choice of councillors and policies, so long as it embraced the *curiales*, continued to make this impossible. Although the summons to the Scottish expedition had been sent to eight earls, including Arundel and Huntingdon, the King was accompanied by only a handful of lords from the border or attached to the household.[3] Edward's return from this largely fruitless journey was marked by a tournament held at Dunstable in

---

[1] We are fortunate in having, in the Winchester Cathedral Cartulary, an eyewitness report of these reconciliations. The text is printed in Appendix A, items ii, iii. Cf. Murimuth, p. 122: 'quo concilio pendente, ad procurationem praelatorum et quorundam comitum, fuit quaedam pax inter regem et archiepiscopum reformata'. The record of the arraignment was formally cancelled in the parliament of 1343 (*Rot. Parl.* ii. 139 (22)). In October 1342 the Exchequer had been ordered to suspend actions of debt against him pending the next parliament (*C.C.R., 1341–3*, p. 662).

[2] *R.D.P.* iv. 537; *C.C.R., 1341–3*, p. 477; Birchington, p. 41.

[3] *R.D.P.* iv. 536; ibid., pp. 353–4. Murimuth, p. 123, says the King was accompanied 'paucis armatis'.

February, immediately prior to the meeting of the great council. There he was joined by the earls of Warwick, Pembroke, Oxford, and Suffolk all of whom, except the last, were of his generation. Gloucester, Warenne, Huntingdon, Arundel, and Devon excused themselves on grounds of age or infirmity.[1] The expedition to Brittany in July under the earl of Northampton comprised much the same group.[2] Kilsby remained in his office as Keeper of the Privy Seal and had accompanied Edward to Scotland, but in June he surrendered the Privy Seal after his rival Zouch secured final confirmation to the see of York. He had passed the zenith of his influence and his presence on Northampton's expedition marked his detachment from the royal councils. His going removed the last barrier to reconciliation with the members of the old home council.[3] The earls of Arundel, Huntingdon, and Warenne did not accompany Edward to Brittany in October 1342 but in November, in response to the King's plea for reinforcements, they joined the council in London under the regent and offered troops.[4]

Thus by the time that Edward returned in January 1343 war and political tact had healed the enmities of the previous five years. Edward had successfully defended his right to rule without constraint; the magnates had successfully asserted their view that he should rule with their co-operation and assent and without arbitrary and vindictive acts. Although the crisis had evoked the language and the remedies of the old Lancastrian tradition, the new political situation offered no ground for their revival.[5] Henceforth though the King made officers and took council of whom he chose, in the great business of the realm he shared his confidence with the magnates. The fact that the principal business was war, that partnership in politics was part of a wider partnership in chivalry and profit, may help to explain why this lasted for a generation. It should not lead us to accept it as inevitable or to underrate the political adaptability or skill with which Edward accomplished his retreat from the policies of 1338.

The reconciliation of the King and the magnate opposition

[1] Murimuth, p. 123.
[2] Baker, p. 76. The earls of Northampton, Oxford, Pembroke, and Devon took part.
[3] Tout, *Chapters*, iii. 162.   [4] *Foedera*, ii. ii. 1213, 1216.
[5] Cf. Wilkinson, *The Chancery under Edward III*, p. 102.

left the Commons to salvage what they could of the concessions of 1341 by their own efforts. In the first place certain safeguards of their liberties had been embodied in statutes; secondly, authority had been given to the peers to exercise constitutional restraints over the King and his ministers. Both had the object of checking administrative and prerogative abuses. When they met in April 1343 the Commons expressed their dismay at the revocation of the statute. They recalled that it had been specifically granted in return for taxation[1] and that the King's promise to hold firm to the concessions of 1341 had been delivered under his seal to the knights of the shires for the assurance of their constituents.[2] Edward was seeking no taxation from the parliament of 1343 and in answering the Commons' protest he affirmed his intention of abiding by the points of the statute that were 'honourable and profitable for the king and his people' to the point of making a fresh statute upon these. Although this never materialized, the King's reply indicated that he was prepared to honour the safeguards of the statute of 1340, which remained unrepealed.[3] Beyond these the Commons in 1341 (as in 1339) had sought protection from the royal commissions of trailbaston.[4] That launched in December 1340 had been one of the most extensive and oppressive investigations of the century, and the Commons had insisted on its abolition and replacement by lawful commissions composed of local men and issued with the assent of parliament.[5] Now the King was again threatening to issue fresh commissions to uncover abuses in the law which had occurred during his absence

---

[1] 'Pur queux Estatutz avoir et meyntenir les Grantz ove les Communes donnerent a nostre Seigneur le Roi les Neofismes pour deux annz' (*Rot. Parl.* ii. 139–140).   [2] Ibid., p. 133; *S.R.* i. 298.

[3] Notably, that is, the confirmation of the Charters and the liberties and customs of cities, and the pardon of debts (*S.R.* i. 295). The revocation of the statute provided that articles contained therein 'which by other of our statutes have been approved, shall according to the form of the said statute in every point . . . be observed' (ibid., p. 297). This suggests that it had not been Edward's original intention to issue a new statute as he now promised, but merely to abrogate what had been novel in that of 1341. In fact, of course, the King did not frame any new statute to replace that of 1341. Cf. Lapsley's discussion of this, loc. cit., pp. 255–8.

[4] Hughes, op. cit., pp. 167 ff.; Lapsley, op. cit., p. 238. *C.C.R.*, *1341–3*, pp. 232, 226. *C.P.R.*, *1340–3*, pp. 259, 219.

[5] 'Et s'il plest a lui d'autres Commissions droitureles par assent de son Parlement isser, selonc ce q'il se sent par ses ministres ou autres estre grevez, que Gentz de Lai, et autres du pays q'ont conussance du port et de les conditions de les officers en diverses parties soient assignez' (*Rot. Parl.* ii. 128 (14)).

in Brittany.[1] Although this was represented as solicitude for law enforcement the Commons were fearful, and sought to impose limitations on the commissioners. They asked that the justices be chosen in parliament with the assent of Lords and Commons, and that before they were sealed the points of the commissions should be shown to the peers 'who have to maintain the laws under you' and to the Commons. Any offences not comprised within the commission were to be dealt with by the courts, and delayed cases were to be referred to parliament. To this the King assented, and the articles of the commissions, having been approved by the Commons, were formally enrolled on the parliament roll.[2] Although the scope of these commissions remained unaltered,[3] in submitting these to parliamentary scrutiny and approval Edward was making a highly significant gesture: nothing less than an admission of the Commons' claim in 1341 that such matters touched the common welfare and should not be issued merely at the King's will. Moreover, in a long sequence of petitions which the Commons presented they sought further curbs on the justices, some of which repeated *verbatim* concessions secured in the parliament of 1341.[4] To most of these the King gave substantial assent and one—limiting the use of exigends—became a statute.[5]

Complaint against the abuse of justice and redress in parliament against the oppressive actions of royal officials had been important and persistent features of the Commons petitions from 1339 through to 1341, and in these matters they had managed to hold on to their most essential gains. For this they had sought support from the peers as guardians of the law; yet it had been the novel role of the peers as a court for redress of

[1] *Rot. Parl.* ii. p. 136 (10).

[2] Ibid., pp. 136–7 (11, 12).

[3] Cf. Putnam, 'The Transformation of the Keepers of the Peace . . .', *Trans. Roy. Hist. Soc.* xii (1929), p. 41. Inquiry was to be made into the chattels of felons and fugitives concealed, into uncustomed wools, the accounts of collectors of the ninth, the bribery of royal officials, the collectors of the wool granted, and the customers and controllers at the ports.

[4] *Rot. Parl.* ii. 136–7. Eight of these petitions (nos. 7, 11, 14, 16, 17, 20, 22, 24) dealt with the powers of the justices, and were repetitions of *Rot. Parl.* ii. 129 (21), 133 (63), 134 (67). Others asked for the payment of wages to the justices; that they should be men of the locality and not baronial or royal officers; that they should bring their record to Westminster in due form.

[5] Ibid., p. 139 (21); *S.R.* i. 299.

breaches of the Charters which, with the provision for the formal
answerability of officers in parliament, had been revoked in
1341 as contrary to the King's oath and a 'blemish' to his
Crown and regality. The Commons made no renewed demand
for these; they merely asked that the Chancellor and Treasurer
should be peers of the land or other wise and sufficient men,
and not royal justices.[1] Despite the evaporation of magnate
opposition, the Commons retained something of their old
Lancastrian attitude. For magnate ministers were in some
degree independent of the Crown; they were not the King's
creatures; the Commons still looked to the Lords to maintain
the laws and liberties of all subjects and in so doing to restrain
the King's ministers and if necessary the King himself. When
Edward, in reply to the Commons' protest, asserted that he
would choose such ministers as he pleased, as he and his
ancestors had in time past, he was bringing to an end a tradition which had embroiled the community in dissent since 1311
and which went back to the reign of Henry III. Edward was
determined that no baronial council should interpose itself between himself and his subjects as the guardian of popular
liberties or the adjudicator of royal acts of government. His
undertaking to make such ministers as were good and sufficient
for him and his people and his protestation that 'it was not his
intention to grieve or oppress his subjects but to rule them by
lenience and gentleness' restated the old ideal of royal government.[2] Magnates and Commons were to be attached to the
Crown by different ties and in different roles; to both the King
would act as a good lord, demanding service and obedience but
affording protection and rewards. But ultimately, if not immediately, the King came to grasp the significance of the Commons' role in the recent crisis. For if he had negated much of
what they had sought and achieved in 1340, and if by 1343
they had retreated from the attempt to determine the structure
of royal government, the new-found status and maturity of the
Commons offered the chance of creating a sense of political
partnership which was to characterize the second half of
Edward's reign.

The crisis had indeed awakened the Commons to political
consciousness. It was they, rather than Stratford or the lay

[1] *Rot. Parl.* ii. 140 (32).   [2] Ibid., p. 140 (32); *S.R.* i. 297.

magnates, who in the early stages had revived the Lancastrian remedies of a council of peers to restrain the King and mitigate the harshness of royal government which was impoverishing and oppressing the land. Derivative though their demands in February 1340 had in this sense been, they signified the emergence of the Commons as a political force behind a definite programme which they looked to enforce through their control of taxation. It was this new corporate self-confidence, the consciousness of a voice and power of their own (though heard and exercised still within a restricted sphere), that proved the substantial legacy of the crisis of 1340–1. For the King's revocation of the statute of 1341 and reconciliation with the magnates, besides undoing the specific achievements of 1340–1, shattered the Commons' own Lancastrian creed of reliance upon the magnates for leadership and support against royal government. They now faced pressure from both King and magnates to provide the services and supplies for a renewed period of war, during which the King's zeal to mobilize the resources of the realm for his enterprise was scarcely less fierce and only somewhat less ambitious than in 1337–40. This situation, which had been tentatively foreshadowed in the years 1332–9, was to persist for the next seventeen years. It was to have profound effects on the development of parliament because henceforth the Commons could hope to limit the King's demands only by their own actions and their own political strength. It finally ensured their emancipation from the Lords in the granting of taxation and in all matters that control of taxation affected, notably the redress of grievances. The history of the Commons as a distinct political entity really starts from 1340.

CHAPTER XIV

The Lay Subsidies, 1344–1360

BOTH in terms of the taxes he obtained and the general support accorded to his war policy, Edward III enjoyed a remarkable degree of success between 1343 and 1360. If the campaigns of 1338–40 had demonstrated the futility of foreign alliances purchased by extensive subsidies, the parliamentary crises of 1340 and 1341 had taught Edward how dangerous popular disaffection could be when harnessed to political opposition in parliament. He profited from both lessons. The expeditions and *chevauchées* of the following two decades were shorter and less expensive than the Netherlands campaign; they gave more scope for the independent initiative of all members of the nobility, avoiding arbitrary division between those with the King and those in England; they were prestigiously successful and highly profitable. This harmony between King and magnates, though it offered some guarantee against arbitrary and oppressive royal government, deprived the Commons of their traditional political leaders. The burdens on the Commons, even during the Crécy–Calais campaign, were never quite so heavy and extensive as in 1338–41, and they had little occasion to criticize the expenditure of the taxes on grounds of military failure. While these considerations reduced the likelihood of major political conflicts, the King himself made pronounced efforts to persuade his subjects that the war was a common concern, waged for the profit and safety of all, for the recovery of just rights against an enemy vowed to the destruction of the realm. Although this was essentially an elaboration of the traditional plea of necessity, its purpose and effect were to win support for royal government as a chivalric enterprise to which the King called his lesser subjects along with his greater.

But although after 1343 the Commons no longer sought the appointment of a magnate council in parliament, nor the appointment of baronial treasurers of the aids, nor the parliamentary audit of accounts, this did not mean that they bore sustained taxation for an ambitious and prolonged war without criticism or complaint. In the twenty years following 1340 they presented, from session to session, a series of demands which came to be procedurally linked with the granting of the subsidy. The extent of the Commons' achievement here will be considered in the next two chapters. Less dramatically but not less effectively the very granting of lay subsidies during this period helped to define and to limit their nature. For eight of the eighteen years between 1342 and 1360 England was engaged in open hostilities with either France or Scotland, the remaining ten years being short periods of truce. Most of the fighting consisted of aggressive English raids on foreign soil. For twelve of these years, and continuously in the decade 1344–54, the realm was paying direct taxation granted specifically for its defence. The implications of these bare facts were momentous. For the first time in English history war taxation had become a normal and apparently permanent feature of government, and this posed some fundamental questions. How could it be justified particularly in time of truce? How could the threat of perpetual taxation be contained? Could taxation for defence of the realm legitimately be used for devastating attacks overseas conducted for personal gain? Simply because they granted taxation, but even more because they wished to avoid granting it, such questions were forced on the Commons. Debate on these questions, amongst themselves and with the King and his councillors, drew attention to the theoretical basis of taxation, helping indeed to disseminate the doctrine of a necessity of the realm but also in some respects to narrow its definition. In this chapter we shall see how the Commons attained a new maturity in defining their responsibilities for the defence of the realm and laid the foundations for their successors to limit their liabilities to taxation on the plea of national necessity.

THE JUSTIFICATION OF TAXATION

The demands of the Hundred Years War made some degree of continuous taxation inevitable, but the particular limitations under which it came to be granted in England were the product of existing precedents and current argument. Elsewhere in Europe there was developing a doctrine of *perpetua necessitas*, which justified the levy of taxes *normaliter* rather than *casualiter*, while some contemporary thinkers held that the plea of necessity enabled the ruler to impose taxation without consent.[1] In England the precedents of 1297 and the practice of the succeeding forty years held such tendencies in check. Edward III inherited a tradition that taxation could only be demanded on the plea of a war in defence of the common safety of all subjects. This plea had to be adjudicated and accepted by the community of the realm in a full parliament of all estates. Moreover, the plea had hitherto always been made with reference to a specific emergency. The existence of a continuous state of war posed a challenge to this tradition. Even if this did not sanction taxation at the will of the ruler, it could be argued that the consent to war given by one parliament bound its successors to grant the means for its continuance. On the other hand it could be questioned whether parliament was obliged to grant taxation during long periods of truce when the realm was not immediately endangered. These posed new and difficult problems.

The parliament rolls record that every tax in this period was demanded and granted for a necessity of the King and kingdom involving the safety and defence of the realm.[2] The scholastic notion of the justice of war waged in self-defence and the obligation upon 'all and singular of the realm to offer themselves and their goods for its defence' had by 1337 been familiarized not merely in parliament but through the writs which royal officers brought to the shires.[3] In a sense this made

---

[1] H. Kantorowicz, *The King's Two Bodies*, pp. 285–8; Gaines Post, *Studies in Medieval Legal Thought*, p. 303. Pierre Jaime, at the end of the thirteenth century, maintained that the King could impose taxation on his subjects *pro defensione regni* even if they refused consent, for in so doing he acted in accordance with the *ius gentium* which obliged all to contribute proportionately to the defence of the fatherland (Gaines Post, op. cit., p. 478). A little later, Fitzralph argued that the King, in virtue of his *dominium*, might impose burdens for the conduct of a common war (cited by C. H. McIlwain, *The Growth of Political Thought in the West*, p. 357). The question is discussed with relation to French practice by J. B. Henneman, *Royal Taxation in Fourteenth Century France*, pp. 22–7.

[2] Thus, in 1339, 'en ceste necessitee'; in January 1340, 'la graunte et chargeaunte necessitee'; in July 1340, 'la grante necessitee q'il avoit'; in 1344, 'pur ce qe la necessite nostre Seigneur le Roi est monstrez a sa commune'; in 1348, 'la grante necessitee nostre Seigneur le Roi'; in 1352, 'en tante necessitee'; in 1359, 'pro necessaria defensione regni nostri' (*Rot. Parl.* ii. 104, 107, 118, 148, 201, 237; *Foedera*, III. i. 503.

[3] '. . . . considerantes quod omnes et singuli de eodem regno pro defensione eiusdem tenentur exponere se et sua' (writ to the sheriff of Bedfordshire and

it harder to justify an aggressive war waged in France. Fear of French invasion was certainly real enough to support the argument that the King should launch an invasion of France as a means of defending the realm of England, and it was in this context rather than as a prelude to a generation of imperialist conquest and profitable venture that parliament had supported the declaration of war in 1337.[1] Throughout the following twenty years the Crown repeatedly recalled this fear. A detailed French plan for the invasion of England in 1339 fell into English hands at the capture of Caen in 1346 and was publicly read out at St. Paul's and later in parliament.[2] Throughout the 1340s the threat from the French, 'to destroy the English tongue and to occupy the realm of England', was rehearsed in the phrases of Edward I's day,[3] despite the fact that the King's victory at Sluys and the Breton and Flemish alliances largely removed the capacity of the French to make further raids. But sometimes the French threats had credibility. The warning delivered to the parliament of 1348, of French preparations 'to destroy and defeat' England echoed the expressed intentions of the French estates in 1347, and in other instances warning of possible invasion was based on alleged evidence of the assembly of ships or troops by the enemy.[4] At other times predictions of the horrors of invasion were disseminated to stiffen public opinion for defensive action. Finally, in 1359 the burning of Winchelsea during the King's absence from the realm aroused

Buckinghamshire, quoted by R. Nicholson, *Edward III and the Scots*, p. 2 n. 3). Compare the King's answer to the men of North Wales in 1336 that all are compelled as a duty to defend the realm against invasion, cited by H. J. Hewitt, *The Organisation of War under Edward III*, p. 41.

[1] See, for instance, Stratford's statement on the origins of the war: 'Philippus de Valesio ad omnes partes maritimas commissiones varias mox transmisit ad interficiendum et destruendum homines et naves Angliae ubicunque in mari poterant inveniri, manum armatam nihilominus ad invadendum terram vestram Vasconie cum omni festinatione mittendo. Sicque per ipsum Philippum et non per vos guerra inchoata juxta deliberationem et consensum parliamenti' (Birchington, in *Anglia Sacra*, p. 30).

[2] *Rot. Parl.* ii. 158; Hewitt, op. cit., pp. 164–5.

[3] *Rot. Parl.* ii. 147.

[4] Ibid. ii. 200; Hewitt, op. cit., pp. 159–60. The Franco-Castilian alliance of 1349–51 revived fears of an invasion and Edward III wrote to the bishops that the Castilians were intending to destroy the English fleet and exterminate the people (*Foedera*, III. i. 201–2). In January 1356, from his winter headquarters at Newcastle upon Tyne, the King alerted the southern coastal shires to the threat of raids in support of the Scots.

a wave of invasion fears similar to that which had gripped public opinion in 1339.[1] Above all the threat of concerted hostilities by the French and the Scots, which would compel the English not merely to fight on two fronts but to face simultaneous invasions when the King himself was fighting overseas, had been deeply embedded in English military thinking by the moment of acute danger in 1297.[2] It prompted the creation of a separate command for the north in 1338, with revenue appropriated to its needs, at a time when the King was otherwise mustering all the resources of the realm for his own expedition. Until the victory of Neville's Cross removed this danger, the defence of the north was a major consideration both in tying up military and financial resources and in limiting support for an aggressive policy in France.[3]

Thus from 1332 to 1360 the heightened tone and increased volume of royal propaganda conditioned the English to living in a state of national emergency.[4] Royal proclamations and royal writs which predicted invasion, ordered measures of defence, arrayed troops, and impounded victuals were issued for different localities in 1345, 1346, 1347, 1351, 1352, 1356, and 1359–60.[5] The obligation on all men to defend the realm was constantly impressed on them by writ and letter and enforced by commissions. Propaganda, both royal and ecclesiastical, was designed to persuade the subject both that his own safety and well-being were at stake and that the King was fighting on his behalf. This strenuous propaganda achieved a substantial measure of success. The Commons avowed that the enmity of the French was directed 'to the overthrow and destruction of our lord the king and his people of England', and that they

---

[1] *Foedera*, III. i. 503, and compare also pp. 468, 471–2, 476–7.

[2] Nicholson, op. cit., p. 105.

[3] The King played on this fear in the parliament of 1352: see *Rot Parl.* ii. 237; *Foedera*, III. i. 315–17. For a discussion of the relation between the defence of the north and the French war, see J. Campbell, 'England, Scotland and the Hundred Years' War', in *Europe in the Late Middle Ages*, esp. pp. 195 ff.

[4] Ever since 1333 Edward had used the threat of Scottish invasion and the evidence of Scottish raids to justify the plea that he was repelling aggression by the Scots (Nicholson, op. cit., p. 112 especially n. 3). The writs to the collectors of the subsidy granted in 1334 declared that 'nobis concesserunt in subvencionem misarum et sumptuum, quos tam pro defensione regni nostri . . . contra Scotorum aggressus qui dicta Regnum et terras hostiliter invadere satagebant et satagunt his diebus' (*Rot. Parl.* ii. 447).

[5] Hewitt, op. cit., pp. 16, 159–60.

would maintain and aid the King's quarrel with all their power.[1] Thanks to the King's victories, the Commons could take pride in their contribution:

> This god commons bi the rode
> I likne hem to the schipes mast
> That with herre catel and here goode
> Maynteyned the werre both furst and last.[2]

It would certainly be a mistake to treat the pleas of necessity recited on the parliament rolls as mere legal phraseology, parliamentary language devoid of actual significance. By the fourteenth century national wars meant at least partial mobilization of the personal and economic resources of the realm, and and this could only be achieved in terms of obligation and consent which had to be practised and accepted at many levels of society. Parliamentary taxation on the plea of necessity formed, as it were, the tip of this iceberg.

Fear of invasion and encirclement undoubtedly provided the most compelling argument for English aggression, but it was bolstered by legal claims and fed by an increasingly militant patriotism. From the early thirteenth century English kings had coupled the defence of the realm with the recovery of their 'rights' in France, and when at length in January 1340 Edward III formally assumed the title to the French throne this feudal and personal conception of the King's war could finally merge with the scholastic doctrine of the just and necessary war fought for national survival.[3] The injury which the French King had inflicted on Edward would 'overthrow him and his realm of England'.[4] The King's plea that he was fighting 'to recover his rights overseas and to save and defend his realm of England' found echoes in the patriotic verses of the time.[5] Where the King's title symbolized the rights and the safety of the realm, his personal danger became a matter of

---

[1] *Rot. Parl.* ii. 237, 227, 136, and see also pp. 104, 107, 147, 264.

[2] Anonymous, 'On the Death of Edward III', in *Historical Poems of the Fourteenth and Fifteenth Centuries*, ed. R. H. Robbins (New York, 1959), p. 105.

[3] On 'Recuperatio' as a justification for war, see J. D. Tooke, *The Just War in Aquinas and Grotius*, p. 181.

[4] *Rot. Parl.* ii. 237.

[5] Thus, in 1340, 'considerantz la pursuite de nostre Droit et de tenir nostre Foi sovereinement'; in 1344, 'en sauvation des Droitz et del'honur nostre Seigneur le Roi et de eux mesmes'; in 1346, 'en pursuite de son querele pur recovrir ses

common, of national concern. It was most evidently so in 1339 when Edward appealed to parliament for aid to release him from his creditors lest he should be 'shamed and dishonoured and he and his people destroyed for ever'.[1] He exploited his personal danger in a message to parliament from the Crécy–Calais campaign,[2] and again in the parliament of 1355 when he sought aid for the mid-winter campaign on the Scottish border.[3] In 1344 the Commons themselves acknowledged 'the hazards which the King and lords faced, at peril of their lives, for the safety of the people of the realm'.[4] Thus both in respect of his title and his personal leadership Edward contrived to make his quarrel that of his subjects.

This commitment of the community to the war was embodied in the promise of parliament in 1337 to maintain the King in an enterprise undertaken with its accord and consent.[5] The emphasis which Edward III placed on this quickly became apparent: first in his demand for a notable subsidy from the parliament of 1339,[6] and later throughout the next two decades when he repeatedly reminded the Commons that he had undertaken the war 'by common assent of them all in parliament, all promising to aid him with their goods and bodies to the best of their power'.[7] This initial assent to the case of

---

droitures par dela et pur sauver et defendre sa terre d'Engleterre' (*Rot. Parl.* ii 118, 147, 157). The lines

> Edward le noble conqueror
> Ki fort et pruz est en estour
> Cil ad grant guere comence
> Pur ses dreitures seu et pene
> Encontre le roi de France en sa terre

quoted by Nicholson, op. cit., p. 2 n. 6, come from B.M. Egerton MS, 3028 fol. 63.

[1] *Rot. Parl.* ii. 103.

[2] Ibid., pp. 157–8.

[3] Ibid., p. 264, 'Q'ils deussent aver regard al grant travail que nostre dit Seigneur le Roi avoit endure pur la defens et salvation de son Roialme et aussint la bone volunte qu'il ad de travailler vers l'Escoce contre ses enemys.'

[4] Ibid., p. 148. For identical propaganda in France in 1338, see Henneman, op. cit., p. 129.

[5] See above, p. 234.

[6] *Rot. Parl.* ii. 103; the 'Libellus Famosus', *Foedera*, ii. ii. 1147–9.

[7] *Rot. Parl.* ii. 157. Thus, too, in 1343, 'par cause que ceste guerre fu emprise et commencee par commune assent des ditz prelatz, grantz et communes . . .'; in 1348, 'par commune assent de tous les grantz et communes de sa terre susdite en diverses parlemens q'ont estez cea en arere come sovent foitz ad este rehercez', and similarly in 1352 (ibid., pp. 136, 165, 237).

necessity undoubtedly made it more difficult for parliament to dispute subsequent demands on the same grounds, and the Commons may have come to feel that they had given hostages to the King by this declaration. In 1340 they secured safeguards against the possibility that in virtue of his new title the King's English subjects would be subject to him as King of France and thus liable to burdens in a double capacity.[1]

Thus Edward, with subtlety and persistence, exploited the plea of necessity to impress on his subjects their inescapable obligation to support the war. Yet however much they rejoiced in his victories and reviled the French, the Commons were never blind to the threat of permanent taxation and were alert to the ways in which royal demands might be restricted. The plea of necessity might be a royal weapon but the definition of necessity contained powerful safeguards for the Commons.

LIMITATIONS ON TAXATION

First, the plea of necessity applied only in time of war. In granting the biennial subsidy of 1346 and the triennial subsidy of 1348, the Commons stipulated that the final year of the tax was to be cancelled if a truce or peace had meanwhile been achieved.[2] A conclusive victory which would bring an end to the war remained their persistent hope, and this, not the continued exploitation of the enemy's country, was the expressed purpose of their grants. Thus the second year of the 1344 subsidy was only granted on condition that the King went overseas in person 'to make an end to the said business',[3] and the victory at Crécy opened the way to what they hoped would be a campaign 'for the final accomplishment of the war'.[4] Edward kept them informed of peace negotiations, insisting that just as he had sought support for the inception of the war, so he would conclude no treaty without their assent.[5] In April 1354, when the conclusion of a peace treaty had advanced as far as

---

[1] *Rot. Parl.* ii. 113. [2] Ibid., pp. 160, 201.

[3] Ibid., p. 148. This condition was rehearsed in the writs to the collectors (*C.F.R., 1337–47*, p. 391). For similar conditions in grants made by Paris in 1340 and Languedoc in 1356, see Hennemann, *Royal Taxation in Fourteenth Century France*, pp. 147, 284.

[4] *Rot. Parl.* ii. 136, 159.

[5] Ibid., pp. 165, 251, 262; Fowler, *The King's Lieutenant*, pp. 129 ff., discusses the draft Treaty of Guines.

an initialled final draft, on being formally asked whether they
would assent to a treaty of perpetual peace, they answered with
one voice 'Yes, Yes'. Nevertheless it was recognized that the
King could not renounce his rights, and the breakdown of
negotiations in 1344, 1352, and 1355 was accepted as evidence
of French perfidy.[1] Having accepted the premisses on which
the war was being fought, parliament could in fact do little to
abbreviate it.

But though the Commons only found final release from the
King's demands with the peace of 1360, they did not necessarily
accept that the state of war of itself justified the demand for a
tax. Taxation had to be sought to meet a specific crisis or
emergency and this enabled parliament to tie its grants to the
achievement of designated objectives. In 1344 they asked that
the subsidy should be safely stored until it could be spent on
the purpose for which it had been asked—the equipment of a
large army to fight in France.[2] In 1348 they asked that the aid
should be safeguarded and assigned solely for the war, and not
for the discharge of old debts;[3] and in 1353 that the tax of the
previous year should be kept for the maintenance of the war
according to the King's intention and not put to other uses.[4]
None of this constituted an illegitimate restraint on the Crown,
for in each case such conditions only elaborated the purpose for
which the tax had been formally asked. But on each of these
occasions the aid had been granted in time of truce and the
Commons' immediate fear was that it might be spent on other
more pressing concerns so that when the designated military
needs matured they would face fresh demands.

Beyond this was the larger and more debatable question of
whether the Commons were obliged to grant taxation in time
of truce. Before the middle of the fourteenth century taxation
had rarely been continuous and had always been demanded for
specific expeditions or invasions. Edward justified his demands
during long periods of truce by warnings that the enemy planned
to resume the war and seems to have convinced the Commons
that the grant of aid was needed to forestall this. He urged this

---

[1] *Rot. Parl.* ii. 147, 237, 264.

[2] Ibid., p. 148. For the operation of a similar condition in France in 1329, see
Henneman, op. cit., p. 77.

[3] *Rot. Parl.* ii. 201.   [4] Ibid., p. 252.

in 1344, 1348, and 1352 to such effect that in 1344 the Commons themselves lamented that the great charges they had sustained for the war had been of no avail because of the enemy's 'feyntes trewes et soeffrances' and urged the King to equip a mighty army for a decisive battle.[1] Thus from September 1347 to early in 1355, although there were only eighteen months of active warfare, the King received lay subsidies for practically the whole period. He collected the final years of the subsidies granted in 1346 and 1348, and was technically within his rights in so doing for in both cases the truce had expired. In 1348 the truce was due to expire in July, within the period covered by the subsidy, and in 1350 the truce lapsed with the death of Philip VI in August and Edward fought a naval action off Winchelsea and conducted a raid from Calais before King John renewed it in September 1351.[2] In both cases there was a hint of opportunism on the part of the King and some discontent in the country. Certainly the conclusion of a truce in September 1347 after the capture of Calais had aroused general expectation that taxation would cease. It was openly said that the King would no longer need the levy of 20,000 sacks of wool which the council of March 1347 had authorized, and Edward had to counteract rumours that it had been suspended.[3] The levy of the second part of the subsidy in October and November encountered more than ordinary opposition, and the issue of further writs in February and March 1348 indicates that in a number of shires there had been refusals to pay.[4] The dislocation caused by the Black Death and the immediate hardship of the heavily depopulated communities led to widespread resistance to the levies of 1349 and 1350,[5] and it is possible that if war had not been renewed in 1350–1 Edward might have remitted the third year of the subsidy, as he did the levy of the *maltolt* and tunnage and

---

[1] *Rot. Parl.* ii. 148, 200, 237.

[2] *Foedera*, iii. i. 230, 232. In May 1351 wardens were appointed in the southern coastal shires and the Isle of Wight was put in a state of defence (ibid., pp. 217, 220).

[3] *C.C.R., 1346–9*, p. 374.

[4] *C.P.R., 1345–8*, pp. 454, 461, 463, 465; *C.P.R., 1348–50*, pp. 67, 77. The King had anticipated refusals to pay the second half of the subsidy granted in 1344 when in November 1345 he ordered it to be collected and stored (*C.P.R., 1345–8*, p. 32).

[5] *C.P.R., 1348–50*, pp. 235–6, 320, 383–4, 389, 519, 526.

poundage.[1] This opposition suggests that the conditions imposed by the Commons in parliament stemmed from their responsiveness to the feelings of the shires. Conscious not merely of the unpopularity of taxation but of the real burden it could impose, yet feeling themselves compelled to grant it for undeniable necessities, they not infrequently sought to appease their constituents by letters patent which recited the plea of necessity and the concessions they had secured in return for the grant.[2] The legalism of the Commons in seeking to limit their obligations in time of truce was thus as expressive of the pressures in the shires as it was of those of the King in parliament. If despite parliamentary reluctance and popular opposition Edward enjoyed continuous taxation between 1344 and 1355, this was due not merely to his popularity or persuasiveness but to the uncertainty which the Commons still felt over the extent of their obligations for defence, which enabled the King to secure the benefit of the doubt.

The Commons' insistence that taxation should be appropriated to specific and immediate needs of war did not so much imply suspicion that the King might spend the tax for his own pleasure as their realization that a ready store of cash could easily be swallowed up in peripheral expenses. At least until 1348 they were convinced that in military terms the subsidies were effectively employed, but they were also intensely suspicious of the King's use of these as security for the loans he contracted with the merchant monopolists. In particular their hostility was focused on the merchants' privilege of buying up the bad debts of other subjects and securing their repayment from the subsidies. At the root of this lay the question of whether taxes became the King's own possession, to be applied to war needs by whatever arrangements he chose to make, or whether they represented public revenues for whose expenditure he was in some way answerable to parliament. The Commons had asserted the latter principle in 1340, and after the royal recovery in 1342–3 they remained watchful of the King's management of the subsidies. This aspect of the King's

---

[1] *C.C.R., 1349–54,* pp. 237, 241. For similar action by the French King in conformity with the principle *cessante causa cessat effectus,* see Henneman, *Royal Taxation in Fourteenth Century France,* pp. 30, 66, 77, 155.

[2] As in 1339, 1340, 1344, and 1348.

dealings with the native merchants was to be an important theme in the parliaments of this decade and we must examine it at least in outline.

Although Edward never resurrected the apparatus of the Walton Ordinances, even for the Calais campaign of 1346–7,[1] he exercised close control over the taxes and continued to use them as the basis for negotiating credit from his financiers. When the first part of the biennial subsidy of 1344 fell due (on 1 November), the truce still held and Edward respected the intention of parliament by ordering the collectors to deposit it in cathedral and priory churches to be kept for the expenses of war.[2] Warrants to the Exchequer in December 1344 for payments from the tax were careful to emphasize that these were connected with the defence of the realm, and prohibited any expenditure of the taxes without the King's express warrant.[3] But already in October Edward had anticipated the tax by a loan of £5,000 from the farmers of the customs, half of which was assigned on these revenues, and in February 1345 the Bardi were receiving payments from the subsidy in discharge of the King's debts.[4] The military expeditions of 1345, of the earl of Northampton to Brittany in June and the earls of Derby, Oxford, and Pembroke to Bordeaux in July brought demands on the stored subsidy which the collectors were ordered to pay in haste.[5] But the summer of 1345 saw the commencement of

---

[1] The administrative arrangements for the King's absence during 1346–8 are described by Tout, *Chapters*, iii. 164–70. Edward had a privy seal of absence and kept in close touch with the home council but never excited the same jealousy as in 1338–40.

[2] *C.C.R., 1343–6*, p. 425; *C.C.R., 1346–9*, p. 18; *C.F.R., 1337–47*, pp. 391, 434.

[3] P.R.O. E 404/5 File 31. Payments were warranted to the Chamberlain of Berwick, to the earl of Lancaster, Bartholomew Burghersh, and the earl of Northampton. The last concludes: 'issint toutes foies que nul assignement se face sur noz custumes ne dismes ne quinzismes a nous grantees ne sur les autres choses reservees pour nous meismes dont vous avez conissaunce saunz expres commaundement de nous' (23 December 1344).

[4] *C.C.R., 1343–6*, pp. 461, 551, 583. These farmers formed the group of seven merchants led by Thomas Melchbourn with the backing of William de la Pole. A larger group had taken over the farm in July 1343 from the Hansards and had been narrowed in August 1344. See Fryde, 'The English Farmers of the Customs, 1343–51', *Trans. Roy. Hist. Soc.* 5th ser. ix (1959).

[5] *C.C.R., 1343–6*, pp. 511, 533. The earl of Derby received £7,825. 14s. as wages and regard for the first six months and the earl of Pembroke £1,989. 5s. 4d. In December 1345 a further £10,200 was sent out to Gascony. See Fowler, *The King's Lieutenant*, Appendix I, pp. 223–4.

a sequence of short-lived companies to farm the customs, from whom the King sought substantial advances on the security of the tax for the great effort of 1346–7. Edward's demand of a loan of 20,000 marks by Michaelmas had precipitated the collapse of Melchbourn and partners, and Wesenham who took over the farm guaranteed this advance on the security of the second year of the subsidy in eleven of the southern shires.[1] At the same time the King extracted a loan of 10,000 marks from the retiring syndicate which was also assigned on the lay subsidy.[2] Nor were these the only loans raised on this security, for in September 1345 William de la Pole advanced 2,000 marks—one of his last loans.[3]

Edward had thus been able to anticipate a large proportion of the subsidy to mount the Crécy campaign, and with the investment of Calais there was an immediate need for even greater sums. The renewal of the subsidy in September 1346 provided the essential security for further loans. Edward's first intention, however, seems to have been to collect the first part, due on 6 December, in cash. On 7 December writs ordered the collectors to bring it to the Exchequer within three days on pain of imprisonment, for the King's pressing business.[4] But as the siege deepened into winter and lack of money brought the threat of desertions the King resorted to more desperate expedients. In February 1347 Chiriton and Wendlingburgh contracted to loan the King £26,000 repayable on the customs on condition that they secured payment from the lay subsidy of old debts (their own or others) up to the value of £20,000.[5] Since most of these were 'hopeless' debts which could be bought up from the King's subjects at a heavy discount this was a profitable speculation for the farmers and a painless way of paying interest by the King.[6] There could be no clearer indication of the King's belief that, once granted to him, the

---

[1] *C.P.R., 1345–8*, p. 100; *C.C.R., 1343–6*, p. 648. Wesenham's farm only lasted until May 1346 when he was ousted by Chiriton and Swanland (*C.C.R., 1346–9*, p. 73; Fryde, op. cit., p. 11).　　[2] *C.C.R., 1343–6*, p. 649.
[3] *C.P.R., 1343–5*, p. 544.　　[4] *C.C.R.*, 1346–9, p. 128.
[5] Ibid., pp. 248–9, 219; *C.P.R., 1345–8*, pp. 277, 569. Special lay and clerical receivers of the tax were appointed to receive the tallies for these debts and charged to make no other payments from the subsidy until these had been satisfied.
[6] Cf. Fryde, 'The English Farmers of the Customs', p. 8. Dr. Fryde has calculated that between 1343 and 1355 royal debts amounting to at least £84,000 were redeemed by the farmers and some other English financiers.

lay subsidy was at his free and personal disposal in the general scheme of war finance. But to treat the subsidy granted for the defence of the realm as part of a commercial bargain designed to bring personal gain to the King's financiers threatened to revive the traditional animus of the taxpayers against royal dealings with the monopolists which had been simmering since 1341. The capture of Calais and the truce of September 1347 brought a respite from war—one, in fact, which was to be prolonged further than could have been anticipated. But the debts from the campaign and the pledges to the merchants help to explain why, despite the truce, Edward was unable to remit the second half of the subsidy and strictly ordered the levy of it in February and March 1348.

Discontent at the King's action and general hostility to royal dealings with the farmers of the customs were manifested in the parliament of March 1348 when the King sought a triennial grant. The Commons imposed a number of conditions on the use of the new subsidy. The prohibition against using it for the repayment of old debts, already noted, was directed against the King's agreement with Chiriton and Wendlingburgh; their ability to purchase these at a discount was the subject of a separate complaint by the Commons in the same parliament.[1] The Commons also prohibited the King from converting the tax into a levy of wool, or raising loans from the taxpayers under general commissions. The council had resorted to both these in raising money for the Calais campaign, and in this parliament the Commons entered protests against a number of its other measures of prerogative finance. Further, they sought to justify their grant of a tax in time of truce by embodying the King's declaration of the necessity, together with their conditions for the grant, in letters patent which could circulate in the shires, and finally they provided for the final year of the grant to be voided if peace or truce still obtained.[2] These proceedings reflected the tensions of a period of intensive war effort, which, as in 1338–40, though on a smaller scale, was marked by a series of prerogative levies and by extensive anticipation of the subsidies through personal contracts between the King and the financiers. The Commons' protests against the former will be discussed in a subsequent chapter; their distrust of the

[1] *Rot. Parl.* ii. 170.   [2] Ibid., pp. 200–1.

King's credit schemes led them to insist on a more rigid appropriation of the tax to the immediate purposes of war, though the circumstances of 1348 made it impracticable as in 1340 to entrust it to special treasurers. For the Commons could no longer look to the lay or ecclesiastical magnates to provide an alternative to royal government; nor were their criticisms grounded on the failure to employ the subsidies profitably in military terms. Their fears were rather that these subsidies would become part and parcel of a prolonged contract with the financiers and would insensibly develop into a permanent element of royal finance. It was this, as we shall see, that inspired their struggle to control the wool subsidy. Against this development the Commons could oppose the two principles inherent in *Confirmatio Cartarum*, on which taxation was granted: first, that inasmuch as the lay subsidies were granted for the benefit and safety of all, they should not provide personal profit to the King's merchants; secondly, that the lay subsidies were granted for a specific emergency and hence for a limited period. Although during the years 1344–51 the Commons were neither able to control the King's expenditure of the tax nor avoid continuous taxation, by granting taxation for limited periods and making their grants conditional on the continuance of open war, they upheld the principle that it served a public necessity which was an occasion rather than a state.

THE PROBLEM OF TAXATION FOR THE STANDING CHARGES OF DEFENCE, 1348–55

The year 1348 brought a different pattern of war policy and war expenditure which offered a new threat to the principle of occasional necessity. Both the effort to capture Calais and the devastation of the plague enforced a respite from the quick succession of aggressive expeditions which had probed and exploited the dissensions of the French from 1342 to 1347. Moreover, the failure of Edward III's attempts to secure the alliance of Louis de Mâle in 1348–50 and of Charles of Navarre in 1354 deprived him of the openings in France which could alone enable him to renew the war on a major scale. Only in areas already under English control, in Brittany, Aquitaine, and Calais, were campaigns conducted, and these were in the nature of a holding operation. There ensued up till 1354–5 long periods of truce punctuated by brief *chevauchées*. In these, and in the warfare of the 1350s in general, the leadership fell less to the King than to his son and other captains. Moreover, the basis of Edward III's war finance was rapidly changing. By 1352 the last of the English syndicates with whom Edward had made personal bargains to exploit the wool trade and supply him with loans had collapsed, and in the following year the trade was regulated by the Ordinance of the Staple and the tax authorized by parliament. Henceforth the King was not merely dependent on parliament for the grant of all forms of taxation but substantially dependent on the Exchequer and his subjects for the speed with which this could be collected and utilized. After almost a century during which the ready availability of loans from Flemish, Italian, and latterly English financiers had enabled vigorous and martial kings to give national war the character of their own personal enterprise, and to plan vast alliances if also to plunge into heedless debt, war finance was henceforth to be dependent wholly on parliament and controlled by the Exchequer; it became in consequence less flexible, less purely royal, more national in character and more limited in scope. To this changing pattern of war finance the new character and extent of English military commitments contributed.

The campaigns of 1342–8 left English forces established in three areas of France. The capture of Calais meant that for the first time in her history England was burdened with something like a paid standing army. A Treasurer of Calais, William de Salopia, was appointed with effect from 1 January 1348 and continued in office until 2 April 1350. During these two and a quarter years his receipts averaged about £10,672 p.a., derived mainly from the Exchequer though some was advanced by Chiriton and Wendlingburgh. From April 1350 until the end of 1351 Henry Tatton and Thomas Baddeby were successive Treasurers, the total of their receipts for this period being £15,824, an average of £9,040 p.a. Again, the farmers of the customs contributed a portion of this, larger in 1350 than in 1351; however, with the commencement of the treasurership of Richard Eccleshall who accounted from 1 January 1352 until 21 February 1361, the whole receipt, apart from the local revenues, was drawn direct from the Exchequer. For the first three years of his account, from the beginning of 1352 to the end of 1354, he received a total of £24,819. 11*s*. 1*d*. from the Exchequer, an average of £8,273 p.a. For the three years 1355 to 1357, marking the projected campaign in the north of France, his receipts soared to £21,579 in 1355 and then fell gradually back to £15,649 in 1356 and £12,378 in 1357. Thereafter for the three years February 1358 to February 1361 his receipt from the Exchequer totalled £38,656. 17*s*. 4*d*., an average of £12,885 p.a. Calais was to continue to cost rather over £12,000 p.a. in the future.[1]

In Gascony military activity was greatest during the lieutenancy of the earl of Lancaster, 1345–50, the repulse of the French attack at Saintes in September 1351, and later during the Black Prince's campaigns of 1355–7. The reorganization of the defences of the Duchy between 1347 and 1350, although it employed troops more effectively in holding and extending the English lands by a succession of short operations, increased the cost, while the granting of lands to local anglophile lords meant a decline in the revenues of the Bordeaux treasury.[2] Gascon defence could not be financed wholly from local sources and became a regular charge on the English Exchequer. Between 1348 and 1361 a total of £86,227 was paid by the Exchequer to the Constable of Bordeaux. Of this £78,459 was paid on the accounts of John Stretele and John Charnels between 1348 and

[1] The following table has been compiled from the enrolled accounts of the Treasurers of Calais, P.R.O., Foreign Accounts.

				Recepta Scaccarii
E 372/194	William de Salopia	1 Jan. 1348–31 Dec. 1348	£11,160. 15*s*. 1*d*.
E 372/194	,,	,,	1 Jan. 1349– 2 Apr. 1350	£12,853. 0*s* 10*d*.
E 372/195	Henry Tatton	2 Apr. 1350– 2 Apr. 1351	£8,382. 1*s*. 8*d*.
E 372/196	Thomas de Baddeby	2 Apr. 1351–30 Dec. 1351	£7,442. 16*s*. 0*d*.
E 372/198	Richard Eccleshall	31 Dec. 1351–28 June 1353	£10,465. 6*s*. 7*d*.
E 372/201	,,	,,	28 June 1353– 9 Feb. 1355	£14,354. 4*s*. 6*d*.
E 372/201	,,	,,	10 Feb. 1355– 8 Feb. 1356	£21,579. 2*s*. 2*d*.
E 372/203	,,	,,	9 Feb. 1356– 8 Feb. 1357	£15,649. 10*s*. 7*d*.
E 372/203	,,	,,	9 Feb. 1357– 8 Feb. 1358	£12,378. 16*s*. 8*d*.
E 372/203	,,	,,	8 Feb. 1358– 9 May 1358	£3,433. 13*s*. 4*d*.
E 372/206	,,	,,	9 May 1358– 9 May 1359	
E 372/206	,,	,,	9 May 1359– 9 May 1360 } £35,223. 4*s*. 0*d*.	
E 372/206	,,	,,	9 May 1360–21 Feb. 1361	

[2] Discussed at length by Fowler, op. cit., chs. iv and vi, and in 'Les Finances et la discipline dans les armées anglaises en France au XIVe siècle', *Les Cahiers Vernonnais*, iv (1964), pp. 59–60. Gascons became a heavy charge after 1337; in 1324 it was expected to yield £13,000 p.a. to the English Exchequer: see below, Appendix B item i.

the end of 1356. Thereafter the cost of maintaining the English hold on Gascony was much reduced, amounting to only £7,262 in the remaining five years, an average of about £1,500 p.a. It is indicative of the extent of Lancaster's operations and of the Exchequer's heavy liabilities that of the £34,675. 18s. which Stretele nominally received between September 1348 and the end of 1350, only £10,097 was actually paid to him at the time. He continued to receive payments with some regularity up till April 1353 by which time a further £12,777 had been discharged, but he was not finally paid in full until July 1358. During the three and a half years from December 1350 to April 1354, which formed an interlude in Stretele's two periods of office, the charge of Gascony was relatively light, in total no more than £10,500 or an average of only £3,000 p.a. On resuming office in April 1354 he secured the payment of the bulk of what was due from before 1350 in two instalments, amounting in all to £11,233. He was fortunate, for almost immediately he had to face the expenses of the Black Prince's campaigns, and in the first three years of his new account, up to January 1357, he acknowledged the receipt from the Exchequer of £33,790. Thereafter as noted, the average annual charge upon the Exchequer was about £1,500 p.a.[1]

The cost of maintaining the English garrisons in Brittany was nowhere near as large as for those in Gascony. Although the original arrangements concluded by Edward in 1343 had provided for all ducal revenues to be handed over for the support of the King's lieutenant, the accounts of successive Treasurers of the Duchy show that these were inadequate and difficult to collect. In consequence, troops serving under the lieutenants had to be paid from England. Gradually, however, many of the fortresses were granted away by Edward III or secured as fiefs and became financially independent, returning

---

[1] The following table has been compiled from the enrolled accounts of the Treasurers of Bordeaux, P.R.O., Foreign Accounts.

			Recepta Scaccarii
E 372/207 John de Stretele	15 Sept. 1348–26 Dec.	1350	£34,675. 18s. 0d.
E 372/198 John de Charnels	27 Dec. 1350– 5 Nov.	1351	£1,191. 13s. 4d.
E 372/207 William de la			
Pomeraye	6 Nov. 1351–16 July	1352	NIL
E 372/199 John de Charnels	17 July 1352– 4 Apr.	1354	£9,307. 17s. 5½d.
E 372/207 John de Stretele	4 Apr. 1354–20 Sept.	1361	£41,052. 6s. 10s.

no revenues to the Treasurer but living off their immediate neighbourhood. This pattern, of supporting garrisons by ransoms from the surrounding area, spread also to the three principal fortresses, Vannes, Bécherel, and Ploërmel. Their ransoms provided the Treasurer with his largest single source of revenue, and though this was insufficient to pay the lieutenant the residual charge to the English Exchequer was not great. Brittany thus became financially almost self-sufficient, though at the cost of limiting the control which the lieutenant could exercise outside the royal garrisons. Moreover, after the battle of Mauron in August 1352 Brittany was not troubled by French attacks.[1]

To maintain these positions on the continent the English needed unimpeded access by sea and the most important battle of these years was in fact fought in the straits in August 1350 under the King's own command. Although the victory was real and twenty years later the Commons in retrospect could celebrate the time when Edward was reputed 'King of the Seas', the price of security was eternal vigilance. Fleets for the west and north were commissioned in March 1351 when French activity in the Channel actually cut off Calais, but in August 1351 the conclusion of a truce with Castile did something to alleviate the threat.[2] Persistent fears of attacks on the southern coast throughout these years gave countenance to the King's financial demands: it was specifically for the defence of Gascony and Brittany and the safeguard of the sea that Edward asked parliament to renew the lay subsidy for a further three years in 1352.[3]

Yet apart from the thirteen months from August 1350 to September 1351 and for the period from the summer of 1352 to the spring of 1353, these were years of virtually continuous truces with the increasing hope that these might be converted into a permanent peace.[4] Embassies to extend the truce and

---

[1] K. Fowler, op. cit., pp. 165–70; also in *Les Cahiers Vernonnais*, iv. 62–3. In 1345 John Charnels accounted for £398. 15s. 4d. paid to men going to Brittany (E 372/199) and Dagworth's account for 1346–7 acknowledged an Exchequer receipt of £2,790. 0s. 11d. (E 372/203).

[2] *Rot. Parl.* ii. 311; *Foedera*, III. i. 215, 245. Cf. Fowler, op. cit., pp. 99–100.

[3] *Foedera*, III. i. 217, 220, 245; *Rot Parl.* ii. 237.

[4] For the renewal of the truce, see *Foedera*, III. i. 225, 230, 232, 254, 260, 262, 266, 276.

explore the terms of peace were numerous and could be expensive if they included the higher nobility. The duke of Lancaster was sent to Guines in July 1353 and again, with the earl of Arundel, to Avignon from August 1354 to January 1355, their joint expenses amounting to £5,648—'the cost of a short campaign'.[1]

Thus the general pattern of expenditure on the continuing commitment overseas showed heavy expenditure up till 1350–1 for the defence of Gascony, the sea, and Calais, followed by a period of more moderate outlay (apart from that for the peace embassies) until the fresh demands made for the campaigns of 1355–7 both in Gascony and the north. But even during the intermediate years the cost of maintaining the English garrisons abroad amounted to not less than £12,000 p.a. In addition to all these the King faced, after 1348, a possibly even greater burden, namely the discharge of the debts of his previous campaigns. When Wetwang closed his account as Keeper of the Wardrobe in November 1347, he owed wages for the Crécy–Calais campaign totalling £16,105.[2] Behind this lay the debts bequeathed by Norwell from the campaigns of 1338–40 which had totalled over £73,000 at the close of his account, and those from the Scottish and Breton campaigns of 1341–3 which Edington left unpaid in April 1344.[3] Payments of sizeable sums were made on all these accounts during the years 1348–55[4] and the surviving warrants for the discharge of wages of war and contributions to ransoms dating from the Crécy–Calais campaign are particularly numerous during 1351.[5] Beyond these again were the substantial sums owed to a number of military commanders such as the earl of Lancaster, the earl of Warwick, Hugh le Despenser, and Edward Prince of Wales.[6]

[1] Fowler, op. cit., p. 137. The account of Lancaster's embassy is published by F. Bock, 'Some New Documents Illustrating the Early Years of the Hundred Years' War, 1353–6', *Bull. John Rylands Library*, xv (1931), pp. 60–99.

[2] Tout, *Chapters*, iv. 118.

[3] Ibid., pp. 105 n. 1, 111–12.

[4] P.R.O., Exchequer Receipt and Issue Rolls, *passim*. Norwell's outstanding debts still totalled at least £7,375 in October 1348 (E 403/344).

[5] P.R.O., Warrants for Issues, E 404/5 File 33. The survival of this series is, of course, very unequal.

[6] Thus the earl of Warwick received £1,457 in Michaelmas term 1348 and £1,342 by Wardrobe bills of the time of Cusance (E 403/344), £666 in the following Easter term (E 403/347), and £333 in Michaelmas 1349 (E. 403/349). Edward Prince of Wales received £3,752 in Easter term 1349 (E 403/347) and

Permanent commitments for defence and past debts, together with expenditure on current expeditions and embassies, thus amounted to at least the equivalent of the annual subsidy which Edward received during these years of predominant truce. Even when the subsidy was renewed in 1352 it was accepted that the posture of defence was itself costly enough to warrant some support from parliament. Yet these years saw the wool subsidies regularized as a *de facto* permanent tax for defence, and this could only reinforce the restiveness of the Commons at the prolongation of the lay subsidies at the full rate during truce and strengthen their conviction that these must be limited to occasions of open war. The emergence of permanent charges for overseas garrisons between 1348 and 1355 thus featured an important change in the relations of King and parliament over war finance. Since they represented a continuing obligation on the realm distinct from any commitment which the Commons had to support the King's personal expeditions, parliament came to shoulder a more habitual responsibility for war finance and eventually to scrutinize more critically its justification and expenditure.

In a further respect, too, these years from 1348 to 1355 marked the beginning of a new relationship between King and Commons. The Black Death brought a radical change in the outlook of the propertied classes. At least up till 1341 the parliamentary Commons identified themselves with the well-being of the whole communities which they represented. In particular they were acutely conscious of the poverty of the rural classes, of the bare economic margin on which many of the poor existed, and of the ways in which royal taxation and prerogative exactions could cause peasants to abandon their lands and even deprive them of the means of subsistence. This theme is familiar not only in the literature of the period and in parliamentary petitions but in the careful provision for exempting the lowest-income groups from taxation and obligatory levies, in the persistent and fierce opposition to prises, and in

the earl of Lancaster £3,333 in the Easter and Michaelmas terms of 1349 (E 403/347, 349). The Executors of Hugh Despenser received £3,858 in two payments in Easter term 1349 (E 403/347) after negotiations with the Crown (*C.C.R.*, *1349–54*, pp. 32–3, 39).

the safeguards sought repeatedly against prerogative taxation during the decade 1338–48. The Commons' attitude was not wholly, or perhaps even primarily, altruistic; the effect of royal exactions might be to disperse their tenants and disrupt the economy of their own estates. But it moulded their attitude into one of natural opposition to the Crown and defence of local interests. The Black Death began their detachment from this patriarchal attitude to their communities. Real poverty still remained but the opportunities for escape were now greater— opportunities which, however, the peasantry could seize only by individual or organized opposition to their masters. King, Lords, and Commons joined in a swift reaction to issue the Ordinance and later Statute of Labourers. The fact that the enforcement of this legislation depended absolutely on the active support of the class from which the parliamentary knights were drawn prompted the first grant of a tax concession in their interests. The triennial subsidies of 1348 and 1351 were both made more palatable by deductions in respect of the fines gathered under the Statute of Labourers. The growing prosperity of the surviving peasantry and the loosening of seigneurial ties, whether by concession or force, encouraged the Commons to think in terms of taxing rather than sparing the lower classes, a trend which culminated in the Poll taxes when the war was renewed after 1369. Equally indicative of the developing alliance between the Commons and the Crown and nobility was the settlement or quiescence after 1350 of the bitterly contested issues of prerogative levies and taxation of wool which had marked the preceding decade, though that was also a consequence of the declining tempo of warfare and particularly of the King's own role in it. The royal complaisance over the anti-papal and treason legislation during the 1350s and the willingness to confer greater power and responsibilities on J.P.s were other aspects of this new identity of outlook of King, Lords, and Commons. Indeed the middle of the century saw the Commons adopt a new and conscious stance as sharers in government rather than as sufferers under it. It signified their emancipation from the Lancastrian tradition which had cast them as attestors of the evils and oppressions of royal misrule.

THE EXPENDITURE OF THE SUBSIDIES, 1348–55

The changing outlook of the Commons, their consciousness of the permanent military burdens overseas, the concession of fines in support of the subsidies, and the decline of contentious royal exactions all help to explain the apparent readiness of the Commons to renew the lay subsidies during the years of truce. That did not mean that they were indifferent to whether the subsidies were truly needed and were properly spent; their provisos that the tax be stored or suspended while the truce continued indicate the contrary. To the question how the subsidies were spent the Exchequer rolls afford only a partial answer since this can only be precisely traced where they were assigned. Most of the first year of the biennial subsidy granted in 1348 and the first half of the second year—up to the Spring of 1350—was received in cash[1] and was not differentiated from other revenue in the Exchequer's general expenditure. But as far as the evidence goes, over the whole period up to 1355, the Commons had substantial justification for suspicions that the lay subsidies were not exclusively used for current war charges.

Some assignments of the tax by letters patent may claim attention first. In September 1348 £4,900 was assigned to Thomas Dagworth and £2,166 to his squire Colkyn de Lovayn for the capture of Charles of Blois whom the King had purchased from them. Payments to both are recorded on the rolls. In October 1348 Henry Picard and his associates acknowledged receipt of £6,100 which on the King's instructions had been assigned to them from the first part of the subsidy due at Michaelmas in repayment of a loan.[2] These were all the result of personal arrangements of the King. The Receipt rolls show that his official claims on the lay subsidies were just as prominent. In every year the domestic offices—Wardrobe, Great Wardrobe, Chamber, Queen's Wardrobe, and Butlery—received substantial assignments: roughly £14,300 in 1348–9, £9,300 in 1349–50, and £13,500 in 1350–1.[3] Most of these

[1] *C.C.R., 1349–54,* pp. 95, 158, 173, 175. Exch. Receipt Rolls, E 401/396, 397, 399.
[2] *C.P.R., 1348–50,* pp. 146, 197, 213; *C.P.R., 1345–8,* p. 441; *C.C.R., 1349–54,* p. 128.
[3] The following discussion is based on an examination of the extant Receipt and Issue rolls between Easter 1348 and Easter 1355. My object has been to ascertain what were the principal assignments on the lay subsidies and what were

assignments were for the current expenses of Clopton, Cusance, and Retford and must largely have been for domestic rather than military needs.[1] The only substantial assignment of the lay subsidy in these years to the Chamber was of £3,800 in Michaelmas term 1348, but on at least four occasions the tax was used to pay Queen Philippa's debts and there were also fairly regular assignments to the King's Butler. In contrast to these substantial assignments for the royal households, the only assignments of the tax for war were of £2,500 in February 1350 to the earl of Lancaster for service in Gascony[2] and some £13,000 in April 1350 as wages for a quarter-year for the Black Prince and other lords accompanying him to Calais.[3] An assignment of 5,000 marks in Michaelmas term 1450–1 to the Sire d'Albret, Bernard Ezii, seneschal of Gascony, probably represented debts to him of some standing.[4] Thus some two-thirds of the first year of the subsidy and almost half the triennial yield was assigned for personal and domestic charges.

After Easter 1350 the Exchequer handled very little of the tax in cash; nevertheless it is necessary to look at the cash payments from the Exchequer as a whole to obtain a balanced picture of the part which the tax palyed in national finance. Apart from some £8,500 paid out to the domestic departments there were four main items of cash expenditure in the first three terms of the subsidy (i.e. Michaelmas 1348–9 to Michaelmas 1349–50 inclusive). The garrison at Calais with the smaller one at Berwick received some £16,500; repayment of loans to Italian merchants totalled £8,666; the discharge of debts from

---

the principal charges on which (when it was received as cash) it may have been spent. The figures cited have been rounded to the nearest £100 and should be treated as indicative of the proportions of different categories of expenditure rather than as the actual sums for specific items.

[1] For the dates and summary totals of these accounts, see Tout, *Chapters* vi. 90.

[2] E 401/399. Some war debts were also assigned on the lay subsidy, e.g. £1,500 to Edward Prince of Wales on 13 October 1349 (ibid.), £233 to the earl of Pembroke on 9 July 1349, and £666 to the earl of Warwick on 12 September 1349 (E 401/397).

[3] The warrant for this was dated 1 April (E 404/5 File 32). On 6 April the Prince was assigned £2,750 and a further £2,755 on 5 May. He was accompanied by the earls of Arundel, Warwick, Huntingdon, and Northampton. Most of this was assigned on the second term of the second year (E 401/401).

[4] The warrant is dated 28 March (E 404/5 File 33) and the assignment similarly (E 401/404). In 1341 he had been owed a total of £14,692: see K. Fowler in *Les Cahiers Vernonnais*, iv. 59.

the accounts of Wetwang and Norwell some £14,000; and about £20,500 was paid to Lancaster on his appointment to Gascony both as wages and in repayment of sums he had lent in 1348. Thus during these three terms, in the liquidation of war debts and the maintenance of war gains the Exchequer discharged in cash and assignment a burden of some £65,500 and at the beginning of the following term gave assignments for a further £13,000 for an expedition. This total equalled approximately the yield of the first two years of the subsidy, but only half of it could have been drawn from that source since one years' yield had been assigned to domestic and personal charges.

In the following three terms (Easter 1350 to Easter 1351 inclusive) little of the tax was received in cash except for some £4,100 from the final instalment of the third year in the summer of 1351. As already noted, the main assignments on the tax were for the Prince of Wales's expedition in the early summer of 1350 and to a much smaller degree for domestic expenses and royal obligations in the term following. Over the three terms the general pattern of expenditure (i.e. cash and assignment from all sources) was heavily weighted towards military charges, if we include under this heading the repayment of debts. Very approximately, military expenditure totalled some £118,000 against £21,000 for domestic charges. But the bulk of the former went not towards current charges, either for expeditions, reinforcements, or standing garrisons, but towards the discharge of the debts of the previous decade. In particular there was a major effort to clear the accounts of former Constables of Bordeaux, Nicholas Usus Maris, John Waweyn, and John Stretele.[1] In Easter term 1351 alone £58,042 was paid out on their accounts, much of it by the hand of Bernard Ezii, the Sire d'Albret. Payments were also made to individual captains like Walter Mauny and Walter Bentley for service in Brittany, but the other substantial repayment was for loans contracted in England and abroad. In January 1351 Henry Picard was repaid a loan of 20,000 marks made in April 1346, and at the same time £1,579 was repaid to Flemish citizens and £1,346 to Tideman de Limburgh.

[1] Their periods of office were: Usus Maris 1335–9, Wawayn 1343–7, Stretele 1348–50.

The Exchequer rolls do not, of course, provide a total picture of English government finance, for some creditors drew revenue directly from the customs under letters patent, but the picture they give of how the Exchequer apportioned its resources is sufficiently definite in outline to indicate the main priorities of the government's expenditure. During the period of this triennial subsidy (1348–51), the bulk of government expenditure had been concentrated on the discharge of its inherited debt, to the extent of perhaps over £150,000. The amounts spent on current military and domestic charges were both very much less, neither of them perhaps much more than a third of this sum. Although the lay subsidy had been principally assigned to these current charges, it must also have contributed substantially to the discharge of debts by cash payments. Thus in the sense that government expenditure in this period remained broadly military in character, the continuous taxation of these years was both justified and used effectively. On the other hand the current charges of defence formed hardly more than half of the yield of the subsidy; nor was the subsidy reserved solely for military expenditure. It is clear that whatever the Commons' views on this situation (and they were not as yet so clearly defined as they were to become later in the century), the King regarded his war obligations as justifying his demand for a tax and regarded the tax as wholly at his disposal as part of the general revenue of government.

The same major elements of expenditure recur in the period covered by the next triennial subsidy, 1352–5, though the repayment of debts shows a decline while domestic charges increase. More than half the lay subsidy during these years was received in cash at the Exchequer and the Issue rolls show a consistent excess of cash over assignment for all classes of expenditure. Assignments on the new lay subsidy to the domestic charges (mainly to the Keeper of the Wardrobe and the Butler) were approximately £7,400 in 1351–2, £4,000 in 1352–3, and £9,500 in 1353–4 with a further £4,000 in the Michaelmas term 1354–5. Apart from an assignment of £1,300 to the Prince of Wales in July 1352 and another of £1,428 to the earl of Lancaster in November 1353 there were no other assignments of any size on the subsidy. There were, in fact, evident administrative advantages in supporting the domestic departments, which operated their own credit system, with assignments on an assured revenue while reserving cash funds for the payment of military wages. The issue rolls of these years show a steady expenditure on the standing charges of defence. The garrisons at Calais and Berwick received about £9,000 p.a. and a further £5,000 was provided in Michaelmas term 1354 for reinforcements sent to Gascony and Brittany. Payments to John Charnels and John Stretele totalled some £25,000 over the whole period and finally liquidated the accumulated arrears for Gascony. Further remaining debts were discharged including £5,300 in 1354 to the marquis of Jülich representing the arrears on his annuity. In June 1352 the earl of Stafford received almost £5,000 for an expeditionary force to Gascony, and in Easter term 1354 the duke of Lancaster received £1,922 for the costs of a small expedition to Normandy and his embassy to Holland and Zeeland, and over £5,000 for the expenses of his embassy to Avignon.

Though not negligible these sums were markedly less than the large totals of the previous three years. With the debts of the previous decade mainly cleared and only slight military activity, expenditure in both categories amounted to not more than half the total of the lay subsidy received. In general terms, at least, the Commons were plainly aware of this, for at the great council of 1353 they asked that the lay subsidy together with the subsidy on wool should be kept safely without being spent or put to any other use but only for the maintenance of the war 'according to the king's good disposition'. In fact the Exchequer had made large assignments on the subsidy to the household and had probably also delivered some of it to the household in cash. Certainly after 1352 the issue rolls record mounting expenditure for the households of the King and Queen. In 1352–3 this totalled £18,500 of which £9,333 was delivered to the King's Chamber 'ad voluntatem regis'. From Michaelmas term 1354 the Chamber was provided with a regular *certum* at the Exchequer amounting to 5,000 marks p.a. and this was shortly to be doubled. In the year 1353–4, when assignments to the domestic departments were some £9,500, cash prests touched £8,500 and in Michaelmas term 1354–5 they stood at over £18,000 of which almost £3,000 went to the Privy Wardrobe and almost £5,000 was in gifts to the

Black Prince and Queen Philippa. Thus as military expenditure both current and for past debts declined, domestic expenditure rose by about a third; from being no more than a quarter of total expenditure in the previous three years it was now equivalent to that on all military charges. The real decline in military expenditure had, of course, come with the discharge of the debts of the previous decade; current charges amounted to no more than half a lay subsidy which was later to be recognized as the appropriate level of taxation in time of truce. Indeed it was even to be urged by the Commons that the cost of garrisons and the guard of the sea should be borne from the wool subsidies alone. Never again, in fact, was any King to be so generously treated as in these years or to encounter such slight opposition to a demand for subsidies for which there was so little immediate justification. The parliament rolls contain hardly more than a hint that the Commons felt reservations about the continuance of the triennial grants, and record no criticism of their expenditure. It is true that the collection of these taxes provoked more than usually violent opposition, but where depopulation had left a few to bear the burden of the tax under the old fixed allocation the attempt to enforce collection was bound to arouse resistance.

CONCESSIONS TO THE TAXPAYERS

The social reasons for the *rapprochement* between the Crown and the Commons have already been indicated. The concessions they purchased by grants of taxation in the matters of wool taxation and the Crown's fiscal prerogatives will be discussed in succeeding chapters. More directly related to the subsidies themselves were the remissions from the fines under the Statute of Labourers. As B. H. Putnam has shown, this scheme was used twice, in relation to the triennial subsidies granted in 1348 and 1352.[1] The concession was first applied to the second instalment of the subsidy in 1349. Probably following representations made to the council, instructions were issued to the collectors in November 1349 to levy from labourers the sums received in excess of their statutory wages in aid of the subsidy. These instructions were embodied in writs to the collectors for

[1] B. H. Putnam, *The Enforcement of the Statute of Labourers* (New York, 1908), pp. 98–149.

the third part of the subsidy in July 1350, which stated that this was being done 'ex populari conquestione' since the excessive wages which were being demanded made it impossible for landlords to pay the subsidy.[1] The fines, on the other hand, were still to be paid direct to the Crown. In some counties there was a vigorous attempt to use the excess wages in relief of the subsidy but the subsidy rolls do not specify what proportion of the subsidy this formed. The evident difficulties encountered in extracting the excess suggest that the effective relief to the taxpayers was probably not very great. In February 1351, when the Ordinance of Labourers was enacted as a statute, the Commons petitioned that the fines and redemptions should be levied in support of the remainder of the tax, and this was included in the statute; fines were thus added to the excess.[2] Following the expiry of the subsidy, these were to be paid to the King.

When the next triennial subsidy was granted, in January 1352, the Commons made it a condition of the grant that all profit from fines, issues, amercements, and excesses should be levied in support of the subsidy, and the King accepted this provided that these were distributed to impoverished places according to their relative needs.[3] Much more care and effort was applied in making this effective; the Commons drew up a schedule for the collection and distribution of the penalties which provided for local adjudication of how the profits were to be distributed. The collectors were to receive the estreats from the justices, levy the penalties, and collect in each district the difference between the amount of the tax and the amount allowed in penalties.[4] The wages of the justices had to be paid out of the penalties as a first charge. The practical difficulties of the scheme and the opportunities it afforded the collectors for embezzlement have been illustrated at length by Miss Putnam;[5] our present concern is with how much relief it afforded to the taxpayer, for it was this which commended it to the Commons. The sums can be traced on the lay subsidy

[1] Ibid., pp. 258–61.
[2] *Rot. Parl.*, ii. 228, 233–5. B. H. Putnam, *Sir William Shareshull* (Cambridge, 1950), p. 55.
[3] *Rot. Parl.* ii. p. 238.
[4] *S.R.* i. 327–8; Putnam, *Sir William Shareshull*, p. 70.
[5] Putnam, *Statute of Labourers*, pp. 208 ff.

rolls and have been tabulated by Miss Putnam.[1] Although the
arrears from the penalties (collected after the tax had ceased)
were to go to the Crown and not the communities, and this
somewhat exaggerates the sums received, these rolls allow 'a
fairly correct calculation as to the sums actually distributed to
the communities as allowances and it is possible therefore to
gauge the measure of success of the scheme from the point of
view of the taxpayers'.[2] The tax was levied in 45 districts for
3 instalments, giving 135 cases for examination. In exactly half
of these—68—a definite sum is reported, and in 64 of these
there was sufficient to distribute to the communities. The total
yield of the tax during the three years was £114,767. 5*s*. 2*d*.
and the total of the penalties £7,747. 14*s*. 2*d*., i.e. about 6 per
cent of the total burden.[3] But in particular localities the proportion was of course higher and in some cases very much
higher. The counties in which the penalties collected amounted
to £200 or over were: Berks; Bucks; Cambridge; Essex; Herts;
Kent; Lancaster; Leicester; Lincoln–Lindsey; Norfolk; Oxford;
Somerset; Wilts; Yorks West Riding. In these counties the
subsidy paid amounted to £53,252. 15*s*. 8*d*. and the sum of the
tax accounted for by penalties amounted to £5,664. 9*s*. 6*d*. or
rather over 10 per cent. This figure, and the evidence produced
by Miss Putnam for the pressure by the local communities for
the holding of assizes by justices and their prosecution of the
collectors for fraud, emphasizes that the concession could be a
major inducement for the enforcement of the statute and a
major contribution to the relief of taxpayers.

B. H. Putnam has brought cogent reasons for crediting the
Chief Justice, Sir William Shareshull, with this scheme which
marked a significant shift in the relationship between the
Crown and the Commons. For over a decade Shareshull had
strenuously and consistently exploited the profits of justice as a
contribution to the Crown's finances, provoking repeated protests from the Commons in parliament who had sought to limit
the scope of the commissions of trailbaston and the eyre. In the
changed social and economic conditions after 1348, as the
Crown came to side with the landowning class as a whole
against the peasantry, landowners were treated as allies rather

---

[1] Putnam, *Statute of Labourers*, pp. 315*–21*.

[2] Ibid., p. 127.   [3] Ibid., p. 128.

than as victims. The Chief Justice showed himself ready to
enlarge their role in law enforcement as justices of labourers
and share with them the profits of the penalties, even to the
point of using in selected counties the whole machinery of the
itinerant King's Bench (Shareshull's favourite device against
which the Commons had repeatedly complained) to demonstrate the truly sensational sums which could be secured from
fines under the statute when this was rigorously enforced.
Finally, after the subsidy had expired, Shareshull was instrumental in favouring the claim by franchise holders to direct
enjoyment of the fines under the statute.[1] Moreover, the principle of inducing the propertied classes to penalize local communities for their own relief and in support of royal justice was
continued in 1357 when fines from the escapes of felons and
fugitives convicted before the justices were similarly applied to
the subsidy. This again had been a fiscal weapon of the Crown
against which the Commons had protested and bargained. If
it proved far less remunerative than the fines of labourers, it
was still indicative of the new mood of the Commons. They
were rapidly coming to regard taxation not so much as something grudgingly paid to the King under an inexorable obligation for purposes which he determined, but as a charge on
communities in the interests of government and the governing
class. The employment of the lesser landlords in enforcing
legislation, the gentry's growing consciousness of being a distinct social order, the linking of numbers of its members with
the enlarging affinities of the great, all induced a more proprietary attitude towards taxation. The taxes became, in a
sense, theirs as well as the King's; in granting them they participated in government and they were beginning to take a
greater interest in their disposal.

The collapse of the Avignon negotiations brought a renewal
of the war in 1355, just as the triennial subsidy expired. Though
Edward planned himself to go to Normandy in support of
Charles of Navarre, and later did conduct a short foray from
Calais, and though the Black Prince was appointed lieutenant
in Gascony in July and sailed in September, parliament was not
summoned to grant a subsidy until after the King's return in
November. If this showed the King's reluctance to plead the

[1] Putnam, *Sir William Shareshull*, p. 72, 75; *Statute of Labourers*, p. 143.

necessities of war after so long a period of taxation in time of truce, his caution was both justified and rewarded; for after Sir Walter Mauny had explained the resumption of war by rehearsing the Avignon negotiations, Sir William Shareshull was able to cap the plea of necessity with the 'hot news' of the Scottish capture of Berwick town and cite the King's own labours for the defence and salvation of the realm.[1] In so undeniable a necessity the Commons could not refuse aid; yet they granted no lay subsidy, but instead renewed the wool tax for six years on condition that the King put no other imposition or charge on the Commons in that period. If this was testimony to their newly established control of indirect taxation, it was also a significant reaction after the continuous taxation of the years of truce. Their assumption was clearly that the accumulated surplus from the subsidies should be available for the immediate expenses of the campaign.

This surplus indeed existed, though it fell far short of the sum required to finance the ambitious operations of 1355–6. Although part of the cost of equipping the Black Prince's expedition to Gascony was met from the Prince's own lands, and he also received contributions directly from the customs and judicial fines,[2] the bulk of it fell on the Exchequer which, during the summer of 1355, paid out over £19,500 in wages for him and his principal commanders. A further 10,000 marks was sent to the Constable of Bordeaux, £4,000 to the Treasurer of Calais, and £3,330 was spent on shipping.[3] Much of this, in fact, must have been drawn from the third year of the subsidy received mainly in cash at the Exchequer in the preceding term. Payments for the King's expedition in November 1355 totalled some £19,666, and the duke of Lancaster received payments of £7,950 for his diplomatic and military services in these terms. Strengthening the crucial garrisons at Calais and Berwick cost £10,600 and £6,333 respectively while £22,800 was

---

[1] *Rot. Parl.* ii. 264–5: 'dont novels lui sont venuz tut chaudes'. The Commons granted the wool subsidy after a brief consultation with the Lords.

[2] The Prince was granted the money from the sessions held in 1354–5 by Sir William Shareshull in the west country, and 1,000 marks from the customs in London. See Hewitt, *The Black Prince's Expedition of 1355–7* (Manchester, 1958), p. 24; Putnam, *Sir William Shareshull*, p. 74.

[3] The decision that the Prince should go to Gascony had been taken in April; his appointment was dated 10 July (Hewitt, op. cit., p. 4; Foedera, III, i. 307). £6,631 was paid in wages in April and the residue on 10 June (E 403/377).

sent out to Gascony for wages in March 1356 and a further £10,000 in September. The total cost of this military effort was not less than £110,000, and since the Exchequer lacked the cash resources to pay this at once, it left a quantity of unpaid debentures many of them still being discharged in 1358–9.[1]

It was not until the Black Prince made his victorious return to England in May 1357, when a truce had already been signed with France, that another parliament, summoned to demonstrate its gratitude, made a grant to discharge his expenses.[2] No roll of its proceedings exists and no document tells us on what ground the formal plea for taxation was made or the terms in which the Commons now granted a single subsidy. All we know is that the grant was made in return for a release of the King's claims to the fines for the escapes and chattels of fugitives and felons and for a pardon of amercements on the counties in future eyres. If the former concession was offered at Shareshull's instigation as some compensation for the loss of the fines under the Statute of Labourers, the Commons were doubtless also aware of the Chief Justice's current series of sessions of the King's Bench in Hertfordshire and were probably anticipating the revival of his policy of financing war expenditure from judicial fines.[3] To have purchased pardon from the eyre may have been the more substantial part of the bargain, for the positive concession of the fines yielded little. The estreats of these were to be delivered by the justices to the collectors so that the fines could be redistributed in support of the taxpayers.[4] The writs to the collectors stated that the King had agreed to this 'on account of the various adversities which he knows the middling men of the realm to have long undergone'.[5] The lay subsidy roll shows that in ten shires nil returns or no returns were made of the receipts from these goods. Thirty-two shires made returns of some amounts received, the total of which was £834. 9s. 4d. Since the tax yielded £38,255. 15s. the

---

[1] These were the main payments recorded on the Issue rolls for Michaelmas and Easter 1355–6 (E 403/379, 380). Warrants for the payment of debentures are in E 404/5 files 34, 35.

[2] About £10,500 was assigned to the Prince, the earls of Warwick, Suffolk, Salisbury, and Oxford, Sir Reginald Cobham, and other lords from the lay subsidy of 1357 in discharge of these debts. The domestic departments received assignments for approximately £9,000 (E 401/443, 446).

[3] *S.R.* i. 352; B. H. Putnam, *Sir William Shareshull*, p. 76.

[4] *C.C.R., 1354–60*, p. 363.   [5] *C.F.R., 1356–68*, p. 44.

relief obtained was just over 2 per cent. However, as with the fines remitted under the Statute of Labourers, this proportion was higher in some counties. In fourteen counties the tax paid totalled £16,568. 7s. 6d. and the remissions were valued at £644. 0s. 6d. or almost 4 per cent. Even so, this was substantially less than the over-all average of 6 per cent and the higher 10 per cent for some counties for the fines under the statute.[1]

If the 1357 subsidy had something of the character of a bargain induced under threat, that of 1360 was an expedient born of imminent danger. It was not, in fact, a parliamentary subsidy and it was not demanded or justified in terms of the King's most ambitious attempt to secure the French Crown. When the failure of negotiations pointed to the resumption of war in June 1359, the mobilization of the realm had already been under way for four or five months, and during August and September Edward gathered for the campaign that was to take him to Rheims (and, as he intended, to his coronation) one of the largest armies of the reign. In the event it was not until 28 October that the King reached Calais, and not until 18 May that he returned to England after a fruitless campaign that resulted in the Treaty of Brétigny. Farley's Wardrobe account, which covers this expedition, records an Exchequer receipt of £108,624, most of which represented wages of war, while beyond this over £31,000 remained to be paid in bills up to 1369.[2] Edward's prodigal expenditure was certainly sup-

---

[1] P.R.O., Exchequer, L. T. R., Enrolled Subsidies, E 359/14. One reason for the poor response was that justices of the peace failed to trouble themselves with the burden of inquiring into escapes and chattels of felons, so that by December 1357 this had to be committed to the tax collectors themselves (*C.F.R., 1356–68*, pp. 56, 63; *C.C.R., 1354–60*, p. 453).

[2] E 101/393/11. Farley's account is discussed by Tout, *Chapters*, iv. 140–7. Several points concerned with it are of interest. Although it covered the period 3 November 1359–7 November 1360, a separate account under Ferriby was instituted after Edward's return and Farley continued to account for the *hospicium* in France. Thus some of his heaviest expenses were incurred during the negotiations at Calais, to which the King returned during September–October 1360. Moreover, both his receipts and expenses were at their lowest during the actual campaign, since wages of war were paid before the start of the expedition and after its close while during the campaign the army lived by booty and ransoms. Nevertheless, the *vadia guerre* in Farley's account total £133,820. 16s. 6½d. and this was substantially borne by the Exchequer. It included the wages of the magnates and captains of the expedition, the Wardrobe acting as the war treasury for the campaign.

ported by his own resources: the ransom of King David of Scotland yielded 10,000 marks and Farley's account records receipts from ransoms extracted during the campaign including that of Burgundy. Yet the duke of Lancaster was undoubtedly correct in warning Edward that the campaign was proving too costly.[1] The receipt rolls show that the Exchequer had been under heavy strain to provide the initial wages of the principal leaders. In July and August it had delivered £28,701 in tallies payable from the customs after Martinmas following, while it had supplemented its meagre cash reserves with over £11,500 raised in loans, the largest of £3,000 from the earl of Arundel.[2] It would scarcely be an exaggeration to say that Edward initiated the supreme campaign of his reign on credit supplied by his nobility. If this was a measure of his and their confidence, it may also reflect the detachment with which the Commons had come to view the ageing King's ambition. The sense of mutual adventure stimulated by the dangers and victories of 1345–56 and nourished by Edward's propaganda was rapidly evaporating. In 1359, with an invasion scare at its height, the mood of the country was defensive. Perhaps Edward had sensed this, for this expedition shares with Henry V's of 1421 the distinction of being the only major campaign of the Hundred Years' War which was not financed from direct taxation.

The tax of 1360 was, in effect, the support charges for troops arrayed in every shire to meet the threat of invasion during Edward's absence from the realm. A detailed discussion of it can be reserved until we examine the problem of arrays and other prerogative levies with which parliament wrestled in this reign.[3] For the present, two features alone need comment. First, this was not a parliamentary grant: the tenth and fifteenth were negotiated at six provincial assemblies which neither constituted parliaments nor were intended as a substitute for parliament. Second, this money was not granted to the King and it was not for national defence in the sense of being at the King's disposal for the defence of the whole realm. It was to remain in the hands of the shire to pay the wages of those arrayed for its defence. In practice it came, ultimately, to be used by the King to equip a fleet for the pursuit of the enemy, but in

[1] Froissart, ed. Luce, vi. 4. Cited by K. Fowler, *The King's Lieutenant*, p. 209.
[2] P.R.O. E 401/452.   [3] See below, ch. xvi. pp. 395–400.

conception it was a striking example of how the lesser landlord class had developed a proprietary attitude towards taxation. The representatives of this class had, on a county basis, authorized the raising of a universal tax and retained it within their own control for expenditure on local defence. Their attitude was historically more characteristic of the French provincial estates than of the English parliament; but it was inspired by imminent invasion rather than local particularism and it was a practical answer to the old problem of payment for compulsory service. None the less it is fitting witness, on the eve of the Treaty of Brétigny, to the degree of political and administrative self-assurance which the Commons had acquired through thirty years of war taxation with its concomitance of frequent parliaments and continuous and increasing responsibilities for the discharge of royal government in the localities.

THE NORTHERN SUBSIDIES

A much more consistent appropriation of taxation for local defence occurred in the north where, between 1337 and 1349, the subsidy from the shires beyond the Trent was placed under special receivers to be reserved for the defence of the border. Throughout the reign of Edward II and during the early campaigns of Edward III the northern counties had been wholly or partly exempt from taxation on account of the devastation of the Scottish raids and the heavy military burdens for their own defence.[1] The extension of the war to France underlined rather than removed the need for a system of organized defence in the north, and Edward's recognition of this was reflected in the Walton Ordinances. These provided the captain of the northern army, the earl of Arundel, with the same direct control over the northern subsidies as the King himself enjoyed, through the privy seal, over the remainder of Exchequer revenues. John Charnels, the deputy receiver at York, probably acted as receiver for this purpose.[2] Although the northern army was not entirely restricted to this revenue, assignments in 1338 for the garrisons at Berwick, Perth, and Carlisle were all drawn on

[1] J. F. Willard, 'The Scotch Raids and the Fourteenth Century Taxation of Northern England', *University of Colorado Studies*, v (1907–8), pp. 237–42; J. Campbell, 'England, Scotland and the Hundred Years' War', in *Europe in the Later Middle Ages*, pp. 191–5.

[2] Tout, *Chapters*, iii. 84; *Foedera*, II. ii. 1029–30.

the northern shires and the reservation of these subsidies was respected by the King when he placed a stop on assignments at the Exchequer in May 1339.[1] But though Edward undoubtedly remained alive to the importance of maintaining supplies to the northern armies, so overwhelming and urgent were his needs in Brabant that the home council found itself forcibly reminding the King that its responsibility for the border compelled it to retain money for its defence.[2] Many of those on the council had personal interests in the north and their concern led them to seek support from the parliamentary knights. Whereas in the parliament of October 1339 the Commons had taken the grudging view that the lords of the marches should protect the border at their own expense, in the January session they supported a comprehensive scheme for the defence of the north. Certain lords were assigned to keep the marches; orders were given for the victualling of Berwick and Edinburgh and payment was provided from the aid granted in the northern shires.[3] This scheme, one of the first fruits of the co-operation of the home council and parliament, was strengthened and elaborated following the grant of the ninth in the final session. John Ellerker replaced John Charnels as receiver of the ninth from the northern shires, and parliament made detailed provision for their defence. The captains of the northern forces, the bishop of Durham, Henry Percy, and Ralph Nevill, were appointed guardians of the ninth with sole authority to warrant payments.[4]

Here, as in other aspects of government, royal authority had been superseded by that of the council, which was firmly pledged to maintain the reservation of the northern subsidies. This appears to have been strictly interpreted. In June 1340 certain Newcastle merchants secured an assignment of £3,233

[1] *C.C.R., 1337–9*, pp. 544, 548, 557. In September 1338 the earl of Arundel had received money from the collectors in Sussex and Shropshire (ibid., p. 448).

[2] P.R.O. S.C. 8/95 n. 4740, quoted in Harriss, 'The Commons' Petitions of 1340', *Eng. Hist. Rev.* lxxviii (1963), p. 632 n. 1. See *C.C.R., 1339–41*, p. 159, for an urgent order of July 1339 to the collectors in Northumberland to gather the tax for the use of a projected campaign in Scotland.

[3] *Rot. Parl.* ii. 104, 109–10.

[4] Ibid., p. 115; *C.F.R.*, v, *1337–47*, p. 178; *C.P.R., 1338–40*, p. 504; *C.C.R., 1339–41*, p. 582. In the same parliament the committee set up to hear the accounts of those who had handled the taxes was instructed to examine that of John Charnels amongst others (ibid., p. 114).

owed to them, on the subsidy in the northern shires, 'notwithstanding any ordinance to the contrary'. They had, in fact,
failed to obtain payment from an earlier assignment in the
East Riding because 'the subsidy is reserved for the war of
Scotland', and subsequently their new assignment was superseded and payment made elsewhere.[1] In September 1340 a
warrant in favour of Thomas Ughtred, keeper of Perth, explicitly acknowledged the appropriation for the Scottish war,
and throughout October and November, when Edward was
urging the council to send every penny to Flanders, the council
steadfastly assigned the ninth in Westmorland, Cumberland,
and Northumberland to northern defence.[2] By November a
short truce was in force on the border and the King requested
the council to use the proceeds of the ninth in Ellerker's hands
for the payment of £5,000 to the earl of Salisbury and £1,000
to the earl of Suffolk for their wages in Flanders, also asking
the guardians of the subsidy to pay £270 to Lord Fauconberg
for his Wardrobe debentures.[3] No action, in fact, seems to have
been taken on these orders and although Edward, following his
sudden return in December, at first continued to recognize the
authority of the guardians,[4] early in 1341 he resumed full
control of the administration and overthrew the arrangements
of 1340. Negotiations were commenced for a truce with Scotland and Ellerker was ordered to pay the earlier assignments
which had not taken effect, together with further sums in discharge of wages owed by the King in Flanders. These comprised £3,617 to the earl of Derby, £550 to John Darcy,
£1,974 to the earl of Northampton, £300 to the earl of Oxford,
and £500 to William Kilsby.[5] Thus much of the accumulated
revenue carefully preserved by the council now went into the
pockets of the King's supporters, though some was used for the
maintenance of the Scottish garrisons.[6] The system itself, however, had not been abrogated and the victory of the opposition
in May 1341 was marked by an order that the ninth in the
north be delivered to Ellerker for the defence of the border in
accordance with the ordinance of the preceding year.[7] A month

---

[1] *C.C.R., 1339–41*, pp. 414, 575–6.   [2] Ibid., pp. 582, 545, 565.
[3] Ibid., pp. 576, 580.   [4] Ibid., p. 597. Writ of 14 January 1341.
[5] Ibid., pp. 522, 608; *C.C.R., 1341–3*, pp. 3–4, 16, 24, 36, 62, 90, 98.
[6] *C.C.R., 1341–3*, p. 22.   [7] Ibid., p. 144.

later the King terminated Ellerker's commission, and he was called to account and returned to his former post as Chamberlain of North Wales.[1] Nevertheless Edward's dissatisfaction was with the official rather than the system. A successor, John Thyngden, was in office by 9 August 1341 and warrants were addressed to him as receiver of the money reserved for the war of Scotland.[2] Throughout the remainder of the year payments from the ninth and the levy of wools were made to various captains and custodians on the border, and in December first the earl of Derby and later the King himself were engaged on a brief campaign along the borders, while plans were made for the maintenance of a permanent force to guard the marches during the summer.[3] The need to reserve the northern subsidies for the Scottish war was thus common ground between the King and his critics, even if Edward's readiness to divert this money to meet his outstanding debts at times when it seemed safe to do so led the Commons to seek the authority of parliament for the enforcement of the appropriation.

The continued concern of the Commons with the defence of the north was shown in their grants of the subsidies of 1344, 1346, and 1348, in all of which they sought to perpetuate the appropriation of the northern subsidy.[4] Though a truce was in force at the time of the 1344 grant, the King agreed to this and in June 1345 John Wodehouse, a canon of York, was appointed receiver not only of the lay but of the clerical subsidy and other aids north of Trent.[5] Although no separate account of Wodehouse for the subsidy has survived, the enrolled accounts of the collectors in the northern shires record a total of £3,772 paid to him.[6] How it was spent is impossible to say, though individual warrants confirm that it was reserved for the defence of the border.[7] In January 1347, as he was rendering his

[1] Ibid., p. 241; *C.F.R., 1337–47*, p. 252.

[2] *C.F.R., 1337–47*, p. 237. Thyngden's commission empowered him to distribute a moiety of his receipts for the wages of those guarding the west march and a moiety for those on the north march 'according to the ordinance made by the king and council'.

[3] *C.C.R., 1341–3*, pp. 186, 235, 238, 298–9, 353.

[4] *Rot. Parl.* ii. 147, 161, 201.

[5] *C.F.R., 1337–47*, p. 474; *C.C.R., 1343–6*, p. 540.

[6] P.R.O. E 359/14 mm. 32d–34.

[7] e.g. P.R.O. E 404/5 File 31 warrant of 26 October 1344 for payment to the chamberlain of Berwick of £859. 5s. 0d. commences: '[Illegible] une aide de

account for this subsidy, Wodehouse was appointed to receive the subsidy in the northern shires granted in the parliament of 1346.[1] The Commons' request that this should be kept for the defence of the north without being assigned elsewhere had met with some reservation from the King, who had replied that he would have regard to the state of these parts and act for their safeguard with the good advice of the council.[2] With the threat to the north removed by the battle of Neville's Cross, the King became increasingly reluctant to pledge money for regional defence. Wodehouse was now to answer for the subsidy 'at the king's orders and as the king shall enjoin upon him'—in other words, he would remain receiver of the northern subsidy though the subsidy might not necessarily be spent on northern defence. In the event most of it seems to have been spent on northern charges. Wodehouse received a total of £5,760. 10s. 5d. from the collectors of the lay subsidy in the north, £3,492. 8s. 3½d. of it between January 1348 and January 1349. During this period he also received £1,699. 13s. 3d. from the first year of the clerical tenth. Wodehouse's own account for this period shows him to have disbursed the greater part of his receipts on Exchequer tallies, totalling £4,308. 5s. 3d., though £795. 6s. 8d. was paid direct to the keeper of Berwick.[3] In the preceding year most of his receipts must have been taken by the payment of £3,222. 3s. 4d. to the King of Scotland and other magnates in the expedition of March 1347.[4] Wodehouse was also appointed receiver of the aid for knighting the King's son granted in September 1346. As elsewhere in England there were long delays in collecting this, and though the collectors in Yorkshire were ordered to pay it to him for the wages of the Scottish expedition of the summer of 1347 he appears to have

disme par les citeyns et Burgeys et de quinzismes par les Communes des Countez-de la Terente nous estoit nadgairs graunte en nostre darrein parlement pour la salvation et defense de nostre roialme et des marches et pour la guerre descoce, vous mandoms qe de la disme et quinzisme desusditz facez faire les assignementz sousescritz.'

[1] *C.C.R., 1346–9*, p. 135; *C.F.R., 1337–47*, p. 495.

[2] *Rot. Parl.* ii. 161.

[3] P.R.O. E 359/14 mm. 34–7. The only surviving account of Wodehouse himself covers the year 22 Ed. III (E 101/676/43).

[4] *Foedera*, III. i. 113. He was also ordered to pay the Clerk of the Avenary a small sum (*C.C.R., 1346–9*, p. 191).

received it only during 1348.[1] In that year he accounted for a receipt of £608. 16s. 4d. from this source together with a further £233 paid by the bishop of St. Andrews for the truce; again most of this was paid to northern lords for their wages of war.[2]

When parliament was called upon to renew the subsidy in 1348, this time for three years, the Commons again asked that the aid beyond Trent should be used for its defence 'if the war springs up again in Scotland'. They were coming to recognize that the appropriation could not be insisted upon in time of truce, and the King's reply assuring them that he would apply that part of the aid, and more, if the need arose, in fact left him a free hand.[3] Yet Wodehouse was again appointed to receive the first part of the subsidy, and it was only in June 1349 that his commission was terminated and the Exchequer was ordered to hear his account.[4] When the Commons renewed the subsidy for a further three years in January 1352 they merely asked that if the King went overseas he would ordain for the safety of the Scottish march. The formal appropriation of the northern subsidies thus ended in 1349; it had been born of the bitter experience of the warfare of the first three decades of the century and the fear of invasion when the King went overseas. It was a recognition that the north was a separate theatre of war in which local resources, military and financial, bore the prime burden of defence. Whereas in 1338–40 the King was ready to override this reservation for his own urgent needs, the home council, strongly impressed by the danger from the north, opposed any violation of the appropriation and secured parliamentary authority to use the subsidies to support a formal organization of defence. Throughout the 1340s the Commons maintained their commitment to northern defence by requiring the appropriation of the subsidy in each of their grants. Only after the battle of Neville's Cross had removed the

---

[1] *C.P.R., 1348–50*, p. 173; *C.C.R., 1346–9*, pp. 305–6; *C.F.R., 1347–57*, p. 44. The enrolled accounts of the collectors of the aid for the northern shires (P.R.O., Enrolled Subsidies E 359/5 mms. 16–21) record the same total of £608. 16s. 4d. paid to Wodehouse as he records among his receipts in his account for 22 Edw. III (E 101/676/43).

[2] Loc. cit. £346. 11s. 5d. was paid on Exchequer tallies and £483. 6s. 8d. as rewards and costs to Percy and Nevill and those involved in the capture of the early of Monteith.

[3] *Rot. Parl.* ii. 201–2.   [4] *C.P.R., 1348–50*, pp. 382, 385.

fear of invasion and the abatement of the demands of war had
brought a more relaxed relationship between the King and his
parliaments were they persuaded to abandon the formal
reservation of the northern subsidies. But though the Commons
had in some measure been in conflict with the King on this
issue, the appropriation of the northern subsidies under a
special receiver had in origin been a royal measure. This
receiver continued to be appointed by the King, not parliament, to disburse money on royal warrant, and to be accountable to the Exchequer. Doubtless such a treasurer of the subsidy
suggested a precedent which in the last decades of the century
the Commons were themselves to use, but in truth the significance of this appropriation was military and administrative
rather than constitutional.

The two decades following the crisis of 1340–1 were the most
formative years for the Commons in the whole medieval period.
At their beginning the Commons had only just emerged as a
coherent political body, voicing a programme which though
derivative was their own, and able to take independent political
action which could compel the King and the Lords to alter or
modify their policies. Not surprisingly such independence of
action was most effective in the field of taxation, and it was
here that, during the next nineteen years until the Treaty of
Brétigny, the Commons would be remorselessly educated in the
doctrines of political obligation and the techniques of political
opposition.
War brought the threat of perpetual taxation: eleven of
these years were marked by the continuous levy of lay subsidies on the plea of necessity which was nourished by persistent royal propaganda. Under this pressure the Commons
sought protection in the very same doctrine, by striving to
limit taxation to times of open war, and ensuring that in
periods of truce it was safeguarded for use in future emergencies. Nothing in fact could limit the King's deployment of
the tax once it was granted, and even in periods of almost
uninterrupted truce the King both received and spent the subsidies. But after 1355 the King could no longer secure the
renewal of lay subsidies, even for open war, with the same ease
as in the preceding twenty years. On a number of grounds the

relationship of King and parliament in the 1350s differed profoundly from that in the preceding decade. In the first place the King had succeeded after the crisis of 1341 in rallying the nobility behind the Crown to a prosecution of the war. The Commons at once faced pressure from above to provide supplies and were at the same time deprived of the baronial leadership against royal exactions under which they had been nurtured. They opposed these with their own ingenuity and resources, and with a degree of bitterness in 1347–8 which was scarcely less marked than in 1340–1. But with the easing of royal demands after 1348 in the relaxed atmosphere of long periods of truce, and even more with the rallying of landlord interests in the aftermath of the Black Death, co-operation between King and Commons gradually replaced exploitation and mistrust. A powerful contribution was made to this by the ending of the King's manipulations of the wool trade through agreements with monopolists which had poisoned relations with parliament since 1339. The decline of war finance, the bankruptcy of the merchants and parliament's victorious struggle to secure control of wool taxation all combined to remove this source of conflict from the politics of the 1350s. Gradually the Commons came to have a more proprietary view of government and taxation as their responsibilities in the shires were increased. The government encouraged this and purchased their complaisance in granting taxes by concessions in their interests. The detachment of the Commons from the King's ambitions in France became pronounced after 1355. Although granting a solitary subsidy in token of the victory at Poitiers, the very completeness of that triumph must have persuaded them that the peace they had always been led to expect was imminent, while the King's own enrichment made it difficult to seek further subsidies for the final campaign. The Commons' only contribution was in fact a tax for home defence, collected and administered themselves. A deep-rooted preoccupation with the defence of the homeland, evident in the insistence by parliament and the home council in 1338–41 on an appropriation for the defence of the north, had here triumphed over the sedulous propaganda for a foreign war. By the time peace came in 1360 the retreat into insularity was well under way.

CHAPTER XV

Parliamentary Taxation and Prerogative Levies, 1343–1362: I Principles and Procedures

THE involvement of the Commons in the political opposition of 1340–1 had profound effects on their role as petitioners. During the first decade of the reign their 'common petition' had become the vehicle for complaint on matters which were recognized as touching the common profit. But while their presentation of the ills of the realm was formally acknowledged to be part of the business of parliament, this still left to the Lords the task of securing redress for these ills and, even more, that of enforcing it on a reluctant or resistant King. For the Commons' formal right to untie the purse-strings was not, of itself, sufficient to compel the King to accept their demands. That depended on the conjunction of a number of other factors. In the first place, discontent in the country had to be sufficiently strong to make it appear impossible to collect a tax without the promise of reform, and such a promise had to be sufficiently definite to enable the Commons to assure the King that the tax could in consequence be collected in the localities. Negotiations at Westminster over grievances and their redress had thus to be realistically related to the position in the shires. But if these grievances touched the scope and authority of royal government—and it was in general only grievances of this kind which provoked fierce and widespread discontent—then the Commons on their own lacked the political stature and power to force concessions from the King and Lords, or to maintain these concessions against the King's will. Only in alliance with at least some of the Lords could they hope to prevail.

It was such an alliance that enabled the Commons to secure concessions in 1340 and 1341 by withholding the grant of taxation. In February 1340 they offered to grant a tax if their petitions were accepted, and in May the conditions on which the tax was granted were given effect in parliament, by letters patent, and by statute. In May 1341 essentially the same procedure was followed: Lords and Commons, separately and conjointly, demanded the acceptance of their petitions as the price of the grant of 30,000 sacks of wool, and the King's concessions were given effect in statute, in an administrative commission, and as conditions attached to the grant of the tax. Thus the distinctive features of these procedures were: the political character of the petitions and the support of both Lords and Commons for them; the negotiation of satisfactory concessions from the King prior to the grant and as the price of it; the joint grant of the tax by Lords and Commons; the assumption by parliament of special responsibility for its collection; the embodiment of the King's concessions in statutes and conditions attached to the grant; the circulation of these conditions in the shires as a guarantee of the settlement and to ensure collection of the tax. All these aspects reflected the depth of the political crisis. They marked an impressive advance in political tactics since 1301 when baronial pressure had been applied to defer the collection of the tax rather than as a preliminary to its grant. In 1340–1 the prolonged negotiations over political grievances reflected the increased authority of the Commons to speak for their communities in parliament, and to bargain with the King over the conditions of a grant. But a conditional offer of taxation could only be an effective weapon when it had the support of the Lords. In this sense it was they who controlled the advances made in 1340–1 for they held the political balance between a restive and assertive Commons and a King resistant to any limitation of royal authority.

These political conditions did not last beyond the end of the crisis. From 1342 to 1348 the King and the nobility were united in their pursuit of war, which in their view the Commons were obliged to support. In these years the Crown's financial demands, if not matching in scale and political ineptitude those of 1337–40, were still sufficient to generate widespread resentment and even hardship in the realm. Within parliament King and Lords pressed the urgent needs of the war with a cogency which made legitimate refusal impossible. Outside parliament they authorized a series of prerogative levies on the same plea of necessity. The Commons made persistent efforts to curb the abuses of prises, military levies, prerogative taxes, judicial exactions, and, above all, indirect taxation. But their petitions were not underwritten by the political support of the Lords and practically their sole sanction was their ability to convince the Crown that the collection of the tax depended on the satisfaction of their grievances. Thus after 1342 the power of the Commons was very limited. The right to petition and the right to assent to taxation did not carry the right to secure remedies or the right to withhold the grant. Nevertheless the Commons had some advantages. From the crisis of 1340–1 they had emerged with greater authority as representatives of the communities and with a more informed appreciation of political and parliamentary tactics. The King's needs remained almost as pressing and the Commons might win concessions by their willingness to meet these even if they could not extort concessions by a refusal to do so. All these enabled them to make tactical gains in the decade of intensive conflict with the Crown over fiscal levies which followed the crisis of 1341. The story of this opposition will be taken up in the following chapter; first we must examine the principles and procedures which governed the Commons' attempt to link the redress of grievances with grants of supply. They afford an interesting commentary on the political aptitude and parliamentary expertise which the Commons possessed at this date.

The parliament rolls leave no doubt that, at least in the eyes of the King and his ministers, the presentation of grievances was a subsidiary function of the Commons. At the beginning of every parliament it was customary to appoint auditors of petitions and to set a day, usually the third after the opening of the session, for the delivery of 'singular' petitions to the Chancellor.[1] The more important 'common petitions' followed a quite distinct procedure. Whether emanating from individuals and communities or from common deliberation once parliament had begun, if they concerned the common profit they were handed by the Commons to the clerk of the parliament and were discussed and answered by the Lords of the council or, if they touched the royal estate, were passed to the King for greater

---

[1] *Rot. Parl.* ii. 201.

deliberation with his council.[1] If we may judge from the parliament rolls, it was only gradually that this procedure secured a fixed place in the routine of parliament. The rolls for the parliaments of 1343 and 1344 give no indication of when the Commons were instructed to present their petitions or when they did so. In the parliament of 1346 and that of April 1348 the rolls record that the Commons were invited to deliver their common petitions to the clerk of parliament following their grant of taxation, while in the January parliament of 1348 when no taxation was granted they delivered their petitions after they had made their answer to the matters on which they had been charged to deliberate.[2] These matters touched only the King's business: primarily the expedition of the war in France for which the Commons were to provide aid, or the negotiations for a settlement which they were asked to approve, but also the internal peace and order of the realm in 1351 and mercantile and monetary problems in 1362. Although the common petitions with the answers had been enrolled, perhaps since 1334,[3] it was not until 1351 that the redress of common grievances was formally acknowledged as one of the causes for the summoning of parliament, after which it continued to figure in the charges delivered to the Commons in the following parliaments of 1352, 1354, and 1355. This development can probably be linked with the appointment of William Shareshull as Chief Justice in 1350, for it was he who pronounced the cause of summons in each of these parliaments.[4]

The inferior importance of this business in the King's eyes meant that it was taken only after the King's matters in the charge had been dealt with. In particular it is clear that the grant of taxation took precedence over the answering of petitions even where these had been presented earlier in the parliament. Thus in the parliament of 1344 the charge was delivered to the Commons on Thursday 10 June when the Lords and Commons requested time to deliberate until Monday the 14th.[5] In fact so keen was the criticism of the Crown and so prolonged was their discussion that the Commons did not make their grant

---

[1] D. Rayner, 'The Forms and Machinery of the Commune Petition in the Fourteenth Century', *Eng. Hist. Rev.* lvi (1941), p. 566.

[2] *Rot. Parl.* ii. 160, 165, 201.   [3] Rayner, op. cit., p. 558.

[4] *Rot. Parl.* ii. 225, 237, 254, 265.   [5] Ibid., p. 147.

until Saturday 26 June, two days before the dissolution of the parliament. In making their grant they asked that the petitions which they had put in earlier in the parliament ('queux ils mettent avant a ce parlement') should be granted.[1] In 1346 and 1348, as we have seen, the invitation to submit their petitions came only after the grant had been made, and in 1352 their petitions were embodied in the same roll as their grant of taxation. The fact that the grant of aid preceded the answering of petitions precluded the Commons from using the former to secure the latter. Under these conditions the Commons could not hope to revive the device (of 1340) of an offer of taxation which could only be transformed into a grant upon the acceptance of their petitions. Nevertheless there were usually in practice opportunities for negotiations on both the tax and their grievances before the grant was made.

It is clear that amongst the Commons themselves discussion of their grievances and the formulation of some of their petitions went on *pari passu* with discussion over the grant of taxation. The long debates in the parliament of 1344 delayed an answer on the aid and the presentation of petitions until two days before the end of parliament; in April 1348 there were again long deliberations before the grant of a tax in a session of only eleven effective days,[2] and in 1352 the roll itself records that the Commons had long treaty and deliberation with certain lords sent to advise them both on the aid and on the compilation of their petitions.[3] Only in 1346 did the grant of a tax follow within a day of the charge, to be followed itself on the next day by the handing in of their petitions. The session of 1346 was exceptionally brief, only seven effective days in all, though even so the Commons seem to have negotiated with the King's emissaries over both aid and petitions.[4] Having assembled their petitions alongside their grant of taxation, it was natural that the Commons should seek to link the two. To overcome the

[1] *Rot. Parl.* ii. 148.

[2] Ibid., p. 200. 'Lesqueux Chivalers et autres des Communes eu ent avisement de jour en autre, au darrein donerent lour Respons'.

[3] Ibid., p. 237: 'Et puis apres longe trete et deliberation eues par les Communes ove la Communalte, et l'avis d'ascuns des Grantz a eux envoiez, si bien pur un Eide . . . come sur la fesance des Petitions touchantes le commune poeple de la terre . . .'

[4] W. N. Bryant, 'Some earlier examples of intercommuning in Parliament, 1340–1348', *Eng. Hist. Rev.* lxxxv (1970), p. 58.

fact that outright grant of the tax had to be made before their petitions were answered (or in most cases even presented) the Commons developed the practice of inserting conditions into the *cedule* of the grant. This *cedule indentee* was the formal instrument by which the Commons granted the tax. It was drawn up by them and specified the tax granted, the cause for which it had been demanded, and the dates at which it was to be paid. It had the force of a legislative act, and was enrolled on the parliament roll. From 1344 the Commons began to preface the grant with a general or particularized complaint about the existing burden of taxes and charges, and to follow the grant with a list of the conditions under which it was made.[1] Thus in 1344 the grant was described as being made 'selonc la forme et conditions contenues en une Cedule' which itself contained the statement that 'Cestui grante vous fait vostre dite Commune sur tiele condicion que . . .' The tax schedule of 1346 did not employ the term condition but appended to the grant a number of clauses, each beginning 'Et que . . .', which learly served as conditions of the grant. The schedule of 1348, which embodied the longest list of specific complaints in the series, also imposed the largest numbers of conditions, the grant being made 'sur cestes conditions desus nomez et autrement nient'. The conditions were to be entered on the parliament roll and both grant and conditions issued as formal letters patent. Finally in 1352 the grant was made 'sur la condition q' ensuyt', this being the whole 'common petition' which was embodied in the tax schedule.[2]

What, then, was the intention and effect of embodying such conditions in the schedule granting the tax? This can best be answered by considering the matters covered by them. Broadly these comprised: stipulations about how the tax was to be collected and spent, provision for answers to petitions, and guarantees about the cessation of various forms of prerogative taxation. The first of these has been covered in the preceding chapter: the stipulations were designed merely to enforce the declared purpose of the tax and to prevent its anticipation. Thus in 1344 and 1346 these conditions laid down the terms of collection, stated that the tax was to be spent on the matters

[1] In 1348 these conditions preceded the grant.
[2] *Rot. Parl.* ii. 148, 159–60, 201, 238.

declared in parliament, that the aid north of the Trent should be employed in the defence of the north, and that the final year of the subsidy should not be collected except for actual war. In 1348 they similarly forbade the tax to be used to discharge ancient debts or to be collected once peace had come. Conditions of this kind could be said to be intrinsic to the purpose of the grant and must have represented terms agreed upon in negotiations with the spokesmen for the Crown. It was otherwise with the conditions relating to the answering of petitions. In 1344 the Commons inserted the condition that all the petitions which they had presented earlier in the parliament should be granted; in 1346 that their petitions should be received in parliament on the morrow and hasty answer given; in April 1348 that a committee of prelates, lords, and judges be appointed to give answers to the petitions presented in the previous parliament and, afforced by the Commons, to deal with those of the present parliament. In 1352, when all their petitions were comprised in the schedule of grant, they asked that all reasonable petitions made by the Commons should be granted, confirmed, and sealed before the end of the parliament.[1]

The Commons' intention was to ensure that an authoritative answer to these petitions was received before the end of the parliament rather than to compel the King's acceptance of their requests. Even in 1344 when the Commons appeared to ask that their petitions be 'granted', they enlarged on this by asking for a committee of Lords and other wise men to examine these and provide remedy before the end of parliament, and it is to this promise of an answer before the end of parliament that the King bound himself in 1346, 1348, and 1352. The complaint that petitions were left unanswered when parliament dissolved had a long history and even in respect of the 'common petition' antedated 1340.[2] It was a frequent if not inevitable consequence of the low priority given to petitions in the parliamentary timetable and it became a particularly acute problem in these years when parliaments were of short duration and met at long intervals. Of the eight parliaments which met between 1343 and 1355 none was in effective session for as long as four weeks and only five lasted longer than a fortnight.

---

[1] *Rot. Parl.* ii. 148, 159–60, 201, 238.   [2] Rayner, op. cit., p. 223.

Two lasted a week or less.[1] It was therefore not surprising that petitions arising from widespread administrative, legal, or financial grievances, which touched the authority and prerogative of the Crown, should have required more deliberation than could be given in time of parliament, or that where an immediate answer was returned it should later have sometimes appeared necessary to amend it.

If this had the mark of a recurring problem, it was aggravated in these years not merely by the fewness and shortness of parliaments but by the absence of the King for fifteen months in 1346–7 and by the vigorous exploitation of the Crown's fiscal prerogatives for war finance which naturally stimulated complaint. Thus the parliament which met in January 1348 was the first assembly able to address to the King complaints arising from the demands for the campaign of 1346–7. Indeed since the summer of 1344 parliament had met only once, in September 1346, for seven days, when the King himself had been absent, and a number of the petitions in that parliament had been referred to him for decision.[2] Not surprisingly, the common petition of January 1348 numbered fifty-seven items against the highest total hitherto of thirty-five. Many of these demanded or implied changes in the law. In such cases, if they were not refused outright, it was common practice to refer them to the justices or to the council, and no fewer than eighteen of these petitions were deferred on this ground.[3] Other items in the common petition were deferred or refused on other grounds, while amongst the singular petitions eighteen from communities complaining about or seeking relief from taxation and other charges were referred 'Coram Rege' since they touched the royal prerogative. These too were remitted to the council with the result that no answers were received before parliament dissolved. Thus although the common petition in this parliament must have been presented about 22 January, much of it

[1] On every occasion the beginning of effective parliamentary business was delayed by the absence of the Lords until at least the third day after the formal opening of parliament. See J. S. Roskell, 'The Problem of the Attendance of the Lords in Medieval Parliaments', *Bull. Inst. Hist. Res.* xxix (1956), especially pp. 166–9.

[2] *Rot. Parl.* ii. 162.

[3] Ibid., pp. 165–74 nos. 7, 9, 10, 13, 21, 23, 25, 29, 35, 36, 46, 47, 50, 52, 53, 56, 62. In a number of cases they were answered with the formula: 'Demoerge entre les autres articles dount la Novelle Lei est demande.'

remained unanswered when parliament ended on 12 February. The summoning of a new parliament within three months and the unlooked-for demand for taxation made the Commons truculent about the postponed petitions, leading them to demand that all petitions from the last parliament be answered. In fact once again substantive answers to all petitions requiring changes in the law were deferred, although the King promised to deal with them after Easter.[1] Thus where an immediate answer could not be given to a petition—because as a matter of law, or prerogative, or technical complexity it required further consideration by the council—the Commons suffered the very real risk of their complaint being pigeon-holed and forgotten. The very pressures of war and government in these years which stimulated grievances also curtailed the opportunities for redressing them.

None the less a body which assembled for so brief a period, never again to meet in the same form, and which did not know when it would next meet, needed to have an immediate answer and an authoritative one, incompatible though these require-ments might be. Thus in January 1348, the Commons had asked that their petitions should be answered and endorsed in parliament before themselves, 'so that they can know the endorsement and have the remedy'.[2] One solution the Com-mons proposed was the appointment of a committee to sit after parliament to continue the adjudication of petitions. Already in 1340 they had asked for and secured a commission of lords and justices to deal with the analogous problem of delayed and difficult judgements, and this must surely have been in their minds when in 1344 they asked that before their departure 'certain men' be ordained to remain until the petitions presented in parliament should have been answered, so that they should not lack remedy.[3] In the April parliament of 1348 they asked for four or six of their number to be elected to pursue their requests before the committee of the Lords who were considering them.[4] Thus the conditions attached to the grant of taxation could largely ensure that the petitions of the Commons received a formal answer before the Commons were dismissed, or before the end of parliament, or at least through

[1] *Rot. Parl.* ii. 201–4. The petitions deferred were no. 5, 8, 10, 14, 16, 17, 24.
[2] Ibid., p. 165.   [3] Ibid., p. 149.   [4] Ibid., p. 201.

a committee which continued to deal with them after parliament. They could not ensure that substantive, let alone affirmative answers would be given to their demands, but so long as the answers which were given were enrolled, as of record, reference back to them would be possible in a subsequent parliament.[1]

Enrolment likewise gave them some support for facing their constituents; here the statute of 1341 provided a valuable precedent. Copies of the statute and conditions with the King's concessions were delivered to the knights of the shires without charge to take back to their constituencies.[2] In 1344 the Commons asked that the schedule of grant and the conditions under which it was made should be enrolled and letters patent issued containing them which could be taken to each county, city, and market town 'to comfort the people'. The grant and the major conditions were in fact enrolled on the Statute Roll.[3] Similarly in April 1348 they required that letters patent should be sent to the shires specifying 'the conditions and the manner of the grant'.[4] The inclusion of the petitions and answers in the form of the grant in 1352, besides ensuring formal answers, may have had the similar purpose of ensuring that conditions written into the tax at Westminster became authoritative and binding in the shires. For although at Westminster taxation and petitioning could be treated as entirely separate functions, of disparate importance, in the shires the difficulties of collecting taxes from an aggrieved populace ensured that they were intimately linked. Nor were the schedules of taxation with their attached conditions mere instruments of propaganda, to pacify popular grievances and ease the path of the collectors. They had the force of statutes, binding upon the King as upon his subjects. In accepting the tax the King accepted the conditions of the grant. If these conditions were fulfilled subjects were bound to pay the tax; if not fulfilled they had legitimate ground for refusal. This was laconically expressed by the Commons in April 1348 when they declared that their grant was made: 'sur cestes conditions dessus nomez et autrement nient'.[5] They did not mean this as a conditional offer of aid for it was in the

[1] In April 1348 the Commons asked that the conditions of the grant 'soient entrez en Roule de Parlement come chose de record, par quoi ils purroient avoir remedie si rien soit attemptez au contraire en temps avenir'. Ibid., p. 201.

[2] Ibid., pp. 131, 133. [3] Ibid., pp. 148, 150; *S.R.* i. 300–1.
[4] *Rot. Parl.* ii. 201. [5] Ibid.

schedule actually granting the tax, and they had then not as yet presented their petitions to the clerk of parliament. It was, in fact, a statement that unless the conditions were observed they would not feel bound to pay the tax. The Commons were pointing to their only, though ultimate, sanction—that they would impede collection. This was, as we have seen, a measure of their isolation from the Lords at Westminster, but in the climate of discontent in the shires in 1344–8 it was a sanction which possessed some credibility.

The indented schedule of taxation could thus be regarded as a compact between the King and the Commons, translating into statutory and binding form the Commons' obligation to grant taxation and the King's obligation to redress his subjects' ills. How then was this compact arrived at? Were the conditions written into the schedule the unilateral work of the Commons; or if not by what process of negotiation were they agreed with the King? This problem is particularly relevant to those conditions which sought to restrain or abolish the exercise of various prerogative levies.

It is thus of some moment whether these 'conditions'
(i) represented unilateral demands by the Commons which the King was bound to accept as the price of the tax; or
(ii) represented concessions agreed after negotiation by which the King agreed to be bound; or
(iii) represented the aspirations of the Commons but had no binding force on the King.

In analysing the evidence of the parliament rolls with these alternatives in mind, it is important to recall the differences in length and routine of these parliaments. The parliaments of 1344 and 1352 lasted three and four weeks respectively, and in both the Commons petitions were presented and discussed before the grant of taxation was made. The parliaments of 1346 and April 1348 lasted one and two weeks respectively, and in both the Commons petitions were not presented until after the tax had been granted. On the basis of this difference we will take first the parliaments of 1344 and 1352 when we know that the Commons demands were under negotiation before the tax was granted. In 1344 the Commons' 'conditions' in their schedule of grant, leaving aside those relating to the administration of the tax, were that all their petitions should be granted, that the 'commune' be discharged of further aids and charges according to the purport of their charter, and that merchants be allowed to trade freely.[1] The first of these was certainly fulfilled for none of their petitions was refused, though one was referred to the justices on a point of law. The King's replies, together with the grant of the tax, were then framed into a statute, described as 'La Chartre ensealee pur la Commune', which was delivered to the knights of the shires.[2] The charter furnished relief for the burdens complained of in the petitions and included a promise of free trade, thus fulfilling the conditions of the grant. The fact that the Commons' demands were known to the King before the grant and that in the charter the Commons' grant to the King was explicitly reciprocated by the King's concessions suggests that the conditions (and hence the petitions) had in practice already been accepted by the King when the grant was made. That this was likewise the case in 1352 is suggested by the fact that the whole common petition was inserted in the grant of the tax and explicitly made the condition of its grant; yet parts of it were refused and others received a qualified reply. Since the tax was none the less granted and collected, it must be assumed that the Commons had already accepted negative replies to some items when they made these a condition of their grant. Indeed the fact that one of the petitions asks for all 'reasonable' petitions to be granted, confirmed, and sealed and that the King termed 'unreasonable' those which he refused, suggests that this saving word had been inserted to meet the King's refusal to be bound in advance by the Commons' demands.[3] Thus in these two parliaments the conditions of the grant certainly represented terms agreed with the King, though in 1352 these may not have been quite as much as the Commons had demanded.

If we turn to the two shorter parliaments, of 1346 and April 1348, at which grants were made before any petitions were presented, it is clear that in both parliaments the Commons were under pressure to grant taxation urgently, though for their part impatient to make vigorous protests about their grievances. Since they had been given no opportunity to present these as petitions, their grants on both occasions were

[1] *Rot. Parl.* ii. 148.   [2] Ibid., p. 150; *S.R.* i. 300–1.
[3] *Rot Parl.* ii. 238–43, petitions nos. ii, xvii, xxv, xxix.

prefaced by complaints about these burdens. Similarly the grant itself was followed by conditions which, besides those governing the levy of the tax, relate to these burdens. In 1346 the conditions were that 'they should not be charged with the burdens above said against the promises and grants of the last parliament', which they regarded the King as having broken, and that 'hasty and good remedy' be given on the matters in their petitions. Both these could be regarded as fulfilled by the responses to the petitions, the first of which formally reaffirmed the royal acceptance of the statute of 1344.[1] At the same time these conditions represented less than what the Commons had complained of in the preface to the grant and what they demanded in their petitions. They had complained that 'such grievances, burdens and oppressions are made from day to day without assent and grant of parliament' and their first petition further asked that commissions of array and purveyances should not be issued 'without assent and grant of parliament'. This requirement of parliamentary assent would have substantially limited the King's prerogative and was refused.[2] So also was much else in their petition. This again may suggest that the Commons were dissuaded from including demands which were known to be unacceptable to the King as part of the condition of the grant. The parliament roll hints that they had received some assurances about the answers to their petitions from the King's emissaries.

If the minimal conditions attached to the grant of 1346 were the consequence of some such arrangement, nothing like that seems to have operated in April 1348. In that parliament, as we have already noted, the Commons were aggrieved not merely at the burdens imposed in the previous two years but at the failure to answer their petitions in January and the unexpected demand for further taxation. They met in an exasperated and truculent mood, prefacing their grant with a long list of their burdens, the cessation of which was made the condition of the grant. These conditions were: that eyres of all kinds should cease; that the *maltolt* be suspended and never more be granted by the merchants; that no charges be imposed

---

[1] *Rot. Parl.* ii. 160.

[2] Ibid. The King in fact argued that such commissions were justified on grounds of necessity. See below, p. 380.

by the council without assent of parliament; that the petitions of this and the preceding parliament be answered; that the merchants who handled the grant of 20,000 sacks of wool be brought to account; that justices inquire into counterfeiting; that the Scottish captives should not be released; that the King restore the 20,000 sacks of wool; that the aid *pur fille marier* cease; that only the King should have a court of Marshalsea.[1] The miscellaneous nature and haphazard order of this list gives the impression of it having been compiled *seriatim* from a number of individual suggestions. Further, only five of these matters appear as items in their preceding common petition.[2] One of these, the cessation of eyres, appears in two petitions and is referred to the King and receives an affirmative answer at his discretion. Three others, on the answerability of merchants for the wool levy, on inquiries into counterfeiting, and on the Scottish prisoners, are answered merely by reference to the replies given in the preceding parliament. Finally the demand for answers to petitions receives a promise that these shall be dealt with after Easter. Important grievances on the aid, the *maltolt*, and the old question of assent to prerogative charges do not figure in the petition. Few, indeed, of the petitions in this parliament receive a fully affirmative answer. Where they revive complaints made in the last parliament they are referred back to the answers then given; where they touch existing legislation, this is reaffirmed; where they require new legislation, they are deferred.

The King and council had plainly summoned the parliament solely to grant taxation; indeed the tactic of holding a previous parliament in January at which the Commons' complaints had been invited while they had been explicitly excused taxation may have been designed to dissociate the redress of contentious grievances from taxation. In April on the other hand the Commons found that the time allowed for petitions was curtailed and that the King's answers were wholly evasive. Probably it was these circumstances which prompted them to attach to their grant a hastily compiled list of conditions embodying their demands and to insist that these be entered on the roll of parliament 'as a matter of record by which they can have remedy if anything be attempted to the contrary in time

---

[1] Ibid., pp. 200–1. [2] Ibid., pp. 201–4, petitions nos. i, ii, iii, v, vi, xv.

to come'. They further stipulated that this record of the grant and their conditions be circulated as letters patent throughout the shires. In these special mention was to be made of the current 'necessity' which had compelled them to make the grant.[1] Evidently the members felt a compelling need to justify to their constituents their grant of a further tax in terms of their attempts to secure redress of grievances. But there is no evidence that such letters patent were issued and it is inconceivable that the King should have lent his authority to a series of demands that (unlike those of 1344) he had not accepted. The conditions embodied in the tax schedule of 1348 must therefore be regarded as an exceptional attempt by the Commons to use the record of the parliament roll to record their aspirations rather than as a statement with binding authority of what was agreed. The parliament of April 1348 thus showed plainly, and probably dramatically, that the Commons could not exploit the King's necessity to require him to satisfy their grievances. Necessity obliged them to grant aid, whereas redress of grievance was a matter of the King's grace. Particularly in the matter of prerogative levies, on which so much of the complaint centred, royal concessions could not be dictated. But when concessions were freely given in answers to petitions, these could be incorporated in the grant of the tax with binding effect as a condition of its payment.

The Commons' opposition to prerogative levies was necessarily framed in constitutional terms. The demands of nationwide wars had led the King to reclothe the ancient rights of the Crown in the new terminology of national emergency. His prerogative authority to take whatever measures were necessary for the preservation of the realm and the common good justified the extension of purveyance and communal service to furnish materials and men for foreign wars. But it was equally on grounds of the common good that subjects demanded that burdens which touched all should be imposed only by common assent. This appeal by both sides to the common profit ensured that the debate on these should be linked with taxation and carried on in parliament. This was especially true of the years 1344–55 when Edward III's second great effort in France depended on a parliament which was now an assured institution

[1] *Rot. Parl.* ii. 201.

with established procedures, and in which the Commons formed an essential and important element, jealous of their own rights against other bodies such as the council and the assembly of merchants. The development of other forms of war taxation in these years such as feudal aids, loans in wool, judicial commissions, and *garde de la mer*, both widened the scope of complaint and underlined the principles which governed all forms of national taxation. Although the Commons possessed in the statute of 1340 a clear declaration of the need for parliamentary assent to the levy of any 'charge', it was not until more than a decade later that any of these particular burdens had been made subject to assent. This was in part at least because the Commons initially strove for the cessation of these charges rather than for the right to grant them. Their first reaction was to emphasize the illegality of such levies, and only in conflict with the prerogative did they define this illegality by asserting the legality of parliamentary assent. The fact that this struggle over extra-parliamentary taxation came to focus upon the question of who was to adjudicate the common good accounts for the signal growth in the political consciousness and sophistication of the Commons in the generation between 1340 and 1370.

The Commons claimed the right to assent to extra-parliamentary forms of war taxation in the parliaments of 1344, 1346, 1348, 1351, and 1352. This was directly related to specific levies authorized by the King and the council, but before considering these, it is worth reviewing the general terms in which the Commons claimed that such charges required parliamentary assent. In 1344 their grant of taxation was made on condition that they should be discharged in future of the 'eides et charges' which they had borne hitherto, 'solonc le purport de lour Chartre'. Despite similarities of language with the statute of 1340, this clearly referred to the 'charter' purchased from the King by their present grant of taxation and enrolled on the statute roll.[1] Indeed neither in their complaints prefacing their grant nor in their petitions did the Commons refer to the requirement of parliamentary assent for charges; in this respect the statute of 1340 was ignored. In 1344 they believed that a

---

[1] *Rot. Parl.* ii. 150–1; *S.R.* i. 300–1. Similarly the eleventh of the Commons petitions asked 'que les Ordinances et Grantes faites a son poeple par sa Chartre soient tenuz'.

charter abolishing these charges was all they needed. By 1346 they had been dis-illusioned. They then complained of new impositions (notably assessments to military service and seizures of victuals) in direct contradiction of the promise made in the previous parliament to abolish these in return for the grant of taxation. Though asserting that such 'grevaunces, duretees et oppressions' had been made without the assent and grant of parliament, they laid more emphasis upon the breaking of the King's promise.[1] Even when the Commons came to write in conditions to their grant they based their prohibition of future charges on the promises and grants made in parliament.[2] Only in their petitions to the King, delivered after their grant had been made, did they ask that no commissions to charge the people should be issued from Chancery without the assent and grant of parliament, and that if such were issued the subject might disobey them.[3] Thus only hesitantly, and as a secondary argument, did the Commons claim that the lack of parliamentary assent might render such impositions illegal. Indeed, the King and his advisers were quick to contest this, claiming both a general assent from parliament (in 1337) to aid the King in the war and a specific consent for these levies from the council, obtained in this time of emergency. The very terms of this rejoinder, which conceded the principle of assent, helped to shift the dispute away from *ex gratia* promises made as part of a bargain over taxation to the question of the circumstances under which consent should be sought and from whom, a fact underlined by the King's promise that the levies thus made should not form a precedent.

The argument over consent figured more prominently in the parliament of January 1348 as a result of the levies authorized by the council in 1347. Although no taxation was sought, the Commons' petitions recalled closely the complaints in the schedule of grant in 1346. They further claimed—though it

---

[1] *Rot. Parl.* ii. 159: 'Lesqueux grevances, duretees et oppressions sount faitz de jour en autre saunz assent ou grante en Parlement et expressement contre Record et grante du dit Parlement publie par tote la terre.'

[2] Ibid., p. 160: 'Et que mes ne soient chargez de grevances et charges susdites contre les promesses et grantz du dit Parlement.'

[3] Ibid. (no. 12). Even this was prefaced by the petition that 'les Ordinances, Promesses et Grantz faitz en Parlement a les dites Communes soient desoreenavant tenuz et gardez'.

was a very dubious interpretation—that in the previous parliament the King and his advisers had accepted that commissions to charge the people should not be issued 'si eles ne feussent grantez en parlement'.[1] They repeated their demand that if such commissions were issued without parliamentary assent subjects might sue writs to suspend them and need not obey. But if the Commons now hoped to secure release from such charges by challenging the legality of non-parliamentary impositions, they would have to accept the legality of such charges as were authorized by parliament. Indeed in a reply couched in very similar terms to that given in 1346, the King claimed that assent had been sought not merely from the Lords but from some members of the Commons present at the same assembly.[2]

With the parliament of March 1348 the Commons came to concentrate their whole demand on the need for assent by parliament and parliament alone to these impositions. They did not cease to complain of the burden of these, but the condition they attached to their grant of taxation in this parliament was that no 'charge' should be imposed by the 'Prive Conseil' without their grant and assent in parliament.[3] The demand for parliamentary assent had plainly been sharpened by the action of the council under Lionel of Antwerp during Edward's absence in levying impositions for the siege of Calais; and it was provision for Calais by large-scale prises which the Commons again attacked in 1351, when, in their petitions, they asked that no such prises should be made without assent of parliament and contrary to the statute.[4] Again, as in 1346 and January 1348, the King pleaded his prerogative of state to act for a necessity of the realm.

Finally in 1352 the King assented to a Commons' petition that no one be compelled to find soldiers unless by common assent and grant in parliament since this was contrary to the law of the realm. At the same time a petition that no tax, tallage, aid, or charge be demanded or levied from the Commons in time

[1] Ibid., p. 166. [2] Ibid., p. 170.

[3] Ibid., p. 201: 'que desore nulle imposition, taillage ne charge d'aprest n'en autre quecumque manere, soit mys part la Prive Conseil nostre Seigneur le Roi saunz lour grante et assent en Parlement'.

[4] Ibid., p. 227: 'la ou la Commune entendi que nulles tiels charges ne prises ne serroient faitz saunz assent du Parlement et encountre l'Estatut'.

to come echoed the earlier hope of securing abolition of levies by an act of grace which may have revived with the decline of the war impetus and the drawing together of King and Commons in the aftermath of the Black Death.[1]

It is clear that throughout the years 1344 to 1352 the ultimate aim of the Commons remained the limitation or abolition of the burden laid upon them by prerogative levies. Their grants of taxation gave them no unilateral power to do this though they could, and did, purchase abolition as an act of grace. This, however, served only as an invitation to the King to reimpose the levies in order to strengthen his own bargaining position when he next demanded taxation, and the Commons quickly came to see that the best hope of limiting prerogative levies was to attack their legality. This confronted them with the King's prerogative claim to override law in case of necessity and with the claims of King and council to impose such 'charges' as the necessity demanded. Their assertion that 'charges' which touched the property of the subject and the law of the realm needed common assent in parliament was an appeal to the principle that underlay national taxation: that what was demanded for the common need and common profit required common assent. But by the same analogy the acceptance of a common necessity carried the obligation to discharge it by common burdens. Common assent provided control of but not escape from such burdens. Caught in the cleft between the royal prerogative to impose 'charges' and communal obligation to grant them as taxation, the Commons still clung to the hope of securing abolition by royal promise. Their claim to give assent was not so much an ultimate objective as an immediate defensive weapon. The ambivalent attitude of the Commons was one reason why the conflict between royal prerogative and parliamentary assent over these levies was never brought to an ultimate, defined solution in the fourteenth century. Another was that just as it was stimulated by the demands of intermittent periods of intensive military activity, so it quickly ceased to be a contentious issue when patterns of warfare changed and new administrative devices developed. But during the decade or so when such levies were contentious, they came to be systematically opposed by the claim that parliament

[1] *Rot. Parl.* ii. 238, 239.

alone could authorize national taxation in any form. The statement of this as a consistent and universal principle was the achievement of these years. How it was applied to each of these levies, and with what effect, we must now examine.

CHAPTER XVI

Parliamentary Taxation and Prerogative Levies, 1343–1362: II Purveyance and Military Service

i. PURVEYANCE

COMPLAINT about purveyance tended to be endemic in medieval parliaments. At every parliament between 1343 and 1355 petitions were presented on purveyance and there were enactments on the statute roll in 1344, 1351, 1354, 1360, and 1362, the last being the principal statute of the Middle Ages on the subject. Evidently the intensive regulation of the activity of royal purveyors by this legislation went only some way to meet the complaints of the Commons, for their petitions repeatedly alleged that the activities of royal purveyors threatened to impoverish and destroy subjects,[1] and in the parliaments of 1344, 1346, 1347, and 1348 the taking of victuals without payment figured among the lists of tallages and charges with which the Commons complained they were wrongfully burdened.[2] In regard to prerogative purveyances for the royal household, the Crown acknowledged this to be an abuse and provided redress and retribution. Though probably ineradicable, it could be contained by administrative action and gave no ground for fundamental controversy between the Crown and the Commons. More contentious was the extension of the Crown's prerogative beyond the limits of domestic purveyances in order to provide victuals and war material for the army. From the latter years of Edward I's reign subjects had treated this as a form of national taxation which only common assent could legitimate. *Confirmatio Cartarum* first required common assent for such national prises, and in petitioning against illicit

---

[1] *Rot. Parl.* ii. 140: 'Qar si Dieux et vous n'y mettez hastive remede, vostre poeple serra nettement destruit'; ibid., p. 149: 'Lesqueux charges emprovrissent le poeple a demesure.'

[2] Ibid., pp. 149, 159, 166, 200.

prises in 1339 the Commons declared that no free man should be assessed or taxed without common assent of parliament.[1] Close regulation by the King of domestic purveyance and the requirement of parliamentary assent for what went beyond this were two strands which, though conceptually different, often intermingled in the Commons' petitions. It will be best, however, if we separate them for this discussion and deal first with the further attempts to regulate legitimate purveyance during the period 1344–62.

The legislation of Edward I had endeavoured on the one hand to regulate and supervise the activities of royal purveyors, and on the other to provide safeguards and even redress for the subjects with whom they dealt. The statute of 4 Edward III, which provided for an appraisal by the constable and other good men of the vill of the price to be paid, had carried this a step further.[2] This body of statute law provided a point of reference both for complaint in parliament and the King's response to it. Both sides appreciated that the answer to abuses practised by royal purveyors was not further legislation but enforcement of the existing law, but on the problem of how to control and punish delinquent royal officials the views of King and Commons diverged. In 1344 Edward ordered that the attention of household officials should be specifically drawn to the statutes, and in 1352 that the statutes should be enrolled in the commissions issued to purveyors.[3] As early as 1338 Edward had ordered investigations into the activities of some notorious purveyors, and throughout the following years, culminating in the large-scale inquiries of 1341, numerous commissions uncovered a variety of abuses of which non-payment was by far the most common.[4] The impetus of these inquiries continued to the eve of the Calais campaign and at other times the King showed himself willing to heed specific complaints of non-payment and to order redress to be made by the household or the Exchequer.[5] But whereas the King was ready to exercise

[1] *Rot. Parl. Hact. Ined.*, p. 269.
[2] These earlier developments are discussed in ch. v.
[3] *Rot. Parl.* ii. 150–1, 265.
[4] See above, ch. x, and also D. Hughes, *The Early Years of Edward III*, pp. 96–8, 204–8, where it is pointed out, however, that presentments against purveyors for the royal household formed only a small part of the inquiries of 1341.
[5] Inquiries into purveyances are recorded on the patent rolls as follows: *C.P.R.,*

authority over his officials to check or redress abuses, his concern to safeguard his prerogative and not impede the enforcement of his rights led him to resist two proposals of the Commons for local control over purveyors although these would have provided more effective sanctions than statutory prohibition or redress of injuries.

The first of these was to place control over the sale of local produce in local hands. Already by the statute 4 Edward III purveyor and vendor were supposed to submit their agreement on the price to be paid to the appraisal of the constable and four good men of the vill, and a petition of 1346 asked that this should be enforced.[1] Two years later the Commons, citing the flagrant misdemeanours of purveyors, asked that two good men of each county should act as intermediaries to sell the produce to purveyors under indenture.[2] This was refused, as was the Commons' suggestion in 1346 that justices of assize and keepers of the peace should be instructed to inquire into breaches of the purveyance statutes.[3] The Commons' other proposal was even less likely to win royal support. Having in mind perhaps the concession in the *Articuli Super Cartas* and subsequent legislation that fraudulent purveyors could be seized and imprisoned by the vill and punished as felons, the Commons in 1344 and 1347 sought to legitimize resistance to a purveyor who took goods without payment after the price had been agreed.[4] In replying to this the King reminded the Commons of his prerogative rights while promising redress against officials who misbehaved. In all this the crux of the Commons' complaints was the failure by either purveyors or the household to make payment, and their most tangible gain was the statute of 1354 which required cash to be paid for all purveyances of less than 20*s*.[5] Finally in 1362 the great Statute of Purveyors, while

---

1340–3, pp. 324, 427, 431, 453, 456; *C.P.R., 1343–5*, pp. 81, 85, 172, 287, 292, 294, 503, 507, 691. For examples of the King ordering redress to individuals, see *Rot. Parl.* ii. 161, 171, 240.

[1] *Rot. Parl.* ii. 161. The statute of 1330 (*S.R.* i. 262) was repeated in 1351 (*S.R.* i. 319).

[2] *Rot. Parl.* ii. p. 203. [3] Ibid., p. 161.

[4] Ibid., pp. 149, 166. The statute was not a dead letter. In July 1342 the royal mandate was issued to the men of Blakeney to arrest two purveyors pursuant to the act of 5 Edward III c. 2 (*C.P.R., 1340–3*, p. 542).

[5] 28 Edward III c. 12. *S.R.* i. 347. This was in response to a Commons' petition in the April parliament (*Rot. Parl.* ii. 258) and perhaps reflects the complaints

restricting the right of purveyance to the royal household and changing the name of purveyors to 'buyers', codified the arrangements for reaching agreement on the price, for ensuring payment, for restricting the amounts purveyed, and for regulating the status and authority of those to whom commissions were issued.[1] Although it related specifically to domestic purveyances and did no more than codify the legislation of the preceding century its very completeness, and the fact that it was issued on the King's mere motion, in time of peace, helped to establish it as the definitive regulation of purveyances for the royal household. Thus the Commons' recognition of the King's prerogative right and the King's recognition of the illegality of non-payment had limited conflict to the question of how purveyors could be disciplined and brought to account. Here the King had successfully resisted proposals to abridge his control over purveyors and had retained power to correct and amend their malpractices.

Purveyances on a national scale posed a different, though concurrent, problem which the King's campaign of 1346–7, the operations of the earl of Lancaster in Gascony in 1350, and the need to victual Calais revived in acute form in the years from 1346 to 1351. Supplies for the besieging army at Calais in 1346–7 were levied through the sheriffs and delivered to a special receiver of victuals at Portsmouth, and a similar system was employed for supplies to the earl of Lancaster's forces in 1350.[2] In January 1351 when Calais itself was under threat of seige, the King ordered large-scale purveyances in most counties for which payment was promised at the Exchequer at

about non-payment for victuals in the Home Counties in October 1353 (*C.P.R.*, *1350–4*, p. 519).

[1] 36 Edward III c. 2. *S.R.* i. 371. This may have been occasioned by renewed complaint over the activities of purveyors, possibly in the parliament of January 1361, for in December 1360 the Steward of the Household was named to lead a commission of oyer and terminer into all felonies, trespasses, and oppressions by purveyors and ministers by colour of their office in all counties of the realm (*C.P.R.*, *1358–61*, p. 517).

[2] For a discussion of the purveyances in the eastern shires in 1346–7 based on the indentures of receipts by the sheriffs, see H. J. Hewitt, *The Organisation of War under Edward III*, pp. 54–8. For supplies to the earl of Lancaster in 1350, see *C.C.R.*, *1349–51*, p. 131. A special feature throughout these years was the numerous commissions to purvey horses. See *C.P.R.*, *1343–5*, pp. 68, 294, 503, 507; *C.P.R.*, *1345–8*, pp. 308, 465.

midsummer and Michaelmas.[1] All these resulted in a good deal of hardship and provoked complaints which were duly investigated by numerous commissions. In May 1346 the Steward of the Household was ordered to investigate complaints in the Midlands that sheriffs had compelled the poor to provide victuals while accepting bribes from the wealthy to be spared.[2] In August and November 1347 commissions in all counties investigated charges of oppressions by purveyors including some specific allegations of extortion in Northamptonshire.[3] This was the background to the complaints in parliament, where such large-scale levies of war supplies were linked with arrays of troops as a form of national taxation which, in the Commons' eyes, required parliamentary assent. Their petitions in the parliaments of 1346 and 1348, after recalling the principles enunciated in 1297 and 1339, asked that commissions for both victuals and arrays should be issued only by the assent of parliament.[4] Again in 1351 when commissioners had been scouring the country for corn to supply the garrison at Calais, the Commons protested that 'nulles tieles charges ne prises ne serroient faitz saunz assent de parlement et encountre l'Estatut'.[5] The King countered this by appealing not so much to his customary prerogative (as with domestic purveyance) as to his wider prerogative to transcend the law in time of common danger or necessity, though coupling this with concessions or promises to redress wrongs. Thus in 1351, while justifying the levies on the ground that 'la necessite est si grande de vitailler la ville de Calais', Edward undertook to reduce the quantity demanded by half in view of the current shortage of corn in England, and also promised that such levies should not constitute a precedent.[6] Writs to this effect went out as early as 23 February 1351, and reductions were certainly made in the demands from some counties, but a petition in the parliament of April 1354 alleged that some sheriffs had still not made payment for these Calais purveyances.[7] It is evident, therefore, that

---

[1] *C.F.R.*, vi, *1347–50*, p. 273. Calais supported a garrison of about one thousand and posed a constant victualling problem throughout the 1350s. See S. J. Burley, 'The Victualling of Calais, 1347–65', *Bull. Inst. Hist. Res.* xxxi (1958), pp. 49–57.

[2] *C.P.R.*, *1345–8*, p. 113.

[3] Ibid., pp. 396, 465–7, 426, 471.

[4] *Rot. Parl.* ii. 159, 166, 200.

[5] Ibid., p. 227.

[6] Ibid.

[7] *C.F.R.*, vi, *1347–56*, p. 288; *C.C.R.*, *1349–54*, pp. 290, 294; *Rot. Parl.* ii. 258.

during these six years of heightened if intermittent campaigning, nation-wide purveyances, handled usually by the sheriffs, were the principal method of furnishing victuals and war supplies for the royal armies. Neither is there any doubt that these were burdensome and bitterly resented, provoking resistance to the point of assaults on royal officials as well as a persistent challenge to their legitimacy in parliament.[1]

Though in no doubt about the extent of the practice and its unpopularity, Edward never conceded the right of parliament to authorize these levies. But as his own military activity lessened, and as a new community of interest between the Crown and the landed classes appeared after the mid-century, commissions for extensive and systematic purveyance to supply armies going overseas became rarer. The principal expeditions of these years were those of the Black Prince to Gascony in 1355, the duke of Lancaster to Normandy in 1356, and those of Lancaster and then the King himself to Calais and Rheims in 1359–60. For all these expeditions, and especially the last which surpassed in size any since the siege of Calais, provisions were required not merely for the period of assembly and transport of the troops, but in varying degrees for their operations in France where the countryside had been ravaged or denuded. That these continued to be provided on a number of occasions by local purveyances is certain. Thus purveyances in the duchy of Cornwall of both victuals and war materials were undertaken by the Black Prince's officials in 1355, and payment was still owing for these two years later.[2] Extensive purveyances by sheriffs in the southern shires of bows and arrows were made in 1355 and the spring of 1356, for the expeditions of both the Black Prince and the earl of Lancaster.[3] More ubiquitous and burdensome than either of these were the purveyances of victuals in all the southern shires in 1360 for the troops arrayed to guard the coasts and for the fleet guarding the seas against invasion.[4] But all these were, in one respect or

---

[1] Assaults on purveyors are recorded in *C.P.R., 1348–50*, pp. 175, 515.

[2] H. J. Hewitt, *The Organisation of War*, p. 170 (citing *The Black Prince's Register*, ii. 86, 103, 107, 116), and *The Black Prince's Expedition of 1355–1357* (Manchester, 1958), p. 93 (citing Gascon Roll 30 Edw. III m. 6).

[3] *C.C.R., 1354–60*, pp. 244, 564, 601; Hewitt, *The Black Prince's Expedition*, pp. 91–2 nn. 44, 48.

[4] *C.P.R., 1358–61*, pp. 349–50, 411; *C.C.R., 1360–4*, p. 9.

another, limited levies. They occasioned little protest in parliament and there is a marked decline in the number of commissions to investigate grievances arising from purveyance.[1] Certainly they did not meet the vast demands made by the operations of the earl of Lancaster and the King, and it seems likely that an alternative was already emerging to the extensive county purveyances by sheriffs as the principal means by which armies were provisioned.

It has been noted that from about 1355 provisions for Calais were mostly supplied by merchant purveyors operating under royal commission.[2] Already in 1355 when a reinforced garrison at Calais was threatened with a shortage of corn, proclamations in all the ports invited merchants to bring supplies to Calais where they would find numerous buyers and prompt payment.[3] The concurrent problem of supplying the Prince in Gascony, particularly with corn, was similarly undertaken by merchants operating under the King's patent.[4] Both at Calais and in the royal household it became established practice to entrust purveyance to a royal official who at the same time had mercantile connections.[5] The appointment of such purveyors for the household for the period of a year, commissioned to supply particular commodities often in large quantities, is noticeable on the patent rolls for these years.[6] Although in 1360 purveyance was used to supply local defence forces in the south-east, and there were seizures of commodities in bulk at some ports,[7] the principal burden of supplying the royal army in France during the expedition seems to have fallen to merchant contractors for wheat, ale, corn, and other victuals, whose patents specifically permitted them to make profit from the transaction.[8]

---

[1] The only ones I have noticed on the patent rolls after 1352 are *C.P.R., 1350–4*, p. 519, and *C.P.R., 1358–61*, pp. 322–3. Illicit purveyances by unauthorized persons of course continued as an administrative abuse and were met by the publication of the names of purveyors in February 1359.

[2] J. S. Burley, op. cit., p. 53.

[3] *C.C.R., 1354–60*, p. 223. In January 1360 a seizure of corn and malt in Lynn for supply to Calais was countermanded after arrangements had been made with John Wesenham and other merchants to supply these commodities to the garrison in bulk: see ibid., p. 607.

[4] *C.P.R., 1354–8*, pp. 467–8, 471–2.

[5] J. S. Burley, op. cit., p. 53.

[6] Examples are in *C.P.R., 1358–61*, pp. 435–6, 437–8, 442, 450–1, 453; *C.C.R., 1354–60*. pp. 544–5.

[7] *C.C.R., 1360–4*, p. 94.   [8] *C.P.R., 1358–61*, p. 312.

The solution which thus emerged to the problem of war purveyance had important political and financial consequences for the Crown. The Crown abandoned in practice (though never in theory) its claim to secure supplies for royal armies by the right of purveyance on the plea of a necessity of the realm. The opposition, both local and parliamentary, which this aroused had tended to unite the countryside against royal officials and by the 1350s the King was ready to welcome a means of removing a contentious issue from the political arena. Victualling by contract was surely more reliable if almost certainly more expensive than purveyance; moreover, it involved the Crown in a closer relationship with the great merchant victuallers, notably those of London, which bred ties both financial and political. The Crown's involvement in London politics, so prominent in the reigns of Richard II and the Lancastrians, was partly at least a product of this change of policy. Edward III's willingness to placate the landowning classes on this issue reflected a general change of attitude which appeared after the middle of the century, deriving in part from the new social and economic situation after 1348. Co-operation with parliament, even at the price of concession, replaced Edward's earlier determination to exploit royal rights to the point of conflict and brought to an end a battle waged vigorously on both sides for half a century. Whether war purveyances needed common assent in parliament or whether they could be levied by royal or conciliar authority on the plea of national necessity was never explicitly resolved. But it could hardly be debated apart from parallel levies of troops nor apart from the whole question of assent to extraordinary taxation and it is as part of the wide-ranging debate over the principles of national taxation that its significance must be assessed. The Commons' tacit victory on this issue helped to substantiate their claim that parliament was the ultimate judge of a necessity of the realm and the sole authority for extraordinary levies which affected the property of subjects.

ii. MILITARY SERVICE

As with purveyance, so too in the case of military service dispute arose when the King's customary rights were adapted and extended to meet the demands of national war. In the first decade of Edward III's reign the Commons had been forced to recognize that their obligations under the Statute of Winchester now extended to service on the borders when the realm was threatened by invasion, while the King had begun to acknowledge, at least in practice, the need for common assent when levying quotas of troops from shires and cities at local cost.[1] But military levies did not always fall clearly into one of these two categories and the requirements of the two decades after 1340 posed many further problems about the nature and limits of the subject's military obligations. Under the persistent threat from the northern border, the arrangements for the array and support of infantry, hobelars, and archers from the northern shires acquired a degree of permanence peculiar to the marches, while the Scottish campaigns of 1346 and 1355 demanded large-scale county levies from well beyond this area. On only two occasions, in 1346 and in 1359–60, were the southern shires fully arrayed against the threat of invasion, and the latter of these generated financial arrangements of an extensive if exceptional character. Continental campaigns, whether conducted by the King or the nobility, were fought increasingly with contract armies, but these were supplemented by archers levied by quotas from local communities whose service overseas for prolonged periods required special negotiation. In some form the King's prerogative to require military service underlay all these diverse levies, but the precise authority for them tended to be subsidiary to the question of whether the cost fell on the King or his subjects. Although all arrays imposed some burden on subjects, the King could usually command service without opposition where he paid the wages. It was when support costs were borne by local communities or charged on a national scale that the demand for common assent in parliament to such levies became vocal.

The other major controversy of these years centred on Edward's attempt to revive the assessment to military service of the landowning class on the basis of income. Derived as it was from the general allegiance of all men to the Crown, this was not easy to challenge; but since commutation effectively transformed this service into a form of graduated taxation, this again raised the question of common assent. The King

---

[1] See above, ch. iv.

justified this extension of his customary prerogative to require service on grounds of national danger and common necessity, but since the effect was to deprive the subject of his property it raised the question of how this necessity and its consequences were to be authorized. Already by 1340 the Commons could appeal to principles and precedents for seeking this authority in common assent of parliament, though it was less clear that they possessed the strength to temper the King's urgent and various military demands during the next decades.

Although the opposition to arrays and opposition to assessments to military service could invoke a common principle, they are sufficiently different issues to be most conveniently discussed apart. During Edward's absence in 1340, parliament had on its own authority organized an extensive scheme of military service for the guard of the north at local cost, but following his return to England arrays of troops were ordered by the King both for the defence of the borders and for service in Brittany.[1] Resistance to this locally took the form of desertion, and the King accused the arrayers of connivance in sending only few and feeble men to the musters.[2] Edward was anxious to make arrays palatable and for the first time authorized payment from royal revenues from the county boundary for troops mustering at Winchelsea for overseas service, while those sent for service on the borders were paid from the muster at Newcastle.[3] Some arrayers did indeed extract money from the localities for the support of these troops, but were subsequently summoned before the council and reprimanded for their action.[4] It was against such unauthorized action by royal officials that the Commons protested in 1344 and sought a firm statutory definition of the liability for wages. They alleged that arrayers had been levying a support charge of 20*s.* or one mark per archer for those arrayed under the wide-scale commission of 13 May ordering the array of 9,000 archers from thirty-two shires for service overseas.[5] The King's response, embodied in

---

[1] *C.C.R., 1341–3*, p. 190.   [2] Ibid., p. 369.

[3] M. R. Powicke, *Military Obligation in Medieval England*, p. 205 (citing C 76/16 m. 15d and m. 17).   [4] *C.C.R., 1341–3*, p. 369.

[5] *Rot. Parl.* ii. 149. For the commissions, see Powicke, op. cit., p. 206 (citing C 76/19 mm. 14–15). An inquisition in June 1345 which found that large sums for wages, clothing, and conduct of archers from Norfolk mustering at Sandwich had been appropriated by the sheriff, may refer to this array (*C.P.R., 1343–5*, p. 516).

more detail in the statute, laid it down that for service overseas wages would be paid by the King from leaving the county boundary.[1] For service on the borders of the realm there was by now a well-established tradition that the county supported the troops until the muster at Newcastle or Carlisle where they received the King's wages. This was once more specifically stated in the writs issued in the northern shires in August 1344 for a muster at Newcastle in September, the array being under the Statute of Winchester.[2] Although definition had been reached between the King and the subjects over the problem of payment, arrays remained highly unpopular and, as in the case of purveyors, commissioners of array not infrequently exceeded their commission and became the object of complaint and even physical attack.[3] It could even happen that archers arrayed for service were themselves assaulted and killed on the way to muster.[4] But henceforth the King's right to military service under the Statute of Winchester and the terms on which payment for this was made ceased to be a matter of dispute and legislation, if not of complaint.

Complaint against arrays of men-at-arms, hobelars, and archers in the parliaments of 1346–8 figured with the taking of victuals amongst the 'grevetees duretees et oppressions' with which the Commons claimed to be burdened. In their petitions in the parliament of 1346 they complained both of arrays by quotas from the shires and the assessments on individuals to provide troops according to the value of their lands. Their main grievance was that these burdens were imposed against the record and assent of the last parliament, but they added that commissions which were in any manner 'chargeant a commune' should not be issued without assent and grant in parliament.[5] In January 1348 their petition, very similar in substance, associated such commissions with those assessing

---

[1] *S.R.* i. 300–1.

[2] *Rot. Scot.* i. 652–3, 657; *C.C.R., 1343–6*, p. 471.

[3] *C.P.R., 1343–5*, pp. 97, 281, 293–4.   [4] Ibid., p. 513.

[5] *Rot. Parl.* ii. 159 (no. 11) refers to 'Commissions d'arraier totes partz en Engleterre Gentz d'armes Hobelours et Archers solonc la Value de lour terres ou de faire gree a la value et auxint archeries chargez sur la Commune'; ibid., p. 160 (no. 12) refers to 'Commissions . . . hors de la Chancellerie come de charger le poeple d'Arrai, des Gentz d'Armes, Hobeleries, archeries, vitailles ou en autre manere chargeant la Commune'; ibid., p. 160 (no. 13) refers to the assessments on individuals according to the value of their lands.

military service on individuals according to their lands, though
the latter was also the subject of a separate and more detailed
petition.[1] In April 1348, although demands for men-at-arms,
hobelars, and archers were again mentioned along with victuals
among the burdens on the Commons, no separate petition
related to them nor was their cessation or regulation even made
a condition of the grant.[2] The pattern of complaint in these
parliaments thus shows an outburst in 1346, which diminishes
and fades away as a grievance by April 1348. Though distinct
from the protest over assessment of individuals, it is associated
with it, notably in the King's answers in 1346 and 1348 which
justified the demands on grounds of the great necessity of the
realm. What occasioned these protests? In particular, to what
extent had the provisions for payment of wages laid down in the
1344 statute been disregarded?

The protest reflected in part the sheer number of arrays
issued during this period. As well as the levies of the northern
counties throughout 1346 and into 1347, quotas of archers were
arrayed from all counties south of the Trent in August 1345,
February and March 1346, and February and September 1347,
for service in France. The types of levies and the basis on which
they were raised were quite distinct for northern and southern
England and it is best to consider them separately. Writs to
call out the levies of the shires north of the Humber were issued
in November 1345 and in February and March 1346, and
extended to the shires north of the Trent in July and September
1346 and again in January 1347.[3] In all these service was
required in virtue of allegiance and was said to be against
invaders, rebels, and contrariants. No payment was offered
since this represented the obligation of all men within these
border counties to defend their homeland. When archers from
Shropshire, Hereford, and Worcester were brought up to
strengthen this force they were promised wages from the point
of leaving their counties.[4] Similarly, when to follow up the
victory at Neville's Cross Balliol and Percy led a raid into the

---

[1] Ibid., p. 166 (no. 16): '. . . ne deussent avoir curreu ne issue commission hors
de la Chauncellerie come de Hobeleries, Archeries, Prises des vitailles ne auxint
commissions d'estendre les terres de certaines gentz outre la some de certeine
value'. For the latter, see also ibid., p. 170 (no. 44).

[2] Ibid., p. 200 (no. 4).

[3] *Rot. Scot.* i. 665–9, 673–5, 682.   [4] Ibid., pp. 666–7.

Lowlands in January 1348, wages were promised to local levies from the point at which they mustered under these captains.[1] Thus the provision of payment was regulated between these three different situations: according to whether men from the north were defending their home territory, or raiding across the border, or whether men from the south were arrayed for service in the north. There is no ground for believing that the complaints in the parliament of September 1346 related to these circumstances.

The case was different for levies from the south where, except in certain seaboard areas, the threat of invasion was less persistent and the King's requirements for overseas service were at once more onerous and more unaccustomed. The only occasion in the south when all men were arrayed for defence of their homelands was in March 1346 when the coastal and certain inland shires were summoned to resist threatened invasion and mustered under regional wardens.[2] Otherwise the demands were for quotas of men-at-arms and archers from cities and shires for service in France. Writs ordering these were first issued in August 1345 to assemble at Portsmouth three weeks after Michaelmas with the intention of accompanying the King; but then in November the departure was postponed until March and new writs were issued in February 1346 for this. Finally the array was postponed until 1 May, and the expedition did not sail until 5 July.[3] Although some writs to the arrayers made no mention of payment of wages, the King seems to have respected the principle that wages should be paid beyond the county border. In Shropshire, Worcester, and Hereford where the arraying official was a *valettus* of the royal household writs were directed to the sheriffs in September 1345 ordering them to pay from the shire revenues the wages of the archers chosen. The array of archers and hobelars ordered through the sheriffs in February 1346 was explicitly stated to be at the King's wages.[4] In February 1347 commissions issued to groups of arrayers (including the sheriff) in all southern shires, to array quotas of

[1] *Rot. Scot.* i. 682.

[2] *Crécy and Calais*, ed. G. Wrottesley (London, 1898), pp. 73–7.

[3] Ibid., pp. 59, 63, 66–8, 72.

[4] Ibid., pp. 61–2; P.R.O. C 47/2/41 no. 1. M. R. Powicke (op. cit., p. 207), however, argues that the silence of the writs about payment implies that the cost of wages was borne by the shire.

archers for service with the King overseas, stated that these were to be at the King's wages, as did those for a similar array ordered in September 'in tam urgente necessitate et periculo'[1] Even so some support charges for these troops seem to have been levied locally,[2] for where the departure of troops from the county was delayed their upkeep fell legitimately on the locality. Moreover, the sheriff might have insufficient money in hand to pay wages between the shire and the muster and might need to levy additional sums if the arrayers were to ensure that their men reached the muster at the port. Arrays, in fact, were sufficiently numerous in these two years to impose burdens on the communities which they might well regard as a form of extra taxation even if these were all technically within the law. The King found it advisable to insert in some writs a disclaimer that his demands 'in the present necessity' would form a precedent. Indeed the abundant evidence of the unpopularity of the array in evasion, desertion, poor equipment, and insufficient numbers would have made it doubly inadvisable for the Crown to flout statutory requirements and thereby provide ground for resistance.[3]

Over the next decade arrays were issued on a number of occasions for service both in the north and overseas. The array of all the northern shires first in July and then in October–November 1355 for the King's winter expedition was, as usual, at the cost of the counties to Newcastle and thereafter at the King's wages, while archers and others from the southern shires received the King's wages from the county border.[4] For all these northern expeditions between 1340 and 1356 wages were

---

[1] *Foedera*, III. i. 107, 135. The writ ordering the muster is in *C.C.R., 1346–9*, p. 374.

[2] M. R. Powicke (op. cit., p. 207 n. 5) cites a case from the array of February 1347; another reference to the embezzlement of money collected for the expenses of archers raised in Essex is in *C.P.R., 1348–50*, p. 453.

[3] Thus the writs of February 1346, while emphasizing 'quod omnes et singuli de eodem regno pro defensione eiusdem tenentur exponere se et sua', went on to disclaim that 'nolumus quod hoc quod sit factum in tanta urgente necessitate stetur in consequencium in futuro' (C 47/2/41 no. 1). Evidence of the unpopularity of arrays may be found in *C.P.R., 1348–50*, p. 112, and *C.P.R., 1354–8*, p. 359.

[4] *Rot. Scot.* i. 776–80, 782–5. Archers were arrayed from Essex and Gloucestershire and miners from the forest of Dean (ibid., p. 785). The Gloucestershire archers, though promised wages, 'contemptuously refused to come' (*C.P.R. 1354–8*, p. 359). Some of the arrays in the south were for the guard of the coasts (P.R.O. C 76/23 m. 1).

paid from the lay subsidies raised in these shires which continued to be administered by a separate treasurer.[1] The long years of crisis on the frontier had produced a stable and workable arrangement for financing its defence.

Arrays of quotas of archers were also issued for royal expeditions to France in 1350, 1352, 1355, and early in 1359 though not all of these eventually took place. In March 1350, citing the assent of the council to his proposed expedition for the defence of the realm, the King demanded quotas of men-at-arms from towns, to muster at Sandwich and go at his wages, and similar writs were issued for county levies then and in June 1351.[2] In May 1352 the counties were arrayed to provide quotas of archers to accompany the King, the writ specifying neither the point of muster nor whether wages were to be paid; but certainly sums were raised locally for the support of these men.[3] For the King's expedition of 1355 to Calais small companies of archers were arrayed in a number of southern shires, where the sheriffs were ordered to pay wages from leaving the county boundary, out of the issues of the shire.[4] In July 1356 orders were sent to sheriffs in thirty-one shires to array archers and summon all royal retainers for an overseas expedition at the King's wages, although the King's commissioners in Norfolk were accused of levying illegally large sums of money for bows and arrows and for clothing these archers.[5] Finally, in January 1359 the King ordered quotas of archers to be arrayed from the southern shires in readiness for his expedition to France. The writs which ordered this gave neither a date nor place of muster but they did make it clear that the men were to be provided with arms and clothing and brought to the King's presence at the expense of the county 'on this occasion, considering the imminent necessity'.[6] The

---

[1] See above, ch. xiv, pp. 348–54.

[2] *Foedera*, III. i. 193; P.R.O. C 76/28, 29.

[3] *Foedera*, III. i. 243. For sums raised in Northamptonshire for their expenses, see *C.P.R., 1350–4*, p. 332.

[4] P.R.O. C 76/29 m. 11.

[5] P.R.O. C 76/34 m. 12, 14; *C.P.R., 1354–8*, p. 610. The occasion of this array is not clear; it may have been that ordered for the guard of the south coast in January 1356 (C 76/33 m. 1).

[6] *Foedera*, III. i. 415. Cf. the array of archers within the county of Chester ordered by the Black Prince in March 1359, *Black Prince's Register*, iii. 331. The archers certainly received the King's wages from the point of muster (C 76/37 m. 8).

inclusion of this requirement and its justification on grounds of urgency suggests very strongly that normal practice was to pay the King's wages to the muster even though the cost of equipment and support of the troops within the shire remained a burden which might be heavy and could easily be exploited by the arrayers. The later arrays of 1359–60 for defence of the realm against invasion were exceptional in being closely linked with the grant of a subsidy and can be left for consideration at a later point.

By 1360 it can be said that the King's right to call upon all subjects for the defence of the realm had been adapted to meet the requirement of a more or less permanent defence of the northern frontier and the sporadic expeditions of the French war. The King exercised his prerogative free of any form of parliamentary assent such as had at one time threatened to become normal, but as a corollary he respected the inviolability of his subjects' property in placing no charge on the community beyond that laid down in statute. The compromise effected in 1344 to meet the new requirements of the foreign wars proved durable. It embodied a principle to which reference was made in the other major issue of military service in these years— the assessment of individuals on the basis of their landed wealth.

The attempt by Edward I to enforce unpaid service on those who held lands of greater value than were comprised in the Statute of Winchester but were below the rank of knights had foundered and had not been seriously revived by Edward II. In 1334–6 Edward III issued writs of arms under the Statute of Winchester for the arming and arraying of all men with lands and rent up to £40 p.a., and summoned all men-at-arms to serve at his wages in the Scottish campaigns of 1334 and 1335 in respect of their allegiance and under penalty of forfeiture.[1] For an unpopular campaign and one which could clearly be represented as in defence of the realm, the enforcement of obligatory service on this section of the landholding class was still of some value; however, as a means of raising troops it was rapidly giving place to contract as being more reliable and popular. Nor had the levy of 1334–5 raised the difficult question

[1] M. R. Powicke, op. cit., pp. 190–1. For the preparations for these campaigns, see Nicholson, *Edward III and the Scots*, chs. xii, xiii, and A. E. Prince, 'The Army', in *English Government at Work, 1327–1336*, i. 351–2, 355–6.

of whether the King could invoke his right to compulsory service for expeditions overseas. In the decade following 1334 there were some limited attempts to extend the obligation to provide a man-at-arms on the basis of each £20 holding,[1] but when late in 1344 Edward revived the idea of an assessment to military service on the basis of wealth, it was new in several important respects.

Firstly it greatly extended the range of landed income within its scope, the commissioners in October 1344 being instructed to return the names of all with an income from 100s. to beyond £1,000 and to assess them to find troops in numbers proportionate to their landed income.[2] For the wealthy this meant a vast increase in their military obligation. Secondly, although the original writs of 9 January ordering men to be assessed to arms on this basis justified the measure in terms of resisting the threat of invasion, writs to the sheriffs in February 1346 ordered these troops to be mustered at Portsmouth where they were to proceed overseas at the King's wages after Easter.[3] Finally it became clear in the course of the summer that instead of this being a means of raising men for the royal expedition it was turning into a form of taxation as individuals and towns commuted their assessed obligation for money fines.[4] Thus what had first appeared in the form of a revised writ of arms intended to have the armed force of the country ready to resist invasion, had turned into a tax to finance the royal expedition to France.

The opposition this aroused is evident in the chronicles (despite the exemption of the lands of the Church) and in the parliament roll. Yet it was not clearly illegitimate. In its original form the array had been authorized 'by advice and assent of prelates, nobles and other men of experience' some of whom might expect to suffer most from the extended assessment. Perhaps as in 1297 its weakest point, as Murimuth suggests, was the demand for overseas service;[5] yet it was undoubtedly

[1] Discussed by M. R. Powicke, op. cit. and pp. 194–5.

[2] *C.P.R., 1343–5*, pp. 414–16; cf. Powicke, op. cit., pp. 195–9.

[3] *C.P.R., 1343–5*, p. 427; *C.P.R., 1345–8*, p. 59; Wrottesley, *Crécy and Calais*, pp. 66, 68, 70.

[4] *C.F.R., 1337–47*, pp. 497–524. In many cases they were allowed to commute part only of the numbers they were assessed to find, and there were certainly efforts to enforce service. See Wrottesley, *Crécy and Calais*, pp. 80–1.

[5] Murimuth, pp. 192, 198.

upon its third aspect, as an additional form of taxation, that the opposition of the Commons was directed. In granting a subsidy in September 1346, the Commons complained that the commission was contrary to the promise of the last parliament and made without grant or assent of parliament,[1] and they asked that those who had still not paid fines should be discharged.[2] The King's reply was given in answer to another petition against arrays and prises; it justified the legal basis of the levy on two grounds.[3] First it cited the general assent given by the Commons to the war and their promise to support the King's quarrel with their goods and bodies. This was a plea which Edward had used on more than one occasion when seeking further taxation from parliament, but thereby he implicitly acknowledged that the levy was a form of national taxation rather than part of the subject's normal military obligation. But secondly, and proceeding from this, the King argued that the necessity to provide for his expedition and the defence of the realm was such that he had ordained this levy of troops on the basis of landed wealth by assent of the Lords; nor, he added, was this to be taken as a precedent.[4] The most controversial aspect of this claim was whether the Lords could sanction a particular form of levy for an imminent emergency under cover of the Commons' earlier pledge to aid the King in his war. Both on theoretical and practical grounds the King's position was strong. The levy was imposed to meet an emergency attested by the Lords; moreover many subjects had already commuted their obligations without question or demur. Yet the exchange in parliament revealed the essential flaw in the King's case. He had acknowledged that the levy was a form of taxation which needed assent of some kind; he had invoked the original assent of parliament to the necessity; yet by analogy with direct taxation common assent would be needed for every particular levy. If it was true that the tax did not touch all laymen, yet its incidence was very wide particularly amongst the class who formed the members of parliament.

The Commons' protests certainly did not cause the King to

---

[1] *Rot. Parl.* ii. 159 (no. 11).   [2] Ibid., p. 160.

[3] Ibid., p. 160 (nos. 12, 13).

[4] The disclaimer of it being a precedent was embodied in the formal discharge given to those who made fine with the King (*C.F.R.*, *1337–47*, p. 514) and it is noted by Murimuth, loc. cit.

cease exacting either service or fines according to the assessment,[1] and it was not surprising that they returned to the charge in January 1348 in two petitions, in one of which they complained of all the 'charges' made without assent or grant of parliament; in the other they specifically recited the assessment of lands and complained that the Exchequer was making excessive demands upon its basis.[2] To both the King made in substance the same reply as in 1346: alleging great necessity and the assent of 'Prelates, Earls, Barons and other Lords and some of the Commons then present' and disclaiming any intention to set a precedent. The King's evident anxiety to claim a wider basis of assent revealed that he was aware of the weakness of his case, though he insisted that the ordinance should be well kept. This tacit admission that the assent of the realm was required for such a levy was underlined when, in making a grant in the April 1348 parliament, the Commons stipulated that no form of taxation ('imposition, taillage ne charge d'apprest') should be levied by the 'Prive Conseil' without their grant and assent in parliament.[3] Although the Commons had in mind primarily the levies made by the council under Lionel of Antwerp in March 1347, there is no doubt that the development of the claim for parliamentary assent to all extraordinary levies in these two years was stimulated by the controversy over the assessment for soldiers. Four years later, when the urgent military demands of 1345–7 were absent and the social repercussions of the plague were beginning to draw King and gentry together, Edward accepted without dissent a petition that no man should be compelled to find soldiers (except for those who held by military tenure) unless by assent and grant in parliament.[4] This was part of the King's general recognition in these years of parliament's exclusive right of assent to extraordinary taxation; and if the enactment of 1352 acknowledged that the experiment of 1345–6 was not to be a precedent, and that necessity had to be sanctioned by common assent, it is possible that Edward did not entirely despair of securing that assent for future levies of this kind. In the event this did not occur, and the only occasion on which common assent was sought in

---

[1] Further fines were made in January and February 1347. See *C.F.R., 1347–57*, pp. 16–17.
[2] *Rot. Parl.* ii. 166, 170.   [3] Ibid., p. 201.   [4] Ibid., p. 239; *S.R.* i. 321.

connection with military obligations was in the exceptional circumstances of the King's last expedition to France in 1359–1360.

Active preparations for Edward's passage to France commenced in the summer of 1359 and the King eventually crossed to Calais on 28 October. On 3 October commissions of array were issued in all shires, including those north of the Trent, to meet the threat of invasion.[1] These recited the Statute of Winchester and thus required all men to arm themselves in accordance with the value of their lands within the range 40s. to £15. It was not until 16 November that a council concerned with the defence of the realm drew attention to the proportionately small contribution from the wealthier gentry under this legislation; but, doubtless with the statute of 1352 in mind, it required those with incomes beyond this limit to supply not additional men but armour and expenses for the troops arrayed according to their estate.[2] The commissioners were to summon the men of the shire to assess and apportion this levy, and were to make their returns by the quinzaine of Hilary. Apparently their efforts were ineffective, and though the council chided them for their lack of diligence it seems probable that there was a good deal of resistance, both passive and active, to the array.[3] Not surprisingly, this centred on the attempt to revive, even in its diluted form, the assessment of the wealthier gentry according to the value of their lands. On 10 February the council disclaimed any intention of using this assessment as a basis for future taxation, asserting that its only concern was that every man should bear a proportionately equal burden in meeting the threat of invasion in this emergency.[4]

---

[1] *C.P.R., 1358–61*, p. 286; *Foedera*, III. i. 449.

[2] *C.P.R., 1358–61*, p. 324; *Foedera*, III. i. 455. For the summons to the council see *C.C.R., 1354–60*, p. 653; *Foedera*, III. i. 456.

[3] Order was subsequently given to release those who had been imprisoned for resistance: see *C.P.R., 1358–61*, p. 324; *Foedera*, III. i. 466. For the council's complaints about the commissioners, see *C.P.R., 1358–61*, pp. 405–7.

[4] *C.P.R., 1358–61*, p. 406: 'Et auxint n'est pas l'entention de nous ne de nostre conseil qe nul homme qi issint irra hors du contee aille a ses custages propres pour le temps qil demeura hors, ne qe vous retournez la value de terres ne de chateaux ne les nouns de nul persone nautre chose paront ceste arrai purra estre traite en ensample n'en consequence d'aucun charge quecounque en temps avenir mes qe soulement soit certifie combien de gentz d'armes et d'archers homme pourra avoir en le dit contee par l'assession et apporcionement avantdites selonc vostre serement, discretion et avis.'

That burden was heavy; throughout December and January the sheriffs were kept busy with purveyances of food and arms, and in new instructions to the arrayers the council gave warning that some of the knights, men-at-arms, and archers would remain to guard the shire but others would be required to go beyond its borders to meet the invader.[1] Here too the council emphasized its intention to adhere to the letter of the law: no man would be compelled to serve outside the border of the shire at his own cost. On the same day as these writs went out to the arrayers—who were now charged to report their figures of the number of troops arrayed by the quinzaine of Easter— the council took steps to secure money for the maintenance of these troops. Writs to the sheriffs of all counties east of a line from the Wash to Southampton ordered that representatives from the shires and boroughs should be elected to come to Westminster on 9 March with full power to treat with the council and agree and consent to what would be ordained for the salvation and defence of the realm. Similar writs ordered representatives from the remaining counties south of the Trent to meet on 18 March at four appointed places: Taunton, Worcester, Leicester, and Lincoln.[2] Finally on 13 March the council commissioned the leading northern magnates to meet the communities of the northern shires locally to treat for an aid.[3] The assembly at Westminster did, in fact, grant a tenth and fifteenth for the expenses of the troops arrayed, and a like grant was made by the local assemblies.

Clearly these assemblies did not constitute a parliament and this term was never used in any document referring to them; nor were they intended even as a substitute for parliament. It is true that in summoning the local assemblies the council emphasized that this had been done because the whole community of the realm could not be gathered in one place in a short time. Moreover the writs which required full powers to

---

[1] *C.P.R., 1358–61*, p. 406.; *C.C.R., 1354–60*, pp. 564, 601; *C.C.R., 1360–4*, pp. 10–11, 94.

[2] *C.P.R., 1358–61*, pp. 404–5; *C.C.R., 1360–4*, p. 94; *Foedera*, III. i. 468; *R.D.P.* iv. 619–21.

[3] *C.P.R., 1358–61*, pp. 414–15. The assembly met at York 'on Monday, the morrow of the close of Easter' and granted likewise a tenth and fifteenth: see ibid., p. 347. It is not clear why T. F. Tout, *Chapters* iii. 223 n. 4, and W. N. Bryant in *Eng. Hist. Rev.*, lxxxiii (1968), p. 768, thought that the tax was not levied north of the Trent.

be given to the representatives provided that their election was to be in an *ad hoc* assembly if the county court could not meet in time.[1] But though procedurally summoned like a parliament, these assemblies were restricted to one particular business. That business was not a grant of national taxation but the provision by each county of the support charge it was obliged to bear for the arrayed men to be sent to defend the realm when the invader landed. Hence these assemblies did not grant the money to the King; they merely gave full power for it to be levied.[2] The money would remain under the control of the shire. It was to be levied in two halves, one immediately, the other as soon as the purpose of the enemy was known; it was first to be deposited in cathedral churches or abbeys under the seals of the collectors and if not required to be returned to those who had paid it. Although the collectors were to be empowered to levy the tax by the authority of Chancery writs, they were chosen by the county and were to render account not to the Exchequer but to the arrayers themselves.[3] These provisions emphasize that the use of the machinery of national taxation was a convenience dictated by the emergency, not an attempt to secure a quasi-legal levy on the plea of necessity. The council faced an almost unprecedented crisis; it knew an invasion to be imminent the strength of which it could probably only guess; its contingency planning had to envisage large-scale and prolonged operations. Already it had been made aware of the difficulties of arraying troops, and in order to keep them in the field over a long period and away from their localities regular payment of wages was essential. That could not be left to the sheriffs, as with the array of a handful of archers in the past. The only organization by which money could be raised within the shire for this purpose was the conventional lay subsidy, and the council in effect invited the shires to make use of this under the cover of royal authority. Its use in this context was an innovation and strikingly underlines how little occasion there had been for Englishmen to develop institutions for

---

[1] This may be deduced from the absence of this phrase in the writs of summons to the central assembly at Westminster. For a parallel discussion, see W. N. Bryant, op. cit., pp. 768–71.

[2] This is explicitly stated in *C.C.R.*, *1360–4*, p. 309.

[3] *C.P.R.*, *1358–61*, pp. 344–6, 415.

warding off a serious threat of invasion during the preceding century.

The action of the council had not been premature; indeed a week before the assembly met at Westminster it had received news that the French were sea-borne and ordered the musters to be taken in every shire.[1] In the interval before the local assemblies met the French had raided Winchelsea on 15 March and the council had immediately dispatched writs ordering arrayers to send troops to London by 21 March.[2] By 18 March it had been decided to fit out fleets for the north and west under Robert de Causton and John de Wesenham to pursue the French, and the arrayers were now ordered to send a quota of knights, men-at-arms, and archers to serve in the fleets. They were to muster at London or, later, Sandwich. Though under compulsion to serve, they were promised wages at the usual rate for five weeks service from the fifteenth and tenth levied in the county.[3] Commissions to the collectors of the tax to pay these troops were issued on 1 April, and included authority to borrow money if their receipts had not materialized.[4]

The impression given by the enrolled writs of swift mobilization paid for by a tax raised in the localities during the latter part of March and early April is illusory. Too few of those summoned reached the ports in time to set sail and in their place others had to be hired to serve at the King's wages.[5] To recover these sums the council at the end of April summoned local collectors from a number of shires to bring varying sums from the tax to be paid to the Exchequer.[6] Further writs on 23 May ordered other counties to pay sums either to the Exchequer or direct to Wesenham.[7] Perhaps the ineffectiveness of the muster had been due to the lack of time to gather the money; certainly some who were sent to sea from the counties had not been paid when they returned and found it impossible to secure their wages from the collectors. At the end of May,

[1] *C.C.R., 1360–4*, pp. 97–9. [2] Ibid., pp. 101, 103.
[3] Ibid., pp. 9–10, 16; *C.P.R., 1358–61*, p. 413.
[4] *C.C.R., 1360–4*, pp. 17, 104–5; *Foedera*, III. i. 480. Payment for victuals and ships for these fleets was also authorized from the tenth and fifteenth by the council: see ibid., p. 29.
[5] Evidence of the delays and default which attended the musters is given in *C.C.R., 1360–4*, p. 104, and *C.P.R., 1358–61*, pp. 415–16.
[6] *C.C.R., 1360–4*, pp. 23–4. [7] Ibid., pp. 35–6.

after he returned, Edward ordered a full-scale inquiry into the collection and payment made in each county. On the basis of this orders were given to the collectors of each shire on 10 July to wind up their accounts, paying the sums due to the King and to the troops, and, after deducting official expenses, to repay the balance (if levied) on a *pro rata* basis throughout the shire.[1] Only £876. 8s. 4d. was paid into the Exchequer by the collectors during the summer and they were again summoned under penalty on 18 September to bring the residue to the Exchequer in the quinzaine of Michaelmas.[2] During that term the Exchequer received a further £2,205. 10s. 3d. from the subsidy and eventually most of the money due to the King and to the seamen and for victuals supplied was paid.[3] Through its officials and those who accounted to it, the Exchequer at different times became involved in this money, though the conditions of the grant were always successfully pleaded to avoid account being rendered to it.

Thus in the event the tenth and fifteenth raised in the counties to support the levies conscripted for local defence was largely used as a tax to pay soldiers and mariners hired by the King to equip a fleet for pursuit of the French. The transformation was dictated solely by military needs. The ineffectiveness of the local array, the inability to move men quickly to the ports, the difficulty and unpopularity of enforcing service on board ships, all emphasized that for meeting invasion on a large scale the legal obligation to compulsory service had little practical value in the age of contract. The incident did indeed show that this could be adapted as the basis of a fiscal obligation, but this had not been the King's original intention. The council had seen the levy of the fifteenth and tenth as the most effective

[1] Ibid., pp. 50–7, 115; *C.P.R., 1358–61*, p. 449; *Foedera*, III. i. 485, 503.

[2] P.R.O. E 401/457; *C.C.R., 1360–4*, pp. 61, 66, 72–3. A complaint that the collector in Nottingham had not repaid the sums to the men of the shire, as ordered, was made in November 1362: see *C.P.R., 1361–4*, p. 293.

[3] P.R.O. E 401/460. For acquittances to John Wesenham and John Buckingham for money received from the collectors for their expenses in setting forth the fleets, see *C.C.R., 1360–4*, pp. 308–9. For payments made to the seamen, see *C.C.R., 1364–8*, pp. 115–16. In 1365 it was alleged against the deputy Treasurer, Richard de Chesterfield, that more than 1,000 (whether pounds or marks is not stated) of the moiety had still not been paid to the King as appeared by the receipt rolls. Richard, however, denied that any but a small proportion of what was due to the King was still uncollected and for this, he claimed, the Exchequer was making distraint on the collectors (ibid., pp. 119–20).

immediate device for enabling the counties to support their men. Though similar in form to the lay subsidy, its different purpose was emphasized by the control which the county retained over its receipt, disbursement, and account. This, and the special circumstances in which it was levied, restricted its usefulness to the King, but the experience of local control over the tax, removed from the Exchequer, may have offered a precedent for future experiments by the Commons in parliament.

CHAPTER XVII

Parliamentary Taxation and Prerogative Levies, 1343–1362: III Judicial and Feudal Dues

i. JUDICIAL PENALTIES

FROM the very outset of his military career Edward III appreciated the contribution which the profits of jurisdiction could make to his war finances. At the beginning of the French war, in October 1337, he had authorized inquiries into the escapes of felons and their chattels with the avowed purpose of raising fines for his expedition, and on his return in December 1340 had launched the notorious trailbaston commissions which provoked widespread condemnation in the parliament of April 1341.[1] Such inquiries into the King's rights and into the defaults and misdeeds of communities and royal officials derived ultimately from the articles of the Eyre. This venerable but obsolescent instrument had been used twice locally in Edward II's reign (1313, 1321) and once on what had been designed as a national scale in 1329. It was to be used in Kent in 1333 and 1348 and for the last time in 1374. Its disappearance marked no lessening of the Crown's concern with the enforcement of order or the profits of jurisdiction, since its omnicompetence became fragmented between numerous more specialized agencies: Justices of Assize, of Gaol Delivery, of the Peace, of Trailbaston, of Oyer and Terminer, and Coram Rege.[2] In the matter of public order the interests of the Crown and its justices were challenged by the claim of the landowning class for a greater share in the legal as well as fiscal and administrative government of the shire.

---

[1] See above ch. xiii. For writs of October 1338 relating to chattels of felons to be levied for war expenses, see *C.F.R., 1337–47*, p. 94.

[2] *Proceedings Before the Justices of the Peace in the Fourteenth and Fifteenth Centuries*, ed. B. H. Putnam (London, 1938), p. xlvi; W. S. Holdsworth, *History of English Law*, 3rd ed. i (London, 1922), pp. 269–92.

The 1330s initiated a prolonged controversy between the Commons and the Government over whether the keeping of the peace should be entrusted to lords and professional judges or to local gentry. Though not of direct concern to the present study, its relevance to the Commons' protests against the fiscal exactions of eyres and trailbaston commissions is twofold. First, the eventual victory of the Commons' view, which gave the landowning gentry penal responsibilities in the shires, made them even less tolerant of the Crown's exploitation of judicial penalties at their expense. Secondly, as this class became increasingly influential in the shires and articulate in parliament, the Crown came to appreciate that judicial penalties could be more easily and less controversially commuted into taxes negotiated in parliament. The Commons, for their part, found that generosity was the best inducement both for securing concessions on their role as keepers of the peace and for purchasing release from commissions of eyre and trailbaston. The desire of the local gentry to undertake the responsibility of local law enforcement was dictated partly by a conviction that their greater knowledge of local matters made them a more effective because more immediate deterrent, and partly by their distrust of the agents of the central government, whether magnates or justices, whose prime interest was oppression or exploitation. The government and the professional justices were divided in their reaction to this. The justices, while appreciative of the role of local keepers of the peace to inform and apprehend, feared their partiality and lack of authority and expertise, and were reluctant to invest them with powers to determine and punish. The central government, apprehensive of the stimulus which the war might give to local disorders in which members of the knightly class had on occasion been conspicuous, was also conscious of the need for the support of this class for its administrative, fiscal, and military plans.[1] During the first two decades of his reign, Edward's unremitting demands on the localities and the authoritarian temper of his rule had severely strained his relations with the shire gentry; after 1348 his demands abated and he increasingly sought co-operation from

---

[1] For examples of bands led by knights and gentry, see D. Hughes, *The Early Years of Edward III*, pp. 219–23, 229. Cf. J. G. Bellamy, *The Law of Treason in England*, pp. 74–5, 90–2.

them in both political and administrative policies. This pattern is reflected in the emergence of the gentry as justices of the peace.[1]

On four occasions during the first decade of the reign the Commons made attempts to secure commissions empowering local gentry to determine felonies and trespasses as keepers of the peace, only to be defeated by the opposition of the justices and magnates. A number of the Commons' demands and protests were closely associated with taxation. In the first parliament of the reign, in September 1327, when they granted a twentieth, they asked that 'bones gentz' be appointed as keepers with power to punish felonies;[2] the keepers appointed were indeed mainly local gentry but their commission was not enlarged beyond the traditional forms of 1326 and 1316. In the parliament of September 1332 which granted the second subsidy of the reign, the Commons protested against the introduction of magnate supervisors of the keepers as part of Chief Justice Scrope's attempt to revive the Eyre for a programme of law enforcement and inquiry into royal rights.[3] Whatever success this protest achieved was again lost when the opponents of gentry keepers secured the reappointment of magnate overseers of counties in February 1333. Not until the Nottingham assembly of 1336, when the fiscal arrangements for the war with France were under discussion, were commissions issued for all counties with powers of hearing and determining felonies and trespasses, and it was only on the eve of the King's departure in 1338 that the keepers were effectually transformed into justices with powers to determine. Moreover, in accordance with the policy of the Walton Ordinances to make communities accountable for locally elected sheriffs and collectors of customs, such keepers were, at least in some counties, nominated locally. If this revealed the King's ambivalent attitude to the gentry, it predictably aroused opposition from the magnates and justices. In the event magnate overseers were also appointed,

[1] This development has been fully treated by B. H. Putnam, loc. cit., and in more detail in 'The Transformation of the Keepers of the Peace into the Justices of the Peace, 1327–1380', *Trans. Roy. Hist. Soc.* 4th ser. xii (1929), pp. 19–48. The following paragraphs are based on this article.

[2] *Rot. Parl.* ii, 11.

[3] Ibid., pp. 66–7; H. M. Cam, 'The General Eyres of 1329–30', *Eng. Hist. Rev.* xxxix (1924), pp. 241–51.

only to be fiercely attacked by the Commons in the critical
parliament of February 1339. The Commons' chance to restate
their faith in gentry keepers of the peace came in the October
parliament when the King coupled his demands for money with
concessions. The Commons claimed that such gentry were the
best instruments for keeping order: where they were not effective
they only needed to be reinforced from among the knights there
present in parliament.[1]

Although the parliaments of 1340 and 1341 did not themselves authorize commissions for keeping the peace, the parliamentary authorization of arrays and purveyances did offer
precedents for the Commons in 1343 to demand that the
justices be chosen in parliament and their commissions approved, and the latter at least seems to have been conceded.[2]
They again expressed their preference for justices who were
'gentz de pays' and asked specifically that sheriffs and seneschals
of lords be excluded.[3] In reply the King insisted that men of
legal ability be included in the commissions and in 1344, when
the grant of a double subsidy accompanied the redress of a
wide range of grievances, their renewed demand for powers was
largely met by a statute which accorded a permanent role to
local men as keepers of the peace and, when afforced by men of
law, conferred powers to determine felonies and trespass.[4] The
commission of the peace with its quorum of justices thus began
to take recognizable shape.[5] The King reaffirmed the statute
in answering a Commons petition in 1346 when, on the occasion
of their grant of a double subsidy, the Commons again pressed
their demand that gentry keepers be given full power to determine;[6] but in the two parliaments of 1348 the Commons themselves seem to have accepted the association of men of law,
changing their request into one for local nomination of the
commission 'since those who live in the shire are better and more
often able to punish felons and trespassers, and with greater
advantage and less grievance to the people than foreign justices'.[7] But it was only in the aftermath of the Black Death,

[1] *Rot. Parl.* ii. 104.   [2] Ibid., p. 136.   [3] Ibid., p. 141.
[4] Ibid., p. 149; *S.R.* i. 300–1; Putnam, *Proceedings*, p. xl.
[5] Commissions of the peace which included men of the shire, with power to
determine felonies and trespasses are recorded in *C.P.R., 1343–5*, pp. 507, 510, 512;
C.P.R., 1345–8, pp. 105, 111, 169–70, 175, 472; *C.P.R., 1348–50*, pp. 64, 75.
[6] *Rot. Parl.* ii. 161.   [7] Ibid., pp. 174, 202.

when they were already on the point of filling wider responsibilities in enforcing the labour legislation, that the commissions
of February 1350 definitively gave the keepers powers of determining and transformed them into justices. Moreover, as with
the justices of labourers, the names of the justices of the peace
were submitted to parliament in 1362 and 1363. When the
statute of 1361 formally constituted the keepers as justices of
the peace, it sanctioned a change that had already been effective
for the previous eleven years. Except for a brief and partial
recession in 1364–8, the authority of local gentry in the enforcement of criminal law was thenceforth progressively
extended.

Against this background of increasing assertion by the local
gentry of responsibility for the government of the shire, their
distrust of visiting commissions of magnates and judges, and
their readiness to utilize their money grants to press their
demands and objections, must be set their opposition to the
fiscal burdens imposed by the punitive inquiries under the eyre
and its lineal descendant, the commissions of trailbaston.
Detached from the function of punishing disorder, and only of
secondary importance as an aid to efficient and honest local
government, such commissions were primarily used by the
government as an opportunity for raising money by individual
and communal amercements and fines. Since their legality was
unchallengeable, their withdrawal could only be secured either
by commutation of a grant of taxation (as in 1340) or by concerted political opposition (as in 1341). But even in his defeat
in that parliament Edward did not surrender his right to these
inquiries and by 1343 the Commons had decided that their best
safeguard lay in attempting to bring the terms of the commissions under parliamentary surveillance and assent.[1] This the
King conceded; nevertheless the commissions issued in midland,
eastern, and southern shires in July 1343 still authorized inquiry
into a formidable and detailed list of misdeeds and defaults by
individuals and communities and soon aroused local protests,
while in January 1344 fresh commissions of inquiry using trailbaston language were issued in both northern and southern
shires.[2] It was probably these that prompted the Commons'

[1] See above, p. 309–10.
[2] *C.P.R., 1343–5*, pp. 97–8; B. H. Putnam, *Sir William Shareshull*, pp. 64–5, for

demand in the parliament of April 1344 that these 'novel enquerees' 'for which outrageous fines and ransoms had been levied, more to the destruction than the amendment of the people', should cease.[1] The King's agreement to this, with certain reservations, was followed by the suspension of proceedings in Northamptonshire and Lancashire. But respites purchased by the inducement of a tax were apt to be of short duration; indeed the Commons may once again have actually approved revised commissions issued in July 1344, as they had in 1343.[2] Certainly the following years saw a number of commissions to magnates and justices to investigate and determine long lists of serious offences. It was the years from 1342 to 1347 that saw the height of Shareshull's activities in obtaining enormous sums for the Exchequer from judicial proceedings against delinquent officials and illegal exporters of wool, first in Suffolk and then in the domains of the Black Prince.[3] Communal penalties might be equally burdensome: in January 1348 the county of Northampton claimed to have compounded for its offence with 4,000 marks.[4]

The effects of these commissions remain to be investigated, but that they made a significant contribution to the war finance of these years seems highly probable.[5] At the first parliament in which the Commons voiced their grievances over the burdens of these years, in January 1348, they asked that 'communes Trailbastoneries ne courgent come autre foitz fut assentuz en Parlement; qar eles furent tout a destruction et anientissement du Poeple, et a moult petit ou nul amendement de la Ley ou de la Pees, ou punissement des Felons ou Trespassours'.[6] Called upon to make a grant in the following parliament in

---

the Commissions of July 1343. Commissions were issued in 1344 into concealments and evasions by those handling the King's money since 1338, and other trespasses are enrolled in *C.P.R., 1343–5*, pp. 281–2, 287, 392, 412, 416. Cf. Putnam, *Trans. Roy. Hist. Soc.* xii. 39.

[1] *Rot. Parl.* ii. 148. Putnam interpreted this protest as directed against the inquiries of 1343 which the Commons had approved: *Trans. Roy. Hist. Soc.* xii. 41; *Shareshull*, p. 49.

[2] Putnam, *Trans. Roy. Hist. Soc.* xii. 41, notes that the warrant for their enrolment was endorsed 'per peticionem de parliamento'.

[3] Putnam, *Proceedings*, p. xl; *C.P.R., 1343–5*, pp. 430, 497; *Shareshull*, pp. 64–8.

[4] *Rot. Parl.* ii. 178.

[5] See the concluding remarks by Putnam, *Shareshull*, p. 78.

[6] *Rot. Parl.* ii. 174.

March, they asked that 'commissions of general enquiries and all manner of eyres cease' during the three years of the grant, writing this petition into the schedule of their grant as a condition.[1] The council recommended acceptance of this demand unless a special emergency intervened. During these years when the magnates' support for the war led them to sanction prerogative levies of many kinds, and while the council was still reluctant to entrust penal powers to the gentry for keeping the peace, the Commons' one hope of relief from such commissions lay in purchasing their suspension. Aided by the concurrence of the Black Death, this was probably achieved for the years 1348–51. By the time the Commons assembled to renew the subsidies in January 1352 the government, faced with an unprecedented crisis of authority in the shires, had accorded them the long-sought powers to act effectually as justices of the peace and now recruited them as justices of labourers with the inducement of levying fines in support of the subsidy. It further bowed to their protests against the extended definition of treason which the justices had been using as a weapon against disorder.

Shareshull, who had become Chief Justice in October 1350 and whose addresses to the parliaments of 1351 and 1352 had laid such stress on the crisis of public order, must be credited with this reversal of royal policy.[2] Its success in consolidating the gentry behind the magnates and the Crown in support of law enforcement permitted him to wield once more the supreme authority of the eyre. As Shareshull told the Commons, he proposed to send the King's Bench wherever there was most need, claiming for it the authority of the Eyre.[3] The itinerary of the King's Bench, which commenced in Buckinghamshire and Warwick in the Trinity Term 1351, took it into eight southern counties before it closed the session at Southwark early in 1354, often sitting at different towns within each shire

---

[1] Ibid., pp. 200, 202.

[2] Putnam, *Shareshull*, pp. 70–2. J. G. Bellamy, *The Law of Treason in England*, pp. 70–80, has shown that the Statute of Treasons was the product of opposition to a policy of changing certain crimes from felony to treason as a means of maintaining law and order by severer punishment. 'Although the mass of the population wanted a decrease in crime, it did not regard the king's solution with any favour and it was Edward who eventually gave way.'

[3] Putnam, *Shareshull*, pp. 110–11; *Proceedings*, pp. lxi–ii.

and moving with a rapidity which could encompass six sessions in one term. The financial success of these sessions is attested by the colossal numbers and amount of the fines enrolled on the King's Bench rolls,[1] but at the next parliament in April 1354 the Commons' complaint of malpractices probably reflected the too vigorous and inequitable efforts of the Chief Justice.[2] For the next two years or more there was a respite from such inquiries. The King's Bench remained predominantly at Westminster until it resumed its itineraries into Hertfordshire, Buckinghamshire, and Bedfordshire early in 1357 and into Somerset and Dorset during the following year.[3] It was perhaps this resumption of activity that prompted the Commons in the parliament of April 1357 once again to purchase exemption from the fiscal penalities of such judicial inquiries. For a whole subsidy payable at Michaelmas 1357 and Easter 1358 they secured release from the King's claims over escapes of felons, chattels of fugitives, and amercements on the counties by future Eyres of justices. The concession, said to be 'on account of the various adversities which the middling men of the realm had long undergone', was probably of more value in respect of the pardon of amercements than of the tax relief yielded from the fines.[4] The Commons had reason to be fearful of the Chief Justice's policy of exploiting the profits of jurisdiction to support the costs of war.

Shareshull's departure in 1361 and the advent of peace together prompted the Commons to try and negotiate with the King a final settlement over their liability to the penalties of the eyre. In the parliament of October 1362 they petitioned for, and the King granted, a pardon for all misprisions and negligences under the articles of the Eyre by which they might incur fines, amercements, or imprisonment, either communal or individual.[5] The Commons emphasized that they did not

---

[1] *Proceedings*, p. 31; *Shareshull*, pp. 72–3, 209–11, 203.

[2] *Rot. Parl.* ii. 259; Putnam, *Shareshull*, pp. 56–7.

[3] Putnam, *Shareshull*, p. 76. General Commissions of oyer and terminer were issued for Kent in March 1356, for Cumberland in November 1356, and for Kent in November 1357 (*C.P.R.*, *1354–8*, pp. 391, 495, 653), for Devon and Cornwall in February 1358, and Berkshire in September 1359 (*C.P.R.*, *1358–61*, pp. 66, 70, 320).

[4] *C.C.R.*, *1354–60*, p. 363; *C.F.R.*, *1356–68*, p. 44. For a discussion of the levying of the fines, see above, ch. xiv pp. 345–6.

[5] *Rot. Parl.* ii. 272; *S.R.* i. 376–8. The King was asked to make out charters of

thereby seek to deprive the King of his feudal or prerogative rights, nor did this prejudice the King's right to hold an Eyre in future. What they received in 1362 was in fact a pardon along rather more extensive lines than those of 1339 and 1357. It was doubtless purchased, together with the Statute of Purveyors, by the renewal of the wool subsidy, and it looked forward to others of a similar kind purchased by the same means in 1371, 1377, 1380, and 1398. Thus a tradition was being established of securing release from judicial penalties by grants of taxation. This reflected, as we have seen, the changing relation of the Crown to the middling men of the shires. Their role as active partners with the King's professional judges in the enforcement of criminal law must have made any attempt to intimidate and mulct them by judicial commissions increasingly anomalous and unwise. To commute these claims by the grant of a tax in parliament must have commended itself to the Crown as a recipe for social harmony. But the Crown's prerogative claims remained in being, and although the eyre was issued locally for the last time in 1374, when it was remitted for a fine,[1] the threat of penal inquiries under its articles was by no means negligible in the hands of a forceful and autocratic ruler.

The exploitation of judicial penalties to provide war revenue could not be attacked by the Commons in the same terms as national purveyances and military obligation. It was not, like those, an extension of the customary prerogative powers of the Crown for the support of an immediate campaign, and could not therefore be directly linked with the taxation granted for that campaign. Since it was less evidently a form of national war taxation, it could not be disputed in terms of national necessity and the common good as could the other levies. The Commons could, of course, cite Eyres amongst the burdens with which they felt oppressed, and appeal to the King's obligation to relieve his subjects from oppressions; but since such Eyres could be represented as fulfilling the King's duty to provide justice and maintain order and his authority to issue them was incontrovertible, there was small scope for argument on their legitimacy. At most the Commons might seek to publicize and

---

pardon to all shires before the end of the parliament. The pardon was confirmed in the parliament of May 1368 (*S.R.* i. 388).

[1] Putnam, *Proceedings*, p. xlvi; *C.P.R., 1370–4*, p. 484.

approve the terms of the commissions in parliament in the hope of tempering their arbitrary character. More effectively they sought to buy release from them through grants of taxation, notably in 1339, 1344, 1348, 1357, and 1362. Although these were bound to be temporary respites, they were indicative of the growing willingness of the King to accommodate the interests of the middling landowners. Moreover, both in undertaking responsibilities for the peace within the shires and in protecting the shires against the incursions of the royal justices, the shire knights were fortifying their position as leaders of the community of the shire and their authority as representatives. Both betoken the steady increase in the political standing of this class within and outside parliament; but this is measured not so much by any challenge to the royal prerogative or constitutional gains at its expense as by the King's willingness to exploit his prerogative in the terms suggested by the Commons—in terms, that is, of parliamentary taxation.

ii. THE FEUDAL AID

Shortly after he landed at La Hogue on 12 July 1346 Edward III knighted his eldest son, Prince Edward. Already in letters patent issued on 22 June on the other side of the Channel he had assigned £6,000 from 'the aid for making the king's first born son a knight, shortly to be levied within the realm' to the Sire d'Albret in payment of debts to him.[1] On 8 September, when the victorious English army had reached Calais, the principal earls and bishops with the King wrote to their peers in England, then assembling for parliament, certifying them of the King's action and their own accord and assent to the levy of an aid at 40s. the knight's fee. At the end of the parliament, when the Commons had already made their grant of a subsidy and had presented their petitions, the Lords acting on the authority of the letters of those absent agreed 'on behalf of themselves and the whole community of the realm' that the aid be put into execution.[2]

It is clear from these proceedings that the Lords had scrupulously followed precedents in accord with the law and custom of the realm. The most important was the *aide pur fille marier*

---

[1] *C.P.R., 1345–8*, p. 136.
[2] *Rot. Parl.* ii. 163; *C.F.R., 1337–46*, p. 490.

granted in 1290 by the magnates 'pro se et tota communitate ejusdem regni' which was likewise levied at the rate of 40*s.* when it was eventually collected in 1302. A previous aid for knighting the King's son had been levied at 40*s.* the fee in 1253. In 1306, however, the aid for knighting Edward of Caernarvon was replaced by the grant of a subsidy of a thirtieth and twentieth, and in 1340 Edward had withdrawn his proposed feudal aid on the grant of the ninth. Neither of these precedents, in the King's view, affected his right to take a feudal aid when future circumstances warranted and that of 1346 was explicitly based on the levy of 1290.[1] Nevertheless the attempt to collect the aid met with immediate and widespread opposition. In January 1347 orders were given to the sheriff of Northampton to arrest all who resisted or refused to pay and those who by armed force frustrated the attempts of collectors and sheriffs to distrain them.[2] Others refused to attend when summoned by the collectors. In March 1347 the Exchequer was inquiring why the aid had not been collected in Herefordshire; in May it was receiving reports of assaults on collectors in Staffordshire, and even by the autumn of 1347 little had been collected in Leicestershire, Warwickshire, and Suffolk.[3] In the northern shires in general, where the proceeds were to be delivered to John de Wodeshouse at what was a critical juncture in the northern war, little or nothing had been collected by July 1347, to the King's anger. The collectors were ordered to levy the aid under pain of forfeiture, to amerce the rebellious, and to have the money ready by 1 August or Michaelmas at latest.[4] The aid from East Anglia had been assigned to the earl of Northampton, and here too the King was writing in September in urgent terms to speed up its collection for fear that the earl would withdraw from the royal army for default of his wages.[5] The same story was repeated in the West Country.[6] Some of these delays were doubtless the fault of the collectors themselves,

[1] *Feudal Aids*, i. xxv; P.R.O. E 359/5 m. 16. For the levy of 1290, see *Rot. Parl.* i. 266.
[2] *C.C.R., 1346–9*, p. 257.
[3] *C.P.R., 1345–8*, pp. 309, 319, 400, 458.
[4] *C.C.R., 1346–9*, p. 356; *C.F.R., 1346–54*, p. 44.
[5] *C.C.R., 1346–9*, p. 317.
[6] In February 1348 the sheriff of Devon was ordered to attach all who had refused to pay: *C.P.R., 1348–50*, p. 70.

who were frequently changed.[1] It is clear too that, coming on top of the collection of the lay subsidy, a levy on wool, arrays, and purveyances, the aid was placing a heavy strain on the revenue-collecting machinery. Nor was it surprising that such a tally of levies should arouse resistance, for the urgency of the King's needs once again gave a peremptory tone to his demands. But beyond these considerations, there were a number of specific objections to the aid of 1346.

Foremost among the burdens of which the Commons complained in the parliament of March–April 1348 was 'le resonable Eide qe fust pardonez par Estatut l'an quatorzisme, dount chescun Fee est chargez de xls., saunz graunt de la Commune; ou par Estatut, le Fee serroit chargez fors qe de xxs., laquele charge est levez de la povere Commune'.[2] Two grievances are here distinguishable. The first, which has attracted most attention, was the pardon given by the statute of 1340. Stubbs cited the Commons' complaint as proof that the aid of 1346 was contrary to the statute of 1340 and that this statute applied to all aids.[3] In fact, the precedents of 1340 seem to have been more ambiguous. In the parliament of October 1339 the Commons had asked to be pardoned the feudal aid which the King had proposed to levy, and Edward had authorized Archbishop Stratford to offer 'pardon and release' of this and other proposed charges in return for a subsidy.[4] The King probably saw this as a remission of his rights on this occasion only, but the concession as it finally appeared in the second statute was made prospective. The omission of this pardon from the first statute of 1340, which comprehended all the other concessions granted in 1339, may suggest that the King and the Commons had failed to agree on the scope of this pardon and release. When it appeared in the third chapter of the second statute which confirmed the first statute in return for the grant of the ninth, the King pardoned and released the Commons from a feudal aid of either kind 'pour tout notre temps'.[5] The Commons could thus sustain their objection by appeal to this statute; nevertheless the King may well have regarded so far-

---

[1] *C.F.R., 1346–54*, pp. 18–22.   [2] *Rot. Parl.* ii. 200.

[3] Stubbs, *Const. Hist.* ii. 415. The statute Stubbs had in mind was 14 Edw. III 2 c. 1 (see his n. 2).

[4] *Rot. Parl.* ii. 105; *Foedera*, ii. ii. 1091. See above, p. 254.

[5] 14 Edw. III 2 c. 3; *S.R.* i. 290.

reaching a concession as going beyond his original intention and constituting an unacceptable limitation of his undoubted feudal prerogative, occasioned only by his financial exigency. King and Lords seem to have had no doubt in 1346 that the King, having knighted his son, was entitled to an aid.

The next point at issue was the rate at which this was to be levied. Here again the Commons appealed to a statute—the first Statute of Westminster of 1281—which had fixed the reasonable aid at 20s. the knight's fee. When Edward I had received the *aide pur fille marier* in 1290 at the rate of 40s., this had been granted by the magnates on behalf of the realm and a similar grant had been made in 1306 when the aid was commuted. In 1340 the Commons had themselves negotiated for the release of the aid. In the second statute of 1340 the King had promised that his subjects should not be charged 'de commune eide faire ou charge sustenir' without common assent in parliament.[1] A 'common aid' would comprise any levy above the defined feudal due which would fall upon the *communitas* as a charge. Hence the Commons could claim the right of assent under the terms of the statute, against the claim of the Lords to grant it on behalf of the whole community as they had done in 1290.[2] Nor was the higher rate of 40s. as against 20s. their only complaint, for there was some dispute about the incidence of the aid. The Commons claimed that it should fall only on tenants in chief and should not be levied from mesne lords and from demesne tenants. Here again the thirteenth-century precedents favoured the King, but the wider the incidence of the tax the less plausible was the narrow basis of consent to it.

Thirdly, the Commons may have been particularly aggrieved at the lack of opportunity for protest or negotiation over the aid in the parliament of 1346. That parliament lasted a bare nine days, from 11 to 20 September, during which they first made their grant of two subsidies and then delivered their petitions and received the replies. It was only after this,[3]

[1] 14 Edw. III 2 c. 1; *S.R.* i. 290.
[2] A reference to the aid may have been comprised in their demand in this parliament 'qe desore nulle imposition, taillage, ne charge d'aprest, n'en autre quecumque manere, soit mys par le Prive Conseil notre Seigneur le Roi sanz lour grante et assent en Parlement': *Rot. Parl.* ii. 201.
[3] *Rot. Parl.* ii. 163: 'Puis porta Mestre Johan de Carleton . . .'

possibly even after the Commons themselves had departed, that the letter from the nobles in Calais was brought into parliament and read and the Lords authorized the levy of the aid. Yet this letter had been written at Calais on 8 September, in time to be available for the meeting of parliament three days later. It is difficult to escape the impression that it had been deliberately held back until the Commons had granted taxation and entered their petitions so that it could not be used by them either as a bargaining counter for the tax or as a matter of complaint, as it had in 1340. The Commons had some reason to feel that the business of parliament had been arranged so as to stifle their complaints.

The Commons could thus raise substantial objections to the aid of 1346; unfortunately by the time they had the opportunity to do so, when asked for further taxation in March 1348, much of it had already been collected. Their demand, made as a condition of the tax, that the *aide pur fille marier* cease during the period of the tax,[1] is puzzling, unless they suspected that the King was contemplating a new levy, while collection of the aid for knighting seems to have proceeded. It was not until 1352, as part of a general settlement of their long-standing grievances over prerogative charges, that the matter was formally settled. One of their petitions asked the King to confirm that the feudal aids should be demanded and levied according to ancient law and custom, at 20*s.* on fees held direct of the King and not from other fees as of late. The King's reply bound him to observe the statutory limitation, and carried the implication that any levy in excess of these would require common assent.[2] This may, indeed, have been made explicit; for among the Commons' petitions in the parliament of November 1355 was a complaint that, whereas they had granted the King an aid of 40*s.* on the fee for knighting his son, the Exchequer was levying this from mesne lords and demesne tenants and imposing a heavy burden on the land.[3] If the Commons had, in the parliament of 1352, formally granted the additional 20*s.* beyond the prerogative levy, they must have done so less for any practical reason (for most of the aid had been collected)

---

[1] *Rot. Parl.* ii. p. 201.   [2] Ibid., p. 240.
[3] Ibid., p. 265. The King's reply was merely that the usage of the Exchequer should be maintained.

than to demonstrate their persistence over a six-year-old grievance and to vindicate the principle that all taxation which fell as a charge on the community, beyond the narrow limits of the prerogative, required the consent of the community in parliament.[1] Whereas in 1290 the Lords could still effectively render that assent, by 1346 this was no longer acceptable to the Commons and by 1352 the King had probably acknowledged the same. The Commons had been forced to admit that, despite the statute of 1340, the King's feudal right to an aid remained unimpaired; the King had accepted that for anything beyond this he would have to secure common assent.

It remains to consider how effective the aid was as a contribution to Edward III's war expenses. The enrolled account shows that the anticipated yield was £11,820. 13s. 4½d. and the total of the clear receipt—deducting the expenses of collection—was £9,003. 8s. 10d.[2] It is not possible to say when this this account was enrolled. No general receiver of the aid was appointed; the individual collectors accounted at the Exchequer at different terms, though in a number of cases their outstanding dues were transferred to the memoranda rolls in 1347, 1348, and 1349. Moreover, from the contemporary account of John de Wodehouse running to January 1349, it is clear that the receipts of the aid from the northern shires had been handed to him by that date.[3] Thus most of the total was probably received during 1347 and 1348, despite protest and obstruction. If this helps to explain why the Commons had so little bargaining power in the parliament of 1348, it is an impressive testimony to the exercise of royal and seigneurial authority in the afterglow of Crécy. What had not been collected by the beginning of 1349 proved harder to obtain. Perhaps following a grant in the

---

[1] Their formal consent at this point may have assisted the collection of arrears of the aid. There are interesting similarities with the exploitation of feudal aids by Philip VI in 1332–4. In France, significantly, the King's rights were defined by an *arrêt* of the *Parlement*. See J. B. Henneman, *Royal Taxation in Fourteenth Century France*, pp. 90–107.

[2] P.R.O. E 359/5 mm. 16–21. The figure of £11,820. 13s. 4½d. is given in some rough notes by a contemporary hand on the dorse of m. 21. An addition of the *Summa Receptae* of the individual collectors gives a total of £11,791. 12s. 11d. The total of £9,003. 8s. 10d. is not given in the account; it is my addition of the items 'in thesauro'.

[3] P.R.O. E 101/676/43. An order to hear Wodehouse's account was made on 20 June 1349: *C.P.R., 1348–50*, p. 385.

parliament of 1352 there was a burst of activity to collect arrears in outlying counties, and those from Lancashire, still owing in 1355, had been paid by the time the account was finally enrolled.[1] By then only the collectors in Northumberland had not been brought to their final account though they had paid in £88. 10s. 10d. out of a total of £290. 6s. 7d. due. Adding their debt to those recorded from other collectors, gives a total of £1,097. 5s. 10d. uncollected.[2] From the King's point of view the aid was an opportune and not unimportant contribution to his war expenses. Much of it, as we have noted, was assigned to discharge debts to the Sire d'Albret and the earl of Northampton, but some was reserved for the King's own use and £608. 16s. 4d. from the northern counties went to local defence.[3]

iii SUMMARY

There is every reason to see the Commons' grievances over purveyance, military service, judicial fines, and the feudal aid as part of a single movement to define the limits of the Crown's fiscal prerogatives during the first phase of the Hundred Years War. For not only had the King consciously exploited these rights as a contribution to war finance but in repeated petitions the Commons had linked them together as 'charges' which they regarded as in some measure illegitimate. The concurrence of all of these in the years 1346–8 provoked violent resistance in the shires and articulate protest in parliament, but this represented only an accentuation of a situation characteristic of the whole war period 1337–60. It was thus natural that protest against these levies should be linked with grants of taxation which involved the King and the Commons in a delicate and sophisticated balance of legal obligation. War gave the King a right to claim taxes from his subjects which they were bound to acknowledge; but it did not give him the right to take taxation without their free assent. The Commons gave their assent as a recognition of the common need and profit of the realm and it

---

[1] *C.F.R., 1346–54*, pp. 367, 403, 425.

[2] It should be noted that a large number of exemptions from the aid were secured by religious houses and others though some of these compounded with smaller payments. See *C.C.R., 1346–9*, index under 'Taxation, exemption from'.

[3] *C.P.R., 1345–8*, p. 452; *C.C.R., 1346–9*, p. 305; *C.F.R., 1346–54*, p. 29. Wodehouse's account records payments to Thomas of York, Henry Percy, and Ralph Nevill.

was in these terms that they likewise presented their petitions of grievances. But while grievances were closely associated with taxation, the Commons could not make the grant of a tax dependent on the redress of their grievances since their grant of taxation was obligatory while the King gave redress as of grace. In practice, moreover, taxation preceded redress in parliamentary procedure. Nevertheless, both because he had to secure their free assent and because he was expected to redress ills which threatened the common weal, the King had to hear and plausibly heed the Commons' grievances. Thus neither King nor Commons had the power to impose their will unilaterally, while the strength and subtlety of these conventions ensured that the conflicting interests of Crown and Commons were framed as constitutional arguments and resolved by compromises formed under the influence of legal definition.

The basic issue was whether the King could authorize levies which were extensions of traditional prerogative rights in virtue of his wider prerogative power to act for the safety and needs of the realm or whether these were forms of extraordinary national taxation needing common assent. When the conflicts finally subsided the traditional prerogatives of the Crown were still secure, but they had been closely defined in a series of statutes, the general effect of which was to confine them to their domestic, local, and feudal character. Purveyance for the royal household, arrays for defence of the locality, and the 'reasonable' feudal aids were all recognized but the subject's liability was in each case closely limited by statute. This meant that any further demand on the subject could only be in the nature of aid, i.e. for a particular necessity to which the subject gave his consent. Nevertheless the conflict between the King and the Commons was rarely fought as a direct issue of principle. In the first place the Commons primarily sought relief from these levies by abolition and were willing to purchase pardon and release by the King's grace even though this left the royal claim untouched and even strengthened. It was only eventually that the Commons came to seek relief by challenging the legality of prerogative levies as lacking the common assent essential for any form of extraordinary taxation. Secondly, as the issue shifted towards the question of assent, there appeared the question of whether this might legitimately be rendered by

the Lords or the council or whether the common assent of
parliament was alone adequate. Thirdly, these issues were
never quite fought out to a finish. The King never admitted
the need for parliamentary assent to national purveyances but
replaced them by merchant contracts. Similarly he resisted
parliamentary right to authorize arrays, though binding himself
to pay for service beyond the locality, and on the one occasion,
in 1359–60, when arrays were on a national scale local assent
was obtained. The King was also brought to acknowledge that
assessment to military service was illegal without assent of
parliament. In both these cases the fact that prerogative levies
were being superseded by contractual service facilitated the
King's *de facto* abandonment of his claims. Likewise the heyday
of the eyre and the feudal aid was already past, and their
occasional and infrequent occurrence made it feasible for the
Commons to purchase pardon from either by the grant of
taxation, though they seem to have successfully asserted their
right of assent to an aid levied in excess of the statutory rate.

This may suggest that these disputes, prolonged and acrimonious though they were, were over forms and shadows rather
than matters of substance. Such would be a fundamental
misreading. Prerogative declaration of a necessity was a potent
weapon in the middle decades of the fourteenth century when a
masterful King, engaged in a massive war effort and solidly
supported by his nobility, was consciously attempting to
mobilize the fiscal and military resources of the realm. The
Commons were instinctively defending their property and their
bodies and were doing so by a conscious appeal to the sole and
supreme authority of parliament to authorize extraordinary
taxation. Moreover, they displayed not merely a fidelity to the
legal principles of taxation but a persistence and single-minded-
ness in opposition which was tribute both to their cohesion and
to their versatility in the techniques of parliamentary opposition. Although at times they mistook their power, endeavouring
to restrict the King's traditional prerogatives or to impose
preconditions on their grants, and though they could still be
out-manœuvred by the King and Lords using their control of
parliamentary business, yet they succeeded in associating the
redress of their grievances with their grants of taxation and
used their authority as representatives to defend the rights of

all subjects. As a result they had by 1360 established parliament as the authority to define and regulate all fiscal levies while they themselves were acknowledged as the sole negotiators and sanctioners of such.

Yet the gains with which the Commons emerged must be credited not only to their acquisition of parliamentary experience but to their increasing status, wealth, and political influence in the shires. It was their value as essential administrators of Edward III's war measures in the shires, as skilled companions in war, and above all as members of the landlord class committed to the maintenance of political and economic stability in the aftermath of the Black Death, that induced the King to turn from exploiting to allying with the gentry. Admission to responsibility in the proliferating offices of shire government made the parliamentary knights agents of the Crown but also more effective defenders of the shire against its incursions. A major shift in political equilibrium was initiated as government became a dialogue between the Crown on the one hand and the governors of the shires on the other. It is in this context that the solution to these prerogative levies must be viewed. The Crown abandoned the attempt to meet the demands of national war by extensions of its prerogative once this could only be enforced against the opposition of a politically important class. It learned to meet the demands of a new age not by updating anachronistic rights but by seeking co-operation in a common enterprise for which subjects were both induced and obliged to contribute.

CHAPTER XVIII

Parliament and Mercantile Taxation:
I The *Maltolt*

THE middle years of the century saw the Commons establish their right of assent to indirect as well as to direct taxation. The constitutional importance of this has never been in doubt, but since the taxation of wool touched primarily the interests of wool merchants and graziers, the impulse of the Commons is held to have been economic rather than political. It will be best, at the start, to summarize this view as presented by Bertie Wilkinson and the late Eileen Power before suggesting some respects in which it appears inadequate.

Wilkinson held that the Commons' victory depended on a change of purpose. As late as 1340 their main object was to abolish the *maltolt*; thereafter they began to look for recognition of their right of assent. The demand for permanent abolition, first heard in 1297, was repeated in 1339, 1343, 1346, 1348, and its echoes could still be traced in the 1360s and 1370s. But by 1348, and conclusively in 1351, the Commons 'fearfully and reluctantly offered in future to vote the tax themselves'. They had slowly come to accept the tax as 'a permanent and inescapable imposition', and in consequence parliamentary consent, not abolition, came to occupy the first place in their demands. This revolution in the Commons' attitude to the customs occurred some time between 1348 and 1350. By 1353 'the mutual recognition of the necessity of the tax in wartime on the one hand and of the necessity of parliamentary consent on the other, was complete'. If recognition of the King's needs was one reason for this, recognition of the true incidence of the tax was another. In their petitions of 1343, 1348, and 1351 the Commons complained that the merchants passed on the tax to the growers, to whom they paid correspondingly lower prices for the wool. As they came to understand that it was not the merchants but the community who paid the tax, so they came to demand that they, who represented the community, should grant it.[1]

This interpretation won acceptance from Eileen Power in all respects save one. In her view the Commons appreciated from the start that the incidence of the tax was on them and not the merchants, and it was this that prompted the demand for abolition. 'If the commons fought the issue on abolition and not on consent, it is because they were in fact more interested in the economic consequences of taxation than in constitutional theory.' Thus economic interests led the Commons, representing the growers, into conflict with the estate of merchants, and it was only the internal dissensions of this body—the conflict of interests between the greater and lesser merchants and the consequent support given by the latter to parliament—that, after 1347 forced the King to seek the tax from parliament, and established the exclusive right of that body to assent. Even so, Power agreed that it was only 'with the utmost reluctance on the part of parliament' that the issue shifted from abolition to control. Not till 1350 did parliament reconcile itself to the tax, grant it, and convert it into a permanent parliamentary subsidy.[2] The elements of this view are, therefore, a primary demand for abolition springing from the necessary incidence of the tax on the producers, and a later conversion to consent springing from the decline of the merchant assembly and the acceptance of the King's need for a permanent tax on wool.

There are, however, difficulties in accepting this account. The allegation that the incidence of the *maltolt* was normally and necessarily on the producer has recently been contested. K. B. McFarlane has argued that in general the graziers were able to profit from the competition between buyers, native and foreign, to resist pressure for lower prices, that to this must be added the competition from native clothiers, and that in the latter part of the century the Commons happily granted the subsidy for long periods at a time.[3] Certainly there is little dispute that after the organization of the Staple at Calais the tax was successfully

---

[1] B. Wilkinson, *Studies in the Constitutional History of the Thirteenth and Fourteenth Centuries* (Manchester, 1937), pp. 72–6.

[2] E. Power, *The Medieval English Wool Trade* (Oxford, 1941), pp. 74–5, 82.

[3] K. B. McFarlane, 'England and the Hundred Years' War', *Past and Present*, 22 (1962), pp. 8–9.

transferred to the purchaser—the Flemish clothiers. Although these arguments must take account of certain specific complaints by the Commons that the merchants were depressing prices to meet the tax, they are sufficiently weighty to compel a fresh examination of Power's thesis.

A further difficulty lies in the timing of the Commons' conversion from abolition to consent which, it is suggested, happened after long years of frustration just when the collapse of the estate of merchants threw the King into the hands of parliament. If, up to 1348, the Commons had made abolition of the *maltolt* the first of their demands, it is a little surprising that by 1350–1, when the King's financiers had all failed, they should forgo their attempt to escape the burden. If they then took occasion of royal weakness to enforce consent, there is some presumption that it was for this that they had striven all along. This brings us to the heart of the problem—what was the nature of the *maltolt*? If it was indeed an imposition, levied by the will of the King alone as were the extensions of the fiscal prerogatives, then parliament had good reason to seek its abolition and, failing that, to try to define its illegality in terms of the necessity of consent. In that case the victor in the struggle was the King, for he had succeeded in converting what had started as a semi-illegal imposition into a permanent tax on wool. As the price of consent, the Commons had accepted the levy and abandoned all hope of securing its abolition. Such seems to be the view advanced by Wilkinson and Power.[1] If, on the other hand, the *maltolt* was an aid or subsidy, the King could claim an indefeasible right to it in a recognized emergency, and any demand for its permanent abolition was not merely unrealistic but unlawful. Equally, however, the *maltolt* could never be accepted as a permanent tax for it was limited by the emergency for which it was demanded. Most important of all, it could only be legitimately authorized by common assent and for the common profit.

Any inquiry into the nature of the *maltolt* must start from the distinction between custom and subsidy.[2] Rigid definitions can-

---

[1] Power, op. cit., p. 85: 'The price of settlement was compromise. The King was left in possession of a high permanent tax on wool, and parliament was left in possession of the power to control it.'

[2] My account of these early customs is based on N. S. B. Gras, *The Early English Customs System* (Cambridge, Mass., 1916), chs. 1, 2; J. R. Strayer, 'Notes on

not be applied before the reign of Edward I, but customs were usually habitual impositions on goods leaving or entering a locality, imposed in the first place by a local authority and not granted to it, and of permanent duration. An export tax which served both to deprive enemies of essential goods and make a profit for the King had appeared during the wars of the Angevins and was first regulated by John in 1203.It was then instituted 'by the advice of our liegemen' and was to endure 'so long as our war lasts';[1] it probably ceased with the truce of 1206. The 'new aid' of 1266, despite its name, was not demanded for a specific emergency, but seems to have resulted from bringing foreign merchants under the protection of the Crown, in this sense anticipating the New Custom of 1303.[2] It led directly to the negotiation with the merchants of the increased custom of 1275. This was granted by the community of merchants with the assent of the great men of the realm. It has been shown that Edward secured acceptance for the new custom by strictly enforcing an embargo on wool exports to Flanders. From the first the custom was committed to the King's bankers, the Riccardi, as the basis for their agreement to fund royal expenses. It was accepted as a permanent, if limited, charge upon major exports which attested both the increasing wealth of the realm and the greater needs of royal government. Thereafter the royal claim that the ancient custom belonged to the Crown as of right and not by grant was never contested.[3]

The subsidy of 1294 (called alternatively 'novum auxilium' and 'custuma in subsidium guerrae') was the first of a series of subsidies in addition to the custom of 1275. Its character is quite clear:

1. It was granted by an assembly of merchants;
2. It was asked and granted for a specific emergency—'in subsidium guerrae suae quam rex pro recuperatione Vasconie

the Origin of English and French Export Taxes', *Studia Gratiana*, xv (1972), pp. 399–422; R. W. Kaeuper, *Bankers to the Crown*, ch. 3.

[1] Gras, op. cit., pp. 53, 218; Strayer, op. cit., pp. 410–11.

[2] Gras, op. cit., pp. 54–8, 78–9; F. M. Powicke, *The Thirteenth Century*, pp. 619, 629; Strayer, op. cit., pp. 414–15. Kaeuper, op. cit., pp. 136–8.

[3] Gras, op. cit., p. 63; Wilkinson, op. cit., pp. 58–9; Power, op. cit., pp. 75–7; Kaeuper, op. cit. pp. 141–7. The King's right to the ancient custom was carefully safeguarded in both *Confirmatio Cartarum* and in the statute 14 Edw. III 2 c. 4.

contra Gallicos intendebat'—as one of a series of proposals for
war finance;

3. It was of limited duration—'for two or three years if the war
lasts as long'.[1]

It thus fulfilled the essential requirements of the aid—consent,
an acknowledged necessity of the realm, and impermanence. It
was an aid to the King in emergency, levied by grant from the
merchants because the wool on which it was charged was in
their hands, but differing in no other way from the aids granted
on lay property by parliament and on clerical wealth by representatives of the clergy. No charge of its illegality was made in
1297 such as was brought against the eighth, though the
Remonstrances did condemn on this ground the summons to
foreign service, the prises, and the breaches of the Forest
Charter. Complaint was made against it as part of the excessive
burden of war taxation, and a specific demand was made for its
cessation. *Confirmatio Cartarum* echoed the Remonstrances when
it declared that 'the greater part of the community of the realm
feel themselves heavily burdened by the *maltolt* on wool'.
Leaving aside for the moment the economic accuracy of this
statement, we should note that this criticism of the *maltolt*
formed part of the complaint against the King's war taxation,
made by the barons not merely on their own behalf but on behalf of the whole community of the realm. They pressed for its
immediate cessation and for the requirement of future consent.
The two were not as irreconcilable as they have been made to
appear. The immediate desire in this, as in other taxes, was for
relief. *De Tallagio* asked that 'nihil capiatur de cetero nomine
vel occasione malae toltae', and in *Confirmatio Cartarum* Edward
stated that 'nous . . . les avuns pleinement relesse'. Thus no
promise was made of permanent remission, no statement that it
would not form a precedent. Had the *maltolt* been an illegal imposition a more strongly worded condemnation and a more permanent prohibition would have been called for.[2]

If the opposition, without challenging the legality of the

[1] Gras, op. cit., p. 79 n. 2; *C.F.R.*, *1272–1307*, p. 347. M. C. Prestwich, *War,
Politics and Finance under Edward I*, p. 195.

[2] In the debate on 'impositions' in 1610 the Crown lawyers pointed out that in
1297 the *maltolt* was said to be burdensome, not illegal. See *Parliamentary Debates in
1610*, ed. S. R. Gardiner (Camden Soc., 1861), pp. 92, 100. Clearly the prohibition
of its future levy in *De Tallagio* went further than the King found acceptable.

maltolt, was concentrating on securing immediate relief on the plea of its being an intolerable burden on the community, it would also wish to stipulate how such a tax should be levied in future for the profit of all. Just as *Confirmatio Cartarum* required that aids, mises, and prises should be levied by common assent and for the common profit of the realm, so it also required common assent for the *maltolt*. Who was to give this? Grammatically, 'leur commun assent' refers back to 'le plus de la communaute del roialme' who felt burdened, but this can hardly be construed as a demand for assent by the Commons. Nor had the baronial opposition ever claimed to give assent to the *maltolt* as they had to aids. It was natural that assent should be sought from the body from whom Edward had obtained the admittedly legal assent in 1294—the merchants; but it was to be given as part of the assent of the whole community. There was no reason to doubt that the merchants would adjudicate the King's plea of necessity in the same terms as did the Commons or the clergy. The opposition in 1297, therefore, had the same aim in regard to the *maltolt* as it had towards other taxes—namely, to assert the right to adjudicate the King's plea of necessity in the light of the common profit of the realm, interpreted as the common weal, and by this criterion and by the right of assent to limit taxation which might ruin and enslave the subject. Its immediate purpose was the cessation of these taxes, its ultimate objective the acknowledgement of taxation as an occasional thing. It did not seek to abolish the *maltolt* permanently, for the wealth of the kingdom should be at the King's service in time of need; it did not seek to remove the right of consent from merchants to parliament, for this was mercantile wealth, and there was little reason to doubt that they were appreciative of the common profit. But it did vindicate the character of the *maltolt* as a temporary aid, granted for an emergency.

If there was no complaint against the illegality of the *maltolt*, and no demand for its permanent abolition, we should expect in the years following 1297 that it would be granted for a limited period by the merchants on those occasions of national emergency when Commons and clergy likewise granted aid to the King. The New Custom of 1303 negotiated with the foreign merchants and never accepted by the denizens need not concern us, for it was a custom, intended as a permanent new rate and accepted as the price of royal protection.[1] The first subsidy on wool after 1294 was that of 1322, but in 1317 the King raised a loan on wool in the form of an additional subsidy for a limited period. It was granted to the King by an assembly of merchants 'in aid of the Scottish war and other urgent and arduous necessities', and in consideration of the aid granted by the clergy and commonalty.[2] In no respect, other than that it was aid by way of a loan, did it depart from the characteristics of the subsidy, and it undoubtedly paved the way for that of 1322. This was granted by native and foreign merchants 'pro defensione ecclesie et populi regni contra hostiles aggressus Scotorum inimicorum regis et regni'; it was made for one year only and in 1323 Edward II disclaimed any intention of retaining it further.[3] In July 1327 the merchants again granted an additional subsidy by way of loan, in view of the King's need for money for the army which he had undertaken to lead against the invasion of the Scots.[4] However, the merchants also secured a concession —the abolition of the Staple instituted in the preceding May; but this, like the loan itself, was of limited duration.[5] No further loans or subsidies on wool were granted before the commencement of the Scottish wars, corresponding to the suspension of lay subsidies in the period of peace between 1327 and 1332.

When Edward III resumed the war against Scotland, Commons, clergy, and merchants were all called upon to contribute. A parliament summoned to meet at York in December 1332 and then prorogued until January granted the King lay and clerical subsidies for the war, and in expectation of a similar demand the merchants, according to a royal writ, had already caused a depreciation in the price of wool.[6] Yet the merchants when approached excused themselves from contributing. Thereupon

[1] Gras, op. cit., pp. 66 ff., 295 ff.; Wilkinson, op. cit., p. 60; F. M. Powicke, op. cit., p. 630.

[2] Wilkinson, op. cit., p. 68; *C.F.R., 1307–19*, p. 335.

[3] Gras, op. cit., p. 521; *C.C.R., 1318–23*, p. 724. A writ to the collectors shows that its yield was specifically earmarked for the payment of victuals purveyed for the Scotch war: *C.P.R., 1321–4*, p. 282.

[4] *C.F.R., 1327–37*, p. 54.

[5] F. R. Barnes, 'The Taxation of Wool, 1327–48', in *Finance and Trade under Edward III*, ed. G. Unwin (Manchester, 1918), p. 139; R. L. Baker, 'The Establishment of the English Wool Staple in 1313', *Speculum*, xxxi (1956), p. 447.

[6] *C.F.R., 1327–37*, p. 342. The King may already have sounded the merchants about a retrospective tax in September 1332. See R. L. Baker, *The English Customs Service 1307–1343*, pp. 28–9.

the King, with the consent of the prelates and magnates of the realm, imposed a subsidy moderate in size (half a mark), limited to one year, and justified by the 'great and endless expenses which the King has been obliged to incur for the defence of the realm against the attacks of the Scots'.[1] The King's action was not arbitrary. The necessity of the realm, which had been accepted by parliament, imposed a clear obligation on the merchants. The King had asked their consent, but this did not confer a right to refuse; faced with their illicit refusal the King had acted with the advice of his natural counsellors for the welfare of the whole community. Nevertheless the King experienced difficulties in securing the subsidy. In March the collectors were authorized to collect the tax direct from the merchants, were put on their guard against fraud and evasions, and were told to justify the exaction on the plea of 'urgent necessity owing to the war against the Scots', while giving assurances that it would not constitute a precedent.[2] By May further negotiations with the merchants enabled the King to recall the levy and receive in its place a grant of a subsidy at the alien rate for the year following 'on account of the great and arduous affairs in defence of the realm against the Scots and other necessary causes'.[3] The subsidy remained unpopular with the merchants who concealed their wool or evaded payment,[4] and there is little reason to doubt that they sought to pass on the tax by lower prices to the growers. The subsidy imposed by the King was recalled on the ground that wool would be sold for less price than it was wont, to the damage of the people of the kingdom, and that granted by the merchants was formally terminated in the parliament of Lent 1334 in very similar phrases.[5]

These early subsidies have an unequivocal character and show how the principles of 1297 were given clear and consistent effect in the following forty years. First the circumstances of

---

[1] *C.F.R. 1327–37*, p. 342; *C.C.R., 1333–7*, p. 60. The tax operated retrospectively from February 1332 to February 1333 (Barnes, op. cit., p. 141). As Baker points out (*English Customs Service*, pp. 28–9), the King had also conceded to the merchants the restoration of home staples from 2 February 1333.

[2] Baker, *English Customs Service*, pp. 28–9; Barnes, op. cit.; *C.F.R., 1327–37*, pp. 353, 355.

[3] *C.F.R., 1327–37*, p. 365; *C.C.R., 1333–7*, pp. 60, 257, 433.

[4] *C.F.R., 1327–37*, pp. 354, 404.

[5] *Rot. Parl. Hact. Ined.*, p. 238; Baker, *English Customs Service*, p. 30.

each grant removes any doubt that these, like the parliamentary subsidies, were aids granted for a specific emergency, and were negotiated with the merchants primarily in terms of political obligation though the Crown might offer subsidiary economic concessions. Secondly, while the merchants were alone thought to be the proper body to make the grant, so that even on their refusal in 1333 consent was not sought from the full parliament, their particular assent was only part of the general assent of the realm to a necessity which touched one and all. The close connection between parliament and merchant assemblies thus existed from the beginning and sprang from the nature of the subsidy. Thirdly, these subsidies were moderate, occasional, temporary, and were granted and used for the common profit. In these respects they stood in contrast to the *maltolt* of 1294–7, and not only vindicated the guarantees of *Confirmatio Cartarum* but helped to establish the character and limitations of taxation on wool. Nevertheless the tax was highly unpopular with the merchants, and its temporary nature enabled them to practise evasion. If a more continuous and effective tax was to be secured, the merchants would have to be given some vested interest in it through beneficial economic or financial concessions. On the other hand, any attempt by the merchants to shift the incidence of the tax on to the growers—of which they were at least widely suspected—was already being resisted on the plea of damage to and impoverishment of the people upon which the Remonstrances and *Confirmatio Cartarum* had been founded. These tensions, foreshadowed in this period of light and occasional taxation of wool, were to develop rapidly when Edward III renewed his grandfather's policy of a continental war fought through expensive alliances. This was to jeopardize the procedure for granting the *maltolt* followed since 1297 and call in question its very nature as an aid or subsidy.

The grant by a merchant assembly in September 1336 of a 20*s.* subsidy on wool opened the series of taxes for the French wars which, like the lay subsidies, became nearly continuous over the next twenty years. If the tax had in this sense become established, there were to be long disputes over its nature. We can best approach these in the light of the conclusions we have formed about the earlier subsidies; asking, that is, on what plea they were demanded; which body gave, or claimed to give,

assent to them; and whether they were regarded as permanent
or temporary taxes. The grant of 1336 had all the characteristics of its predecessors. It was made 'for the expedition of
arduous and urgent business touching the King and the safety
and defence of the realm', and was paralleled by the concurrent grant of a lay subsidy in parliament.[1] It was probably
for a limited period.[2] By May 1338 the subsidy had been raised
to 40s. as part of the King's agreement with the Contract
Merchants whose monopoly of exports would enable them to
recover their loans to the Crown from the additional subsidy
more speedily. Although termed a subsidy the tax was to run
until these loans were repaid, and it was still being taken when
parliament met in October 1339 and demanded its cessation.[3]
In the later sessions of this parliament in 1340 the King conceded for the first time the right of parliament to grant the
maltolt, which it proceeded to do for a limited period from
Easter 1340 to Pentecost 1341. The statute of 1340 recited how
this grant was made: 'the king prayed the prelates, earls,
barons and all the commonalty for the great business which he
hath now in hand, that they would grant him some aid upon the
wools, leather, woolfells and other merchandise to endure for a
small season'.[4] This first grant by parliament, therefore, embodied all the characteristics of the aid. Again, in the parliament of April 1343, having heard of the progress of the war and
the prospects of peace, the Commons undertook, if the King
failed to secure an honourable peace, 'de lui eider a meyntenir
sa querele ove tote lour poiar' and granted the *maltolt* from Midsummer 1343 to Michaelmas 1346.[5] The next occasion on
which parliament authorized the *maltolt* was in the March
parliament of 1348, when it accepted a prospective grant for
three years from the Michaelmas following, previously made by
the council.[6] In the parliament of February 1351 the subsidy

---

[1] *C.F.R., 1337–47*, p. 50. Baker, *English Customs Service*, p. 35 n. 11.

[2] There is no precise evidence of its duration but the *Scalacronica*, p. 102, assumes
that it was for a limited period and complains that it was kept on thereafter.

[3] Barnes, op. cit., p. 144, suggests that this was granted in March but the first
firm evidence found by Fryde is in an agreement of 4 May. See Fryde, 'The
Financial Resources of Edward III in the Netherlands, 1337–40', p. 1151 n. 1,
and p. 441 n. 1 below quoting E 159/117 m. 185.

[4] *S.R.* i. 291.   [5] *Rot. Parl.* ii. 136–8.

[6] Ibid., pp. 200–1. There seems to be no record of a separate grant by parliament itself on this occasion, and the Commons had probably little alternative but

was renewed in terms which echoed the statute of 1340 and linked it with the grant of 1348. The Commons offered 'en cas q'il plese a notre dit Seigneur le Roi en ceste sa grante necessitee la subside de xl s. avandit un demi an ou un an avoir lui plese a les Piers et commune de la terre sa volunte monstrer', and the grant was made 'pur grante necessitee laquele uncore dure et se monstre plus grant de jour en jour', to run for two years from Michaelmas following.[1] When this was due to expire, the King asked the October parliament of 1353 to renew it 'pur un temps', 'en eide de la meintenance de sa dite guerre'. The Commons, in agreeing to this, made its levy after the first year conditional on the continuance of the war and stipulated that the money from the subsidy should be safely guarded for the war and not applied to any other purpose.[2] These conditions they had already imposed on the lay subsidies. Finally, in 1356, faced with the King's demand for aid to meet the Scottish invasion, parliament granted not a lay subsidy but the wool subsidy for six years to come.[3]

On six occasions between 1340 and 1356—every time, that is, when it had the opportunity—parliament had authorized the grant of the *maltolt*. It had never excused itself from so doing, and it had consistently done so in terms of a grant of aid for the necessities of the kingdom, for a specific period. As granted by parliament, at least, the *maltolt* retained the character it had had since 1294—an aid granted for a common necessity. On two occasions in this period, however, the *maltolt* was authorized by a non-parliamentary assembly. In July 1342 a full assembly of merchants—as comprehensive as that of 1336—granted the subsidy until Midsummer 1343. This might appear to be a revival of the earlier tradition; but as well as the fact that the statute of 1340 now required parliamentary assent, the grant was made not as an aid to the King in necessity, but as part of a bargain or treaty with him for the restoration of a measure of free trade.[4] But though the merchants were no longer acting as

---

to accept the council's 'grant' since the repayment of the loan of wool was charged upon the subsidy. See below, pp. 450–55. In granting the concurrent triennial subsidy the Commons laid stress on their obligation to aid the King in the present necessity.   [1] Ibid., p. 229.
    [2] Ibid., pp. 251–2.   [3] Ibid., 265.
    [4] It was, however, claimed to be of common benefit to the King, the merchants, and the people: see *R.D.P.* iv. 540; G. Unwin, 'The Estate of Merchants, 1337–

judges of the necessity of the realm, another body might claim in an emergency to do so. In February 1346 Edward, on the eve of sailing for France, secured the prolongation of the *maltolt* for two years from a great council. This was done because

veantz la necessitee qe le Roil avoit d'estre eidez avant son passage par dela pur y recovrir ses droitures et pur defendre son Roialme d'Engleterre assenterent par acorde des Marchantz q notre dit Seigneur le Roi avereit la eide de sa dite guerre et pur defens de sa dite terre[1]

In the following year the council authorized a prospective renewal of the *maltolt* from Michaelmas 1348 together with other emergency levies which Edward later justified on the plea of necessity and promised not to treat as precedents. The dangerous plausibility of the claim that the council was the natural judge of necessity was shown in the parliament of January 1348 when the King, answering the Commons' protests, declared that when the current *maltolt* expired he would 'take advice with his good council and do what was best for the profit of the people'.[2]

We have been brought to the question why, after 1340, parliament should have regarded itself, rather than the merchants or the great council, as the proper adjudicator of the necessity which obliged the grant of a subsidy on wool. But it will perhaps be of benefit to defer this a moment while we consider some other aspects of the consistency of parliament's attitude to wool taxation in these years.

Parliament's readiness to grant the *maltolt* throughout the 1340s was matched by a determined hostility to the claims of other bodies. Already in 1339 the Commons complained that the *maltolt* had been (in 1338) 'enhauncee saunz assent de la commune et des Grandz',[3] and in the following years they took their stand on the requirement of parliamentary consent embodied in the statute of 1340. Thus in 1343 the Commons complained that the grant by the merchants (in July 1342) had been 'sanz assent des communes' in violation of the statute,[4] and

---

1360', in *Finance and Trade under Edward III*, pp. 209–10. The 'agreements' or 'Treaties' of the merchants with the King are given in *C.C.R., 1341–3*, p. 553, and *C.P.R., 1340–3*, p. 415.

[1] *R.D.P.* iv 556–7; *Rot Parl.* ii. 161.   [2] *Rot. Parl.* ii. 168.

[3] Ibid., p. 105.   [4] Ibid., p. 140.

in the parliament of September 1346 they similarly challenged the grant by the great council in the preceding February as being 'saunz assent ou grante en parlement' and expressly against the promise given in 1343.[1] Again in the January parliament of 1348 they complained that the continued levy of the *maltolt* was contrary to the statute of 1340, and when in the following March parliament sanctioned its renewal for three years as previously granted by the council, they sought guarantees that in future 'nulle tiele grante se face par les Marchantz', and that no other imposition or charge should be made by the Council without the assent of parliament.[2] Finally, in granting the tax in 1351, they explicitly designated as illegal any grants made outside parliament, asking 'qe commissions ne soient faites sur tieles grantes singulers s'il ne soit en plein parlement. Et si nul tiel grant soit fait hors du parlement soit tenuz pur nul.'[3]

On every occasion when the wool tax was under discussion in these years parliament insisted on its exclusive right of assent, and granted it whenever it had the opportunity. What then becomes of its 'conversion' to consent in 1348–51? The argument for this rests on the dying away of the demand for abolition, and underlying this is the presumption that what the Commons had primarily sought was permanent release from the tax. We have already seen that there is no compelling evidence for interpreting the demand of 1297 in this sense, and that such a demand would be difficult to reconcile with the nature of the *maltolt* as an aid. Likewise in the 1340s the demand for abolition must be related to the insistence on parliament's exclusive right of assent. The demands by the Commons in 1340, 1343, 1346, and 1348 that the *maltolt* be 'abatue' or 'ouste' and that the ancient custom of half a mark should be restored were on each occasion connected with their attack on the recent grant by the merchants or the council.[4] Their final demand in 1351 that 'les ditz xls ne sount mes demandez ne levees desorenavant' likewise referred to its grant by the merchants.[5] What the Com-

---

[1] *Rot. Parl.* ii. 159.

[2] Ibid., pp. 168, 201.   [3] Ibid., p. 229.

[4] Ibid., pp. 104–5, 140, 161, 168. On each occasion they appealed to the statute of 1340.

[5] Ibid., p. 229. The subsequent demands for the 'abolition' of the subsidy may be dealt with here. In 1362 the Commons were insisting on the occasional character

mons were demanding, in short, was the abolition of a subsidy illegally granted by another body, not the abolition of all wool subsidies *tout court*. With it went the assertion that parliament was the rightful body to grant any subsidy beyond the ancient custom and willingness to translate this into effect.

Thus the Commons' aim did not change from abolition of the *maltolt* to assent and control of it, but exhibited after 1340 a marked consistency of purpose. They and they alone would grant the tax. But this insistence on the sole legality of their assent was something so new in 1340, so different from the accepted practice up to 1336, that the problem of explaining why, in this short period, a complete and important change of attitude took place may seem to present even greater difficulty.

The hostility of the Commons to the *maltolt* has been attributed to the fact that whereas it was granted by the assembly of merchants its incidence fell upon the graziers whose interests the Commons represented. Though the ability of the merchants to pass on the tax has been challenged as a general theory, and though it could hardly explain a change of attitude which we have located in a space of four years, it derives its authority from some explicit statements by the Commons in parliament which cannot be overlooked. In 1343 the Commons complained that the grant of the *maltolt* by the merchants was 'en charge et meschief de voz communes . . . qar ce est encontre reson qe la commune de lour biens soient par Marchandz chargez.' In reply the King asserted that the guaranteed minimum price afforded adequate safeguard.[1] In 1348 the Commons again demanded that no grant should be made by the merchants 'de sicome ce est soulement en grevance et charge de la commune en noun par des marchantz qi achatent de tant les leines au meyns'.[2] In 1351 the Commons complained that a grant by the merchants 'chiet en charge du poeple et nemy des marchantz', and asked that such be forbidden 'qar par cause des ditz xl s. les mar-

---

of the grant as well as on their exclusive right of assent (ibid., p. 271; *S.R.* i. 374); in 1371 they simply asked that no subsidy should be placed on wool other than that to which they had assented (*Rot. Parl.* ii. 308; *S.R.* i. 393), and in 1377 they were again reaffirming the principle of parliamentary assent and reciting the statute of 1340 which forbade its levy without the assent of the Lords and community of the realm. The King's reply shows that he understood this (*Rot. Parl.* ii. 365–6).

[1] *Rot. Parl.* ii. 140. [2] Ibid., p. 201.

chauntz achatent les leynes par tant le meyns et les vendent a chier'.[1] So consistent and definite an assertion, together with the provision of minimum prices as a remedy in 1336 and 1343, clearly had some foundation in fact. But these protests can be read in two ways. They can be read as an assertion that because the incidence of any *maltolt* fell inevitably on the 'community' (i.e. the graziers) in the form of lower prices, parliament, should grant it; or they can be read as an assertion that whereas the *maltolt* when granted by the merchants fell on the community, when granted by parliament it did not. Although the first has been the preferred interpretation, it seems very probable that it was their conviction of the second that stimulated the vehement protests of the Commons in these years and explains their eagerness to grant the tax themselves. If this were so we could expect to find some change in the nature of the grants by merchant assemblies which would account for the animus which the Commons developed against them between 1336 and 1340.

We must start with the period before 1336 since this provides some further evidence of complaint against a depression of prices consequent on the *maltolt*. That prices paid for wool were depressed during the years 1294–7 seems fairly certain, though it is less certain that this was due to price-cutting by the merchants. These years saw the first general fall in prices after a steady rise for more than a decade. Wool prices were particularly affected, very probably by the uncertainties of the market (the volume of wool exports dropped) and of the government's intentions (there were seizures of wool in 1294 and 1297) as much as by the effects of the *maltolt*.[2] In the absence of any specific figures or even contemporary opinions about the incidence of the tax in these years it seems safest to assume that the burden was distributed between graziers, merchants, and foreign consumers. The sole beneficiary was the King. The first explicit statement that the *maltolt* caused a fall in prices paid for wool in England is found in a letter sent by the King to the Treasurer and Barons of the Exchequer in January 1333 in

---

[1] *Rot. Parl.* ii. 229.

[2] For a discussion of the evidence which presents a somewhat different conclusion, see M. Prestwich, *War, Politics and Finance under Edward I*, pp. 195–9. E. B. Fryde emphasizes the effect of the war in disorganizing trade and credit facilities as a cause for the decline of exports in 1294–6 ('Financial Resources of Edward I', p. 1179).

which he explained the reasons for levying a subsidy on wool
after the merchants had refused to grant it. The King alleged
that they had publicized the King's intention in order to depress
the price of wool in England. All that we are entitled to say
about this is that the King must have thought the charge would
have some credibility.[1] On the other hand it is clear that even if
true, it did not render a subsidy more acceptable to the merchants, who refused to grant it even when they had obtained a
concession which truly did put them in a position to depress
prices to the graziers. For Edward had already promised to re-
establish home staples which effectively excluded aliens from
buying wool direct from the producers, and it was the effect of
this, as much as of the subsidy, which produced complaints
from the Commons in the parliament of 1334 that their profits
from the sale of wool had been cut.[2] It would seem therefore
that although some of the burden of the *maltolt* fell on the
graziers, they were not at the mercy of the merchants so long as
they could sell their wool competitively in a free market. It was
the restrictions placed on this, by an embargo on exports in
August 1336 and the subsequent establishment of a monopoly
to handle the purchase, export, and sale of wool, rather than
the grant of the subsidy itself, which necessitated the fixing of
minimum prices in the Nottingham assembly of September
1336.

Edward III's schemes for mobilizing the wool revenue to
finance his continental alliances in the years 1337–40 have been
intensively investigated and have already been considered in
outline in a previous chapter.[3] Our concern here is with their
effect on the body of merchants and upon the relations of this
body with the government and the graziers between 1336 and
1340. The scale of Edward's plans required not merely a tax on
wool, but a share in the profits from its sale, together with the
anticipation of both by loans. For this he needed to construct a

[1] *C.F.R., 1327-37*, p. 342. Cf. Baker, op. cit., p. 29; Power, op. cit., p. 72.

[2] *Rot. Parl. Hact. Ined.*, p. 238: 'les bones gentz de vostre commune se sentent
durement greve de ce qils ne poent vendre lour leines a lour profit, come ils
soleient faire, pur ce que les estranges marchantz neviegnent de achatre leines, come
ils soleient faire, par tote la terre, et de ceo qe la custume est encrue'. Cf. Baker,
loc. cit.

[3] See above, ch. x, and the works by Barnes, Unwin, Power, and Fryde already
cited.

monopoly of the wool trade in conjunction with a group of merchants who would make advances to the Crown. The mechanism for creating a monopoly lay with the King through prerogative pre-emption, an embargo placed on exports for a specified period, and the restriction of the sale to a designated staple. The scarcity thus created would produce a steep rise in price from which the maximum benefit might be secured by the controlled release of the wool on a favourable market. All these elements had been previously employed in isolation; what was new in 1337 was firstly their combination in a carefully timed plan, and secondly the partnership between the King and a group of merchants small enough to enforce the monopoly rigidly, and wealthy enough to sustain the delay between purchase and sale, while concurrently making large advances to the Crown on the expected profit. The 'Contract Merchants', led by Pole and Conduit who agreed in July 1337 to handle the Dordrecht venture, comprised a largish group of some 250, but the effective leadership lay with an inner circle of about 50 merchants who commanded the greatest resources. For these, as for their successors, the attraction of the scheme lay not merely in the promise of substantial profits, but in the enjoyment of an exclusive relationship with the Crown from which privileges might flow. Once this group had become involved in royal finance, their recovery of debts from the Crown depended on their willingness to continue as the King's factors in further agreements. Hence it was that the construction of a narrow monopoly based on the King's administrative authority and the merchants' resources and experience was a recurrent feature of these years. A very high rate of profit—perhaps as much as 200 per cent—could be expected if all went according to plan. In 1337 Edward secured from the Contract Merchants a loan of £200,000 and the promise of half the profits on the wool. On paper the scheme looked promising, but it had a number of serious defects which time and again in the following years were to cripple its operation.

In the first place the merchants lacked sufficient capital, not indeed to endure the delays, but to sustain the King's demand for loans together with his default of repayment. Frequent transferences of the monopoly from one group of merchants to another marked these years: following the seizure of Dordrecht in 1338 to the Bardi and Perucchi, and thence to William de la Pole; in 1343–4 to a narrow monopoly of thirteen led by William Melchbourn, and thence again with the backing of Pole to syndicates led by Melchbourn (1344–5), Wesenham (1345–6), and Chiriton and Swanland (1346–9). The English companies which undertook the farm of the customs between 1344 and 1349 enjoyed for long periods the monopoly of wool exports (and in 1347 the handling of the forced loan in wool); however, even thus bolstered, and given the opportunity to realize on Crown debts which they purchased at discount, they had to borrow much of their capital on short-term loans, and after 1347 they were in no position to make further advances to the King.[1]

Secondly, the vesting of all the profits from the wool trade in the hands of the King and a small group of monopolists antagonized other parties who were excluded. These were the lesser merchants and the growers. Although the King had secured the consent of the lesser merchants to the Contract scheme in July 1337, the gap between them and the monopolists rapidly widened under the stresses of the following year. The seizure at Dordrecht in March 1338 produced a permanent division between the monopolists, who by their participation in subsequent schemes were enabled to recover the King's debts to them, and the lesser merchants whose exclusion from the trade rendered their Dordrecht bonds largely worthless. Though there were some attempts to heal this division—in 1339 by Pole, and notably in the assembly of July 1342—the reconstruction of narrow monopolies after 1343 and particularly the opportunities these provided of purchasing Dordrecht bonds at discount led to a prolonged and embittered estrangement between these two sectors in the merchant body.[2] The lesser merchants did not content themselves with a barren hostility to the monopolists. They sought their own interests first in a widening of the monopoly to include themselves, and then, when the events of 1342–3 showed this to be a delusion, in the demand for free trade in wool. While as participators in the extended monopoly of 1342–3 they had accepted the Staple as a means of maintaining the price to the consumer, they tended thereafter to

[1] Fryde, 'The English Farmers of the Customs', pp. 3–7.
[2] Unwin, *Finance and Trade*, pp. 196–7, 215–17; Fryde, op. cit., p. 3.

view it as an instrument of monopoly, and to seek its abolition. But at all times they were agreeable to a *maltolt* on wool from which they might be able, through personal exemptions, to secure payment of their old debts. Broadly speaking, therefore, the lesser merchants were opposed to monopolies, but only because they were excluded from them by the great monopolists.

The other interest outraged by the royal monopolies was that of the growers. A free market in wool, in which native and foreign buyers competed, helped to protect them against any attempt by the merchants to pass on the tax by forcing down the price. But such a free market was destroyed by the general embargo on exports and prerogative pre-emption, out of which the privileged position of the monopolists was constructed. Moreover, not only was the producer thus forced to sell to the monopolists, but in 1337 he was required to part with his wool on credit.[1] The guaranteed minimum prices which were offered to him in 1336, 1341, and 1343 may have secured his basic livelihood (so long as he could cash his debentures) but the monopolist schemes necessarily excluded him from all share in the profits which the joint exploitation of the trade by King and monopolists secured. It was thus the enforcement of a monopoly rather than the levy of the *maltolt*, which enabled the King's merchants to hold down the price of wool. In any case the King's merchants were hardly in a position to pay high prices to the graziers. Their commitments to the King and the King's own commitments to his allies and troops were so great that they could or would not sustain any sharing of the profits with the producers; moreover the delays and frustrations of the scheme eventually produced such a glut of wool in the Netherlands markets that prices after 1338 were severely depressed. The opposition of the graziers was thus directed against all monopolies, and their support for free trade in wool concentrated on a free market for its sale. Unlike the lesser merchants who were excluded from the trade, the graziers were being compelled to participate to their disadvantage, and this gave them a

---

[1] Six months' credit for one half and twelve months' credit for the other. The fact that this credit was given not to the King but to the monopolists, together with the fact that the growers received only a small proportion of the £65,000 to which their credit was pledged, explains the hatred of the monopolists which these arrangements engendered. Unwin, op. cit., pp. 190–6.

simple remedy. They opted out. Resistance to the collection of
wool, evasion by concealment and smuggling took a toll of each
of these schemes which at times proved fatal.[1]

Thirdly, in giving rise to these dissensions, the royal monopolies destroyed the accepted basis of the system of taxation. In
1336 the estate of merchants was still recognized as the proper
body to grant a tax on wool. Its assent was part of that common
assent of the realm which adjudicated the King's plea of necessity for which the tax was granted. The tax was asked for the
common profit and was expected to be used for this. By 1340 all
this was in ruins. The estate of merchants was no longer a
coherent body, for the interests of the monopolists were irrecon-
cilably set against those of the lesser merchants, and its position
as one of the estates of the nation—comparable to the commons
and the clergy—was destroyed. It could no longer claim to
grant national taxes, and it was not as the grantors of a national
tax that the great merchants negotiated with the King. The
various contract schemes were not conceived as part of the
common responsibility for aiding the King in a common peril,
and for the common profit, but were bargains between partners
in a commercial enterprise from which each hoped to draw
equal gain. Their nature was in this sense individual and
economic rather than political. They arose from a war conducted in defence of the realm but they appeared to operate not
to the profit of the realm but to that of the King and his agents.
Indeed the working of these schemes injured other interests to
such a degree that they might be said to impair the common
profit of the realm. Such agreements, moreover, threatened the
occasional nature of the tax, for it was now not granted for an
emergency but for the sake of prolonged economic advantages
which both parties hoped might be permanent.

Thus it came about that the estate of merchants found its
authority to tax and regulate the trade in wool challenged by
parliament to whom the graziers and lesser merchants turned.
Under their influence the Commons became opposed to monopolies and hostile to all monopolists. In so far as they voiced
the particular interests of lesser merchants and graziers, they

[1] Certainly in 1337–8, 1340, and 1341–2: see Unwin, op. cit., p. 193, 197, 204,
208. Barnes, op. cit., p. 161. On the whole question of enforcement, see Baker,
The English Customs Service.

demanded free trade and were generally suspicious of an organized Staple. They would oppose the levy of a *maltolt* as part of a monopolistic contract which enriched the great merchants but held down prices paid to graziers, but neither merchants nor graziers opposed a *maltolt* granted by parliament as part of an agreement for free trade, for this guaranteed a market price to the grazier and provided lesser merchants with an opportunity to recover some of their claims from the Crown. To these interests free trade was of more immediate concern than parliamentary control of the *maltolt* and was often made the condition of the grant of the tax by parliament. Moreover, in voicing their opposition to a *maltolt* as part of a monopolistic contract, the Commons could appeal forcibly to the principle of 'quod omnes tangit' which was integral to the grant of a public aid. In identifying the *maltolt* as granted by parliament in the context of free trade as an aid for the common profit, parliament drew on a firm political tradition which, as much as its appreciation of the economic consequences of monopoly agreements, enabled it to oppose the powerful interests of King and merchants with such consistency and eventual success. And once parliament had asserted the public character of the tax the King could only construct monopolies to exploit it by either prolonging it at will or securing assent to it from other assemblies.

With this general pattern of interests in mind, we can trace the development of parliament's concern with wool taxation in the years following the Contract Scheme of 1337. Already in the parliament of February 1338, when the collapse of the Dordrecht venture was imminent, the King was forced to take account of the resistance of the graziers to the extent of conceding free export of half the wool of the kingdom after 1 August if the other half could be secured to the King's merchants be pre-emption. In August he negotiated with a great council a satisfactory basis for making deferred payment from the fifteenth for the pre-empted wool.[1] Edward hoped to offset the effects of this relaxation of the embargo on exports by increasing the subsidy to 40s., and secured agreement to this by May from the original body of Contract Merchants who could hope to

[1] Fryde, 'The English Farmers of the Customs', pp. 3–7; Unwin, op. cit., pp. 198–9.

recover the Crown's debts to them by exemption from the duty.[1]

Although the first half of 1338 thus produced a new attempt to combine guarantees to the graziers with retention of the King's right to make profit from the pre-emption and export of wool through his agents, this foundered as the King's predicament in Brabant became acute. Unable to wait for the full benefit of these schemes, Edward readily granted licences to export wool duty-free to all who would lend or contribute troops for his campaign. The stimulus provided by export licences and the eventual ending of the embargo produced a glut of wool in Antwerp which depressed the price of sale.[2] In the general collapse of the market, it was those handling the King's wool and those who could export duty-free who could survive, and the year 1339 saw the strengthening of the monopolists headed by William de la Pole who became mayor of the Antwerp Staple. The graziers, who had suffered the effects first of compulsory purchase and then of depressed prices, and the lesser merchants who had suffered first the embargo and then the full brunt of the additional subsidy which eliminated their profits, both turned on the monopolists as the agents of the King's policy and its supposed beneficiaries. Well-grounded suspicions that the King's merchants had defrauded the King while failing to provide sufficient resources to carry on the campaign lent substance to the Commons' charges in 1340. Their petition complained that the taxes granted to the King in the past had failed to reach him, to the hindrance of his plans,

---

[1] Fryde, 'The Financial Resources of Edward III', pp. 1150–1; Unwin, op. cit., p. 198. There is some uncertainty about the body who granted this increase. Barnes thought that it was a merchant assembly held in March, but the first notice of it found by Fryde is in the agreement with the contract merchants in May. This agreement refers to 'quadraginta solidos quos iidem mercatores de singulis saciis lane sue que extra regnum nostrum educerent nomine subsidii nobis per ipsos concessi et custume inde debite solvere tenentur in eisdem subsidio et custuma de ipsis lanis suis a festo Sancti Petri ad Vincula proxima futuro usque festum Sancti Michaelis proxime sequente et , . . post idem festum Sancti Michaelis educendis allocari quosque eis de summis sibi sic debitis satisfactum fiunt' (P.R.O. E 159/117 m. 185).

[2] The evidence for the price at which wool sold in the Netherlands in these years has been investigated in detail by E. B. Fryde in *The Wool Accounts of William de la Pole*, pp. 12–15 and Appendix. Fryde emphasizes that the 40s. subsidy from the autumn of 1338 'was likely to take away most of the normal profits of the English merchants'.

and asked the council to investigate where this money had gone and require account of it. Merchants, collectors, and ministers, great and small, who had handled the King's money since 1336 should be brought to account.[1] Accordingly a parliamentary committee was set up to hear the accounts of William de la Pole, John Charnels, Paul of Monteflorum, the Bardi, William Melchbourn, and all others who had received the King's wool and goods. Pole appeared before this committee on 5 April and days were assigned to him and the others to come to account. He was still doing so on 21 July when he was removed from the office of second baron of the Exchequer.[2] Finally the Commons required that in future taxes should not be handled by the financiers but by lords named by and answerable to the council, and this was done in regard to the ninth which, on the King's acceptance of these demands, the Commons proceeded to grant. This assertion of parliament's concern for war finance helped to vindicate the traditional nature of the wool tax as an aid granted to the King for a necessity of the realm. Their petition demanded that such taxation should serve the profit of the King and the relief of his people; it had therefore to be reserved for the use of the King and the defence of the land, entrusted to councillors and ministers not merchants and financiers. Parliament's indictment of the King's merchants for using taxation to serve their private advantage rather than the common profit signalized the end of the pretensions of the estate of merchants to grant taxation for the common profit of the realm and converted the Commons to the demand for parliamentary assent as part of their hostility to royal monopolists. This provided the context for the Commons' petition in October 1339 for the restoration of the old rate of the *maltolt*, 'since it has been increased without the assent of either the Commons or the Lords' by the King's agreement with the merchants in 1338.[3]

In 1340 the Commons granted the *maltolt* for the first time. Although they had taken pains to destroy the monopolists' position, they were eager to acknowledge and meet the King's

---

[1] Winchester Cathedral Cartulary. See Appendix A item i.

[2] *Rot. Parl.* ii. 114; *C.P.R., 1338–40*, p. 551. Pole's dismissal from this office was in accordance with the clause in the Commons' petition asking that those chargeable to account for the King's money should not hold any office until their account had been rendered. See Harriss, 'The Commons Petitions of 1340', p. 644

[3] *Rot. Parl.* ii. 105.

needs, and offered to grant a tax in wool. The first such offer, of 30,000 sacks in January 1340, was superseded by the grant of the ninth on wheat, fleeces, and lambs in the following April. Then in July 1340, following Edward's urgent appeal for money after his victory at Sluys, parliament granted a loan of 20,000 sacks to be repaid from the second year of the ninth. The loan was testimony to Stratford's pledge to finance the King's expedition by parliamentary control of the wool trade; but the promise proved impossible to keep, and Edward took his revenge by a personal attack on the archbishop. The failure to enforce collection of the grant of wool even when authorised by parliament itself did not mark the end of such levies, as might have been expected. Parliament's determination to prevent the recurrence of royal monopolies produced one final attempt to collect wools, by the weapon of pre-emption. In April 1341 parliament granted 30,000 sacks to the King, appointing special collectors and renewing the guaranteed minimum prices. It even accompanied this by an embargo on export until Michaelmas to facilitate collection, but with a promise thereafter of free export at the ancient custom.[1] Despite these inducements to the growers and merchants, this scheme too foundered on the stubborn opposition of the growers, and only a small proportion of the wool was ever collected. This brought to an end the attempt by parliament to operate on its own authority a scheme for the pre-emption and export of wool. It had been inspired by determination to release the trade from the grip of the monopolists, and it had imposed itself on the King by combining an attack on his agents with an undertaking to fulfil his needs. This it had failed to do, and the King, embittered by his military failures, turned on its instigators. When he renewed the attempt to exploit the wool trade in 1342 it was once more with the aid of the merchants.

Already in July 1341 Edward had started to rebuild a monopoly of English and foreign merchants who were prepared to pay high prices to handle the wool pre-empted by parliament, and the necessary corollary of this was the embargo on exports imposed in January 1342. But as the wool grant came to an end the King returned to the plan of financing his projected campaign in Brittany with a heavy export tax. The *maltolt*

[1] Ibid., p. 133.

authorized by parliament in 1340 had been illegally prolonged and in July 1342 Edward struck a bargain with a large assembly of 142 merchants to authorize this tax afresh in return for the free sale of their wool through the Staple at Bruges.[1] This enlarged monopoly comprised many who hoped to secure repayment from the subsidy for their Dordrecht bonds. If this agreement had been successful, the full assembly of merchants might have been permanently reconstituted and parliamentary control of the wool tax might never have been established. That it failed was due less to any hostility from parliament than to the King's need for a more direct and profitable exploitation of the wool trade, obtainable only through agreement with the great merchants. It was fear of the renewal of a narrow monopoly wielding prerogative pre-emption which induced both the merchants and parliament to negotiate in April 1343 to fortify and safeguard the agreement of the previous year.

The assent which the King secured from the merchants and the Commons to the continuance of the *maltolt* for three years from Michaelmas 1343 was obtained by formal concessions to both. The merchants were allowed a measured repayment of their Dordrecht bonds and to enforce a cartel at Bruges to keep the price of wool high, while the Commons secured for the graziers a revision of the minimum prices and a pledge that the King would not grant exemption to anyone either to buy wool below the legal price or export it without payment of the subsidy.[2] Although the King had secured prior assent to this from the merchant assembly and though the Commons protested against the grant 'made by the merchants without assent of the Commons',[3] any friction between the Commons and the merchants on this score was outweighed by their mutual fears of the recrudescence of prerogative monopolies. The King's willingness to make such concessions was testimony to the increasing authority of parliament's claim to grant the *maltolt*. But once this authoritative grant had been secured, Edward was free to use it to negotiate in July 1343 a loan of 10,000 marks per annum from a group of 34 (of the 142) under the

---

[1] Unwin, op. cit., pp. 205–12. The agreements are in *C.P.R., 1340–3*, p. 415, and *C.C.R., 1341–3*, p. 553.

[2] Unwin, op. cit., p. 214; *C.C.R., 1343–6*, p. 217; *Rot. Parl.* ii. 138.

[3] *Rot. Parl.* ii. 140.

leadership of Thomas Melchbourn, and by March 1344 only 13 of these remained effective as King's merchants. For the next five years the King was able to sustain an effective monopoly of the trade. By March 1345 the first group of English merchants secured the farm of the custom, which passed in August of that year to John Wesenham and thence, in October 1346, to Chiriton and Swanland who held it till 1349.[1] It was the renewal of this strict monopoly of export, fortified by long periods of embargo, and above all perhaps the permission for these financiers to cash Dordrecht bonds purchased at discount that was finally to bring the lesser merchants to use parliament in their demand for free trade.

This now became the theme of parliament's struggle against the King's merchants. In 1344 the Commons petitioned for the free sale of wool, the abolition of fixed prices, and the opening of the sea to all merchants, making the last demand a condition of granting a lay subsidy.[2] But the needs of the Crécy war enforced the King's attachment to his great merchants and before the *maltolt* was due to expire in Michaelmas 1346 Edward had secured its renewal by a great council on the plea of urgent necessity. This was done with the connivance of the monopolists, notably Chiriton and Co., who were financing the enterprise. Edward later defended the action as having been by agreement with the Merchants who on the security of the tax 'ount faitz plusours chevances a nostre dit seigneur le Roi en aide de sa dite guerre'. On these grounds he resisted demands for the cessation of the *maltolt* by the parliament of 1346. It was Chiriton and Swanland who handled—on very favourable terms—the levy of 20,000 sacks of wool authorized by the great council of March 1347.[3] Thus the King had succeeded in rebuilding a narrow monopoly to exploit the wool trade based not merely on prerogative authority and private agreement but on disregard of parliament's claim to authorize the levy of the *maltolt*. Hence the January parliament of 1348 saw such a wholesale attack on the King's merchants—on their monopoly, their buying up of Dordrecht bonds, their imposition of

[1] Fryde, 'The English Farmers of the Customs', pp. 3–7; Unwin, op. cit., p. 215.
[2] *Rot. Parl.* ii. 148, 151.
[3] Ibid., p. 161. For the council of 1347, see *C.C.R., 1346–9*, pp. 290–1; *C.P.R., 1345–8*, pp. 264, 326, 438, and in general for the levy of wool, below, pp. 450–55.

additional charges, and their enforcement of the Bruges Staple—
that it provoked a reply from Chiriton and Swanland.[1] This
animus against 'les faux jettes des Marchantz' was repeated in
the March parliament in the demand for the free passage of
wools and for calling the merchants to account for their handling of the levy of 20,000 sacks. Finally the Commons, in reasserting their claim and their readiness to grant the *maltolt*,
demanded that no future grant of the tax should be made by
the merchants who 'achatent de tant les leyns au meins'.[2]

   The King's eventual recognition of parliament's right to
grant the *maltolt* was itself a sign that both his need and the
opportunity for monopolistic exploitation of the wool trade
were passing. Already by the summer of 1348 Chiriton and
Swanland were in difficulties, and by April 1349 they were
bankrupt. Though Malwayn's group took over the sureties of
Chiriton in 1349 and carried on till 1351 they did not farm the
customs and the real period of monopolistic control of the wool
trade had ended. Edward made one final attempt in Easter
1349 to revert to a quasi-monopoly along the lines of 1343, but
its failure threw him back on parliament and ensured the
triumph of its persistent demand for free trade.[3] As Unwin
pointed out, the free trade enactments of the parliament of 1351
were not merely a condemnation of the past but 'safeguards
against the repetition of these expedients in the future'. Once
again, it is in the light of this long struggle for free trade against
the royal monopolists that the petition touching the *maltolt* must
be read. Its theme is the legitimacy of the grant of the tax by
parliament for the common need of the realm and the illegality
of 'grantes singulers' by the merchants outside parliament. It
demands that all merchants should have access to the wool
trade 'saunz estre restreint des marchantz qi se disent estre
merchantz le roi'.[4] It was thus the triumph over the monopolists which at once secured free sale for the growers, free trade
for the merchants, and the exclusive right of assent to the
maltolt for parliament. Granted by parliament within the con-

---

[1] *Rot. Parl.* ii. 165–6, 169 (nos. 38, 39), 173 (no. 68).

[2] Ibid., pp. 200, 201 (nos. 5, 8).

[3] Fryde, 'The English Farmers of the Customs', pp. 13–16; Unwin, op. cit.
p. 222.

[4] *Rot. Parl.* ii. 229.

text of free trade the *maltolt* could not be used to depress prices to the growers—indeed the organization of the Company of the Staple as a cartel enabled the tax to be passed on in the selling price to the consumer. It was when the *maltolt* operated as part of a monopoly which, by embargoes and prerogative buying, put the grower at the mercy of the monopolist, that the tax might be passed on in lower prices than the graziers would have obtained on a free market.

The victory over the monopolists was consolidated in the great council of 1353 by the Ordinance of the Staple and the formal exclusion of English merchants from the export trade. Only with the end of the war and the consequent absence of any need to exploit the trade did parliament in 1362 finally remove the disability on English merchants and pave the way for the formation of the English Company of the Staple at Calais.[1] Even so, this same parliament was careful to insist that no grant of a wool tax should be made by the merchants without the assent of parliament. There could be no clearer evidence that in the mind of the Commons the true objection to a grant by the merchants was that it formed part of an agreement to exploit monopoly profits.

We may now summarize the previous discussion. From its origin the subsidy on wool was recognized as an aid granted to the King for a limited period on the plea of specific necessity. Since it was levied on mercantile wealth, the assent given to the King's plea of common need was that of the merchants, and formed, in its coincidence with similar assent to the royal demands from Commons and clergy, part of the common assent of the realm. As such it was to be used for the common profit. In all these respects the practice of taxation up to 1336 was faithful to the principles of *Confirmatio Cartarum*. Thenceforward the tax, though initially granted in conformity with these conditions, became an element in the construction of a narrow monopoly of powerful merchants who under royal authority exploited the wool trade to the profit of the King and themselves. Lesser merchants were largely excluded from the trade and the

---

[1] Unwin, op. cit., pp. 231, 243; Fryde, 'The English Farmers of the Customs,' p. 17; Power, op. cit., p. 98; *C.P.R.*, *1358–61*, p. 564; *Rot. Parl.* ii. 271.

growers of wool compelled to part with their produce at less than the free market price. As such, the tax lost its public character as an aid, for it formed part of an economic bargain, for the private profit of the parties, and might be continued beyond the specific emergency for as long as the contract proved profitable. The Commons' attack on the monopolists in 1340 in the name of the common profit sought parliamentary control over the expenditure of this and other taxes and, as a natural consequence of these developments, advanced parliament's claim to give that common assent which the estate of merchants had now forfeited. But parliament was also induced by the King's needs and the desire to wean him from the monopolists to use its own authority to pre-empt wool, and the failure of this encouraged the King once again to negotiate with the merchants. The agreement of 1342 marked the attempt by the lesser merchants to serve the King's needs while preserving their own interests through an enlarged monopoly, again with a *maltolt* as part of the bargain. But fortified with the parliamentary grant of the *maltolt*, the King had by 1343 returned to a narrow monopoly, while the lesser merchants were constrained to throw their support behind parliament's demand for free trade. The failure of their independent bargain with the King meant that parliament's exclusive right to grant the subsidy now became the sole weapon with which to compel the King to forgo monopolies. Hence on every occasion in the following years parliament insisted on this right and on the illegality of grants by other bodies which, since they were 'singular' in character and yet fell upon the community, fulfilled neither the requirement of common assent nor that of common profit. Likewise, on every occasion when it had the opportunity, it granted the tax on the condition of the restoration of free trade, and in terms of an aid for a limited period to cover the King's needs. Parliament's claim to the exclusive right of assent became steadily more authoritative; even so, the King's final acceptance of parliament's claim and the safeguards for opening the trade to all merchants probably owed more to the internal failure of monopolies in wool, together with the cessation of open war, than to parliamentary resistance. Parliament, which remained fearful of the re-emergence of the monopolists, readily granted the subsidy on the plea of necessity, emphasizing its nature by formally appropriating it to war, limiting it to times of open conflict, and remaining watchful lest other bodies should grant it. Although, therefore, the main energies of parliament in these years were directed against the control of the wool trade by royal monopoly, in which its claim to grant the *maltolt* proved the principal weapon, it was the fact that this claim was based on a clear and traditional concept of the nature of the tax which parliament was alone competent to fulfil, that explains both the strength and endurance of the parliamentary opposition and the significance of its ultimate victory.

CHAPTER XIX

Parliament and Mercantile Taxation: II Other Levies

i. THE LOAN OF 20,000 SACKS OF WOOL (1347–8)

ATTEMPTS to collect levies in wool in the years 1336–41, whether under prerogative pre-emption or parliamentary authority, had been attended by political and administrative difficulties, and had left the King unfavourable towards their repetition. It was a measure of the desperate need to mobilize revenue of any kind for the Calais war that on 3 March 1347 a great council meeting at Westminster authorized a new levy in wool. Those present, who gave assent on behalf of the community after deliberation on the state of the war, were the King's nobles and 'fideles'. It was argued that unless the King could continue the war throughout the summer he would lose all that he had spent thereon, just when he hoped to bring it to a speedy and successful conclusion. This was to be an exceptional levy, and care was taken to ensure that it applied to both lay and ecclesiastical landlords, did not favour the rich by exemptions, and did not burden the very poor. The 20,000 sacks were to be loaned, repayment being promised by tallies and letters patent on the wool subsidy for the three years Michaelmas 1348–51 granted in the same council. The wool was to be priced at the Nottingham rates and the quantity to be levied divided between the shires, as in the last grant of wool. Answer was to be made by the collectors to the King before 1 August 1347, and any refusing to yield their wool were to be compelled to pay treble what they had been assessed.[1]

An assembly of merchants met at Westminster on 7 March, and a further seventy-nine merchants from thirteen counties were summoned individually to appear before the council on 27 April.[2] Between these dates, on 2 April, indentures had been

[1] *C.F.R., 1347–56*, pp. 1–10; *C.C.R., 1346–9*, pp. 290–1.
[2] *H.B.C.*, p. 523 nn. 2, 3.

sealed between the King and John Wesenham, Walter Chiriton, and other merchants for the disposal of this wool. The merchants were to pay the King for the wool at 23*s*. 4*d*. below the Nottingham price in four instalments (£40,000 by the quinzaine of midsummer; £10,000 by Michaelmas; £16,666. 13*s*. 4*d*. by Christmas; and the balance by Purification 1348). They were to appoint the collectors of the wool and to enjoy a monopoly of wool exports until Easter 1348; if by Easter they had not succeeded in shipping all the wool they could secure repayment from the wool subsidies thereafter.

The effect of this arrangement was that the King would receive £66,666. 13*s*. 4*d*. by Christmas 1347 together with a final instalment early in the new year. To repay the loan to the graziers he would have to find £23,333. 6*s*. 8*d*. beyond this sum and he would further lose whatever profit could be made on the sale of the wool abroad. The merchants, having brought the wool cheaply, hoped to sell it dear with the aid of their monopoly. Since the King's merchants were to be repaid from the customs if they failed to ship any part of the wool, it was thus essential for them to control the wool subsidies, and by the same agreement they took the farm of these for three years from Michaelmas at £50,000 p.a., less £4,000 p.a. which they could deduct in payment of previous royal debts to them.[1] The clear yield of this farm of the customs and subsidies would thus be £46,000 p.a. or £138,000 over the three years, less any recompense the merchants might claim for the wool they failed to ship. Moreover, on these revenues, as the agreement recognized, Walter Chiriton and Gilbert Wendlingburgh had claim for the balance of a loan of 40,000 marks made to the King in Flanders in February 1347. Thus if the repayment of the loan of the wool was to be charged on the farm of the customs, only a small proportion of this would ever reach the King.[2] Only the

---

[1] Chiriton and Swanland held the farm of the customs on similar terms for two years from Michaelmas 1346 and, with Wendlingburgh, secured an extension of this for a further three years in May 1348 when they advanced the King the custom and subsidy on 12,000 sacks at 46*s*. 8*d*. per sack, i.e. £28,000 (*C.P.R.*, *1348–50*, p. 145). This would appear therefore to supersede the arrangement of April 1347 and the preference accorded to Chiriton and Swanland over all other assignments on the customs must have deferred any expectation of the wool growers for repayment.

[2] *C.C.R.*, *1346–9*, pp. 248–9. In fact E. B. Fryde has calculated that between Michaelmas 1346 and October 1347 Edward borrowed from Chiriton and Co.

urgency of the King's needs and the discouraging precedents for levies of this kind can account for the King's sacrifice of the profits he might have expected from collecting and market-ing the wool through a contract arrangement on the lines of that of 1336–7. But the failure of that scheme, the odium it had brought, and the enfeebled position of the English com-panies all made it necessary to provide special safeguards for the merchants. Their profit depended on the speedy collection and marketing of the wool while the embargo on exports by other merchants remained in force. It is easy to see how the constraints of an embargo and the hazards of securing repayment prejudiced the lesser merchants and graziers against monopolists whose contracts seemed to secure the profit from the wools to them-selves rather than to the King.

With the experience of the levies of 1340–1 in mind the government was well aware of the vulnerability of the scheme. The King's writs provided penalties for refusals to part with wool while the indenture with the merchants took account of the practice of substituting inferior wools to those grown locally. The collectors did, indeed, meet both evasion and fraud, but in the early part of the summer—in June and July, the shearing time—a sequence of writs strictly enjoined the collectors to penalize severely those guilty of fraud or contumacy.[1] Those who were lax were threatened with imprisonment in the Tower and the seizure of their lands, and by early August the sheriffs were instructed to compile lists after the octave of the Assump-tion of all who refused to pay and to seize their goods and chat-tels to triple the value.[2] Evidently there was disaffection among the collectors as well as the vendors: some are alleged to have said that the wool was to be levied to the use of the merchants and not to that of the King, 'to his deception and the delay of the war', and the writ countered this by affirming that it was to be sent to Flanders for the King's use.[3] In some places the wool was to be delivered to the merchants; in others stored in

at least £55,000 and probably more, most of which the merchants borrowed at a heavy interest in Flanders. He also reckons that the customs were yielding at least £60,000 p.a. and possibly well over £70,000 p.a. Fryde, 'The English Farmers of the Customs', pp. 6, 12.

[1] *C.F.R., 1347–56*, pp. 11–15; *C.C.R., 1346–9*, pp. 227–8, 386.
[2] *C.C.R., 1346–9*, p. 374.   [3] *C.F.R., 1347–56*, p. 11.

religious houses.[1] Some communities and individuals received remissions on account of poverty; and in outlying counties —Northumberland and Cornwall—wool was still being collected in December 1348 and June 1355.[2] But in general the effort of the summer of 1347 seems to have been reasonably successful, and the resistance of the vendors to have been overcome by the exercise of firm authority.

Resistance of another kind was experienced from the lesser merchants. Finding that wool was still being bought and shipped by merchants, Edward on 24 June ordered that no wool was to be purchased until the 20,000 sacks had been collected.[3] A month later, when this had brought the local cloth trade to a standstill, a proclamation in all shires permitted the purchase of wool but forbade its export, and the embargo in favour of the monopolists was reinforced by writs of 1 August.[4] Perhaps partly owing to the successful collection of the wool, Edward on his return to England in October 1347 was willing to listen to the complaint which these actions had produced. After representations by the merchants to the council, the embargo on exports was lifted late in November 1347 and free trade was restored.[5]

The resentment stirred up by these proceedings was shown in the parliament of January 1348. Recalling that divers aids had been granted to and taken by the King from his poor Commons in aid of his war, to be used entirely for his profit, the Commons complained that the merchants were turning the present levy in wool to their own profit and the King's loss. They had, 'en coverte et coloure manere de usure, bargainez ove le Roi et cheviz sur meismes les Biens' to the excessive damage of him and the great impoverishment of his people in

[1] *C.P.R., 1345–8*, pp. 362, 438; *C.C.R., 1346–9*, pp. 293, 363.
[2] *C.C.R., 1346–9*, pp. 321–2, 333–4, 578; *C.F.R., 1347–56*, p. 431.
[3] *C.C.R., 1346–9*, p. 282. [4] Ibid., pp. 304, 357.
[5] Ibid., p. 416, writ of 26 November, 1347, and cf. the letter patent of 17 January 1348 granting Chiriton and Wendlingburgh leave to export 5,000 sacks of wool and reciting that of their free will they have agreed to the free passage of wool from all ports notwithstanding the previous embargo (*C.P.R., 1345–8*, p. 453). Fryde (op. cit., p. 13) says that the embargo lasted from October 1347 to October 1348 except for certain privileged associates of Chiriton and Co. and that no considerable sums were collected in customs until the autumn of 1348 nor much wool shipped apart from the 20,000 sacks. It may be that the King's measures in the summer had left the other merchants with little wool to ship despite the formal raising of the embargo.

divers ways, which the petition now specified. It complained of the 23s. 4d. per sack which the merchants had been excused in their payment to the King and of the opportunity given them to buy up the King's debts for 1s. or 2s. in the pound, to set against their farm of the custom;[1] it alleged that by the embargo on exports the King had lost in customs and subsidies as much or almost as much as the sum which was advanced to him, whereas the Commons, by reason of this embargo, had not been able to sell the wool wherewith to pay their fifteenths. It further complained of extortions and deceits by the collectors of the wool in using false weights, and of illicit seizures. The petition concluded by asking for these charges to be examined during the present parliament by a commission including members of the Commons, so that the goods of his subjects should reasonably and fully come to the King's profit. In reply the King promised to assign some of his council to inquire into the charges, invited representations by the Commons, and ordered the justices investigating false monies to inquire into the excesses of officials.[2] The Commons' insistence on judging the handling of the wool aid in terms of the common profit, their suspicions of the honesty of the King's merchants, and their call for a parliamentary commission of inquiry are all strongly reminiscent of the petition of 1340. Complaint was not directed against the loan itself but against the contract with the merchants and against the activities of the collectors. How far the commission they asked for was implemented in this parliament is not clear; however, in May 1348, on the ground that the Commons had not been cognizant of the King's arrangements with the merchants and in view of the merchants' offer to answer before the council, the King absolved the merchants from answering either in parliament or before his justices.[3]

Before this, the Commons had returned to their complaint in the parliament of March 1348. Although they numbered the loan of 20,000 sacks among the burdens which impoverished the commonalty, their specific grievances were of extortions by the collectors and of the restraint on the passage of wools until

---

[1] On this, see Fryde, op. cit., p. 8. The complaint in the petition probably related to the loan of 40,000 marks in February 1347 for which the merchants were allowed to enter debts of £20,000 owed to them or others to cash them on the tenth and fifteenth.

[2] *Rot. Parl.* ii. 170 (no. 49).   [3] *C.P.R., 1348–50*, p. 104.

the King's wools had been sold, by which the Commons could only sell their wools at half-value. They remarked that the King had had little advantage from the loan of wool and in the first of their common petitions they asserted that through the false tricks of the merchants the King had lost all but a third of the profit. They asked that in each county justices should be elected by the Commons with powers to inquire into and determine all extortions and frauds in the collection of the wool before the aid should be collected. In making their grant, moreover, the Commons inserted conditions requiring the merchants to answer before the justices in the shires and requiring the King to restore the 20,000 sacks taken as a loan.[1] All this is unmistakable evidence of the strength of feeling in the parliaments of 1348 against the handling of the wool levy, but the King gave little heed to either the petitions or the conditions of the grant. The merchants were absolved from the inquiry and the loan was never repaid.

There was one further levy arising from the farm of the customs and the subsidies granted to the monopolists which fortified the resentment against them and became a matter of complaint in parliament. This was a loan to the King of two marks per sack of wool, imposed by the farmers apparently on their own authority. It was paid to them by all whom they permitted to export wool during the embargo which accompanied the loan of 20,000 sacks. This levy—described in a petition in January 1348 as an 'outrage et duresse'—had perhaps been the subject of complaint before the council leading to the lifting of the embargo in November 1347. However, in the January parliament of 1348 the Commons, recalling the King's concession of free trade, complained of this as a continuing charge, and the King agreed to summon the merchants before parliament to hear their answer.[2] Yet the Commons repeated their petition for freedom of passage for all merchants and the consequent abolition of this extra loan in the March parliament, and freedom of passage was again conceded by the King in his reply.[3] Chiriton's accounts appear to confirm that this levy

[1] *Rot. Parl.* ii. 200–1 (nos. 4, 5). They accused the merchants of levying wool in excess and of impeding the sale of the remainder of the crop.

[2] Ibid., p. 169 (no. 38).

[3] Ibid., p. 201 (no. 8).

had been charged.¹ Two petitions in the parliaments of 1351
and 1352, both in the name of the merchants, sought redress
against Chiriton and Co. for the sums exacted under this
arrangement. In both petitions it was asserted that the loan
had been authorized by royal writs to the collectors of customs
in the ports, but in view of other inaccuracies in the petitions
it remains uncertain how official such a levy was.²

The farmers of the customs, it has been remarked, 'assumed
that they could do as they liked with the customs as long as they
paid the fixed annual rent for them'.³ This was a source of
grievance and loss to other merchants, but also a matter of
wider political concern. A loan in wool should aid the King
in time of necessity, without being to his subjects' loss. For
such a loan to be a source of loss to the King and profit to
other subjects was not merely something which aroused the
jealousy and envy of those who lent but a violation of a political
principle. The King, however, persisted in regarding his
dealings with the merchants as a private contract for which he
need not answer. Once the wool was loaned to him under
legitimate authority—and the Commons never questioned the
legitimacy of the loan however much they may have complained
of its burden⁴—he considered that he could use and dispose
of it as he pleased, reckoning that his arrangements with the
merchants offered the most profitable means of meeting his
urgent military needs. Undoubtedly the Commons saw the
force of this argument—it is noticeable that in the March
parliament they were much more muted in criticism of the
contract itself than in January for in the interval they had
discussed it with the council—but all along their principal
complaint was of the profit to the merchants and the loss
sustained by the King and his subjects, though they also
complained of illegal extortions by the collectors. To the extent

¹ Fryde, op. cit., p. 7.
² *Rot. Parl.* ii. 230, 241. The first petition says that the King issued writs for the
levy at Michaelmas 23 Edw. III (1349) but by then Chiriton was no longer
farming the customs, and the second petition dated this in Michaelmas 1348
though it probably meant 1347.
³ Fryde, op. cit., p. 7, who cites the illegal rebates they approved.
⁴ The authority to sanction a public loan rested with the King's council since
a loan, as distinct from a tax, did not (in theory) deprive the subject of his property.
The council attested the case of necessity and the assent of the community of the
realm to the necessity was not required.

that the merchants or collectors had been guilty of false and
oppressive dealing with his subjects Edward was prepared to
offer redress and inquiry; but the commercial terms on which he
disposed of the wool he regarded as his own affair. The Commons might criticize in the name of the profit of the realm and
the King's profit; they could make their demand in a common
petition linked to the grant of taxation; they could seek to bring
the merchants to account. In all this they showed themselves
mindful of their achievements in 1340, but the different answer
they received was eloquent of the political consolidation and
military triumphs by which Edward had strengthened his
position in the interval.

ii. THE TAXATION OF CLOTH

The great council of 3 March 1347 also imposed, for the first
time, a custom on the export of cloths by natives—aliens had
been paying a custom of 12*d.* on imported or exported cloth as
part of the *Nova Custuma*. The cloth custom of 1347 was of
14*d.* upon broadcloths or cloths of assize exported by denizens
and 21*d.* (in addition to the 12*d.*) on those exported by aliens.
Scarlets were charged at 2*s.* 4*d.* and 3*s.* 6*d.* respectively and
worsteds at 1*d.* and 1½*d.* for the entire cloth. The reason given
in the writs which ordered its collection was the decline of
wool exports and growth of cloth exports. Its collection was
to be under the authority of John Wesenham as King's Butler,
who was to answer at the Exchequer, and on 28 April he
appointed collectors in each port of the realm.[1]

In the parliament of January 1348 the Commons presented
two petitions which had been combined. Both complained of
the effect of the new custom and asked that it should be
abolished, the first alleging that it discouraged alien merchants
and impoverished native merchants, the second that the tax on
worsteds was a great damage to the labourers. The answer
made was that it pleased the King and Lords that this should
remain in force since it was reasonable that the King should
derive profit from the export of cloths as much as from wool.[2]
The Commons in no way challenged the legality of the grant
by the council, nor did the King defend it as an emergency

[1] *C.P.R., 1348–50*, pp. 6, 276; *C.F.R., 1347–56*, p. 28.
[2] *Rot. Parl.* ii. 168 (no. 31); Gras, *The Early English Customs System*, p. 72.

measure or on ground of necessity. It was presented as an equitable, permanent tax to take account of a change in the pattern
of wealth. As such it stood in the same category as the wool
'custom' of half a mark and assent by the Commons was thus
neither sought nor demanded.[1] The tax continued to be collected
at this rate and remained under the authority of the Butler
until after 1350 when it was joined to the remnant of the New
Custom of 1303.[2]

In the great council held at Westminster on 23 September
1353, at which representatives attended, the magnates and
Commons drew attention to the discouragement of cloth sales
from the seizures by royal aulnagers of all cloths not attaining
the assised length and breadth. They asked that the office of
aulnager be abolished and that in its place the King should
receive a subsidy of 4*d.* per cloth charged on the seller. In
his answer to this petition the King told the Commons to
negotiate with the Chancellor and Treasurer as to what should
be done for the King's profit and the result was the grant of a
tax of 4*d.* on cloth without grain, 5*d.* on half grain, and 6*d.* on
grain. Cloth duly charged was to be sealed with the coket
seal for petty customs and unsealed cloth offered for sale was
to be forfeit. The levy of this tax was recorded in the aulnage
accounts, which were attached to the customs accounts from
December 1353 to 1358.[3]

In 1358 the step was taken of farming this new subsidy instead of collecting it directly. For the years 1353–8 it could not
have yielded much over £250 p.a. and at Michaelmas John
Malwayn and Adam de Bury took out a farm for four years.[4]
When this expired in 1362 a new policy was adopted of farming
the subsidy on the basis of the shires. Individuals or groups of

---

[1] It was said in 1353 to have been 'lately ordained by the common assent of the
prelates, earls, barons, magnates and other the King's lieges', i.e. the same kind
of formal assent as was given to the custom of 1275 (*C.F.R., 1347–56*, p. 368).

[2] Ibid., pp. 253, 368; *C.P.R., 1348–50*, pp. 201, 424–5; Gras, loc. cit.

[3] *Rot. Parl.* ii. 252 (no. 34); *S.R.* i. 330–1; *C.F.R., 1347–56*, p. 385. H. L. Gray,
'The Production and Export of English Woollens in the Fourteenth Century',
Eng. Hist. Rev. xxxix (1924), p. 19.

[4] *C.P.R., 1358–61*, pp. 138–9. Collectors in the ports were to pay their receipts
direct to the farmers and no longer rendered account at the Exchequer. The commissions to the collectors continued to be enrolled on the patent rolls (ibid., pp.
332, 434). I have not been able to ascertain for what sum the subsidy was farmed,
but the receipt rolls record payments from the farmers in these years.

two and three took the farm of the subsidy in particular shires for periods of two or three years.[1] Thus Warwickshire was farmed at £30 p.a., Somerset, Gloucester, and Dorset by a consortium for £150 p.a., Oxfordshire and Berkshire for £10 p.a., and so on. The farm of London was taken for one year only at £120, though in February 1363 it was transferred to Peter Sterre for a term of three years at £80 p.a. These leases were renewed throughout the 1360s at the same rents or with minor variations (though the farm of London went down to 100 marks in 1366) and yielded a total of approximately £600 p.a.[2] For the remainder of the century (except possibly 1394–8), the subsidy on the sale of cloth seems to have been regularly farmed. The agreement of 1353 thus effected a permanent change in the tax structure, but since it was the conversion of a customary and prerogative right to a money payment by negotiation with the King, there was no reason for the Commons' assent to this to be regularly renewed.

Thus neither of these taxes on cloth was an aid, levied like the tenths and fifteenths and the *maltolt* for the necessities of the King and the realm in time of war. They were permanent dues, derived from the prerogative, and of light incidence. The King made no attempt to secure a heavy subsidy on cloth, perhaps because up to 1350 he was engaged in dispute with the Commons over the right of assent to the *maltolt* and thereafter because financial needs were secondary to the desire for political accommodation with parliament.

ii. THE SUBSIDIES FOR ARMING SHIPS

The campaigns of 1345–7 in northern France followed by the defence of Calais in 1350–1 prompted both the King and the merchants to give protection to English shipping. This could be done either by the creation of a naval force to act as an armed escort or by arming merchantmen themselves. These methods were employed successively when the problem was first tackled in 1345–6. Some time in 1345 Edward instituted a levy, probably by the advice of the council, of 1s. per sack of wool or 300 woolfells and 1d. on the pound of general merchandise to be

---

[1] *C.C.R., 1360–4*, pp. 432–4, 436, 517–20.
[2] *C.C.R., 1364–8*, pp. 70, 281; *C.P.R., 1364–7*, pp. 130, 232–3, 398. The farms of thirty counties named in 1362 amount to £532 p.a.

paid to the King's Butler, John de Wesenham. This was to be spent on wages of mariners staying at sea in special ships for the guard of merchandise. Early in 1346 by advice of the council and with the assent of the merchants this was changed. By an order to all collectors on 10 January 1346 the King instructed them to retain these moneys in their hands and themselves to pay the wages of men-at-arms and archers with which every ship laden with wool was to be armed. At the same time the poundage charge was dropped.[1] It was perhaps because this measure was haphazard and largely ineffective and because the King's siege of Calais was now entering its decisive phase that the council in England under Lionel of Clarence, probably on the advice of the lords with the King, reverted to the policy of providing a royal fleet. On 3 March 1347 the council authorized an additional and much heavier tax of 2s. on the sack of wool, 2s. on the tun of wine, and 6d. in the pound on general merchandise to provide 120 great ships of war for the convoy of merchandise and the guard of the coast. The admiral of this fleet, John de Montgomery, was ultimately to receive and spend this subsidy for which a London merchant, Peter Sterre, was appointed controller. The subsidy was to be levied from 18 March until the morrow of Michaelmas.[2] This was in force throughout the summer of 1347 and shortly after Michaelmas the collectors were ordered to present their accounts at the Exchequer despite their earlier instructions to render them to the admiral.[3] In fact although the subsidies on wine and poundage had ceased to be levied by 25 November, that on wool was continued on the King's plea that the passage of wools had been delayed. In the parliament of January 1348 the Commons petitioned for this to cease, and though Edward protested that in view of the heavy expenditure for the safe conduct of merchandise its prolongation was no great charge, he agreed that it should cease at Easter.[4] When further taxation was asked from the parliament in March following, the Commons secured a reaffirmation of the King's promise that this levy on wool would not be demanded after Easter. This was adhered to.[5]

---

[1] C.C.R., 1343–6, p. 632; C.P.R., 1348–50, p. 76.
[2] C.P.R., 1345–8, p. 264; Rot. Parl. ii. 166; Gras, op. cit., p. 81.
[3] C.C.R., 1346–9, p. 394.   [4] Rot. Parl. ii. p. 166.
[5] Ibid., p. 202; Gras, op. cit., p. 522.

The parliament of January 1348 had also seen a petition from 'all the merchants of England' about the 1s. on the sack of wool authorized in 1346. In 1346 when the merchants had agreed to this levy, certain of them had entered into bonds to provide safe conduct for merchants who paid the subsidy by hiring men-at-arms and archers for the wool ships. The petition now alleged that those who had received the subsidy had failed to provide safe conduct so that some merchants had been killed and others had lost goods to the value of £2,000; it asked that the merchants should be summoned to answer before the King in parliament for what they had received. The King agreed to appoint commissioners to inquire on oath who had received the subsidy and what losses had been sustained, and these were named on 12 March.[1] There is no record of their proceedings or of any further complaint about the subsidy.

In considering the complaints voiced about these taxes the differences in their character need to be borne in mind. The shilling on the sack of wool of 1346, authorized by the council with the assent of the merchants, was handled and spent by the merchants for their own safety, and the complaint of its misappropriation in January 1348 was made in a bill in the name of the merchants. The King's authority was here only implicated to a very limited extent. The levy on wool, wine, and merchandise, on the other hand, was imposed by the council of absence in March 1347 as part of a series of emergency measures which were generally unpopular and against which the Commons protested. It had a wider purpose—the maintenance of a fleet—and a wider incidence. Although the council may have claimed to act for the whole community—as it did in levying the loan in wool—and may have secured a *post facto* consent from a subsequent assembly of merchants, in January 1348 the Commons' petition noted that it 'estoit assiz sanz assent de votre Commune'.[2] Their main complaint, however, was that the levy on wool was being prolonged beyond the term for which it had been authorized.

The next levy, imposed on 28 February 1350, consisted of a subsidy of 2s. on the sack of wool, 1s. on the tun of wine, and 6d. poundage. It was 'unanimously and spontaneously granted by

---

[1] *Rot. Parl.* ii. 171; *C.P.R., 1348–50*, p. 76.
[2] *Rot. Parl.* ii., p. 166.

all the merchants of the realm' for a period of one year to fit out armed ships to suppress piracy.[1] Collectors of the subsidy were appointed under the authority of King and council and once again Peter Sterre of London was appointed controller of the tax.[2] However, when a truce was concluded with France in June 1350 the King ordered the levy to be suspended,[3] and in July orders were sent to all collectors to account with John de Buckingham, Keeper of the Great Wardrobe, for their receipts, which they were to deliver to him by indenture. In fact little money from this reached the Great Wardrobe.[4] Then on 24 September 1350 the King, having learned as he said of the activities of French and Spanish ships in the Channel, declared his intention of instituting convoys, to sustain which he ordained a tax of 2s. on the sack of wool, 4s. on every last of hides, 40d. on a tun of wine, and 6d. poundage for the period of one year.[5] Although the writ for collection represents this as an emergency measure along the lines of that of 1347, a petition in the parliament of 1351 says that it was granted by the merchants.[6] Early in October Peter Sterre was appointed controller of this subsidy, which was collected throughout the following year until 28 September 1351, although it legally expired on 24 September.[7] In the parliament of February 1351 the Commons complained that no safe conduct had been afforded for merchants by this measure and asked that the tax be abolished and the merchants allowed to provide safe conduct themselves.[8] This the King refused, the tax continued to be levied, and at least £700 of it was paid out as wages to mariners in the Easter term 1351.[9]

Thus although the Commons in 1348 noted that the tax of 1347 had been imposed without their assent, and protested against its continuation beyond the appointed period, there was

[1] *C.F.R., 1347–56*, p. 217.

[2] *C.C.R., 1349–54*, p. 167; *C.P.R., 1348–50*, p. 481.

[3] *C.C.R., 1349–54*, p. 241.

[4] Ibid., p. 192. Buckingham was 'to do therewith as the king has enjoined him, so that the king's affairs which depend on the sending of the money be not endangered by default'. Buckingham's account shows that he received no more than £197. 14s. 2d. from the subsidy (E 361/3 m. 48).

[5] *C.F.R., 1347–56*, p. 252.   [6] *Rot. Parl.* ii. 229.

[7] *C.P.R., 1348–50*, p. 574; *C.C.R., 1349–54*, pp. 254, 259, 288, 297, 323, 327; *C.F.R., 1347–56*, p. 311. The Exchequer expressed misgivings about exacting it beyond 24 September.

[8] *Rot. Parl.* ii. 229.   [9] P.R.O. E 403/356.

no opposition to taxes of this kind granted by the merchants for a limited duration and applied to the defence of shipping. Misapplication of the taxes did arouse protest—in 1348 and 1351—and behind this lay the crux of the divergence between the merchants and the King. The former wanted to make their own arrangements for the defence of shipping—with themselves handling the tax and preferably hiring troops to arm their own vessels. The King on the other hand regarded the subsidy as prompted by the current necessity, to be handled through one of his own officials—the Butler, Admiral, or Keeper of the Great Wardrobe—with an official controller and Exchequer audit, and used to finance a fleet of royal vessels for the convoy of merchantmen and the guard of the coast. But unless the operations of such a fleet were effective, the matter of the application of this national tax would be raised in parliament, and raised as a matter which touched the commune as a whole (as in 1351) and not merely on behalf of the merchants (1348). Suspicion that the King had used the money for his own purposes, whether well founded or not, only encouraged the merchants to press for their own control; but if they failed to secure this, their best hope of ensuring the effectiveness of a subsidy under royal control was to see that it was granted and appropriated by parliament where its expenditure could be subject to criticism. It was this logic that eventually made tunnage and poundage part of the parliamentary grant.

On the expiration of the tax in Michaelmas 1351 it was apparently not renewed and the next notice that appears of a tax in this form is at the end of 1359. Before Edward sailed to France on 28 October the council took steps to provide for a fleet to transport the King's army, to safeguard the coast in his absence, and to maintain communications with France. The magnates 'with the consent of the merchants' therefore granted 6*d.* in the pound on all merchandise imported and exported from 1 December 1359 until Michaelmas 1360. The money was to be collected in each port by two men of the town elected for the purpose, and was to be despatched every six weeks to the mayor and sheriffs of London under whose supervision it was to be spent on the costs of the ships of war, by advice of the council. The collectors were to be accountable solely to the mayor and sheriffs, and they were charged to use the money only for the

defined purpose, not converting it to other uses.[1] This applied,
if on a smaller scale, the same principle of autonomous local
control of a tax raised for local defence as that levied in support
of the archers for defence of the coasts. A national tax authorized by the council was thus entirely removed from Exchequer
control. In the course of December and January elections
accordingly took place in a number of ports and were reported
to the council.[2] Towards the end of January, however, the
council authorized—apparently on its own—an additional tax
of 2*s.* on the sack of wool and 2*s.* on the tun of wine.[3] Fresh
commissions for the collection of the new tax were sent out in
February 1360 and on 20 February the collectors in every port
were charged to attend in London with their revenue at dates to
be appointed by the two captains of the fleets for the west and
the north, Philip Witton and John Wesenham respectively. The
money was to be applied, by the King's direction, to the expenses of these fleets, but account was still to be rendered for it
to the mayor and sheriffs of London.[4]

The subsidiary mercantile taxes considered in this chapter
were all initiated during 1346–7. Although authorized by the
council alone in response to a particular emergency, with the
exception of the subsidy for arming ships in 1347 their legitimacy was not challenged by the Commons. The wool levy was
accepted as a loan (which the council was recognized as competent to authorize) and the cloth tax as an additional custom;
even the subsidy for arming ships was acceptable when granted
by the merchants as in 1346 and 1350. Parliamentary assent was
thus not an issue with regard to these levies and criticism
centred rather on the use to which they were put. For even
though they were not granted by parliament, these taxes were
public in character since they were levied for the common
profit. Thus a loan was akin to an aid in being levied for the
profit of the King and the realm, and with memories of 1340
still fresh and the current struggle over the *maltolt* at its height, it
was scarcely surprising that the King's arrangements with the
greater merchants for handling the loan evoked criticism in

---

[1] *C.C.R., 1354–60*, p. 600.   [2] *C.P.R., 1358–61*, pp. 319, 330.
[3] *C.C.R., 1354–60*, p. 601.
[4] *C.P.R., 1358–61*, pp. 331, 410. No account of this tax appears to survive among
the archives of the city of London.

terms of the common good. For however necessary such arrangements were to enable the King to benefit from the loan, they involved some measure of loss to the Crown and corresponding private gain to the merchants. If such criticism contributed towards aligning the interests of the lesser merchants with parliament as a whole, so in another way did the new subsidy for arming ships. For when it became clear that the Crown's interest in the effective application of these subsidies would lead it to insist that they should be handled by royal officials, the merchants saw in parliament the best guarantee that these taxes would be properly applied.

CHAPTER XX

King, Parliament, and Public Finance in Time of Peace, 1360–1369

THE Treaty of Brétigny initiated a longer period of peace than the century had yet seen. For both the King and his subjects disengagement from the demands and achievements of the previous decades was neither easy nor complete. Although the Chancellor could picture the King 'dwelling in his own land in the seat of peace, desiring above all the quiet and tranquillity of nobles, lords and commons', and the Commons give thanks that the King 'had removed them from the bondage of other lands and the many charges they had sustained in time past', these years were not entirely free of either domestic tensions or military burdens.[1] At home plague and bad harvests deepened the growing social and economic rift between landlords and peasants, whilst among the ruling class a confident imperialism found expression in vociferous anti-papalism and in the effort to consolidate and extend English control in the overseas dependencies of Ireland, Gascony, Brittany, and Ponthieu. Nevertheless both the Crown and its subjects looked to enjoy the fruits of victory—the King by indulgence in conspicuous display, his subjects by relief from taxation.

In 1360 there was no precedent for peacetime taxation. Direct and indirect subsidies had both come to be recognized as parliamentary aids, to be granted by the common assent of the realm in virtue of a common necessity and to be used for the common profit. For twenty-three years the occasion of this necessity had been a war waged for the defence of the realm and the vindication of the King's claim to the throne of France. When the Treaty of Brétigny provided for the renunciation of that claim the obligation to grant taxation ceased; to demand it for the continuing charges of defence during peacetime the established obligation would have to be extended or redefined. The solution was found in a compromise which satisfied both

[1] *Rot. Parl.* ii. 283, 276.

the King and the Commons and which carried profound consequences for the government of England for three centuries to come. By renewing the wool subsidy in 1362, 1365, 1368, and 1369, parliament effectively converted this into a permanent peacetime tax, though one for which its recurrent assent was necessary. Equally important was the corollary that direct taxation could only be sought for a dire necessity of the realm identified with war. That no direct taxation was sought or granted during this decade was a striking vindication of the safeguards embodied in the legal doctrine of necessity. On what grounds, then, were the Commons and Lords persuaded to grant this indirect taxation?

When parliament met in October 1362 the wartime grant of the wool subsidy at 40s. the sack had already expired, and the Commons may have expected that they would henceforth pay only the customary half-mark. The Chancellor's charge contained no mention of the need for taxation, and it was only in the course of the parliament that the council approached the Commons with a statement of the King's needs.[1] Whether this took the specific form of estimates of revenue and expenditure or was couched in general terms is not clear; the Commons in any case accepted it as demonstrating the existence of a 'grande necessitee' and renewed the wool subsidy at half the usual rate retrospectively from its expiry last Michaelmas. Both King and Commons were at pains to emphasize its temporary nature. The King had asked for the subsidy 'pur un temps', and the Commons extracted a specific promise that it should run for only three years after which the custom of half a mark would be restored. Their grant was not to set a precedent nor was it to be turned into a permanent tax by subsequent negotiations between the King and the merchants which might prolong it without assent of parliament. These provisos reflected ancient fears which Edward's tentative approach to the body of merchants to establish a foreign staple at Calais had revived.[2] While the King was thus able to exercise indirect pressure on

---

[1] Ibid., p. 271 (no. 26).
[2] Edward's scheme for establishing the Calais staple may have merged into the wider prospect of creating a self-supporting appanage for Edmund, earl of Cambridge, from a union of Calais and Ponthieu with the county of Flanders. See G. Unwin, *Finance and Trade under Edward III*, pp. 243-6.

the Commons, they were able to use their grant to secure substantial concessions on purveyances and eyres. Such bargains, however, were incidental to the fact that the Commons had accepted the King's plea of necessity and had taken the first step—the one that counted—towards making the wool subsidy into a recurrent peacetime tax.

In the parliament of January 1365, well before this grant was due to expire, the King asked for its renewal at a higher rate. Again the Chancellor's charge contained no reference to financial matters although he acknowledged the King's gratitude for the great and frequent aids to maintain the war. Ten days after the beginning of parliament, when the legislation for the statute of Praemunire had been agreed, the Chancellor initiated a discussion among the Lords on the state of the royal finances.[1] He explained how a select number of peers had been in the presence of the King where 'lui estoit pleinement monstre son Estat'. This statement or *monstrance* showed that all the revenues of the land would not suffice to meet half the King's expenses. The Chancellor therefore appealed to them in the King's name, as those from whom the King had always had aid and succour in salvation of his estate and honour which they had always held in regard, to consider some way in which he could be aided with the least burden to his people. His speech, though evocative of occasions such as that of 1339, was careful to avoid any hint of obligation and any reference to the doctrine of necessity. It was framed in altogether more personal terms, as an appeal to the good will of the subject to save the King's honour and estate. In response all the Lords and the Commons restored the wool subsidy to 40*s.* and granted it for three years from the following Michaelmas. Thus, as in 1362, the council had taken the initiative in approaching parliament for aid to meet a deficit in Crown revenues which had been demonstrated by a written statement and attested by the Lords. On both occasions the Commons had been won over by substantial concessions, while the government's uncertainty of its case was reflected in the absence of all mention of taxation in the Chancellor's charge and the construction of a plea of financial need as an appeal to save the King's 'estate and honour'.

[1] *Rot. Parl.* ii. 285.

The same pattern recurred in the parliament of May 1368. On this occasion the Chancellor's charge was more suggestive: he paralleled the great benefits of victory and peace which the King had received from God with those received from his subjects in their bodies and goods, and his declaration of the King's intention to guard and preserve the realm in peace and tranquillity carried a strong suggestion of an appeal to subjects for aid.[1] At the beginning of the second week the Lords held a discussion by themselves about finance. Archbishop Langham showed how the revenue from the subsidy was expended on various charges, emphasizing that the King received little or nothing to his own 'profit and increase' and requesting its renewal, burdensome to the people though it was. Lords and Commons then granted the King 'in aid of his estate and to save and guard his honour' a wool subsidy of 36s. 8d. per sack for two years from the following Michaelmas.[2] In fact it lasted for one year only, for in May 1369 the Prince of Wales was formally summoned to Paris to answer appeals against him, and in June the English parliament advised Edward to resume the title of King of France. Perhaps because no immediate military activity was foreshadowed the short parliament of barely one week saw no grant of direct taxation. But immediately following the resumption of the title, Lords and Commons were shown 'the estate of the king'. They were told that the war would bring great costs and expenses which the King could not sustain without the aid of his subjects, and thereupon they renewed the wool subsidy for a further three years at the increased rates of 43s. 4d. for denizens and 53s. 4d. for aliens.[3]

Thus until the last year of this decade taxation was sought not on the occasion and for the needs of war but to meet a deficit arising from the expenses of government, which was demonstrated by statements of varying degrees of detail laid before the Lords and presumably the Commons. The grants made were all of indirect taxation, at levels which varied according to the degree of the royal needs. They were made jointly by Lords and Commons and were (after 1362) to safeguard the estate and honour of the King. They were not rendered obligatory by any 'necessity' and were usually purchased by extensive concessions

[1] Ibid., p. 294. [2] Ibid., p. 295. [3] Ibid., p. 300.

to the Commons; but for what expenses were they asked and how were they justified? In 1365 and 1368 Langham specified the charges upon the King for which taxation was implicitly sought. In 1365 he listed these as fees and annuities; the maintenance of the 'establishments' in Calais, Gascony, the Scottish border, and Ireland; costs and gifts for foreign visitors (ambassadorial expenses). In 1368 he mentioned Calais and Guisnes, Ponthieu, and other lands overseas, Ireland, and the Scottish march where the reopening of war seemed possible.[1] In 1369 the Commons' greatest fear was of renewed attacks on Calais and the coast. Taxation was thus demanded as a benevolent contribution towards a general deficit and more especially for the maintenance of the frontiers and outposts of the realm. This was a burden for which the King might plausibly seek support from his subjects in their own interest, but the repeated designation of these grants as made for 'the estate and honour of the king' showed that there was as yet no acknowledged obligation on the Commons to support the standing charges of defence in peacetime.

For a number of reasons the wool subsidy was well suited to become a permanent peacetime tax. As such it would help to confine direct taxation to times of war and even particular emergencies. It equally served to affirm that the wool subsidy was a national tax, to be granted only by parliament for the needs of the realm. It was, moreover, fitting that the defence of the English markets in Calais and Gascony should be met from a tax on wool, and advantageous that the burden of this should fall at least partly on England's customers. Finally, since as a peacetime tax it was not obligatory, it provided an effective bargaining counter for the redress of grievances. All these reasons facilitated its establishment as a recurrent tax, a development of which the Commons may only gradually have become aware. But the justification for this was the existence of a permanent deficit between the Crown's revenue and expenditure, demonstrated by official statements in council and parliament. The evidence for this deficit has survived in several documents produced by the Exchequer which T. F. Tout and Dorothy Broome (who published them) accepted as sufficiently trustworthy to show that the aftermath of the war had produced

[1] *Rot Parl.* ii. 285, 294.

a great gulf between revenue and expenditure which the King was justified in asking his subjects to bridge by taxation.[1] That, certainly, was what parliament was told, but before accepting this official version it will be advisable to inquire into the accuracy of the figures, to establish the causes and nature of the deficit, and to discover how it was met. For the comprehensive picture of national finance which these statements purport to give not only provides a unique chance of assessing the financial viability of the English state in this brief moment of peace; such statements are also evidence of the Exchequer's capacity to analyse and predict the extent of its financial liabilities and its capacity to meet them, and of the priorities which guided the King and his councillors in framing financial policy. A close examination of this unique evidence will provide a fitting con- clusion to our study of the evolution of national finance in terms of the interests of Crown, parliament, and Exchequer.

Before embarking on an analysis of these documents a word must be said about their character. The largest group is formed by the two documents designated by Tout and Broome AII and AIII and two further documents in the Public Record Office (which they did not cite) which we may call D and E. All these are described as 'Remembrances' and basically list the pay- ments actually made at the Exchequer for a stereotyped list of charges during defined periods within the span Michaelmas 1362 to February 1364. The earliest (D) must have been com- piled soon after May 1363 and the remainder during the autumn and winter of 1363–4, the latest some time after Feb- ruary.[2] In addition, AII, AIII, and E include a short statement of annual revenue, substantially the same in each document, which has been appended to the more detailed statement of expenditure. The only summary of actual receipts occurs in D for the short period February–May 1363. The only estimate of

---

[1] T. F. Tout and Dorothy M. Broome, 'A National Balance Sheet for 1362–3', *Eng. Hist. Rev.* xxxix (1924), pp. 404–19. Tout's discussion of the financial crisis is in *Chapters in Medieval Administrative History*, iii. 240 ff.

[2] The two additional statements are P.R.O., Exchequer of Receipt Miscellanea, E 407/5 roll 115; and Exchequer K.R., E 101/399/13. These are printed below as Appendix B iv, v. The Issue Roll for the Easter term 1363 records additional payments to the principal ministers of the receipt (the two Chamberlains and the Treasurer's Clerk) and others totalling £79. 13s. 4d. for their expenses in remain- ing in London during the summer vacation 'pro expedicione negotio Regis et examinacione rotolorum de eadem Recepta' (E 403/415).

future expenditure occurs in E as a prediction covering the remainder of the Michaelmas term 1363-4 following the Christmas recess. Nearest in form to this group of documents is C, a summary of expenditure under very similar headings covering a period of almost three years in the earlier part of Langham's treasurership (1359–62).[1] It lacks any summary or estimate of revenue. The remaining two documents are both distinct from those already discussed, though in different ways. AI is a summary statement of revenue and expenditure for 37 Edward III (presumably the Exchequer year Michaelmas 1362-3) which omits non-recurrent items and seems designed to give a brief conspectus of the Exchequer's liabilities and resources for the purpose of prediction. Some of its figures correspond with those in AII and its estimate of revenue is basically that used in AII, AIII, and E. A statement in this form could be easily comprehended by the council; it represented the traditional 'state' of the finances of the realm of which a previous example exists from 1319, and which the Walton Ordinance charged the Treasurer to prepare annually. All these documents, with the exception of C (the earliest to be compiled), reveal a concern to demonstrate a deficit between revenue and expenditure, and this seems to be the purpose of the final document, B. This is entitled 'La remembrance de les despens nostre seignour le Roi qe enbusoignent annuelment estre faitz en temps de peez'. It is not, like the other documents, a statement of actual expenditure during a particular year but an estimate of the annual recurrent charges of peacetime and of the revenue to meet them. Its arrangement shows some similarity with the estimate of expenditure for the half-term Christmas to

---

[1] This was suggested by Tout and Broome (op. cit., p. 406) although the reference to the earl of March would seem to date it before the beginning of Langham's treasurership in November 1360. To judge from the sum paid on the Chamber *certum*, the period covered was rather under three years (Langham's treasureship lasted for 2¼ years) and I have averaged out the particular items on the basis of a quotient of 2⅔. This seems to work reasonably for most items but it cannot be applied to the figures for household expenses. These are given under the names of different Keepers of the Wardrobe in the previous decade, but cannot represent either their total or average prests as Tout appears to assume. They look more like the residual debts on their accounts discharged within this period. Walton's account, the last mentioned, was presented in January 1361. But if these were Wardrobe debts, the statement lacks any item for prests for the household during this period.

Easter 1364 in E. Its relevance to the discussion in the parliament of January 1365 is obvious and it was probably compiled during the preceding months, thus being the latest of the documents in the collection. This review of these documents, as summarized in the following table, suggests some preliminary conclusions.

	Expenditure	Revenue	Statement of Deficit	Suggested Date of Composition
AI	Summary statement for Mich. 1362–Mich. 1363	Summary statement Mich. 1362–Mich. 1363	Yes	Autumn 1363
AII	Detailed statement Mich. 1362–Mich. 1363	As in AI	Yes	Autumn 1363
AIII	Detailed statement for Feb. 1363–Feb. 1364	As in AI	No	Spring 1364
B	Estimate of annual peacetime expenditure	Estimate of annual peacetime revenue	Yes	Uncertain; ? latter half of 1364
C	Detailed statement for ?1359–62	None	No	Uncertain; ? 1362/3
D	Detailed statement for Feb.–May 1363	Statement for Feb.–May 1363	No	Summer 1363
E	Detailed statement for Mich.–Christmas 1363 and Estimate for Christmas 1363–Easter 1364	As in AI	Yes	Christmas Recess 1363–4

The composition over a period of one and a half years of a succession of statements following a basic model indicates that this was an exercise in which the Exchequer was well versed. The fact that they covered different periods which did not all coincide with the Exchequer year suggests that the Exchequer may well have kept running totals of its payments on recurrent charges, perhaps in the form of files of warrants. Intended primarily for the information of the Treasurer (as were D and AIII), they could form the basis for reports to the council and for any attempt to estimate future expenditure. The Exchequer's motives in compiling these statements seem firstly to have been a concern from the early summer of 1363, and then more particularly in the winter following, to establish and analyse the level of its expenditure; secondly in the winter of 1363–4 a need to counterbalance this analysis of expenditure with an assessment of annual revenue in order to demonstrate the existence of a deficit. Probably later in 1364 it then produced a general assessment of annual revenue and expenditure.

We must now try to establish the accuracy of these documents, taking the more detailed statements of expenditure first. Internal evidence gives a strong presumption that the statements of actual expenditure (i.e. excluding B) were compiled from Exchequer records. Thus they contain no suspiciously rounded figures, the variations between them can be related to the different periods which they cover, and a note on C suggests that it was compiled from the files of warrants for issues.[1] The list of expenses in AI is the least satisfactory, being incomplete both in relation to its own total and to the lists in AII–III from which it clearly derives.[2] By taking from C a rough annual average of the items of expenditure, we can check the levels in the documents covering 1362–4. The main test of the accuracy of these statements, however, must be from the Exchequer accounts, where such are available.

We may begin with the costs of defence since it was upon these that the Chancellor laid emphasis in seeking taxation. In

---

[1] The only common figure in the periods covered by AII and AIII is for payment 'pur deniers appromptez devant le temps susdit'. D, which overlaps the first half of AII and AIII, has the same figure as AII for the wages for Gascony and the payments to the earls of Cambridge and Pembroke. These must have been paid early in 1363 as they do not figure in E. E has the same figure as AIII for additional prests to the Chamber. The item given in C as 'Paiementz faitz par garaunt qe ne purrount plenement estre espresses' recall the instruction in the Walton Ordinances 'qe mesmes les garantz facent expresse mencion de la cause pur quei celles dettes, obligacions, assignementz, paiementz, douns, ou regardz sont faitz' and that this information should be enrolled.

[2] For its arithmetical inconsistency, see Tout and Broome, op. cit., p. 407.

AII–III the costs of the garrisons at Calais, Dover, Berwick, Roxburgh, and elsewhere are given as £4,023. 6s. 8d. in AII, as £3,890. 11s. 3d. in AIII, and as £4,003. 14s. 4d. in B. A first impression is that these figures seem remarkably low. In the decade before 1360 Calais alone had cost some £12,000 p.a., and even in C the annual average is £12,231. The accounts of the Treasurer of Calais show that payments in 1360–1 reached this figure in an attempt to clear Eccleshall's debts before he surrendered the office in February. But under his successor Brantingham the annual charge of Calais to the Exchequer dropped dramatically, to £3,329 in 1361–2, and then to about £1,500 p.a. in the succeeding years. This was mainly because the garrison was placed on a peacetime footing but partly also because the Treasurer was receiving some revenue from Ponthieu.[1] The cost of the Scottish garrisons followed a similar decline from wartime levels. In 1355–7 Henry Percy had been retained as sheriff and castellan of Roxburgh for £500 p.a., but his successor Richard Tempest received a total of £1,179 for the three years from 1358 to February 1361 when he entered a new indenture to keep Roxburgh for £200 p.a. in war and £100 p.a. in peace.[2] In 1362 Tempest indented to keep Berwick for two years at a fee of £500 p.a., though his receipts in fact fell short of this and in March 1364 Percy replaced him as custodian for two years at a fee of 200 marks p.a.[3] Thus whereas over the period covered by statement C, the costs of Berwick and Roxburgh had averaged £1,722 p.a., by 1364 they were costing no more than 500 marks. The figures given in the statements for the cost of the garrisons therefore seem realistic.[4]

[1] Eccleshall's account records a receipt of £14,003, 14s. in Michaelmas 1358–9, £4,163 in 1359–60, and £11,334 in 1360–1 with a further payment of £1,050 after its close (E 372/206). Brantingham's account records receipts from the Exchequer of £3,329. 13s. 8d. for the year February 1361–2; of £1,527. 11s. 5d. for Feb. 1362–3; of £1,756. 16s. 3d. for Feb. 1363–4; of £493. 6s. 8d. for Feb. 1364–5; and of £1,014. 9s. 7d. for Feb. 1365–6. Brantingham showed a modest but persistent deficit on all his accounts after the first (E 372/207, E 372/208, E 372/209, E 372/210).

[2] J. Bain, *Calendar of Documents Relating to Scotland* iii, *1307–1357* (Edinburgh, 1887), p. 304 no. 1655; E 372/207; E 404/8/40.

[3] Bain, op. cit. iv. 17 no. 69; E 101/27/12; E 101/29/13.

[4] Additional to the retaining fee was the cost of repairs. Dover (included in these statements) received no prests from the Exchequer between January 1364 and July 1365 (E 101/29/12).

More burdensome than the garrisons was the cost of maintaining armies in the overseas dependencies of Gascony,
Ponthieu, Brittany, and Ireland. Payments from the English
Exchequer to the Constable of Bordeaux had fallen steeply
after 1356 to an average of no more than £1,500 p.a., although
wages for reinforcements from England could more than
double this sum.[1] The agreement in the Treaty of Brétigny to
recognize English sovereignty over the enlarged duchy gave
Edward the opportunity to confer it on the Black Prince as a
fief in July 1362,[2] thereby absolving the English Exchequer
from financial responsibility for its defence and administration.
After the initial expense of equipping the Prince's army the
financial responsibility for the defence of the duchy was thrust
upon the Estates of Bordeaux who made grants of taxation for
its defence. The only charge upon the Exchequer in these years
was the setting out of the Prince's expedition which sailed in
February 1363, itemized at £2,662. 6s. 8d. in AII and £2,452 in
AIII.[3] Gascony was not listed as a recurrent charge in statement B and neither, for similar reasons, was Ponthieu. Here too
the English developed the practice of securing grants of taxation
from local Estates which not only paid the cost of local administration but provided a surplus to finance the garrisons at
Calais and Crotoy and even to yield an increasing revenue

[1] Above, p. 344. C gives the total payment for the Seneschal, Constable, and
other ministers in Gascony as £1,383. 15s., an average of about £500 p.a. The
cost of the forces sent to Gascony in the same period is stated as £8752. 19s. 1d.,
averaged out at £3,282 p.a.

[2] *Foedera*, III. ii. 667.

[3] William Farley was the last Constable of Bordeaux appointed by the Crown
(resigned July 1362). He received a total of £2,528. 18s. 2½d. during the preceding
year (P.R.O. E 372/210). His successor John Harewell (1362–4) was the Black
Prince's official (Tout, *Chapters*, vi. 70). He is recorded as receiving £17,476. 10s. 8d.
from the English Exchequer in the account of the Seneschal Richard of Fylongley.
No further receipts from England are recorded before 1370 (E 101/177/1).
Bernard Brocas was appointed receiver of the King's money in Aquitaine until
10 April 1363. Brocas's account is solely for money supplied by the Exchequer for
the Prince's expedition (Tout, *Chapters*, vi. 70) and his succeeding account until
9 December 1364 shows receipts solely from the duchy (E 101/177/3). Thereafter
the Exchequer had no financial responsibilities in Aquitaine until 1372. Further
'prests' paid to the duke of Lancaster, the Prince, the duke of Brittany, and others
are recorded on membranes 3 and 5 of E 101/394/17 (Tout and Broome, op cit.,
p. 413 n. 8, p. 415 n. 7). These are recorded on the Issue rolls for 26 July 1362
and 3 June 1363 and were from money received from the French ransom. See
The Ransom of John II, ed. D. Broome (Camden Soc. xiv), pp. 17–18, and below,
pp. 494–5.

(from £428 in 1361–2 to over £1,000 in 1366–7) to be paid into
the English Exchequer.[1] In Brittany likewise English responsibility for administration and defence ceased when the battle of
Auray finally established Jean IV as duke. Between 1362 and
1364 Brest, which had anyway ceased to be a financial liability,
was given into Breton hands while the duke's financial obligations towards Edward III and the English captains induced
him to take a leaf from the book of the Black Prince, his friend
and ally, and develop the *fouage* as an extraordinary tax for
defence of the duchy.[2] But if by 1363–4 the English Crown had
shaken off the financial incubus of its continental possessions, in
Ireland it faced heavy and sustained expenditure.

This was not entirely a matter of choice. The Gaelic revival had not merely dangerously attenuated the area under
the political control of the English, it had progressively reduced
the revenue from which English rule was maintained. The peace
with France provided the opportunity of large-scale intervention in Ireland to re-establish the position. Initially this would
be costly, but once the authority of the English Crown was
acknowledged, Ireland like the continental dependencies might
be made to pay its way whether or not it ever again yielded a
profit to the Crown.[3] The policy was initiated in September

[1] The following payments were made by the receiver of Ponthieu and Montreuil
Easter–Easter

	1361–2	1362–3	1363–5	1365–7
	£	£	£	£
Receipts:	1,729	1,786	3,921	7,273
Payments:				
To Exchequer	428	511	1,535	2,083
To Calais	350	394	106	
To Crotoy				2,955

Compiled from P.R.O. E 372/206, 207, 208, 212.

[2] M. Jones, *Ducal Brittany, 1364–1399* (Oxford, 1970), pp. 32–3, 44, 146, 161.

[3] H. G. Richardson and G. O. Sayles have shown that in the thirteenth century
Ireland yielded substantial revenue to Henry III and Edward I, and though the
decline had started by 1300 it was Bruce's invasion of 1315 which precipitated
the real loss of control. In the first half of the fourteenth century Irish revenue was
never more than half the average for the thirteenth and the surplus available to the
English Crown must have been negligible. 'Irish Revenue 1278–1384', *Proceedings
of the Royal Irish Academy*, lxii (1962), pp. 87–99. Compare the statement of the
clear profit from Ireland as £2,120 in 1292–3 and £1,424 in 1324 in the estimates
in Bodleian MS North C.26 (Appendix B i). J. F. Lydon, 'William of Windsor
and the Irish Parliament', *Eng. Hist. Rev.* lxxx (1965), p. 256 discounts the feasi-
bility of Ireland becoming profitable again. But revenue did increase markedly

1361 when Clarence was sent to Ireland to remain there with one short interval until November 1366. Up to that point the cost of Ireland had been small—in statement C wages of war totalled no more than £556—but between July 1361 and the beginning of 1364 the payments for Clarence's troops amounted to over £22,000.[1] AII gives expenditure on wages in Ireland as £7,504 and AIII as £12,688 with additional payments for shipping in both cases.[2] Since these were occasional, non-recurrent payments, the variation between the two overlapping accounts need not cause worry, but the figure in B of £4,000 p.a. must be an estimate based on the largely misplaced optimism for a quick military victory which would enable the reduction of forces to a near-peacetime level.[3] Certainly the English government hoped to reintroduce and extend the system of direct taxation to support the cost of the English troops, but it was not until William of Windsor became lieutenant in 1369 with a further £20,000 provided for his army that there began an intensive programme of taxation which—as in Aquitaine—was to erupt in political opposition to English rule.[4]

A further charge mentioned by the Chancellor in 1365 was the gifts and expenses for foreign visitors. The entry 'gifts to strangers and denizens' in AII is costed at £866 17s. 4d., in AIII at £1,170. 13s. 4d. (with the addition of rewards to custom officials), and in B the item is estimated at £1,000. No external check can be provided for these figures, but they seem consistent and reasonable. An allied charge in all three documents

---

under Clarence's rule (Richardson and Sayles, loc. cit.) and a belief in the profitability of Ireland remained an article of faith for the author of *The Libelle of English Polyce*. Clarence's appointment is in *Foedera*, III. ii. 622.

[1] P.R.O. E 101/28/22, cited by Lydon, op. cit., p. 256 n. 1. Walter Dalby's account is for wages paid during the period 10 July 1361–13 February 1364. It is not totalled. A. J. Otway-Ruthven, *A History of Medieval Ireland* (London, 1968), pp. 289–91.

[2] In AI the payments for Gascony and Ireland are lumped together as a total of £15,000.

[3] Yet on 13 February 1365, precisely when parliament was discussing these charges, the King wrote to the Chancellor and Treasurer of Ireland forecasting that 'a great outpouring of money is needed if the necessary resistance to his Irish enemies is to be made' (*C.F.R., 1356–68*, p. 308).

[4] Lydon, op. cit.; M. V. Clarke, 'William of Windsor in Ireland, 1369–76', in *Fourteenth Century Studies*, gives the details of the earlier Irish parliamentary subsidies. See likewise H. G. Richardson and G. O. Sayles, *The Irish Parliament in the Middle Ages* (London, 1952), pp. 80–1, 113–14.

concerning foreign missions (messageries) cost £1,751. 6s. 7d. in
AII, £3,345. 14s. 3½d. in AIII, and was estimated at £1,000 in
B. Neither of these two items appears in AI. As with the cost of
military expeditions, such a charge might easily be increased by
an important embassy, and it seems possible that the enlarged
figure in AIII, paralleled by that in statement E covering the
period Michaelmas–Christmas 1363, reflected the preparations for King John's return to England in January 1364.[1] If all
the foregoing are reckoned as comprising the foreign charges on
the Exchequer, the total of these in AII is £14,144, in AIII
£21,093, and in AI (confined to military expenditure) £19,023.
As we have said, large variations between different periods in
expenditure of this type are not surprising, and in so far as the
figures can be tested against external evidence, they appear
realistic.

Akin to this were the war debts on the accounts of previous
Keepers of the Wardrobe. AI and AII record a payment of
£5,594. 10s. 3d. on these and AIII of £6,309. 10s. 3d. The
estimate in B, of 10,000 marks, seems realistic particularly
since Farley alone left debts of £31,303 in May 1361 and his
account shows that the greatest effort to discharge these took
place between 1363 and 1365.[2]

The domestic departments listed in AII–III were the household and Butlery, the Great Wardrobe, and the Works. In AII
and AIII the expenses of the *Hospicium* and Butlery together
were £18,694 and £17,708. The Wardrobe accounts for these

---

[1] None of the embassies during the period covered by these statements as listed
from the accounts in the Public Record Office were prolonged or expensive
(L. Mirot, *Les Ambassades anglaises pendant la Guerre de Cent Ans, Bibl. de l'École des
Chartes*, lx (1899), pp. 180–1). It was not until the summer and autumn of 1364
that embassies of the bishop of London, the earl of Salisbury, and the duke of
Lancaster went to Flanders to negotiate the marriage of Edmund, earl of Cambridge
(E 101/314/32–4), and the cost of these did not exceed £500. The only payments
of this kind recorded on the Issue roll for Michaelmas 1363–4 were £249. 4s. 8d.
to Roger de Beauchamp and William de Burton for a journey to Holland and
Zeeland and £230 to two esquires sent on secret business to the papal court
(E 403/417).

[2] E 101/393/11. Discussed also by Tout, *Chapters*, iv. 144. The Exchequer had
made a vast effort to discharge the residual debts on these Wardrobe accounts in
1360–2 when, according to document C, a total of £53,266 was paid on the
accounts of Farley's predecessors. This is fully borne out by the Issue rolls,
particularly that for Michaelmas 1360–1 (E 403/402). Farley's own debts included £16,627. 7s. 4d. to five members of the upper nobility (the Black Prince,
the duke of Lancaster, the earls of Northampton, March, and Warwick).

years, which run from November, show an Exchequer receipt of
£15,866 for November 1362–3 and of £20,465 for the year
following, which gives almost exactly the same average of
£18,200.[1] Document B, on the other hand, estimates this charge
as £9,333 p.a. Why this was set so low is difficult to understand. The *Hospicium* expenses had never fallen below £12,000
during the reign and in the fifteenth century this was to be considered a reasonable level for the maintenance of a dignified
household. Household expenditure had indeed been running at
this level in 1360–2, since when it had suddenly increased, and
B may reflect the hope or expectation of a return to the more
moderate level. For the Great Wardrobe AII and AIII give
£8,000 and £8,692 respectively while the accounts of the
Keeper, running from June each year, record an Exchequer
receipt of £5,305 for 1362–3 and £8,490 for 1363–4. This increase was part of a steeply rising curve which had started from
the figure of £3,950 in 1360 and 1361 and was to culminate in
totals of £9,485 in 1365–6 and £17,020 in fifteen months of
1366–7.[2] In C the average figure comes out at £5,833. Thus
B's estimate of £4,000 clearly looked back to the beginning of
the decade and it was to this level that the Great Wardrobe in
fact returned in 1367–70. A similar if even greater disparity
between actual expenditure and the estimate in B occurs for the
King's Works. AII and AIII record expenditure of £14,312 and
£15,378 respectively; B gives an estimate of £5,000 p.a. Unfortunately the total annual charge for the King's Works cannot be ascertained for the years before 1378 but in the century
following that date the average for any group of years is less
than half the sum of £5,000.[3] Similarly the total expenditure
recorded in C if averaged out gives a figure of £2,963. AII–III
thus reflect the vast building programme which is well documented for these years and B, though substantially lower, was
still larger than the normal expenditure of this department.
Finally there were the expenses of the King's stud and stable,
given as £690 in AII and estimated at 1,000 marks in B. Over-
all there was thus a very considerable disparity between the

---

[1] Tout, *Chapters*, vi. 92–3; discussed ibid. iv. 164 ff.

[2] Ibid. vi. 107; discussed ibid. iv. 423.

[3] H. M. Colvin (ed.), *The History of the King's Works* (London, 1963), ii. Appendix A, table 2, p. 1024. By 1369–70 expenditure had apparently returned to this
level (£2,373). See J. H. Ramsay, *Revenues*, ii. 293.

totals of AII–III and B on the main domestic departments; the former being £41,006–£41,778, the latter £18,333. 6s. 8d. AI was more closely related to AII–III: its total of £43,333. 6s. 8d. comprising 40,000 marks for the household and Great Wardrobe and 25,000 marks for the Works. The estimates in B are thus not realistic but notional: they appear to represent the conventional or traditional scale of costs. This will be relevant when we try to decide for what purpose B was produced.

Our next section of expenses comprises fees and annuities. These appear under three heads in AII–III. First come the fees of justices, barons of the Exchequer, and other ministers. AII–III give these as £1,761 and £1,554, the calculated average in C gives £1,849, and B reproduces the figure of AII. For annuities granted by patent from the customs and subsidies AII gives £6,300, a figure repeated in B, while AI, AIII, and E adopt the slightly larger total of £6,933.[1] For life annuities by patents payable at the Exchequer, the figure of £6,450 in AI and AII also shows a slight increase in AIII to £7,170 and a marked increase over the averaged figure of £4,125 in C, though this may be distorted by being based on a total of less than three full years.[2] There is probably insufficient evidence from which to check these figures, but their general consistency is convincing. The total given in B, of £13,000, can only be explained as a conflation of annuities on both customs and Exchequer revenues, despite the fact that the customs were already listed separately and thus figure twice. Here again, therefore, B gives an unrealistic picture, though not one related to a traditional figure.

The final major group of expenses can best be described as the personal expenses of the royal family. In AII–III these included the *certum* for the Chamber and Queen Philippa's personal annuity at the Exchequer, and purchases 'al oeps le roy' of silver, jewels, lands, prisoners, and horses. The Chamber *certum* of 10,000 marks had been instituted in 1355–6 when the last Chamber manors were given to the King's daughter Isabella and the Queen's annuity was £1,756.[3] AII and B give

---

[1] On this difference, see Tout and Broome, op. cit., p. 417 n. 3.

[2] Document E gives a payment for the Michaelmas term 1363–4 of £3,447. 15s. and an estimate for the Easter term of £3,000.

[3] Tout, *Chapters*, iv. 314.

these figures though AIII has an additional payment of £336 to the Queen and the repayment of a loan from the Chamber of £812 (also recorded in document E). Additional payments to the Chamber beyond the *certum* and to Queen Philippa, as the King's gift for the discharge of her debts, appear in the expenses listed in C averaged out at £2,067 and £2,015 respectively. Although these additional payments were frequent during the decade, they are not listed in B.[1] The item in AII–III for the purchase of silver, jewels, and lands figures at £4,068 and £5,623[2] and appears also in D and E, being linked in the former with the purchase of prisoners. This occurs as a separate item in AII–III, set down at £600 and £300. Three years and more after the battle of Poitiers the Exchequer is recorded as spending a total of £30,853 on prisoners during the period covered by C, though such expenditure was clearly diminishing rapidly by 1364. As we would expect, all these additional purchases are omitted in AI and B and in the estimate in E. Hence, whereas in AII–III the personal expenses of the royal family totalled £13,781 and £13,828, in B they amounted to no more than £8,422, comprising merely the annuities for the Chamber and the Queen.

From this review of the expenditure side of these documents we may draw two sets of conclusions: first, as to the different nature of AII–III and B; secondly, as to the pattern of expenditure. The major difference between the two types of document is, of course, that whereas AII–III give the full range of actual payments by the Exchequer within their appointed periods (as do D and E), B (like the estimate in E) is a forecast of necessary or predictable charges. Whereas the expenditure in AII–III is given in precise figures, a number of those in B are in rounded numbers. Tested against Exchequer evidence, the figures in AII–III can be accepted as realistic, and there is no reason to doubt that they were compiled from the Exchequer's record of issues. In B the estimates for defence and foreign expenditure

---

[1] For additions to the *certum*, see Tout, *Chapters*, iv. 316–17; also warrants for £200 in 1359, 2,000 marks in October 1366, and £300 in February 1367 (P.R.O. E 43/636, E 404/8/51, 52). In 1369–70 its total receipt was almost £2,000 above the *certum* (Ramsay, *Revenues*, ii. 293), a figure similar to that at the beginning of the decade.

[2] This figure in AIII includes purchases of horses which in AII is separately reckoned at £690 and in B at 1,000 marks.

stand close to those of AII–III on which they must in some measure have been based since the pattern of this expenditure had changed only recently. The exception, Ireland, can justifiably be regarded as a special case. But the estimates for the domestic departments are always well below actual expenditure and appear to represent a conventional peacetime level. Its estimates of the King's personal expenses omit entirely the large occasional expenditure in AII–III. B therefore presents neither the full range of actual expenditure nor the full total of expenditure on the range of charges which it contains. It is a distorted estimate, the purpose of which we shall have to consider later. The pattern of expenditure revealed by AII–III has one very striking feature, namely that the defence and 'foreign' charges were about half those of the domestic departments even without counting the King's personal expenses. If this mirrored the shift from war to peace, it contrasted with the emphasis placed upon the maintenance of defence in the Chancellors' speeches. In this connection we should observe that the much smaller estimates for domestic expenditure in B give proportionately greater significance to the external costs.

Before we leave the expenditure side of these statements we may look in a little more detail at the areas on the domestic side where expenditure was most conspicuous. The cost of the Wardrobe itself, though high, was not excessive;[1] it was in the Great Wardrobe and the Works that expenditure had significantly increased. The figures for 'purchases' in the Great Wardrobe accounts reflect a sustained programme of refurnishing of the King's residences. From the beginning of 1363 to the end of 1367 this item was never less than £7,000 p.a., reaching a peak of almost £11,000 for such purchases in 1365–6 and only declining to the more modest level of £3,000 in 1369–70 when Queen Philippa's death confirmed the King's

---

[1] Tout, *Chapters*, iv. 173–5. The increase in the consumption of the household seems to have begun with Buckingham's treasureship after 1353, rising from an average of £12,000 to £17,000 p.a. This was at a time when war expenditure had declined and many of the debts of the Crécy–Calais campaign had been discharged. The rise continued under Buckingham's successor, Retford, and on the eve of Edward's last campaign the *hospicium* expenses stood at over £20,000, though they had returned to £13,226 for the year 1361–2. After 1363 the Queen's household was amalgamated with that of the King and before her death the joint *hospicium* expenses never fell below £17,500 p.a.

growing retirement.[1] Equally symptomatic of the King's indulgence in conspicuous display was the passion—which he shared with his captains—for building. Edward in these years of peace betrayed a compulsive urge to embellish and construct in every royal residence, partly from prestige but partly in response to his increasing need for domestic comfort as old age approached. Although he was responsible for 'the only wholly new royal castle built in the Later Middle Ages',[2] at Sheppey, more characteristic were the works at Windsor where the new college and the extensive remodelling of the royal lodgings were but the largest of a type of operation carried out in many other royal residences. Most of this work was undertaken after 1353. From 1353 to 1361 the sums spent on these projects were substantial but not excessive. The fact that each undertaking was separately accounted for, by the clerk of the works in charge, makes it impossible to give a final total for royal expenditure. Besides £6,500 for the new college at Windsor Castle, they included £500 and more on improvements at Easthampstead, £847 at Henley, and £1,064 at Rotherhithe.[3] But after 1361 the King's projects became far more ambitious and costly. The reconstruction of Windsor between 1362 and 1365 cost £15,028; the building of Sheppey castle (1361–9) £24,772; and improvements to the King's hunting lodges and favourite resting places like Moor End in Northamptonshire (£1,000 between 1363 and 1365), Gravesend (£1,350 between 1362 and 1368), King's Langley (nearly £3,000 between 1360 and 1377), and Sheen (£1,700 between 1363 and 1368) brought expenditure on the King's works to a total higher than at any time since the reign of Edward I, though Edward III's building lacked the military and national justification of his grandfather's.[4]

While the expenditure of the domestic departments represented a major modernization programme for all the King's palaces, the Exchequer was also charged with sustained expenditure on various forms of investment. Soon after the

[1] P.R.O. E 361/4 mm. 12–16.
[2] Colvin, *The King's Works*, ii. 793.
[3] Ibid., pp. 875, 926, 961, 992. The works at Rotherhithe which had been completed by 1355 were paid for from the Chamber (ibid., p. 990).
[4] Ibid., i. 162; ii. 878–9, 794 n. 3, 744, 946, 974, 995. In the single term Easter 1363 £2,500 was spent on work at Sheppey, Windsor, and other residences (E 403/415).

Treaty of Brétigny the King began to buy land, paying £1,000 to the executors of John Beauchamp in 1361 for property in Baynard's Castle, and later that year 500 marks to Walter Mauny for land in Sheppey and 3,000 marks for the lordship of Leybourne from Juliana, Countess of Huntingdon.[1] Later in the decade he bought Salden in Buckinghamshire from John Nowers for 1,000 marks, and in 1369–70 the Exchequer was paying for the King's purchases in Eltham, Bermondsey, Rotherhithe, and Greenwich.[2] Investment of a different kind, but which might also amplify the royal patrimony, was the purchase of the marriage of the young son of the earl of March, Edmund, who provided a husband for Lionel of Clarence's daughter Philippa, his only issue, for which the Exchequer paid 5,000 marks.[3] Edward was also quick to purchase jewels and plate as they came on the market, notably from the executors of Henry, duke of Lancaster, and John Beauchamp in 1361 and from those of Humphrey Bohun, earl of Hereford, in 1366.[4] Above this the Exchequer purchased jewels for gifts to the King of France (2,800 marks in 1360) and for a succession of royal marriages including those of the Prince of Wales in 1361 (£1,478) and Isabella (£2,370) in 1365–6.[5] But Edward's preferred investment was prisoners of war. The sum of almost £31,000 spent on this in statement C is easily verifiable. In 1359 the King acknowledged that he owed the Black Prince £20,000 for the purchase of three prisoners taken at Poitiers, and he subsequently took over from him five others of note to the value of perhaps half this sum. Edward purchased five further prisoners from other captains for 8,500 marks as well as

---

[1] P.R.O. E 404/6/40 (30 Jan. 1361), E 403/402 (12 Feb.), E 403/408 (15 June); *Issues of the Exchequer, Henry III–Henry VI*, ed. F. Devon (London, 1835), p. 175. For the purchase of Leybourne which yielded £636. 10s. p.a. in leases, see B. P. Wolffe, *The Royal Demesne*, p. 62. It was paid for initially by the Chamber, which recovered the money from the Exchequer (E 403/412, 29 Oct.).

[2] P.R.O. E 404/9/59, 24 Feb. 1369; E 404/9/63, 22 Nov. 1369; E 404/9/65, 18 Feb. 1370. Colvin, op. cit. ii. 992 n. 8. In 1363 Edward also bought land from Edward Balliol in Ponthieu: see Devon, *Issues*, p. 178. These were all, apparently, for the King's use. His only major endowment, of Windsor College, had been completed with the grant of lands from alien priories in 1360 (*C.P.R., 1358–61*, pp. 362, 364).

[3] Devon, *Issues*, p. 171; E/404/6/36, 28 Jan. 1359.

[4] Devon, *Issues*, p. 175; E 404/6/40, 30 Jan. 1361; E 404/7/49, 8, 9 June 1366.

[5] Tout, *Chapters*, iv. 317; E 404/8/53, 17 May 1367; Devon, *Issues*, pp. 170–2; E 403/402, 17 Nov. 1360, 19 Jan. 1361; E 403/409, 15 Oct. 1361.

a number of others of lesser importance.[1] Throughout the decade the Exchequer was paying instalments on these purchases, none of them of less than 500 marks, and as late as 1369–70 the Exchequer was ordered to pay Sir Nicholas Loraine 10,000 marks from the clerical tenth for the purchase of Hugh de Chatillon.[2] Moreover, some of those who sold prisoners to the King received payment in the form of a life annuity charged on a royal manor or an alien priory.[3] What return the King secured from these ransoms cannot be known since whatever was received went into the Chamber.[4]

Finally each of these statements contains a substantial sum paid in annuities for which the figure of £13,000 in B seems to represent an agreed estimate. How far this was a recent development is very difficult to say. Amongst the first annuities on the customs and subsidies was one of £1,000 p.a. in 1348 to Queen Philippa, in lieu of the Honour of Pontefract which she surrendered to the earl of Lancaster;[5] this was followed by a number of very substantial life annuities granted between 1354 and 1359 to the King's family and immediate associates. By that date £5,000 had been granted from the customs to five known recipients, and there were probably others.[6] Life grants

[1] H. J. Hewitt, *The Black Prince's Expedition of 1355–7*, pp. 156–9; *C.P.R., 1358–61*, p. 300; Devon, *Issues*, pp. 174, 177. £6,000 of the £20,000 was paid in July 1362 (E 403/410). The Prince bound himself for 3,000 florins for the Count of Vendosme, 15,000 florins for the Count of Joigny, and 25,000 crowns for James de Bourbon (*Foedera*, III. ii. 599, 635; E 404/6/40, 4 Feb. 1361). Payment of £1,293. 15*s*. to the Captal de Buch and others for James de Bourbon was made on 15 February (E 403/402).

[2] P.R.O. E 404/6/36, 12 Feb. 1359; E 404/6/41, 12 Mar. 1361, payment of £600, part of a larger sum to Arnold Lebret; E 404/9/59, 12 Feb. 1369, 500 marks instalment on the count of Eu; E 404/10/64, 9 Feb. 1370, warrant for 10,000 marks for the purchase of Hugh de Chatillon and payments of this recorded on the Issue roll (F. Devon, *Issue Roll of Thomas de Brantingham* (London, 1835), pp. 5, 445, 450). For other examples of the King purchasing prisoners through the Exchequer see *C.P.R., 1354–8*, pp. 635–6; *C.P.R., 1358–61*, pp. 63, 300, 440; *Foedera*, III. ii. 796.

[3] e.g. *C.P.R., 1358–61*, pp. 63, 440. E 404/6/38, 23 Nov. 34 Ed. III, records the grant of 100 marks p.a. to John de Podenhale for a prisoner taken at Calais and the subsequent conversion of this to an annuity from the farm of the alien priory of St. Faith.

[4] The only record of such a payment on the Exchequer rolls relates to 500 marks, part of the £1,000 ransom paid by the archbishop of Sens, the residue of which was paid as a retaining fee to the count of Tankerville (E 401/467; E 403/410, June 1362).

[5] *C.P.R., 1348–50*, p. 217.

[6] The Black Prince had 1,000 marks from the customs of London (*C.P.R.*,

of this kind were personal favours and accorded ill with the character of a subsidy which was granted for a limited period and for the needs of the realm.

From this survey it will have become clear that the very high level of expenditure which was causing concern in the Exchequer in the latter part of 1363 was the product not of residual war obligations nor of any peacetime necessities but mainly of the gratification of the King's personal tastes and the enlargement of his private wealth. Whereas the total expenditure listed in AII was £98,929, a calculation of normal expenditure on the basis of the figure and items included in B suggests a total of about £55,000 p.a.[1] Thus about 40 per cent of the Exchequer's expenditure was in the King's private interest. If this novel and extraordinary situation was one cause for concern, hardly less was that on the receipt side.

The statements of revenue are never as detailed as those of expenditure, being invariably in the form of revenue from the customs on the one hand and all other revenues 'received at the Exchequer' on the other, except in AI where the revenue from the Hanaper is differentiated. But there is no consistent rule about whether these figures are shown as gross or as net after payment of fees and annuities. For the customs and subsidies AI and AIII give a figure of £38,206. 13s. 4d. as the gross yield with £6,933. 6s. 8d. charged as annuities and a net yield of £31,273. 6s. 8d., and E clearly accords with this. AII gives merely a gross total of £38,000 in its statement of receipt but the expenditure side records £6,300 as charged upon this for annuities. On this basis the figure of £30,000 from customs and subsidies given in B is presumably net, yet annuities are entered on the expenditure side using the figure of £6,300 in AII. Thus B must be regarded as far less realistic than AI and AII, whose figures may well have been based on an actual calculation for the year February 1363–4. According to J. H. Ramsay's totals compiled from the enrolled customs accounts,

1354–58, p. 255); the earls of Warwick and Stafford had 1,000 marks each from the customs of Boston, Hull, and London (*C.C.R., 1354–60*, p. 149; *C.C.R., 1364–8*, p. 318); Edward Balliol had £2,000 from the same (*C.C.R., 1354–60*, p. 345).
[1] The basis of this calculation is the figures given in B except that a figure of £12,000 has been taken for the Wardrobe, a figure of £4,000 for Works, a figure of £13,000 for all annuities, and the item of debts on previous Wardrobe accounts has been omitted.

the yields for the years Michaelmas 1362–3 and 1363–4 were respectively £43,421 and £38,409.[1] On the other hand these were only about half the yield of the customs throughout the previous decade. Partly this was the effect of halving the rate of the subsidy in the parliament of 1362, but these two years also saw a marked slump in exports of wool from an average of 32,655 sacks to 29,244 in 1362–3 and 19,218 in 1363–4.[2] The trade was in fact to recover in the following three years to its former level only to make a comparable decline in the last three years of the decade. But in the autumn of 1364 the Exchequer could only report to the council that the wool revenue was down to half its former yield. In fact the restoration of the subsidy to 40*s.* from Michaelmas 1365 and the recovery of trade in the years 1364–7 brought this revenue back to near the habitual level of the previous decade, at an average of £72,661 for these years.[3] Thereafter it declined (with the volume of exports) to over £64,000 in 1367–9, before the outbreak of war and plague brought another disastrous slump in exports which even the heaviest subsidy yet imposed could not raise to over £49,000. The figures for customs revenue in AI–AIII were therefore realistic but untypical.

It is less easy to assess the reliability of the figures for the other revenues received at the Exchequer. For these AI and AIII give a gross total of £8,724. 18*s.* 9*d.*, which after the deduction of wages and annuities becomes £4,256. 8*s.* 4*d.* E employs this net figure and AII one very close to it. B gives a (presumably gross) total of £10,000 but this must be regarded as notional. AI makes a division of these revenues between 'sheriffs, farms, and other revenues of England through the Exchequer' (£6,458. 5*s.* 5*d.* gross, £2,656. 8*s.* 4*d.* net) and the Hanaper revenue (£2,266. 13*s.* 4*d* gross, £1,600 net). The accounts of the Keeper of the Hanaper for the two years 1362–4 substantially confirm the latter, showing a gross receipt of £2,184 and £1,538. 19*s.* 3*d.* paid 'in thesauro'. Any attempt to assess the statement of the remaining revenues can only be

---

[1] J. H. Ramsay, *Revenues*, ii. 292. The concurrence of the estimate and the enrolled account may suggest that the statements of revenue were appended to these lists of expenses only at the end of 1364, although this presents severe difficulties in regard to document E.

[2] E. M. Carus-Wilson and O. Coleman, *England's Export Trade, 1275–1547* (Oxford, 1963), p. 48.   [3] Ramsay, loc. cit.

in respect of their net yield as recorded on the receipt rolls. An analysis of the receipt rolls for Michaelmas 1362–3 shows that there was available to the Exchequer from sheriffs, escheators, farmers and the exchanges a total of £8,867. 4s. 3d.[1] Moreover beyond this there were other classes of revenue which regularly yielded substantial sums. Fines and casualties in this year were worth £1,878. 9s. 4d.; temporalities £1,087. 16s. 11d. and alien priories £568. 5s. 7d. Some additional revenues from the overseas territories brought the annual total recorded on the rolls to £14,013. 17s. 2d. from all sources other than taxation, ransoms, and loans, i.e. some £10,000 more than that given in the statements. There is no reason to suppose that this was untypical. Indeed the statement of revenue received in the three months February to May 1364 in document D shows that these revenues produced £3,051. 5s. 10d. It is true that this total was some £5,000 less than that recorded from the same sources twenty years earlier, owing mainly to the fact that the peace with France had drastically reduced the revenue from alien priories. On this comparison the revenue from sheriffs, escheators, and farmers had fallen by some £700 and that from fines and casualties by almost £2,000, but these were almost offset by increases in revenue from the Hanaper, Mints and Exchanges, and Temporalities. On the whole it cannot be said that the intervening period had seen a marked fall in the ordinary revenues of the Exchequer, which remained more substantial than would appear from statements AI–AIII. Thus a realistic figure for total revenue in these years would have been about £52,000 p.a. with the prospect of slightly more in a normal year as wool exports revived.

We can now turn to the deficits which are given in the statements AI, AII, and AIII as £55,264. 1s. 9d., £56,674. 17s. 6d., and £64,768. 17s. 1d., while at Christmas 1363 E was predicting that by the following Easter expenditure would already have exceeded the whole year's income by £17,279. 13s. 4d. Even though these statements appear to have substantially under-estimated the normal revenue of the Exchequer, the existence of a very large imbalance between the figures for revenue and expenditure is undeniable. This was almost wholly the product of the King's personal demands. How in practice had the

[1] Appendix B table iii.

Exchequer managed to meet them? The answer is provided by a note appended to AII that this deficit was 'received and paid from the ransoms of France and Burgundy and the revenues of Ponthieu and Calais'. Ponthieu and Calais might yield £1,000 p.a. at most, so that the greater part of this deficit could only have been paid from the ransoms. Yet only in the statement of receipts between February and May 1363 in D is this revenue included, amounting in these months to £7,387. 4s. 4d. The fact that the ransom money provides the missing element in these statements is illuminating, but no less so is the question of why it does not figure in them. What was the nature and size of these ransoms; were they received at the Exchequer, and how were they used?

The first ransom to be received was that of Charles of Blois finally negotiated in 1356 nine years after his capture. Of the total ransom of 700,000 *écus*, or £116,666. 13s. 4d., only the first 100,000 *écus* (25,000 marks) was ever paid. This was delivered in two equal instalments in July and November 1357 although it was not recorded on the Receipt roll until October 1357 and June 1358.[1] Both appear as cash receipts and were added into the totals of the rolls. Serious negotiations for the ransom of David II of Scotland had begun in 1351 but it was not until the Treaty of Berwick in October 1357 that the terms were finally settled. David was to be liberated for a ransom of 100,000 marks payable in ten years by equal instalments each midsummer. The first instalment was delivered in June 1358 to the lords guarding the marches and entered on the receipt roll under 6 August.[2] The second instalment was paid at Bruges where Edward appointed as receivers John Malewayn, governor of the English merchants, and Richard Eccleshall Treasurer of Calais. Edward, who arrived at Calais in October, gave acquittance there for £2,000 and for a further 2,500 marks at Bruges in December. By then the whole of the 10,000 marks

---

[1] *Foedera*, III. i. 336, 360, 382. P.R.O. E 401/443, E 401/446. For this and the subsequent history of the ransom of Jean de Bretagne, see Michael Jones, 'The Ransom of Jean de Bretagne, Count of Penthièvre: an Aspect of English Foreign Policy 1386–8', *Bull. Inst. Hist. Res.* xlv (1972), pp. 7–26.

[2] For the ransom of King David see *The Exchequer Rolls of Scotland*, ed. G. Burnett, ii (Edinburgh, 1878), pp. xxxvii–xlv; E. W. M. Balfour-Melville, *Edward III and David II* (Historical Assoc., 1954), pp. 14–22. The payment of the first instalment is recorded in *Foedera*, III. i. 397 and E 401/446.

had been delivered to either William Farley or Richard
Eccleshall for the wages of the troops with the King or in the
Calais garrison. But it was not until long after, when Eccleshall
and Malewayn rendered account in February 1361, that it was
formally entered on the Receipt roll.[1] Although arrangements
were made to receive the third instalment in June 1360, neither
this nor any further instalments of the Scottish ransom were
paid before a new arrangement in May 1365 reduced the
annual instalments to 6,000 marks while raising the total sum
to £100,000.[2]

Malewayn and Eccleshall also became receivers of the ransom of Burgundy, totalling 200,000 *moutons d'or* or approximately £40,000, by which Philip de Rouvre bought off the
English invasion of 1359. They were authorized to receive the
first instalment of 50,000 *moutons* in June 1360 and in February
1361 this was formally entered on the Receipt roll of the
Exchequer.[3] In fact a memorandum of their payments from
this sum, which probably accompanied their account, shows
that the whole of this sum had already been expended when the
formal entry of its receipt was made. Among the larger items
were £3,134 delivered to Eccleshall for the wages of troops at
Calais and just under £1,000 to William Farley for the safeguard
and expenses of King John of France at Calais during Edward's
campaign. A sum of 2,500 marks had been sent back to England
to be paid into the Chamber for Edward himself, £1,600 was paid
to John Newmarch for the duke of Lancaster, and a number of
payments were made to foreign captains and nobility who had
probably accompanied the King. All these payments were made
on the authority of privy seal writs directed to the two receivers
and were subsequently entered on the Issue rolls.[4] From this it
is clear that Edward was using the ransom money in their hands
as a separate fund under his immediate control for the payment
of urgent commitments. It was entirely removed from the hands
of the Treasurer and Chamberlains and was only entered as an

[1] *Foedera*, III, i. 397, 453, 465. P.R.O. E 401/461; E 403/402 (15 Feb.);
E 372/206; C 76/40 m. 2.
[2] An acquittance for the third instalment was made out (*Foedera*, III. i. 500) but
it is not recorded on the Receipt roll and is not reckoned in the revised arrangements
for payment of the residue in 1369.
[3] Ibid., pp. 498, 500; E 401/461.
[4] P.R.O. E 101/27/35; E 403/402.

Exchequer receipt to provide the King's receivers with a formal acquittance when they accounted for it at the Exchequer. The device had doubtless been prompted by the King's need for ready cash at Calais during the 1359–60 campaign, but when in October 1360 the terms of payment were revised,[1] the new Treasurer of Calais, Thomas Brantingham, was appointed 'receiver of the King's money' and the ransom continued to be administered as a separate fund.

Instalments of the ransom were paid until May 1363 when a total of £16,041 had been entered on the Receipt rolls since October 1361.[2] Most of these entries are recorded as cash receipts, but under the corresponding dates on the Issue rolls are recorded payments of the equivalent sums by the hands of Brantingham which show how the money was expended. Thus on 27 October 1361 the large sum of £7,800 from the ransom was almost certainly part of the £9,350 delivered to the Constable of Bordeaux for the retinue of the Prince just as the £2,000 paid in on 18 December must have been the same sum credited to Chandos, lieutenant in Normandy, on the same day. Brantingham himself received the wages of his retinue at Calais from this money on three occasions. The ransom was also used to pay important retainers in France. The Burgundian Walter de Graunson received his annuity of 190 marks from this source in December 1362 and the lord of Berghes received £150 in the following May. It is clear that all the above payments were made in France, usually at Calais, and that the Exchequer neither received the money nor authorized its disbursement through its own instruments. So far was it from being Exchequer revenue that what Edward did not need for his continental projects was deposited in the special treasury in the Tower.[3] That the Exchequer was used solely to preserve a record for account was further shown in October 1363 when Edward appointed four other receivers for the current instalment of the ransom. Their surviving account of the £2,000 which they handled shows a payment of £1,800 to Florentine merchants

[1] *Foedera*, III. i. 549, 553.
[2] Ibid., pp. 612–13; E 401/465, 467, 470, 472.
[3] The entries relating to the Burgundy ransom can be traced on the receipt and Issue rolls under the following dates: 27 Oct., 18 Dec. 1361; 14 June, 21 June 1362; 9 Dec. 1362; 10 May 1363. The payment of £1,264. 14s. 9½d. into the Tower was made on 9 Dec. 1362.

even though the Receipt roll records the whole sum as received in cash.[1]

The largest of these ransoms, that from France, was treated in the same way.[2] The Treaty of Brétigny had obliged King John to pay a total of 3,000,000 *écus* or £500,000 in annual instalments of 400,000 *écus* (£66,666. 13*s*. 4*d*.) after an initial payment of 600,000 *écus*. Of this sum about £166,666. 13*s*. 4*d*. had been paid by King John's death in 1364 and a further £48,666. 13*s*. 4*d*. and possibly as much as £100,000 was delivered by Charles V before the outbreak of hostilities in January 1369. From the first it is clear that Edward III regarded the ransom as the most notable of his spoils of war and reserved it for his personal disposal. The first payment, made in October 1360, was of 400,000 *écus* which, by the King's oral command, was stored in the treasury at the Tower without any record of it being made at the Exchequer. This treasury was to be used as the receptacle for the major part of the ransom received before John's death. It was under the King's immediate control and from the money accumulated there Edward ordered disbursements to be made as he thought fit. Once again, it was merely the need to record these payments and to ensure that the recipients could be called to account for their receipts that caused Edward to enter it on the Exchequer rolls. Beginning in March 1361 disbursements from the Tower hoard were made through the Exchequer every few months. A similar procedure was adopted for an instalment of £18,133. 6*s*. 8*d*. in May 1362 and for another of £17,833. 6*s*. 8*d*. in February 1364. For the £15,000 which was the papal contribution to the ransom, levied by a tax on the clergy in 1362, a special collector was appointed who paid the tax into the Treasury of Receipt, although of this £6,000 was immediately transferred to the Tower on the King's command. The balance due on the initial payment amounting to 200,000 *écus* (50,000 marks) was received in December 1360 and March 1361 at Bruges by Edward's personal attorneys, John Malewayn and Richard

---

[1] *Foedera*, III. i. 711; P.R.O. E 101/28/29.

[2] The complicated story of the payment of King John's ransom has been worked out and fully documented by Dorothy M. Broome, 'The Ransom of John II, 1360–70' in *Camden Miscellany*, xiv (Camden, Soc., 1926). The following discussion is based almost entirely on that study, though the Issue rolls record some additional small payments from the ransom which are not noted by Miss Broome.

Eccleshall. On the King's instructions they paid £31,333. 6s. 8d. into the Treasury of Receipt where £11,666. 13s. 4d. was assigned to the Black Prince and the duke of Lancaster, but the remaining £2,000 was, on Edward's order, received by Chandos and paid into the Chamber. The payments of the ransom received between July 1362 and July 1363, totalling 93,400 écus (£15,566. 13s. 4d.), were used to support the English military commitments in France, being paid directly to the Black Prince (£10,000), Sir John Chandos (£5,000), le Maréchal Audrehem (£500), and the Chancellor of Normandy (£66. 13s. 4d.). Thus the ransom was handled in broadly three ways: it was stored in the treasury at the Tower until disbursed at the King's order; it was paid into the Receipt of the Exchequer; and it was assigned directly on royal orders. The King adopted whichever procedure best suited his or his creditors' immediate needs, for it is clear that he regarded this as his private wealth and repudiated any claim by the Exchequer to receive and disburse this as part of the national revenue. If he found it convenient to use the Exchequer as an office of record for disbursement of the ransom, the payments themselves make it clear that these were for persons and projects close to his heart.

How had the instalments up to April 1364 been used? Leaving aside the £47,171. 1s. 4d. which remained unspent in the Tower, the £15,566. 13s. 4d. delivered directly to four creditors, and the £2,000 paid by Chandos into the Chamber all the remainder had been paid out through the Exchequer on the King's instructions. The payments were predominantly for the military exploits of the King's sons and the small circle of upper nobility and war captains. The Black Prince himself received £25,000, partly in discharge of his debts for the 1359–60 campaign, but mainly to equip himself for his command in Gascony, and to this must be added a further £10,000 assigned direct to him in 1362–3. Edward thus invested heavily in setting-up the Prince's rule in Gascony; indeed a further £3,820 is recorded as paid to the earl of Warwick and for the wages of shipping their expedition. Next in size was the £6,740 delivered to the King's lieutenant in Normandy, Sir John Chandos, in 1362–3. Other large payments were the £5,000 paid in 1361 to Henry, duke of Lancaster, for the 1359 campaign and the £4,000 paid in 1363 to his successor John of Gaunt, though this was subsequently repaid. 2,000 marks was received by the duke of Brittany, £1,225 by Guichard d'Angle, and £1,312 by the King's merchant, a Genoese John de Mare, mainly for jewellery, while retaining fees were paid to the Comte de Tankerville (£675) and Jean le Maingre (£459). Finally the King had just under £2,000 paid to his Chamber and just over £3,000 to the Wardrobe, Great Wardrobe, and Works.

Thus of the whole ransom some £47,171 remained in the Tower; £4,000 had found its way to the Chamber; £64,437 had been paid in different ways to various creditors, but preponderantly for the Prince and other commanders; and £46,154 had been spent by the Exchequer in ways which cannot now be traced. A general indication of what these were can, of course, be obtained from the statements of expenses which we have considered. The summary of expenditure in C (for *c.* 1359–62) reflects very clearly the large payments made through the Exchequer to the Black Prince, the payments for the English presence in Brittany and Normandy, the repayment of the debts of 1359–60, and the purchase of prisoners. The later statements, as we have noted, reveal heavy expenditure on the domestic charges. Thus it seems that, up to the end of 1364, the King's expenditure of the ransoms was very largely controlled in his own interests and that much of it was invested either in establishing his son in Gascony or in his more personal gratification. The investment of part in further profits of war and part in stone and movable wealth and personal dignity adhered faithfully to a pattern which all his captains and nobility were familiarizing at the time. The King was perhaps setting a standard which few could compete with, but he was none the less following the dictates of fashion and common sense.

To return to the statements AI–AIII with this evidence in mind is to view very differently the picture they present. For it is clear that much of the expenditure which they record was of ransom monies which, though entered on the Exchequer rolls for the purpose of record, represented expenditure of the King's personal treasure. Since the statements omitted to balance this by recording the receipt of the ransom money, the resultant deficit was artificial. But if they do not demonstrate a deficit in the national finances as Tout and Broome believed, what was their purpose and significance?

It has been seen that the Exchequer had first in 1363 produced a full statement of expenditure and that only subsequently in the winter of 1363/4 did it produce the summary of
annual revenue from which a deficit could be deduced. The
figures showed that the level of expenditure to which the
Exchequer was committed by the King's programme of building, improvement and investment in overseas ventures could
not be supported from its normal revenues. So long as there
were ransoms to finance it this was well enough, and it was no
concern of the Exchequer how much of his wealth the King
spent in this way. But in March 1364 the final instalment of the
ransom of Burgundy was paid and in April King John died.
Charles V was in no hurry to renegotiate the payment of
further instalments. No payments had been received on the
Scottish ransom since 1360 and the ransom of Charles of Blois
had long been in suspense. At the same time wool exports, as
we have seen, were showing a further decline for the second year
running. By the Spring of 1364 the Exchequer thus faced the
prospect of becoming actually (and not merely formally)
responsible for paying for the King's expenditure without
money from ransoms and with a shrinking ordinary revenue.
Thus the Exchequer's statements were designed not to analyse
a current crisis but to illustrate the size of that which faced it
in the year ahead.

While the Exchequer could alert the King and the council
to this situation it had no authority either to reduce expenditure
or to increase revenue. It took a number of measures which
would help to see it through, but these were limited expedients.
A restraint on annuities seems to have operated during 1364
and into 1365, for there are a few preferential warrants while
large numbers of arrears were paid at the end of 1365.[1] The
Exchequer was also able to borrow from the Chamber. Up till
1364 the loans from the Chamber had been few and small. But
on 20 February it received £1,200 and in the months following
loans totalled £817 in April, £3,603. 10s. 8d. in June and July,
£530 in December, and £1,000 in May 1365.[2] Predictably

[1] Thus a number of writs for payment of annuities during 38 Edward III conclude with the phrase 'niencontrestant aucune defense faite a contraire' (E 404/7
file 45) while the files for April and May 1366 contain very large numbers of writs
for payments of annuities in arrears (E 404/7 file 47, 48).

[2] E 401/475, E 401/477, E 401/479, E 401/481.

almost all these Chamber loans were earmarked for the King's own concerns like the building of Sheppey, the purchase of plate, and the payment of his particular creditors. Repayment was mostly made late in 1365. Did the Exchequer make any plea for retrenchment, and specifically for the cutback of the King's domestic and personal expenditure? Neither the accounts of the Wardrobe and Great Wardrobe nor the level of building activity reveal a significant decline in 1364–5. Nevertheless we must consider in this connection the one document the purpose of which has hitherto remained obscure.

The picture given in B differs so profoundly from that in the other documents that unless some details of it were plainly derived from AII it would be difficult to assign it to the same years. As its title indicates, it was not a record of actual payments in any year but an estimate of the annual inescapable expenditure in time of peace, and followed closely the form of the estimate in document E. It might thus be expected to provide for a reduction of excessive costs. This in a sense it does, for its figures for the Great Wardrobe and the Works probably represent the conventional norms while that for the Wardrobe itself is considerably lower even than this. Moreover, the fact that, apart from the *certum* of the Chamber and Queen, B omits all items relating to the King's investments may indicate that these were considered neither certain nor necessary charges. While the figures for the domestic departments are reduced to a conventional level those for administrative costs and the payment of debts follow very closely the actual totals in AII and so do those for the wages of the garrisons. All these charges were moderate. For Ireland the substantially lower figure may equally reflect a guess at the cost of maintaining the army after the current operations. This general scaling down to conventional figures of those items where expenditure had noticeably soared in the current accounts was designed to produce an equally conventional final total. Expenditure came out at a contrived sum of 100,000 marks with revenue at £40,000 and the resultant deficit of 40,000 marks. But this general picture of B as a blueprint for retrenchment and frugality is seriously impaired by the items relating to annuities. This, as we have seen, gives the figure of £13,000 for annuities from the Exchequer revenues (which is approximately the

total for all annuities in AI–III) with a further £6,300 for
those from the customs, and then follows this on the receipt
side by giving the net instead of gross figure for the customs.
The result was to inflate the total burden of annuities to
£12,600 beyond the figures in AI–III. Was this by accident
or design?

Negligence or oversight is scarcely consistent with the
careful structuring of a document which produces such well-
rounded totals. Both the conventional low estimates for the
domestic expenses and the exaggerated figures for annuities
must have had the same purpose. In terms of the financial
situation in 1364 there were only two possible purposes which
such a document could serve—it could either justify a reduction
of expenditure or an increase in revenue. In discussing this
document hitherto, the former has seemed more plausible and
the figures for domestic expenditure may indeed have been
used to urge economies in this field. But rulers usually prefer
to think in terms of fresh taxes rather than of strict retrenchment,
and we have already noticed that the title of B suggests a close
link with the parliament of 1365. In that parliament the
Chancellor laid emphasis upon the burden of annuities,
together with the fortresses and diplomatic presents, suggesting
that the King could not bear these from his revenues. Moreover,
many of the Commons must have known of and perhaps suffered from the restraint upon annuities during the past year. A
tax which would replenish the royal treasury might also aid
their individual pockets. Again, the low conventional estimates
of domestic expenditure and the omission of the King's personal
investments can be explained as designed to preclude criticism
of royal extravagance. In fact the contrived moderation of the
expenditure side would have yielded an insufficient deficit to
justify the government's demand had not the burden of
annuities been equally artifically inflated. Moreover, the
estimate was designed to show that the domestic departments
and administrative costs could be met from existing revenues
while the total of defence, annuities, and diplomatic gifts (just
over £28,000) effectually matched the deficit of 40,000 marks.
Such a sum was also approximately what the doubling of the
rate of the wool subsidy could be expected to produce. We
may fairly surmise therefore that document B was carefully

constructed in order to present a demand for taxation to the parliament of January 1365.

By the end of that year the anticipated 'crisis' had passed. A strong revival of wool exports, together with the increased subsidy granted by parliament, brought in ample revenue to cover royal expenditure. Moreover, Edward had been busy reactivating the obligations of his principal captives and clients. In the course of 1365 he had negotiated with Charles V the repayment of the remainder of the ransom, and the first of the new instalments (of 25,000 marks) was received at the Exchequer in January 1366. Further sums of 25,000 marks and 23,000 marks were received in 1367 and 1368. Charles claimed that a further 393,800 *écus* (98,450 marks) were paid by him on Edward's assignment, and though no evidence can be found to substantiate this, it is not improbable that Edward should have sought to use the ransom to support the Prince's operations in Gascony and Spain.[1] The Scottish ransom had likewise been resuscitated by an agreement of May 1365 which reduced the annual instalments to 6,000 marks while raising the total sum to £100,000. These instalments were paid regularly from February 1366 to February 1369 when 54,000 of the original 100,000 marks remained outstanding.[2] Payments were also received in these years from Jean IV, duke of Brittany, who in 1362 had acknowledged a debt to Edward of 64,000 nobles (£21,333. 6s. 8d.) for the military help he had received. Only 2,000 marks of this had been paid by the beginning of 1366 but within the next three years Edward received a further £13,437.[3] This reactivation of the outstanding obligations to Edward III thus yielded not less than £84,103. 13s. 4d. in the years 1366–9.

The suspension of receipts from the ransoms had prompted an investigation into the sums received from France which led to changes in the procedure for handling the renewed payments. The record on the Receipt rolls of the payments made from the Tower treasury was checked and where necessary rectified and the unspent residue in the Tower was assigned to the

[1] The account of Richard Fylongley, Seneschal of Guienne from 19 July 1362 to Michaelmas 1370, records a receipt during the period of £20,767. 10s. 9d. from the French ransom by the hands of William Felton, John Roches, and others, but it does not specify the dates of these payments. E 101/177/1.

[2] *Foedera*, III. ii. 785, 818, 841, 856, 877–8.

[3] Ibid., pp. 837, 885, 858; M. Jones, *Ducal Brittany, 1364–69*, Appendix B (1).

Chamber. Future instalments were recorded on the Receipt rolls but then transferred to the Chamber. Miss Broome regarded these happenings as a successful protest by the Exchequer against the King's autocratic disregard of its rules, but the Exchequer was not attempting to claim control of this revenue itself and they more probably reflect a deliberate change in royal policy. In the years before 1364, when Edward was spending the ransoms on a variety of projects mainly designed to strengthen his position in France, there were obvious advantages in having special receivers overseas and a separate treasury in the Tower from both of which payments could be made and then formally recorded in the receipt. But by 1366 his liabilities in Gascony and Brittany had ceased, his purchases of prisoners had largely finished, and even much of his building had been completed. The sudden stringency of the years 1364–5 may also have given him pause. After 1366 he became more concerned to build up his reserves, and for this the Chamber, traditionally the storehouse of the King's wealth rather than a spending agency, was appropriate. Into this he paid not merely the French ransom but the receipts from Brittany and Scotland.[1] Even so these ransoms seem to have been under the control not of the keeper of the Chamber, Helming Leget, but of masters of the King's money in the Tower, John Thorp and Walter Bardi. Certainly the ransom money was jealously preserved; it is doubtful whether even the loans made by the Chamber to the Exchequer in these years, totalling £8,046. 16s. 2d. between November 1367 and November 1368, came from this store.[2] Thus the effect of the Exchequer inquiry in 1365 was to affirm even more explicitly that the ransoms were the King's personal wealth. Not until the beginning of 1369 was this wealth tapped. In the first three months of that year a total of £41,975. 6s. 4d. was delivered into the Exchequer from the King's Chamber, representing money from the French

[1] For the Breton money see M. Jones, loc. cit. The receipts from the Scottish ransom are recorded as *sol* payments on the Receipt rolls but the Issue roll for 3 March 1367 (E. 403/429) records the payment of this instalment to the Chamber by the hand of John Thorp, Keeper of the King's Money in the Tower.

[2] E 101/396/8, printed in Tout, *Chapters*, iv. 347–8, records the loan of £6,277. 16s. 2d. between November 1367 and Easter 1368, and the Receipt roll for Michaelmas 1367 records further loans of £1,759 (E 401/495). These loans were spent on buildings, gifts, jewels, and plate, and were all quickly repaid to the Chamber.

ransom, from the duke of Brittany, and from the Duke of Bourbon. To this can be added the current instalment of £4,000 from Scotland. There followed in June the unspent residue from the first phase of the French ransom, totalling £41,171. 1*s*. 4*d*. In all Edward released £87,146. 7*s*. 8*d*., of which £11,870 was delivered to William of Windsor for the Irish expedition and some £26,000 to the Black Prince. Thus Edward showed himself ready to commit his gains of war once more to the hazard, to lose all or to win again.[1]

It is certain that these sums represented only a proportion—possibly even the lesser proportion—of what Edward had accumulated in his Chamber. The total sum received from the lesser ransoms we cannot guess though some individual payments were impressive;[2] we do know that for a time the English occupancy of northern France was exploited for the King's personal gain. From 1358 Brest and certain other castles in Normandy and Brittany with their surrounding ransom districts were farmed by English captains who made payments into the Chamber. By 1362 there were twenty-five such castellanries besides Brest in English hands, and though after his recovery of the duchy Jean IV slowly endeavoured to replace these by Bretons, the changeover was incomplete even by 1370.[3] By then their payments had been transferred to the Exchequer. Beyond these profits of war were the personal and prerogative revenues which any King might exploit for his profit. Entries on the Chancery rolls recording payments of forfeitures, fines, licences to alienate, and recognizances into

[1] D. Broome, 'The Ransom of John II', pp. 12, 37, 38.

[2] In 1361 the King's attorneys, Eccleshall and Malewayn, received 3,000 crowns from the bishop of Noyon's ransom and in 1362 6,000 crowns were paid by the archbishop of Sens (*Foedera.* III, ii. 607, 647). Whereas these were used by the King for current payments, the money from the duke of Bourbon, 40,000 crowns, was paid into the Chamber in two instalments in 1367 and 1368 (ibid., pp. 837, 841). It was only handed over to the Exchequer in the following March along with the other revenue in the Chamber (E 401/491).

[3] Tout, *Chapters*, iv. 250–1, 317–18; Jones, op. cit., pp. 64, 146, 161. Some examples of the size of these payments were the 5,333 gold crowns, £800, and 2,000 florins recorded in 1361 (*C.P.R., 1361–4*, pp. 122, 126; *C.C.R., 1360–4*, p. 195); the 500 marks (not 5,000 marks as Tout, loc. cit.) in 1365 and the £200 in 1366 (*C.C.R., 1364–8*, pp. 145, 223). In 1361 Knolles was paying 2,000 marks into the Chamber for his castles in Normandy and as late as 1365 John Buckingham, bishop of Lincoln, paid 500 marks into the Chamber for his keeping of some Breton castles (*Foedera*, III. ii. 623, 776).

the Chamber seem to be particularly numerous during the decade 1356–66.[1] Such sums were rarely under £100 or over £500 though they might reach large figures like the fine of 3,600 marks imposed in 1361 on Sir Matthew Gourney and Sir John St. Loo.[2] Where circumstances were favourable the King might exploit his prerogative, as when the executors of the duke of Lancaster paid in £2,760. 19*s*. in February 1362 or when in 1366 William of Wykeham paid 'a great sum' into the Chamber for the restoration of the temporalities of Winchester.[3] By 1369 the Chamber had become the custodian of a treasure which—though its dimensions are shadowy—must certainly rank Edward III among the richest of the medieval English kings. In the main this had come from the only source possible, the gains of war; moreover, it represented the residue after what the King considered prudent and necessary reinvestment in the same field, as well as expenditure on the fruits of peace. Edward was no hoarder. Yet this accumulation of personal wealth was not merely kept distinct from national finance; it brought no diminution of the Chamber's demands on the Exchequer, both for its *certum* of 10,000 marks p.a. and for occasional payments 'for the king's secret business' and the purchase of jewels. The King had made himself the personal beneficiary not only of national war but of a peacetime tax on wool justified by the maintenance of national defence.

At the conclusion of this lengthy investigation into the nature of the 'crisis' of the mid-sixties, we may return to its effects on the relations between the King and his parliaments. The coming of peace had dissolved the close association of monarch and people in a common obligation to ensure the defence of the realm. Subjects no longer felt bound to grant taxation for this purpose, while the King felt free to employ the profits which

---

[1] *C.P.R., 1354–8*, pp. 183, 213, 643; *C.P.R., 1358–61*, p. 341; *C.P.R., 1361–4*, p. 440; *C.P.R., 1364–7*, p. 643; *C.P.R., 1367–70*, p. 359; *C.C.R., 1360–4*, pp. 421, 524, 562; *C.C.R., 1364–8*, pp. 28, 223; *C.C.R., 1369–74*, pp. 222, 228. A total of £4,373. 6*s*. 8*d*. is recorded in these entries as paid into the Chamber, but such revenue might also be assigned to the Chamber by tally—as for instance was £607 from fines before the Justices in February 1360 (E 401/454), while 400 marks was paid in as a fine for the appropriation of a church in July 1362 (E 403/410).

[2] *C.P.R., 1361–4*, pp. 144, 186; *C.C.R., 1358–61*, pp. 299, 300.

[3] Issue Roll Mich. 1366 (E 403/429); *C.P.R., 1364–7*, pp. 353.

war had brought him for his private gain and pleasure. With the expiry of the wool subsidy in 1362 the Commons could at most be expected to renew it at half the wartime rate, and this indeed, was sufficient to maintain English military commitments overseas. It was only the momentary prospect of paying for the King's military investments and personal projects from national revenue, rather than from ransoms, that prompted the Exchequer to lay before parliament evidence of a financial deficit on which the Crown could build a demand for taxation to meet the standing charges of defence. Artificial and contrived though the crisis in a sense was, it reflected the fundamental change which taxation had wrought in the attitude of subjects to royal government. Parliament had long come to accept an obligation to grant taxation for the defence of the realm in time of war or even truce; now this obligation was being extended in time of peace. The basis for this was the deficit between national revenue and expenditure. Although an analogy with the needs of war could be pleaded if this deficit could be shown to arise from the standing charges of defence, it introduced a new principle. The solvency of royal government was now asserted to be the responsibility not merely of the King but of the whole realm. In the novel circumstances of this decade such concepts were only beginning to emerge, and the government's own uncertainty was reflected in the wording of its demands for taxation and the financial statements it prepared in their support. Already it faced more intensive bargaining with the Commons over these demands even though the full logic of their concern with the solvency of the realm was not felt until the following decade. We may therefore conclude this chapter by looking at the concessions which the Commons obtained and the indications these provide of their strength and interests.

Six parliaments were held between 1362 and 1369, and apart from those of 1366 and 1369 which lasted barely a week, all were in session for between three and five weeks. The frequency of parliament during this period of peace is only partly explained by the need to renew the wool subsidy. This was granted in four of these parliaments, but in most of them finance came second in importance to the problems of relations with Scotland and the papacy, the organization of the wool staple, and legislation on social and economic problems. War itself dominated only the final short parliament. Parliament therefore met without the twin pressures of the preceding twenty-five years to grant taxation for the common enterprise and to protest against prerogative levies harmful to the common good. To that extent there was less direct encouragement to associate the redress of grievances closely with taxation. Common petitions are recorded in five of these parliaments including all of those in which taxation was granted, but in no case were the Commons' grievances formally made the conditions of the grant of the tax. There may have been procedural difficulties in so doing for in the grant of the wool subsidies the Lords were associated with the Commons; certainly there was nothing in the political situation to warrant an alliance of the two against the Crown. Indeed the keynote of this decade remained the enforced solidarity of the propertied classes in the face of the economic and social uncertainties which the recurrence of the plague in 1361-2 and 1369 underlined.

As already noted, taxation did not figure explicitly in the charges to the parliaments of these years although it may have been deduced therefrom when the charge was explained in detail to the separate assemblies of Lords and Commons.[1] But precedence was always given to the great matters of royal policy, such as the Scottish Treaty and the anti-papal legislation. Following debate and resolution on these matters came the financial demands, usually in the context of a statement and debate about the whole financial situation of the realm. It is clear that in 1362, 1365, and 1368 this demand was made before the Commons put in their common petition,[2] though only in the exceptionally short parliament of 1369, overshadowed by the reassumption of the French title, is it certain that taxation (in fact the raising of the existing rate) was

---

[1] The exposition of the charge in detail is made clear in the parliaments of 1365 and 1366 and can be inferred in 1362 (*Rot. Parl.* ii. 283-4, 289-90).

[2] Ibid., pp. 271 (no. 26), 285, 295. In 1365 parliament began on 20 January and was occupied for ten days with royal business. The discussion on finance took place on 30 January and the Commons' petitions were discussed during the following week. In 1368 parliament began on 1 May and spent the first week on royal business. On Saturday 6 May the Commons were told to put in their petitions by the following Wednesday and the debate on finance began on Monday the 8th.

granted before petitions were received.[1] In the preceding parliaments it seems that negotiation on the Commons' grievances continued during the remainder of the session with direct reference to the tax until, on the final day of the parliament, first the King's answers to the petitions and then the tax grant were formally read and approved. That final sequence was of no practical importance for both had been previously determined.

The only explicit evidence connecting the grant of the tax with the King's answers to the petitions comes from 1362. The parliament roll in fact records no formal request for a subsidy, merely its grant on the final day. Amongst the common petitions one appears to be a series of provisos to be appended to the grant similar in form to the conditions entered on the rolls in the 1340s.[2] These stipulated that the ancient custom should be restored after the term of the grant, that the grant should not form a precedent, that free trade be assured for denizen merchants, and that no tax should be placed on wool by the merchants. As Unwin made clear, these represented an attempt to restrain the King from implementing his policy of reconstituting the Company of the Staple at Calais as a monopoly body through which indirect taxation might be levied.[3] The project had already been discussed at a merchant assembly in the previous year, but amongst the general class of merchants some favoured and others opposed it, and the Commons themselves in 1362 found that they could render no united answer.[4] All their petition did was to reiterate the principles fought for and secured in the decade 1342–52, notably of free trade and parliamentary authority over all taxation. Edward formally accepted these though this did not prevent him from instituting the Calais staple by royal ordinance in March 1363. Further, in 1362 the Commons sought to restrict the scope of the eyre to the common law pleas, *quo warranto*, treason, robbery, and

---

[1] In 1369 parliament began on Sunday 3 June. The decision to resume the title was taken on the following Wednesday and the discussion and grant of taxation took place on Thursday. Only then were the Commons invited to put in their petitions, to be answered on Saturday, although they may well have been formulating them in the preceding days.

[2] *Rot. Parl.* ii. 271 (no. 26).

[3] Unwin, *Finance and Trade under Edward III*, pp. 244–6.

[4] *Rot. Parl.* ii. 269.

other felonies. The council opposed this as a limitation of the
prerogative, and the Commons finally agreed to purchase a
royal pardon from many of the articles of the eyre as the price
of the subsidy.[1] Here too it is clear that an acceptable bargain
had been reached during a period when both petition and tax
were under consideration. The only other instance in which a
concession was specifically purchased by the grant of taxation
was the pardon for trespasses in 1369, granted out of regard for
the great aids and charges which the Commons had sustained.

The relative freedom of the Commons to grant or refuse
taxation in this decade encouraged them to demand and obtain
concessions on a number of substantive issues. Thus in 1362
they secured the most complete definition of royal rights of
purveyance in the Middle Ages. Although Edward was stated
to have granted the petition for this 'de sa benignite et de sa
propre volonte, saunz motion de grantz ou communes', it
was stated elsewhere that there had been great clamour in this
parliament about abuses by purveyors and commissions to
investigate those relating to the royal households were issued
immediately after its close.[2] In the following parliament of
1363, at which no taxation was sought, their protests were far
less effective. The March Ordinance of the Staple had established a market due of 40d. per sack of wool and the Commons
were quick to petition for its abolition.[3] All they secured was a
general promise of investigation and redress, and it was not
until the parliament of 1365 when opposition to the Staple
had hardened and its own defects had become apparent that
—by the grant of a much higher rate of subsidy—they secured
the repeal of the Ordinance and with it the 40d. duty on sale
of wool in Calais. Abolished likewise in this parliament was
the restrictive sumptuary and mercantile legislation of the preceding parliament.[4] The Commons then also secured the repeal
of general commissions of oyer and terminer into goods forfeited to the King which had been issued with the provision
that the Commissioners could take for themselves a third of the
amercements—in the words of the Commons, 'en manere

[1] *Rot. Parl.* ii. 272–3.

[2] *Rot. Parl.* ii., pp. 270, 272; *C.P.R., 1361–4*, p. 294.

[3] *Rot. Parl.* ii. p. 276.

[4] Ibid., pp. 285–7. The Receipt roll for 22 July 1364 records a payment of
£239. 13s. 4d. from the Calais staple in respect of this levy (E 401/477).

Champertours par la Lei'.[1] The revival of these commissions must have been particularly odious after the pardon of such liabilities under the articles of the eyre in 1362. With it went a renewal of their petition in the parliament of 1343 that justices of the peace should be elected in parliament. The King refused this, but it is a measure of the confidence with which the gentry were now claiming a share in the rule of the shire that .they were emboldened to press for a concession to which the Lords and judiciary were notoriously opposed. In the parliament of 1368 the Commons again championed the rights and interests of the gentry of the shires against those of the royal government on the one hand and the labouring classes on the other. Their petitions began with an appeal to the Charters and demands for good government and the formal affirmation by the King of the validity of the pardon granted in 1362.[2] The Commons were disturbed about the use of criminal procedures to forward private interests, whether through accusations by approvers or through commission of inquiry issued to indi-viduals which should properly be restricted to the justices; they also sought protection from the abuse of levies of estreats by sheriffs and tighter control over the qualifications and opera-tions of the escheators. With equal confidence they voiced the interests of that middle class which drew its livelihood from land and commerce but had no seigneurial rights. One petition demanded the enforcement of the Statutes of Labourers while another in the name of London and other civic corporations asked for the enforcement of the restriction to the freemen of retailing.[3]

The growing assurance with which the parliamentary Com-mons voiced the distinctive interests of the middling propertied classes of the realm marked the increase of their political in-fluence beyond their traditional concern with assent to taxa-tion. In matters touching the realm they spoke with a unique authority. Their advice was now separately taken on great issues and their support specifically secured when relations with the papacy or foreign states touched the rights and in-

[1] Ibid., p. 286. [2] Ibid., p. 295; *S.R.* i. 388.
[2] *Rot. Parl.* ii., 296. For comment on the labour legislation, see E. A. Kosminsky, *Studies in the Agrarian History of England in the Thirteenth Century* (Oxford, 1956), p. 258.

terests of the realm at large. Their criticism in the name of the common good of the realm had to be heeded and their particular grievances had to be answered and in some measure redressed. The King asked them for taxation for the common good of the realm but the Commons were not uncritical of this plea and the Crown had taken the step of proving its needs as well as merely stating them. By 1369 the Commons had been admitted to the threshold of the ark of government; in the years ahead they were to venture to probe its secrets. It was symbolic of their status that when, at the close of the last parliament of the years of peace, the King entertained its members to a great and solemn feast, members of the Commons were among his guests.

Retrospect

THE emergence of a system of public finance in England,
which has been the theme of this volume, was an essential
feature of the early nation state. It was during the century and
a half preceding the Treaty of Brétigny that most of the
institutions of early modern England took recognizable form.
The Crown as the symbol of national identity and the focus of
national loyalty, the council advising and restraining the King,
parliament as the voice of the community of the realm, the
Exchequer controlling national finance, all bore witness to the
new dimensions of national government. Patriotism manifested
itself externally in national war and incipient chauvinism while
internally royal government ramified within the shires, using
new classes as its agents and helping to create from the hitherto
locally orientated communities a new political society in the
nation as a whole. This new 'community of the realm' found
that it had obligations to sustain for its common safety as well
as rights and liberties to maintain for its common welfare.
Public finance embraced each of these aspects. The new concepts of Crown and realm imposed fiscal obligations on subjects,
the new fiscal administration facilitated the collection and
spending of national resources, the new political community
claimed a voice in the use of its wealth for the common good.
Public finance thus reflects the authority of the state to command the wealth of its subjects and the acknowledgement by
subjects of their obligation to contribute to the preservation of
the state. In this sense it lies at the heart of the political relationship on which the early modern state was built.

Such changes had roots in English society well before this
period began, but it was in the first half of the fourteenth
century that they gathered to a peak, acquiring momentum
under the stimulus of war, political opposition, and social
upheaval. If England had not faced the demands of national
war it is difficult to see how the idea or system of public finance
could have developed. The sense of unity and common vulnerability which the defence of an island coastline induced, and the

existence of a common enemy on the northern and southern frontiers, made a doctrine of national danger a reality, whereas in France such danger was experienced only in regional terms. There could be no more powerful obligation than to provide for the common defence, but the embodiment of this obligation in the grant of parliamentary taxation drew on a long history of political evolution. The concept of the realm as a political community was the product of new techniques of government and the new authority and status of the ruler. From the end of the twelfth century the Crown became the symbol of the realm, uniting ruler and ruled in the service of the common good, which it was the object of the state to promote. Parliament emerged as an instrument of government for the common profit, but also as the institutional expression of the community of the realm. For that common profit—which under the pressure of war came to be identified with the preservation of the state from danger—the Crown could require taxation from its subjects. Because the danger touched the whole realm, and parliament represented the whole realm, parliament alone could assent to the necessity and authorize taxation to meet it; thereupon the obligation became universally binding. This assent was political in character, an expression of the *concordia* or unity of Crown and subjects. It had to be freely given, for it affirmed a common unity and obligation; it could embrace bargaining over the nature, quantity, and use of the tax; but it could not admit a complete or free refusal of the obligation, for that would be contrary to the common profit and mark a repudiation of political authority on which the state rested. The granting of taxation by parliament was thus in part at least ritualistic, but since it deprived subjects, from the highest to the lowest, of their property it tested political authority and could involve conflict.

There is no doubt that the Crown's ability to require taxation for war brought a vast increase in its resources and authority. English Kings had not neglected their hereditary fiscal rights; indeed the enlargement and exploitation of their domainal and prerogative revenues as appurtenances of the Crown had been one of the fields where the new legal doctrines of the state had been vigorously applied. As, during the thirteenth century, the Crown came to embody the identity of the state, kings were able to insist that their *regalia* were perpetually immune from encroachment by subjects. At the same time they were strengthening and elaborating the machinery of the Exchequer to deal with the new dimensions of national finance. Even so the thirteenth century offered merely a foretaste of the growth of national finance under the pressures of war. For a national war the King could identify his own ambitions and interests with those of the realm; he could mobilize the resources of the realm on an unheard-of scale; he could enlarge the territorial bounds of his rule and penetrate deeper into the political life of his people. In financial terms direct taxation at least doubled and indirect taxation could quadruple the King's normal peacetime income. That war costs were correspondingly heavy did not matter; for the Crown the fruits of war were primarily military and political, though war might also bring enormous personal wealth to the King. War finance on this scale transformed royal ambitions and authority. Although bound to use taxation for the common defence, the King could deploy it as he thought best. Assured of taxation and of the control of national finance exercised through the Exchequer, the King could exploit the opportunities offered by the development of credit to secure the utmost flexibility in financial planning. Through the Wardrobe he could anticipate revenue and ensure its availability to match his immediate strategic and tactical needs. Although under the stresses of war the relations between Wardrobe and Exchequer could get out of balance, especially if the King's ambitions outstripped his resources, yet within the terms of his age and by comparison with other rulers, the English King could claim to have the wealth of his kingdom at his immediate disposal. Thus was kingship given a new dimension—its resources and authority becoming truly national.

The enlargement of the Crown's authority, to act and speak on behalf of the realm, involved embracing the interests and purposes of the realm and thus giving them a place alongside its own. If in the English system of centralized government parliament was the instrument through which King and subjects co-operated most effectively for the common profit of the realm, it was also the place where criticism and opposition could be most effective. Resistance to taxation locally could be vigorous and might reduce its yield, but the King and central administration were tenacious and rarely if ever retracted their commands. Hence because the assent of parliament carried such authority in the localities, it became the responsibility of those who rendered that assent to ensure that their undertakings to the King could be performed. If the exception of 1339 underlined the rule that English representatives never referred back to their constituencies, it also demonstrated the need for the King never to press his demands beyond what the realm could bear. The representative quality of the Commons lent authority both to their assent to the necessity and to their criticism in the name of the common profit. It was this sense of a double responsibility, to the Crown and the community, that emboldened the Commons to criticize royal government or check royal demands. Thus did their authority to adjudicate the common profit enable them to associate the granting of taxation with complaint against illegal levies which impoverished or ruined the subject. The close association between the grant of taxation and the redress of the ills of the community was explicitly affirmed in the crises between 1297 and 1311. Further, the King had a duty to see that what was granted for the common profit should be used for it; that the aid should neither be misused so that the common profit was not advanced, nor abused so that it served the private or 'singular' profit of subjects.

All this furnished parliament with a powerful critique of royal government at a time when, under the pressures of war, the Crown was invoking the case of necessity to extend ancient rights or advance new claims. In time of truce, or even in time of peace, the maintenance of garrisons or fleets for defence was represented as a continuing need for which taxation could legitimately be sought. Traditional rights to purveyance and military service, unquestioned within a domestic or local context, were being extended on the plea of necessity to support and compose national armies. The King's need to increase the yield and availability of the wool tax was undermining the traditional character of the *maltolt* as an aid, making it part of a commercial agreement with the merchant monopolists which could be prolonged indefinitely to their mutual profit. The King, finally, was led to exploit his feudal and judicial rights to raise money for war. Prerogative taxation became under the stress of war not merely a threat but a reality—vivid testimony to the strength of royal authority when fortified by the existence of national emergency. Criticism or limitation of royal actions was effective only through parliament, but even there the Commons' range of weapons was strictly limited. They could not withhold their grants to compel the Crown's submission, nor could they impose conditions as a price of their grants; for necessity, if proved, imposed an inescapable obligation, while remedy for complaint was at the King's grace. In the business of parliament taxation preceded complaint, and the tax once granted became the King's property for which he could not be called to account. The Crown's traditional prerogatives could not be challenged nor could its power to govern be legitimately restrained.

Direct assaults on such bastions of royal authority could prove vain. Yet the Commons were answerable to the communities of the shires who could not be indefinitely outraged. If they looked naturally to the Lords to present and endorse their grievances, and even force redress and reform upon the Crown, the Lords themselves were ultimately bound to protect the King's prerogatives and generally to support his policies. For the most part therefore the Commons were forced to conduct a dialogue with the Crown over their political obligations, and to conduct it on the Crown's terms. Any limitation they sought to impose on the Crown's demands, and any objections they made to prerogative levies, had to be within the framework of their acknowledged obligation. They had to limit the King's demands by casuistry and compel him to heed their grievances by exploiting parliamentary procedure. They thus sought ways of distinguishing between their obligations in open war and times of truce, of defining the purpose of their grants by conditions, of bargaining for redress of grievances, of purchasing release from burdens and defining their illegality by appeal to the need for assent. In substance they had achieved little by 1350. By 1360 their gains were greater: the cessation of continuous direct taxation in time of truce; parliamentary assent to indirect taxation; strict statutory control of purveyors, and a decline of war purveyances; payment for arrays and the proscription of assessments of the wealthy to military service; the beginning of a tradition of purchasing exemption from the penalties of the eyre, and a right to assent to extensions of feudal aids. Even so, these were all essentially defensive achievements. The Commons had reasserted the principles of common assent and common profit against the almost overwhelming royal pressure to finance the war, but they had not negated any legitimate royal demand or prerogative right.

What they had gained was something just as significant if more intangible. Most of the conditions, limitations, and objections which the Commons voiced to taxation were also employed by their contemporaries in the towns and local estates in France, often to greater effect. But the very fact that in the English parliament the Commons found evasion of national taxation less possible forced them to develop corporate identity as a political body representing the realm, to evolve political techniques, and to employ the concepts of political obligation in argument among themselves and with the Crown. By 1369 the Commons had thus attained a degree of political organization and political identity; they had secured all the powers they were to enjoy for the next 200 years; they had established precedents whose relevance was to be tested anew in the seventeenth century; and they stood poised to probe the defects of royal government and demand reform and accountability in the name of the common profit.

This emergence of the Commons as a political force in their own right owed much to the example of and association with the Lords. The Lords exercised more influence on the development of the Commons than did the King, for they fulfilled the role of arbiters between the claims of Crown and people. During the thirteenth century, while they could still claim to represent the community of the realm, they criticized the King's plea of necessity in terms of the necessities of the kingdom and the common profit. Later, in the crisis of 1297, they vindicated the need for common assent and questioned the plea of necessity as applied to the Flanders expedition and in its effects upon the welfare of subjects. By 1311, under the stress of heavy burdens of war and weak royal leadership, they directly restrained the King's power to make war, brought his financial agents under investigation, reasserted the control of the Exchequer over national finance, and claimed that the fisc should contribute to public expenditure to relieve the subject. It was the Ordinances of 1311 which first revealed the political implications of a doctrine of public finance. The King was required to answer for his use of both taxation and the revenues of the fisc in terms of the common profit, and both were brought under baronial restraint. Likewise it was the Ordainers' citation of the burdens and grievances of the realm, to attest the King's misrule and justify their restraint of royal power, that gave the Commons a function of their own, albeit subordinate, in the political arena. Since the crisis of 1297 they had indeed served as the agents of the magnate opposition in parliament, in the presentation of petitions of grievances, and in the linking of these with grants of taxation. However opportunist the purposes of the magnates, this all proved a potent stimulus to the awareness of the Commons. They were made partners and later heirs of the tradition of constitutional opposition to the Crown in its more radical manifestation. The stimulus given to their sense of identity as representatives is visible in the *Modus Tenendi Parliamentum*; their debt to the Lancastrian critique in formulating a coherent programme of reform of royal government is plain from their petitions of 1340. There they boldly attested the evils of the realm as contrary to the common profit, attacked evil counsellors and ministers for their handling of public revenues, demanded resumption of the fisc to support the King's estate and relieve his people, and appealed to a magnate council to redress these ills of the realm and control royal government for the common profit.

In fact the crisis of 1340–1 saw the last expression of the alliance of Lords and Commons against the Crown in this period. Influential as were the effects of this alliance and dramatic as was its expression, it was exceptional rather than normal. With regard to taxation, the Lords were the natural allies of the King rather than of the Commons. Even under Edward II the periods of baronial control of government proved more burdensome than those in which the King ruled alone. From 1332 to 1336 King and baronage shared a common purpose to subdue Scotland, and when Edward had repaired the breaches of the crisis of 1339–41, the combined pressures of King and Lords to exploit the wealth of the kingdom for the war against France brought prolonged periods of taxation. It was because the King's plea of necessity was endorsed by the Lords that it was so irresistible; because the Lords connived at the extensions of the prerogatives, at the impositions of the *maltolt* by the merchants or council, at the levy of feudal aid and the loan in wool, that the Commons were forced to frame and present their own petitions in the name of the commonalty, to define and limit their obligations, and to evolve their own parliamentary tactics. Thus whether in opposition to or alliance with the Crown the Lords, as the greatest of the King's subjects, set a course for the Commons' own actions and aspirations.

Feudal war was by its nature aristocratic, and even as it was acquiring a national character, the King and the magnates retained their traditional attitude of exploiting the realm to serve their military ambitions. Politically, this set the pattern of their relations with parliament until the end of the Crécy–Calais campaign. The Commons, while defending the particular interests of their class, seem to have felt a responsibility to protect the poor of the shire from impoverishment by the demands of war whether through purveyance, arrays, or taxation. But from the middle of the century changes took place in the attitudes of both Crown and Commons which reflected changes in society at large. In the first place the 1350s saw a marked lessening of pressure on the Commons and a greater readiness by the Crown to give safeguards for their rights and recognition of their claims. This partly reflected the decreasing pressure of war itself and the King's active participation in campaigns. More fundamentally it marked the change in society wrought by the Black Death. The sudden opportunity given to the poorer classes to secure higher wages and personal and tenurial freedom at the expense of their social betters rallied all ranks of the landlord class to a policy of legislative suppression. Almost overnight the Commons became the allies of King and Lords and their necessary agents for the enforcement of this policy in the shires. They were recruited as justices of labourers, they won their long-waged battle for punitive powers on the commissions of the peace, they received inducements in the form of rebatement of taxation from the fines on their poorer neighbours. Soon indeed they were to seek new forms of taxation to tap the new prosperity of the labouring class. War itself assisted this change, for as companions in arms of both King and magnates, respected for their proven abilities to lead and fight in the contract companies, the shire gentry were more readily embraced by their political and social superiors. Thus recruited into the political government of the shires, and increasingly identified with the aims and assumptions of royal government, the parliamentary Commons gradually began to adopt the proprietary attitude to public finance of the King and the Lords. In the last year of war they were given control of the subsidy raised for the defence of the shires and in the brief interval of peace which followed the finances of the kingdom were set before them in successive parliaments. Royal finance had become truly public: revenue from both the fisc and taxation had a public function, to maintain the Crown and to defend the realm. Monarch and people each contributed their goods for the common profit, and if it remained the monarch's right and responsibility to spend revenue for this purpose, there were now good grounds for claiming that it fell to the Commons, representing the community of the realm, to criticize the King and even to call him to account in the same terms. As a corollary the monarchy had developed its own sphere of private and personal wealth, immune from the charges and obligations of state. This creation of a new, private 'own' sat uneasily alongside the public 'own' of the royal fisc, the line between them never being clearly defined.

In these ways the parliamentary Commons and the classes from which they were drawn were becoming part of an 'establishment' within the shires and within the nation as a whole. From the middle of the fourteenth century we begin to discern a political society, composed of King and nobility (in its widest sense), whose community of interests and common assumptions were to ensure the stability of English political life until the seventeenth century. The unity of that society was attested by the notion of 'the Crown in parliament', and in parliament the conflicts of political society were ritualized and for the most part resolved. To the formation and definition of parliament's role the pressure of national war and the disputes over financial obligation had made a decisive contribution.

Documents in the Winchester Cathedral Cartulary[1]

i. THE COMMONS' PETITIONS OF 1340 (Item 297)

Fol. 35ᵛ. Tales erant articuli et peticiones communitatis regni Anglie a domino Edwardo tercio Rege regni predicti Anno quarto-decimo et regni Francie primo petiti et in pleno parliamento die mercurii proxima post primam dominicam quadragesime apud Westmonasterium Anno predicto celebrato propositi. De quibus dominus Edwardus Rex predictus ex assensu Prelatorum Comitum Baronum et communitatis quosdam articulos in precedenti processu expressos concessit et stabiliuit.

Fol. 36ʳ. [1] Al comencement prie la dite commune qe seint Esglise eit ses Fraunchises en touz pointz. Et si null' extorsion ou grevaunce ou null' mal soit fait encountre la Fraunchise de seint Esglise qil soit redresse par parlement a la siwte de chescun qi pleindre se vodra resonablement, et qe la graunt Chartre et la Chartre de Foreste et toutes aultres estatuz faites devant ces houres soient tenuz en touz pointz qe cherrount en amendement a ceste parlement.

[2] Item pur ceo qe diverses taillages ount este graunteez a nostre seignour le Roi avant ces houres dount la commune de sa terre sont issint enpoiriz qe a graunt peine poont ils vivere, les queux biens de graunt partie ne sount pas venuz a nostre dit seignour le Roi a graunt areresse de lui et de ses bosoignes, prie la dite commune qe par parlance de soen bon consail soit enquis ou les ditz biens sont devenuz et leaux acompte soit rendue, issint qe le Roi puisse estre servi al profist de lui et descharge de soen pople, et qe tiel punicement soit fait ou le mal serra trovez auxibien des marchants com de quillours et daltres ministres grauntz ou altres de quel condicion qils soient qi les biens avaunditz se sount medles puis lan disme. Issint qe le chastiement qenserra faite soit ensaumple en temps avenir, et qe nul acquitance ensoit faite a nulle de eaux, et si

---

[1] These documents are printed by kind permission of the Dean and Chapter of Winchester Cathedral.

nulle soit faite avant ces hores puis le taxe triennalle et les leines furent grauntez a nostre seignour le Roi puis soen aler outre la meer soit repelle et tenu pur nulle, et la exacion des touz les pointz avantditz soit faite et surveu par ascuns certeins des grauntz esluz et ordinez a cest parlement par touz les grauntz de la commune, et ceux qe sount chargables en cel accompte ne soient en nulle office tanqe la dite acompte soit rendue.

[3] Item prie la dite commune qe toutes maners des profitz auxibien taxes custumes graundes maritages eschetes et totes maners altres profitz sourdantz de Roialme seiont reservus au poeple, et saunz nulle part aillours assignee durant sa guerre, a graunte aide de lui et en descharge de seon popele, et qe certeins Pieris de la terre seient ordinez a cest parlement pur cestes choses garder ordiner recevre et liverer a les opes le Roi et en defence de sa terre, et nomement de ceo qe serra hore grauntee a cest parlement par la commune. Car la dite commune ne porra desoremes nulles tieles charges endurer, et qe touz les groses bosoignes de la terre soient par les ditz Pieris, appelez ceux justices et autre quant ils lour plerra, ordinez triez et juggez et movez et par nulles autres, issint qe des aides grauntes a nostre seignour le Roi riens ne soit donez assigne ne en nulle part liveree si noun par lour ordinaunce des Peirs, auxint come eux voillent respoundre en plein parlement.

[4] Item prie la dite commune qentre issit et la proscheine parlement briefs soient maundez a touz les viscountes Dengleterre denquere par auncienz remembrauncez qe terres ount esteez du temps dount il en adz memorie qe ne sount des cheites ne des pourchaz des Rois qe sont donez venduz ou aloignez de la Corone puis le temps le Roi Edward laiel, issint qen le proschein parlement ore avenir le douns et ventes de tout tel temps soient iuggez et triez par parlement issint qe les leies nient resonables soient defaitz pour touz jours et reseisez en la main le Roi, issint qe le Roi puisse vivere de soen saunz charge de soen poeple.

[5] Item prie la dite Commune qe sicom nostre seignour le Roi est tut prest afaire et adeste quanque soen bon consail voudra ordiner saunz aver regard au travail de soen corps ou a nulle autre meschif, qe tieux gentz seiont ordinez de lui consailler et de soen Roialme governer qe soient bones et leaux de la terre et nulles autres, eslutz ore a ceo parlement et de parlement en parlement, et qe voillent et tiegnent les bosoignes de la terre come desuz est et en tiel maner come ils voudrent respoundre en plein parlement, issint qe les dites Peirs ou ascuns de eux ou ceux qi sount ordinez par lour Commune

assent pour qi ils voillent respoundre et puissent continuelement
scer sur les bosoignes le Roi et du Roialme en la forme susdite.
Issint qe les juggementz qe sount pendantz en nulle des places par
difficulte en awer des justices et qe le cas et les roules soient faitz
venir ou les justices des places devant ditz Piers et mys en certein.
Issint qe ceo qe nest point fait devant eaux soit parfait au plein
parlement ensiwant par assent du parlement. Issint qe les parties qi
pleidont ne seient deslaiez ne en cas desheritez par la cause ou
contrariouse opinion des justices et les ditz Peirs eiont plain poiar as
tote le foithe qils soient assis en la forme susdit de mettre a respouns
touz les ministres le Roi, Justices Barouns et Clerks de Escheqir et
Clerks de la Chauncellerie et toutes altres ministres, de lour poorts
auxibien a la sywete de dite partie com a la suyte le Roi, par
enqueste devant eux prise, issint qe ceux qi feussent de nulle mailfait
atteints ou qi eussent riens pris malement pur faire lour office fuissent
duement puniz par la garde des ditz Peirs et qe ceo qe nest point
parfait devant eux soit parfait al proschein parlement ensiwant. Et
soit ordine par parlement qe tiels ministres eiont feodz suffisauntz
du Roi, issint qils ne soi puissent par cele veie excuser a rien prendre
a grevance du poeple, et qe nulle qe soit chief Justice de la place le
Roi ne soit Justice assignez de prendre assises en pais ne neit poiar
par patent forsqe en sa chief place de mesme, desicom mal avient
de ceo qar il ne voet point reverser ses propres iuggementz. Et qe
tous les Justices [*erasure*] clerks de la Chauncellerie Barons del
Escheqir et tous altres ministres de chescun place soient iurez afaire
droit a chescun saunz delaier et saunz rien prendre des parties pur
faire lour office, et qe le serment soit devant les Peirs de la terre et
pronouncement ordinez en parlement sour ceux qe seront trovez
coupables en tiel cas. Et qe nulle proces des pleez soit descontinuez
en nulle place pur defaute de une lettre ou de une silable, et qe
nullep eticion soit grauntee encountre launcien lei de la terre sil ne
soit par agard des ditz Piers et qe nulle brief ne soit graunte desoremes qe hon appele non obstante.

qe soit encountre commune droit

ii. A REPORT OF ARCHBISHOP STRATFORD'S RECONCILIATION WITH WILLIAM KILSBY (Item 517)

fol 120. [*Mutilated*] scire velitis inter dominum Regem et dominum meum
Cantuar' [*mutilated*] et obs . . . alibus utriusque ut forsitan audistis
pacem esse reformatam et lic [*mutilated*] iuxta vultum eiusdem
multum visa cordialis in principio non fuisset seq [*mutilated*] tractatibus quos postmodum frequentes habebant quanto sepius con-
ferebat tanto Rex graciosiorem et illariorem vultum exhibuit eidem.

Cum multis et onera [*mutilated*] Regalibus consiliariis venit de
Londonie dominus Willelmus de Kylseby apud Otteford qui
Rogaverunt ex parte Regis et idem dominus W. rogavit devote
benivolenciam domini mii predicti qui variis habitis tractatibus
hinc et inde concordes finaliter sunt effecti et mutuo datis osculis
idem Dominus W. et ceteri venientes in mensa cum domino remanserunt. Materiam quorum et formam seriose gestam in his inter-
clusis dominacioni vestre transmitto dominacionem vestram altis-
simus dirigat in agendis feliciter sicut opto. Scriptum apud Mansfeld
iii die Novembris.

iii. THE RECONCILIATION OF EDWARD III AND ARCHBISHOP
   STRATFORD (Item 518)

Concordia inter Regum et Archiepiscopum Johannem
Memorandum quod die Martis proxime post festum Sancte Luce
Evangeliste fuerat pax inter Regem et dominum Cantuar' reformata
in Aula Magna Westmonasterie tanta ex parte Regis plebe congrega-
tur et exire non valente quanta quia dicta aula poterat continere,
Rege vestibus regalibus indicto super altius scannum domino Cantuar subtus ad inferiorem gradum ac aliis prelatis ad consilium
congregatis ibidem stantibus in pressura, Comite de Derby qui erat
mediator dicte pacis ac aliis magnatibus proceribus et popiliaribus
in magno silencio astantibus tunc ibidem. In primis dixit dominus
Cantuar' Regi 'Domine mi ad vestram veni presenciam de vestra
tollerancia unde vobis regracior ad faciendum vobis reverenciam et
obedientiam quas possum et ut vestram benevolenciam et dominacionem bonam captem viis et modis quibus scio et possum statu
ecclesie dignitatis mee ac meo semper salvis, et ulterius adiecit et
duxit et certi articuli crimina ecclesiam et defectus tangentes michi
nuper ex parte vestra imponebantur quorum occasione moti erga
me graviter eratis. Unde desiderans ut plus possim vestram benevolenciam attingere et habere vestre dominacioni supplico quod
responsiones et excusaciones mee ad dictos articulos coram prelatis
et aliis nobilibus quos ad hoc deputare volueritis audiantur et si
reperiar quod non contingat deo dante in defectum emendas com-
petentes vobis offero iuxta posse ecclesie et meo semper salvis.'
Quibus dictis super duobus articulis maioris ponderis premissorum.
120d. vidilicet de litteris declaracionis homagii facti sub verbo [*mutilated*]
plus ex parte Regis et remissionis ducentorum milium [*mutilated*]
... ennium Rex Francie debuit invenisse Regi Anglie per quandam
[perfidiam] [*mutilated*] magnam factam nuper Regi Francie. Dominus
Cantuar optulit suam innocentiam [coram] Rege declarare iura-
mento quod illas huiusmodi litteras non consignavit nec [assenciit]

consignari malitiose dolose vel sediciose in Regis aut corone sue prejudicium scienter protestacione premissa quod hoc non faceret coram Rege ut iudice suo set in hac parte dictaxat se innocentem detegeret et immunem, et hoc iuravit ad sancta Dei Evangilia tunc ibidem, et promisit et quod numquam prosequeretur contra illium de consilio aut officiariis Regis per viam punicionis in iudicio vel extra occasione articulorum predictorum nec pro dissencionibus motis a tempore quo Rex sibi indignacionem ostendit, Statu dignitate ecclesie et suo semper salvis. Iuravit eciam pro posse suo statum salvare regalem, regis honorem et iura corone quatenus pertinet ad eum, iuribus statu ecclesie et suo semper salvis. Subsequenter vero die lune ante festum Omnium Sanctorum venerunt de Londonie ad dominum Cantuar' apud Otteforde dominus de la Bret', dominus J. de Montgomery et dominus Robertus de Lecheburi milites, magistri J. de Offord et J. Thoresburi et alii multi regales rogantes instanter et petentes ex parte Regis et sua quod idem dominus Cantur' ad suam benevolenciam dominum W. de Kilesbi acceptaret, asserent hanc Regi esse peticionem et affectuosam voluntatem, et tandem post varios tractatus in hac parte habitos dominus Cantuar eorum annuit peticioni qui leti exeuntes dictum dominum W. secum ad presenciam Archiepiscopi adduxerunt, quem ad suam et aliorum instantem requisicionem et devotam ad suam graciam et benivolenciam admisit, et sibi mutuo oscula adinvicem dederunt et ibidem una cum aliis regalibus cum dicto domino in prandio remanserunt.

Exchequer Revenues and Expenditure under Edward II and Edward III

i. TABLE OF ESTIMATED REVENUE, 1324, BASED ON BODLEIAN MS. NORTH C.26

	£	s.	d.	
Shire revenues (sheriffs, farms, fee farms, etc.)	11,742	12	3	
Ancient Custom[1] (clear value	mutilated			
New Custom[1] (clear value)	mutilated			
Fines and amercements in the courts (omitting eyres)	mutilated			
Reliefs, fines for marriages, and attermined debts	mutilated			[£19,496. 12s. 5d.]
North Wales and West Wales	mutilated			
Exchanges of London and Canterbury	————[2]			
Mines in Devonshire	————[3]			
Stanneries in Devonshire (at farm)	mutilated			
Escheatries north and south of Trent	700	0	0	
Forests	333	6	8	
Prise of wine	400			
Gauge of wine (at farm)	200			
Gascony (clear receipt)	13,000	0	0	
Total	45,872	12	4	

[1] In 1284 the ancient custom was estimated at £8,000 p.a. (*Eng. Hist. Rev.* xl. 233), and M. Prestwich gives a figure of £18,000 p.a. as the average yield of the old and new customs in the period 1303–7 (*War, Politics and Finance*, p. 199).

[2] Not estimated, in the absence of figures of receipts in the previous 3 years; but valued at £500 earlier in Edward II's reign and estimated at this figure in 1284.

[3] Not estimated, since valued earlier in the reign at 400 marks but subsequently farmed at 200 marks and then released.

	£	s.	d.
Ireland[1]	1,424	0	0
Fines and amercements before the Seneschal and Marshal and Clerk of the Market	300	0	0
Issues of the Great Seal (clear receipt)	300	0	0
Contrariants' lands in England still in the King's hand	12,652	0	0
Contrariants' lands in Wales and Ireland	——————— 2		
Forfeitures of wool per aulnagers	——————— 3		
Total	60,549	0	0

ii. TABLE OF REVENUES RECEIVED AT THE EXCHEQUER, MICHAELMAS 1342–MICHAELMAS 1343, COMPILED FROM RECEIPT ROLLS E 401/370, 371

This and the following table, for 1362–3, include both revenue received in cash and revenue assigned. Although the figures do not therefore represent what was actually received during this period, they broadly represent revenue available to the Exchequer for the discharge of its obligations during the year. Assignments which have been subsequently cancelled have been omitted, as have all *prestita restituta*, loans, and other items not representing real revenue. All revenue from taxation, including sales of wool, is omitted. The section 'Fines and Casualties' embraces both judicial fines (including those arising from the eyre) and fines for licences and for the King's grace (including payments for wardships, marriages, and reliefs).

[1] Said to be worth £2,120 p.a. clear under Edward I on the basis of accounts of 1292–3.
[2] Not estimated, in the absence of figures for earlier receipts.
[3] Not estimated, since this revenue, valued at £700 p.a., was paid to the Wardrobe.

	Michaelmas 1342–3	Easter 1343	Totals
	£ s. d.	£ s. d.	£ s. d.
Sheriffs	2,926 18 10	2,752 19 5	5,679 18 3
Escheators	73 15 2	85 17 11	159 13 1
Hanaper	153 7 2	343 7 9	496 14 11
Mint and exchanges	—	316 19 4	316 19 4
Farms and fee farms	1,023 13 9	1,877 8 1	2,901 1 10
Fines and casualties	1,569 4 5	2,179 10 5	3,748 14 10
Alien priories	2,597 18 11	2,706 8 8	5,304 7 7
Temporalities	626 6 1	92 0 2	718 6 3
Totals	8,971 4 4	10,354 11 9	19,325 16 1

iii. TABLE OF REVENUES RECEIVED AT THE EXCHEQUER, MICHAELMAS 1362–MICHAELMAS 1363, COMPILED FROM RECEIPT ROLLS E 401/470, 472

	Michaelmas 1362–3			Easter 1363			Totals		
	£	s.	d.	£	s.	d.	£	s.	d.
Sheriffs	2,920	18	10	1,721	15	0	4,642	13	10
Escheators	814	8	1	133	19	3	984	7	4
Hanaper Clerk of the Market	459 260	12 0	3 0	519	16	10	1,239	9	1
Mint and exchanges	632	2	3	187	13	0	819	15	3
Farms and fee farms	1,859	3	10	597	4	0	2,456	7	10
Fines and casualties	923	3	10	955	5	6	1,878	9	4[1]
Alien priories	394	13	5	173	12	2	568	5	7
Temporalities	680	3	7	407	13	4	1,087	16	11
Totals	8,944	6	1	5,069	11	1[2]	14,013	17	2

[1] £615. 1s. 9d. of this total came from fines for the purchase of wardships and marriages.

[2] Additional revenue from Ireland, Calais, and Ponthieu totalled £372. 12s. in this term.

P.R.O., EXCHEQUER OF RECEIPT
MISCELLANEA, E 407/5/115[1]

Fait a remembrer des deniers receuz a la Receit et paiementz del xx[e] iour de Feverer lan xxxvii[e] que iour levesque de Wircestre rece [ut son office tanqe a le][2] xvi[e] iour de Maii proschein ensuant lun et lautre iour acomptez

La Summe totale Receu £21,504. 0s. 6½d. dount

	£	s.	d.
De ce qe Remanoit le xx[e] iour de Feverer susdit	4,102	13	8
De les Custumes de touz les portz Dengleterre	6,962	16	8½
dount in Berewyk en assignement £723 0. 1½d.			
De les x[es] grauntez par le pape en partie de la Raunceoun de Fraunce	£1,550.		
De deniers appromptez de la Raunceoun deinz la Tour	3,737	4	4
De la Raunceon de Burgoyne	2,100		
Des viscountz, temporaltez, estallementz et autre revenues par leschequier	1,243	6	6
Et par assignementz de mesmes les revenues	1,807	19	4
La Summe des Paiementz £20,553. 18s. 1d. dount			
Au Roi pour sa Chaumbre	2,500 marcarum		
A ma dame la Roigne de ses certeines et d'apprest	1,083	10	1
Pur despens del hostiel le Roi	2,644	4	0
Pur la graunde Garderobe	502	19	0
Pur les overeignes le Roi et pour Plumb	3,047	4	1
Pur le Prince et le Count de Warr' vers Gascoigne	2,452		
Pur gages vers Irland'	2,136	5	6
Pur gages des Mariners et serieantz darmes	1,185	17	0½
Pur Caleys, Berewyk et Rokesburgh'	1,708	13	4
Pur Feez et gages par patentz	1,831	11	3
Fez des Justices, Barons, et autres Ministres	518	4	4
Messageries vers la Court et aillours pardela et vers Caleys pour les houstages	445	6	8
Pur vitailles, gages et robes par billes Farle, Buk', Walton et Neubury	505	8	3½
Pur Freres et aumoignerye	110	11	2

---

[1] Printed by permission of the Controller of H.M. Stationery Office.
[2] Tear in the manuscript. Words supplied from E 101/394/17 m. 6.

	£	s.	d.
Pur le Count de Cant', le Count de Pembr,' la Duchesse de Bretagne	181	6	8
Pur douns as estranges et denzeins	147	4	0
Pur prisoners, vessel dargent, terres et une Corone achatez	326	13	4
Pur Dettes la Roigne Descoce	23	13	4
Commune Messagerie, acat de parchemyn et autres menues paiementz	36	12	8

v. 'STATEMENT E'

P.R.O., EXCHEQUER K.R., ACCOUNTS VARIOUS, E 101/399/13[1]

La Remembrance des deniers[2] paiez a la Receit pour les despens nostre Seignour le Roi del fest de Seint Michel darrein passe tanqe a la fest de Nowel proschein ensuant

cestassavoire

A nostre seignour le Roi pour sa chaumbre

4,500 marcarum dount dict' term' de Sanct Johann' 2000 marcarum et pour la Sanct Mich' 2500 marcarum

	£	s.	d.
Item Au Chaumbre le Roi pour deniers apprestez	812	10	0
A ma dame la Roigne de ceo qele prent a lescheqier et pour acquiter ses dettes	509	8	5
Pur les despens del hostiel le Roi	3,961	5	3
Pur la graunde Garderobe	2,783	2	2

Et outre ceo sount duez pour cire et espicerie appromptez encontre la Noel £800

Pur loffice de la Botillarie

Rienz puys la Seint Michel par cause qyl estoit assigne devant

---

[1] Printed by permission of the Controller of H.M. Stationery Office.
[2] deniers paiez a la Receit pour *written above the line*

	£	s.	d.
Pur les overeignes le Roi	3,934	0	7
Pur Gages de guerre vers Irlande	8,483	2	1½
Pur Caleys, Dovor', Berewyk, Rokesburgh et autres Chasteux le Roi	914	4	7
Pur terres et chivaux achatez	1,594	4	1
Pur feez et gages grauntez par patentz as diverses gentz a term de lour vie	3,477	15	0
Pur feez des Justices, Barons et autres Ministres	511	0	0
Pur Messageries vers la Court et aillours pardela et vers Caleys pour les houstages	1,480	11	5
Pur gages de guerre, vitailles et robes par billes Buk', Walton, Farle, Feriby et Neubury et autres	2,203	11	4½
Pur Freres et autre Aumoignerie	279	1	4
Pur douns as estraunges et denzeins et regards des Custumers	497	9	8½
Pur dettes la Roigne descoce	61	18	8
Commune Messagerie, acat de parchemyn et autres menues paiementz	67	14	8
Item deniers paiez a les escoce en monoie et en pris de vesseill' dargent	1,130	2	4
Item sount paiez puys la Seint Michel a ma dame la Roigne et ceux qe sount assignez sur la custume de Loundres par patentz	826	1	11

La Summe Totale paie puys la Seint Michel £36,527 3 7½
qe fount 54,790 marcarum 10s. 3½d.

Et fait a remembrer de ceo qe covient estre paie de la Noel tanqe a les octaves de Pasc'

cest assavoir

Au Roi en sa Chaumbre	5,800 marcarum
A ma dame la Roigne de ceo qele prent de les custumes et a Lescheqier	£1,250
Item pur lostiel le Roi outre les £10 par le iour paiez par ma dame la Roigne par eyme	3,600
Item pur la grande Garderobe par eyme	3,000
Item pur la Butillarie par eyme	2,500
Item pur les overeignes le Roi le Simeigne a £300 par eyme	3,600
Item pur achate de plomb qest due et sera pourveu devant la Pasque pur les ditz overaignes par eyme	1,000

	£	s.	d.

Item pur gages de monsieur de Clarence et autres
pur cest quartier outre ceo qest paie a monsieur
William de Wyndesore par eyme   1,000

Item sount duez a monsieur John Cobham fitz au
Countesse Mareschall   1,000 marcarum

Item pur Caleys, Dovyre, Berewyk, Rokesburgh'
et autres chasteux le Roi par eyme   £2,000

Item pur feez grauntez par patentz qe serront
duez a la Pasque par eyme   3,000

Item pur feez des Justices, Barons et autres a la
Pasque par eyme   500

Item pur Freres et aumoignerie le Roi tanque la
Pasque   292

Item pur dettes ma dame la Roigne Descoce qe
serra paie devant la Pasque   400

La Summe qe covient estre paie a la Pasque et devant par eyme
£26,675. 6s. 8d. qe fount 40,013 marcarum

Et fait a remembrer des coustages et douns qe serront faitz par
cause de la venue le Roi de France

La Somme totale des despens par entre la Seint Mich et les
Octaves de Pasq par eyme
94,803 marcarum 10s. 3½d. qe fount £63,202 10s. 3½d.

Et Fait a remembrer qe les custumes dengleterre
amountent par un an au Roi   57,500 marcarum
dount 10,400 marcarum assignez a ma dame
la Roigne et autres par patentz

Item Viscountez, Fermes, la Haneper, les
eschaunges et toutes autres revenues par
lescheqier amountent par un an par eyme
outre les assignementz faitz par patentes et
gages des venours et fauconers   6,384 marcarum

La Summe   63,884 marcarum

Et issint passent les despenses le Roi par entre la
Seint Michel et les octaves de Pasque outre toutes
les revenues Dengleterre d un an entier   25,919 marcarum

List of Sources Cited

A. MANUSCRIPT SOURCES

Bodleian Library, Oxford:
MS. North C.26

Public Record Office:
C 47   (Chancery Miscellanea)
C 49   (Parliament and Council Proceedings)
C 76   (Treaty Rolls)
C 81   (Chancery Warrants)
E 43   (Exchequer Treasury of Receipt, Ancient Deeds, Series WS)
E 101   (Exchequer, King's Remembrancer, Various Accounts)
E 159   (Exchequer, King's Remembrancer, Memoranda Rolls)
E 359   (Exchequer, Lord Treasurer's Remembrancer, Enrolled Subsidies)
E. 361 (Exchequer, Lord Treasurer's Remembrancer, Enrolled Accounts, Wardrobe and Household)
E 372   (Exchequer, Lord Treasurer's Remembrancer, Pipe Rolls)
E 401   (Exchequer of Receipt, Receipt Rolls)
E 403   (Exchequer of Receipt, Issue Rolls)
E 404   (Exchequer of Receipt, Warrants for Issues)
E 407   (Exchequer of Receipt, Miscellanea)
SC 8   (Ancient Petitions)

Winchester, Dean and Chapter Muniments:
Cartulary

Westminster Abbey Muniments:
No. 12195

B. PRINTED SOURCES

i. CHRONICLES

Annales Monastici, ed. H. R. Luard, vol. iv, *De Oseneia, Chronicon Thomae Wykes et de Wigornia* (R.S., 1869).
Bartholomei de Cotton, Historia Anglicana, ed. H. R. Luard (R.S., 1859).
Chronica Adae Murimuth et Roberti de Avesbury, ed. E. M. Thompson (R.S., 1889).
Chronica Johannis de Oxenedes, ed. Sir H. Ellis (R.S., 1859).
Chronica Monasterii de Melsa, ed. E. A. Bond, 3 vols. (R.S., 1866–8).

Chronica Rogeri de Hovedene, ed. W. Stubbs, 4 vols. (R.S., 1868–71).
Chronica Rogeri de Wendover, ed. H. G. Hewlett, 3 vols. (R.S., 1886–9).
'Chronicle of the Civil Wars of Edward II', ed. G. L. Haskins, *Speculum*, xiv (1939).
Chronicle of Pierre de Langtoft, ed. T. Wright, 2 vols. (R.S., 1866–8).
Chronicle of Walter of Guisborough, ed. H. Rothwell (Camden Soc. lxxxix, 1957).
Chronicles of the Reigns of Edward I and Edward II, ed. W. Stubbs (R.S., 1882–3), vol. i, *Annales Londonienses and Annales Paulini*; vol. ii, *Gesta Edwardi de Carnarvon Auctore Canonico Bridlingtoniensi*.
Chronicon Galfridi le Baker de Swynbroke, ed. E. M. Thompson (Oxford, 1889).
Chronicon Henrici Knighton, ed. J. R. Lumby, 2 vols. (R.S., 1889).
Croniques de London, ed. G. J. Aungier (Camden Soc., 1844).
Gervase of Canterbury, Opera Historica, ed. W. Stubbs, 2 vols. London, 1879–80).
Gesta Regis Henrici Secundi Benedicti Abbatis, ed. W. Stubbs, 2 vols. (R.S., 1867).
Giraldus Cambrensis, Opera, ed. J. Brewer, 8 vols. (R.S., 1861–91).
Johannis de Trokelowe et Henrici de Blaneforde Chronica et Annales, ed. H. T. Riley (R.S., 1865).
Matthaei Parisiensis, Chronica Majora, ed. H. R. Luard, 7 vols. (R.S., 1872–84).
Scalacronica of Thomas Grey, ed. J. Stevenson (Maitland Club, Edinburgh, 1836).
Vita Edwardi Secundi, ed. N. Denholm-Young (London, 1957).

ii. PUBLISHED AND CALENDARED DOCUMENTS

Anglia Sacra, ed. H. Wharton, 2 vols. (London, 1691).
Anglo-Norman Political Songs, ed. I. Aspin (Anglo-Norman Text Soc., 1953).
AQUINAS, Thomas, *Selected Political Writings*, ed. A. P. D'Entrèves (Oxford, 1948).
Black Book of the Admiralty, ed. Sir T. Twiss, 4 vols. (R.S., 1871–6).
Book of Prests of the King's Wardrobe for 1294–5, ed. E. B. Fryde (Oxford, 1962).
BRACTON, *De Legibus Angliae*, ed. G. D. G. Hall (London, 1965).
Calendar of Chancery Warrants, 1244–1326.
Calendar of Close Rolls.
Calendar of Documents relating to Scotland, ed. J. Bain, 3 vols. (Edinburgh, 1887).
Calendar of Fine Rolls.
Calendars of Letter Books of the City of London: Letter Books A–G, ed. R. Sharpe (London, 1899–1905).

Calendar of Memoranda Rolls (Exchequer), 1326–7.
Calendar of Patent Rolls.
Calendar of Papal Letters.
Catalogue des rolles gascons, normans et francois, ed. T. Carte, 2 vols. (London, 1743).
Chartulary of Winchester Cathedral, ed. A. W. Goodman (Winchester, 1927).
Crécy and Calais, ed. G. J. Wrottesley (William Salt Soc., 1898).
De Speculo Regis Edwardi Tertii, ed. J. Moisant (Paris, 1891).
Dialogus de Scaccario, ed. C. Johnson (London, 1950).
Documents Illustrative of English History in the Thirteenth and Fourteenth Centuries, ed. H. Cole (London, 1844).
Documents of the Baronial Movement of Reform and Rebellion 1258–1267, ed. R. F. Treharne and I. J. Sanders (Oxford, 1973).
Early Taxation Returns, ed. A. C. Chibnall (Buckinghamshire Record Soc. xiv, 1966).
Exchequer Rolls of Scotland, ii, *1359–79,* ed. G. Burnett (Edinburgh, 1878).
Feudal Aids, 6 vols. (H.M.S.O., 1899–1920).
Die Gesetze der Angelsachsen, ed. F. Liebermann, 3 vols. (Halle, 1903).
Historical Poems of the XIV and XV Centuries, ed. R. H. Robbins (New York, 1959).
Issue Roll of Thomas Brantingham, 1370, ed. F. Devon (London, 1835).
Issues of the Exchequer, Henry III–Henry VI, ed. F. Devon (Record Comm., 1847).
Lancashire Lay Subsidies, ed. J. A. C. Vincent (Record Soc. for Lancashire and Cheshire, xxvii 1893).
Liber Quotidianus Contrarotulatoris Garderobe Anno Regni Regis Edwardi Primo Vicesimo Octavo, ed. J. Nichols (Soc. of Antiquaries, 1787).
Lincolnshire Assize Roll for 1298, ed. W. S. Thomson (Lincoln Record Soc. xxxvi, 1944).
Litterae Cantuarienses, ed. J. B. Sheppard, 2 vols. (R.S., 1888).
Litterae Walliae, ed. J. G. Edwards (Cardiff, 1940).
Memoranda de Parliamento, ed. F. W. Maitland (R.S., 1893).
Minot, L., *Poems,* ed. J. Hall (Oxford, 1897).
Mirror of Justices, ed. W. J. Whitaker (Selden Soc. vii, 1895).
Parliamentary Writs, ed. F. Palgrave, 2 vols. in 4 (London, 1827–34).
Pipe Rolls, Henry II, Richard I, John (Pipe Roll Soc., 1884–1954).
Pipe Roll for 1295, Surrey Membrane, ed. M. Mills (Surrey Record Soc. vii, 1924).
Political Songs of England, ed. T. Wright (Camden Soc., 1839).
Proceedings before the Justices of the Peace in the Fourteenth and Fifteenth Centuries, ed. B. H. Putnam (Selden Soc., 1938).

534   *List of Sources Cited*

Ransom of John II, 1360–70, ed. D. M. Broome (Camden Soc. xiv, 1926).
Red Book of the Exchequer, ed. H. Hall, 3 vols. (R.S., 1897).
Register of the Black Prince, 4 parts (London, 1930–3).
Register of St. Osmund, ed. W. H. R. Jones, 2 vols. (R.S., 1883–4).
Registrum Roberti de Winchelsey, ed. Rose Graham, 2 vols. (Canterbury and York Soc. li–lii, 1952).
Report from the Lords' Committees . . . for all matters touching the Dignity of a Peer, 4 vols. (London, 1820–9).
Rotuli Litterarum Clausarum in Turri Londinensi asservati, 1204–27, ed. T. D. Hardy, 2 vols. (Record Comm., 1833–44).
Rotuli Parliamentorum, vols. i, ii.
Rotuli Parliamentorum Angliae Hactenus Inediti, ed. H. G. Richardson and G. O. Sayles (Camden Soc. li, 1935).
Rotuli Scotiae, 2 vols. (Record Comm., 1814–19).
RYMER, T., *Foedera, Conventiones, Litterae*, ed. A. G. Clarke and F. Holbrooke, vols. i–iii (Record Comm., 1816–30).
Select Cases in the Court of King's Bench, iv, Edward II, ed. G. O. Sayles (Selden Soc. lxxiv, 1957).
Song of Lewes, ed. C. L. Kingsford (Oxford, 1890).
Statutes of the Realm, vol. i (Record Comm., 1810).
Surrey Taxation Returns, ed. J. F. Willard and H. C. Johnson (Surrey Record Soc. xviii, 1922).

iii. SECONDARY SOURCES

BAKER, R. L., 'The Establishment of the English Wool Staple in 1313', *Speculum*, xxxi (1956), pp. 444–53.
——, *The English Customs Service 1307–1343, a Study of Medieval Administration* (Philadelphia, 1961).
BALDWIN, J. F., *The King's Council in England in the Later Middle Ages* (Oxford, 1913).
BALFOUR-MELVILLE, E. W. M., *Edward III and David II* (Historical Association, London, 1954).
BARNES, F. R., 'The Taxation of Wool, 1327–48', in *Finance and Trade under Edward III*, ed. G. Unwin (Manchester, 1918).
BEAN, J. M. W., *The Decline of English Feudalism* (Manchester, 1968).
BELLAMY, J. G., *The Law of Treason in England in the Later Middle Ages* (Cambridge, 1970).
BISSON, T. N., 'Negotiations for Taxes under Alphonse of Poitiers', *XIIe Congrès Internationale des Sciences Historiques* (Paris–Louvain, 1966), pp. 75–102.
BOCK, F., 'Some New Documents Illustrating the Early Years of the Hundred Years' War, 1353–6', *Bulletin of the John Rylands Library*, xv (1931), pp. 60–99.

BOCK, F., *Das Deutsche–Englische Bundnis von 1335–1342* (Munich, 1956).

BOND, A., 'Extracts from the Liberate Rolls Relative to Loans Supplied by Italian Merchants', *Archaeologia*, xxviii (1840), 261–326.

BROOME, D., and TOUT, T. F., 'A National Balance Sheet for 1362–3', *Eng. Hist. Rev.* xxxix (1924), pp. 404–19.

BROWN, R. Stewart, 'The End of the Norman Earldom of Chester', *Eng. Hist. Rev.* xxxv (1920), pp. 26–54.

BRYANT, W. N., 'The Financial Dealings of Edward III with the County Communities, 1330–60', *Eng. Hist. Rev.* lxxxiii (1968), pp. 760–71.

——, 'Some Earlier Examples of Intercommuning in Parliament', *Eng. Hist. Rev.* lxxxv (1970), pp. 54–8.

BURLEY, S. J., 'The Victualling of Calais, 1347–65', *Bull. Inst. Hist. Res.* xxxi (1958), pp. 49–57.

CAM, H., *The Hundred and the Hundred Rolls* (London, 1930).

——, 'The General Eyres of 1329–30', *Eng. Hist. Rev.* xxxix (1924), pp. 241–51.

——, 'The *Quo Warranto* Proceedings', *History*, xi (1926), pp. 143–8.

CAMPBELL, J., 'England, Scotland and the Hundred Years' War in the Fourteenth Century', in *Europe in the Later Middle Ages*, ed. J. R. Hale, J. R. L. Highfield, and B. Smalley (London, 1965), pp. 184–216.

CARUS-WILSON, E. M., and COLEMAN, O., *England's Export Trade, 1275–1547* (Oxford, 1963).

CAZEL, F. A., 'The Fifteenth of 1225', *Bull. Inst. Hist. Res.* xxxiv (1961), pp. 67–81.

——, 'Royal Taxation in Thirteenth Century England', in *L'impot dans le Cadre de la Ville et de l'État* (Brussels, 1966).

CHEW, H. M., 'Scutage in the Fourteenth Century', *Eng. Hist. Rev.* xxxviii (1923), pp. 19–41.

CHRIMES, S. B., *An Introduction to Medieval Administrative History* (Oxford, 1952).

CLARKE, M. V., *Medieval Representation and Consent* (London, 1936).

——, *Fourteenth Century Studies*, ed. M. McKisack and L. S. Sutherland (Oxford, 1937).

COLVIN, H. M. (ed.), *The History of the King's Works*, 3 vols. (H.M.S.O., London, 1963).

CRAIG, J., *The Mint* (Cambridge, 1953).

CRONNE, H. A., *The Reign of Stephen* (London, 1970).

CUTTINO, G. P., 'A Reconsideration of the *Modus Tenendi Parliamentum*', in *The Forward Movement of the Fourteenth Century*, ed. F. L. Utley (Columbus, 1961), pp. 31–60.

Davies, J. C., *The Baronial Opposition to Edward II* (Cambridge, 1918).
——, 'The First Journal of Edward II's Chamber', *Eng. Hist. Rev.* xxx (1915), pp. 662–80.
Deighton, H. S., 'Clerical Taxation by Consent, 1279–1301', *Eng. Hist. Rev.* lxviii (1953), pp. 161–92.
Denholm-Young, N., 'The Paper Constitution Attributed to 1244', *Eng. Hist. Rev.* lviii (1943), pp. 401–23.
——, *Collected Papers on Medieval Subjects* (Oxford, 1946).
——, *History and Heraldry* (Oxford, 1965).
Deprez, E., *Les Préliminaires de la Guerre de Cent Ans* (Paris, 1902).
Dupont-Ferrier, G., 'Histoire et signification du mot "Aides" dans les institutions financieres de la France', *Bibl. École des Chartes*, lxxxix (1928), pp. 53–69.
Edwards, J. G., 'The Negotiating of the Treaty of Leake, 1318', in *Essays Presented to R. Lane Poole* (Oxford, 1927), pp. 260–87.
——, 'The *Plena Potestas* of English Parliamentary Representatives', in *Oxford Essays in Medieval History Presented to H. E. Salter* (Oxford, 1934), pp. 141–54.
——, '*Confirmatio Cartarum* and Baronial Grievances in 1297', *Eng. Hist. Rev.* lviii (1943), pp. 147–71, 273–300.
——, 'Justice in Early English Parliaments', *Bull. Inst. Hist. Res.* xxvii (1954), pp. 35–53.
Ehrlich, L., 'Exchequer and Wardrobe in 1270', *Eng. Hist. Rev.* xxxvi (1921), pp. 553–4.
Favier, J., *Finance et fiscalité au Bas Moyen Âge* (Paris, 1971).
Fowler, K., 'Les Finances et la discipline dans les armées anglaises en France au XIVᵉ siècle', *Les Cahiers Vernonnais*, iv (1964), pp. 55–84.
——, *The King's Lieutenant* (London, 1969).
Fraser, C. M., *A History of Antony Bek* (Oxford, 1957).
Fryde, E. B., 'Edward III's Wool Monopoly of 1337', *History*, xxxvii (1952), pp. 8–24.
——, 'The English Farmers of the Customs, 1343–51', *Trans. Roy. Hist. Soc.* 5th ser. ix (1959), pp. 1–17.
——, 'The Last Trials of Sir William de la Pole', *Econ. Hist. Rev.* xv (1962), pp. 17–30.
——, 'The Financial Resources of Edward I in the Netherlands, 1294–8', *Revue Belge de Philologie et d'Histoire*, xl (1962), pp. 1168–87.
——, and Fryde, M. M., 'Public Credit with Special Reference to North West Europe', in *The Cambridge Economic History of Europe*, iii, ed. M. M. Postan, E. E. Rich, and Edward Miller (Cambridge, 1963).

FRYDE, E. B., *Wool Accounts of William de la Pole* (Borthwick Institute, York, 1964).

——, 'The Financial Resources of Edward III in the Netherlands, 1337–40', *Revue Belge de Philologie et d'Histoire*, xlv (1967), pp. 1142–93.

——, 'Parliament and the French War, 1336–40', in *Essays in Medieval History Presented to Bertie Wilkinson* (Toronto, 1969), pp. 250–69.

——, 'Parliament and the Revolt of 1381', in *Liber Memorialis Georges de Lagarde* (Paris–Louvain, 1970), pp. 75–88.

——, and MILLER, E., *Historical Studies of the English Parliament*, 2 vols. (London, 1971).

GALBRAITH, V. H., *Studies in the Public Records* (London, 1948).

——, 'The *Modus Tenendi Parliamentum*', *Journal of the Warburg and Courtauld Institutes*, xvi (1953), pp. 81–99.

GIESEY, R. E., *The Juristic Basis of Dynastic Right to the French Throne* (Philadelphia, 1961).

GRAS, N. S. B., *The Early English Customs System* (Cambridge, Mass., 1916).

GRAVES, E. B., 'Circumspecte Agatis', *Eng. Hist. Rev.* xliii (1928), pp. 1–20.

GRAY, H. L., 'The Production and Export of English Woollens in the Fourteenth Century', *Eng. Hist. Rev.* xxxix (1924), pp. 13–35.

——, *The Influence of the Commons on Early Legislation* (Cambridge, Mass., 1932).

HARRIS, B. E., 'King John and the Sheriffs' Farms', *Eng. Hist. Rev.* lxxix (1964), pp. 532–42.

HARRISS, G. L., 'Preference at the Medieval Exchequer', *Bull. Inst. Hist. Res.* xxx (1957), pp. 17–40.

——, 'Parliamentary Taxation and the Origins of Appropriation of Supply in England, 1207–1340', in *Gouvernés et Gouvernants* (Société Jean Bodin, Brussels, 1965), pp. 165–79.

——, 'The Commons' Petitions of 1340', *Eng. Hist. Rev.* lxxxviii (1963), pp. 625–54.

HARTUNG, F., 'Die Krone als Symbol der Monarchischen Herrschaft im Ausgehenden Mittelalter', *Abhandlungen der Preussischen Akademie der Wissenschaften*, xiii (1940).

HARVEY, P. D. A., 'The English Inflation of 1180–1220', *Past and Present*, lxi (1973), pp. 3–30.

HARVEY, S., 'The Knight and the Knight's Fee in England', *Past and Present*, xlix (1970), pp. 3–43.

HASKINS, G. L., 'The Doncaster Petition of 1321', *Eng. Hist. Rev.* liii (1938), pp. 478–85.

HENNEMAN, J. B., *Royal Taxation in Fourteenth Century France* (Princeton, 1971).

HEWITT, H. J., *The Black Prince's Expedition of 1355–7* (Manchester, 1958).

——, *The Organisation of War under Edward III* (Manchester, 1966).

HOFFMAN, H., 'Die Unveraüslichkeit der Kronrechter im Mittelalters', *Deutsches Archiv fur Erforschung des Mittelalters*, xx (1964), pp. 389–474.

HOLT, J. C., *The Northerners* (Oxford, 1961).

——, 'Politics and Property in Early Medieval England', *Past and Present*, lvii (1972), pp. 3–52.

——, *Magna Carta* (Cambridge, 1965).

HOWELL, M., *Regalian Right in Medieval England* (Oxford, 1962).

HOYT, R. S., 'Royal Demesne, Parliamentary Taxation and the Realm, 1294–1322', *Speculum*, xxiii (1948), pp. 58–69.

——, 'Royal Taxation and the Growth of the Realm in Medieval England', *Speculum*, xxv (1950), pp. 36–48.

——, *The Royal Demesne in English Constitutional History, 1066–1272* (New York, 1950).

——, 'The Coronation Oath of 1308: the Background of "Les Leys et Les Custumes" ', *Traditio*, xi (1955), pp. 235–57.

HUGHES, D., *A Study of Social and Constitutional Tendencies in the Early Years of Edward III* (London, 1915).

JAMES, M. E., 'Obedience and Dissent in Henrician England; the Lincolnshire Rebellion of 1536', *Past and Present*, xlviii (1970), pp. 3–78.

JOHNSON, C., 'The System of Account in the Wardrobe of Edward I', *Trans. Roy. Hist. Soc.* 4th ser. vi (1923), pp. 50–72.

JOHNSTONE, H., 'The Parliament of Lincoln, 1316', *Eng. Hist. Rev.* xxxvi (1921), pp. 53–7.

——, *Edward of Carnarvon* (Manchester, 1946).

JOLLIFFE, J. E. A., 'The Chamber and Castle Treasuries under King John', in *Studies in Medieval History Presented to F. M. Powicke* (Oxford, 1948), pp. 117–42.

——, 'The *Camera Regis* under Henry II', *Eng. Hist. Rev.* lxviii (1953), pp. 1–21, 337–62.

——, *Angevin Kingship* (London, 1955).

JONES, M., *Ducal Brittany, 1364–1399* (Oxford, 1970).

KAEUPER, R. W., Bankers to the Crown (Princeton, 1973).

KANTOROWICZ, E. H., *The King's Two Bodies* (Princeton, 1957).

——, 'Inalienability; a Note on Canonical Practice and the English Coronation Oath in the Thirteenth Century', *Speculum*, xxix (1954), pp. 488–502.

KEENEY, B. C., 'Military Service and the Development of Nationalism in England, 1272–1327', *Speculum*, xxii (1947), pp. 534–49.

KERSHAW, I., 'The Agrarian Crisis in England, 1315–22', *Past and Present*, lix (1973), pp. 3–50.

KOSMINSKY, E. A., *Studies in the Agrarian History of England in the Thirteenth Century* (Oxford, 1956).

LAPSLEY, G., *Crown, Community and Parliament*, ed. H. Cam and G. Barraclough (Oxford, 1951).

LEWIS, N. B., 'The Recruitment and Organisation of a Contract Army, May to November 1337', *Bull Inst Hist Res.* xxxvii (1964), pp. 1–19.

LIEBERMANN, F., *Über die Leges Anglorum Saeculo XIII ineunte Londoniis Collectae* (Halle, 1894).

——, 'A Contemporary Manuscript of the Leges Anglorum Londoniis Collectae', *Eng. Hist. Rev.* xxviii (1913), pp. 732–45.

LYDON, J. F., 'William of Windsor and the Irish Parliament', *Eng. Hist. Rev.* lxxx (1965), pp. 252–67.

McFARLANE, K. B., 'England and the Hundred Years' War', *Past and Present*, xxii (1962), pp. 3–13.

——, 'Had Edward I a "Policy" towards the Earls?', *History*, l (1965), pp. 145–59.

McILWAIN, C. H., *The Growth of Political Thought in the West* (New York, 1932).

McKISACK, M., *The Fourteenth Century* (Oxford, 1959).

MADDICOTT, J. R., *Thomas of Lancaster, 1307–1322* (Oxford, 1970).

MADOX, T., *History and Antiquities of the Exchequer*, 2 vols., 2nd ed. (London, 1769).

MARONGIU, A., *Il Parlamento in Italia* (Milan, 1962); *Medieval Parliaments*, trans. S. J. Woolf (London, 1968).

MILLS, M., 'Adventus Vicecomitum, 1258–1272', *Eng. Hist. Rev.* xxxvi (1921), pp. 481–96.

——, 'Adventus Vicecomitum, 1272–1307', *Eng. Hist. Rev.* xxxviii (1923), pp. 331–54.

——, 'Exchequer Agenda and Estimates of Revenue, Easter Term 1284', *Eng. Hist. Rev.* xl (1925), pp. 229–34.

——, 'Experiments in Exchequer Procedure (1200–1232)', *Trans. Roy. Hist. Soc.* 4th ser. viii (1925), pp. 151–70.

——, 'The Reforms at the Exchequer (1232–42)', *Trans. Roy. Hist. Soc.* 4th ser. x (1927), pp. 111–33.

MIROT, L., 'Les Ambassades anglaises pendant la Guerre de Cent Ans', *Bibliothèque de l'École des Chartes*, lix (1898), pp. 550–77, lx (1899), pp. 177–214.

MITCHELL, S. K., *Studies in Taxation under John and Henry III* (New Haven, 1914).

MITCHELL, S. K., *Taxation in Medieval England* (New Haven, 1951).

MORRIS, J. E., *The Welsh Wars of Edward I* (Oxford, 1901).

MORRIS, W. A., 'The Date of the *Modus Tenendi Parliamentum*', *Eng. Hist. Rev.* xlix (1934), pp. 407–22.

——, 'Magnates and Community of the Realm in Parliament, 1264–1327', *Mediaevalia et Humanistica*, i (1943), pp. 58–94.

——, and WILLARD, J. F., *The English Government at Work, 1327–1336*, vol. i (Cambridge, Mass., 1940).

——, and STRAYER, J. R., *The English Government at Work, 1327–1336*, vol. ii (Cambridge, Mass., 1947).

——, WILLARD, J. F., and DUNHAM, W. H., *The English Government at Work, 1327–1336*, vol. iii (Cambridge, Mass., 1950).

NICHOLSON, R., *Edward III and the Scots* (Oxford, 1965).

OTWAY-RUTHVEN, J., *A History of Medieval Ireland* (London, 1968).

PAINTER, S., *Studies in the History of the English Feudal Barony* (Baltimore, 1943).

——, *The Reign of King John* (Baltimore, 1949).

PASQUET, D., *An Essay on the Origins of the House of Commons*, trans. R. G. D. Laffan (Cambridge, 1925).

PATOUREL, J. LE, 'Edward III and the Kingdom of France', *History*, xliii (1958), pp. 173–89.

PETIT-DUTAILLIS, Ch., *Studies and Notes Supplementary to Stubbs' Constitutional History*, 3 vols (Manchester, 1930).

PHILLIPS, J. R. S., *Aymer de Valence* (Oxford, 1972).

——, 'The Middle Party and the Treaty of Leake, 1318', *Bull. Inst. Hist. Res.* xlvi (1973), pp. 11–27.

POST, G., '*Plena Potestas* and Consent in Medieval Assemblies', *Traditio*, i. (1943), pp. 355–408.

——, *Studies in Medieval Legal Thought* (Princeton, 1964).

POWELL, J. E., and WALLIS, K., *The House of Lords in the Middle Ages* (London, 1968).

POWER, E., *The Medieval English Wool Trade* (Oxford, 1941).

POWICKE, F. M., *Stephen Langton* (Oxford, 1928).

——, *King Henry III and the Lord Edward*, 2 vols. (Oxford, 1947).

——, *The Thirteenth Century* (Oxford, 1953).

POWICKE, M. R., *Military Obligation in Medieval England* (Oxford, 1962).

PRESTWICH, J. O., 'War and Finance in the Anglo-Norman State', *Trans. Roy. Hist. Soc.* 5th ser. iv (1954), pp. 19–44.

PRESTWICH, M. C., *War, Politics and Finance under Edward I* (London, 1972).

——, 'Exchequer and Wardrobe in the Later Years of Edward I', *Bull. Inst. Hist. Res.* xlvi (1973), pp. 1–10.

PRINCE, A. E., 'The Payment of Army Wages in Edward III's Reign', *Speculum*, xix (1944), pp. 137–60.

PRONAY, N., 'The Hanaper under the Lancastrian Kings', *Proceedings of the Leeds Philosophical and Literary Society*, xii (1967), pp. 73–86.

PUGH, R. B., *The Crown Estate, an Historical Essay* (H.M.S.O., London, 1960).

PUTNAM, B. H., *The Enforcement of the Statute of Labourers* (New York, 1908).

——, 'The Transformation of the Keepers of the Peace into the Justices of the Peace, 1327–1380', *Trans. Roy. Hist. Soc.* 4th ser. xii (1929), pp. 19–48.

——, *The Place of Sir William Shareshull in Legal History* (Cambridge, 1950).

RAMSAY, J. H., *The Genesis of Lancaster*, 2 vols. (Oxford, 1913).

——, *A History of the Revenues of the Kings of England*, 2 vols. (Oxford, 1925).

RAYNER, D., 'The Forms and Machinery of the Commune Petition in the Fourteenth Century', *Eng. Hist. Rev.* lvi (1941), pp. 198–233, 549–70.

RHODES, W. E., 'The Italian Bankers in England and their Loans to Edward I and Edward II', in *Owens College Historical Essays*, ed. T. F. Tout and J. Tait (Manchester, 1902), pp. 137–167.

RICHARDSON, H. G., 'The English Coronation Oath', *Speculum*, xxiv (1949), pp. 44–75.

——, 'The Chamber under Henry II', *Eng. Hist. Rev.* lxix (1954), pp. 596–611.

——, 'The Coronation in Medieval England', *Traditio*, xvi (1960), pp. 111–202.

——, and SAYLES, G. O., 'The Early Records of the English Parliaments' *Bull. Inst. Hist. Res.* v (1928), pp. 129–54, vi (1928–9), pp. 71–88, 129–55.

——, ——, 'The Parliaments of Edward III', *Bull. Inst. Hist. Res.* viii (1930–1), pp. 65–82; ix (1931–2), pp. 1–18.

——, ——, 'The Clergy in the Easter Parliament, 1285', *Eng. Hist. Rev.* lii (1937), pp. 220–34.

——, ——, *The Irish Parliament in the Middle Ages* (London, 1952).

——, ——, 'Irish Revenue, 1278–1384', *Proceedings of the Royal Irish Academy*, lxii (1962), pp. 87–99.

——, ——, *The Governance of Medieval England* (Edinburgh, 1963).

RIESENBERG, P. N., *Inalienability of Sovereignty in Medieval Political Thought* (New York, 1956).

ROSKELL, J. S., 'A Consideration of Certain Aspects and Problems of the English *Modus Tenendi Parliamentum*', *Bull. of the John Rylands Library*, l (1968), pp. 411–42.

ROTHWELL, H., 'The Confirmation of the Charters, 1297', *Eng. Hist. Rev.* lx (1945), pp. 16–35, 177–91.

——, 'Edward I and the Struggle for the Charters', in *Studies in Medieval History Presented to F. M. Powicke* (Oxford, 1948), pp. 319–32.

ROUND, J. H., *Domesday Studies*, 2 vols. (London, 1888).

——, *Feudal England* (London, 1895).

SANDERS, I. J., *Feudal Military Service in England* (Oxford, 1936).

SAYLES, G. O., 'Representation of Cities and Boroughs in 1268', *Eng. Hist. Rev.* xl (1925), pp. 580–5.

——, 'The Seizure of Wool at Easter 1297', *Eng. Hist. Rev.* lxviii (1952), pp. 543–6.

SOMERVILLE, R., *History of the Duchy of Lancaster*, vol. i (London, 1953).

SOUTHERN, R. W., 'The Place of Henry I in English History', *Proceedings of the British Academy*, xlviii (1962), pp. 127–69.

STEPHENSON, C., 'The Seignorial Tallage in England', in *Mélanges d'Histoire Offerts a Henri Pirenne*, ii (Brussels, 1926), pp. 465–474.

——, *Borough and Town* (Cambridge, Mass., 1933).

——, *Medieval Institutions* (New York, 1954).

STRAYER, J. R., 'Defence of the Realm and Royal Power in France', in *Studi in Onore di Gino Luzzato* (Milan, 1948), pp. 289–296.

——, *On the Medieval Origins of the Modern State* (Princeton, 1970).

——, 'Notes on the Origin of English and French Export Taxes', *Studia Gratiana*, xv (1972), pp. 399–422.

——, and TAYLOR, C. H., *Studies in Early French Taxation* (Cambridge, Mass., 1938).

STUBBS, W., *Constitutional History of Medieval England*, 3 vols. 4th ed. (Oxford, 1883).

——, *Select Charters of English Constitutional History*, revised ed. by H. W. C. Davis (Oxford, 1929).

SUTHERLAND, D. W., *Quo Warrants Proceedings in the Reign of Edward I* (Oxford, 1963).

TAIT, J., 'On the Date and Authorship of the *Speculum Edwardi Regis*', *Eng. Hist. Rev.* xvi (1901), pp. 110–15.

TAYLOR, J., 'The Manuscripts of the *Modus Tenendi Parliamentum*', *Eng. Hist. Rev.* lxiii (1968), pp. 673–88.

TOOKE, J. D. *The Just War in Aquinas and Grotius* (London, 1965).

TOUT, T. F., *Chapters in Medieval Administrative History*, 6 vols. (Manchester, 1920–33).

Tout, T. F., *The Place of Edward II in English History*, 2nd ed. rev. by H. Johnstone (Manchester, 1936).

Treharne, R. F., *The Baronial Plan of Reform, 1258–1263* (Manchester, 1932).

Turner, G. J., 'The Sheriff's Farm', *Trans. Roy. Hist. Soc.* n.s. xii (1898), pp. 117–49.

Ullmann, W., *Principles of Government and Politics in the Middle Ages* (London, 1961).

Unwin, G., *Finance and Trade under Edward III* (Manchester, 1918).

Warren, W. L., *Henry II* (London, 1973).

Whitwell, R. J., 'Italian Bankers and the English Crown', *Trans. Roy. Hist. Soc.* n.s. xvii (1903), pp. 175–233.

Wilkinson, B., *The Chancery under Edward III* (Manchester, 1929).

—— 'The Protest of the Earls of Arundel and Surrey in the Crisis of 1341', *Eng. Hist. Rev.* xlvi (1931), pp. 181–93.

—— *Studies in the Constitutional History of the Thirteenth and Fourteenth Centuries* (Manchester, 1937).

——, 'The Sherburn Indenture and the Attack on the Despensers, 1321', *Eng. Hist. Rev.* lxiii (1948), pp. 1–28.

—— 'The Negotiations Preceding the Treaty of Leake, August 1318', in *Studies in Medieval History Presented to F. M. Powicke* (Oxford, 1948), pp. 333–53.

——, *Constitutional History of England, 1216–1399*, 3 vols. (London, 1948–58).

Willard, J. F., 'Edward III's Negotiations for a Grant in 1337', *Eng. Hist. Rev.* xxi (1906), pp. 727–31.

——, 'The Scottish Raids and the Fourteenth Century Taxation of Northern England', *University of Colorado Studies*, v (1907–8), pp. 237–42.

——, 'An Exchequer Reform under Edward I', in *Essays Presented to D. C. Munro* (New York, 1928).

——, 'Ordinances for the Guidance of a Deputy Treasurer 22 October 1305', *Eng. Hist. Rev.* xlviii (1933), pp. 84–9, 352.

——, 'The Taxes upon Movables of the Reign of Edward I', *Eng. Hist. Rev.* xxviii (1913), pp. 517–21.

—— *Parliamentary Taxes on Personal Property, 1290–1334* (Cambridge, Mass., 1934).

Wolffe, B. P., *The Royal Demesne in English History* (London, 1971).

Index

Kilsby, William, Keeper of the Privy
Seal, 246, 284, 295, 303, 306–8,
350, 520–2
King's Langley (Herts.), 484
Knaresborough (Yorks.), 156
Knolles, Thomas, 501n.

Lacy, Henry de, Earl of Lincoln
(1272–1311), 107, 167
— family of, 150, 154, 156
La Hogue (Calvados), 410
Lancaster, Duke of, see Henry 'of
Grosmont', John 'of Gaunt'
— Earl of, see Edmund 'Crouchback',
Henry, Henry 'of Grosmont',
Thomas
Langham, Simon, Archbishop of
Canterbury (1366–8), 469–70, 472
Langley Marsh (Bucks.), 157
Langton, John, 221
Langton, Stephen, Archbishop of
Canterbury (1207–28), 33
— Walter, Treasurer of England, 203,
207, 211
Lapsley, G., 271–2
Leake, Treaty of (1318), 78, 91, 173–7,
262
Lechbury, Robert de, 522
Leges Edwardi Confessoris, 9, 22, 135
Leget, Helming, 500
Leicester, 174, 396
— Earl of, see Edmund 'Crouchback',
Montfort
Leybourne (Yorks.), 485
Libellus Famosus, 289, 294n., 295n.
Lincoln, 223, 396
— Bishop of, see Buckingham,
Burghersh
— Earl of, see Lacy
— earldom of, 143n.
Lionel 'of Antwerp', Duke of Clarence
(1362–8), 373, 394, 460, 478, 485,
530
Llewellyn ap Gruffydd, Prince of
Wales (d. 1282), 43
Llewellyn ap Iorwerth (d. 1240),
197
London, 13–14, 19n., 27, 34, 121, 135n.,
215, 237, 283, 295–383, 398,
521–2
— Bishop of, see FitzNeal
— loans from city of, 212, 277n.
— Tower of, 139, 492–5, 499–500
Lorraine, Nicholas, 486

Louis IX, King of France (1226–70),
(as Prince) 15, 28n.–29n., 33, 36,
135; (as King) 137
Louis de Male, Count of Flanders, 327
Louis II, Duke of Bourbon, 501
Louth, William, 202
Louvain, 288
Lovayn, Colkyn de, 335

McFarlane, K. B., 421
Magna Carta, 8n., 11, 20, 25, 27–8, 61,
73, 111, 120n., 518
Maingre, Jean le, 495
Malines, 281–2, 306
Malwayn, John, 446, 458, 490–3,
501n.
March, Earl of, see Mortimer
Marchia, William de, 72
Mare, John de, 495
Margaret, Queen of England (1299–
1307), 149–50, 173
Marshal, Richard, Earl of Pembroke
(1231–4), 28
Mauny, Walter, 277, 337, 343, 485
Meaux, chronicle of, 125
Melchbourn, Thomas, 324n.–5, 445
— William, 263n., 437, 442
Meopham, Simon, Archbishop of
Canterbury (1328–33), 180n.
Merchant Assemblies: (1322) 426;
(1327) 426; (1332) 426–8; (1336)
235, 428–9, 435; (1338) 238;
(1340) 279; (1342) 430, 444, 448;
(1347) 450
Mills, M., 145
Mint, 147, 192, 196
Mirror of Justices, 114
Mitchell, S. K., vii, 17, 20–1, 28, 32
Modus Tenendi Parliamentum, 81–4, 108,
117, 123, 268–9, 515
Molyns, John de, 286n.
Montague, William, Earl of Salisbury
(1337–44), 234, 246, 294–5n.,
297n., 305n.
— William, Earl of Salisbury (1349–
1397), 345n., 479n.
— family of, 154
Montalt, Robert, de, 155
Monteflorum, Paul de, 239, 263n.,
299n., 442
Montfort, Simon de, Earl of Leicester
(1231–65), 45, 142
Montgomery, Sir John de, 460, 522
Montreuil, county of, 149n., 477n.